READINGS IN THE HISTORY OF CIVILIZATION

READINGS IN THE HISTORY OF CIVILIZATION

EDITED BY
GERRIT P. JUDD

THE MACMILLAN COMPANY, NEW YORK
COLLIER-MACMILLAN LIMITED, LONDON

Third Printing, 1967

Library of Congress catalog card number: 66–15370

The Macmillan Company, New York
Collier-Macmillan Canada, Ltd., Toronto, Ontario

Printed in the United States of America

PREFACE

This book of readings is designed mainly for college students in Western civilization courses. The inclusion of material dealing with Asia and Africa makes it also suitable for courses in world civilization.

Undergraduates in Western or world civilization courses, who are usually freshmen, often have difficulty with documents. The solution to this problem seems to lie neither with long introductions nor with extended annotation. Undergraduates have been known to rely on the introduction and slight the text. Undergraduates also generally dislike footnotes, possibly from the experience of studying Shakespeare in heavily annotated high-school editions. Accordingly, except where required by holders of the copyright to print excerpts in full, the present editor has reduced annotation to a minimum, and has provided comparatively short introductions in order to focus attention on the readings themselves.

The heart of the problem is not the presentation of the readings, but their selection. This book has only twenty sources, but has almost twice that number (36, to be precise) of selections from secondary works.

The word *source,* like its first cousin *document,* has a forbidding overtone to beginners in college history. In choosing these materials, I have kept in mind not only their historical significance but also their attractiveness as literary records. The "sources" include Plato's account of the death of Socrates, the funeral oration of Pericles, the lightly accented monastic gossip of Jocelin of Brakelond, Boccaccio's somber description of the Black Death in Florence, Voltaire's telling wit in the *Philosophical Dictionary,* Burke's fulminations against the French Revolution, Disraeli's sharp attack on the horrors of industrialism, and two great speeches by Winston Churchill made in June 1940, when seemingly invincible Nazi armies were overrunning France.

But the major part of this book consists of selections from historians and others who have a story to tell or an analysis to make, and who narrate or analyze (and sometimes do both) not only with insight but also with memorable language. I have read from many of these selections (along with the "sources" mentioned above) in crowded lecture halls, sometimes with the rare and wonderful reward of pindrop silence. It has been gratifying to group together between covers so many favorites. For the Middle Ages, these authors include Henry Adams, Marc Bloch, George Coulton, and Sidney Painter, with Johan Huizinga for the late medieval period. Others, no less honored, include Garrett Mattingly on Renaissance diplomacy, John E. Neale on Elizabeth I's "queencraft," Herbert Butterfield on modern science, and Lord David Cecil's astute and beautifully written description of the English governing class of the early nineteenth century.

Throughout, I have stressed variety in primary and secondary works alike. The subject matter ranges from technology, economic analysis, and institutional history to devotional literature, political theory, social criticism, and the arts. The selections themselves come from media ranging from the formal treatise and historical biography to memoirs, the essay, and (in one case) the novel.

This volume is designed to be a "teaching" book, with the first lesson written plainly. In the experience of the present editor, the first duty of a teacher is to interest his students. With interest once aroused, the rest is comparatively easy, especially after students wander into the library to teach themselves. Hopefully, with this book students may begin to realize that history is, after all, a record of life, filled with all the challenges, vexations, and delights of being alive in the transient present. With such awakened interest, students may also realize that, to paraphrase a celebrated statement, history is a mirror held up to life, and that there is no such thing as dull history, only (regrettably) some dull historians.

Acknowledgment is gratefully made to the many publishers who have kindly granted permission to reprint copyrighted material. Specific acknowledgment appears in notes to the pertinent selections.

I wish also to thank Mr. Robert J. Patterson, history editor of The Macmillan Company, for much needed help and encouragement in this project.

G. P. J.

CONTENTS

❧ READINGS IN THE HISTORY OF CIVILIZATION

I

THE ANCIENT WORLD

PART ONE

☙ THE ANCIENT WORLD

Mediterranean civilization from about 3000 B.C. to the fall of the Roman Empire in the West in the fifth century A.D. is traditionally known as the Ancient World. Here civilization originated on the planet, from stimuli and circumstances that still remain obscure. In Mesopotamia and Egypt, humanity experimented with forms of government and left written records, sketchy at first, on stone and clay. A priestly class and a codification of law slowly took form. Religion flourished and moved toward ethical monotheism, an achievement of the Hebrews in the sixth century B.C. About this time the Greeks, one of the most talented peoples of the Ancient World, began their spectacular advances in literature and the arts. The Greeks also formulated systems of science and philosophy, as the terms are commonly understood, and some Greek city-states briefly achieved a limited form of democracy.

In the third century B.C. the center of Mediterranean power began to pass westward to Rome, which absorbed Greek civilization and spread its forms as far north as Scotland, and so became the biggest empire yet known in the Mediterranean world. Christianity appeared in the Roman empire, as a minority movement at first, drawing heavily on both Hebrew and Greek elements. What is traditionally known as Ancient Civilization continued in the Byzantine empire, but in western Europe it lapsed into almost total darkness with the fall of Roman power there.

ONE

THE ORIGIN OF CIVILIZATION

Civilization originated about 3000 B.C. *in Egypt and Mesopotamia, perhaps in Mesopotamia first. Fragmentary evidence indicates that in its formative period Egyptian civilization received a stimulus from Mesopotamia. But in any case the two regions developed separately, for the most part, until about 1500* B.C. *Exactly how and why civilization arose from the Neolithic (New Stone Age) substructure presents a continuing and perhaps unsolvable problem. Historians and other scholars have long wondered why civilization first appeared in the Near East instead of in some other place. This question is part of a larger and still puzzling question, namely, the dynamics of human society: the forces and circumstances governing the emergence, rise, and decline of civilization itself. A wide variety of tentative answers to this puzzle has appeared, for example, in the lengthy works of Spengler and Toynbee. Among the more provocative shorter discussions of the early development of civilization in recent historical research is that of Robert J. Forbes, whose primary concern is technology and engineering.*

ROBERT J. FORBES

MAN THE MAKER *

After 3000 B.C. the papyri and clay tablets, the leather rolls and pottery shards, and the inscriptions on monuments and temples allow us direct contact with ancient civilizations. A wealth of historical and religious documents, contracts, laws, registers, and bookkeeping records are now available, and many more await publication and translation. They show us the great social effects of the discoveries and inventions of predynastic times. They reveal the basic structure of the early empires of Egypt, Mesopotamia, and the Indus valley as they emerge from the mists of prehistory.

These early empires are typical urban civilizations. From the mass of villages of the early peasant civilization in the river valleys, towns crystallized as centers to harbor the new classes of craftsmen, scribes, and merchants, soldiers and sailors, public servants and officials who ran the state. Inroads of nomad warriors during the Late Stone Age not only introduced war as an activity of the state, but in certain cases these warriors conquered the new states and settled in their main cities as permanent rulers. In their wake a new class emerged, that of the slaves, usually war captives bound to the harshest forms of labor in mines, quarries, and fields.

The cities harbored the new classes whose food came from the surplus that the great mass of farmers produced. In these cities the crafts and sciences were concentrated. They were based on the advances in the fields of geology, chemistry, natural history, astronomy, agriculture, mechanics, metallurgy, and architecture that had been achieved in earlier periods.

The structures of these new empires differed widely. In Mesopotamia we find an agglomeration of small city-states, each concentrated in a major town. The chief priest of the temple ruled this parcel of the land as the steward of the god who was supposed to be the creator and owner. The organization of the city-state seems to have been a kind of state communism. The products of farms and crafts were brought to the temple where they were registered and stored. The temple issued food and raw materials to the citizens, farmers, and craftsmen.

In Egypt the power was concentrated in the hands of the king, who himself was a god and who administered Upper and Lower Egypt through two separate organizations of officials.

Science and the Craftsmen

As specialization increased, most of the craftsmen of antiquity began to be organized into guilds. The greater part of these guilds were closely associated with the temples or were in some way directed by the state. The "overseers" of the guilds were often of priestly rank. They were scribes who had mastered the mysteries of language and writing. But this does not mean that they were priests in our modern sense of the word, for most officials and noblemen who were believed to have mastered some special

* Reprinted from *Man the Maker,* pp. 39–51, by R. J. Forbes by permission of Abelard-Schuman Ltd.

field of knowledge had such priestly rank. They might have been educated in the temple schools which, as was later true in the Middle Ages, were then the centers of education. In ancient Assyria the guilds were often headed by an official, usually someone of high rank, who bore a title that meant "one who gives instructions." This and other evidence proves that the crafts through their leaders were in touch with the science of the day.

Science in the period under consideration (3000–600 B.C.) had a completely different structure from the science of today. We moderns, having collected and analyzed all the relevant data, synthesize these into our scheme of nature. This synthesis then provides us with the means of using nature for our own purposes. Antiquity, especially during the pre-Hellenic period, knew nothing of such procedures. For ancient man there was no clear-cut distinction between the separate fields of religion, philosophy, or science. All these aspects of the world were molded into one encompassing scheme of thought. Ancient man had not yet learned to think in terms of abstract principles and had no concept of the inner meaning of individual phenomena. Such "divine curiosity about the essence of things," as the Greek natural philosophers expressed it, did not yet exist.

The educated man of the ancient world had a firm belief that everything in the universe had been created "in the beginning" by the gods. The cosmic order as originally established by the gods existed as a stable scheme from the beginning of time. He had no desire to inquire why or how the observed phenomena of nature worked. He knew that everything had its assigned place in a world that had been molded by the gods on the Day of Creation. He had only to find the place in this cosmic order of anything he was confronted with. Naming a thing meant knowing its place in the cosmos, or putting it in the "net of the world," as the Egyptians expressed it. No further logical reasoning was required. Naming a thing was the same as recognizing its magical links and potencies in the cosmos. Magic, not logic, governed the natural phenomena.

We need not outline these ancient scientific views in detail. The practical result was that though the learned leaders of the guilds did use the observations of the craftsmen, their theories were of no use to the development of the crafts. The ancient scientific leaders were considered an absolute necessity only because they had to put the finishing touches to the work of the craftsmen. For example, when the sculptor, whom the ancient Egyptians picturesquely called "he who makes alive," had finished his stone or wooden statue, it was not fit to serve in the temple or tomb until the priestly overseer of the guild of sculptors had applied the rite of the "opening of the mouth" to it to give it the magical power of housing the soul of the dead man it represented.

Hence the observations of the technologists were embodied in the ancient philosophy of life, but not a single natural phenomenon served to guide scientific theory directly. Today research is considered to be the lifeblood of technology and industry, neither of which can thrive on rules deduced from trial and error alone. This lack of theoretical background explains why, after the astonishing strides made in the latter part of the New Stone Age, so little progress was made in ancient technology. What progress there was emerged very slowly. Technology, unsupported by science, had to go the long way of experience. The very practical technology and engineering of those days seems to have had no connection with the magical philosophy of life which permeated antiquity. The bond is hidden because the connection is one-sided. By imperceptible degrees this magical world became a logical one. Gradually certain aspects of nature became the subject of scientific speculation without interference from philosophical or religious dogmas. Eventually a real natural science arose that could guide and help clever practical engineers and craftsmen.

We know that science was organized even in preclassical times. Both Egypt and Mesopotamia had groupings of learned men—we might call them scientific societies today—that possessed libraries and collected all the scientific observations. These societies advised the kings and priests on problems that were both practical (the construction of temples, for example) and religious or philosophical (the correct date of religious festivals, the calendar, ceremonial, and the interpretation of dreams). As centers of scientific research in the modern sense of the word, however, they remained completely barren.

The Earliest Architects

We rightly admire the very practical achievements of the early technologists and engineers. Their huge pyramids and temples still fill us with admiration for the men who planned and carried through these astonishing technical feats. Slave power alone did not account for these structures. Technical skill and organization were required as well. It is certain that structural drawings of the pyramids existed. The stone of these huge graves was quarried on the side of the Nile opposite the building site. The blocks were cut to the correct size and marked with the name of the gang of quarrymen, the date, and the place where they were to be fitted into the pyramid.

No less than 2,300,000 blocks of limestone were used in erecting the Great Pyramid, which was designed as the tomb-monument for King Khufu or Cheops in the 29th century B.C. Many more blocks and slabs of granite and other casing stones were imported from quarries in the south of Egypt by floating them down the Nile on rafts. The pyramid covers an area of thirteen acres, and the sides at the base are 756 feet long. Herodotus, the Father of History, tells us that an army of 100,000 workmen worked on this project for twenty years, and his account is believed to be substantially accurate. The workmen were not all slaves, as is popularly believed, but mostly craftsmen and farmers, the latter working on the job in payment of taxes during the season of the inundation, when agricultural work was impossible anyway. One third of this large number of workers were busy erecting the body of the pyramid, another third quarried and transported the stones and other materials required, and the rest were needed to supply food and to build sheds and sleeping quarters for the laborers. An ancient Egyptian title of those days can be translated only by our modern word "organizer." Surely the organizers of those days knew their job, for even today the handling of such a great mass of people is no simple feat.

This high architectural skill was the achievement of only a few generations; the Great Pyramid was built only about 150 years after the very first stone building had been erected. In predynastic times, natural stone was first employed in lining graves and making floors of important buildings. The art of quarrying was perfected. The old "fire and water" method of disintegrating rocks was superseded by careful drilling of holes and the use of copper wedges and copper saws, aided by emery or sand, to produce blocks and slabs of natural stone. Great stone slabs and obelisks still partly attached to the living rock show how daring the Egyptian engineers were. Egypt was particularly fortunate in having many quarries of all kinds of natural stone suitable for building and decoration.

In Mesopotamia this art was never properly developed. There we find bricks as the principal building material. These bricks, of a type also used in Egypt, were formed from the clay abundantly available in the river valleys. This clay was sometimes reinforced by mixing it with chopped straw and reeds. The shaped bricks were then dried in the heat of the sun. As fuel was scarce in the ancient Near East, and only such inferior fuel as straw, dung, and brushwood was available, the use of burnt bricks was restricted to important buildings like temples, palaces, and graves.

Architecture in natural stone was an Egyptian achievement. The oldest surviving building of stone masonry in the world is the "step" pyramid of Sakkarah. During the excavations of the stores and temples within the wall enclosing this pyramid, which was erected for the Pharaoh Zoser (about 2940 B.C.), it was found that his prime minister, Imhotep, was the architect and builder of this first example of natural-stone architecture.

The earlier buildings in this area show a peculiar technique. With the experience gained in building with timber, bundles of reeds, and bricks, Imhotep tried a more permanent material. He had large-size bricks quarried from the natural stone, and after assembling them into crude shapes like walls and pillars, had them cut to look like the older wooden ceilings and pillars of reed bundles, or shaped to give the impression of an opened wooden gate. During these experiments he gradually conceived the idea of assembling smaller stone bricks and slabs so that the resulting architectural forms were no longer an imitation of older structures made of wood or other materials. In some cases he preshaped the stone bricks or slabs to build up stone pillars according to the method that has been used ever since.

We have here a complex of structures which were more or less the experimental field of a builder who was trying to find the proper forms inherent in a new material, natural stone. And so developed the purely Doric columns and other forms which we had always believed to be original Greek inventions. In this complex of buildings we find the experimental series that served to teach the great pyramid builders of generations to follow, who learned to appreciate the forms that were more natural to this new building material. We need not wonder that Imhotep was revered in Egyptian tradition as one of the wisest men of their early days. About 2,000 years after his death he was apotheosized as a god of medicine, a profession that he probably never practiced—at least his original titles do not indicate that he did.

Aqueducts and Canals

In the field of engineering this period did not bring many important new inventions except the aqueduct. However, this does not mean that nothing spectacular was done in irrigation and canal building. Irrigation was very much the principal interest of the governments both in Egypt and in Mesopotamia. But the system used in each country was different.

In Egypt the rise of the Nile occurs in the right season for the farmer, from August until early October. Hence he has time to sow winter or spring crops after working the fields. The system adopted in ancient Egypt was basin irrigation. In each of the irrigation areas built up by cooperative labor, the dikes were cut at the proper moment as determined by the rise of the Nile. The water was conducted over the total area and given time to precipitate its enriching silt. Then the necessary cuts were made in the dikes downstream and the water left to flow back into the river. The Nile has an adequate amount of silt for the fields, but not so much that canals will silt up too quickly. Nature made it easy for the Egyptians. Hapi, the god of the Nile, was a friendly deity.

The situation in Mesopotamia was quite different. Here the sudden, irregular rise of the Euphrates and Tigris rivers came between April and June, and the rivers carried a fivefold amount of silt compared to that of the Nile. The waters came too late for the winter crops and too early for the spring crops. The inhabitants of these plains had to store this water in special basins, but this enabled them, on the other hand, to water their fields at will. This so-called perennial irrigation system required an immense amount of labor, but it allowed the ancient Babylonians to harvest three crops every two years. The gods of the floods were often destructive, and had to be propitiated. The bountiful harvests of Mesopotamia have frequently attracted the attention of classical authors. It is logical therefore to find Mesopotamian city-despots frequently boasting about the canals they dug or put in order again by removing the accumulated silt.

The "steward" of Lagash, Entemanna, built the Shatt-el-Hai, which conducted the waters of the high-level Tigris through the plains to the lower Euphrates at Ur. Another canal took off from the Tigris near Samarra and was led through an aqueduct over the river Diyalah to the regions north of the Tigris. The Hindia barrage or dam restored by Alexander the Great was much older and had impounded the waters of the Euphrates so that they could be distributed through the area around Babylon. The existence of so many small city-states without a strong central government did not promote extreme efficiency of irrigation in these valleys. We also hear of ancient bankers speculating in canal building and in the sale of irrigated fields. But the general scheme remained in good order until the Mongols in their destructive wars of the thirteenth century A.D. depopulated these lands, whereupon the irrigation system fell to ruin through sheer neglect.

The Egyptians were not content with the basin irrigation system they had built up and therefore they extended it considerably. About 2000 B.C. a series of strong kings, the so-called Twelfth Dynasty—notably King Amenemhet III—extended the branch of the Nile called Bahr-el Jusef (Joseph's Canal) until it reached the desert depression called the Fayyum. At the entrance to this oasis Amenemhet built a large dam. Thus he not only led the rich silt of the Nile into this new province, which has flourished ever since, but he also introduced perennial irrigation in a part of Egypt, for the Fayyum could be used as a storage basin and its waters could be led back into the basin system of the valley at will. This system demanded proper and constant care. During subsequent periods of Egyptian history it was neglected and had to be restored by succeeding generations, but it still was widely used until late Roman times, when neglect caused its complete breakdown and the resultant evaporation of Lake Fayyum.

The ancient Egyptians were great builders of canals. At Elephantine, shipping was hindered by the first cataract of the Nile. Here, about 1875 B.C., King Sesostris built a canal 260 feet long, 35 feet wide, and 26 feet deep, to provide his ships with a means of avoiding the dangerous natural course of the Nile. The Greek Ptolemies reigned in Egypt during the last three centuries B.C., and documents on civil engineering jobs dating from this period are quite detailed. We read about the construction of dikes and their foundations, and about the use of reeds, mats, and stones to protect them.

It seems that the irrigation units of those days were about 100 acres, which is one tenth of the present unit. On the other hand, we have contracts for the reclamation of 7,000 acres for the state Secretary of Finance, Apollonius (260 B.C.). The architect Cleon had to build 50 miles of dikes! We also hear of the contractors, who in a series of eight contracts had to move over 10 million cubic feet of earth; another contract mentions 1.7 million cubic feet that had to be moved. These contracts show that part of the fee was prepaid and that tools were furnished by the state. Even labor was often put at the disposal of the contractors when there were plenty of state slaves.

Another important engineering feat of the Egyptians was the canal connecting the Mediterranean and the Red Sea. This forerunner of the modern Suez Canal was used for over a thousand years. The Egyptians never were great sailors. Their trade with Arabia and Somaliland consisted of shipping their merchandise along the coast to Myos Hormos, a point about halfway along the Red Sea, where the trade route went overland through the valley of Hammamat to Coptos on the Nile. They avoided the northern part of the Red Sea, where there were many shoals and treacherous winds. The canal that was constructed consisted of two parts. The west-east stretch was a canal running from Bubastis on the eastern branch of the Nile delta through the Tumilat depression to Lake Timsah. It was really an irrigation canal which watered what in ancient times was the valley of Goshen—the region that harbored the Israelites when they lived in Egypt.

The second part of the canal ran north and south from Lake Timsah through the so-called Bitter Lakes to a point just north of the present Suez Canal. The total length was slightly less than 100 miles.

We have sound reasons for believing that this canal was constructed by the same kings who incorporated the Fayyum into their irrigation system. It certainly existed in the later period of Egyptian history when King Necho II (600 B.C.) sent an expedition to circumnavigate Africa. The Persian king, Darius, had the canal desilted so that it would serve his policy of creating sea trade between Egypt, India, and Persia. It was then about 200 feet wide and 40 feet deep. According to the memorial tablets erected by him along this canal, he had a fleet of 24 ships sailing through it to Persia. Alexander the Great and certain Roman emperors are known to have deepened and used it, but it was neglected after the fourth century A.D. and silted up completely.

The aqueduct, so important in water supply, was a Persian invention. From time immemorial the plains of Persia were irrigated by water drawn from the foothills of the mountain ranges. "Qanats" or tunnels were dug into these hills and the tapped water led through drains to the fields. Such tunnels were fairly common in the ancient Near East.

Jerusalem had an important water supply of this kind which played a part in the Old Testament story of the Pool of Shiloah; so had Megiddo. These achievements of mining and architecture set an example for the earliest dated Assyrian aqueduct. It was built about 700 B.C. and led the waters of a mountain river impounded by a barrage at Bavian through a 70-foot drain to Nineveh, 20 miles south. There the waters are used to irrigate the palace gardens and fields of the kings of Assyria. This huge structure is the first of a series of ingenious aqueducts built mainly by Greeks and Romans. The first of these to be constructed at Megara and on the island of Samos date about 100 years later.

It is interesting to note that the great works of the engineers find their expression in early mathematics. The achievements of Egyptians and more particularly Sumerians and Assyrians in mathematics and astronomy were closely linked with practical engineering. We have no theoretical discussion of any mathematical problem but only a series of practical solutions for certain typical problems. They deal with the areas of fields, the slopes of pyramids, the quantity of stone needed for a cylindrical well, masses of earth to be removed in canal building, and similar practical problems. Even astronomy was primarily used to predict the rise of the rivers.

TWO

CIVILIZATION IN ANCIENT EGYPT

Even the main outline of the dawning of civilization in Egypt may never be known. It is, of course, well established that Egyptian civilization evolved with extraordinary speed and with even more extraordinary creativity. But how civilization emerged there is a tale only partly told, for the surviving written records are scanty. Nonwritten remains such as the pyramids, although vastly impressive, reveal a society already in a comparatively advanced stage of organization, yet they give little clue as to how that organization developed. Toynbee tried to solve the riddle of Egyptian civilization with his well-known formula of challenge and response. Childe found in Egypt's urbanization a useful field of inquiry, while Redfield viewed early Egyptian civilization in terms of what he called a "folk society." In his stimulating study of early Egyptian history, Professor John A. Wilson has reviewed the theories of Toynbee, Childe, and Redfield, and has decided that none of the three has presented an entirely satisfactory explanation of this fascinating and possibly unsolvable problem.

JOHN A. WILSON

THE BURDEN OF EGYPT*

. . . Alluvial soil has tantalizingly covered and hidden some of the most interesting evidence of all: the data on man's final settlement along the banks of the Nile as a relatively sedentary creature, the first evidence of his transition from a life based on pursuing food or gathering it in transit to a life based on nurturing food in the place where he lived. In the gap of evidence, we are limited to speculation. Desiccation of the desert must have cut off plant foods except at the margin of the River. The animals of the upland, including man, were thus herded down to the river bank, pursuing plant food and pursuing each other. A much closer juxtaposition meant greater acquaintance: man found that it was advantageous to keep certain animals close at hand for his future food supply; he found that certain plants could be teased into greater productivity for his feeding and the feeding of those animals which he was holding beside him. Slowly—probably without invention but with unconscious transition—food-gathering gave way to food-production, the essential element of historical life. But the evidence on this transition is lost to us beneath the alluvium.

* Reprinted from *The Burden of Egypt,* pp. 20–36, by John A. Wilson by permission of The University of Chicago Press. Copyright 1951 by The University of Chicago Press.

When finally the curtain does rise again for a few scattered views of man, he has his feet firmly planted in the black alluvial mud along the Nile, he has domestic animals, and he is cultivating plants. In his dietary essentials and in the physical bases of life, he is modern man—or, at least, man as he was up to the industrial revolution. He still had a long way to go in achieving the full physical values of the life he had, and he still had to work out his new social organization, and he still had vast unexplored stretches in his intellectual and spiritual life. But the gap in our evidence hides a major revolution—the transition from the food-gathering economy of hunters, fishers, trappers, and grubbers for roots and pluckers of berries to the food-producing economy of farming and herding cattle. In the food-gathering economy the social unit had necessarily been limited to the family or tribe, ranging over a considerable area of land and necessarily limited to light, portable equipment. Now man was settled, and he could begin to accumulate goods in greater quantity. He was more definitely in control of his food, since he himself produced it, so that there could be more food. More people could live within any given area, so that the family or tribe need not be the essential element. Unrelated families could live side by side, without difficult competition, perhaps even to mutual advantage. Such a transition must have taken long thousands of years. It was still incomplete when our evidence begins once more.

Diligent search along the margins of the cultivated land, in the Faiyum, on the edges of the Delta, and in pockets of land in Middle Egypt, has given us some incomplete evidence on prehistoric man's dim gropings for a fuller life. Roving food-gatherers came out of the north African prairie and paused at the margins of the Faiyum lake. Before they departed again, they left a kitchen midden of elephant or hippopotamus bones, with scanty traces of their simple artifacts: microlithic flints, with little or no pottery. At a later stage—probably many centuries later—the inhospitable desert cast them forth, and they settled down at the edge of the jungle swamps which lined the Nile Valley. The artifacts were somewhat more numerous, but still primitive and crude. We have tools and weapons, beads, baskets, pottery, granaries, and the bones of domestic animals. The last two are very important because they show that man no longer roamed in pursuit of his food but stayed in one place to produce his food. At Merimdeh Beni-Salameh at the southwestern margin of the Delta, there was even a village of crude oval huts made of big lumps of mud. It was no garden city. The entire village covered about six acres, and the ungainly huts were of a single, smoke-filled room about fourteen by nine feet. There was a jar sunk into the flooring to drain off the rain water coming through the roof. It was not a cheery place.

The village had a communal granary, consisting of woven baskets sunk into the ground. The individual huts had no granaries beside them. Apparently the first attempts at village life retained some of the elements of tribal custom: the individual sense of property had not yet replaced the community sense of property. The cereals included the same kind of barley as is grown today, emmer wheat, and a common vetch. Flax was also grown, spun into thread, and woven into linen on some kind of crude loom. So we have already had the revolution in life produced by the discovery that certain kinds of wild plants could be protected, nurtured, and teased into greater productivity for man's food and clothing. The other discovery had also taken place: that certain kinds of animals could be held close beside man and cultivated for their meat, hides, or wool. However, the Merimdeh village and the Faiyum middens show an incomplete transition to food-producing. The small amount of grain indicated by the granaries and the profusion of bones of wild animals suggest that the cereals of his fields and the meat of his cattle and pigs did not yet provide a sufficient diet for man. The jungle and the desert were still close at hand, and man was still animated by a primitive restlessness; he went hunting and fishing for additional food.

Probably his fields were tiny pockets of soil, adventitiously watered by the Nile, and he had not yet set himself to the formidable tasks of draining the jungle marshes and then channeling water to the cleared fields. That was to be a long, slow process, still incomplete at the time when history began. For the moment he took what was easiest to his hand.

If we jump all the way down into historic times and look at the wall carvings of the Old Kingdom, we can see that the process of domestication was still uncompleted after some two thousand years. These Old Kingdom scenes show the nobles of historic times hunting in lush swamps teeming with wild life: hippopotamus, crocodile, and wild fowl. To be sure, the ancient artist may have allowed himself the luxury of exaggeration; but he must have had models upon which to draw, the models of a land not yet completely drained and tamed. Further, such scenes show a continuing experimentation in the domestication of wild animals. There are stables containing gazelles and hyenas, fattened by forcible feeding. Man did not give up the attempt to add new animals to his domestic menage until history had run a full millennium and the strong hand of tradition halted further experimentation.[1]

We return to the primitive and prehistoric. It is not the purpose of this book to detail the successive cultures of predynastic Egypt, with the elements of change in each. We wish only to make a few points. The first is that the struggle was a native struggle within Egypt and—until the end of the predynastic period—not affected to any appreciable degree by stimuli from outside. Long, slow change of culture may be a matter of unconscious inner drive, without invasion of "superior" or of goading peoples from abroad. We do not know very much about race in predynastic Egypt. What we do know is chiefly negative, that changes of race in the early Nile Valley were negligible in quantity or quality. For the most part, there was an "Egyptian," short, slight, long-headed, and dark, a mongrel of Africa, Asia, and the Mediterranean. Whatever motivation there was toward civilization burned deep within him, a slow fire of which he was quite unconscious. Gradually, without deliberate invention on his part and without any early stimulation from abroad, he was to grope his way upward toward a life of greater maturity, of greater physical comfort, and of greater interdependent complexity. Until the very end of the predynastic period, the process was unconscious and terribly slow. Man's feet were mired in the mud of the river banks, and he had to move deliberately.

And so the archeologist lists a series of successive predynastic cultures with formidable names: Tasian, Badarian, Amratian, Gerzean, and Semainean; and he lists the physical phenomena which appear in each culture: flints, pottery, the earliest metal, amulets, graves, houses, and works of art. There was constant change, and—with qualifications—there was constant enrichment. Certain forms, such as houses and metal implements, became more numerous, larger, and more varied. Other forms, however, suffered through competition with new elements; flint weapons and decorated pottery reached climaxes of achievement at an early stage and then faded away in quality as man's energies were diverted into other lines. This was particularly true of pottery, where man's creative artistry produced ware of the greatest skill, beauty, and utility; but then his craftsman's impulse was drawn into other channels, and the pottery became dull and merely utilitarian.

Before we discuss art further, perhaps we should gain a clearer picture of the artist. What do we know about the predynastic Egyptian, since he has left us no writing and we have to learn about him through the objects he left buried in Egyptian soil? The pic-

[1] J. H. Breasted in *Scientific Monthly,* November, 1919, pp. 416 ff.

ture is, of course, quite incomplete, but it does have contours. Let us pick a point toward the end of the predynastic stretch, but before the final transition into history, and set down what we know about the man who lived along the Nile.

To begin with, he was no physical giant. The men stood less than five feet six inches in height, the women were closer to five feet tall. They were slight, but strong-boned, with relatively long heads and oval, rather birdlike faces. The men had no great amount of hair on face or body and probably had slight or patchy beards. Their clothing was relatively scanty but was of linen. For dress occasions they wore strings of simple beads and adorned their faces with an eye cosmetic, preferably green. Physically, as in other respects, they showed relations to the Hamites, the Semites, and the Mediterraneans.

Those crude oval huts of rough lumps of mud had now become rectangular houses of shaped mud bricks. One model house which has come down to us has a door lined with wood and small windows framed in wood. Its original must have been large enough for inner partitioning into rooms, with a central timber supporting a flat roof. Most of the essentials of the historical house were present.[2]

This man was a farmer, but he probably had little to sell or trade, so that each domestic unit must have been self-sufficient in the necessities of life. Armed with a homemade hoe of wood and a sickle set with flint teeth, he cultivated barley, emmer wheat, vetch, a few vegetables, and flax. The cereals gave him bread and beer; the flax gave him the linen which was spun and woven into cloth.

Perhaps every family had a domestic animal or two, which might be pooled into a village herd. It must have been a rarely wealthy man who had a herd of his own. The animals were the African long-horned cattle, the sheep, the goose, the goat, the donkey, and—chiefly in the north—the pig. Perhaps we may credit the prehistoric Egyptian with the selective breeding of two animals, a naturally hornless kind of cattle and the Egyptian greyhound.[3] Despite the presence of domestic animals, it is a fair assumption that meat was not a normal element of diet but was reserved for feasts and sacrifices. Fishing, fowling in the marshes, and hunting in the desert supplemented the meat provision.

Although this man was self-sufficient for his domestic and field tools, there was one category of goods which he probably could secure only by trading, and that embraced the implements of metal. Metallurgy must have been a skilled craft confined to a few technicians. The smelting of copper required great heat in a closed space, and it has been assumed that some of the techniques were the same as in the fusing of sands and ores for glazing.[4] The copper was cast in a mold, and the closed mold was shortly to replace the open mold. Having conquered metal, man was now able to bend it to his needs and make knives, daggers, axes, chisels, etc., with the metal assuming a shape for its necessary function and not following the old shapes set by stone implements. Stone tools and weapons were on the way out, no longer able to compete with copper; but, before the stone disappeared, it had a final triumph of technical skill, particularly because religious custom eschewed the new medium and clung to stone for such practices as sacrifice or circumcision. The final flint blades are superb pieces, thin, beautifully ground, and rippled to perfection. Such delicately beautiful flints may have been purely show-pieces. The ordinary farmer had to content himself with wooden tools or with implements of wood set with flint points or edges. Metal and the finest flints belonged to the community or to the overlord.

[2] D. Randall-MacIver and A. C. Mace, *El Amrah and Abydos* (*EES,* Vol. XXIII [1902]), p. 42, Pl. X; H. Schäfer and W. Andrae, *Die Kunst des alten Orients* (3d ed., Berlin, 1942), p. 173.

[3] E. O. Orenander in *Sphinx,* XXII (1931), 8 ff.; M. Hilzheimer in *Antiquity,* VI (1932), 411 ff.

[4] A. Lucas in *Jea,* XXXI (1945), 96 f.

This little Egyptian had his times of aggressiveness and adventure. Archeology produces a great amount of arrowheads and mace-heads, and the skeletons of the predynastic Egyptians show an extraordinary number of broken bones. Apparently, communities had come into competitive contact with other communities, so that there was already that warfare which built little states into larger states and was ultimately to produce a nation. We do not know anything about the authority under whom the Egyptian fought. Theoretically, there were already local rulers of small states, distinct from the tribal chieftains of an earlier stage.

If we define a "machine" as an instrument which unites two distinct elements for a single merged force, this man commanded several simple machines. Of course, he had inherited the bow and arrow from long-distant ancestors. He had also the harpoon with attached cord, the hoe, the spindle, the loom, and—most complicated of all—the drill for hollowing out stone vases or for piercing small beads. These are all of a fairly elementary mechanical nature, but they have advanced beyond a club or a hand ax or a digging stick.

In one respect this late predynastic Egyptian had fallen short of the achievements of his ancestors, and that was in the craftsmanship of containers, vessels of pottery and stone. His loving artisanry had been diverted to other channels. The pottery had declined in the fineness of the ware, in the boldness of the form, and in the pains taken with decoration. The stone vessels were not so commonly in the very refractory materials, nor were they so successful in form; it was now sufficient to make a container of routine shape out of soft stone. Artistic talents had gone into the shaping of figurines or into the decoration of ceremonial slate palettes, an artistry which required the new technique of relief sculpture. To a degree, art was separating itself from function and was becoming a skilled craft for the purposes of the state or the overlord.

This man was earth-bound to his little fields, except at such times as he was led forth to war. However, he was not cut off from contact with distant regions. The boats which plied the Nile now carried sails, and some of them may have adventured out into the "Great Green" Sea, hugging the coast as long as possible. There was commerce the whole length of Egypt, and somehow goods trickled in from other areas: gold and copper from the eastern mountains, ivory and myrrh from the distant south, olive oil from Libya and from Palestine, cedar woods from the Phoenician coast, lapis lazuli and obsidian from lands far to the east. Such goods may have passed only from community to community, but the means were already present, in shipping, for more direct contact and thus for greater influence of one culture on another. It is already possible to see a remarkable similarity of form between Egypt and Palestine in the shapes of pots, stone vessels, and stone palettes.[5]

We know very little about the religion of this man. Most of what we list we guess from his burials. Certainly, a belief in some kind of future life was important to him. His graves became increasingly elaborate, and increasingly he took goods with him into his grave. Food and drink were most important; but clothing, ornamentation, cosmetics, weapons, and tools accompanied him to the next world. Sometimes such objects were broken or pierced and thus "killed," so that they might share their owner's fate. At times dogs were buried with their masters. Whether servants were killed and buried at the same time as their masters we do not know. This was a practice which disappeared early in historical times, and one assumes that it was a prehistoric practice, in order to maintain a lord's household in the future life. The predynastic evidence for the custom is, however, lacking. We shall revert presently to the other evidence on religion as shown by art.

Was life a grim business for this predynastic Egyptian, with his back bent to the

[5] H. J. Kantor in *JNES*, I (1942), 174 ff.

hoe or the loom? Yes, it must have been drudgery, but the monotony was relieved by the celebration of feasts, which surely marked the fortunes of the Nile and the agricultural year. There were fishing and hunting and warring. There were even games. Excavation has produced a crude kind of checkerboard. It is a table of unbaked clay with four stumpy legs, its surface divided into eighteen squares, and accompanied by about a dozen game pieces of clay coated with wax.[6] Such an apparatus for amusement is significant. There must already have been the slight surplus of wealth which relieved the pressure of endless toil; there must already have been the leisure time for entertainment. Such a transitional point and such a state of mind are also indicated by the development of an art for its own sake. Let us go back and look at the art of earlier predynastic times.

The urge toward beauty appeared first in the manufacture of useful things, such as a graceful pot with an applied decoration or a stone jug which made skilful use of the natural graining of the stone. A rounded pot offered an irresistible surface for the early artist. He could build up the form with applied clay, he could incise the pot when it was still damp, he could fire the vessel in such a way as to give two tones, he could apply a shiny slip or burnish his ware, or he could paint the surface. Thus we have a great variety of wares, decorated with a great variety of motifs. A bowl may show a primitively blocked-out painting of a hunter with his hounds on leash, while a jug may depict an adorned boat plying the waters of the Nile. This repertoire of paintings on pottery offers a great deal of our information on the culture of predynastic Egypt. It certainly affords plenty of speculation for the prehistorian. Are the connections of this "Cross Lined" ware with Africa to the south and the Sahara to the west? Does this "Decorated" ware derive from the northern part of Egypt? Just how are these "Wavy Handled" pots related to Palestine? Such questions illustrate again the variety of contacts possible in a relatively primitive culture. It is easy to say that Egypt's early development was essentially internal, without important outside inffuence, but it is also clear that there were outside contacts which must have been mutually refreshing to both parties.

The pots which show pictures of boats are especially important as indicating a river commerce from one end of Egypt to the other. The boats carry simple ensigns which probably give the place of origin, that is, the home port. In so far as we can identify these ensigns, they show that there was river commerce along the entire course of the Nile from the Mediterranean to the First Cataract, at a time long before Egypt was a unified nation.[7] Under relatively primitive conditions, with local rule only, the river merchants of Egypt were able to move about freely with their wares. Nor was trading contact restricted to the Nile Valley alone. The presence in predynastic Egyptian graves of foreign materials, such as lapis lazuli, obsidian, ivory, and olive oil, shows that there was a range of commerce extending ultimately to lands as distant as Persia. This does not imply caravans of Egyptians ranging hundreds of miles away from Egypt or merchants from Iran bringing their wares to the Nile Valley, nor does it mean commercial ships plying the Mediterranean several centuries before history. It is more likely that distant wares were passed from one area to another by immediate, rather than long-range, contact. Nevertheless, the closed tube of the Nile Valley was not hermetically sealed against all contact, and outside influences would have some slow cumulative pressure as time went on.

It is difficult to talk about the religion of predynastic Egypt because the evidence is

[6] Of middle predynastic times (E. R. Ayrton and W. L. S. Loat, *Pre-dynastic Cemetery at El Mahasna* [*EES,* Vol. XXXI (1911)], p. 30, Pl. XVII).

[7] P. E. Newberry in *Annals of Archaeology and Anthropology,* V (Liverpool, 1912–13), 132 ff.; in *Ancient Egypt* (1914), pp. 5 ff.

so slight and because the modern concept of religion fits the ancient scene so imperfectly. With ancient man, religion permeated every part of life and yet was hardly formalized into a theological system. Predynastic Egypt has left us no writings, so that we must make our guesses from the few material remains and on the supposition that the later theological system had had its prehistoric beginnings. This is insecure ground for speculation. The Egyptian graves have provided art objects which are undoubtedly connected with a belief in unseen and powerful forces. This is particularly true of figurines of humans, animals, and standardized symbols. Arguing from the analogy of primitive peoples known to the anthropologist today, one assumes that religion held three strong forces: protection from known and unknown perils, success in the enterprise of food-gathering or food-producing, and the enlargement and continuance of one's own people. The Egyptians were agricultural and must have invoked the forces promoting growth of their crops and enlargement of their herds. They must have given consideration to the force of reproduction of their own kind. And they must have offered fearful propitiation to the vast perils of a great world. These attitudes toward mysteries which were partly within their control but were largely controlled by the unknowable whims of nature would make up the beginnings of their religion. We can see a few of their attitudes in the figurines of females or of animals having to do with reproduction. But other figurines or amulets are less meaningful and may have been forces which would protect them from the many perils of existence. Their religion was as simple in essential elements and as complicated in daily and hourly forms as are the observances of most primitive peoples.

We cannot know what political struggles went on in predynastic Egypt. Beyond doubt, there was a reaching-out for power on the part of small units, and the process of conquest and assimilation built up constantly larger units. In theory there would be an evolutionary process, with the village-state growing into a district-state and the district-state growing into a large province; ultimately, at the beginning of history, a full nation would have come into being. We do not know that this expansive process moved according to such a theory. Certainly, there was a governmental change when men settled down to agriculture, won some surplus, and engaged in a struggle for larger territory. The tribal unit of most primitive times, a unit related by blood or immediate intimacy, certainly gave way to a wider governmental unit, in which people were not necessarily related by blood, did not necessarily know one another, but had sufficient economic and social interests in common that they were willing to act under one ruler. However, it is possible that the unit of rule was still relatively small only a few centuries before dynastic times and that the large provincial state came into being rather suddenly and only in the latest predynastic period.

This question about the size of the governmental and social and economic unit is linked with another problem which is equally a matter of speculation: When did large-scale irrigation works come into Egypt? It has been suggested that the first settlers in the Nile Valley lived on the edge of a thick jungle swamp and cultivated such pockets of land as were readily available. Such a location and such a life would provide small and unrelated communities, confined in size by limited food. The initial draining of the swamps would be the prerequisite to the gaining of greater agricultural territory, and this process of cutting away and draining the jungle may well have been a constant one. There is, however, a second step which was the essential for the winning of the fullest possible agricultural territory, and that was the bringing of major irrigation works to the land—large catch basins or canals which cut across miles of land and brought the Nile waters to the edge of the desert hills. The draining of the swamps won fertile soil for agriculture, but that soil could be kept fertile and extended in area only by large-scale irrigation. Large-scale irrigation demands planning and agency by a strong governmental organization, and, when once undertaken, it maintains and fosters that strong governmental unit.

The question is then: At what stage in the long centuries of predynastic process did the Egyptian attain such a degree of widespread co-operation, such an ability to plan ahead and carry out his plans, and such an ambition for more power, land, and food that he was able to undertake large irrigation projects? The answer to that question must be personal and subjective because we have no data to permit more than speculation. We can see man's abilities through his artifacts—pots and stone vessels, stone and copper implements, amulets and ornaments, houses and clothing—and we still do not have the answer. How intelligent was he, in our critical terms? The former assumption that the ancient Egyptian invented a 365-day calendar several centuries before dynastic times has been shown to be untenable. That calendar was initiated after the dynasties had begun. To be sure, such a calendar had to be based on a long period of observation, on recording by some kind of notation, and on the ability to work out the records into a consistent system. But if this 365-day calendar was initiated sometime in the first three dynasties, the preceding period of observations and records need not have extended very far into the late predynastic period. The invention of the calendar cannot be used for the argument that the Egyptian of the middle predynastic period had extraordinary intellectual powers.[8]

What can we say about his abilities, beyond the observed facts of skill in local arts and crafts and the acceptance of a widespread commerce? He had a number of simple skills, which involved logical process and experimentation along new lines. As a biologist, he was able to bring into being new species of plants and animals. As a chemist, he could make bread, brew beer, and mix paints or clays. As a geologist, he sought out the stones for knives and jars, mineral compounds for cosmetics, gold, and copper. As a physicist, he could work exquisite flint knives, drill small beads, glaze stone or pottery surfaces, and smelt and cast copper. As a mathematician, he could lay out fields and construct huts. At some time in his prehistoric career he had advanced to the stage of using machines, that is, instruments which combined more than one principle of force. A drill for hollowing out stone vessels is a machine in this sense, for it combines the cutting point, the downward pressure, and a rocking or rotary motion, all for a single purpose. This drill must have come in quite early in the predynastic period, if we may judge from the magnificent stone vessels. On the other hand, the potter's wheel apparently did not enter Egypt until historic times. We do not know when such machines as the plow and the standing loom appeared in Egypt. It is possible that the plow was a late predynastic development, depending upon that other unsettled problem of the time when large-scale irrigation and agriculture began.

At any rate, it is correct to say that our Egyptian primitive had latent abilities and a willingness to experiment along modest lines. If he must be called a "barbarian" because he was not yet literate and civilized, he was not a doltish savage; he was an earthbound peasant of limited range and imagination, but his gaze was sometimes raised above the mud, and vaguely he pressed toward the enrichment of his life. Even so, we do not have enough data to decide at what point he took the two major steps of extensive irrigation works and government of a far-reaching and impersonal nature. The dynasties begin with a union of the parts of Egypt into a single nation. At about the same time we

[8] O. Neugebauer in *Acta orientalia,* XVII (Copenhagen, 1938), 169 ff.; A. Scharff in *Historische Zeitschrift,* CLXI (Munich and Berlin, 1940), 3 ff.

have pictorial evidence that the king of Egypt was interested in irrigation and would take ceremonial part in the opening of a new canal.[9] It is a personal judgment that large governmental units and large irrigation projects were relatively new at the time and that the slow processes of building ever larger communities and of clearing the jungle had gone on very deliberately for a long time and then had a final spurt of energy, a spurt which flung man into history itself.

As we have pointed out above, the wall reliefs of historical times show a clear vestige of jungle conditions, suggesting that the complete clearing of the swamps had not yet been effected. Further, it is possible to argue that irrigation works on a grand scale were a concomitant of an important social revolution: some pressure of population demanded more land; more land was won by irrigation; increased crops permitted a much greater population; and greater population produced profound political, economic, and social changes in life. This is the kind of revolution which starts very slowly, finally picks up momentum, and then accelerates rapidly. It cannot be proved or disproved at present, but it is possible that the important changes in agriculture through irrigation were an immediate forerunner of historic times and, in fact, produced the historic times. This does not mean that the digging of large canals produced history; the process was far more complex than that. It does mean that man reached a certain stage of maturity or of internal pressure when he was moved to undertake such a co-operative activity and that his maturity, interacting with the products of irrigation, won for him a new kind of life.

What was that new kind of life? In attempting to answer that question, one must consider certain concepts suggested by certain scholars. Toynbee has laid down the principle of "Challenge and Response" for the evocation of ancient Egyptian society.[10] For him, the first challenge was a physical one: the clearing of the river jungle along the Nile, the taming of the fertile black soil, and the extension and control of the river floodwaters. Through such a response of activity, a uniform culture was constructed, and the energies of the responders continued unabated into historic times, with the great achievements of the Pyramid Age.

Beyond doubt, there is an important principle here. Nevertheless, it would still seem to leave a number of unanswered questions. Why did the prehistoric people of Egypt respond to the challenge, whereas their southern neighbors in the Sudan did not respond? Did the prehistoric Egyptians ignore the challenge of a fertile soil blanketed by jungle marshes for a long period of time; and, when they finally responded positively to the challenge, what new factors made them respond? Obviously, we are dealing with a spiritual agent which can be seen and described after the fact but which cannot be predicted before the fact. It would seem that an environment might offer opportunities which could be ignored until some catalytic force precipitated the energies of a people in a useful way. What could such a catalyst

[9] J. E. Quibell, *Hierakonpolis,* I ("Egyptian Research Account," Vol. IV [London, 1900]), Pl. XXVI, *c;* Schäfer and Andrae, *op. cit.,* p. 188.

[10] Arnold J. Toynbee, *A Study of History,* I (Oxford University Press, 1935), 302–15; or one-volume abridgment (Oxford Press, 1947), pp. 68–73. In subsequent chapters it may be noted that we have not found some of Toynbee's concepts or principles sufficiently applicable to ancient Egypt to warrant detailed discussion. For example, we have difficulty in accepting the sequence of "time of troubles" (First Intermediate Period), "universal state" (Middle Kingdom), "interregnum" (Hyksos invasion), and "universal state" reasserted (Empire); for us, the effectively disturbing troubles which wrecked Egyptian culture grew out of the Empire and the attempt to maintain it. Even less valid seems the concept of the worship of Osiris as a kind of "universal church created by an internal proletariat"; the Osirian religion was mortuary and could not be the genesis of a "new society," and it was originally created by and for Toynbee's "dominant minority." These criticisms do scant justice to Toynbee's enormously refreshing influence in assailing formerly fixed ideas. The thinking of this book owes much to him, even though his societal pattern for Egypt is rejected.

be—the product of gradual economic change, the product of gradually increasing population, a stimulus from abroad, or a gradual spiritual maturing? Perhaps there was no one catalyst but rather a combination of some of these suggested forces. If so, the slow change of past ages would become a rapid change of late predynastic into dynastic times.

Another concept which should be considered at this point is Childe's "urban revolution."[11] This view would see the beginning of history as marked by a basic social change, in which the undifferentiated agricultural society came to cluster around villages which were agricultural, political, and economic centers. In a very general sense every man in the preceding society had been his own self-sufficient master, producing his own food and clothing; making his own tools, weapons, and containers; building his own hut; and trading his own goods directly. With Childe's urban revolution, there came specialization of function. Instead of the farmer's undertaking a whole series of domestic avocations, certain men embraced the professions of weapon-maker, potter, weaver, builder, sailor, merchant, etc. This theory would see agricultural improvement as producing both a surplus of wealth and a surplus of population. The surplus of wealth created a ruling class with leisure time and an interest in the arts, and the surplus of population provided the specialists who would serve each need of the crafts and arts as a main vocation. Further, the larger communities were based on interdependent, but impersonal, interests instead of a single common interest of a personally related group. Thus there was a need for new sanctions to control such impersonally organized communities, so that there was a growth of governmental organization, of impersonal law, and of the constraints of a national religion. Thus Childe's urban revolution called into being an elaborated state, with a civil and ecclesiastical bureaucracy and a police force to elicit conformance to the ritual of religion and law. Ultimately, the professionalization of the government and of commerce would produce a final by-product of the urban revolution, since the necessity for keeping administrative and business records demanded writing.

The urban revolution contained two apparently conflicting currents. On the one hand, the individual had become a specialist in some vocation, and higher talents were called forth from him as a specialist. On the other hand, as society moved away from the smaller community, which had been intimate and related, and became a large state, with the awful impersonality of formalized law and religious dogma, there was a depersonalization of the individual, who became, as it were, a mere statistic of the state. That conflict between individual and group was present at the beginning of history, just as it is today.

What can one say about this theory of the urban revolution? Obviously, as a theory it has much that is acute and just. Yet it is too absolute. It has two essentials: markedly increased population, tending toward an urban economy, and specialization of function. The term "urban," however, implies too much; it seems to say that agriculture ceased to be basic and that commerce replaced agriculture in importance. Actually, agriculture did not lose its essential importance, and one may doubt whether any community in earliest Egypt deserved the term "city." They were all agricultural villages of greater or less degree. Probably one would have to come far down into history —possibly down to the Eighteenth Egyptian Dynasty—before one could be sure of a city in the modern sense. Further, specialization of profession had surely been present in the earlier economy, even though in a lesser degree. The small tribal community must have had its farmer who was more skilful than any other in making weapons, its farmer

[11] V. Gordon Childe, *Man Makes Himself* (London, 1936), pp. 157–201, and *What Happened in History* (Penguin Books, 1946), pp. 106–17.

whose hand turned more readily to painting, and its farmer who was a priest and medicine man. The differences between the earlier agricultural period and the historical period are not differences of kind but differences of degree. Thus one may accept a truth in Childe's "urban revolution," provided that it is understood that it was not "urban" and was not a "revolution." There was a change in the direction of greater concentration of population in centers, there was a change toward greater professionalism, there was an increase in wealth, and there was an elaboration of administrative machinery to control the new elements.

Let us consider one more concept, Redfield's "folk society." [12] This is an abstraction, constructed for the purpose of understanding modern urban society in contrast to a simpler and more primitive society. This ideal folk society is homogeneous, small, and has a strong sense of community. It is nonliterate, and its economy is one of self-sufficiency rather than of buying and selling. In general, the ties of family provide the community. The society is deeply rooted in religious belief and custom, and relations are personal, so that the secular and impersonal have not yet come into being. The behavior of such a society is strongly traditional, so that there is no encouragement to speculation or to experimentation, since sanctified tradition has provided all the answers. Such a folk society could exist as a pure culture only if the conditions of its maintenance and security from disturbance were assured.

Over against the abstraction of the folk society is placed the concept of its opposite —modern urban society, large, amorphous, heterogeneous, and lacking a sense of community. Urban society is secular, highly impersonal in relationships, and very complicated in its interdependence of commercial transactions. Family and tradition are of little importance. The society is, of course, literate and, at its ideal best, speculative, experimental, and fluid.

How did ancient Egypt at its crucial point between prehistory and history fit into the concept of the folk society or of the urban society? Clearly, it was in a transitional stage between the two. In its entire historical course ancient Egypt never reached the full urban stage. It was always strongly agricultural. Although increasingly secularized, it always had a strongly controlling element of the sacred. In few other cultures was the force of tradition so binding, and after its first historical spurt of energies it dropped any dangerous tendencies toward speculation or experimentation. Despite its practices of a semisecular government, of an intricate interdependence of economics, of literacy, and of the union of two disparate sections of Egypt under a single rule, ancient Egypt was always at heart a sacred society, clinging passionately to hallowed tradition.

Even in the predynastic period, however, it seems clear that Egypt was not a pure folk society. It was relatively fluid and was willing to try out new methods of plant or animal breeding, of architecture, or of art. In fact, there may have been less hostility to change in the prehistoric than there was in historic times, when a codified and enforced dogma began to set its disapproval upon deviations from the traditional. Further, predynastic Egypt saw an increasing amount of commerce and thus an increasing interweaving of persons and communities which were not related by blood. Basically, the economy of any one unit was that of self-sufficiency, but the role of the market was already strong, and the essential element of the folk culture—a strong sense of group solidarity as over against outsiders—had already weakened. Whether in the predynastic or the dynastic period, ancient Egypt was transitional between the folk society and urban society, and no sharp break appeared at the beginning of history.

Thus the three concepts of challenge and

[12] Robert Redfield, "The Folk Society," *American Journal of Sociology,* LII (1947), 293–308.

response, the urban revolution, and the folk society are useful and instructive about that important transition between prehistoric "barbarism" and historic "civilization," but none of them provides a full and satisfying explanation of the phenomenon of such a transition within a comparatively brief time. No one can give that satisfying explanation, first, because our information is too slight on the times and, second, because there were certain spiritual imponderables at which we can only guess. It would provide a certain satisfaction if we could lay down a series of observations on economic, social, and political changes, add them up, and achieve a result which was clearly determinant: here were the forces which brought man into civilization, which gave him a maturity of mind and outlook, which produced national governments, which called forth writing, which gave the rudiments of science, and which produced a sophisticated world outlook, art, and literature. Perhaps we simply do not know enough to list such visible determinants of historical change, but we suspect that we shall never know enough because the essential motivating forces will always be invisible, the outreaching of man's mind and spirit. Those spiritual and intellectual impulses would never be recorded because they lie too deep in the human heart and mind; early man was quite unconscious of them.

The phenomenal determinants of economics, environment, diet, and governmental and social organization seem to produce different results in different places. The civilization which emerged in Egypt was different from that which emerged in Mesopotamia, or the Indus Valley, or China, or Yucatan. The physical cultures of these different areas were distinct, and their spiritual settings were markedly varied. Further, there were some barbarisms—as in the Sudan—which were given a whole series of favorable determinants and still did not emerge into civilized life. It is possible to argue that each case is extraordinarily complex and that the series of phenomenal determinants is different in each case, so that—if we could know enough—we could explain the differences in each civilization or each barbarism on the basis of a highly complicated mathematical equation. But we suspect that every equation would contain an unknown value, the *x* of the mind and spirit of man. The totality of our visible observations would still leave us short of a historical or sociological answer to the phenomenon of the emergence of a culture into civilization.

THREE

GREEK RELIGION AND PHILOSOPHY

Like other early peoples, the ancient Greeks developed polytheism to explain both nature and human life. Readers of Homer are familiar with the charming Greek pantheon of male and female deities, each with fallible human characteristics. But at a somewhat later stage in Greek civilization, noticeably from the sixth century B.C. *onward, Greek thinkers became increasingly dissatisfied with traditional polytheism as an explanation of reality and as a guide to conduct. Scientists and philosophers created new explanations and guides in rational, as opposed to fanciful, terms. In a series of clear and sympathetic essays, the eminent classical scholar G. Lowes Dickinson has traced the Greek transition from polytheism to philosophy. His work underscores the central Greek tendency, still a mainspring in Western civilization, to trust reason in humanity's continuing search for truth and the good life.*

G. LOWES DICKINSON

THE GREEK VIEW OF LIFE*

In approaching the subject of the religion of the Greeks it is necessary to dismiss at the outset many of the associations which we are naturally inclined to connect with that word. What we commonly have in our mind when we speak of religion is a definite set of doctrines, of a more or less metaphysical character, formulated in a creed and supported by an organization distinct from the state. And the first thing we have to learn about the religion of the Greeks is that it included nothing of the kind. There was no church, there was no creed, there were no articles. Priests there were, but they were merely public officials, appointed to perform certain religious rites. The distinction between cleric and layman, as we know it, did not exist; the distinction between poetry and dogma did not exist; and whatever the religion of the Greeks may have been, one thing at any rate is clear, that it was something very different from all that we are in the habit of associating with the word.

What, then, was it? It is easy to reply that it was the worship of those gods—of Zeus, Apollo, Athene, and the rest—with whose names and histories everyone is familiar. But the difficulty is to realize what was implied in the worship of these gods; to understand that the mythology which we regard merely as a collection of fables was to the Greeks actually true; or at least that to nine Greeks out of ten it would never occur that it might

* Reprinted from *Man the Maker,* pp. 39–51, 1–60 *passim,* by G. Lowes Dickinson, Methuen & Co. Ltd., London, 1896.

be false, might be, as we say, mere stories. So that though no doubt the histories of the gods were in part the inventions of the poets, yet the poets would conceive themselves to be merely putting into form what they and everyone believed to be essentially true.

But such a belief implies a fundamental distinction between the conception, or rather, perhaps, the feeling of the Greeks about the world, and our own. And it is this feeling that we want to understand when we ask ourselves the question, what did a belief in the gods really mean to the ancient Greeks? To answer it fully and satisfactorily is perhaps impossible. But some attempt must be made; and it may help us in our quest if we endeavour to imagine the kind of questionings and doubts which the conception of the gods would set at rest.

When we try to conceive the state of mind of primitive man, the first thing that occurs to us is the bewilderment and terror he must have felt in the presence of the powers of nature. Naked, houseless, weaponless, he is at the mercy, every hour, of this immense and incalculable Something so alien and so hostile to himself. As fire it burns, as water it drowns, as tempest it harries and destroys; benignant it may be at times, in warm sunshine and calm, but the kindness is brief and treacherous. Anyhow, whatever its mood, it has to be met and dealt with. By its help, or, if not, in the teeth of its resistance, every step in advance must be won; every hour, every minute, it is there to be reckoned with. What is it then, this persistent, obscure, unnameable Thing? What is it? The question haunts the mind; it will not be put aside; and the Greek at last, like other men under similar conditions, only with a lucidity and precision peculiar to himself, makes the reply, "It is something like myself." Every power of nature he presumes to be a spiritual being, impersonating the sky as Zeus, the earth as Demeter, the sea as Poseidon; from generation to generation, under his shaping hands, the figures multiply and define themselves; character and story crystallize about what at first were little more than names; till at last, from the womb of the dark enigma that haunted him in the beginning, there emerges into the charmed light of a world of ideal grace a pantheon of fair and concrete personalities. Nature has become a company of spirits; every cave and fountain is haunted by a nymph; in the ocean dwell the Nereids, in the mountain the Oread, the Dryad in the wood; and everywhere, in groves and marshes, on the pastures or the rocky heights, floating in the current of the streams or traversing untrodden snows, in the day at the chase and as evening closes in solitude fingering his flute, seen and heard by shepherds, alone or with his dancing train, is to be met the horned and goat-footed, the sunny-smiling Pan.

Thus conceived, the world has become less terrible because more familiar. All that was incomprehensible, all that was obscure and dark, has now been seized and bodied forth in form, so that everywhere man is confronted no longer with blind and unintelligible force, but with spiritual beings moved by like passions with himself. The gods, it is true, were capricious and often hostile to his good, but at least they had a nature akin to his; if they were angry, they might be propitiated; if they were jealous, they might be appeased; the enmity of one might be compensated by the friendship of another; dealings with them, after all, were not so unlike dealings with men, and at the worst there was always a chance for courage, patience and wit.

Man, in short, by his religion has been made at home in the world; and that is the first point to seize upon. . . .

And as with the external world, so with the world within. The powers of nature were not the only ones felt by man to be different from and alien to himself; there were others, equally strange, dwelling in his own heart, which, though in a sense they were part of him, yet he felt to be not himself, which came upon him and possessed him without his choice and against his will. With these, too, he felt the need to make himself at home, and these, too, to satisfy his need, he shaped into creatures like himself. To the whole range of his inner experience he gave definition and life, presenting it to himself in a series of spiritual forms. In Aphrodite, mother of Eros, he incarnated the passion of love, placing in her broidered girdle "love and desire of loving converse that steals the wits even of the wise"; in Ares he embodied the lust of war; in Athene, wisdom; in Apollo, music and the arts. The pangs of guilt took shape in the conception of avenging Furies; and the very prayers of the worshipper sped from him in human form, wrinkled and blear-eyed, with halting pace, in the rear of punishment. Thus the very self of man he set outside himself; the powers, so intimate, and yet so strange, that swayed him from within he made familiar by making them distinct; converted their shapeless terror into the beauty of visible form; and by merely presenting them thus to himself in a guise that was immediately understood, set aside, if he could not answer, the haunting question of their origin and end.

Here then is at least a partial reply to our question as to the effect of a belief in the gods on the feeling of the Greek. To repeat the phrase once more, it made him at home in the world. The mysterious powers that controlled him it converted into beings like himself; and so gave him heart and breathing space, shut in, as it were, from the abyss by this shining host of fair and familiar forms, to turn to the interests and claims of the passing hour an attention undistracted by doubt and fear.

But this relation to the world of nature is only one side of man's life; more prominent and more important, at a later stage of his development, is his relation to society; and here too in Greek civilization a great part was played by religion. For the Greek gods, we must remember, were not purely spiritual powers, to be known and approached only in the heart by prayer. They were beings in human form, like, though superior to ourselves, who passed a great part of their history on earth, intervened in the affairs of men, furthered or thwarted their undertakings, had begotten among them sons and daughters, and followed, from generation to generation, the fortunes of their children's children. Between them and mankind there was no impassable gulf; from Heracles the son of Zeus was descended the Dorian race; the Ionians from Ion, son of Apollo; every family, every tribe traced back its origin to a "hero," and these "heroes" were children of the gods, and deities themselves. Thus were the gods, in the most literal sense, the founders of society; from them was derived, even physically, the unit of the family and the race; and the whole social structure raised upon that natural basis was necessarily penetrated through and through by the spirit of religion.

We must not therefore be misled by the fact that there was no church in the Greek state to the idea that the state recognized no religion; on the contrary, religion was so essential to the state, so bound up with its whole structure, in general and in detail, that the very conception of a separation between the powers was impossible. If there was no separate church, in our sense of the term, as an independent organism within the state, it was because the state, in one of its aspects, was itself a church, and derived its sanction, both as a whole and in its parts, from the same gods who controlled the physical world. Not only the community as a whole but all its separate minor organs were under the protection of patron deities. The family centred in the hearth, where the father, in his capacity of priest, offered sacrifice and prayer to the ancestors of the house; the various corporations into which families were grouped, the local divisions for the purpose of taxation, elections, and the like, derived a spiritual unity from the worship of a common god; and finally the all-embracing totality of the state itself was explained and justified to all its members by the cult of the special protecting deity to whom its origin and prosperous continuance were due. The sailor who saw, on turning the point of Sunium, the tip of the spear of Athene glittering on the Acropolis, beheld in a type the spiritual form of the state; Athene and Athens were but two aspects of the same thing; and the statue of the goddess of wisdom dominating the city of the arts may serve to sum up for us the ideal of that marvellous corporate life where there was no ecclesiastical religion only because there was no secular state.

Regarded from this point of view, we may say that the religion of the Greeks was the inner aspect of their political life. And we must add that in one respect their religion pointed the way to a higher political achievement than they were ever able to realize in fact. One fatal defect of the Greek civilization, as is familiar to students of their history, was the failure of the various independent city states to coalesce into a single harmonious whole. But the tendency of religion was to obviate this defect. We find, for example, that at one time or another federations of states were formed to support in common the cult of some god; and one cult in particular there was—that of the Delphian Apollo—whose influence on political no less than on religious life was felt as far as and even beyond the limits of the Greek race. No colony could be founded, no war hazarded, no peace confirmed, without the advice and approval of the god—whose cult was thus at once a religious centre for the whole of Greece, and a forecast of a political unity that should co-ordinate into a whole her chaos of conflicting states.

The religion of the Greeks being thus, as we have seen, the bond of their political life, we find its sanction extended at every point to custom and law. The persons of heralds, for example, were held to be under divine protection; treaties between states and contracts between individuals were confirmed by oath; the vengeance of the gods was invoked upon infringers of the law; national assemblies and military expeditions were inaugurated by public prayers; the whole of corporate life, in short, social and political, was so embraced and bathed in an idealizing element of ritual that the secular and religious aspects of the state must have been as inseparable to a Greek in idea as we know them to have been in constitution. . . .

And now let us turn to a point for which perhaps some readers have long been waiting, and with which they may have expected us to begin rather than to end. So far, in considering the part played by religion in Greek life, we have assumed the position of orthodoxy. We have endeavoured to place ourselves at the standpoint of the man who did not criticize or reflect, but accepted simply, as a matter of course, the tradition handed down to him by his fathers. Only so, if at all, was it possible for us to detach ourselves from our habitual preconceptions, and to regard the pagan mythology not as a graceful invention of the poets, but as a serious and, at the time, a natural and inevitable way of looking at the world. Now, however, it is time to turn to the other side, and to consider the Greek religion as it appeared to contemporary critics. For critics there were, and sceptics, or rather, to put it more exactly, there was a critical age succeeding an age of faith. As we trace, however imperfectly, the development of the Greek mind, we can observe their intellect and their moral sense expanding beyond the limits of their creed. Either as sympathetic, though candid, friends, or as avowed enemies, they bring to light its contradictions and defects; and as a result of the process one of two things happens. Either the ancient conception of the gods is transformed in the direction of monotheism, or it is altogether swept away, and a new system of the world built up, on the basis of natural science or of philosophy. These tendencies of thought we must now endeavour to trace; for we should have formed but an imperfect idea of the scope of the religious consciousness of the Greeks if we confined ourselves to what we may call their orthodox faith. It is in their most critical thinkers, in Euripides and Plato, that the religious sense is most fully and keenly developed; and it is in the philosophy that supervened upon the popular creed, rather than in the popular creed itself, that we shall find the highest and most spiritual reaches of their thought. . . .

The attitude of Euripides towards the popular religion is so clearly and frankly critical that a recent writer has even gone so far as to maintain that his main object in the construction of his dramas was to discredit the myths he selected for his theme. However that may have been, it is beyond controversy true that the deep religious sense of this most modern of the Greeks was puzzled and repelled by the tales he was bound by tradition to dramatize; and that he put into the mouth of his characters reflexions upon the conduct of the gods which if they may not be taken as his own deliberate opinions, are at least expressions of one aspect of his thought. It was, in fact, impossible to reconcile with a profound and philosophic view of the divine nature the intrigues and amours, partialities, antipathies, actions and counter-actions of these anthropomorphic deities. Consider, for example, the most famous of all the myths, that of Orestes. . . . the son of Agamemnon and Clytemnestra. Agamemnon, on his return from Troy, was murdered by Clytemnestra. Orestes escapes; but returns later, at the instigation of Apollo, and kills his mother to avenge his father. Thereupon, in punishment for his crime, he is persecuted by the Furies. Now the point which Euripides seizes here is the conduct of Apollo. Either it was right for Orestes to kill his mother, or it was wrong. If wrong, why did Apollo command it? If right, why was Orestes punished? Or are there, as Æschylus would have it, two "rights," one of Apollo, the other of the Furies? If so, what becomes of that unity of the divine law after which every religious nature seeks? The dilemma is patent; and Euripides makes no serious attempt to meet it. . . .

The myths, but not religion! The criticism certainly of Plato and probably of Euripides was prompted by the desire not to discredit altogether the belief in the gods, but to bring it into harmony with the requirements of a more fully developed consciousness. The philosopher and the poet came not to destroy, but to fulfil; not to annihilate, but to transform the popular theology. Such an intention, strange as it may appear to us with our rigid creeds, we shall see to be natural enough to the Greek mind, when we remember that the material of their religion was not a set of propositions, but a more or less indeterminate body of traditions capable of being presented in the most various forms as the genius and taste of individual poets might direct. And we find, in fact, that the most religious poets of Greece, those even who were most innocent of any intention to innovate on popular beliefs, did nevertheless unconsciously tend to transform, in accordance with their own conceptions, the whole structure of the Homeric theology. Taking over the legends of gods and heroes, as narrated in poetry and tradition, Æschylus and Sophocles, as they shaped and reshaped their material for the stage, were evolving for themselves, not in opposition to but as it were on the top of the polytheistic view, the idea of a single supreme and righteous God. The Zeus of Homer, whose superiority, as we saw, was based on physical force, grows, under the hands of Æschylus, into something akin to the Jewish Jehovah. The inner experience of the poet drives him inevitably to this transformation. Born into the great age of Greece, coming to maturity at the crisis of her fate, he had witnessed with his own eyes, and assisted with his own hands the defeat of the Persian host at Marathon. The event struck home to him like a judgment from heaven. The Nemesis that attends upon human pride, the vengeance that follows crime, henceforth were the thoughts that haunted and possessed his brain; and under their influence he evolved for himself out of the popular idea of Zeus the conception of a God of justice who marks and avenges crime. . . .

While thus, on the one hand, the Greek religion by its inner evolution was tending to destroy itself, on the other hand it was threatened from without by the attack of what we should call the "scientific spirit." A system so frankly anthropomorphic was bound to be weak on the speculative side. Its appeal, as we have seen, was rather to the imagination than to the intellect, by the presentation of a series of beautiful images, whose contemplation might offer to the mind if not satisfaction, at least acquiescence and repose. A Greek who was not too inquisitive was thus enabled to move through the calendar of splendid festivals and fasts, charmed by the beauty of the ritual, inspired by the chorus and the dance, and drawing from the familiar legends the moral and æsthetic significance with which he had been accustomed from his boyhood to connect them, but without ever raising the question, Is all this true? Does it really account for the existence and nature of the world? Once, however, the spell was broken, once the intellect was aroused, the inadequacy of the popular faith, on the speculative side, became apparent; and the mind turned aside altogether from religion to work out its problems on its own lines. We find accordingly, from early times, physical philosophers in Greece free from all theological preconceptions, raising from the very beginning the question of the origin of the world, and offering solutions, various indeed but all alike in this, that they frankly accept a materialistic basis. One derives all things from water, another from air, another from fire; one insists upon unity, another on a plurality of elements, but all alike reject the supernatural, and proceed on the lines of physical causation. . . .

The argument is an old one into whose merits this is not the place to enter. But one thing is certain, that the sceptical spirit which was invading religion, was invading also politics and ethics; and that towards the close of the fifth century before Christ, Greece and in particular Athens was overrun by philosophers, who not only did not scruple to question the foundations of social and moral obligation, but in some cases explicitly taught that there were no foundations at all; that all law was a convention based on no objective truth; and that the only valid right was the natural right of the strong to rule. It was into this chaos of sceptical opinion that Plato was born; and it was the desire to meet and subdue it that was the motive of his philosophy. Like Aristophanes, he traced the root of the evil to the decay of religious belief; and though no one, as we have seen, was more trenchant than he in his criticism of the popular faith, no one, on the other hand, was more convinced of the necessity of some form of religion as a basis for any stable polity. The doctrine of the physicists, he asserts, that the world is the result of "nature and chance" has immediate and disastrous effects on the whole structure of social beliefs. The conclusion inevitably follows that human laws and institutions, like everything else, are accidental products; that they have no objective validity, no binding force on the will, and that the only right that has any intelligible meaning is the right which is identical with might. Against these conclusions the whole soul of Plato rose in revolt. To reconstruct religion, he was driven back upon metaphysics; and elaborated at last the system which from his day to our own has not ceased to perplex and fascinate the world, and whose rare and radiant combination of gifts, speculative, artistic, and religious, marks the highest reach of the genius of the Greeks, and perhaps of mankind.

FOUR

THE DEATH OF SOCRATES

Socrates (469–399 B.C.*) was one of the most stimulating and influential philosophers of ancient Greece. His method of inquiry was dialectic, a search for knowledge through logical discourse in the form of cross examination. By professing to know nothing, Socrates cast doubt on many traditional attitudes and beliefs. His teachings provoked intense hostility from conservatives. As one reflection of this hostility, Aristophanes satirized him in the* Clouds. *Finally, in a time of turmoil following the ruinous Peloponnesian War, Socrates was brought to trial on the charge of demoralizing the youth of Athens and was condemned to death. Though he could have saved himself by going into exile he refused to do so on the ground that such action would be contrary to reason. Instead he calmly drank the cup of poisonous hemlock and thus became an early martyr to the cause of freedom of thought and speech. His teachings and martyrdom had a profound effect on Plato, his great pupil. In the* Phaedo *Plato describes the last hours and death of Socrates in a passage justly considered to be a masterpiece of world literature. The passage further reveals the reverence for reason which is one of the greatest contributions of ancient Greece to civilization.*

DIALOGUES OF PLATO*

I am convinced, Socrates, said Cebes, and have nothing more to object; but if my friend Simmias, or any one else, has any further objection to make, he had better speak out, and not keep silence, since I do not know to what other season he can defer the discussion, if there is anything which he wants to say or to have said.

But I have nothing more to say, replied Simmias; nor can I see any reason for doubt after what has been said. But I still feel and cannot help feeling uncertain in my own mind, when I think of the greatness of the subject and the feebleness of man.

Yes, Simmias, replied Socrates, that is well said: and I may add that first principles, even if they appear certain, should be carefully considered; and when they are satisfactorily ascertained, then, with a sort of hesitating confidence in human reason, you may, I think, follow the course of the argument; and if that be plain and clear, there will be no need for any further enquiry.

Very true.

But then, O my friends, he said, if the soul is really immortal, what care should be taken of her, not only in respect of the portion of

* From *Dialogues of Plato,* II, 255–266, translated by Benjamin Jowett, Oxford University Press, 1892.

time which is called life, but of eternity! And the danger of neglecting her from this point of view does indeed appear to be awful. If death had only been the end of all, the wicked would have had a good bargain in dying, for they would have been happily quit not only of their body, but of their own evil together with their souls. But now, inasmuch as the soul is manifestly immortal, there is no release or salvation from evil except the attainment of the highest virtue and wisdom. For the soul when on her progress to the world below takes nothing with her but nurture and education; and these are said greatly to benefit or greatly to injure the departed, at the very beginning of his journey thither.

For after death, as they say, the genius of each individual, to whom he belonged in life, leads him to a certain place in which the dead are gathered together, whence after judgment has been given they pass into the world below, following the guide, who is appointed to conduct them from this world to the other: and when they have there received their due and remained their time, another guide brings them back again after many revolutions of ages. Now this way to the other world is not, as Aeschylus says in the Telephus, a single and straight path—if that were so no guide would be needed, for no one could miss it; but there are many partings of the road, and windings, as I infer from the rites and sacrifices which are offered to the gods below in places where three ways meet on earth. The wise and orderly soul follows in the straight path and is conscious of her surroundings; but the soul which desires the body, and which, as I was relating before, has long been fluttering about the lifeless frame and the world of sight, is after many struggles and many sufferings hardly and with violence carried away by her attendant genius; and when she arrives at the place where the other souls are gathered, if she be impure and have done impure deeds, whether foul murders or other crimes which are the brothers of these, and the works of brothers in crime—from that soul every one flees and turns away; no one will be her companion, no one her guide, but alone she wanders in extremity of evil until certain times are fulfilled, and when they are fulfilled, she is borne irresistibly to her own fitting habitation; as every pure and just soul which has passed through life in the company and under the guidance of the gods has also her own proper home.

Now the earth has divers wonderful regions, and is indeed in nature and extent very unlike the notions of geographers, as I believe on the authority of one who shall be nameless.

What do you mean, Socrates? said Simmias. I have myself heard many descriptions of the earth, but I do not know, and I should very much like to know, in which of these you put faith.

And I, Simmias, replied Socrates, if I had the art of Glaucus would tell you; although I know not that the art of Glaucus could prove the truth of my tale, which I myself should never be able to prove, and even if I could, I fear, Simmias, that my life would come to an end before the argument was completed. I may describe to you, however, the form and regions of the earth according to my conception of them.

That, said Simmias, will be enough.

Well then, he said, my conviction is, that the earth is a round body in the centre of the heavens, and therefore has no need of air or of any similar force to be a support, but is kept there and hindered from falling or inclining any way by the equability of the surrounding heaven and by her own equipoise. For that which, being in equipoise, is in the centre of that which is equably diffused, will not incline any way in any degree, but will always remain in the same state and not deviate. And this is my first notion.

Which is surely a correct one, said Simmias.

Also I believe that the earth is very vast, and that we who dwell in the region extending from the river Phasis to the Pillars of Heracles inhabit a small portion only about the sea, like ants or frogs about a marsh, and that there are other inhabitants of many other like places; for everywhere on the face of the earth there are hollows of various forms and sizes, into which the water and the mist and the lower air collect. But the true earth is pure and situated in the pure heaven—there are the stars also; and it is the heaven which is commonly spoken of by us as the ether, and of which our own earth is the sediment gathering in the hollows beneath. But we who live in these hollows are deceived into the notion that we are dwelling above on the surface of the earth; which is just as if a creature who was at the bottom of the sea were to fancy that he was on the surface of the water, and that the sea was the heaven through which he saw the sun and the other stars, he having never come to the surface by reason of his feebleness and sluggishness, and having never lifted up his head and seen, nor ever heard from one who had seen, how much purer and fairer the world above is than his own. And such is exactly our case: for we are dwelling in a hollow of the earth, and fancy that we are on the surface; and the air we call the heaven, in which we imagine that the stars move. But the fact is, that owing to our feebleness and sluggishness we are prevented from reaching the surface of the air: for if any man could arrive at the exterior limit, or take the wings of a bird and come to the top, then like a fish who puts his head out of the water and sees this world, he would see a world beyond; and, if the nature of man could sustain the sight, he would acknowledge that this other world was the place of the true heaven and the true light and the true earth. For our earth, and the stones, and the entire region which surrounds us, are spoilt and corroded, as in the sea all things are corroded by the brine, neither is there any noble or perfect growth, but caverns only, and sand, and an endless slough of mud; and even the shore is not to be compared to the fairer sights of this world. And still less is this our world to be compared with the other. Of that upper earth which is under the heaven, I can tell you a charming tale, Simmias, which is well worth hearing.

And we, Socrates, replied Simmias, shall be charmed to listen to you.

The tale, my friend, he said, is as follows: —In the first place, the earth, when looked at from above, is in appearance streaked like one of those balls which have leather coverings in twelve pieces, and is decked with various colours, of which the colours used by painters on earth are in a manner samples. But there the whole earth is made up of them, and they are brighter far and clearer than ours; there is a purple of wonderful lustre, also the radiance of gold, and the white which is in the earth is whiter than any chalk or snow. Of these and other colours the earth is made up, and they are more in number and fairer than the eye of man has ever seen; the very hollows (of which I was speaking) filled with air and water have a colour of their own, and are seen like light gleaming amid the diversity of the other colours, so that the whole presents a single and continuous appearance of variety in unity. And in this fair region everything that grows—trees, and flowers, and fruits—are in a like degree fairer than any here; and there are hills, having stones in them in a like degree smoother, and more transparent, and fairer in colour than our highly-valued emeralds and sardonyxes and jaspers, and other gems, which are but minute fragments of them: for there all the stones are like our precious stones, and fairer still. The reason is, that they are pure, and not, like our precious stones, infected or corroded by the corrupt briny elements which coagulate among us, and which breed foulness and disease both in earth and stones, as well as in animals and plants. They are the jewels of the upper earth, which also shines with gold and silver and the like, and they are set in the light of day and are large and abundant and in all places, making the earth a sight to gladden the beholder's eye. And there are animals and men, some in a middle region, others dwelling about the air as we dwell about the sea; others in islands which the air flows round, near the continent; and in a word, the air is used by them as the water and the sea are by us, and the ether is to them what the air is to us. Moreover, the temperament of their seasons is such that they have no disease, and live much longer than we do, and have sight and hearing and smell, and all the other senses, in far greater perfection, in the same proportion that air is purer than water or the ether than air. Also they have temples and sacred places in which the gods really dwell, and they hear their voices and receive their answers, and are conscious of them and hold converse with them; and they see the sun, moon, and stars as they truly are, and their other blessedness is of a piece with this.

Such is the nature of the whole earth, and of the things which are around the earth; and there are divers regions in the hollows on the face of the globe everywhere, some of them deeper and more extended than that which we inhabit, others deeper but with a narrower opening than ours, and some are shallower and also wider. All have numerous perforations, and there are passages broad and narrow in the interior of the earth, connecting them with one another; and there flows out of and into them, as into basins, a vast tide of water, and huge subterranean streams of perennial rivers, and springs hot and cold, and a great fire, and great rivers of fire, and streams of liquid mud, thin or thick (like the rivers of mud in Sicily, and the lava streams which follow them), and the regions about which they happen to flow are filled up with them. And there is a swinging or see-saw in the interior of the earth which moves all this up and down, and is due to the following cause:—There is a chasm which is the vastest of them all, and pierces right through the whole earth; this is that chasm which Homer describes in the words,—

> 'Far off, where is the inmost depth beneath the earth;'

and which he in other places, and many other poets, have called Tartarus. And the see-saw is caused by the streams flowing into and out of this chasm, and they each have the nature of the soil through which they flow. And the reason why the streams are always flowing in and out, is that the watery element has no bed or bottom, but is swinging and surging up and down, and the surrounding wind and air do the same; they follow the water up and down, hither and thither, over the earth—just as in the act of respiration the air is always in process of inhalation and exhalation;—and the wind swinging with the water in and out produces fearful and irresistible blasts: when the waters retire with a rush into the lower parts of the earth, as they are called, they flow through the earth in those regions, and fill them up like water raised by a pump, and then when they leave those regions and rush back hither, they again fill the hollows here, and when these are filled, flow through subterranean channels and find their way to their several places, forming seas, and lakes, and rivers, and springs. Thence they again enter the earth, some of them making a long circuit into many lands, others going to a few places and not so distant; and again fall into Tartarus, some at a point a good deal lower than that at which they rose, and others not much lower, but all in some degree lower than the point from which they came. And some burst forth again on the opposite side, and some on the same side, and some wind round the earth with one or many folds like the coils of a serpent, and descend as far as they can, but always return and fall into the chasm. The rivers flowing in either direction can descend only to the centre and no further, for opposite to the rivers is a precipice.

Now these rivers are many, and mighty, and diverse, and there are four principal ones, of which the greatest and outermost is that called Oceanus, which flows round the earth in a circle; and in the opposite direction flows Acheron, which passes under the earth through desert places into the Acherusian lake: this is the lake to the shores of which the souls of the many go when they are dead, and after waiting an appointed time, which is to some a longer and to some a shorter time, they are sent back to be born again as animals. The third river passes out between the two, and near the place of outlet pours into a vast region of fire, and forms a lake larger than the Mediterranean Sea, boiling with water and mud; and proceeding muddy and turbid, and winding about the earth, comes, among other places, to the extremities of the Acherusian lake, but mingles not with the waters of the lake, and after making many coils about the earth plunges into Tartarus at a deeper level. This is that Pyriphlegethon, as the stream is called, which throws up jets of fire in different parts of the earth. The fourth river goes out on the opposite side, and falls first of all into a wild and savage region, which is all of a dark blue colour, like lapis lazuli; and this is that river which is called the Stygian river, and falls into and forms the Lake Styx, and after falling into the lake and receiving strange powers in the waters, passes under the earth, winding round in the opposite direction, and comes near the Acherusian lake from the opposite side to Pyriphlegethon. And the water of this river too mingles with no other, but flows round in a circle and falls into Tartarus over against Pyriphlegethon; and the name of the river, as the poets say, is Cocytus.

Such is the nature of the other world; and when the dead arrive at the place to which the genius of each severally guides them, first of all, they have sentence passed upon them, as they have lived well and piously or not. And those who appear to have lived neither well nor ill, go to the river Acheron, and embarking in any vessels which they may find, are carried in them to the lake, and there they dwell and are purified of their evil deeds, and having suffered the penalty of the wrongs which they have done to others, they are absolved, and receive the rewards of their good deeds, each of them according to his deserts. But those who appear to be incurable by reason of the greatness of their crimes—who have committed many and terrible deeds of sacrilege, murders foul and violent, or the like—such are hurled into Tartarus which is their suitable destiny, and they never come out. Those again who have committed crimes, which, although great, are not irremediable—who in a moment of anger, for example, have done some violence to a father or a mother, and have repented for the remainder of their lives, or, who have taken the life of another under the like extenuating circumstances—these are plunged into Tartarus, the pains of which they are compelled to undergo for a year, but at the end of the year the wave casts them forth—mere homicides by way of Cocytus, parricides and matricides by Pyriphlegethon—and they are borne to the Acherusian lake, and there they lift up their voices and call upon the victims whom they have slain or wronged, to have pity on them, and to be kind to them, and let them come out into the lake. And if they prevail, then they come forth and cease from their troubles; but if not, they are carried back again into Tartarus and from thence into the rivers unceasingly, until they obtain mercy from those whom they have wronged: for that is the sentence inflicted upon them by their judges. Those too who have been pre-eminent for holiness of life are released from this earthly prison, and go to their pure home which is above, and dwell in the purer earth; and of these, such as have duly purified themselves with philosophy live henceforth altogether without the body, in mansions fairer still, which may not be described, and of which the time would fail me to tell.

Wherefore, Simmias, seeing all these things, what ought not we to do that we may obtain virtue and wisdom in this life? Fair is the prize, and the hope great!

A man of sense ought not to say, nor will I be very confident, that the description which I have given of the soul and her mansions is exactly true. But I do say that, inasmuch as the soul is shown to be immortal, he may venture to think, not improperly or unworthily, that something of the kind is true. The venture is a glorious one, and he ought to comfort himself with words like these, which is the reason why I lengthen out the tale. Wherefore, I say, let a man be of good cheer about his soul, who having cast away the pleasures and ornaments of the body as alien to him and working harm rather than good, has sought after the pleasures of knowledge; and has arrayed the soul, not in some foreign attire, but in her own proper jewels, temperance, and justice, and courage, and nobility, and truth—in these adorned she is ready to go on her journey to the world below, when her hour comes. You, Simmias and Cebes, and all other men, will depart at some time or other. Me already, as a tragic poet would say, the voice of fate calls. Soon I must drink the poison; and I think that I had better repair to the bath first, in order that the women may not have the trouble of washing my body after I am dead.

When he had done speaking, Crito said: And have you any commands for us, Socrates—anything to say about your children, or any other matter in which we can serve you?

Nothing particular, Crito, he replied: only, as I have always told you, take care of yourselves; that is a service which you may be ever rendering to me and mine and to all of us, whether you promise to do so or not. But if you have no thought for yourselves, and care not to walk according to the rule which I have prescribed for you, not now for the first time, however much you may profess or promise at the moment, it will be of no avail.

We will do our best, said Crito: And in what way shall we bury you?

In any way that you like; but you must get hold of me, and take care that I do not run away from you. Then he turned to us, and added with a smile:—I cannot make Crito believe that I am the same Socrates who have been talking and conducting the argument; he fancies that I am the other Socrates whom he will soon see, a dead body—and he asks, How shall he bury me? And though I have spoken many words in the endeavour to show that when I have drunk the poison I shall leave you and go to the joys of the blessed,—these words of mine, with which I was comforting you and myself, have had, as I perceive, no effect upon Crito. And therefore I want you to be surety for me to him now, as at the trial he was surety to the judges for me: but let the promise be of another sort; for he was surety for me to the judges that I would remain, and you must be my surety to him that I shall not remain, but go away and depart; and then he will suffer less at my death, and not be grieved when he sees my body being burned or buried. I would not have him sorrow at my hard lot, or say at the burial, Thus we lay out Socrates, or, Thus we follow him to the grave or bury him; for false words are not only evil in themselves, but they infect the soul with evil. Be of good cheer then, my dear Crito, and say that you are burying my body only, and do with that whatever is usual, and what you think best.

When he had spoken these words, he arose and went into a chamber to bathe; Crito followed him and told us to wait. So we remained behind, talking and thinking of the subject of discourse, and also of the greatness of our sorrow; he was like a father of whom we were being bereaved, and we were about to pass the rest of our lives as orphans. When he had taken the bath his children were brought to him—(he had two young sons and an elder one); and the women of his family also came, and he talked to them and gave them a few directions in the presence of Crito; then he dismissed them and returned to us.

Now the hour of sunset was near, for a good deal of time had passed while he was within. When he came out, he sat down with us again after his bath, but not much was said. Soon the jailer, who was the servant of the Eleven, entered and stood by him, saying:—To you, Socrates, whom I know to be the noblest and gentlest and best of all who ever came to this place, I will not impute the angry feelings of other men, who rage and swear at me, when, in obedience to the authorities, I bid them drink the poison—indeed, I am sure that you will not be angry with me; for others, as you are aware, and not I, are to blame. And so fare you well, and try to bear lightly what must needs be—you know my errand. Then bursting into tears he turned away and went out.

Socrates looked at him and said: I return your good wishes, and will do as you bid. Then turning to us, he said, How charming the man is: since I have been in prison he has always been coming to see me, and at times he would talk to me, and was as good to me as could be, and now see how generously he sorrows on my account. We must do as he says, Crito; and therefore let the cup be brought, if the poison is prepared: if not, let the attendant prepare some.

Yet, said Crito, the sun is still upon the hill-tops, and I know that many a one has taken the draught late, and after the announcement has been made to him, he has eaten and drunk, and enjoyed the society of his beloved; do not hurry—there is time enough.

Socrates said: Yes, Crito, and they of whom you speak are right in so acting, for they think that they will be gainers by the delay; but I am right in not following their example, for I do not think that I should gain anything by drinking the poison a little later; I should only be ridiculous in my own eyes for sparing and saving a life which is already forfeit. Please then to do as I say, and not to refuse me.

Crito made a sign to the servant, who was standing by; and he went out, and having been absent for some time, returned with the jailer carrying the cup of poison. Socrates said: You, my good friend, who are experienced in these matters, shall give me directions how I am to proceed. The man answered: You have only to walk about until your legs are heavy, and then to lie down, and the poison will act. At the same time he handed the cup to Socrates, who in the easiest and gentlest manner, without the least fear or change of colour or feature, looking at the man with all his eyes, Echecrates, as his manner was, took the cup and said: What do you say about making a libation out of this cup to any god? May I, or not? The man answered: We only prepare, Socrates, just so much as we deem enough. I understand, he said: but I may and must ask the gods to prosper my journey from this to the other world—even so—and so be it according to my prayer. Then raising the cup to his lips, quite readily and cheerfully he drank off the poison. And hitherto most of us had been able to control our sorrow; but now when we saw him drinking, and saw too that he had finished the draught, we could no longer forbear, and in spite of myself my own tears were flowing fast; so that I covered my face and wept, not for him, but at the thought of my own calamity in having to part from such a friend. Nor was I the first; for Crito, when he found himself unable to restrain his tears, had got up, and I followed; and at that moment, Apollodorus, who had been weeping all the time, broke out in a loud and passionate cry which made cowards of us all. Socrates alone retained his calmness: What is this strange outcry? he said. I sent away the women mainly in order that they might not misbehave in this way, for I have been told that a man should die in peace. Be quiet then, and have patience. When we heard his words we were ashamed, and refrained our tears; and he walked about until, as he said, his legs began to fail, and then he lay on his back, according to the directions, and the man who gave him the poison now and then looked at his feet and legs; and after a while he pressed his foot hard, and asked him if he could feel; and he said, No; and then his leg, and so upwards and upwards, and showed us that he was cold and stiff. And he felt them himself, and said: When the poison reaches the heart, that will be the end. He was beginning to grow cold about the groin, when he uncovered his face, for he had covered himself up, and said—they were his last words—he said: Crito, I owe a cock to Asclepius; will you remember to pay the debt? The debt shall be paid, said Crito; is there anything else? There was no answer to this question; but in a minute or two a movement was heard, and the attendants uncovered him; his eyes were set, and Crito closed his eyes and mouth.

Such was the end, Echecrates, of our friend; concerning whom I may truly say, that of all the men of his time whom I have known, he was the wisest and justest and best.

FIVE

GREEK DEMOCRACY: THE FUNERAL ORATION OF PERICLES

The Greek city-states developed a high degree of civic pride. In addition, Athens developed a distinctive system of limited democracy, a noteworthy achievement for the ancient world and further proof that the ancient Greeks were indeed a remarkable people. One of the most eloquent Greek statements of civic pride and democracy was the funeral oration, attributed by Thucydides to Pericles, for those Athenians who had died in the first year (431 B.C.) *of the Peloponnesian War. Thucydides composed many fictitious speeches. But Pericles, the leading Athenian statesman of the fifth century* B.C. *was a gifted orator, and the speech attributed to him by Thucydides may well have represented the actual oration. Thucydides was one of the greatest of the ancient Greek historians—impartial, accurate, and a firm believer in the theory that events proceeded from human motives and acts rather than from supernatural forces.*

THUCYDIDES

HISTORY OF THE PELOPONNESIAN WAR*

Most of my predecessors in this place have commended him who made this speech part of the law, telling us that it is well that it should be delivered at the burial of those who fall in battle. For myself, I should have thought that the worth which had displayed itself in deeds, would be sufficiently rewarded by honours also shown by deeds; such as you now see in this funeral prepared at the people's cost. And I could have wished that the reputations of many brave men were not to be imperilled in the mouth of a single individual, to stand or fall according as he spoke well or ill. For it is hard to speak properly upon a subject where it is even difficult to convince your hearers that you are speaking the truth. On the one hand, the friend who is familiar with every fact of the story, may think that some point has not been set forth with that fulness which he wishes and knows it to deserve; on the other, he who is a stranger to the matter may be led by envy to suspect exaggeration if he hears anything above his own nature. For men can endure to hear others praised only so long as they can severally persuade themselves of their own ability to equal the actions re-

* From Thucydides, *History of the Peloponnesian War,* II, 35–46, translated by Richard Crawley, Longmans, Green. London, 1874.

counted: when this point is passed, envy comes in and with it incredulity. However, since our ancestors have stamped this custom with their approval, it becomes my duty to obey the law and to try to satisfy your several wishes and opinions as best I may.

I shall begin with our ancestors: it is both just and proper that they should have the honour of the first mention on an occasion like the present. They dwelt in the country without break in the succession from generation to generation, and handed it down free to the present time by their valour. And if our more remote ancestors deserve praise, much more do our own fathers, who added to their inheritance the empire which we now possess, and spared no pains to be able to leave their acquisitions to us of the present generation. Lastly, there are few parts of our dominions that have not been augmented by those of us here, who are still more or less in the vigour of life; while the mother country has been furnished by us with everything that can enable her to depend on her own resources whether for war or for peace. That part of our history which tells of the military achievements which gave us our several possessions, or of the ready valour with which either we or our fathers stemmed the tide of Hellenic or foreign aggression, is a theme too familiar to my hearers for me to dilate on, and I shall therefore pass it by. But what was the road by which we reached our position, what the form of government under which our greatness grew, what the national habits out of which it sprang; these are questions which I may try to solve before I proceed to my panegyric upon these men; since I think this to be a subject upon which on the present occasion a speaker may properly dwell, and to which the whole assemblage, whether citizens or foreigners, may listen with advantage.

Our constitution does not copy the laws of neighbouring states; we are rather a pattern to others than imitators ourselves. Its administration favours the many instead of the few; this is why it is called a democracy. If we look to the laws, they afford equal justice to all in their private differences; if to social standing, advancement in public life falls to reputation for capacity, class considerations not being allowed to interfere with merit; nor again does poverty bar the way, if a man is able to serve the state, he is not hindered by the obscurity of his condition. The freedom which we enjoy in our government extends also to our ordinary life. There, far from exercising a jealous surveillance over each other, we do not feel called upon to be angry with our neighbour for doing what he likes, or even to indulge in those injurious looks which cannot fail to be offensive, although they inflict no positive penalty. But all this ease in our private relations does not make us lawless as citizens. Against this fear is our chief safeguard, teaching us to obey the magistrates and the laws, particularly such as regard the protection of the injured, whether they are actually on the statute book, or belong to that code which, although unwritten, yet cannot be broken without acknowledged disgrace.

Further, we provide plenty of means for the mind to refresh itself from business. We celebrate games and sacrifices all the year round, and the elegance of our private establishments forms a daily source of pleasure and helps to banish the spleen; while the magnitude of our city draws the produce of the world into our harbour, so that to the Athenian the fruits of other countries are as familiar a luxury as those of his own.

If we turn to our military policy, there also we differ from our antagonists. We throw open our city to the world, and never by alien acts exclude foreigners from any opportunity of learning or observing, although the eyes of an enemy may occasionally profit by our liberality; trusting less in system and policy than to the native spirit of our citizens; while in education, where our rivals from their very cradles by a painful discipline seek after manliness, at Athens we live exactly as we please, and yet are just as ready to encounter every legitimate danger. In proof of this it may be noticed that the Lacedæmonians do not invade our country alone, but bring with them all their confederates; while we Athenians advance unsupported into the territory of a neighbour, and fighting upon a foreign soil usually vanquish with ease men who are defending their homes. Our united force was never yet encountered by any enemy, because we have at once to attend to our marine and to despatch our citizens by land upon a hundred different services; so that, wherever they engage with some such fraction of our strength, a success against a detachment is magnified into a victory over the nation, and a defeat into a reverse suffered at the hands of our entire people. And yet if with habits not of labour but of ease, and courage not of art but of nature, we are still willing to encounter danger, we have the double advantage of escaping the experience of hardships in anticipation and of facing them in the hour of need as fearlessly as those who are never free from them.

Nor are these the only points in which our city is worthy of admiration. We cultivate refinement without extravagance and knowledge without effeminacy; wealth we employ more for use than for show, and place the real disgrace of poverty not in owning to the fact but in declining the struggle against it. Our public men have, besides politics, their private affairs to attend to, and our ordinary citizens, though occupied with the pursuits of industry, are still fair judges of public matters; for, unlike any other nation, regarding him who takes no part in these duties not as unambitious but as useless, we Athenians are able to judge at all events if we cannot originate, and instead of looking on discussion as a stumbling-block in the way of action, we think it an indispensable preliminary to any wise action at all. Again, in our enterprises we present the singular spectacle of daring and deliberation, each carried to its highest point, and both united in the same persons; although usually decision is the fruit of ignorance, hesitation of reflexion. But the palm of courage will surely be adjudged most justly to those, who best know the difference between hardship and pleasure and yet are never tempted to shrink from danger. In generosity we are equally singular, acquiring our friends by conferring not by receiving favours. Yet, of course, the doer of the favour is the firmer friend of the two, in order by continued kindness to keep the recipient in his debt; while the debtor feels less keenly from the very consciousness that the return he makes will be a payment, not a free gift. And it is only the Athenians who, fearless of consequences, confer their benefits not from calculations of expediency, but in the confidence of liberality.

In short, I say that as a city we are the school of Hellas; while I doubt if the world can produce a man, who where he has only himself to depend upon, is equal to so many emergencies, and graced by so happy a versatility as the Athenian. And that this is no mere boast thrown out for the occasion, but plain matter of fact, the power of the state acquired by these habits proves. For Athens alone of her contemporaries is found when tested to be greater than her reputation, and alone gives no occasion to her assailants to blush at the antagonist by whom they have been worsted, or to her subjects to question her title by merit to rule. Rather, the admiration of the present and succeeding ages will be ours, since we have not left our power without witness, but have shown it by mighty proofs; and far from needing a Homer for our panegyrist, or other of his craft whose verses might charm for the moment only for the impression which they gave to melt at the touch of fact, we have forced every sea and land to be the highway of our daring, and everywhere, whether for evil or for good, have left imperishable monuments behind us. Such is the Athens for which these men, in the assertion of their resolve not to lose her, nobly fought and died; and well may every one of their survivors be ready to suffer in her cause.

Indeed if I have dwelt at some length upon the character of our country, it has been to show that our stake in the struggle is not the same as theirs who have no such blessings to lose, and also that the panegyric of the men over whom I am now speaking might be by definite proofs established. That panegyric is now in a great measure complete; for the Athens that I have celebrated is only what the heroism of these and their like have made her, men whose fame, unlike that of most Hellenes, will be found to be only commensurate with their deserts. And if a test of worth be wanted, it is to be found in their closing scene, and this not only in the cases in which it set the final seal upon their merit, but also in those in which it gave the first intimation of their having any. For there is justice in the claim that steadfastness in his country's battles should be as a cloak to cover a man's other imperfections; since the good action has blotted out the bad, and his merit as a citizen more than outweighed his demerits as an individual. But none of these allowed either wealth with its prospect of future enjoyment to unnerve his spirit, or poverty with its hope of a day of freedom and riches to tempt him to shrink from danger. No, holding that vengeance upon their enemies was more to be desired than any personal blessings, and reckoning this to be the most glorious of hazards, they joyfully determined to accept the risk, to make sure of their vengeance and to let their wishes wait; and while committing to hope the uncertainty of final success, in the business before them they thought fit to act boldly and trust in themselves. Thus choosing to die resisting, rather than to live submitting, they fled only from dishonour, but met danger face to face, and after one brief moment, while at the summit of their fortune, escaped, not from their fear, but from their glory.

So died these men as became Athenians. You, their survivors, must determine to have as unfaltering a resolution in the field, though you may pray that it may have a happier issue. And not contented with ideas derived only from words of the advantages which are bound up with the defense of your country, though these would furnish a valuable text to a speaker even before an audience so alive to them as the present, you must yourselves realise the power of Athens, and feed your eyes upon her from day to day, till love of her fills your hearts; and then when all her greatness shall break upon you, you must reflect that it was by courage, sense of duty, and a keen feeling of honour in action that men were enabled to win all this, and that no personal failure in an enterprise could make them consent to deprive their country of their valour, but they laid it at her feet as the most glorious contribution that they could offer. For this offering of their lives made in common by them all they each of them individually received that renown which never grows old, and for a sepulchre, not so much that in which their bones have been deposited, but that noblest of shrines wherein their glory is laid up to be eternally remembered upon every occasion on which deed or story shall call for its commemoration. For heroes have the whole earth for their tomb; and in lands far from their own, where the column with its epitaph declares it, there is enshrined in every breast a record unwritten with no tablet to preserve it, except that of the heart. These take as your model, and judging happiness to be the fruit of freedom and freedom of valour, never decline the dangers of war. For it is not the miserable that would most justly be unsparing of their lives; these have nothing to hope for: it is rather they to whom continued life may bring reverses as yet unknown, and to whom a fall, if it came, would be most tremendous in its consequences. And surely, to a man of spirit, the degradation of cowardice must be immeasurably more grievous than the unfelt death which strikes him in the midst of his strength and patriotism!

Comfort, therefore, not condolence, is what I have to offer to the parents of the dead who may be here. Numberless are the chances to which, as they know, the life of man is subject; but fortunate indeed are they who draw for their lot a death so glorious as that which has caused your mourning, and to whom life has been so exactly measured as to terminate in the happiness in which it has been passed. Still I know that this is a hard saying, especially when those are in question of whom you will constantly be reminded by seeing in the homes of others blessings of which once you also boasted: for grief is felt not so much for the want of what we have never known, as for the loss of that to which we have been long accustomed. Yet you who are still of an age to beget children must bear up in the hope of having others in their stead; not only will they help you to forget those whom you have lost, but will be to the state at once a reinforcement and a security; for never can a fair or just policy be expected of the citizen who does not, like his fellows, bring to the decision the interests and apprehensions of a father. While those of you who have passed your prime must congratulate yourselves with the thought that the best part of your life was fortunate, and that the brief span that remains will be cheered by the fame of the departed. For it is only the love of honour that never grows old; and honour it is, not gain, as some would have it, that rejoices the heart of age and helplessness.

Turning to the sons or brothers of the dead, I see an arduous struggle before you. When a man is gone, all are wont to praise him, and should your merit be ever so transcendent, you will still find it difficult not merely to overtake, but even to approach their renown. The living have envy to contend with, while those who are no longer in our path are honoured with a goodwill into which rivalry does not enter. On the other hand, if I must say anything on the subject of female excellence to those of you who will now be in widowhood, it will be all comprised in this brief exhortation. Great will be your glory in not falling short of your natural character; and greatest will be hers who is least talked of among the men whether for good or for bad.

My task is now finished. I have performed it to the best of my ability, and in word, at least, the requirements of the law are now satisfied. If deeds be in question, those who are here interred have received part of their honours already, and for the rest, their children will be brought up till manhood at the public expense: the state thus offers a valuable prize, as the garland of victory in this race of valour, for the reward both of those who have fallen and their survivors. And where the rewards for merit are greatest, there are found the best citizens.

And now that you have brought to a close your lamentations for your relatives, you may depart.

SIX

THE ROMAN MASSES

In theory, history treats the life of the whole community. But because of the one-sided nature of most historical records, the emphasis in historical research usually falls on the governing classes, that fraction of the community which dominates public life. Most written history is in fact the history of leadership, or, in other terms, the history of power relationships. Such history has comparatively little to say about the inarticulate bulk of humanity which comprises the majority of any community. Yet to ignore this majority is to ignore the main segment of human experience.

Present day democracy has focussed new attention on the masses of antiquity. Research dealing with the masses is difficult because of the fragmentary nature of the records, but it is rewarding to be able to modify many conventional judgments about the past. In particular, research in Roman social history diminishes much of the glory associated with Roman rule, even for Rome's best periods. Such research, including the penetrating analysis of Frank R. Cowell, reveals the miserable conditions of life among the Roman lower classes and forces a reassessment of the standard of living of Roman civilization and of ancient civilization as a whole.

FRANK R. COWELL

CICERO AND THE ROMAN REPUBLIC *

The developed and modern way of life of cultivated Roman society did not extend at all deeply. The voice of the common man and woman finds little or no echo in the pages of Cicero or of his contemporaries. Such references as are made to them are rarely respectful, often contemptuous. Millions of Romans and Italians around Cicero, peopling the soil of Italy, working in the fields, vineyards and olive plantations, crowding the market-places, marching to wars, laughing, cheering and yelling in the public circuses and theatres, jostling in the streets as they watched the triumphant processions of their victorious generals, have vanished, leaving no account of their daily lives, their loves, hates, hopes and fears.

Although they made up the Roman Republic, their fate seems to have been of scant concern to the men who depended upon their votes for the privilege of ruling over them. Despite the fine stoic sentiments he was fond of uttering about the dignity and brotherhood of mankind, Cicero, the most urbane of men (to use a favourite word of his own invention), in his more intimate and candid moments called the masses the scum of the earth.

Their condition was indeed unenviable.

* From *Cicero and the Roman Republic,* pp. 326–34, by Frank R. Cowell. Reprinted by permission of Penguin Books Inc., Baltimore. Copyright, 1956.

What little we are able to piece together about the life of the common people of Rome shows a depressing picture of poverty and neglect. Life, while it lasted, was supported at a minimum cost. Their food was of the plainest—wheat porridge or simple wheat cakes flavoured, if at all, by a few herbs or vegetables and an occasional cheese, dried salt fish and olive oil. Sugar was unknown and honey was probably beyond their means. They did not drink milk, but cheap wine, mixed perhaps with water. Coffee and tea were of course not known until eighteen hundred years later. Meat they saw so rarely that masses of the Romans never seem to have acquired much taste for it. On one of Caesar's campaigns it was apparently accounted a hardship when Roman soldiers were forced to eat meat because their corn supplies had been exhausted. A little higher in the social scale, however, there was more meat-eating; mainly of pork. Poultry was also available for the better-off classes.

The needy Roman citizen was, however, assured of free water and cheap corn. From 58 B.C. to 46 B.C. corn was supplied free to all Roman citizens who cared to go to get it. A public water supply has never been thought to make men less inclined to work for their own support. But free bread raises different emotions, and any suggestion of it has always met violent opposition. Roman experience is very often quoted in evidence of the evils to which it may be expected to lead. 'Bread and circus-races' has become a by-word in referring to the degeneracy and corruption of the Roman proletariat. But it has been suggested above that cheap or free bread was not so much the cause of the rot in Roman life as merely one of its symptoms. Cicero did not object to a well-managed corn supply. If it was not likely to exhaust the Treasury, he thought it 'both practicable for the State and necessary for the common man . . . a blessing therefore both to the citizens and the State'.

The violence and unrest which made life in Rome so unpleasant for Cicero were certainly not caused by free corn doles. All alike were symptoms of a great evil calling aloud for firm treatment. The corn dole naturally did not improve matters and it alone became a serious financial problem. No doubt it was for this reason that Cicero referred to the masses of Rome as 'the wretched starveling mob, the bloodsucker of the Treasury'. Leeches they were indeed, but it must not be forgotten that the hand that applied them to the body politic of Rome was that of Caesar's agent, Clodius. Was it a deliberate move to drain the Treasury so that Caesar's senatorial opponents should find themselves without the wherewithal to equip armies against Caesar? Whether so intended or not, the free corn policy undoubtedly added heavily to the embarrassments of the Senate.

The shattered condition of public affairs was such that when Caesar eventually fought his way through chaos to supreme control of the Republic he reaped the whirlwind he had himself stirred up, and among many other worries he inherited the unpleasant responsibility of finding grain for about two-thirds of the free population of the city of Rome. This probably required about 300 tons out of the 500 tons of wheat needed to feed the population every day. Suddenly to reduce this tremendous outlay was an unpleasant task, and the man who undertook it obviously had to be sure of his own position. Caesar in 46 B.C. was the first man to have achieved such security since the retirement of Sulla in 79 B.C. He dared not do what Sulla had done and abolish the dole, but he cut down the names on the free list for corn to 150,000—eloquent testimony to the shallowness of the devices by which, as leader of the *populares,* he rose to power. In this way he was able to halve the annual cost to the Treasury of 72 million sesterces on the corn dole. The free corn policy had been Caesar's in opposition. He did not intend it to be more than a means of gaining power. No doubt he then realized that unless the supply of free wheat in Rome was drastically reduced, his policy of large-scale emigration for Rome's unemployed would be all the more difficult to achieve.

The great mass of the poor had nothing resembling the home over which Cicero waxed so eloquent when on his return from exile he claimed compensation for the destruction of his fine house. There, he said, had been his household gods and the family divinities of his hearth, and what could be more holy or more fitting a subject for religious respect than the house of a Roman citizen? However florid and artificial his language seems to our ear, and however convincing it no doubt was to thousands of Roman householders, it must have sounded somewhat hollow to the thousands of destitute Romans whose home was at the best some mean room in one of the many-storied lodging-houses crowded together in the depressions between the hills which were reserved for the better homes. To build within the protecting walls of Rome the Romans were forced to run the tenements as high as they dared. There the masses were huddled together, many without heat, water, or adequate light, often lucky if they were able to retain a roof over their heads, for there were frequent collapses of some of the crazy structures, and others often caught fire. Free corn may well have meant the difference between life and death from starvation to many of the poverty-stricken inhabitants of Rome's teeming tenements. No wonder therefore that the management of the public wheat was high up on the list of burning political questions.

Of course not all the citizens and electors of Rome were on the margin of starvation. There were grades among the totally unemployed. Some would be clients of the well-to-do, paying an obsequious call every morning which, for the price of servility to the rich man's door-keepers and personal servants, might yield a coin or two to satisfy their landlord, as well as a few scraps of food. Among this crowd would be many former slaves who had been given their freedom. Within one generation, in Cicero's lifetime between 81 B.C. and 49 B.C., it has been estimated that half a million slaves were freed and let loose in Rome. There was therefore a vast recruiting-ground for private bands of thugs and bullies. Most poor Romans were probably not unemployed but made up the hard-working artisans and shopkeepers who kept alive the free commerce and industry of the city; bakers who were also the millers, leather workers, shoemakers, fullers who were the only laundrymen and dyers, as well as makers of cheap clothes—for the old days were long past when every Roman girl and woman from the highest to the lowest spent hours spinning and weaving. There must also have been thousands of porters and carriers. The Roman masses, like the masses in all ages, worked largely for each other, no doubt on very slender margins of profit. The rich provided so much for themselves by the work of their slaves that the small artisan, unless he was an exceptionally skilled worker or engaged in some luxury trade like jewellery, did not have wealthy clients. The average Roman could truly have been called 'the man in the street'. For the masses escaped from their cramped, dirty and inconvenient homes as often as they could by living on the street and in the Forum. There was no Sunday or 'week-end' but there were about one hundred public holidays every year. Hence the demand for public games, the 'circus-races'. Because these events provided the one staple means of temporary escape from the sordid realities of daily life, they were immensely popular and filled much more of the waking thoughts of the average Roman than we can now easily imagine. The crowded, cheap public baths that were to form a second relief from the boredom and tedium of poverty had not attained their full development during the Republic, but already in Cicero's lifetime they were becoming popular. Open from sunrise to sunset at a very low fee, they provided a public resort and meeting-place of a type unknown to dwellers in our modern cities. Daily life on this level was not likely to breed conservative opinions in politics.

Over all these struggling folk hung the constant fear of great discomfort from bad seasons, a cold winter, drenching rain or torrid summer heat, as well as the more serious menace of sudden catastrophe: illness, loss of a patron, robbery and violence against which there was no police protection, sudden collapse of the market, failure of the free wheat, as well as less frequent but by no means unknown risks of the collapse of their crazy tenements or their destruction by fire, against which also there was no public fire brigade to fight for them. Among Cicero's property were some shops, two of which had entirely collapsed, and the rest seemed likely soon to follow them. He regarded the matter with what he considered philosophic detachment, refused to be annoyed and jokingly remarked that not the tenants alone but the very mice had migrated.

Shops below, crowded tenements above, narrow busy streets, were the setting for the feverish life of the city. Parts of it devoted to public affairs had a dignity and spaciousness contrasting all the more vividly with the squalor and uneasiness of the poorer quarters. They had one source of satisfaction denied to the dwellers in most of our industrial towns. The sight of some of the temples, public buildings, statuary and memorial buildings was free of cost to all whose eye delighted in beauty. But the Roman people were to benefit more in this respect from rulers who came after Cicero and Caesar than they had ever done under the Republic. The 'puritan tradition' of the Roman Republic is seen in Cicero's opinion that the expenditure of public money was justified 'when it is made for walls, docks, aqueducts, harbours, and all those works which are of service to the community'. But, despite his friend Pompey's initiative in providing new public buildings, Cicero confessed at the end of his life to doubts about the propriety of building 'theatres, colonnades and new temples'.

The cost of living for the poorer classes was very low. Vegetables, a little cheese, some dried salt fish, dried beans and olive oil were a cheap addition to the free or low-priced public wheat. The cheaper grades of wine mixed with water furnished a very popular and inexpensive drink.

In this way the masses struggled to keep body and soul together, although on a style of life that seems miserable enough to us today, if we could forget the years in Europe after 1940 when hundreds of thousands were forced by the miseries of war and invasion to reduce their level of consumption even below that of the dregs of society in ancient Rome.

Low State of Public Health

Little enough is known about the more serious epidemic diseases of Rome; still less has survived from which it would be possible to get a reliable picture of the general level of public health. It is difficult to believe that it was good. The low state of medical knowledge and above all ignorance of the elements of hygiene combine to forbid optimism on the subject. The mere lack of soap alone must have been an immense disadvantage. Handicapped in the effort to clean dirt from their bodies and their clothes, they were equally hard put to it to clear the dirt, refuse and sewage from their dwellings, their towns and cities. Everyone in Rome was vulnerable to dirt and disease; some classes were more affected than the rest. Ignorance of the way to avoid maladies arising from the various trades and industrial processes undoubtedly carried off thousands of Romans at an early age. Some occupations were so notoriously unhealthy that they were reserved for criminals and slaves. Such were the metal mines. Before any mechanical aids in ventilating and draining were invented, work in quarries and in underground mines was necessarily particularly dangerous. Explosives were unknown, so that the only method of shifting huge rocks and stones was to crack them by lighting great fires. The heat and fumes of the fires, apart from any poisonous gases they might create by acting on metal ores, were alone a sufficient hazard. Lead workers and sulphur workers were also dangerously exposed and their expectation of life was small. So also was that of workers in stone and marble. Silicosis, against which it has not yet been found possible to protect workers completely, found them defenceless.

Trades which would not now be regarded as dangerous then held many risks. The peculiar processes of the fullers have been mentioned. Their work in confined small rooms must have been extremely unpleasant from the smells and from the possibly infected nature both of their materials and of the clothes they had to clean. To be exposed to burning sulphur, as they were in their bleaching processes, was an additional danger.

There were more offensive trades than the fullers', particularly that of the tanners and leather-makers, and efforts were made to segregate them beyond the Tiber. Candle-makers and oilmen, whose oil came from olives, no doubt also deserved to be included in this class.

The millers and bakers had a less pleasant occupation than they mostly have today. Nearly 200,000 tons of wheat consumed in Rome every year had to be carried at some stage in sacks on the workers' backs. To this exhausting toil must be added the hard work of grinding corn by hand in the days before water-mills and windmills were common. No true Roman would endure to see his wife at a grinding-mill. The threat of being sent to work at grinding corn was sufficient to make most slaves tremble. Covered in perspiration and flour, the millers and bakehouse workers needed frequent baths which it is very questionable whether many were able to get. The unpleasant association of lice with the milling and baking trade endured long enough in Italy to make it probable that it also existed in Cicero's Rome. Before the public-bath habit became regular, the resources of such citizens as believed in cleanliness was a daily wash of the arms and legs and a weekly bath in the scullery. It was a possibility open to few of the poorer tradesmen and to fewer still of the more numerous slaves.

It has taken a new form of warfare to bring home to the city-dwellers of today what they owe to modern sanitation and to supplies of water, soap, gas and electricity. Not until such services, formerly taken for granted, are suddenly interrupted or destroyed, does their vital link with civilization become evident. In ancient Rome there was of course neither gas nor electricity. Sanitary services left much to be desired; none of the appliances to which we are accustomed had then been invented.

It is important, therefore, not to assume that life in Republican Rome had anything like a modern physical background. Our standards of public health and cleanliness are on a vastly better scale.

Just as we are apt to forget the low standards of public health and cleanliness in Rome, so in this age of machines it is difficult to realize what life was like when all work had to be done by human muscles aided to some extent by the help of animals. Not merely the loading, unloading and distribution of the tremendous tonnage of food and supplies but all forms of manufacturing and construction depended upon the physical strength of the men of Rome. What that means in carpentry and woodwork alone is sufficiently obvious when it is realized how much hard work is involved in the various processes between felling a tree and the production by hand of the planed and polished woodwork required in furniture and building.

The sheer physical burden of all this toil, apparent in the strained muscles, arteries and hearts of the labouring classes, their premature ageing and death, would have been a melancholy commentary upon the pleasing delusion of some contemporary moralists that nobody has ever been killed by overwork. Death, when it came, increased the hazards of the survivors. Burial was indeed forbidden within the precincts of the city, but immediately beyond were the vast common graves into which the dead bodies of the poor were thrown indiscriminately at night. In their funeral customs the Romans further sharpened the contrast between rich and poor. The magnificent torchlight processions accompanying the funeral train of the rich and powerful, the musicians, the mourning women, and above all the men impersonating the deceased's ancestors, on their way to the magnificent tombs lining the wayside on the main approaches to the city, all threw into sharp relief the social gulf between the best people and the dregs of the city.

This would not be the only shock for us if we could visit Cicero's Rome. We should find it crowded, noisy, dirty, with unusual and forbidding stenches, swarming with vast crowds of people, many of whom would seem almost sub-human types marked by disease, mental deficiency, malformation and mutilation, and all under the threat of sudden death. The general impression of Rome might well have been sickening, even frightening. Very little of the glib cynicism which amuses itself by throwing doubt upon the reality of modern material progress would be likely to survive such an experience.

When the masses lived or rather existed in such conditions, it is not surprising to learn that no provision was made for educating them. By Cicero's time also, compulsory army service had begun to be of less importance to the State than the professional army; so the average Roman missed this opportunity of being taken out of their sordid surroundings and being given some form of organized training. The growing race of slaves and descendants of slaves in any case would never have had this experience of corporate life and discipline in the service of a great cause. They were therefore entirely and, for an imperial race with responsibilities towards a vast subject world, shamefully ignorant, neglected and uncontrolled. Not benefiting, as did the Romans of the heroic age, from a firm family and social discipline, not the bearers of that high tradition of self-control, self-discipline and devotion to public duty, they were but poor stuff. Yet into their unskilled and incompetent hands was committed the great heritage of the golden age of the Republic.

If, as Samuel Johnson believed, one test of a civilization is the way in which it treats its poor, it is indeed difficult to take a rosy view of the quality of life in the Roman Republic. There are other measures of the relative standard of material civilization in different countries. In modern times it has been well said that the average expectation of life is one good measure. It is a figure which varies today from less than thirty years of life in India to nearly seventy years in New Zealand. The lack of adequate actuarial statistics in the ancient world, where life assurance was an unknown science, makes it impossible to apply this modern test to Ancient Rome.

SEVEN

ROME'S DECLINE AND FALL

The decline and fall of the Roman Empire in the West (the Greek-speaking eastern, or Byzantine, Empire survived until A.D. *1453) has appalled and fascinated successive generations of thoughtful people. Rome's fall to barbarians in the fifth century* A.D. *plunged western Europe into five centuries of darkness (the so-called early Middle Ages), darkness unrelieved except for some comparatively small areas of light. Some scholars have insisted that it is possible to overstate Rome's "fall," because some civilization continued even into the early Middle Ages and because the West ultimately made contact with the brilliant traditions of the Ancient World. Nonetheless, with the barbarian invasions the once-strong Roman organization in western Europe, with its orderly government, its system of law, and its well-trained legions, simply disappeared. By far, the greater part of western Europe reverted to barbarism. The city of Rome, once the proud center of Roman glory, became a pathetic ghost town, with only a fragment of its former population living miserably in almost deserted neighborhoods while cattle grazed in the once-busy forum. The spectacle of such fallen glory has reminded later generations that civilization, the product of human effort, may not only rise but also fall. The problem of Rome's fall has evoked much discussion and much dissent. Scholars have not agreed about the causes of ancient Rome's decline, just as they disagree about the causes of the origin of civilization. Edward Gibbon, the great English historian of the late eighteenth century, concluded that Rome was at its apex in the century preceding the death of Marcus Aurelius in* A.D. *180 and emphasized the role that Christianity played in Rome's later decline. More recent scholars, among them Frank W. Walbank, have questioned Gibbon's interpretation by pointing out that Rome suffered from serious internal dislocation long before* A.D. *180. From this point of view, Rome's decline extended over many centuries and proceeded from a number of complex internal ailments which the Romans themselves did not comprehend.*

FRANK W. WALBANK

THE DECLINE OF THE ROMAN EMPIRE IN THE WEST*

The *pax Augusta* brought prosperity to a wide area of the earth's suface; but it completely failed to release new productive forces. As in the century after Alexander's death in 323 B.C.—a century in many ways comparable to the early Empire—the step to industrialisation and the factory was never taken. Indeed, except for a few new devices like the mill-wheel, the level of technique inside the Roman Empire never surpassed that already reached at Alexandria. Nor was this due to any special Roman foible; on the contrary it continued the classical tradition of the Alexandrines, who could find no better use for many of their mechanical devices than to impress the ignorant congregations in the Egyptian temples and to bolster up their religion with sham miracles. For the origins of this tradition one must go back to the Greek city-state.

From its outset classical civilisation inherited a low level of technical skill, judged by the part Greece and Rome were destined to play in history. The Greek tribes settled in a poor and rocky land; only by incessant labour could Hesiod wring a livelihood from the soil of Boeotia. Consequently, the leisure which was to bring forth the Ionian Renaissance and the fine flower of Periclean Athens could only be purchased at a price. The temples on the Acropolis, the plays in the theatre of Dionysus, the speculations of Plato, were only possible because an army of women, resident foreigners, slaves and imperial subjects supported by their toil a leisured minority of full citizens. The position at Rome was similar. There the wealth of the late republic was built up, as we saw, on the sweat of the provinces, the loot of many wars, and the sufferings of countless slaves enduring abject misery on the plantations of aristocratic landowners, resident in Rome. This relationship of absentee landlord and plantation slave reproduced in an accentuated form that contrast which underlay ancient civilisation, between the leisured class of the city and the multitude labouring to support it on the land—a contrast which evoked a famous criticism of the cities of the Empire as 'hives of drones'.

This antithesis was no new thing; like the low level of classical technique, it had been characteristic of the ancient civilisations which sprang up in the river valleys of Egypt, Mesopotamia and the Punjab round about the third millennium B.C. Common to the east too was the institution of slavery, which spread from the home to the mine and the plantation, to become the basis of Greek and Roman civilisation, a cancer in the flesh of society which grew with society itself. Slavery was never effectively challenged. Aristotle (384–322 B.C.), one of the most acute philosophers and students of political science who ever lived, laid it down as axiomatic that 'from the hour of their birth some are marked out for subjection, others for rule'

* Reprinted from *The Decline of the Roman Empire in the West,* pp. 22–33, by Frank W. Walbank by permission of Abelard-Schuman Ltd.

(*Politics,* I, 5, 2. 1254*a*); 'the art of war' he wrote 'is a natural art of acquisition, for it includes hunting, an art which we ought to practise against wild beasts and against men who, though intended by nature to be governed, will not submit; for war of such a kind is naturally just' (*Politics,* I, 8, 12. 1256*b*). It is perhaps not strange that a philosopher who so faithfully reflects the practice of his own society in framing his definition of a just war should also have sought to demonstrate the natural inferiority of woman to man.

After Aristotle another school of philosophers arose, the Stoics, who for a short time asserted the equality of slaves and free men; but they never passed from this to the obvious conclusion that slavery should be abolished. Very soon they too lapsed back into the easier Aristotelian view. Meanwhile slavery was spreading both geographically and in the number of human beings which it enveloped in its folds. The wars of Alexander's successors and of the Roman republic brought a constantly increasing supply; especially on the plantations and sheep ranches and in the mines they formed an indispensable source of labour. At Rome 'Sardinians for sale' became a proverb for anything in cheap supply; and Strabo has left us a picture of the famous slave-market of Delos in the late second century B.C. (XIV, 668); 'the island', he writes 'could admit and send away tens of thousands of slaves in the same day. . . . The cause of this was the fact that the Romans, having become rich after the destruction of Carthage and Corinth (146 B.C.), used many slaves; and the pirates, seeing the easy profit therein, bloomed forth in great numbers, themselves not only going in quest of booty, but also trafficking in slaves.'

It was this slavery at the root of society which controlled the general pattern of classical civilisation. For it split up every community into two kinds of human beings—the free man and the slave; and it ordained that those who did the basic work of society should not be those to benefit from it. The natural outcome was that the slave lacked the incentive to master and improve the technique of the work he was doing. Equally disastrous was the effect upon the slaveowners themselves. Because it became normal to associate manual labour with slaves, Greek culture began to draw a line between the things of the hand and the things of the mind. In the *Republic,* Plato (*c.* 429–347 B.C.) pictured a utopian community divided into three sharply differentiated classes, endowed each with some imaginary 'metallic' quality —Guardians with a golden cast of mind, to govern; Auxiliaries with an admixture of silver, to fight and police the state; and finally Workers, sharing in the base metals, to do the work of society and to obey. Aristotle, with an equal contempt for manual work, writes: 'Doubtless in ancient times the artisan class were slaves or foreigners, and therefore the majority of them are so now. The best form of state will not admit them to citizenship' (*Politics,* III, 5. 3. 1278*a*). 'Certainly the good man . . . and the good citizen ought not to learn the crafts of inferiors except for their own occasional use; if they habitually practise these, there will cease to be a distinction between master and slave' (*Politics,* III, 4. 13. 1277*b*).

The Roman attitude varied no whit from this. Cicero's formulation deserves to be quoted in full. 'Public opinion' he writes (*De Officiis,* I. 150-51) 'divides the trades and professions into the liberal and the vulgar. We condemn the odious occupation of the collector of customs and the usurer, and the base and menial work of unskilled labourers; for the very wages the labourer receives are a badge of slavery. Equally contemptible is the business of the retail dealer; for he cannot succeed unless he is dishonest, and dishonesty is the most shameful thing in the world. The work of the mechanic is also degrading; there is nothing noble about a workshop. The least respectable of all trades are those which minister to pleasure, as Terence tells us, "fishmongers, butchers, cooks, sausage-makers." Add to these, if you like, perfumers, dancers, and the actors of the gaming-house. But the learned professions, such as medicine, architecture and the higher education, from which society derives the greatest benefit, are considered honourable occupations for those to whose social position they are appropriate. Business on a small scale is despicable; but if it is extensive and imports commodities in large quantities from all over the world and distributes them honestly, it is not so very discreditable; nay, if the merchant, satiated, or rather satisfied, with the fortune he has made, retires from the harbour and steps into an estate, as once he returned to harbour from the sea, he deserves, I think, the highest respect. But of all the sources of wealth farming is the best, the most able, the most profitable, the most noble.'

Government at Rome throughout the period of the republic was in the hands of an aristocratic clique whose wealth was derived from land and which had debarred itself from commerce by a self-denying ordinance. This caste was the natural opponent of any economic improvement which challenged its own position. After the conquest of Macedonia in 168 B.C. it closed down the Macedonian mines lest they should strengthen the commercial elements which would have worked them; and once current needs could be met from the Spanish mines, the Senate practically stopped mining in Italy. 'This maintained Senatorial authority beyond challenge: but it also checked the economic expansion which might have restored the balance in the country.' [1]

It was this landed class which peopled the countryside of Italy and Sicily with the slave gangs which later threatened Rome's very existence in the revolt of Spartacus (73–71 B.C.). Meanwhile the towns and cities were filling up with eastern slaves, who not only undertook all kinds of manual work, but also acted as teachers, doctors, architects and professional men. The consequence was that socially these activities were ill thought of. 'The meaner sort of mechanic has a special and separate slavery,' wrote Aristotle (*Politics,* I. 13. 13. 1260*a*); and similarly the Romans despised the free artisan as one doing work proper to a slave. Thus the atmosphere was wholly unfavourable to technical progress in a field for which anyone of any consequence had nothing but contempt. When labour is cheap and worthless, why conserve it? So the classical world perpetuated that technical retardation which had been one of the most paradoxical features of the civilisations of the Nile and Euphrates—paradoxical because it was thanks to a unique crop of technical inventions—the plough, the wheeled cart, the sailing boat, the solar calendar, the smelting of copper ores, the use of the power of oxen and the harnessing of the winds with sails—that these civilisations had come into being. In both instances the cause of retardation was the same—the bisection of society into classes with contrary interests.

Economically, this division of society ensured that the vast masses of the empire never tasted the fruits of their labour; and this meant a permanently restricted internal market. Because wealth was concentrated at the top, the body of society suffered from chronic under-consumption. Accordingly industry had to seek its market either in the limited circle of the middle and upper class, together with the army (which therefore had considerable economic significance), or else outside the Empire, where of course there were even fewer markets for mass-produced goods. Consequently, the economic basis for industrialisation was not to hand. The expansion of the Empire brought new markets, which staved off the problem for a time; but, as we shall see, the effects of this expansion were soon cancelled out by the decentralisation of production and were never radical enough to carry a large-scale industry, using all the resources of advanced technique and advanced forms of power.

[1] A. H. McDonald, *The Rise of Roman Imperialism,* Sydney, 1940, p. 12.

On the other hand, because of the social structure, Greece and Rome never even considered the possibility of catering for the proletariat and peasantry, and so creating a deeper, instead of a wider, market. What expansion the Empire brought proves on closer examination to be 'a matter of greater extension, not of greater depth'. The *pax Augusta* removed many handicaps and much wastage; goods circulated with greater ease and over wider areas. But there was no qualitative change in the nature of classical economy. In one field alone were there notable technical achievements—in that of building and engineering, where the Hellenistic Age had already given a lead, under the stimulus of interstate warfare; but even here the Romans were concerned with the amplifying and application of old processes rather than with the creation of new. Thus behind the rosy hues of Gibbon's picture of a prosperous Antonine world we are now in a position to detect at least one fatal weakness—the complete stagnation of technique.

It has been suggested above that in the long run the expansion of the Roman Empire could bring only a temporary fillip to its economy. The reason why this was so deserves special attention, for it illuminates a factor of some importance for our central problem. Modern investigation has revealed in the Roman Empire the operation of an economic law which finds its application equally in our own society—the centrifugal tendency of industry to export itself instead of its products, and of trades to migrate from the older areas of the economy to the new.

The operation of this law has been felt with full force in this country, since India began to satisfy its own needs with cotton manufactured in Bombay; here the lesson has been underlined by mass unemployment in the cotton towns of Lancashire. Today this movement to the periphery is usually connected with the establishment of the capitalistic form of production in colonial and backward areas and, as such areas become independent states, these states use political methods to assert an economic independence based on local industry. 'Autarky' as a feature of the national state is a characteristic of modern times. In the Roman Empire the factors were somewhat simpler and more primitive.

Perhaps the most important reason for moving industry as near as possible to the new market was the weakness of ancient communications. Judged by preceding ages, Roman communications were highly developed; but in relation to the tasks the Empire set, they were still far too primitive. Mechanically the vehicles used on land were very inefficient; for the ancient world never discovered the horse-collar, but employed a form of harness which half-strangled the beast every time it tried to drag a load along. A sea voyage was always chancy, and overseas-trade a hazardous business. Even by the time of Augustus the task of maintaining imperial communications was beginning to weigh as an intolerable burden upon the inhabitants of the Empire. The cost of the Imperial Post, the upkeep of the roads, the housing of travelling officials—all these fell upon the provincial. And in spite of police and river flotillas, brigandage had not been wholly eliminated; the inns too were often poor and unevenly distributed. The difficulties of a voyage in the first century A.D. are illustrated by the story of St. Paul's adventures (including a shipwreck) on board the three vessels which were necessary to bring him from Palestine to Rome. In short, the best transport system of the ancient world was inadequate to cope with a relatively high circulation of consumers' goods; and to make matters worse there is evidence that deterioration had set in from the time of Augustus onwards.

A second factor which impelled industry outwards towards its markets was the insecurity of ancient credit. Because of the risks entailed, it was always costly to raise capital for a trading venture; interest rates were high because the risk run was personal. There was no ancient equivalent of the joint-stock company with limited liability to ensure corporate responsibility for financial ventures; and banking itself remained primitive. The Empire saw no further development of the Ptolemaic system of a central bank with branch establishments; on the contrary, in Egypt there are signs of regression to a system of independent local banks.

Furthermore, the fact that ancient industry was based on slavery also influenced the movement of decentralisation. For slavery as an institution was adversely affected by the Augustan peace. The steps the Emperors took to end war and piracy caused a drying-up of the main source of supply. The great days of the Delian slave market were gone for ever; and, though under the more humane conditions of the early Empire the number of home-reared slaves was quite considerable, they were not sufficient to fill the gap, so that increasingly the Roman world had to fall back on the small trickle from outside the frontiers. Besides this, the growth of humanitarian sentiment, already mentioned in chapter two, led to a widespread movement of slave-manumission. Yesterday's slave was tomorrow's freedman; and his grandsons would be full Roman citizens. Clearly the normal basis of ancient capitalistic activity was being undermined. And this led to a shifting of industry to more primitive lands where, as in Gaul, industry had available, if not new slaves, what was perhaps better, a free proletariat willing to turn its hands to manual labour. In the Celtic lands, as in Ptolemaic Egypt, we find free workers engaged in industrial production. Whereas in the potteries of Arretium in Italy, before A.D. 25, 123 out of 132 known workers were slaves, there is no evidence for the employment of slaves in the potteries of Gaul and the Rhine valley; and inscriptions from Dijon refer to stoneworkers and smiths as 'free dependents' (*clientes*) of a local *seigneur*—an interesting sidelight on the break-up of the tribal system and the growth of social classes in Gaul. This shifting of industry contributed to the already mentioned urbanisation of these backward parts; and here we may note that the new municipalities in such areas as Gaul and Spain inherited what the Italian municipalities had largely lost—a hinterland inhabited by peasants. It has been argued that by becoming each a little Rome in exploiting the dwellers in its own countryside the municipalities contributed on a long-term view to their own subsequent ruin.

Another important feature of industry based on slavery was that concentration brought no appreciable reduction of overhead expenses, as happens where power-machines are employed. Hence there was no incentive to develop the old centres rather than expand to new. Moreover, the simple nature of ancient equipment, the absence of complicated machinery, made it a comparatively easy business to move. Usually it would merely be a question of a few simple tools and the skill carried in a man's own fingers. On the other hand, the restricted internal market, which necessarily drove the merchant farther and farther afield, combined with the constant demands of a relatively prosperous army along the frontiers to reinforce the general centrifugal tendency of industry. Incidentally, the army had changed its economic role since the days of the republic. Then, as the source of valuable plunder, it had paid its way over and over again; now, as a peaceful garrison force, rarely fighting, and then against poor barbarians, it was an economic liability, some 250,000 to 300,000—rising later to 400,000 and more—idle mouths to feed—an item which must certainly figure among the causes of Roman decline.

All these tendencies did not operate at once nor to the same extent; but over a period of years they resulted in a clear movement of industry outwards from the old centres of the Empire. One of the earliest developments was that trade became local and provincial instead of international; though, significantly, the drop in long-distance trade in mass-produced goods did not apply to luxury articles, which still travelled virtually any distance to meet the demands of the wealthy few. Over the whole Empire there was a gradual reversion to small-scale, hand-to-mouth craftsmanship, producing for the local market and for specific orders in the vicinity. Often the movement of decentralisation had two stages. Thus the manufacture of *terra sigillata,* the universal redware pottery of the early empire, shifted first from Italy to Graufesenque in the Cevennes and thence, in the course of the second century A.D., to Lezoux in the Allier basin, to eastern Gaul, Rhaetia and Alsace, and finally to Rheinzabern near Speyer. 'In the African lamp industry Italian wares gave place to Carthaginian, which themselves lost the market to lamps of purely local manufacture.' [2]

The progress made by the various provinces was naturally uneven; sometimes the first result of decentralisation was to locate some important manufacture in particularly favourable surroundings; in which case the decentralised industry might for a time capture the international market. This happened to Gallic wine and pottery, which were exported from Narbonne and Arles to the east, until the middle of the third century; pottery from Gaul is found throughout this period in Italy, Spain, Africa, Britain and even in Syria and Egypt. But on the whole this was exceptional, and in the case of Gaul and Germany was probably due to geographical factors, especially the excellent water-transport system, and also to the existence of cheap labour, conditions which were not reproduced in the older provinces of the east.

Progress in such areas as Gaul and Roman Germany was balanced by the decay of Italy. During the second century A.D. this one-time kernel of the Empire lost increasingly its predominant position. Northern Italy remained prosperous for a longer period, thanks to its links with the Danube provinces. But in the rest of the peninsula from the end of the first century A.D. onwards there appear signs of depopulation and a marked decline in the export of both agricultural and industrial products. As the trend towards decentralisation developed, and as the Gallic wine-trade grew, the vineyards and olive fields of Italy shrank, making place increasingly for the cultivation of corn on large estates, farmed with serf-labour. Italy became an incubus, supported by invisible exports—officials' salaries and the Emperor's private income.

Simultaneously, at the opposite extreme, in the lands outside the frontiers, and especially to the north and northeast, among the Gauls, the Germans and the Scythians, the outward expansion of Roman trade and influence was inducing a ferment, which was to have the most far-reaching effects. Already the Gauls whom Caesar conquered (59–50 B.C.) and the Germans whom Tacitus described in his *Germania,* published in A.D. 98, had to some degree modified their earlier tribal organisation; in both lands there were considerable differences of wealth, and rich counts had each their retinues of followers. But from the time of Augustus the natural development of these peoples was accelerated by the impact of Romanisation. Increasingly they became involved in imperial trade-currents, buying and selling across the frontiers. Increasingly they enlisted in the Roman armies as mercenaries, and on retirement took their Roman habits back to their tribes like New Guinea natives returning home from Rabaul or Sydney. Romanised chieftains employed their new culture in the service of Rome, or like Arminius, against her. In short, the centrifugal economic movement did not and could not stop at the frontiers; but overflowing into the barbarian world beyond, it carried the virtues and vices of civilisation like a strong wine to unaccustomed heads. Thus it was the Romans themselves who taught the northern barbarians to look with interest and envy at the rich spoils of the Empire.

Meanwhile the process of decentralisation and subdivision into smaller and smaller

[2] F. Oertel in *Cambridge Ancient History,* Vol. XII (1939), p. 241.

local economic units could have only one ultimate result—provincial autarky and the decomposition of the Empire. As one might expect, this economic tendency found its political reflection in the division of the Empire, first of all in the four-fold administration of Diocletian and his three colleagues (A.D. 286), later, after Constantine had transferred the capital to Byzantium (A.D. 330), in the permanent division into an eastern and western Empire, which laid the foundations of mediaeval Europe.

EIGHT

THE RISE OF CHRISTIANITY

In historical terms, the rise of Christianity has presented many baffling problems. Much of the history of early Christianity is obscure. Roman sources give little information about it. Historians of Christianity, therefore, have had to treat its rise mainly in general terms based on an intimate understanding of philosophy and religion in the Greek-Roman world. One such analysis, short but penetrating, is that of Professor Erwin R. Goodenough. His analysis treats the dissatisfaction which people of antiquity had with rational philosophy as a guide to truth. His analysis also treats the special appeal which Christianity had over other contemporary religions.

ERWIN R. GOODENOUGH

THE CHURCH IN THE ROMAN EMPIRE*

No religion can have any general appeal which does not at least seem to offer to men what they feel they deeply need. Christianity was and is no exception to the rule. It succeeded at first fundamentally because it offered to the Græco-Roman world into which it came, and of which it was largely a product, the kind of comfort and inspiration which men were seeking. When the Greeks were at the height of their powers they had taught that the universe is a great ordered system of which man is a part, and hence that the only right way to live is first to try to understand this ideal order of nature, and then to make one's life fit into it. In public life that meant the most thoughtful coöperation in affairs of state; in private it meant the organization of body and mind in such a way that each part of one's being had its place, yet so that man's natural guide, his reason, kept all other parts from overstepping their proper bounds. In the Hellenistic Age, that is, during the centuries between Alexander and the beginnings of Christianity, this ideal had been interpreted by leaders of thought as a demand that man so rationalize his life that he be completely independent of fortune, even indifferent as to the outcome of his endeavors, an ideal which man hoped to achieve by simplifying his desires so that he would expect to find happiness not in the acquisition and enjoyment of external goods, but in the ability to be content with what he happened to have. The

* *The Church in the Roman Empire,* by Erwin R. Goodenough, Copyright ©, 1931 by Henry Holt and Company, Inc.; copyright renewed 1958 in the name of Erwin R. Goodenough. Reprinted by permission of Holt, Rinehart and Winston, Inc.

supreme virtue was thus the dominance of reason in one's life, resulting in contentment with life as it comes. Such at least was the ideal life as described by philosophic writers of almost every Hellenistic school, and with them, while frequently only a pose, it was for many a passionate quest; and yet that it had much appeal to ordinary men may seriously be doubted.

In any case by the beginning of the first century before Christ a great mass of men were finding increasing help in the teaching of those who confessed the inability of man, as he naturally is, to keep his passions and desires always subject to his reason, and who sought to discover in some form of religion a door to a larger life, in which his reasoning faculty, too weak to control his life, might be enlarged and strengthened. For the various philosophies which were monotheistic had taught that the mind or reason of man was a bit of God living in him. Why not then appeal to God to give more of Himself, to make the reason fragment in man larger and stronger? If such an addition to one's natural powers could be achieved, that would be truly salvation, as the age called it, by which was meant an assurance of safety in the vicissitudes of this world, as well as in that next world to which all men were looking with restless expectation. It was thought that this divinity, which man hoped to find revealed in religion so that he could take it into himself, was not so much God himself as a radiation out from God. The ancient world was still full of sun-worship, or of figures and conceptions derived from sun-worship, so that God was thought of as the sun sending out to men God-rays, as the sun radiates sun rays. Now as the sun warms and brings life into the physical world, so, it was thought, these God-rays, coming into men's lives, warm and enliven their minds, making them grow and become strong, until men can meet the trials of life with happy security. This radiating aspect of deity was called by many names, Word, Spirit, Savior, Creator, Lord, Divine Law, Natural Law, Power of God, Reason, Wisdom, all of which suggest slightly different aspects of a conception which properly included them all and many more.

The expansion of one's own reason, or spirit, by the incoming of this Divine Spirit, then, to use the only term of the lot which has kept any of its original meaning, was regarded as the solution of life's problems. But how was it to be accomplished? Where could the Spirit be found? The majority of men thought like their primitive ancestors that they could secure and use spiritual power by means of magical charms, passwords, and incantations. Others had a higher and more mystical aspiration, to find it by direct action of God in their own hearts. But all regarded its coming as marking the victory of the higher spiritual part of man over the material and bodily, and as a sure guarantee of happy existence after death. And all people of the age, barring only a few of the most severe thinkers, hoped to find this Spirit not by unaided rational or mystical efforts, but with the help of some divinely revealed external rite or sacred book which would show timid and heart-hungry humanity the Way, the Road, to Life. That is, the Hellenistic Age witnessed one of the most momentous changes of history: men lost the reliance of thoughtful Greeks of the Classical Age upon the accumulation of truth by human reason and investigation, and turned instead to ask God to reveal the truth to them. The imparting of this revelation was regarded as a divine illumination, or, as they sometimes called it, a new spiritual birth, and it would come as the reward not of the exertion but of the prostration of human effort. If ever mankind could be convinced that such a revelation had been found, human effort and cares in this life must be completely and permanently subordinated to the higher world and its demands.

This great new emphasis upon the value of external revelation arose partly because of the breakdown of philosophic initiative and moral courage, but also because the Greek world discovered in the Orient and Egypt many religions, themselves age-old though new to the Greeks, which suggested the possibility of discovering such a revelation. In many oriental countries sacred rites of majestic dignity and mystery celebrated the deities who had for centuries, if not millenniums, been represented as meeting halfway the same feeling of human helplessness and guilt as that which the Hellenistic peoples were experiencing. Most of these religions had also a sacred book or literature which seemed to reveal unplumbed depths of wisdom when expounded by those who understood them. These books, it was thought, had been dictated by the Spirit to some holy man or men who had written them down without error, so that they were a valid guide to spiritual things, were, indeed, the truth direct from God.

The first important religion of this type in the Greek world was Orphism, which from the sixth century B.C. had been growing from a small beginning to great influence. It taught the uselessness of this life, man's sinfulness and need of redemption because of his inability to save himself without divine help; and it solved its own problem in an elaborate ritual in which the believer became "enthusiastic," that is, filled with the saving deity. Long before the beginning of the Christian Era the sacred stone and rites of the Great Mother, a religion of Asia Minor, had been taken to Rome, as well as the Sibylline Oracles, supposed utterances of inspired women. Two other religions, that of the saving Mithra from Persia, and of Isis, Mother of Heaven and the Gods, from Egypt, were making a deep mark upon the life of the entire civilized world, for the devotees of both insisted that in their rites, scriptures, and pass-words the desire of the Hellenistic Age for a saving revelation of deity had been met. The "saving deity" in all these religions was interpreted as a personalized symbol for the Spirit which men were seeking, so that union with the special "savior" in a rite meant union with God's beneficent Spirit.

Everywhere still another religion, Judaism, was exciting interest, though the Jews were only just beginning to rise above their racial prejudices. Many Jews still wanted to keep their religion to themselves, or to require of all converts a strict observance of the Jewish customs and taboos which would make them ridiculous in the eyes of their Greek and Roman fellow citizens. Yet other Jews, especially many who lived out in the Græco-Roman world, themselves affected by the spirit of the times, were not slow to see the advantage they had in their Scripture, and to represent it to all men as the ancient and only genuine revelation of God. Since approximately 400 B.C. Judaism had become, especially in Egypt under the Ptolemies, a missionary religion, "compassing sea and land to make one convert," and apparently presenting itself in Greek terms, like the other oriental religions, as the Way to the Spirit.

Each of these religions, as well as many others, had its special appeal. Orphism offered the Spirit through ancient rites and enthusiasm. The beautiful Sun-God Mithra had his atoning slaughter of a sacred bull, by which his devotees might be benefited. In the ceremony of initiation into another mystery, that of Cybele, a bull was butchered in such a way that its blood streamed down over the initiate, making him a partaker in the very life and spirit of the god himself. These mysteries, then, released for men the purifying and saving forces of the universe. Isis, the lovely distraught mother, who found and collected the scattered pieces of her beloved's slaughtered body, and brought him back to life, represented the deeply desired compassion and love of God for men, God's philanthropy, as they called it, which would heal their broken lives and assure them a happy life after death. Demeter, seeking her daughter Persephone, was the saving *mater dolorosa* of antiquity. And Jews, who had the most magnificent body of revealed writing of any religion, had with it an ability to dominate the material environment which excited the envy of those who ridiculed them for their peculiarities. Yet all these religions by their ritual and moral discipline rather led the initiate up to deity than brought the deity down to men. Or perhaps the two might be regarded as meeting half-way. But the deity did not come down and dwell with men in any permanently accessible form. He or she remained remote, approachable only by mystery and rite, and, as a result of the expense of initiation, frequently accessible not at all to the poor. If, then, there should come a religion which would offer such Scriptures and moral achievement as Judaism, such enthusiasm as Orphism, such vividly enacted dispensation of spiritual rebirth as Cybele and Eleusis, such passionate yearning love in deity as Demeter and Isis, together with magnificent ritual in which the lower classes might participate, it would be a great religion indeed. But if to these it could add a concreteness of conviction, a belief that deity, in his love of men, had actually come down in the flesh and lived with men, loved the poor, helped the suffering, and then had died an agonizing death for mankind, but had conquered that death by coming back to life afterwards; and that now, having gone back to reign with God as before, he was acting as mediator and helper for men; and that he had left behind on earth his Spirit in which men could be reborn and live, die and rise again: could such a story be told by men who could say "I saw him with my own eyes, touched him with my own hands," then the religious need of the age would be met. The story of early Christianity is the story of the rise and conquest of a religion which offered just this appeal.

II

THE MIDDLE AGES

PART TWO

⟳§ THE MIDDLE AGES

After the fall of the Roman Empire in the West in the fifth century, western Europe entered a period of five centuries of almost total darkness, after which it began a fast and widespread recovery and growth which lasted about 300 years. The two centuries of comparative stagnation which followed were brightened mainly by the Italian Renaissance. The millennium after the fall of Rome in the West is traditionally known as the Middle Ages, specifically the middle period between the fall of the Roman empire in the West and the age of exploration and Protestantism that is usually associated with the "modern" world. Some specialists have subdivided this millenium into the early Middle Ages (500–1000), the Middle Ages (1000–1300), and the Late Middle Ages (1300–1500).

Cogent reasons exist to follow this classification. After Rome's fall in the West, the Greek tradition flourished in Byzantium and, with modifications, in the Moslem world. But the West languished for five centuries or so before it began to regain its classical heritage. In the early Middle Ages, and indeed long after, disorder prevailed, and only slowly did the West build toward security. Peasants, the inarticulate majority of Western humanity, toiled in the fields, while knights, only slightly more articulate, fought and administered. Meanwhile churchmen prayed and studied Christian theology as well as classical writings, which helped to set the tone of a higher value system. Medieval life shows an extreme range of contrasts, from utter brutality on the one hand to exquisite gentility on the other. And herein lies one of its many fascinations for students of history.

NINE

THE RISE OF ISLAM

After the fall of the Roman Empire in the West, Hellenistic civilization survived in the Eastern Mediterranean world. The Byzantine (east Roman) Empire, which lasted until A.D. *1453, nourished the Greek tradition and was particularly creative in architecture, law, and ecclesiastical literature. From the seventh century onward Islam challenged Byzantium and spread westward through Egypt into Spain. But the Moslem conquest did not destroy the Greek heritage. Instead, the Moslem world absorbed the Greek tradition in philosophy and science (although not in literature), preserved it, and added to it important ingredients, among them the zero and considerable medical lore. For about 500 years the Moslem world was the most creative successor of Mediterranean civilization, and in time it transmitted its expanded classical heritage to western Europe. In full recognition of the vital role of Islam, Philip K. Hitti has analyzed the rise of Moslem civilization and its spread westward.*

PHILIP K. HITTI

HISTORY OF THE ARABS*

The two cardinal events of late ancient times are the Teutonic migrations resulting in the disruption of the venerable Roman empire, and the Arab conquests which demolished the Persian empire and shook the Byzantine power to its very foundation. Of these two, the Arab conquests culminating in the occupation of Spain marked the beginning of the Middle Ages.[1] If someone in the first third of the seventh Christian century had had the audacity to prophesy that within a decade some unheralded, unforeseen power from the hitherto barbarous and little-known land of Arabia was to make its appearance, hurl itself against the only two world powers of the age, fall heir to the one—the Sāsānid—and strip the other—the Byzantine—of its fairest provinces, he would undoubtedly have been declared a lunatic. Yet that was exactly what happened. After the death of the Prophet sterile Arabia seems to have been converted as if by magic into a nursery of heroes the like of whom both in number and quality is hard to find anywhere. The military campaigns of Khālid ibn-al-Walīd and 'Amr ibn-al-'Āṣ which ensued in al-'Irāq, Persia, Syria and Egypt are among the most brilliantly executed in the history of warfare and bear favourable comparison with those of Napoleon, Hannibal, or Alexander.

The enfeebled condition of the rival Byzantines and Sāsānids who had conducted internecine wars against each other for many generations; the heavy taxes, consequent upon these wars, imposed on the citizens of both empires and undermining their sense of loyalty; the previous domestication of Arabian tribes in Syria and Mesopotamia, and particularly along the borders; the existence of schisms in the Christian church resulting in the establishment of Monophysite communities in Syria and Egypt and Nestorian congregations in al-'Irāq and Persia, together with the persecution by the orthodox church—all these paved the way for the surprisingly rapid progress of Arabian arms. The Byzantines had neglected the frontier forts. After their victory of Mu'tah, in the land of ancient Moab, over the column sent by the Prophet (Sept. 629), Heraclius stopped the subsidies which the Syro-Arab tribes south of the Dead Sea and on the Madīnah-Ghazzah route had regularly received.[2] The native Semites of Syria and Palestine as well as the Hamites of Egypt looked upon the Arabian newcomers as nearer of kin than their hated and oppressive alien overlords. In fact the Moslem conquests may be looked upon as the recovery by the ancient Near East of its early domain. Under the stimulus of Islam the East now awoke and reasserted itself after a millennium of Western domination. Moreover, the tribute exacted by the new conquerors was even less than that exacted by the old, and the conquered could now pursue their religious practices with more

* From *History of the Arabs,* 6th ed., 1956, pp. 142–46, 174–75, by Philip K. Hitti. Reprinted by permission of Macmillan and Co., Ltd. and St. Martin's Press, Inc., and The Macmillan Co. of Canada, Ltd.

[1] Henri Pirenne, *Mahomet et Charlemagne,* 7th ed. (Brussels, 1935).

[2] Theophanes, pp. 335–6.

freedom and less interference. As for the Arabians themselves, they represented a fresh and vigorous stock fired with new enthusiasm, imbued with the will to conquer and emboldened by the utter contempt of death inculcated by their new faith. But no small share of their seemingly miraculous success was due to their application of a military technique adapted to the open steppes of Western Asia and North Africa —the use of cavalry and camelry—which the Romans never mastered.

The "clerical" interpretation of the Islamic movement, emphasized in Arabic sources, makes it entirely or primarily a religious movement and lays no stress on the underlying economic causes. The corresponding and equally discredited hypothesis held by many Christians represents the Arabian Moslems as offering the Koran with the one hand the sword with the other. Outside of the Arabian peninsula and especially in the instance of the *ahl al-kitāb* (Christians and Jews) there was a third and, from the standpoint of the conquerors, more desirable choice besides the Koran and the sword—tribute. "Make war . . . upon such of those to whom the Book has been given until they pay tribute offered on the back of their hands, in a state of humiliation." [3] This third choice was later by the necessity of circumstances offered to Zoroastrians and heathen Berbers and Turks; in the case of all of these theory gave way to expediency. Islam did provide a new battle-cry, a convenient rallying-point and a party watchword. It undoubtedly acted as a cohesive and cementing agency for the heterogeneous masses never before united and furnished a large part of the driving force. But it is hardly in itself enough to explain the conquests. Not fanaticism but economic necessity drove the Bedouin hordes, and most of the armies of conquest were recruited from the Bedouins, beyond the confines of their arid abode to the fair lands of the north. The passion to go to heaven in the next life may have been operative with some, but the desire for the comforts and luxuries of the civilized regions of the Fertile Crescent was just as strong in the case of many.

This economic aspect of the interpretation of the conquests, worked out by Caetani,[4] Becker [5] and other modern critical scholars, was not entirely ignored by the Arab chroniclers of old. Al-Balādhuri, the most judicious of the historians of the conquest, declares that in recruiting for the Syrian campaign abu-Bakr "wrote to the people of Makkah, al-Tā'if, al-Yaman and all the Arabs in Najd and al-Hijāz summoning them to a 'holy war' and arousing their desire for it and for the booty to be got from the Greeks." [6] Rustam, the Persian general who defended his country against the Arab invasion, made the following remark to the Moslem envoy: "I have learned that ye were forced to what ye are doing by nothing but the narrow means of livelihood and by poverty." [7] A verse in the *Hamāsah* of abu-Tammām [8] has put the case tersely:

> No, not for Paradise didst thou the nomad
> life forsake;
> Rather, I believe, it was thy yearning after
> bread and dates.

Envisaged in its proper setting, the Islamic expansion marks the final stage in the agelong process of gradual infiltration from the barren desert to the adjacent Fertile Crescent, the last great Semitic migration.

The chroniclers, all of whom viewed the events of the conquest in the light of their subsequent developments, would also have us believed that these campaigns were conducted through the sagacity of the first caliphs, particularly abu-Bakr and 'Umar, in accordance with carefully prearranged plans.

[3] Sūr. 9 : 29.

[4] *Annali,* vol. ii, pp. 831–61.
[5] In *Cambridge Medieval History* (New York, 1913), vol. ii, ch. xi.
[6] *Futūh,* p. 107 = Hitti, p. 165.
[7] Balādhuri, pp. 256–7 = Hitti, pp. 411–12.
[8] P. 795.

History shows but very few cases in which the course of great events was foreseen by those who launched them. Far from being entirely the result of deliberate and cool calculation, the campaigns seem to have started as raids to provide new outlets for the warring spirit of the tribes now forbidden to engage in fratricidal combats, the objective in most cases being booty and not the gaining of a permanent foothold. But the machine so built soon got beyond the control of those who built it. The movement acquired momentum as the warriors passed from victory to victory. It was then that the systematic campaigns began, and the creation of the Arab empire followed inevitably. Its creation was therefore due less to early design than to the logic of immediate circumstances.

The clerical or theological view favouring a providential interpretation of Islamic expansion, corresponding to the Old Testament interpretation of the Hebrew history and to the medieval philosophy of Christian history, has a faulty philological basis. The term Islam may be used in three senses: originally a religion, Islam later became a state, and finally a culture. Unlike Judaism and the old Buddhism, the religion of Islam proved as much of an aggressive and missionary religion as Christianity. Subsequently it built up a state. The Islam that conquered the northern regions was not the Islamic religion but the Islamic state. The Arabians burst forth upon an unsuspecting world as members of a national theocracy. It was Arabianism and not Muhammadanism that triumphed first. Not until the second and third centuries of the Moslem era did the bulk of the people in Syria, Mesopotamia and Persia profess the religion of Muhammad. Between the military conquest of these regions and their religious conversion a long period intervened. And when they were converted the people turned primarily because of self-interest—to escape tribute and seek identification with the ruling class. As for Islam as a culture, it developed slowly after the military conquests on a substratum composed of the core and heritage of the Syro-Aramaean, Persian and Hellenistic civilizations which had preceded it. With Islam the Near Orient not only recaptured the whole of its former political domain but regained in the realm of culture its ancient intellectual preeminence. . . .

By the conquest of the Fertile Crescent and the lands of Persia and Egypt the Arabians came into possession not only of geographical areas but of the earliest seats of civilization in the whole world. Thus the sons of the desert fell heir to these hoary cultures with their long traditions going back to Greco-Roman, Iranian, Pharaonic and Assyro-Babylonian times. In art and architecture, in philosophy, in medicine, in science and literature, in government, the original Arabians had nothing to teach and everything to learn. And what voracious appetites they proved to have! With an ever sharp sense of curiosity and with latent potentialities never aroused before, these Moslem Arabians in collaboration with and by the help of their subject peoples began now to assimilate, adapt and reproduce their intellectual and esthetic heritage. In Ctesiphon, Edessa, Nisibis, Damascus, Jerusalem and Alexandria they viewed, admired and copied the work of the architect, the artisan, the jeweller and the manufacturer. To all these centres of ancient culture they came, they saw and were conquered. Theirs was another instance in which the victor was made captive by the vanquished.

What we therefore call "Arab civilization" was Arabian neither in its origins and fundamental structure nor in its principal ethnic aspects. The purely Arabian contribution in it was in the linguistic and to a certain extent in the religious fields. Throughout the whole period of the caliphate the Syrians, the Persians, the Egyptians and others, as Moslem converts or as Christians and Jews, were the foremost bearers of the torch of enlightenment and learning just as the subjugated Greeks were in their relation to the victorious Romans. The Arab Islamic civilization was at bottom the Hellenized Aramaic and the Iranian civilizations as developed under the ægis of the caliphate and expressed through the medium of the Arabic tongue. In another sense it was the logical continuation of the early Semitic civilization of the Fertile Crescent originated and developed by the Assyro-Babylonians, Phoenicians, Aramaeans and Hebrews. In it the unity of the Mediterranean civilization of Western Asia found its culmination.

TEN

THE CHRONICLE OF JOCELIN OF BRAKELOND

The lopsided documentation of the Middle Ages, heavily weighted toward theology and other ecclesiastical matters, along with the obvious domination of the higher value system by the Church, has led many historians to consider the medieval period as an Age of Faith. The soaring magnificence of the cathedrals has reinforced this view. Some scholars have taken literally the otherworldly emphasis of the ecclesiastical documents, and have concluded, with varying degrees of reservation, that Christian idealism dominated the period. A few, dazzled by the later glamour of the Italian Renaissance, have denied that much, if any, appreciable individualism or secularism existed in the Middle Ages. Both views are unrealistic. The Middle Ages were secular as well as ecclesiastical, and people with fully developed personalities lived, loved, worked, and quarreled in this allegedly "otherworldly" time. The Chronicle of Jocelin of Brakelond offers an intensely human corrective to the caricature of existence which the lopsided medieval documentation as a whole has produced.

Jocelin became a monk in the great monastery of Bury St. Edmunds in Norfolk, England, in 1173. His Chronicle, which begins with the death of Abbot Hugh in 1180 and ends abruptly in 1203, is mainly in praise of Abbot Samson (1135–1211). Old Abbot Hugh, Samson's predecessor, had let the affairs of the monastery fall into laxity, and Samson, appropriately named, undertook a reformist regime after his election in 1182. The Chronicle, first published in Latin in 1840, attracted the attention of Thomas Carlyle, who made it the central subject of his Past and Present *(1843). English translations followed. Carlyle described Jocelin as "an ingenious and ingenuous, a cherry-hearted, innocent, yet withal shrewd, noticing, quick-witted man."*

The selection from the Chronicle, which follows, describes the events preceding Samson's election and reveals in authentic tones the electioneering and gossip of the monks, not as spiritual superfolk in an earnestly otherworldly and austere time, but as flesh-and-blood people with weaknesses and foibles characteristic of human beings in any historical period.

JOCELIN OF BRAKELOND

THE ELECTION OF AN ABBOT*

Hugh the abbot being buried, it was ordered in chapter that some one should give intelligence to Ranulf de Glanville, the justiciar of England, of the death of the abbot. Master Samson and Master R. Ruffus, our monks, quickly went beyond seas, to report the same fact to our lord the King, and obtained letters that those possessions and rents of the monastery, which were distinct from those of the abbot, should be wholly in the hands of the prior and convent, and that the remainder of the abbey should be in the hands of the King. The wardship of the abbey was committed to Robert of Cockfield and Robert of Flamville, the steward, who forthwith put by gage and safe pledges all those servants and relatives of the abbot to whom the abbot had, after the commencement of his illness, given anything, or who had taken anything away belonging to the abbot, and also the abbot's chaplain (a monk of the house), whom the prior bailed. Entering into our vestiary, they caused all the ornaments of the church to be noted down in an inventory.

During the vacancy in the abbacy, the prior, above all things, studied to keep peace in the convent, and to preserve the honour of the church in entertaining guests, being desirous of irritating no one, of not provoking anybody to anger; in fact, of keeping all persons and things in quietude. He nevertheless winked at some acts in our officials which needed reformation, and especially in the sacrist, as if he cared not how that officer dealt with the sacristy. Yet during the vacancy, the sacrist neither satisfied any debt nor erected any building, but the oblations and incomings were foolishly frittered away.

Wherefore the prior, who was the head of the convent, seemed by the greater part to be highly censurable, and was said to be remiss; and this thing our brethren called to mind among themselves, when it came to the point of making choice of an abbot.

Our cellarer entertained all guests, of whatsoever condition they were, at the expense of the convent. William the sacrist, on his part, gave and spent as he chose, kind man! giving alike what he should and should not; "blinding the eyes of all with gifts."

Samson the sub-sacrist, being master over the workmen, did his best that no breach, chink, crack or flaw should be left unrepaired so far as he was able; whereby he acquired great favour with the convent, and especially with the cloister monks. In those days our choir was erected by Samson's exertion; and he arranged the order of the paintings, and composed elegiac verses for them. He also made a great draught of stone and sand for building the great tower of the church. Being asked whence he procured the money for his work, he answered that certain of the burgesses had privily given him moneys for building and completing the tower.

Nevertheless, certain of our brethren said that Warin, a monk of our house and keeper of the shrine, together with Samson the sub-sacrist, had conspired to remove some por-

* From *The Chronicle of Jocelin of Brakelond*, pp. 12–33, edited by Sir Ernest Clarke. Alexander Moring, The De La More Press. London, 1903.

tion of the offerings to the shrine, in order that they might disburse the same for the necessary purposes of the church, and in particular for the building of the tower; being the more ready to believe this when they saw that the offerings were expended for extraordinary purposes by others, who, to speak plainly, stole them. And these before-named two men, in order to remove from themselves the suspicion of any such pious theft, made a certain hollow trunk, with a hole in the middle or at the top, and fastened with an iron lock. This they caused to be set up in the great church, near the door without the choir, where the common people usually pass, so that persons should put their contributions therein for the building of the tower.

Now William the sacrist had a jealousy of his companion Samson, as had many others who took part with the same William, Christians as well as Jews; the Jews, I say, to whom the sacrist was said to be father and protector, whose protection they indeed enjoyed, having free ingress and egress, and going all over the monastery, rambling about the altars and by the shrine while high mass was being celebrated. Moreover, their moneys were kept safe in our treasury, under the care of the sacrist, and, what was still more improper, their wives with their little ones were lodged in our pittancy in time of war. His enemies or opponents having, therefore, consulted together how they might suddenly overcome Samson, they conferred with Robert of Cockfield and his colleague, who were wardens of the abbey, and persuaded them to this—that they should, on behalf of the King, forbid any one to erect any fabric or building so long as the abbacy was vacant; but that, on the other hand, the moneys from the offerings should be collected, and kept for the purpose of discharging some debt.

And thus was Samson beguiled, and his "strength departed from him," nor could he from thenceforth labour as he had desired. Indeed, his opponents were able to delay, but not annul, his purpose; for having regained his strength, and "pulled down the two pillars," that is, having removed the two wardens of the abbey, upon whom the malice of others relied, the Lord gave him, in process of time, the means of fulfilling his desire of building the aforesaid tower, and of finishing it even as he wished. And so it was, as if it had been said to him from above, "Well done, thou good and faithful servant; thou hast been faithful over a few things, I will make thee ruler over many things."

During the time that the abbacy was vacant we oftentimes, as was our duty, besought God and the holy martyr St. Edmund that they would vouchsafe to us and our church a meet shepherd, thrice every week singing the seven penitential psalms prostrate in the choir, after going forth from chapter. There were some amongst us who, had it been known who was to be abbot, would not have prayed so devoutly.

As concerned the choice of an abbot, assuming the King gave us free election, divers men spoke in divers ways—some publicly, some privately; and "so many men, so many opinions."

One said of another, "That brother is a good monk, a likely person; he is well conversant with the Rule and custom of the house; although he may not be so perfect a philosopher as certain others, he would make a very good abbot. Abbot Ording was not a learned man, and yet he was a good abbot, and governed this house wisely: we read, too, in the fable, that it had been better for the frogs to have chosen a log for a king, upon whom they might rely, than a serpent, who venomously hissed, and after his hisses devoured his subjects."

Another would answer, "How may this be? How can an unlearned man deliver a sermon in chapter, or to the people on festivals? How can he who does not understand the Scriptures attain the knowledge of 'binding and loosing'? seeing that the cure of souls is the art of arts and science of sciences. God forbid that a dumb image should be set up in the Church of St. Edmund, where many learned and studious men are well known to be."

Also said one of another, "That brother is a good clerk, eloquent and careful, strict in the Rule; he has much loved the convent, and has undergone many hardships in respect of the possessions of the church: he is worthy to be made abbot." Another answered, "From good clerks, Good Lord, deliver us: that it may please Thee to preserve us from the barrators of Norfolk, we beseech Thee to hear us, good Lord." Moreover, one said of another, "That brother is a good manager, which is proved from his department, and from the offices which he has well served, and by the buildings and reparations which he has performed. He is able to travail for and defend the house, and is, moreover, something of a clerk, although 'much learning has not made him mad': he is worthy to be made abbot." Another answered, "God forbid that a man who can neither read nor chant, nor perform Divine service—a wicked and unjust man, and a grinder of the faces of the poor—should be abbot."

Also said one of another, "That brother is a kind man, affable and amiable, peaceful and well-regulated, open-hearted and liberal, a learned man and an eloquent, a proper man enough in looks and deportment, and beloved by many, indoors as well as out; and such a man might, with God's permission, become abbot to the great honour of the church." The other answered, "It is no honour, but rather a burden, to have a man who is too nice in his meat and drink; who thinks it a virtue to sleep long; who is expert in spending much, and yet gets little; who is snoring when others are awake; who always is desirous to be in plenty, nor yet cares for the debts which increase from day to day, nor considers the means of discharging expenses; hating anxiety and trouble; caring for nought so long as one day comes and another goes; a man cherishing and fostering flatterers and liars; a man who is one thing in name and another in deed. From such a prelate defend us, O Lord!"

Also said a certain one of his fellow, "That man is almost wiser than all of us put together, both in secular and ecclesiastical matters; a wonderful counsellor, strict in rule, learned and eloquent, and of proper stature; such a prelate would do honour to our church."

The other answered, "True, if he were of known and approved reputation. His character is questionable; report may lie, or it may not. And although the man you mean is wise, of lowly carriage in chapter, devout in psalmody, strict in the cloister whilst he is in the cloister, yet it is mere outward show with him. What if he do excel in any office? He is too scornful, lightly esteems the monks, is closely intimate with secular persons; and should he be angry, scarcely returns an answer with a good grace to any brother, or to one even asking a question of him."

I heard in like manner one brother disparaged by some, because he was slow of speech; of whom it was said that he had paste or malt in his mouth when he was called upon to speak. And as for myself, being at that time a youth, "I understood as a youth, I spoke as a youth;" and said I never could consent that any one should be made abbot unless he knew somewhat of dialectics, and knew how to discern truth from falsehood. Again, a certain person, who in his own eyes seemed very wise, said, "May the almighty Lord bestow on us a foolish and simple shepherd, so that it should be the more needful for him to get help from us!"

I heard in like manner a certain studious and learned man, and honourable by the nobility of his family, disparaged by some of our seniors merely for this reason—because he was a novice. The novices, on the other hand, said of the elders, that old men were valetudinarians, by no means fit to govern a monastery. And thus many persons spoke many things, "and each was fully persuaded in his own mind."

I observed Samson the sub-sacrist as he

was sitting along with the others at blood-letting season (at which time monks are wont to reveal to each other the secrets of the heart, and to talk over matters with each other). I saw him, I say, sitting along with the others, smiling and saying nothing, but noting the words of each, and after a lapse of twenty years calling to mind some of the before-written opinions. In whose hearing I used to reply to these critics, that if we were to put off the choice of an abbot until we found one who was above disparagement or fault, we never should find such a one, for no one alive is without fault, and "no estate is in all respects blessed."

Upon one particular occasion I was unable to restrain myself, but must needs blurt out my own private opinion, thinking that I spoke to trusty ears. I then said that a certain person who formerly had a great regard for me, and had conferred many benefits upon me, was unworthy of the abbacy, and that another was more worthy; in fact, I named one for whom I had less regard.

I spoke according to my own conscience, rather considering the common weal of the church than my own advancement; and what I said was true, as the sequel proved. And, behold, one of the sons of Belial disclosed my saying to my friend and benefactor; for which reason, even to this day, never could I since, neither by entreaty nor good offices, regain his goodwill to the full. "What I have said I have said." "And the word once spoken flies without recall."

One thing remains, that I take heed to my ways for the future; and if I should live so long as to see the abbacy vacant, I shall consider carefully what, to whom, and when I speak on such a matter, lest I either offend God by lying, or man by speaking unreasonably. I shall then advise (should I last so long), that we choose not too good a monk, nor yet an over-wise clerk, neither one too simple nor too weak; lest, if he be over wise in his own conceit, he may be too confident in his own judgment, and contemn others; or, if he be too boorish, he may become a byword to others; I know that it has been said, "In the middle you will be safest," also that "Blessed are they who hold a middle course."

Perhaps, after all, it may be the best course to hold my peace altogether, and say in my heart, "He that is able to receive it, let him receive it."

The abbacy being vacant, Augustine, the Archbishop of Norway, took up his abode with us, in the house of the abbot, receiving by the King's precept ten shillings a day from the revenues of the abbey. He was of considerable assistance in obtaining for us our free election, bearing witness of what was well, and publicly declaring before the King what he had seen and heard.

At that time the holy child Robert suffered martyrdom, and was buried in our church; and many signs and wonders were wrought among the people, as we have elsewhere written.

ELEVEN

THE PEASANTS

Probably ninety per cent of medieval people were peasants. But astonishingly little is known about them. Universally illiterate, like prehistoric people they left no documents of their own. Literate members of medieval society, mainly churchmen, either ignored the peasants, or, in most cases, mentioned them with contempt. To reconstruct the life of peasants, not only their economic condition but also their customs, attitudes, and inner experience, presents an almost impossible challenge. Such reconstruction must come from a hodgepodge of fragments, many satiric rather than sympathetic in mood. George Coulton, one of the world's foremost medievalists, brought his unusually deep insight to this unusually difficult problem.

G. G. COULTON

THE MEDIEVAL VILLAGE*

The medieval peasant was, essentially, the kind of man who still meets us by the thousand in outlying districts of the Continent, and by handfuls even in Great Britain. He lacked some very important things which his descendants now enjoy even in the remotest corners of Europe; yet, in the main, his existence was what may still be found here and there. Looking closely at him and his village, we see the rough life of labouring folk hardened by their constant fight against land and weather; we see taskmasters whose interests necessarily conflicted with the needs of those elementary breadwinners; yet who, to their credit be it said, did not always enforce every advantage that the strict law might have given them. Our general impression will be that of a society very engaging in its old-world simplicity, but with much to learn before it can struggle through into modern civilization, whether we take that word in Richard Cobden's sense or in the sense of those romantics who picture an ideal society enjoying all modern material gains, yet purged from the dross of Reformation and Capitalism. No thoughtful and unprejudiced reader, however unfamiliar with special medieval conditions, is likely to go far wrong in his judgement on what we find (for instance) in the Durham and Halesowen Rolls. He will probably conclude, as Berthold concluded nearly seven centuries ago, that it will need the experience of many generations to teach these men an efficient sense of social solidarity. And the real tragedy is that so much truth should be in Berthold's words, and that so much of the peasant's degradation should be accountable to all rich folk, from that day to our own. As the operative

* From *The Medieval Village,* pp. 390–93, by G. G. Coulton. Reprinted by permission of Cambridge University Press. Cambridge, 1925.

Higgins says to Margaret Hale in *North and South*: "If I'm going wrong when I think I'm going right, it's their sin who ha' left me in my ignorance. I ha' thought till my brains ached." The medieval peasant was what he was, and the modern is what he is, partly because the sifting process of civilization has left him at the bottom, but partly also because luckier folk have pushed him down. His annals are short and simple; the ploughman does not wade through slaughter to a throne, but all the cruellest elements of tragedy may be found in his village, as Turgenieff shows in his *King Lear of the Steppe,* and Gottfried Keller in *Romeo und Julia auf dem Dorfe*. There was much real neighbourly kindness; but there were also desperate jealousies and feuds, with crimes which seem all the more sordid when so little is at stake. The medieval peasant shows us mankind in the making, human nature in its elementary aspects. If we try to reckon up the things which he most truly enjoyed, we shall find that all, or nearly all, are common to all countries and ages—earth's bosom, the sun and clouds and rain, the inexhaustible love and endurance of the human heart:

> I said it in the meadow path,
> I said it on the mountain stairs—
> The best things any mortal hath
> Are those which every mortal shares.[1]

Those simple things the peasant enjoyed as we do; and, if this simplicity shows his faults naked and unabashed, it is equally transparent of courage and moral beauty. That the life of the medieval village had a true dignity at its best, and even a true glory in the highest sense of that word, no man can doubt who reads Chaucer's brief description of the Ploughman. Here we have the least cultured stratum of society in that day, even though the Ploughman was, by his calling, near the top of that lowest stratum. We cannot escape from the significance of that public judgement, all the more damning because of its impersonal and unconscious character, which has transmuted *villanus* into *villain,* and *Bauer* into *boor*. Polite speech, as early as the thirteenth century, used the word *village* to characterize coarseness of thought and deed.[2] Yet nobody who knows the modern peasant can doubt that, if we could travel back, we should find many comparisons humiliating to ourselves in the lives of these "poor folk in cottages, charged with children and chief lord's rent." This sort of family, in quite recent times, has begun to supply the universities with some of their best stuff; and this sort, in the Middle Ages, formed a village aristocracy not of rank but of merit. Here and there the medieval peasant bought his freedom and took to learning; it is possible, though far from certain, that this happened even more frequently than in the seventeenth century, when so many yeomen's sons did the like. But, in the vast majority of cases, these medieval peasants pursued the even tenor of their way, from cradle to grave, along their native fields and lanes. We may conclude—and to me no other conclusion seems possible—that the modern labourer is better off, even materially, than these men, and incomparably superior in social, political and religious liberty; but this should not make us forget how truly, in every age, the Kingdom of Heaven is within a man. We may keep our thoughts sweet by reading and re-reading what Chaucer tells us concerning the Poor Parson's brother:

> With him ther was a Plowman, was his brother,
> That hadde y-lad of dong ful many a fother,
> A trewë swinker and a good was he,
> Livinge in pees and parfit charitee.
> God loved he best with al his holë herte
> At allë tymes, thogh him gamëd or smerte,
> And thanne his neighëbour right as himselve.

[1] Lucy Larcomb, in *Songs of Faith, Nature, and Comradeship,* No. 36. The writer is a manual worker, who in Chaucer's day would probably have been what the present writer and reader might also have been, a serf.

[2] Alwin Schultz, *Höfisches Leben,* 2nd ed. 1889, 1, 156. *Dörperie* was used in the language of German chivalry as *villenie* in French.

He woldë thresshe, and therto dyke and
delve,
For Cristës sake, for every poorë wight,
Withouten hyre, if it lay in his might.
His tythës payëd he ful faire and wel,
Bothe of his proprë swink and his catel.
In a tabard he rood upon a mere.

For the land is eternally healthy, and we suffer when we feel the least divorce or estrangement from it. But, so long as urban life and village life exist, the peasant will always be a child compared with the city-dweller. The contrast was clearly marked even 600 years ago, in spite of what Maitland has taught us concerning the strong agricultural elements in the urban civilization of those days. This gulf has since widened, and it becomes enormous if we regard the medieval village solely through modern spectacles. It was W. H. Riehl, I think, who made exhaustive researches and found that the German peasant-farmer of about 100 years ago had a vocabulary of only 600 words, all told. Mr. Tawney suggests that most medieval villagers saw no more than a hundred separate individuals in the course of their whole lives.[3] There is a deep abyss between these men and the modern villager with his bicycle and picture-palace, and perhaps with his memories of strange lands and folk in the Great War. As compared with him, we must repeat the word, medieval peasants were children. We should find even Chaucer's Ploughman a child in his serene unconscious conservatism and dead-weight of inattention, concentrated on his own things in his own little corner, while we vainly dangle a crown of more complicated civilization over his head—yet childlike, again, in his divine receptivity at sudden moments, and in his resolve to take the kingdom of glory by force. We should find in him the child's April moods of sunshine and shower; a nature sometimes hidebound and selfish and narrow to the last degree, and sometimes generously impulsive; with the child's pathetic trust at one moment, and unreasonable distrust at another; and, above all, with a child's fear of the dark. . . .

[3] *L.c.* p. 264. The isolation may be exaggerated in this sentence, but not much.

TWELVE

THE KNIGHTS

If peasants were universally illiterate, medieval knights were seldom literate and seldom left records of their own. What may be known of them comes mainly from fragments, not only stirring descriptions in chronicles but also from more fanciful descriptions in epics. As that part of medieval society which fought, while churchmen prayed and peasants tilled the fields, knights embodied the standard virtues of warriors—strength, courage, and loyalty—as modified somewhat by the gentler values of chivalry. Nonetheless, they were fundamentally fighters in times of widespread disorder and in many ways were a rude and rough lot. They also served as rural administrators, the ancestors of the country gentry. To reconstruct their daily lives, not only what they did but also, equally importantly, what they thought (thinking being a part of and a motive for doing), demands a high degree of creative imagination. Sidney Painter, one of America's greatest and best beloved medieval scholars, included among his many writings a unique reconstruction of the life and attitudes of this important segment of medieval society.

SIDNEY PAINTER

A HISTORY OF THE MIDDLE AGES*

The feudal male had one primary function: fighting. His education and his way of life were aimed at fitting him for this occupation. At the age of seven or eight he was sent away from home lest the indulgence of his parents, especially his mother, might soften him. He received his education at some friendly feudal court, usually that of his father's lord or of a relative. For some years he was a page serving the lady of the castle. Any nonmilitary talent he acquired, such as playing a musical instrument or singing, was likely to be gained in these years. At fourteen or fifteen he became a squire and served the lord. He cared for the horses, polished armor, and served his lord at table. He was hardened to the wearing of armor and trained in the use of knightly equipment. When he was considered old enough and adequately prepared, usually when he was about twenty, he was given arms, armor, and horse of his own, and solemnly made a knight. In its simplest form, before the development of chivalric ideas, this ceremony consisted of putting on his new armor, kneeling before a knight—usually the lord who had trained him—and receiving a terrific blow from the knight's fist or the flat of his sword. Once the feudal male had been knighted he became of age. He could do homage and rule his fief.

The knight's principal occupation and favorite amusement was fighting. If he were a baron, he fought to keep his vassals in hand and to gain what he could from his neighbors. The simple knight who held a fief followed his lord to battle because it was his duty and in the hopes of sharing in the booty. The landless knight fought for his living. War could be extremely profitable. Although plundering peasant villages could rarely have yielded much booty, there was always the chance of capturing another knight and ransoming him. Gerard de Furnival, a simple knight who followed King John, captured a Breton noble and received enough money to buy for his son the heiress to an English barony. But entirely apart from the chance of profit it is important to remember that fighting was a delightful sport. And it was little more dangerous than football. The knight's armor protected him from the weapons of anyone who was not a knight and fairly well from the knightly sword and lance. Moreover no knight wanted to kill another, for a corpse was of no value. If a feudal lord went to war with a neighbor and killed him, he found the slain man's heir in his place ready to continue the struggle. But if he captured his foe, he could ransom him for a rich manor or even a strong castle. Even when kings and feudal princes fought supposedly serious wars in the early Middle Ages, they were not bloody. In the great and decisive battle of Lincoln in 1217, where some 600 knights on one side fought 800 on the other, only one knight was killed, and everyone was horrified at the unfortunate accident.

When he was living peacefully at home the knight rose well before dawn, commonly as early as two or three o'clock, heard mass in his chapel, and got the business of the day out of the way. He consulted with his officials, judged cases, and generally saw to the business of his fief. By dawn he was ready for the really important occupation of the day—hunting. This could take many forms. The most highly esteemed—because it was most like war—was the pursuit on horseback of a stag or wild boar and the slaying of the quarry when the chase was over. Deer, wolves, and wildcats were hunted in the same manner. A more gentle form of hunting, considered peculiarly suitable for ladies but practiced avidly by their lords as well, was hawking. Here one rode through the green meadows beside a stream with a trained hawk on one's wrist and sent it in pursuit of any game bird that appeared. Hunting formed an extremely important part of a noble's life, and he kept great packs of hunting dogs and many trained hawks, or more properly falcons.

About two or three o'clock in the afternoon the knight settled down to a good solid meal consisting of course after course of meat and poultry well reinforced with bread and pastry, and washed down with incredible quantities of ale or wine, according to the custom of the country. When he finished this repast, he was in the mood to be entertained. Here tastes differed. King John of England considered a hanging a suitable after-dinner entertainment, but others preferred less gruesome forms. Wandering minstrels came by ready to display their varied talents. Some were merely storytellers, with a magnificent supply of the types of tale that have amused men of all epochs. Others had with them tumblers, dancing bears, or dancing girls. A few had learned long narrative poems that they recited. As the only artificial light available was smoky torches, the knight was likely to go to bed soon after darkness set in.

Needless to say, the knight of the eleventh and early twelfth centuries was no model of gentleness and refinement. He drank himself into a stupor with considerable regularity. His castle was usually filled with prostitutes. If he got annoyed with his opponent during a chess game, he was inclined to brain him with one of the massive chessmen of the day. When a servant was slow in bringing his wine, he threw a javelin at him to speed his steps. If his wife annoyed him, he beat her savagely. In one contemporary tale there is a scene where a wife suggests to her husband that it is not quite the thing to murder a guest while he is taking a bath. She is promptly knocked down for her trouble. In the fourteenth century, when ways had grown gentler, the Knight of La Tour Landry wrote a book of advice for his daughters. He told them of a wife who was accustomed to contradict her husband. One day her husband lost patience, knocked her flat on the floor, and kicked her face until her looks were permanently destroyed. That was what happened to wives who contradicted their husbands.

There was little or no legal restraint on the personal behavior of a member of the feudal class. While he was bound not to injure his lord, his lord's immediate family, his vassal, or his vassal's family, and might have to answer in his lord's court for an offense against a fellow vassal, the feudal system left him entirely free in regard to all other persons. Before the thirteenth century only feudal custom had any vitality in France; public law was practically nonexistent in so far as nobles were concerned. In an attempt to reduce the disorder in Normandy in 1091, William Rufus and his brother Robert issued a decree directing that if a man wanted to slay his enemy, he should give him fair warning by blowing his horn before attacking him.

In England there was an effective public law before which all freemen were equal in theory. In practice, however, the royal officials ignored offenses committed by men of importance unless someone equally important complained. As a rule the nobleman's crime was blamed on his men. Thus we hear in the records of a band of armed men plundering a village and carrying off some of the inhabitants to the castle of a great baron, Roger de Clifford. Roger in person set the amount of their ransoms, but there is no suggestion that he should be accused of any crime. A girl is abducted on the highway, taken to a knight's house, and raped by the knight and his men. The court solemnly accepted the statement of the knight that he was horrified to hear that she had not been in his house of her own free will. In short, even in England if a member of the feudal class committed his crimes against anyone other than the king or a great lord, he was fairly safe from prosecution, or at least from punishment.

The knight was religious in the sense that he accepted without question the basic teachings of the church and followed the prescribed forms of observance. He heard mass and confessed regularly. According to his means he gave alms and made donations to religious corporations. He was careful always to have at hand a private chaplain dependent on him to hear his confession: he would go to great trouble to avoid having to confess to a comparatively independent parish priest. In general he was inclined to feel that repentance and atonement were far easier than virtue. He did much as he pleased and made generous gifts to the church. Perhaps he even went on a long pilgrimage or a crusade. There were few feudal families of any importance that did not found a religious house, and a great baron might have four or five such houses endowed by his family and its vassals. It is impossible to question the knightly zeal for religion and devotion to the church and its teachings, but faith does not seem to have interfered with personal conduct to any great extent.

The women of the feudal class shared the characteristics of the men. If we are to believe preachers and storytellers, they were far too fond of drink. In fact, a not uncommon description of a lady in contemporary tales is "the fairest woman who ever drained a bottle." They beat their maid servants, sometimes to the point of death. Of course their ordinary daily life was less violent. Their work was spinning, weaving, sewing, and supervision of their households. When they hunted, it was usually in the form of falconry.

The status of women in feudal society was extremely complex. Since a woman could not fight, she was always treated as a minor by early feudal custom. She was always in the custody of some man. Before she was married she was in the care of her father. Afterwards she passed under the authority of her husband. When her husband died, she was in the custody of his lord or her eldest son. She had no rights whatever against her husband, and her person and property were completely under his control. While the church tried to limit the brutality of husbands to their wives by restricting the size of the stick with which they beat them, its teachings did not improve woman's status. She was the source of all evil: Eve's sin had banished man from Paradise. She was in herself a weak vessel given to sin. Moreover, the church insisted on the wife's subordination to her husband. The husband was to the wife as God was to him. But before bemoaning too much the status of woman in the early feudal epoch one should compare it with her position in other contemporary societies. The Moslem women were confined in a harem under the supervision of servants, and the Byzantine noblewomen were little freer. The feudal lady was completely at the mercy of her husband, but against all others she enjoyed his rank. When a knight was away, his wife ruled his household and his fief. Despite their handicap women could and did play an important part in feudal society.

The life of the feudal class was simple and crude and its members enjoyed little more luxury than the peasants who tilled their fields. A knight had at his disposal a plentiful supply of whatever his lands produced. He could have all the bread and game he could eat and all the ale or wine he could drink. But although his food was unlimited in quantity, it was far from varied. He could also have all the woolen clothes he could wear, but they were fashioned by the comparatively unskilled hands of his wife and her maids. In short, he had more food and clothing than a peasant, but they were of the same general quality.

The knight's castle was extremely simple and must have been most uncomfortable. There were usually two rooms: the hall and the chamber. In the hall the knight did his business with his officials, his vassals, and his peasants. There he ate, on tables made of planks laid across sawhorses. The hall must have been a scene of wild confusion, filled with servants, men-at-arms, prostitutes, guests, and the lord and his family. At night the servants slept in the hall, either on the tables or the floor. The chamber was the private room of the lord and his family. There he entertained guests of high rank. At night the lord, his lady, and their children slept in beds, while their personal servants slept on the chamber floor. Sometimes a very great lord had a chapel in his castle. By the twelfth century a few were so luxurious as to have a dressing-room called a wardrobe attached to the chamber. The castles were cold and drafty. The windows were covered by boards, or open. If the castle was of wood—as most were before the thirteenth century—the knight could not have a fire. In a stone castle one could have fire, but as chimneys did not appear until the late twelfth century, the smoke must have been almost unbearable. It seems likely that if one of us were offered the choice between spending a winter night with the lord or his serf, he would choose the comparatively tight mud hut with the nice warm pigs on the floor.

THIRTEEN
SOME MEDIEVAL ATTITUDES

One of the most elusive problems of the Middle Ages is the reconstruction of medieval attitudes toward life. Otherworldliness, as a counsel of perfection, existed side by side with gross cynicism. The extent to which medieval society accepted Christianity remains unknown and possibly unknowable. Medieval attitudes toward everyday affairs still present many puzzles to historians. Medieval attitudes particularly fascinated Marc Bloch, one of the greatest medieval historians of the twentieth century. By using techniques from anthropology, he asked a series of new questions about medieval mentality and found new and exciting answers; for example, the nature of the medieval image of time and nature. Such new reconstruction of medieval attitudes reveals previously unexplored areas of medieval experience and goes a long way toward clarifying some motivations of medieval behavior.

MARC BLOCH
FEUDAL SOCIETY*

The men of the two feudal ages were close to nature—much closer than we are; and nature as they knew it was much less tamed and softened than we see it today. The rural landscape, of which the waste formed so large a part, bore fewer traces of human influence. The wild animals that now only haunt our nursery tales—bears and, above all, wolves—prowled in every wilderness, and even amongst the cultivated fields. So much was this the case that the sport of hunting was indispensable for ordinary security, and almost equally so as a method of supplementing the food supply. People continued to pick wild fruit and to gather honey as in the first ages of mankind. In the construction of implements and tools, wood played a predominant part. The nights, owing to the wretched lighting, were darker; the cold, even in the living quarters of the castles, was more intense. In short, behind all social life there was a background of the primitive, of submission to uncontrollable forces, of unrelieved physical contrasts. There is no means of measuring the influence which such an environment was capable of exerting on the minds of men, but it could hardly have failed to contribute to their uncouthness.

A history more worthy of the name than

* Reprinted from pp. 72–87 of *Feudal Society* by Marc Bloch by permission of The University of Chicago Press. Copyright 1961 by the University of Chicago Press. Published in England by Routledge and Kegan Paul Ltd., London.

the diffident speculations to which we are reduced by the paucity of our material would give space to the vicissitudes of the human organism. It is very naive to claim to understand men without knowing what sort of health they enjoyed. But in this field the state of the evidence, and still more the inadequacy of our methods of research, are inhibitive. Infant mortality was undoubtedly very high in feudal Europe and tended to make people somewhat callous towards bereavements that were almost a normal occurrence. As to the life of adults, even apart from the hazards of war it was usually short by our standards, at least to judge from the records of princely personages which (inexact though they must often be) constitute our only source of information on this point. Robert the Pious died at about the age of 60; Henry I at 52; Philip I and Louis VI at 56. In Germany the first four emperors of the Saxon dynasty attained respectively the ages of 60 (or thereabouts), 28, 22 and 52. Old age seemed to begin very early, as early as mature adult life with us. This world, which, as we shall see, considered itself very old, was in fact governed by young men.

Among so many premature deaths, a large number were due to the great epidemics which descended frequently upon a humanity ill-equipped to combat them; among the poor another cause was famine. Added to the constant acts of violence these disasters gave life a quality of perpetual insecurity. This was probably one of the principal reasons for the emotional instability so characteristic of the feudal era, especially during its first age. A low standard of hygiene doubtless also contributed to this nervous sensibility. A great deal of effort has been expended, in our own day, in proving that baths were not unknown to seignorial society. It is rather puerile, for the sake of making this point, to overlook so many unhealthy conditions of life: notably under-nourishment among the poor and overeating among the rich. Finally, we must not leave out of account the effects of an astonishing sensibility to what were believed to be supernatural manifestations. It made people's minds constantly and almost morbidly attentive to all manner of signs, dreams, or hallucinations. This characteristic was especially marked in monastic circles where the influence of mortifications of the flesh and the repression of natural instincts was joined to that of a mental attitude vocationally centred on the problems of the unseen. No psychoanalyst has ever examined dreams more earnestly than the monks of the tenth or the eleventh century. Yet the laity also shared the emotionalism of a civilization in which moral or social convention did not yet require well-bred people to repress their tears and their raptures. The despairs, the rages, the impulsive acts, the sudden revulsions of feeling present great difficulties to historians, who are instinctively disposed to reconstruct the past in terms of the rational. But the irrational is an important element in all history and only a sort of false shame could allow its effects on the course of political events in feudal Europe to be passed over in silence.

These men, subjected both externally and internally to so many ungovernable forces, lived in a world in which the passage of time escaped their grasp all the more because they were so ill-equipped to measure it. Water-clocks, which were costly and cumbersome, were very rare. Hourglasses were little used. The inadequacy of sundials, especially under skies quickly clouded over, was notorious. This resulted in the use of curious devices. In his concern to regulate the course of a notably nomadic life, King Alfred had conceived the idea of carrying with him everywhere a supply of candles of equal length, which he had lit in turn,[1] to mark the passing of the hours, but such concern for uniformity in the division of the day was exceptional in that age. Reckoning ordinarily —after the example of Antiquity—twelve hours of day and twelve of night, whatever

[1] Asser, *Life of King Alfred,* ed. Stevenson, c. 104. According to L. Reverchon, *Petite histoire de l'horlogerie,* p. 55, a similar system was still employed by Charles V of France.

the season, people of the highest education became used to seeing each of these fractions, taken one by one, grow and diminish incessantly, according to the annual revolution of the sun. This was to continue till the moment when—towards the beginning of the fourteenth century—counterpoise clocks brought with them at last, not only the mechanization of the instrument, but, so to speak, of time itself.

An anecdote related in a chronicle of Hainault illustrates admirably the sort of perpetual fluctuation of time in those days. At Mons a judicial duel is due to take place. Only one champion puts in an appearance—at dawn; at the ninth hour, which marks the end of the waiting period prescribed by custom, he requests that the failure of his adversary be placed on record. On the point of law, there is no doubt. But has the specified period really elapsed? The county judges deliberate, look at the sun, and question the clerics in whom the practice of the liturgy has induced a more exact knowledge of the rhythm of the hours than their own, and by whose bells it is measured, more or less accurately, to the common benefit of men. Eventually the court pronounces firmly that the hour of 'none' is past.[2] To us, accustomed to live with our eyes turning constantly to the clock, how remote from our civilization seems this society in which a court of law could not ascertain the time of day without discussion and inquiry!

Now the imperfection of hourly reckoning was but one of the symptoms, among many others, of a vast indifference to time. Nothing would have been easier or more useful than to keep an accurate record of such important legal dates as those of the births of rulers; yet in 1284 a full investigation was necessary to determine, as far as possible, the age of one of the greatest heiresses of the Capetian realm, the young countess of Champagne.[3] In the tenth and eleventh centuries, innumerable charters and memoranda were undated, although their only purpose was to serve as records. There are exceptional documents which are better in this respect, yet the notary, who employed several systems of reference simultaneously, was often not successful in making his various calculations agree. What is more, it was not the notion of time only, it was the domain of number as a whole which suffered from this haziness. The extravagant figures of the chroniclers are not merely literary exaggeration; they are evidence of the lack of all awareness of statistical realities. Although William the Conqueror certainly did not establish in England more than 5,000 knights' fees, the historians of a somewhat later time, and even certain administrators (though it would certainly not have been very difficult for them to obtain the right information), did not hesitate to attribute to him the creation of from thirty-two to sixty thousand of these military tenements. The period had, especially from the end of the eleventh century, its mathematicians who groped their way courageously in the wake of the Greeks and Arabs; the architects and sculptors were capable of using a fairly simple geometry. But among the computations that have come down to us—and this was true till the end of the Middle Ages—there are scarcely any that do not reveal astonishing errors. The inconveniences of the Roman numerical system, ingeniously corrected as they were by the use of the abacus, do not suffice to explain these mistakes. The truth is that the regard for accuracy, with its firmest buttress, the respect for figures, remained profoundly alien to the minds even of the leading men of that age.

Expression

On the one hand, the language of the educated, which was almost uniformly Latin; on the other, the variety of tongues in everyday use: such is the singular dualism which prevailed almost throughout the feudal era. It was peculiar to Western civilization properly

[2] Giselbert of Mons, ed. Pertz, pp. 188–9 (1188).
[3] *Les Établissements de Saint-Louis,* ed. P. Viollet, III, p. 165, n. 8.

so called and helped to distinguish it sharply from its neighbours—from the Celtic and Scandinavian worlds with their rich poetic and didactic literatures in the national languages; from the Greek East; and, at least in the really Arabized zones, from the world of Islam.

In the West itself, it is true, one society long remained an exception. This was Anglo-Saxon Britain. Not that Latin was not written there and written very well, but it was by no means the only language written. The old English tongue was elevated at an early date to the dignity of a literary and legal language. It was King Alfred's wish that young people should learn it in the schools before the more gifted passed on to Latin.[4] The poets employed it in their songs, which were set down in writing as well as recited. It was also used by the kings in their laws; by the chanceries in the legal documents drawn up for kings or magnates; and even by the monks in their chronicles. This was something unique in that age, a culture that was able to keep in touch on its highest levels with the medium of expression employed by the mass of the population. The Norman Conquest cut short this development. Between William's letter to the people of London, written soon after the battle of Hastings, and a few occasional administrative instructions in the late twelfth century, there was not a single royal deed that was not drawn up in Latin. With virtually only one exception, the Anglo-Saxon chronicles are silent from the middle of the eleventh century. As for those writings which may, by stretching a point, be called "literature," they were not to reappear till shortly before the year 1200 and then at first only in the form of a few minor works of edification.

On the continent the fine cultural effort of the Carolingian renaissance had not wholly neglected the national languages. True it occurred to no one in that age to consider the Romance tongues as worthy of being put into writing; they were regarded merely as a highly corrupt form of Latin. The German dialects, on the other hand, invited the attention of many men, at court or in the ranks of the higher clergy, whose mother-tongue they were. Old poems, hitherto purely oral, were transcribed and new ones, mainly on religious themes, were composed; manuscripts in *lingua theotisca* (Germanic) figured in the libraries of the great. But here again political events—this time the dismemberment of the Carolingian empire, with the troubles which followed—interrupted the trend. From the end of the ninth century to the end of the eleventh, a few pious poems and some translations comprise the meagre treasure which the historians of German literature must be content to record. In comparison with the Latin writings composed on the same soil and during the same period, we may as well admit that both in quantity and in intellectual quality it is negligible.

We must be careful, moreover, not to think of this Latin of the feudal era as a 'dead language', with all that the epithet implies of the stereotyped and uniform. In spite of the taste for correctness and purism re-established by the Carolingian renaissance, there was much which tended to produce to a greater or lesser extent, according to the environments and the persons concerned, new words and new turns of phrase. One of these circumstances was the need to describe facts unknown to the Ancients or to express thoughts which, in the sphere of religion especially, had been foreign to their ideas; another was the infectious influence of the logical process (very different from that embodied in the traditional grammar) to which people's minds grew accustomed through the use of the vernacular; finally, there were the effects of ignorance or half-knowledge. Moreover, if books tend to impede change, does not speech always favour it? Now men did not confine themselves to writing Latin. They sang it—witness the abandonment by poetry (at least in those forms of it most imbued with true feeling) of the classical prosody of long and short

[4] *Pastoral Care,* ed. Sweet, p. 6.

syllables in favour of accented rhythm, the only music henceforth perceptible to the ear. They also spoke it. It was for a solecism committed in conversation that a cultivated Italian, summoned to the court of Otto I, found himself cruelly mocked by a little monk of St. Gall.[5] In preaching, Bishop Notker of Liège, if he was addressing laymen, used Walloon; on the other hand, if he was preaching to his clergy he used Latin. Undoubtedly many ecclesiastics, especially among the parish priests, would have been incapable of imitating him, or even of understanding him. But for educated priests and monks the old *κοινή* of the Church retained its function for oral communication. Without Latin, how would it have been possible, at the Curia, in the great councils or in the course of their wanderings from abbey to abbey, for these men from different countries to communicate with each other?

Of course, in almost every society, the modes of expression vary, sometimes very considerably, according to the use which it is desired to make of them or the class to which the people concerned belong. But the contrast is limited, as a rule, to slight variations in grammatical exactitude or quality of vocabulary. In feudal society it was incomparably more profound. In a great part of Europe, the common languages, which were connected with the Germanic group, belonged to quite another family from the language of the educated. The Romance tongues themselves were so far removed from their common ancestor that to pass from them to Latin involved long training at school.

Thus the linguistic separation was reduced, in the long run, to the division between two human groups. On the one hand there was the immense majority of uneducated people, each one imprisoned in his regional dialect, limited, so far as literary culture was concerned, to a few secular poems transmitted almost exclusively by word of mouth, and to those pious cantilenas which well-meaning clerics composed in the vulgar tongue for the benefit of simple folk and which they sometimes committed to parchment. On the other hand, there was the little handful of educated people who, constantly alternating between the local everyday speech and the universal language of learning, were in the true sense bilingual. To them belonged the works of theology and history, invariably written in Latin; the knowledge of the liturgy; even the understanding of business documents.

Latin was not only the language in which teaching was done, it was the only language taught. To be able to read was simply to be able to read Latin. Though there were exceptional cases, in legal documents, of a lapse into the vernacular, this anomaly, where it occurs, must be simply regarded as a sign of ignorance. If, from the tenth century, certain charters of southern Aquitaine are full of Provençal terms, in the midst of a more or less incorrect Latin, it is because the monasteries of Rouergue or Quercy, situated away from the great centres of the Carolingian renaissance, could count very few literate monks. Because Sardinia was a poor country whose inhabitants, after their flight from the coastal region ravaged by pirates, lived in quasi-isolation, the first documents written in Sardinian are much older than the earliest Italian texts of the Peninsula.

The most immediately perceptible result of this hierarchic division of languages is that the picture of itself left by the first feudal age is exasperatingly blurred. Acts of sale or donation, of bondage or enfranchisement, judgments of the courts, royal privileges, written records of homage—the legal documents of everyday life—are the most valuable sources for the historian of society. If they are not always honest, they have at least, unlike the narrative texts intended for posterity, the merit of having been at worst designed to deceive only contemporaries, whose credulity had other limits than ours. Now, with very few exceptions which have just been explained, they were, till the thir-

[5] Gunzo Novariensis in Migne, *P. L.*, CXXXVI, col. 1286.

teenth century, invariably drawn up in Latin. But this was not the way in which the realities they were intended to record were first expressed. When two lords debated the price of an estate or the clauses of a contract of subjection they certainly did not talk to each other in the language of Cicero. It was the notary's business later to provide, as best he could, a classical vestment for their agreement. Thus every Latin charter or notarial record is the result of a work of translation, which the historian today, if he wishes to grasp the underlying truth, must put back, as it were, into the original.

This would be well enough if the process had always followed the same rules. But this was by no means the case. From the schoolboy exercise, clumsily reproducing an outline mentally projected in the vernacular, to the Latin oration, carefully polished by a learned clerk, all stages are to be found. Sometimes—and it is incontestably the most favourable case—the current word is simply disguised, as well as may be, by the addition of a pseudo-Latin termination: for example, *hommage* is scarcely concealed as *homagium*. In other cases, there was an endeavour to use only strictly classical terms, to the point of writing—by an almost blasphemous *jeu d'esprit* assimilating the priest of the Living God to the priest of Jupiter—*archiflamen* for archbishop. The worst of it was that, in the search for parallelisms, the purists did not hesitate to be guided by the analogy of sounds rather than of meanings. Because, in French, the nominative case of *comte* was *cuens,* it was translated as *consul;* or *fief* might be rendered as *fiscus*. It is true that general systems of translation were gradually established, some of which shared the universalist character of the learned language: *fief,* which was called *Lehn* in German, had as regular equivalents, in the Latin charters of Germany, words coined from French. But nothing was ever translated into notarial Latin, even when most skillfully handled, without being slightly deformed.

Thus, the technical language of law itself was handicapped by a vocabulary that was at once too archaic and too unstable to come really close to reality. As for the vulgar tongue, it had all the want of precision and the instability of a purely oral and popular vocabulary. As regards social institutions, confusion in words inevitably involved confusion of things. If only by reason of the imperfection of their terminology, a great uncertainty beset the classification of human relations. But this was not all. To whatever purposes it was applied, Latin had the advantage of providing the intellectuals of the age with an international medium of communication. On the other hand, to most of the men who made use of it, it presented the grave inconvenience of being radically divorced from the inner word—the term that stood naturally, in their minds, for the concept—so that they were forced to resort to perpetual approximations in the expression of their thoughts. Among the multiple causes that doubtless combine to explain the absence of mental precision, which was, as we have seen, one of the characteristics of those times, should we not include this incessant movement to and fro between the two planes of language?

Culture and Social Classes

To what extent was the language of the educated, medieval Latin, also the language of the aristocracy? To what extent, in other words, can the group of *literati* be identified with the ruling class? So far as the Church is concerned, the answer is clear. It is of no great consequence that the pernicious system of nominations had resulted, here and there, in the appointment of ignorant men to the highest posts. The episcopal courts, the great monasteries, the chapels royal, in a word, all the headquarters of the ecclesiastical army, never lacked educated clergy who, while often of noble or knightly origin, had been brought up in the monastic and especially the cathedral schools. But as soon as we come to the lay world, the problem becomes more complex.

Let us not imagine that, even in the darkest times, this society was positively hostile to all learning. That it was commonly deemed proper that a leader of men should have access to the treasure-house of thoughts and memories to which the written word, that is to say Latin, alone provided the key is most clearly shown by the importance attached by many sovereigns to the education of their heirs. Robert the Pious, 'king learned in God', had been the pupil of the illustrious Gerbert at Rheims; William the Conqueror gave his son Robert a cleric as tutor. Among the great of the earth, there were to be found genuine book-lovers: Otto III, brought up, it is true, by his mother who, as a Byzantine princess, had brought from her native country the customs of a much more refined civilization, spoke Greek and Latin fluently; William III of Aquitaine had assembled a fine library where he was sometimes to be found reading far into the night.[6] To these examples may be added the cases, by no means exceptional, of those princes who, intended originally for the Church, had retained some of the learning and some of the tastes proper to the clerical world; such a one was Baldwin of Boulogne—a rough soldier, nevertheless—who became king of Jerusalem.

But an education of this type was possible only in the atmosphere of a great dynasty, already firmly based on their hereditary power. Nothing is more significant in this respect than the almost regular contrast in Germany between the founders of dynasties and their successors. Both Otto II, the third Saxon king, and Henry III, the second of the Salians, were carefully educated, in contrast with their fathers—Otto the Great, who learned to read at the age of thirty, and Conrad II, whose chaplain avows that he 'knew not his letters'. As often happened, both the fathers were thrown too young into a life of adventure and peril to have had time to prepare themselves, otherwise than by practical experience or oral tradition, for their profession as rulers. Still more was this true of the lower ranks of the nobility. The relatively brilliant culture of a few great royal or noble families should not deceive us; nor should the exceptional fidelity with which the knightly classes of Italy and Spain held to pedagogic traditions, somewhat rudimentary though these were: the Cid and Ximenes, if their knowledge perhaps did not extend much farther, at least knew how to sign their names.[7] But north of the Alps and the Pyrenees at least the majority of the small or medium lords who exercised most authority at this time were illiterates in the full sense of the word. So much was this the case that in the monasteries into which some of them precipitately retreated in the evening of their days, the terms *conversus,* that is to say one who comes late to the monk's vocation, and *idiota,* which designated the monk incapable of reading the Holy Scriptures, were treated as synonymous.

This neglect of education among the laity explains the rôle of the clergy both as interpreters of the ideas of the great and as depositaries of political traditions. The princes were obliged to rely on the clerical element among their servants for services that the rest of their entourage would have been incapable of rendering. About the middle of the eighth century the last lay referendaries of the Merovingian kings had disappeared; in April 1298, Philip the Fair handed over the seals to the knight Pierre Flotte. Between these two dates more than five centuries elapsed, during which the chancelleries of the sovereigns who reigned over France had at their head churchmen exclusively. It was the same elsewhere, on the whole. It is important to realize that the decisions of the powerful of this world were sometimes suggested and always expressed by men who, whatever their national or class

[6] Adhemar of Chabannes, *Chronique,* ed. Chavanon, III, c. 54. The emperor Henry III, to whom reference is made below, had manuscripts copied for him by the monks: *Codex epistolarum Tegernseensium* (*M.G.H., Ep. Selectae,* III), no. 122.

[7] Menendez Pidal, *La España del Cid,* II, pp. 590 and 619.

allegiances, none the less belonged by their whole training to a society by nature universalist and founded on spiritual things. Beyond question they helped to maintain, above the confusion of petty local strife, a concern for certain wider issues. When required, however, to give written form to acts of policy, they felt impelled to justify them officially by reasons drawn from their own moral code. Thus there came to be diffused over the documents of almost the entire feudal era that veneer of disingenuousness the evidence of which is to be seen in particular in the preambles of so many enfranchisements masquerading as pure gifts, though they were in fact purchased for money, or in so many royal grants of privileges, invariably made to appear as inspired by simple piety. Since for a long period the writing of history itself, with accompanying value-judgments, was also in the hands of the clergy, the conventions of thought as much as the conventions of literature combined to hide the cynical reality of human motives behind a sort of veil which was only to be finally torn asunder, on the threshold of modern times, by the harsh hands of a Commynes and a Machiavelli.

The laity, however, remained in many respects the active element in secular society. Undoubtedly the most illiterate of them were not on that account ignorant men. Apart from the fact that they were in a position, when necessary, to have translated for them what they could not read themselves, we shall see presently to what an extent tales told in the vernacular could transmit both memories and ideas. Still, we must never forget that the majority of lords and many great barons were administrators incapable of studying personally a report or an account, judges whose decisions were recorded (if at all) in a language unknown to the court. Is it surprising that these leaders, who were ordinarily obliged to reconstitute their past decisions from memory, should often have totally lacked the sense of continuity which, quite erroneously, some historians of today are at great pains to ascribe to them?

Almost strangers to writing, they tended to be indifferent to it. After Otto the Great had received the imperial crown in 962, he allowed a privilege to be issued in his name which was inspired by the 'pacts' of the Carolingian emperors and perhaps by certain historical writings; granting to the popes, 'till the end of time', the possession of an immense territory. By thus denuding himself of territory, the king-emperor would have abandoned to the Patrimony of St. Peter the greater part of Italy and even the control of some of the most important Alpine routes. Certainly Otto never dreamed for one moment that these dispositions, though very precise, would in fact be carried out. It would be less surprising if it were a question of one of those dishonest agreements which at all times, under pressure of circumstances, have been signed without the least intention of executing them. But absolutely nothing, save perhaps an imperfectly understood historical tradition, obliged the Saxon prince to make such a pretence. On the one hand, there is the parchment with the ink on it; on the other—quite unconnected with it—what was actually done; such was one particularly flagrant example of a typical dichotomy. A great many people in a position to direct human affairs did not understand the only language deemed worthy to record, not only the knowledge most useful to man and his salvation, but even the results of all social activity.

THE RELIGIOUS MENTALITY

'Ages of faith,' we say glibly, to describe the religious attitude of feudal Europe. If by that phrase we mean that any conception of the world from which the supernatural was excluded was profoundly alien to the minds of that age, that in fact the picture which they formed of the destinies of man and the universe was in almost every case a projection of the pattern traced by a Westernized Christian theology and eschatology, nothing could be more true. That here and there doubts might be expressed with regard to the 'fables' of Scripture is of small significance; lacking any rational basis, this crude scepticism, which was not a normal characteristic of educated people, melted in the face of danger like snow in the sun. It is even permissible to say that never was faith more completely worthy of its name. For the attempts of the learned to provide the Christian mysteries with the prop of logical speculation, which had been interrupted on the extinction of ancient Christian philosophy and revived only temporarily and with difficulty during the Carolingian renaissance, were not fully resumed before the end of the eleventh century. On the other hand, it would be wrong to ascribe to these believers a rigidly uniform creed.

Catholicism was still very far from having completely defined its dogmatic system, so that the strictest orthodoxy was then much more flexible than was to be the case later on, after scholastic philosophy and the Counter-Reformation had in turn exercised their influence. Moreover, in the ill-defined border land where Christian heresy degenerated into a religion actively opposed to Christianity, the old Manichaeanism retained a number of votaries in various places. Of these it is not precisely known whether they had inherited their religion from groups who had remained obstinately faithful to this persecuted sect since the first centuries of the Middle Ages, or had received it, after a long interval, from Eastern Europe. But the most notable fact was that Catholicism had incompletely penetrated among the common people. The parish clergy, taken as a whole, were intellectually as well as morally unfit for their task. Recruited with insufficient care, they were also inadequately trained; most commonly instruction consisted in casual lessons given by some priest, himself poorly educated, to a youth who was preparing himself for orders while serving the mass. Preaching, the only effective means of making accessible to the people the mysteries locked up in the Scriptures, was but irregularly practised. In 1031 the Council of Limoges was obliged to denounce the error which claimed that preaching was the prerogative of the bishops, for obviously no bishop would have been capable by himself of preaching the Gospel to the whole of his diocese.

The Catholic mass was recited more or less correctly in all parishes, though sometimes the standard was rather low. The frescoes and bas-reliefs on the walls or the capitals of the principal churches—'the books of the unlettered'—abounded in moving but inaccurate lessons. No doubt the faithful nearly all had a superficial acquaintance with the features most apt to strike the imagination in Christian representations of the past, the present, and the future of the world. But their religious life was also nourished on a multitude of beliefs and practices which, whether the legacy of age-old magic or the more recent products of a civilization still extremely fertile in myths, exerted a constant influence upon official doctrine. In stormy skies people still saw phantom armies passing by: armies of the dead, said the populace; armies of deceitful demons, declared the learned, much less inclined to deny these visions than to find for them a quasi-orthodox interpretation.[8] Innumerable nature-rites, among which poetry has especially familiarized us with the May-day festivals, were celebrated in country districts. In short, never was theology less identified with the popular religion as it was felt and lived.

Despite infinite variations according to environment and regional traditions, some common characteristics of this religious mentality can be discerned. Although it will mean passing over various deep and moving features and some fascinating problems of permanent human interest, we shall be obliged to confine ourselves here to recalling those trends in thought and feeling whose

[8] Cf. O. Höfler, *Kultische Geheimbünde der Germanen,* I, 1934, p. 160.

influence on social behaviour seems to have been particularly strong.

In the eyes of all who were capable of reflection the material world was scarcely more than a sort of mask, behind which took place all the really important things; it seemed to them also a language, intended to express by signs a more profound reality. Since a tissue of appearances can offer but little interest in itself, the result of this view was that observation was generally neglected in favour of interpretation. In a little treatise on the universe, which was written in the ninth century and enjoyed a very long popularity, Rabanus Maurus explained how he followed his plan: 'I conceived the idea of composing a little work . . . which should treat, not only of the nature of things and the properties of words . . . , but still more of their mystic meanings.' [9] This attitude explains, in large part, the inadequacy of men's knowledge of nature—of a nature which, after all, was not regarded as greatly deserving of attention. Technical progress—sometimes considerable—was mere empiricism.

Further, this discredited nature could scarcely have seemed fitted to provide its own interpretation, for in the infinite detail of its illusory manifestations it was conceived above all as the work of hidden wills—wills in the plural, in the opinion of simple folk and even of many of the learned. Below the One God and subordinated to his Almighty Power—though the exact significance of this subjection was not, as a rule, very clearly pictured—the generality of mankind imagined the opposing wills of a host of beings good and bad in a state of perpetual strife; saints, angels, and especially devils. 'Who does not know,' wrote the priest Helmold, 'that the wars, the mighty tempests, the pestilences, all the ills, indeed, which afflict the human race, occur through the agency of demons?' [10] Wars, we notice, are mentioned indiscriminately along with tempests; social catastrophes, therefore, are placed in the same class as those which we should nowadays describe as natural. The result was a mental attitude which the history of the invasions has already brought to notice: not exactly renunciation, but rather reliance upon means of action considered more efficacious than human effort. Though the instinctive reactions of a vigorous realism were never lacking, a Robert the Pious or an Otto III could nevertheless attach as much importance to a pilgrimage as to a battle or a law, and historians who are either scandalized by this fact or who persist in discovering subtle political manœuvres in these pious journeys merely prove thereby their own inability to lay aside the spectacles of men of the nineteenth and twentieth centuries. It was not merely the selfish quest of personal salvation that inspired these royal pilgrims. From the patron saints whose aid they went to invoke, they expected for their subjects as well as for themselves, not only the promise of rewards in heaven, but the riches of the earth as well. In the sanctuary, as much as on the field of battle or in the court of law, they were concerned to fulfil their function as leaders of their people.

The world of appearances was also a transitory world. Though in itself inseparable from any Christian representation of the Universe, the image of the final catastrophe had seldom impinged so strongly on the consciousness of men as at this time. They meditated on it; they assessed its premonitory signs. The chronicle of Bishop Otto of Freising, the most universal of all universal histories, began with Creation and ended with the picture of the Last Judgment. But, needless to say, it had an inevitable *lacuna:* from 1146—the date when the author ceased to write—to the day of the great catastrophe. Otto, certainly, expected this gap to be of short duration: 'We who have been placed at the end of time . . .' he remarks on several occasions. This was the general conviction among his contemporaries as it had been in earlier times, and

[9] Rabanus Maurus, *De Universo libri XXII,* in Migne, *P. L.,* CXI, col. 12.
[10] Helmold, *Chronica Slavorum,* I, 55.

it was by no means confined to the clergy; to suppose so would be to forget the profound interpenetration of the two groups, clerical and lay. Even among those who did not, like St. Norbert, go so far as to declare that the event was so close that the present generation would witness it no one doubted of its imminence. In every wicked prince, pious souls believed that they recognized the mark of Anti-christ, whose dreadful empire would precede the coming of the Kingdom of God.

But when in fact would it strike—this hour so close at hand? The Apocalypse seemed to supply an answer: 'and when the thousand years are expired . . . ' Was this to be taken as meaning a thousand years after the death of Christ? Some thought so, thus putting back the great day of reckoning—according to the normal calculation—to the year 1033. Or was it rather to be reckoned from his birth? This latter interpretation appears to have been the most general. It is certain at any rate that on the eve of the year one thousand a preacher in the churches of Paris announced this date for the End of Time. If, in spite of all this, the masses at that time were not visibly affected by the universal terror which historians of the romantic school have mistakenly depicted, the reason is above all that the people of that age, though mindful of the passage of the seasons and the annual cycle of the liturgy, did not think ordinarily in terms of the numbers of the years, still less in figures precisely computed on a uniform basis. How many charters lack any trace of a date! Even among the rest, what diversity there is in the systems of reference, which are mostly unconnected with the life of the Saviour—years of reigns or pontificates, astronomical indications of every kind, or even the fifteen-year cycle of the indiction, a relic of Roman fiscal practices! One entire country, Spain, while using more generally than elsewhere the concept of a definite era, assigned to it—for reasons that are somewhat obscure—an initial date absolutely unrelated to the Gospel, namely the year 38 B.C. It is true that legal documents occasionally and chronicles more frequently adhered to the era of the Incarnation; but it was still necessary to take into account the variations in the beginning of the year. For the Church excluded the first of January as a pagan festival. Thus, according to the province or the chancellery, the year designated the thousandth began at one or other of six or seven different dates, which ranged, according to our calendar, from 25th March 999 to 31st March 1000. What is worse, some of these initial dates, being essentially moveable since they were linked with a particular liturgical moment of the Easter period, could not be anticipated without tables, which only the learned possessed; they were also very apt to lead to permanent confusion in men's minds by making some years longer than others. Thus it was not unusual for the same day of the month, in March or April, or the feast of the same saint to occur twice in the same year. Indeed, for the majority of Western men this expression, 'the year 1000', which we have been led to believe was charged with anguish, could not be identified with any precise moment in the sequence of days.

Yet the notion of the shadow cast over men's minds at that time by the supposed imminence of the Day of Wrath is not altogether wrong. All Europe, it is true, did not tremble with fear towards the end of the first millennium, to compose itself suddenly as soon as this supposedly fateful date was past. But, what was even worse perhaps, waves of fear swept almost incessantly over this region or that, subsiding at one point only to rise again elsewhere. Sometimes a vision started the panic, or perhaps a great historic calamity like the destruction of the Holy Sepulchre in 1009, or again perhaps merely a violent tempest. Another time, it was caused by some computation of the liturgists, which spread from educated circles to the common people. 'The rumour spread through almost the whole world that the End would come when the Annunciation coincided with Good Friday,' wrote the abbot of

Fleury a little before the year 1000.[11] Many theologians, however, remembering that St. Paul had said: 'the day of the Lord cometh like a thief in the night', condemned these indiscreet attempts to pierce the mystery in which the Divinity chose to veil his dread purpose. But is the period of waiting made less anxious by ignorance of when the blow will fall? In the prevailing disorders, which we should unhesitatingly describe as the ebullience of adolescence, contemporaries were unanimous in seeing only the last convulsions of an 'aged' humanity. In spite of everything, an irresistible vitality fermented in men, but as soon as they gave themselves up to meditation, nothing was farther from their thoughts than the prospect of a long future for a young and vigorous human race.

If humanity as a whole seemed to be moving rapidly towards its end, so much the more did this sensation of being 'on the way' apply to each individual life. According to the metaphor dear to so many religious writers, the true believer was in his earthly existence like a pilgrim, to whom the end of the road is naturally of more importance than the hazards of the journey. Of course, the thoughts of the majority of men did not dwell constantly on their salvation. But when they did, it was with deep intensity and above all with the aid of vivid and very concrete images, which were apt to come to them by fits and starts; for their fundamentally unstable minds were subject to sudden revulsions. Joined to the penitent mood of a world on the verge of dissolution, the desire for the eternal rewards cut short more than one leader's career by voluntary withdrawal to the cloister. And it ended for good and all the propagation of more than one noble line, as in the case of the six sons of the lord of Fontaines-lès-Dijon who eagerly embraced the monastic life under the leadership of the most illustrious of their number, Bernard of Clairvaux. Thus, in its way, the religious mentality favoured the mixing of the social classes.

[11] *Apologeticus,* in Migne, *P.L.,* CXXXIX, col. 472.

Many Christians, nevertheless, could not bring themselves to submit to these austere practices. Moreover, they considered themselves (and perhaps not without reason) to be incapable of reaching heaven through their own merits. They therefore reposed their hopes in the prayers of pious souls, in the merits accumulated for the benefit of all the faithful by a few groups of ascetics, and in the intercession of the saints, materialized by means of their relics and represented by the monks, their servants. In this Christian society, no function exercised in the collective interest appeared more important than that of the spiritual organizations, precisely in so far—let us make no mistake about this—as they were spiritual. The charitable, cultural and economic rôle of the great cathedral chapters and of the monasteries may have been considerable: in the eyes of contemporaries it was merely accessory. The notion of a terrestrial world completely imbued with supernatural significance combined in this with the obsession of the beyond. The happiness of the king and the realm in the present; the salvation of the royal ancestors and of the king himself throughout Eternity: such was the double benefit which Louis the Fat declared that he expected from his foundation when he established a community of Canons Regular at the abbey of St. Victor in Paris. 'We believe', said Otto I, 'that the protection of our Empire is bound up with the rising fortunes of Christian worship.' [12] Thus we find a powerful and wealthy Church, capable of creating novel legal institutions, and a host of problems raised by the delicate task of relating this religious 'city' to the temporal 'city'; problems ardently debated and destined to influence profoundly the general evolution of the West. These features are an essential part of any accurate picture of the feudal world, and in face of them who can fail to recognize in the fear of hell one of the great social forces of the age?

[12] Tardif, *Cartons des rois,* no. 357; *Diplom. regum et imperatorum Germaniae,* I, Otto I, no. 366.

FOURTEEN

MEDIEVAL ARCHITECTURE

Architecture was the greatest art form of the Middle Ages. The best of the medieval Romanesque or Gothic styles rivals the architecture of any period in any civilization. Henry Adams (1838–1918), one of America's most distinguished historians, wrote a glowing account of medieval civilization, with special attention to architecture. His book Mont-Saint-Michel and Chartres, *privately printed in 1905 and published in 1913, begins with the Romanesque abbey church, Mont-Saint-Michel, built in Normandy between 1020 and 1135. This majestic structure, which glorifies the archangel St. Michael, embodies the militant energy of the Normans, that same energy which made possible their conquest of England in 1066. After describing Mont-Saint-Michel, Adams turns his attention to the Gothic cathedral at Chartres, which glorifies the Virgin Mary. He ends his account with an extraordinarily perceptive analysis of medieval philosophy.*

HENRY ADAMS

MONT-SAINT-MICHEL AND CHARTRES*

The Archangel loved heights. Standing on the summit of the tower that crowned his church, wings upspread, sword uplifted, the devil crawling beneath, and the cock, symbol of eternal vigilance, perched on his mailed foot, Saint Michael held a place of his own in heaven and on earth which seems, in the eleventh century, to leave hardly room for the Virgin of the Crypt at Chartres, still less for the Beau Christ of the thirteenth century at Amiens. The Archangel stands for Church and State, and both militant. He is the conqueror of Satan, the mightiest of all created spirits, the nearest to God. His place was where the danger was greatest; therefore you find him here. For the same reason he was, while the pagan danger lasted, the patron saint of France. So the Normans, when they were converted to Christianity, put themselves under his powerful protection. So he stood for centuries on his Mount in Peril of the Sea, watching across the tremor of the immense ocean—*immensi tremor oceani*—as Louis XI, inspired for once to poetry, inscribed on the collar of the Order of Saint Michael which he created. So soldiers, nobles, and monarchs went on

* Reprinted from *Mont-Saint-Michel and Chartres,* pp. 1–13, by Henry Adams by permission of Houghton Mifflin Co. Copyright 1905 by Henry Adams and 1933 by Charles Francis Adams.

pilgrimage to his shrine; so the common people followed, and still follow, like ourselves.

The church stands high on the summit of this granite rock, and on its west front is the platform, to which the tourist ought first to climb. From the edge of this platform, the eye plunges down, two hundred and thirty-five feet, to the wide sands or the wider ocean, as the tides recede or advance, under an infinite sky, over a restless sea, which even we tourists can understand and feel without books or guides; but when we turn from the western view, and look at the church door, thirty or forty yards from the parapet where we stand, one needs to be eight centuries old to know what this mass of encrusted architecture meant to its builders, and even then one must still learn to feel it. The man who wanders into the twelfth century is lost, unless he can grow prematurely young.

One can do it, as one can play with children. Wordsworth, whose practical sense equalled his intuitive genius, carefully limited us to 'a season of calm weather,' which is certainly best; but granting a fair frame of mind, one can still 'have sight of that immortal sea' which brought us hither from the twelfth century; one can even travel thither and see the children sporting on the shore. Our sense is partially atrophied from disuse, but it is still alive, at least in old people, who alone, as a class, have the time to be young.

One needs only to be old enough in order to be as young as one will. From the top of this Abbey Church one looks across the bay to Avranches, and towards Coutances and the Cotentin—the *Constantinus pagus*—whose shore, facing us, recalls the coast of New England. The relation between the granite of one coast and that of the other may be fanciful, but the relation between the people who live on each is as hard and practical a fact as the granite itself. When one enters the church, one notes first the four great triumphal piers or columns, at the intersection of the nave and transepts, and on looking into M. Corroyer's architectural study which is the chief source of all one's acquaintance with the Mount, one learns that these piers were constructed in 1058. Four out of five American tourists will instantly recall the only date of mediaeval history they ever knew, the date of the Norman Conquest. Eight years after these piers were built, in 1066, Duke William of Normandy raised an army of forty thousand men in these parts, and in northern France, whom he took to England, where they mostly stayed. For a hundred and fifty years, until 1204, Normandy and England were united; the Norman peasant went freely to England with his lord, spiritual or temporal; the Norman woman, a very capable person, followed her husband or her parents; Normans held nearly all the English fiefs; filled the English Church; crowded the English Court; created the English law; and we know that French was still currently spoken in England as late as 1400, or thereabouts, 'After the scole of Stratford atte bowe.' The aristocratic Norman names still survive in part, and if we look up their origin here we shall generally find them in villages so remote and insignificant that their place can hardly be found on any ordinary map; but the common people had no surnames, and cannot be traced, although for every noble whose name or blood survived in England or in Normandy, we must reckon hundreds of peasants. Since the generation which followed William to England in 1066, we can reckon twenty-eight or thirty from father to son, and, if you care to figure up the sum, you will find that you had about two hundred and fifty million arithmetical ancestors living in the middle of the eleventh century. The whole population of England and northern France may then have numbered five million, but if it were fifty it would not much affect the certainty that, if you have any English blood at all, you have also Norman. If we could go back and live again in all our two hundred and fifty million arithmetical ancestors of the eleventh century, we should find ourselves doing many surprising things, but among the rest we should pretty certainly be ploughing most of the fields of the Cotentin and Calvados; going to mass in every parish church in Normandy; rendering military service to every lord, spiritual or temporal, in all this region; and helping to build the Abbey Church at Mont-Saint-Michel. From the roof of the Cathedral of Coutances over yonder, one may look away over the hills and woods, the farms and fields of Normandy, and so familiar, so homelike are they, one can almost take oath that in this, or the other, or in all, one knew life once and has never so fully known it since.

Never so fully known it since! For we of the eleventh century, hard-headed, close-fisted, grasping, shrewd, as we were, and as Normans are still said to be, stood more fully in the centre of the world's movement than our English descendants ever did. We were a part, and a great part, of the Church, of France, and of Europe. The Leos and Gregories of the tenth and eleventh centuries leaned on us in their great struggle for reform. Our Duke Richard-Sans-Peur, in 966, turned the old canons out of the Mount in order to bring here the highest influence of the time, the Benedictine monks of Monte Cassino. Richard II, grandfather of William the Conqueror, began this Abbey Church in 1020, and helped Abbot Hildebert to build it. When William the Conqueror in 1066 set out to conquer England, Pope Alexander II stood behind him and blessed his banner. From that moment our Norman Dukes cast the Kings of France into the shade. Our activity was not limited to northern Europe, or even confined by Anjou and Gascony. When we stop at Coutances, we will drive out to Hauteville to see where Tancred came from, whose sons Robert and Roger were conquering Naples and Sicily at the time when the Abbey Church was building on the Mount. Normans were everywhere in 1066, and everywhere in the lead of their age. We were a serious race. If you want other proof of it, besides our record in war and in politics, you have only to look at our art. Religious art is the measure of human depth and sincerity; any triviality, any weakness cries aloud. If this church on the Mount is not proof enough of Norman character, we will stop at Coutances for a wider view. Then we will go to Caen and Bayeux. From there, it would almost be worth our while to leap at once to Palermo. It was in the year 1131 or thereabouts that Roger began the Cathedral at Cefalu and the Chapel Royal at Palermo; it was about the year 1174, that his grandson William began the Cathedral of Monreale. No art—either Greek or Byzantine, Italian or Arab—has ever created two religious types so beautiful, so serious, so impressive, and yet so different, as Mont-Saint-Michel watching over its northern ocean, and Monreale, looking down over its forests of orange and lemon, on Palermo and the Sicilian seas.

Down nearly to the end of the twelfth century the Norman was fairly master of the world in architecture as in arms, although the thirteenth century belonged to France, and we must look for its glories on the Seine and Marne and Loire; but for the present we are in the eleventh century—tenants of the Duke or of the Church or of small feudal lords who take their names from the neighbourhood—Beaumont, Carteret, Gréville, Percy, Pierpont—who, at the Duke's bidding, will each call out his tenants, perhaps ten men-at-arms with their attendants, to fight in Brittany, or in the Vexin toward Paris, or on the great campaign for the conquest of England which is to come within ten years—the greatest military effort that has been made in western Europe since Charlemagne and Roland were defeated at Roncesvalles three hundred years ago. For the moment, we are helping to quarry granite for the Abbey Church, and to haul it to the Mount, or load it on our boat. We never fail to make our annual pilgrimage to the Mount on the Archangel's Day, October 16. We expect to be called out for a new campaign which Duke William threatens against Brittany, and we hear stories that Harold the Saxon, the powerful Earl of Wessex in England, is a guest, or, as some say, a prisoner or a hostage, at the Duke's Court, and will go with us on the campaign. The year is 1058.

All this time we have been standing on the *parvis,* looking out over the sea and sands which are as good eleventh-century landscape as they ever were; or turning at times towards the church door which is the *pons seclorum,* the bridge of ages, between us and our ancestors. Now that we have made an attempt, such as it is, to get our minds into a condition to cross the bridge without breaking down in the effort, we enter the church and stand face to face with eleventh-century architecture; a ground-plan which dates from 1020; a central tower, or its piers, dating from 1058; and a church completed in 1135. France can offer few buildings of this importance equally old, with dates so exact. Perhaps the closest parallel to Mont-Saint-Michel is Saint-Benoît-sur-Loire, above Orléans, which seems to have been a shrine almost as popular as the Mount, at the same time. Chartres was also a famous shrine, but of the Virgin, and the west porch of Chartres, which is to be our peculiar pilgrimage, was a hundred years later than the ground-plan of Mont-Saint-Michel, although Chartres porch is the usual starting-point of northern French art. Queen Matilda's Abbaye-aux-Dames, now the Church of the Trinity, at Caen, dates from 1066. Saint Sernin at Toulouse, the porch of the Abbey Church at Moissac, Notre-Dame-du-Port at Clermont, the Abbey Church at Vézelay, are all said to be twelfth-century. Even San Marco at Venice was new in 1020.

Yet in 1020 Norman art was already too ambitious. Certainly nine hundred years leave their traces on granite as well as on other material, but the granite of Abbot Hildebert would have stood securely enough, if the Abbot had not asked too much from it. Perhaps he asked too much from the Archangel, for the thought of the Archangel's superiority was clearly the inspiration of his plan. The apex of the granite rock rose like a sugar-loaf two hundred and forty feet (73.6 metres) above mean sea-level. Instead of cutting the summit away to give his church a secure rock foundation, which would have sacrificed about thirty feet of height, the Abbot took the apex of the rock for his level, and on all sides built out foundations of masonry to support the walls of his church. The apex of the rock is the floor of the *croisée,* the intersection of nave and transept. On this solid foundation the Abbot rested the chief weight of the church, which was the central tower, supported by the four great piers which still stand; but from the croisée in the centre westward to the parapet of the platform, the Abbot filled the whole space with masonry, and his successors built out still farther, until some two hundred feet of stonework ends now in a perpendicular wall of eighty feet or more. In this space are several ranges of chambers, but the structure might perhaps have proved strong enough to support the light Romanesque front which was usual in the eleventh century, had not fashions in architecture changed in the great epoch of building, a hundred and fifty years later, when Abbot Robert de Torigny thought proper to reconstruct the west front, and build out two towers on its flanks. The towers were no doubt beautiful, if one may judge from the towers of Bayeux and Coutances, but their weight broke down the vaulting beneath, and one of them fell in 1300. In 1618 the whole façade began to give way, and in 1776 not only the façade but also three of the seven spans of the nave were pulled down. Of Abbot Hildebert's nave, only four arches remain.

Still, the overmastering strength of the eleventh century is stamped on a great scale here, not only in the four spans of the nave, and in the transepts, but chiefly in the triumphal columns of the croisée. No one is likely to forget what Norman architecture was, who takes the trouble to pass once through this fragment of its earliest bloom. The dimensions are not great, though greater than safe construction warranted. Abbot

Hildebert's whole church did not exceed two hundred and thirty feet in length in the interior, and the span of the triumphal arch was only about twenty-three feet, if the books can be trusted. The nave of the Abbaye-aux-Dames appears to have about the same width, and probably neither of them was meant to be vaulted. The roof was of timber, and about sixty-three feet high at its apex. Compared with the great churches of the thirteenth century, this building is modest, but its size is not what matters to us. Its style is the starting-point of all our future travels. Here is your first eleventh-century church! How does it affect you?

Serious and simple to excess! is it not? Young people rarely enjoy it. They prefer the Gothic, even as you see it here, looking at us from the choir, through the great Norman arch. No doubt they are right, since they are young: but men and women who have lived long and are tired—who want rest—who have done with aspirations and ambition—whose life has been a broken arch—feel this repose and self-restraint as they feel nothing else. The quiet strength of these curved lines, the solid support of these heavy columns, the moderate proportions, even the modified lights, the absence of display, of effort, of self-consciousness, satisfy them as no other art does. They come back to it to rest, after a long circle of pilgrimage—the cradle of rest from which their ancestors started. Even here they find the repose none too deep.

Indeed, when you look longer at it, you begin to doubt whether there is any repose in it at all—whether it is not the most unreposeful thought ever put into architectural form. Perched on the extreme point of this abrupt rock, the Church Militant with its aspirant Archangel stands high above the world, and seems to threaten heaven itself. The idea is the stronger and more restless because the Church of Saint Michael is surrounded and protected by the world and the society over which it rises, as Duke William rested on his barons and their men. Neither the Saint nor the Duke was troubled by doubts about his mission. Church and State, Soul and Body, God and Man, are all one at Mont-Saint-Michel, and the business of all is to fight, each in his own way, or to stand guard for each other. Neither Church nor State is intellectual, or learned, or even strict in dogma. Here we do not feel the Trinity at all; the Virgin but little; Christ hardly more; we feel only the Archangel and the Unity of God. We have little logic here, and simple faith, but we have energy. We cannot do many things which are done in the centre of civilization, at Byzantium, but we can fight, and we can build a church. No doubt we think first of the church, and next of our temporal lord; only in the last instance do we think of our private affairs, and our private affairs sometimes suffer for it; but we reckon the affairs of Church and State to be ours, too, and we carry this idea very far. Our church on the Mount is ambitious, restless, striving for effect; our conquest of England, with which the Duke is infatuated, is more ambitious still; but all this is a trifle to the outburst which is coming in the next generation; and Saint Michael on his Mount expresses it all.

Taking architecture as an expression of energy, we can some day compare Mont-Saint-Michel with Beauvais, and draw from the comparison whatever moral suits our frame of mind; but you should first note that here, in the eleventh century, the Church, however simple-minded or unschooled, was not cheap. Its self-respect is worth noticing, because it was short-lived in its art. Mont-Saint-Michel, throughout, even up to the delicate and intricate stonework of its cloisters, is built of granite. The crypts and substructures are as well constructed as the surfaces most exposed to view. When we get to Chartres, which is largely a twelfth-century work, you will see that the cathedral there, too, is superbly built, of the hardest and heaviest stone within reach, which has nowhere settled or given way; while, beneath, you will find a crypt that rivals the church above. The thirteenth century did not build so. The great cathedrals after 1200 show economy, and sometimes worse. The world grew cheap, as worlds must.

You may like it all the better for being less serious, less heroic, less militant, and more what the French call *bourgeois,* just as you may like the style of Louis XV better than that of Louis XIV—Madame du Barry better than Madame de Montespan—for taste is free, and all styles are good which amuse; but since we are now beginning with the earliest, in order to step down gracefully to the stage, whatever it is, where you prefer to stop, we must try to understand a little of the kind of energy which Norman art expressed, or would have expressed if it had thought in our modes. The only word which describes the Norman style is the French word *naïf.* Littré says that *naïf* comes from *natif,* as *vulgar* comes from *vulgus,* as though native traits must be simple, and commonness must be vulgar. Both these derivative meanings were strange to the eleventh century. Naïveté was simply natural and vulgarity was merely coarse. Norman naïveté was not different in kind from the naïveté of Burgundy or Gascony or Lombardy, but it was slightly different in expression, as you will see when you travel south. Here at Mont-Saint-Michel we have only a mutilated trunk of an eleventh-century church to judge by. We have not even a façade, and shall have to stop at some Norman village—at Thaon or Ouistreham—to find a west front which might suit the Abbey here, but wherever we find it we shall find something a little more serious, more military, and more practical than you will meet in other Romanesque work, farther south. So, too, the central tower or lantern—the most striking feature of Norman churches—has fallen here at Mont-Saint-Michel, and we shall have to replace it from Cérisy-la-Forêt, and Lessay, and Falaise. We shall find much to say about the value of the lantern on a Norman church, and the singular power it expresses. We shall have still more to say of the towers which flank the west front of Norman churches, but these are mostly twelfth-century, and will lead us far beyond Coutances and Bayeux, from *flèche* to *flèche,* till we come to the flèche of all flèches, at Chartres.

We shall have a whole chapter of study, too, over the eleventh-century apse, but here at Mont-Saint-Michel, Abbot Hildebert's choir went the way of his nave and tower. He built out even more boldly to the east than to the west, and although the choir stood for some four hundred years, which is a sufficient life for most architecture, the foundations gave way at last, and it fell in 1421, in the midst of the English wars, and remained a ruin until 1450. Then it was rebuilt, a monument of the last days of the Gothic, so that now, standing at the western door, you can look down the church, and see the two limits of mediaeval architecture married together—the earliest Norman and the latest French. Through the Romanesque arches of 1058, you look into the exuberant choir of latest Gothic, finished in 1521. Although the two structures are some five hundred years apart, they live pleasantly together. The Gothic died gracefully in France. The choir is charming—far more charming than the nave, as the beautiful woman is more charming than the elderly man. One need not quarrel about styles of beauty, as long as the man and woman are evidently satisfied and love and admire each other still, with all the solidity of faith to hold them up; but, at least, one cannot help seeing, as one looks from the older to the younger style, that whatever the woman's sixteenth-century charm may be, it is not the man's eleventh-century trait of naïveté; —far from it! The simple, serious, silent dignity and energy of the eleventh century have gone. Something more complicated stands in their place; graceful, self-conscious, rhetorical, and beautiful as perfect rhetoric, with its clearness, light, and line, and the wealth of tracery that verges on the florid.

The crypt of the same period, beneath, is almost finer still, and even in seriousness stands up boldly by the side of the Romanesque; but we have no time to run off into the sixteenth century: we have still to learn the alphabet of art in France. One must live deep into the eleventh century in order to understand the twelfth, and even after passing years in the twelfth, we shall find the thirteenth in many ways a world of its own, with a beauty not always inherited, and sometimes not bequeathed. At the Mount we can go no farther into the eleventh as far as concerns architecture. We shall have to follow the Romanesque to Caen and so up the Seine to the Île de France, and across to the Loire and the Rhone, far to the South where its home lay. All the other eleventh-century work has been destroyed here or built over, except at one point, on the level of the splendid crypt we just turned from, called the Gros Piliers, beneath the choir.

There, according to M. Corroyer, in a corner between great constructions of the twelfth century and the vast Merveille of the thirteenth, the old refectory of the eleventh was left as a passage from one group of buildings to the other. Below it is the kitchen of Hildebert. Above, on the level of the church, was the dormitory. These eleventh-century abbatial buildings faced north and west, and are close to the present parvis, opposite the last arch of the nave. The lower levels of Hildebert's plan served as supports or buttresses to the church above, and must therefore be older than the nave; probably older than the triumphal piers of 1058.

Hildebert planned them in 1020, and died after carrying his plans out so far that they could be completed by Abbot Ralph de Beaumont, who was especially selected by Duke William in 1048, 'more for his high birth than for his merits.' Ralph de Beaumont died in 1060, and was succeeded by Abbot Ranulph, an especial favourite of Duchess Matilda, and held in high esteem by Duke William. The list of names shows how much social importance was attributed to the place. The Abbot's duties included that of entertainment on a great scale. The Mount was one of the most famous shrines of northern Europe. We are free to take for granted that all the great people of Normandy slept at the Mount and, supposing M. Corroyer to be right, that they dined in this room, between 1050, when the building must have been in use, down to 1122 when the new abbatial quarters were built.

How far the monastic rules restricted social habits is a matter for antiquaries to settle if they can, and how far those rules were observed in the case of great secular princes; but the eleventh century was not very strict, and the rule of the Benedictines was always mild, until the Cistercians and Saint Bernard stiffened its discipline toward 1120. Even then the Church showed strong leanings toward secular poetry and popular tastes. The drama belonged to it almost exclusively, and the Mysteries and Miracle plays which were acted under its patronage often contained nothing of religion except the miracle. The greatest poem of the eleventh century was the 'Chanson de Roland,' and of that the Church took a sort of possession. At Chartres we shall find Charlemagne and Roland dear to the Virgin, and at about the same time, as far away as at Assisi in the Perugian country, Saint Francis himself—the nearest approach the Western world ever made to an Oriental incarnation of the divine essence—loved the French *romans,* and typified himself in the 'Chanson de Roland.' With Mont-Saint-Michel, the 'Chanson de Roland' is almost one. The 'Chanson' is in poetry what the Mount is in architecture. Without the 'Chanson,' one cannot approach the feeling which the eleventh century built into the Archangel's church. Probably there was never a day, certainly never a week, during several centuries, when portions of the 'Chanson' were not sung, or recited, at the Mount, and if there was one room where it was most at home, this one, supposing it to be the old refectory, claims to be the place.

III

THE LATE
MIDDLE AGES

PART THREE

☙ THE LATE MIDDLE AGES

During the greater part of the last two medieval centuries, Western civilization to the north of Italy lost the full-blown creativity which had transformed the Romanesque style into the Gothic and which had transformed vague and sometimes contradictory Church traditions into the well-reasoned body of Scholasticism. The Black Death of 1348 and thereafter, along with wars and local insurrections, led to vast distress and disillusion. This atmosphere of restlessness and gloom, intensified by civil and ecclesiastical dislocation, later became a major force in precipitating the Protestant Reformation.

FIFTEEN

THE BLACK DEATH

In the 150 years or so after 1300, medieval civilization lost much of its former vigor, and in some respects declined. The Church had a continuing administrative crisis, climaxed by the Great Schism of 1378–1417, and a theological crisis in the heresies of Wycliffe and Hus. With few exceptions, scholars in this period were generally inferior to the great theologians of the two preceding centuries. After about 1300, Gothic architecture produced no important new forms, and in the flamboyant style tended to sacrifice majesty to ornamentation. In general, the climate of expressed European opinion moved toward hysteria and despair. A major force in the stagnation of late medieval civilization was the Black Death (bubonic plague) of 1348, which in its successive visitations reduced Europe's population by about one third. In terms of social and psychological impact on European civilization, the Black Death is comparable to the highly destructive World Wars of the twentieth century. One of the most moving contemporary descriptions of the Black Death is by the Italian poet and novelist Giovanni Boccaccio (1313–75). His Decameron, *a collection of witty and occasionally coarse stories supposedly told by refugees from the Black Death, opens with a somber and frightening account of the plague in Florence.*

GIOVANNI BOCCACCIO

THE DECAMERON *

As often, most gracious ladies, as I bethink me, how compassionate you are by nature one and all, I do not disguise from myself that the present work must seem to you to have but a heavy and distressful prelude, in that it bears upon its very front what must needs revive the sorrowful memory of the late mortal pestilence, the course whereof was grievous not merely to eyewitnesses but to all who in any other wise had cognisance of it. But I would have you know, that you need not therefore be fearful to read further, as if your reading were ever to be accompanied by sighs and tears. This horrid beginning will be to you even such as to wayfarers is a steep and rugged mountain, beyond which stretches a plain most fair and delectable, which the toil of the ascent and descent does but serve to render more agreeable to them; for, as the last degree of joy brings with it sorrow, so misery has ever its sequel of happiness. To this brief exordium of woe—brief, I say, inasmuch as it can be put within the compass of a few letters—succeed forthwith the sweets and delights which I have promised you, and which, perhaps, had I not done so, were not to have been expected from it. In truth, had it been honestly possible to guide you whither I would bring you by a road less rough than this will be, I would gladly have so done. But, because without this review of the past, it would not be in my power to shew how the matters, of which you will hereafter read, came to pass, I am almost bound of necessity to enter upon it, if I would write of them at all.

I say, then, that the years of the beatific incarnation of the Son of God had reached the tale of one thousand three hundred and forty-eight, when in the illustrious city of Florence, the fairest of all the cities of Italy, there made its appearance that deadly pestilence, which, whether disseminated by the influence of the celestial bodies, or sent upon us mortals by God in His just wrath by way of retribution for our iniquities, had had its origin some years before in the East, whence, after destroying an innumerable multitude of living beings, it had propagated itself without respite from place to place, and so, calamitously, had spread into the West.

In Florence, despite all that human wisdom and forethought could devise to avert it, as the cleansing of the city from many impurities by officials appointed for the purpose, the refusal of entrance to all sick folk, and the adoption of many precautions for the preservation of health; despite also humble supplications addressed to God, and often repeated both in public procession and otherwise, by the devout; towards the beginning of the spring of the said year the doleful effects of the pestilence began to be horribly apparent by symptoms that shewed as if miraculous.

Not such were they as in the East, where an issue of blood from the nose was a manifest sign of inevitable death; but in men and women alike it first betrayed itself by the emergence of certain tumours in the groin or

* Reprinted from *The Decameron,* pp. 4–12, translated by J. M. Rigg, George Routledge and Sons, Ltd., London, 1905.

the armpits, some of which grew as large as a common apple, others as an egg, some more, some less, which the common folk called gavoccioli. From the two said parts of the body this deadly gavocciolo soon began to propagate and spread itself in all directions indifferently; after which the form of the malady began to change, black spots or livid making their appearance in many cases on the arm or the thigh or elsewhere, now few and large, now minute and numerous. And as the gavocciolo had been and still was an infallible token of approaching death, such also were these spots on whomsoever they shewed themselves. Which maladies seemed to set entirely at naught both the art of the physician and the virtues of physic; indeed, whether it was that the disorder was of a nature to defy such treatment, or that the physicians were at fault—besides the qualified there was now a multitude both of men and of women who practised without having received the slightest tincture of medical science—and, being in ignorance of its source, failed to apply the proper remedies; in either case, not merely were those that recovered few, but almost all within three days from the appearance of the said symptoms, sooner or later, died, and in most cases without any fever or other attendant malady.

Moreover, the virulence of the pest was the greater by reason that intercourse was apt to convey it from the sick to the whole, just as fire devours things dry or greasy when they are brought close to it. Nay, the evil went yet further, for not merely by speech or association with the sick was the malady communicated to the healthy with consequent peril of common death; but any that touched the clothes of the sick or aught else that had been touched or used by them, seemed thereby to contract the disease.

So marvellous sounds that which I have now to relate, that, had not many, and I among them, observed it with their own eyes, I had hardly dared to credit it, much less to set it down in writing, though I had had it from the lips of a credible witness.

I say, then, that such was the energy of the contagion of the said pestilence, that it was not merely propagated from man to man, but, what is much more startling, it was frequently observed, that things which had belonged to one sick or dead of the disease, if touched by some other living creature, not of the human species, were the occasion, not merely of sickening, but of an almost instantaneous death. Whereof my own eyes (as I said a little before) had cognisance, one day among others, by the following experience. The rags of a poor man who had died of the disease being strewn about the open street, two hogs came thither, and after, as is their wont, no little trifling with their snouts, took the rags between their teeth and tossed them to and fro about their chaps; whereupon, almost immediately, they gave a few turns, and fell down dead, as if by poison, upon the rags which in an evil hour they had disturbed.

In which circumstances, not to speak of many others of a similar or even graver complexion, divers apprehensions and imaginations were engendered in the minds of such as were left alive, inclining almost all of them to the same harsh resolution, to wit, to shun and abhor all contact with the sick and all that belonged to them, thinking thereby to make each his own health secure. Among whom there were those who thought that to live temperately and avoid all excess would count for much as a preservative against seizures of this kind. Wherefore they banded together, and, dissociating themselves from all others, formed communities in houses where there were no sick, and lived a separate and secluded life, which they regulated with the utmost care, avoiding every kind of luxury, but eating and drinking very moderately of the most delicate viands and the finest wines, holding converse with none but one another, lest tidings of sickness or death should reach them, and diverting their minds with music and such other delights as they could devise. Others, the bias of whose minds was in the opposite direction, maintained, that to drink freely, frequent places of public resort, and take their pleasure with song and revel, sparing to satisfy no appetite, and to laugh and mock at no event, was the sovereign remedy for so great an evil: and that which they affirmed they also put in practice, so far as they were able, resorting day and night, now to this tavern, now to that, drinking with an entire disregard of rule or measure, and by preference making the houses of others, as it were, their inns, if they but saw in them aught that was particularly to their taste or liking; which they were readily able to do, because the owners, seeing death imminent, had become as reckless of their property as of their lives; so that most of the houses were open to all comers, and no distinction was observed between the stranger who presented himself and the rightful lord. Thus, adhering ever to their inhuman determination to shun the sick, as far as possible, they ordered their life. In this extremity of our city's suffering and tribulation the venerable authority of laws, human and divine, was abased and all but totally dissolved, for lack of those who should have administered and enforced them, most of whom, like the rest of the citizens, were either dead or sick, or so hard bested for servants that they were unable to execute any office; whereby every man was free to do what was right in his own eyes.

Not a few there were who belonged to neither of the two said parties, but kept a middle course between them, neither laying the same restraint upon their diet as the former, nor allowing themselves the same license in drinking and other dissipations as the latter, but living with a degree of freedom sufficient to satisfy their appetites, and not as recluses. They therefore walked abroad, carrying in their hands flowers or fragrant herbs or divers sorts of spices, which they frequently raised to their noses, deeming it an excellent thing thus to comfort the brain with such perfumes, because the air seemed to be everywhere laden and reeking with the stench emitted by the dead and the dying, and the odours of drugs.

Some again, the most sound, perhaps, in judgment, as they were also the most harsh in temper, of all, affirmed that there was no medicine for the disease superior or equal in efficacy to flight; following which prescription a multitude of men and women, negligent of all but themselves, deserted their city, their houses, their estates, their kinsfolk, their goods, and went into voluntary exile, or migrated to the country parts, as if God in visiting men with this pestilence in requital of their iniquities would not pursue them with His wrath wherever they might be, but intended the destruction of such alone as remained within the circuit of the walls of the city; or deeming, perchance, that it was now time for all to flee from it, and that its last hour was come.

Of the adherents of these divers opinions not all died, neither did all escape; but rather there were, of each sort and in every place, many that sickened, and by those who retained their health were treated after the example which they themselves, while whole, had set, being everywhere left to languish in almost total neglect. Tedious were it to recount, how citizen avoided citizen, how among neighbours was scarce found any that shewed fellow-feeling for another, how kinsfolk held aloof, and never met, or but rarely; enough that this sore affliction entered so deep into the minds of men and women, that in the horror thereof brother was forsaken by brother, nephew by uncle, brother by sister, and oftentimes husband by wife; nay, what is more, and scarcely to be believed, fathers and mothers were found to abandon their own children, untended, unvisited, to their fate, as if they had been strangers. Wherefore the sick of both sexes, whose number could not be estimated, were left without resource but in the charity of friends (and few such there were), or the interest of servants, who were hardly to be had at high rates and on unseemly terms, and being, moreover, one and all, men and women of gross understanding, and for the most part unused to such offices, concerned themselves no further than to supply the immediate and expressed wants of the sick, and to watch them die; in which service they themselves not seldom perished with their gains. . . .

It had been, as to-day it still is, the custom for the women that were neighbours and of kin to the deceased to gather in his house with the women that were most closely connected with him, to wail with them in common, while on the other hand his male kinsfolk and neighbours, with not a few of the other citizens, and a due proportion of the clergy according to his quality, assembled without, in front of the house, to receive the corpse; and so the dead man was borne on the shoulders of his peers, with funeral pomp of taper and dirge, to the church selected by him before his death. Which rites, as the pestilence waxed in fury, were either in whole or in great part disused, and gave way to others of a novel order. For not only did no crowd of women surround the bed of the dying, but many passed from this life unregarded, and few indeed were they to whom were accorded the lamentations and bitter tears of sorrowing relations; nay, for the most part, their place was taken by the laugh, the jest, the festal gathering; observances which the women, domestic piety in large measure set aside, had adopted with very great advantage to their health. Few also there were whose bodies were attended to the church by more than ten or twelve of their neighbours, and those not the honourable and respected citizens; but a sort of corpse-carriers drawn from the baser ranks, who called themselves becchini and performed such offices for hire, would shoulder the bier, and with hurried steps carry it, not to the church of the dead man's choice, but to that which was nearest at hand, with four or six priests in front and a candle or two, or, perhaps, none; nor did the priests distress themselves with too long and solemn an office, but with the aid of the becchini hastily consigned the corpse to the first tomb which they found untenanted. The condition of the lower, and, perhaps, in great measure of the middle ranks, of the people shewed even worse and more deplorable; for, deluded by hope or constrained by poverty, they stayed in their quarters, in their houses, where they sickened by thousands a day, and, being without service or help of any kind, were, so to speak, irredeemably devoted to the death which overtook them. Many died daily or nightly in the public streets; of many others, who died at home, the departure was hardly observed by their neighbours, until the stench of their putrefying bodies carried the tidings; and what with their corpses and the corpses of others who died on every hand the whole place was a sepulchre.

It was the common practice of most of the neighbours, moved no less by fear of contamination by the putrefying bodies than by charity towards the deceased, to drag the corpses out of the houses with their own hands, aided, perhaps, by a porter, if a porter was to be had, and to lay them in front of the doors, where any one who made the round might have seen, especially in the morning, more of them than he could count; afterwards they would have biers brought up, or, in default, planks, whereon they laid them. Nor was it once or twice only that one and the same bier carried two or three corpses at once; but quite a considerable number of such cases occurred, one bier sufficing for husband and wife, two or three brothers, father and son, and so forth. And times without number it happened, that, as two priests, bearing the cross, were on their way to perform the last office for some one, three or four biers were brought up by the porters in rear of them, so that, whereas the priests supposed that they had but one corpse to bury, they discovered that there were six or eight, or sometimes more. Nor, for all their number, were their obsequies honoured by either tears or lights or crowds of mourners; rather, it was come to this, that a dead man was then of no more account than a dead goat would be to-day. From all which it is abundantly manifest, that that lesson of patient resignation, which the sages were never able to learn from the slight and infrequent mishaps which occur in the natural course of events, was now brought home even to the minds of the simple by the magnitude of their disasters, so that they became indifferent to them.

As consecrated ground there was not in extent sufficient to provide tombs for the vast multitude of corpses which day and night, and almost every hour, were brought in eager haste to the churches for interment, least of all, if ancient custom were to be observed and a separate resting-place assigned to each, they dug, for each graveyard, as soon as it was full, a huge trench, in which they laid the corpses as they arrived by hundreds at a time, piling them up as merchandise is stowed in the hold of a ship, tier upon tier, each covered with a little earth, until the trench would hold no more. But I spare to rehearse with minute particularity each of the woes that came upon our city, and say in brief, that, harsh as was the tenor of her fortunes, the surrounding country knew no mitigation; for there—not to speak of the castles, each, as it were, a little city in itself—in sequestered village, or on the open champaign, by the wayside, on the farm, in the homestead, the poor hapless husbandmen and their families, forlorn of physicians' care or servants' tendance, perished day and night alike, not as men, but rather as beasts. Wherefore, they too, like the citizens, abandoned all rule of life, all habit of industry, all counsel of prudence; nay, one and all, as if expecting each day to be their last, not merely ceased to aid Nature to yield her fruit in due season of their beasts and their lands and their past labours, but left no means unused, which ingenuity could devise, to waste their accumulated store; denying shelter to their oxen, asses, sheep, goats, pigs, fowls, nay, even to their dogs, man's most faithful companions, and driving them out into the fields to roam at large amid the unsheaved, nay, unreaped corn. Many of which, as if endowed with reason, took their fill during the day, and returned home at night without any guidance of herdsman. But enough of the country! What need we add, but (reverting to the city) that such and so grievous was the harshness of heaven, and perhaps in some degree of man, that, what with the fury of the pestilence, the panic of those whom it spared, and their consequent neglect or desertion of not a few of the stricken in their need, it is believed without any manner of doubt, that between March and the ensuing July upwards of a hundred thousand human beings lost their lives within the walls of the city of Florence, which before the deadly visitation would not have been supposed to contain so many people! How many grand palaces, how many stately homes, how many splendid residences, once full of retainers, of lords, of ladies, were now left desolate of all, even to the meanest servant! How many families of historic fame, of vast ancestral domains, and wealth proverbial, found now no scion to continue the succession! How many brave men, how many fair ladies, how many gallant youths, whom any physician, were he Galen, Hippocrates, or Æsculapius himself, would have pronounced in the soundest of health, broke fast with their kinsfolk, comrades and friends in the morning, and when evening came, supped with their forefathers in the other world!

SIXTEEN

THE VIOLENT TENOR OF LIFE

In his justly famous book The Waning of the Middle Ages *Johan Huizinga (1872–1945), probably the greatest Dutch historian of the twentieth century, delineates "the forms of life, thought, and art" in France and the Netherlands in the fourteenth and fifteenth centuries. Fully at home in works of literature as well as in more conventional historical sources, Huizinga stresses the violence and uncertainty of life in the Late Middle Ages. He pays particular attention to the pessimism, decadence, and religiosity of this hard-to-characterize period. Huizinga also points out its extremes of cruelty and tenderness, which had, as he puts it, "the mixed smell of blood and of roses."*

JOHAN HUIZINGA

THE WANING OF THE MIDDLE AGES*

To the world when it was half a thousand years younger, the outlines of all things seemed more clearly marked than to us. The contrast between suffering and joy, between adversity and happiness, appeared more striking. All experience had yet to the minds of men the directness and absoluteness of the pleasure and pain of child-life. Every event, every action, was still embodied in expressive and solemn forms, which raised them to the dignity of a ritual. For it was not merely the great facts of birth, marriage and death which, by the sacredness of the sacrament, were raised to the rank of mysteries; incidents of less importance, like a journey, a task, a visit, were equally attended by a thousand formalities: benedictions, ceremonies, formulæ.

Calamities and indigence were more afflicting than at present; it was more difficult to guard against them, and to find solace. Illness and health presented a more striking contrast; the cold and darkness of winter were more real evils. Honours and riches were relished with greater avidity and contrasted more vividly with surrounding misery. We, at the present day, can hardly understand the keenness with which a fur coat, a good fire on the hearth, a soft bed, a glass of wine, were formerly enjoyed.

Then, again, all things in life were of a proud or cruel publicity. Lepers sounded their rattles and went about in processions,

* From *The Waning of the Middle Ages,* pp. 1–21, by Johan Huizinga. Reprinted by permission of Edward Arnold (Publishers) Ltd., London, 1924.

beggars exhibited their deformity and their misery in churches. Every order and estate, every rank and profession, was distinguished by its costume. The great lords never moved about without a glorious display of arms and liveries, exciting fear and envy. Executions and other public acts of justice, hawking, marriages and funerals, were all announced by cries and processions, songs and music. The lover wore the colours of his lady; companions the emblem of their confraternity; parties and servants the badges or blazon of their lords. Between town and country, too, the contrast was very marked. A medieval town did not lose itself in extensive suburbs of factories and villas; girded by its walls, it stood forth as a compact whole, bristling with innumerable turrets. However tall and threatening the houses of noblemen or merchants might be, in the aspect of the town the lofty mass of the churches always remained dominant.

The contrast between silence and sound, darkness and light, like that between summer and winter, was more strongly marked than it is in our lives. The modern town hardly knows silence or darkness in their purity, nor the effect of a solitary light or a single distant cry.

All things presenting themselves to the mind in violent contrasts and impressive forms, lent a tone of excitement and of passion to everyday life and tended to produce that perpetual oscillation between despair and distracted joy, between cruelty and pious tenderness which characterize life in the Middle Ages.

One sound rose ceaselessly above the noises of busy life and lifted all things unto a sphere of order and serenity: the sound of bells. The bells were in daily life like good spirits, which by their familiar voices, now called upon the citizens to mourn and now to rejoice, now warned them of danger, now exhorted them to piety. They were known by their names: big Jacqueline, or the bell Roland. Every one knew the difference in meaning of the various ways of ringing. However continuous the ringing of the bells, people would seem not to have become blunted to the effect of their sound.

Throughout the famous judicial duel between two citizens of Valenciennes, in 1455, the big bell, "which is hideous to hear," says Chastellain, never stopped ringing. What intoxication the pealing of the bells of all the churches, and of all the monasteries of Paris, must have produced, sounding from morning till evening, and even during the night, when a peace was concluded or a pope elected.

The frequent processions, too, were a continual source of pious agitation. When the times were evil, as they often were, processions were seen winding along, day after day, for weeks on end. In 1412 daily processions were ordered in Paris, to implore victory for the king, who had taken up the oriflamme against the Armagnacs. They lasted from May to July, and were formed by ever-varying orders and corporations, going always by new roads, and always carrying different relics. The Burgher of Paris calls them "the most touching processions in the memory of men." People looked on or followed, "weeping piteously, with many tears, in great devotion." All went barefooted and fasting, councillors of the Parlement as well as the poorer citizens. Those who could afford it, carried a torch or a taper. A great many small children were always among them. Poor country-people of the environs of Paris came barefooted from afar to join the procession. And nearly every day the rain came down in torrents.

Then there were the entries of princes, arranged with all the resources of art and luxury belonging to the age. And, lastly, most frequent of all, one might almost say, uninterrupted, the executions. The cruel excitement and coarse compassion raised by an execution formed an important item in the spiritual food of the common people. They were spectacular plays with a moral. For horrible crimes the law invented atrocious punishments. At Brussels a young incendiary and murderer is placed in the centre of a circle of burning fagots and straw, and made fast to a stake by means of a chain running round an iron ring. He addresses touching words to the spectators, "and he so softened their hearts that every one burst into tears and his death was commended as the finest that was ever seen." During the Burgundian terror in Paris in 1411, one of the victims, Messire Mansart du Bois, being requested by the hangman, according to custom, to forgive him, is not only ready to do so with all his heart, but begs the executioner to embrace him. "There was a great multitude of people, who nearly all wept hot tears."

When the criminals were great lords, the common people had the satisfaction of seeing rigid justice done, and at the same time finding the inconstancy of fortune exemplified more strikingly than in any sermon or picture. The magistrate took care that nothing should be wanting to the effect of the spectacle: the condemned were conducted to the scaffold, dressed in the garb of their high estate. Jean de Montaigu, grand maître d'hôtel to the king, the victim of Jean sans Peur, is placed high on a cart, preceded by two trumpeters. He wears his robe of state, hood, cloak, and hose half red and half white, and his gold spurs, which are left on the feet of the beheaded and suspended corpse. By special order of Louis XI, the head of maître Oudart de Bussy, who had refused a seat in the Parlement, was dug up and exhibited in the market-place of Hesdin, covered with a scarlet hood lined with fur "selon la mode des conseillers de Parlement," with explanatory verses.

Rarer than processions and executions were the sermons of itinerant preachers, coming to shake people by their eloquence. The modern reader of newspapers can no longer conceive the violence of impression caused by the spoken word on an ignorant mind lacking mental food. The Franciscan friar Richard preached in Paris in 1429 during ten consecutive days. He began at five in the morning and spoke without a break till ten or eleven, for the most part in the cemetery of the Innocents. When, at the close of his tenth sermon, he announced that it was to be his last, because he had no permission to preach more, "great and small wept as touchingly and as bitterly as if they were watching their best friends being buried; and so did he." Thinking that he would preach once more at Saint Denis on the Sunday, the people flocked thither on Saturday evening, and passed the night in the open, to secure good seats.

Another Minorite friar, Antoine Fradin, whom the magistrate of Paris had forbidden to preach, because he inveighed against the bad government, is guarded night and day in the Cordeliers monastery, by women posted around the building, armed with ashes and stones. In all the towns where the famous Dominican preacher Vincent Ferrer is expected, the people, the magistrates, the lower clergy, and even prelates and bishops, set out to greet him with joyous songs. He journeys with a numerous and ever-increasing following of adherents, who every night make a circuit of the town in procession, with chants and flagellations. Officials are appointed to take charge of lodging and feeding these multitudes. A large number of priests of various religious orders accompany him everywhere, to assist him in celebrating mass and in confessing the faithful. Also several notaries, to draw up, on the spot, deeds embodying the reconciliations which this holy preacher everywhere brings about. His pulpit has to be protected by a fence against the pressure of the congregation which wants to kiss his hand or habit. Work is at a stand-still all the time he preaches. He rarely fails to move his auditors to tears. When he spoke of the Last Judgment, of Hell, or of the Passion, both he and his hearers wept so copiously that he had to suspend his sermon till the sobbing had ceased. Malefactors threw themselves at his feet, before every one, confessing their great sins. One day, while he was preaching, he saw two persons, who had been condemned to death—a man and a woman—being led to execution. He begged to have the execution delayed, had them both placed under the pulpit, and went on with his sermon, preaching about their sins. After the sermon, only some bones were found in the place they had occupied, and the people were convinced that the word of the saint had consumed and saved them at the same time.

After Olivier Maillard had been preaching Lenten sermons at Orléans, the roofs of the houses surrounding the place whence he had addressed the people had been so damaged by the spectators who had climbed on to them, that the roofer sent in a bill for repairs extending over sixty-four days.

The diatribes of the preachers against dissoluteness and luxury produced violent excitement which was translated into action. Long before Savonarola started bonfires of "vanities" at Florence, to the irreparable loss of art, the custom of these holocausts of articles of luxury and amusement was prevalent both in France and in Italy. At the summons of a famous preacher, men and women would hasten to bring cards, dice, finery, ornaments, and burn them with great pomp. Renunciation of the sin of vanity in this way had taken a fixed and solemn form of public manifestation, in accordance with the tendency of the age to invent a style for everything.

All this general facility of emotions, of tears and spiritual upheavals, must be borne in mind in order to conceive fully how violent and high-strung was life at that period.

Public mourning still presented the outward appearance of a general calamity. At the funeral of Charles VII, the people are quite appalled on seeing the cortège of all the court dignitaries, "dressed in the deepest mourning, which was most pitiful to see; and because of the great sorrow and grief they exhibited for the death of their master, many tears were shed and lamentations uttered throughout the town." People were especially touched at the sight of six pages of the king mounted on horses quite covered with black velvet. One of the pages, according to a rumour, had neither eaten nor drunk for four days. "And God knows what doleful and piteous plaints they made, mourning for their master."

Solemnities of a political character also led to abundant weeping. An ambassador of the king of France repeatedly bursts into tears while addressing a courteous harangue to Philip the Good. At the meeting of the kings of France and of England at Ardres, at the reception of the dauphin at Brussels, at the departure of John of Coïmbre from the court of Burgundy, all the spectators weep hot tears. Chastellain describes the dauphin, the future Louis XI, during his voluntary exile in Brabant, as subject to frequent fits of weeping.

Unquestionably there is some exaggeration in these descriptions of the chroniclers. In describing the emotion caused by the addresses of the ambassadors at the peace congress at Arras, in 1435, Jean Germain, bishop of Chalons, makes the auditors throw themselves on the ground, sobbing and groaning. Things, of course, did not happen thus, but thus the bishop thought fit to represent them, and the palpable exaggeration reveals a foundation of truth. As with the sentimentalists of the eighteenth century, tears were considered fine and honourable. Even nowadays an indifferent spectator of a public procession sometimes feels himself suddenly moved to inexplicable tears. In an age filled with religious reverence for all pomp and grandeur, this propensity will appear altogether natural.

A simple instance will suffice to show the high degree of irritability which distinguishes the Middle Ages from our own time. One can hardly imagine a more peaceful game than that of chess. Still like the *chansons de gestes* of some centuries back, Olivier de la Marche mentions frequent quarrels arising over it: "le plus saige y pert patience."

A scientific historian of the Middle Ages, relying first and foremost on official documents, which rarely refer to the passions, except violence and cupidity, occasionally runs the risk of neglecting the difference of tone between the life of the expiring Middle Ages and that of our own days. Such documents would sometimes make us forget the vehement pathos of medieval life, of which the chroniclers, however defective as to material facts, always keep us in mind.

In more than one respect life had still the colours of a fairy-story; that is to say, it assumed those colours in the eyes of contemporaries. The court chroniclers were men of culture, and they observed the princes, whose deeds they recorded, at close quarters, yet even they give these records a somewhat archaic, hieratic air. The following story, told by Chastellain, serves to prove this. The young count of Charolais, the later Charles the Bold, on arriving at Gorcum, in Holland, on his way from Sluys, learns that his father, the duke, has taken all his pensions and benefices from him. Thereupon he calls his whole court into his presence, down to the scullions, and in a touching speech imparts his misfortune to them, dwelling on his respect for his ill-informed father, and on his anxiety about the welfare of all his retinue. Let those who have the means to live, remain with him awaiting the return of good fortune; let the poor go away freely, and let them come back when they hear that the count's fortune has been re-established: they will all return to their old places, and the count will reward them for their patience. "Then were heard cries and sobs, and with one accord they shouted: 'We all, we all, my lord, will live and die with thee.' " Profoundly touched, Charles accepts their devotion: "Well, then, stay and suffer, and I will suffer for you, rather than that you should be in want." The nobles then come and offer him what they possess, "one saying, I have a thousand, another, ten thousand; I have this, I have that to place at thy service, and I am ready to share all that may befall thee." And in this way everything went on as usual, and there was never a hen the less in the kitchen.

Clearly this story has been more or less touched up. What interests us is that Chastellain sees the prince and his court in the epic guise of a popular ballad. If this is a literary man's conception, how brilliant must royal life have appeared, when displayed in almost magic splendour, to the naïve imagination of the uneducated!

Although in reality the mechanism of government had already assumed rather complicated forms, the popular mind pictures it in simple and fixed figures. The current political ideas are those of the Old Testament, of the romaunt and the ballad. The kings of the time are reduced to a certain number of types, every one of which corresponds, more or less, to a literary motif. There is the wise and just prince, the prince deceived by evil counsellors, the prince who avenges the honour of his family, the unfortunate prince to whom his servants remain faithful. In the mind of the people political questions are reduced to stories of adventure. Philip the Good knew the political language which the people understands. To convince the Hollanders and Frisians that he was perfectly able to conquer the bishopric of Utrecht, he exhibits, during the festivities of the Hague, in 1456, precious plate to the value of thirty thousand silver marks. Everybody may come and look at it. Amongst other things, two hundred thousand gold lions have been brought from Lille contained in two chests which every one may try to lift up. The demonstration of the solvency of the state took the form of an entertainment at a fair.

Often we find a fantastic element in the life of princes which reminds us of the caliph of the *Arabian Nights*. Charles VI, disguised and mounted with a friend on a single horse, witnesses the entrance of his betrothed and is knocked about in the crowd by petty constables. Philip the Good, whom the physicians ordered to have his head shaved, issues a command to all the nobles to do likewise, and charges Pierre de Hagenbach with the cropping of any whom he finds recalcitrant. In the midst of coolly calculated enterprises princes sometimes act with an impetuous temerity, which endangers their lives and their policy. Edward III does not hesitate to expose his life and that of the prince of Wales in order to capture some Spanish merchantmen, in revenge for deeds of piracy. Philip the Good interrupts the most serious political business to make the dangerous crossing from Rotterdam to Sluys for the sake of a mere whim. On another occasion, mad with rage in consequence of a quarrel with his son, he leaves Brussels in the night alone, and loses his way in the woods. The knight Philippe Pot, to whom fell the delicate task of pacifying him on his return, lights upon the happy phrase: "Good day, my liege, good day, what is this? Art thou playing King Arthur, now, or Sir Lancelot?"

The custom of princes, in the fifteenth century, frequently to seek counsel in political matters from ecstatic preachers and great visionaries, maintained a kind of religious tension in state affairs which at any moment might manifest itself in decisions of a totally unexpected character.

At the end of the fourteenth century and at the beginning of the fifteenth, the political stage of the kingdoms of Europe was so crowded with fierce and tragic conflicts that the peoples could not help seeing all that regards royalty as a succession of sanguinary and romantic events: in England, King Richard II dethroned and next secretly murdered, while nearly at the same time the highest monarch in Christendom, his brother-in-law Wenzel, king of the Romans, is deposed by the electors; in France, a mad king and soon afterwards fierce party strife, openly breaking out with the appalling murder of Louis of Orléans in 1407, and indefinitely prolonged by the retaliation of 1419 when Jean sans Peur is murdered at Montereau. With their endless train of hostility and vengeance, these two murders have given to the history of France, during a whole century, a sombre tone of hatred. For the contemporary mind cannot help seeing all the national misfortunes which the struggle of the houses of Orléans and of Burgundy was to unchain, in the light of that sole dramatic motive of princely vengeance. It finds no explanation for historic events save in personal quarrels and motives of passion.

In addition to all these evils came the increasing obsession of the Turkish peril, and the still vivid recollection of the catastrophe of Nicopolis in 1396, where a reckless attempt to save Christendom had ended in the wholesale slaughter of French chivalry. Lastly, the great schism of the West had lasted already for a quarter of a century, unsettling all notions about the stability of the Church, dividing every land and community. Two, soon three, claimants contending for the papacy! One of them, the obstinate Aragonese Peter of Luna, or Benedict XIII, was commonly called in France "le Pappe de la Lune." What can an ignorant populace have imagined when hearing such a name?

The familiar image of Fortune's wheel from which kings are falling with their crowns and their sceptres took a living shape in the person of many an expelled prince, roaming from court to court, without means, but full of projects and still decked with the splendour of the marvellous East whence he had fled—the king of Armenia, the king of Cyprus, before long the emperor of Constantinople. It is not surprising that the people of Paris should have believed in the tale of the Gipsies, who presented themselves in 1427, "a duke and a count and ten men, all on horseback," while others, to the number of 120, had to stay outside the town. They came from Egypt, they said; the pope had ordered them, by way of penance for their apostasy, to wander about for seven years, without sleeping in a bed; there had been 1,200 of them, but their king, their queen and all the others had died on the way; as a mitigation the pope had ordered that every bishop and abbot was to give them ten pounds tournois. The people of

Paris came in great numbers to see them, and have their fortunes told by women who eased them of their money "by magic art or in other ways."

The inconstancy of the fortune of princes was strikingly embodied in the person of King René. Having aspired to the crowns of Hungary, of Sicily, and of Jerusalem, he had lost all his opportunities, and reaped nothing but a series of defeats, and imprisonments, chequered by perilous escapes. The royal poet, a lover of the arts, consoled himself for all his disappointments on his estates in Anjou and in Provence; his cruel fate had not cured him of his predilection for pastoral enjoyment. He had seen all his children die but one, a daughter for whom was reserved a fate even harder than his own. Married at sixteen to an imbecile bigot, Henry VI of England, Margaret of Anjou, full of wit, ambition and passion, after living for many years in that hell of hatred and of persecution, the English court, lost her crown when the quarrel between York and Lancaster at last broke out into civil war. Having found refuge, after many dangers and suffering, at the court of Burgundy, she told Chastellain the story of her adventures: how she had been forced to commit herself and her young son to the mercy of a robber, how at mass she had had to ask a Scotch archer a penny for her offering, "who reluctantly and with regret took a groat scots for her out of his purse and lent it her." The good historiographer, moved by so much misfortune, dedicated to her "a certain little treatise on fortune, based on its inconstancy and deceptive nature," which he entitled *Le Temple de Bocace*. He could not guess that still graver calamities were in store for the unfortunate queen. At the battle of Tewkesbury, in 1471, the fortunes of Lancaster went down for ever. Her only son perished there, probably slaughtered after the battle. Her husband was secretly murdered; she herself was imprisoned in the Tower of London, where she remained for five years, to be at last given up by Edward IV to Louis XI, who made her renounce her father's inheritance as the price of her liberty.

An atmosphere of passion and adventure enveloped the lives of princes. It was not popular fancy alone which lent it that colour.

A present-day reader, studying the history of the Middle Ages based on official documents, will never sufficiently realize the extreme excitability of the medieval soul. The picture drawn mainly from official records, though they may be the most reliable sources, will lack one element: that of the vehement passion possessing princes and peoples alike. To be sure, the passionate element is not absent from modern politics, but it is now restrained and diverted for the most part by the complicated mechanism of social life. Five centuries ago it still made frequent and violent irruptions into practical politics, upsetting rational schemes. In princes this violence of sentiment is doubled by pride and the consciousness of power, and therefore operates with a twofold impetus. It is not surprising, says Chastellain, that princes often live in hostility, "for princes are men, and their affairs are high and perilous, and their natures are subject to many passions, such as hatred and envy; their hearts are veritable dwelling-places of these, because of their pride in reigning."

In writing the history of the house of Burgundy, the *leitmotiv* should constantly keep before our minds the spirit of revenge. Nobody, of course, will now seek the explanation of the whole conflict of power and interests, whence proceeded the secular struggle between France and the house of Austria, in the family feud between Orléans and Burgundy. All sorts of causes of a general nature—political, economic, ethnographic—have contributed to the genesis of that great conflict. But we should never forget that the apparent origin of it, and the central motive dominating it, was, to the men of the fifteenth century and even later, the thirst for revenge. To them Philip the Good is always, in the first place, the avenger, "he who, to avenge the outrage done to the person of Duke John, sustained the war for sixteen years." He had undertaken it as a sacred duty: "with the most violent and deadly hatred he would give himself up to revenge the dead, as far as ever God would permit him, as he would devote to it body and soul, substance and lands, submitting everything to Fortune, considering it more a salutary task and agreeable to God to undertake it, than to leave it."

Read the long list of expiatory deeds which the treaty of Arras demanded in 1435—chapels, monasteries, churches, chapters to be founded, crosses to be erected, masses to be chanted—then one realizes the immensely high rate at which men valued the need of vengeance and of reparations to outraged honour. The Burgundians were not alone in thinking after this fashion; the most enlightened man of his century, Aeneas Sylvius, in one of his letters praises Philip above all the other princes of his time, for his anxiety to avenge his father.

According to La Marche, this duty of honour and revenge was to the duke's subjects also the cardinal point of policy. All the dominions of the duke, he says, were clamouring for vengeance along with him. We shall find it difficult to believe this, when we remember, for instance, the commercial relations between Flanders and England, a more important political factor, it would seem, than the honour of the ducal family. But to understand the sentiment of the age itself, one should look for the avowed and conscious political ideas. There can be no doubt that no other political motive could be better understood by the people than the primitive motives of hatred and vengeance. Attachment to princes had still an emotional character; it was based on the innate and immediate sentiments of fidelity and fellowship, it was still feudal sentiment at bottom. It was rather party feeling than political. The last three centuries of the Middle Ages are the time of the great party struggles. From the thirteenth century onward inveterate party quarrels arise in nearly all countries: first in Italy, then in France, the Netherlands, Germany and England. Though economic interests which sometimes have been at the bottom of these quarrels, the attempts which have been made to disengage them often smack somewhat of arbitrary construction. The desire to discover economic causes is to some degree a craze with us, and sometimes leads us to forget a much simpler psychological explanation of the facts.

In the feudal age the private wars between two families have no other discernible reason than rivalry of rank and covetousness of possessions. Racial pride, thirst of vengeance, fidelity, are their primary and direct motives. There are no grounds to ascribe another economic basis to them than mere greed of one's neighbour's riches. Accordingly as the central power consolidates and extends, these isolated quarrels unite, agglomerate to groups; large parties are formed, are polarized, so to say; while their members know of no other grounds for their concord or enmity than those of honour, tradition and fidelity. Their economic differences are often only a consequence of their relation towards their rulers.

Every page of medieval history proves the spontaneous and passionate character of the sentiments of loyalty and devotion to the prince. At Abbeville, in 1462, a messenger comes at night, bringing the news of a dangerous illness of the duke of Burgundy. His son requests the good towns to pray for him. At once the aldermen order the bells of the church of Saint Vulfran to be rung; the whole population wakes up and goes to church, where it remains all night in prayer, kneeling or prostrate on the ground, with "grandes allumeries merveilleuses," while the bells keep tolling.

It might be thought that the schism, which had no dogmatic cause, could hardly awaken religious passions in countries distant from Avignon and of Rome, in which the two popes were only known by name. Yet in fact it immediately engendered a fanatical hatred, such as exists between the faithful and infidels. When the town of Bruges went over to the "obedience" of Avignon, a great number of people left their house, trade or prebend, to go and live according to their party views in some diocese of the Urbanist obedience: Liège, Utrecht, or elsewhere. In 1382 the oriflamme, which might only be unfurled in a holy cause, was taken up against the Flemings, because they were Urbanists, that is, infidels. Pierre Salmon, a French political agent, arriving at Utrecht about Easter, could not find a priest there willing to admit him to the communion service, "because they said I was a schismatic and believed in Benedict the anti-pope."

The emotional character of party sentiments and of fidelity was further heightened by the powerfully suggestive effect of all the outward signs of these divergences: liveries, colours, badges, party cries. During the first years of the war between the Armagnacs and the Burgundians, these signs succeeded each other in Paris with a dangerous alternation: a purple hood with a cross of Saint Andrew, white hoods, then violet ones. Even priests, women and children wore distinctive signs. The images of saints were decorated with them; it was asserted that certain priests, during mass and in baptizing, refused to make the sign of the cross in the orthodox way, but made it in the form of a Saint Andrew cross.

In the blind passion with which people followed their lord or their party, the unshakable sentiment of right, characteristic of the Middle Ages, is trying to find expression. Man at that time is convinced that right is absolutely fixed and certain. Justice should prosecute the unjust everywhere and to the end. Reparation and retribution have to be extreme, and assume the character of revenge. In this exaggerated need of justice, primitive barbarism, pagan at bottom, blends with the Christian conception of society. The Church, on the one hand, had inculcated gentleness and clemency, and tried, in that way, to soften judicial morals. On the other hand, in adding to the primitive need of retribution the horror of sin, it had, to a certain extent, stimulated the sentiment of justice. And sin, to violent and impulsive spirits, was only too frequently another name for what their enemies did. The barbarous idea of retaliation was reinforced by fanaticism. The chronic insecurity made the greatest possible severity on the part of the public authorities desirable; crime came to be regarded as a menace to order and society, as well as an insult to divine majesty. Thus it was natural that the late Middle Ages should become the special period of judicial cruelty. That the criminal deserved his punishment was not doubted for a moment. The popular sense of justice always sanctioned the most rigorous penalties. At intervals the magistrate undertook regular campaigns of severe justice, now against brigandage, now against sorcery or sodomy.

What strikes us in this judicial cruelty and in the joy the people felt at it, is rather brutality than perversity. Torture and executions are enjoyed by the spectators like an entertainment at a fair. The citizens of Mons bought a brigand, at far too high a price, for the pleasure of seeing him quartered, "at which the people rejoiced more than if a new holy body had risen from the dead." The people of Bruges, in 1488, during the captivity of Maximilian, king of the Romans, cannot get their fill of seeing the tortures inflicted, on a high platform in the middle of the market-place, on the magistrates suspected of treason. The unfortunates are refused the deathblow which they implore, that the people may feast again upon their torments.

Both in France and in England, the custom existed of refusing confession and the extreme unction to a criminal condemned to death. Sufferings and fear of death were to be aggravated by the certainty of eternal damnation. In vain had the council of Vienne in 1311 ordered to grant them at least the sacrament of penitence. Towards the end of the fourteenth century the same custom still existed. Charles V himself, moderate though he was, had declared that no change would be made in his lifetime. The chancellor Pierre d'Orgemont, whose "forte cervelle," says Philippe de Mézières, was more difficult to turn than a mill-stone, remained deaf to the humane remonstrances of the latter. It was only after Gerson had joined his voice to that of Mézières that a royal decree of the 12th of February, 1397, ordered that confession should be accorded to the condemned. A stone cross erected by the care of Pierre de Craon, who had interested himself in the decree, marked the place where the Minorite friars might assist penitents going to execution. And even then the barbarous custom did not disappear. Etienne Ponchier, bishop of Paris, had to renew the decree of 1311 in 1500.

In 1427 a noble brigand is hanged in Paris. At the moment when he is going to be executed, the great treasurer of the regent appears on the scene and vents his hatred against him; he prevents his confession, in spite of his prayers; he climbs the ladder behind him, shouting insults, beats him with a stick, and gives the hangman a thrashing for exhorting the victim to think of his salvation. The hangman grows nervous and bungles his work; the cord snaps, the wretched criminal falls on the ground, breaks a leg and some ribs, and in this condition has to climb the ladder again.

The Middle Ages knew nothing of all those ideas which have rendered our sentiment of justice timid and hesitating: doubts as to the criminal's responsibility; the conviction that society is, to a certain extent, the accomplice of the individual; the desire to reform instead of inflicting pain; and, we may even add, the fear of judicial errors. Or rather these ideas were implied, unconsciously, in the very strong and direct feeling of pity and of forgiveness which alternated with extreme severity. Instead of lenient penalties, inflicted with hesitation, the Middle Ages knew but the two extremes: the fulness of cruel punishment, and mercy. When the condemned criminal is pardoned, the question whether he deserves it for any special reasons is hardly asked; for mercy has to be gratuitous, like the mercy of God. In practice, it was not always pure pity which determined the question of pardon. The princes of the fifteenth century were very liberal of "lettres de rémission" for misdeeds of all sorts, and contemporaries thought it quite natural, that they were obtained by the intercession of noble relatives. The majority of these documents, however, concern poor common people.

The contrast of cruelty and of pity recurs at every turn in the manners and customs of the Middle Ages. On the one hand, the sick, the poor, the insane, are objects of that deeply moved pity, born of a feeling of fraternity akin to that which is so strikingly expressed in modern Russian literature; on the other hand, they are treated with incredible hardness or cruelly mocked. The chronicler Pierre de Fenin, having described the death of a gang of brigands, winds up naïvely: "and people laughed a good deal, because they were all poor men." In 1425, an "esbatement" takes place in Paris, of four blind beggars, armed with sticks, with which they hit each other in trying to kill a pig, which is a prize of the combat. On the evening before they are led through the town, "all armed, with a great banner in front, on which was pictured a pig, and preceded by a man beating a drum."

In the fifteenth century, female dwarfs were objects of amusement, as they still were at the court of Spain when Velazquez painted their infinitely sad faces. Madame d'Or, the blond dwarf of Philip the Good, was famous. She was made to wrestle, at a court festival, with the acrobat Hans. At the wedding-feasts of Charles the Bold, in 1468, Madame de Beaugrant, the female dwarf of Mademoiselle of Burgundy, enters dressed like a shepherdess, mounted on a golden lion, larger than a horse; she is presented to the young duchess and placed on the table. As to the fate of these small creatures, the account-books are more eloquent for us than any sentimental complaint could be. They tell us of a dwarf-girl whom a duchess caused to be fetched from her home, and how her parents came to visit her from time to time and receive a gratuity. "Au père de Belon la folle, qui estoit venu veoir sa fille. . . . 27*s.* 6*d.*" The poor fellow perhaps went home well pleased and much elated about the court function of his daughter. That same year a locksmith of Blois furnished two iron collars, the one "to make fast Belon, the fool, and the other to put round the neck of the monkey of her grace the Duchess."

In the harshness of those times there is something ingenuous which almost forbids us to condemn it. When the massacre of the Armagnacs was in full swing in 1418, the Parisians founded a brotherhood of Saint Andrew in the church of Saint Eustache: every one, priest or layman, wore a wreath of red roses, so that the church was perfumed by them, "as if it had been washed with rose-water." The people of Arras celebrate the annulment of the sentences for witchcraft, which during the whole year 1461 had infested the town like an epidemic, by joyous festivals and a competition in acting "folies moralisées," of which the prizes were a gold fleur-de-lis, a brace of capons, etc.; nobody, it seems, thought any more of the tortured and executed victims.

So violent and motley was life, that it bore the mixed smell of blood and of roses. The men of that time always oscillate between the fear of hell and the most naïve joy, between cruelty and tenderness, between harsh asceticism and insane attachment to the delights of this world, between hatred and goodness, always running to extremes.

After the close of the Middle Ages the mortal sins of pride, anger and covetousness have never again shown the unabashed insolence with which they manifested themselves in the life of preceding centuries. The whole history of the house of Burgundy is like an epic of overweening and heroic pride, which takes the form of bravura and ambition with Philippe le Hardi, of hatred and envy with Jean sans Peur, of the lust of vengeance and fondness for display with Philip the Good, of foolhardy temerity and obstinacy with Charles the Bold.

Medieval doctrine found the root of all evil either in the sin of pride or in cupidity. Both opinions were based on Scripture texts: *A superbia initium sumpsit omnis perditio.* —*Radix omnium malorum est cupiditas.* It seems, nevertheless, that from the twelfth century downward people begin to find the principle of evil rather in cupidity than in pride. The voices which condemn blind cupidity, "la cieca cupidigia" of Dante, become louder and louder. Pride might perhaps be called the sin of the feudal and hierarchic age. Very little property is, in the modern sense, liquid, while power is not yet associated, predominantly, with money; it is still rather inherent in the person and depends on a sort of religious awe which he inspires; it makes itself felt by pomp and magnificence, of a numerous train of faithful followers. Feudal or hierarchic thought expresses the idea of grandeur by visible signs, lending to it a symbolic shape, of homage paid kneeling, of ceremonial reverence. Pride, therefore, is a symbolic sin, and from the fact that, in the last resort, it derives from the pride of Lucifer, the author of all evil, it assumes a metaphysical character.

Cupidity, on the other hand, has neither this symbolic character nor these relations with theology. It is a purely worldly sin, the impulse of nature and of the flesh. In the later Middle Ages the conditions of power had been changed by the increased circulation of money, and an illimitable field opened to whosoever was desirous of satisfying his ambitions by heaping up wealth. To this epoch cupidity becomes the predominant sin. Riches have not acquired the spectral impalpability which capitalism, founded on credit, will give them later; what haunts the imagination is still the tangible yellow gold. The enjoyment of riches is direct and primitive; it is not yet weakened by the mechanism of an automatic and invisible accumulation by investment; the satisfaction of being rich is found either in luxury and dissipation, or in gross avarice.

Towards the end of the Middle Ages feudal and hierarchic pride had lost nothing, as yet, of its vigour; the relish for pomp and display is as strong as ever. This primitive pride has now united itself with the growing sin of cupidity, and it is this mixture of the two which gives the expiring Middle Ages a tone of extravagant passion that never appears again.

A furious chorus of invectives against cupidity and avarice rises up everywhere from the literature of that period. Preachers, moralists, satirical writers, chroniclers and poets speak with one voice. Hatred of rich people, especially of the new rich, who were then very numerous, is general. Official records confirm the most incredible cases of unbridled avidity told by the chronicles. In 1436 a quarrel between two beggars, in which a few drops of blood had been shed, had soiled the church of the Innocents at Paris. The bishop, Jacques du Châtelier, "a very ostentatious, grasping man, of a more worldly disposition than his station required," refused to consecrate the church anew, unless he received a certain sum of money from the two poor men, which they did not possess, so that the service was interrupted for twenty-two days. Even worse happened under his successor, Denys de Moulins. During four months of the year 1441, he prohibited both burials and processions in the cemetery of the Innocents, the most favoured of all, because the church could not pay the tax he demanded. This Denys de Moulins was reputed "a man who showed very little pity to people, if he did not receive money or some equivalent; and it was told for truth that he had more than fifty lawsuits before the Parlement, for nothing could be got out of him without going to law."

A general feeling of impending calamity hangs over all. Perpetual danger prevails everywhere. To realize the continuous insecurity in which the lives of great and small alike were passed, it suffices to read the details which Monsieur Pierre Champion has collected regarding the persons mentioned by Villon in his *Testament,* or the notes of Monsieur A. Tuetey to the diary of a Burgher of Paris. They present to us an interminable string of lawsuits, crimes, assaults and persecutions. A chronicle like that of Jacques du Clercq, or a diary such as that of the citizen of Metz, Philippe de Vigneulles, perhaps lay too much stress on the darker side of contemporary life, but every investigation of the careers of individual persons seems to confirm them, by revealing to us strangely troubled lives.

In reading the chronicle of Mathieu d'Escouchy, simple, exact, impartial, moralizing, one would think that the author was a studious, quiet and honest man. His character was unknown before Monsieur du Fresne de Beaucourt had elicited the history of his life from the archives. But what a life it was, that of this representative of "colérique Picardie." Alderman, then, towards 1445 provost, of Péronne, we find him from the outset engaged in a family quarrel with Jean Froment, the city syndic. They harass each other reciprocally with lawsuits, for forgery and murder, for "excès et attemptaz." The attempt of the provost to get the widow of his enemy condemned for witchcraft costs him dear. Summoned before the Parlement of Paris himself, d'Escouchy is imprisoned. We find him again in prison as an accused on five more occasions, always in grave criminal causes, and more than once in heavy chains. A son of Froment wounds him in an encounter. Each of the parties hires brigands to assail the other. After this long feud ceases to be mentioned in the records, others arise of similar violence. All this does not check the career of d'Escouchy: he becomes bailiff, provost of Ribemont, "procureur du roi" at Saint Quentin; he is ennobled. He is taken prisoner at Montlhéry, then comes back maimed from a later campaign. Next he marries, but not to settle down to a quiet life. Once more, he appears accused of counterfeiting seals, conducted to Paris "comme larron et murdrier," forced into confessions by torture, prevented from appealing, condemned; then rehabilitated and again condemned, till the traces of this career of hatred and persecutions disappear from the records,

Is it surprising that the people could see their fate and that of the world only as an endless succession of evils? Bad government, exactions, the cupidity and violence of the great, wars and brigandage, scarcity, misery and pestilence—to this is contemporary history nearly reduced in the eyes of the people. The feeling of general insecurity which was caused by the chronic form wars were apt to take, by the constant menance of the dangerous classes, by the mistrust of justice, was further aggravated by the obsession of the coming end of the world, and by the fear of hell, of sorcerers and of devils. The background of all life in the world seems black. Everywhere the flames of hatred arise and injustice reigns. Satan covers a gloomy earth with his sombre wings. In vain the militant Church battles, preachers deliver their sermons; the world remains unconverted. According to a popular belief, current towards the end of the fourteenth century, no one, since the beginning of the great Western schism, had entered Paradise.

IV

THE RENAISSANCE
PART FOUR

☙ THE RENAISSANCE

During the Late Middle Ages and extending into the post-medieval period, the city-states of the Italian peninsula entered a vigorous era known as the Renaissance. Literally, Renaissance means "rebirth," and is used broadly in the sense of a revival of classical learning and civilization. To Jacob Burckhardt, the Swiss historian of the nineteenth century, the classical revival combined with strong native tendencies in Italy and led to highly creative activity which centered on worldliness and individualism as opposed to the otherworldliness and the community-centered way of life of the Middle Ages. Revisionist scholars question Burckhardt's view and find the Renaissance somewhat less glamorous than he supposed, particularly because many allegedly new tendencies of the Renaissance had long before appeared in the Middle Ages. But little question can exist about the vigor of the Italian Renaissance in classical scholarship, statecraft, economics, and the arts. Among historians, the era of the Renaissance remains a distinct period, though somewhat less clearly defined than Burckhardt and his followers believe it to have been. In any case, the Renaissance formed one of the main bridges between the era called "medieval" and the era called "modern."

SEVENTEEN

BURCKHARDT'S THESIS

In his monumental essay The Civilization of the Renaissance in Italy, *first published in 1860, the great Swiss scholar Jacob Burckhardt (1818–97) formulated the basic concept of the Renaissance. Burckhardt regarded the Italian Renaissance as, in his famous phrase, "the discovery of the world and of man," that is, the development of secularism and individualism after the "faith, illusion, and childish prepossession" of the Middle Ages. According to Burckhardt, the Renaissance first flowered in Italy in the fourteenth century as a result of many causes, among them the despotism of the Italian city-states, which put a high premium on personality and personal talent, and the revival of the Greek-Roman classics, which provided a form and a channel for the Italian spirit once freed of its medieval bonds. Many of Burckhardt's followers overstated his thesis, and many modern historians believe that Burckhardt himself overstated it. Nonetheless, in the present state of historical scholarship, Burckhardt's thesis still provides an indispensable starting point for Renaissance studies.*

JACOB BURCKHARDT

THE CIVILIZATION OF THE RENAISSANCE IN ITALY*

In the character of these states, whether republics or despotisms, lies not the only but the chief reason for the early development of the Italian. To this it is due that he was the first-born among the sons of modern Europe.

In the Middle Ages both side of human consciousness—that which was turned within as that which was turned without—lay dreaming or half awake beneath a common veil. The veil was woven of faith, illusion, and childish prepossession, through which the world and history were seen clad in strange hues. Man was conscious of himself only as member of a race, people, party, family, or corporation—only through some general category. In Italy this veil first melted into air; and *objective* treatment and consideration of the State and of all the things of this world became possible. The *subjective* side at the same time asserted itself with corresponding emphasis; man became a spiritual *individual,* and recognized himself as such. In the same way the Greek had once distinguished himself from the barbarian, and the Arabian had felt himself an individual at a time when other Asiatics knew themselves only as members of a race. It will not be difficult to show that this result was owing, above all, to the political circumstances of Italy.

In far earlier times we can here and there detect a development of free personality which in Northern Europe either did not occur at all or could not display itself in the same manner. The band of audacious wrongdoers in the sixteenth century described to us by Luidprand, some of the contemporaries of Gregory VII, and a few of the opponents of the first Hohenstaufen, show us characters of this kind. But at the close of the thirteenth century Italy began to swarm with individuality; the charm laid upon human personality was dissolved, and a thousand figures meet us each in its own special shape and dress. Dante's great poem would have been impossible in any other country of Europe, if only for the reason that they all still lay under the spell of race. For Italy the august poet, through the wealth of individuality which he set forth, was the most national herald of his time. But this unfolding of the treasures of human nature in literature and art—this many-sided representation and criticism—will be discussed in separate chapters; here we have to deal only with the psychological fact itself. This fact appears in the most decisive and unmistakable form. The Italians of the fourteenth century knew little of false modesty or of hypocrisy in any shape; not one of them was afraid of singularity, of being and seeming unlike his neighbours.

Despotism, as we have already seen, fostered in the highest degree the individuality not only of the tyrant or *condottiere* himself, but also of the men whom he protected

* Reprinted from Jacob Burckhardt, *The Civilization of the Renaissance in Italy,* Part II, chs. 1–2, and Part III, ch. 1, translated by S. G. C. Middlemore, 1878.

or used as his tools—the secretary, minister, poet, and companion. These people were forced to know all the inward resources of their own nature, passing or permanent; and their enjoyment of life was enhanced and concentrated by the desire to obtain the greatest satisfaction from a possibly very brief period of power and influence.

But even the subjects whom they ruled over were not free from the same impulse. Leaving out of account those who wasted their lives in secret opposition and conspiracies, we speak of the majority who were content with a strictly private station, like most of the urban population of the Byzantine Empire and the Mohammedan states. No doubt it was often hard for the subjects of a Visconti to maintain the dignity of their persons and families, and multitudes must have lost in moral character through the servitude they lived under. But this was not the case with regard to individuality; for political impotence does not hinder the different tendencies and manifestations of private life from thriving in the fullest vigour and variety. Wealth and culture, so far as display and rivalry were not forbidden to them, a municipal freedom which did not cease to be considerable, and a Church which, unlike that of the Byzantine or of the Mohammedan world, was not identical with the State—all these conditions undoubtedly favoured the growth of individual thought, for which the necessary leisure was furnished by the cessation of party conflicts. The private man, indifferent to politics, and busied partly with serious pursuits, partly with the interests of a *dilettante,* seems to have been first fully formed in these despotisms of the fourteenth century. Documentary evidence cannot, of course, be required on such a point. The novelists, from whom we might expect information, describe to us oddities in plenty, but only from one point of view and in so far as the needs of the story demand. Their scene, too, lies chiefly in the republican cities.

In the latter circumstances were also, but in another way, favourable to the growth of individual character. The more frequently the governing party was changed, the more the individual was led to make the utmost of the exercise and enjoyment of power. The statesmen and popular leaders, especially in Florentine history, acquired so marked a personal character that we can scarcely find, even exceptionally, a parallel to them in contemporary history, hardly even in Jacob van Artevelde.

The members of the defeated parties, on the other hand, often came into a position like that of the subjects of the despotic states, with the difference that the freedom or power already enjoyed, and in some cases the hope of recovering them, gave a higher energy to their individuality. Among these men of involuntary leisure we find, for instance, an Agnolo Pandolfini (d. 1446), whose work on domestic economy is the first complete programme of a developed private life. His estimate of the duties of the individual as against the dangers and thanklessness of public life is in its way a true monument of the age.

Banishment too has this effect above all, that it either wears the exile out or develops whatever is greatest in him. "In all our more populous cities," says Gioviano Pontano, "we see a crowd of people who have left their homes of their own free-will; but a man takes his virtues with him wherever he goes." And, in fact, they were by no means only men who had been actually exiled, but thousands left their native place voluntarily, because they found its political or economical condition intolerable. The Florentine emigrants at Ferrara and the Lucchese in Venice formed whole colonies by themselves.

The cosmopolitanism which grew up in the most gifted circles is in itself a high stage of individualism. Dante, as we have already said, finds a new home in the language and culture of Italy, but goes beyond even this in the words "My country is the whole world!" And when his recall to Florence was offered him on unworthy conditions he wrote back: "Can I not everywhere behold the light of the sun and the stars; everywhere meditate on the noblest truths, without appearing ingloriously and shamefully before the city and the people? Even my bread will not fail me!" The artists exult no less defiantly in their freedom from the constraints of fixed residence. "Only he who has learned everything," says Ghiberti, "is nowhere a stranger; robbed of his fortune and without friends, he is yet the citizen of every country, and can fearlessly despise the changes of fortune." In the same strain an exiled humanist writes: "Wherever a learned man fixes his seat there is home."

An acute and practised eye might be able to trace, step by step, the increase in the number of complete men during the fifteenth century. Whether they had before them as a conscious object the harmonious development of their spiritual and material existence is hard to say; but several of them attained it, so far as is consistent with the imperfection of all that is earthly. It may be better to renounce the attempt at an estimate of the share which fortune, character, and talent had in the life of Lorenzo the Magnificent. But look at a personality like that of Ariosto, especially as shown in his satires. In what harmony are there expressed the pride of the man and the poet, the irony with which he treats his own enjoyments, the most delicate satire, and the deepest goodwill!

When this impulse to the highest individual development was combined with a powerful and varied nature, which had mastered all the elements of the culture of the age, then arose the "all-sided man"—*l' uomo universale*—who belonged to Italy alone. Men there were of encyclopædic knowledge in many countries during the Middle Ages, for this knowledge was confined within narrow limits; and even in the twelfth century there were universal artists, but the problems of architecture were comparatively simple and uniform, and in sculpture and painting the matter was of more importance than the form. But in Italy at the time of the Renaissance we find artists who in every branch created new and perfect works, and who also made the greatest impression as men. Others, outside the arts they practised, were masters of a vast circle of spiritual interests.

Dante, who even in his lifetime was called by some a poet, by others a philosopher, by others a theologian, pours forth in all his writings a stream of personal force, by which the reader, apart from the interest of the subject, feels himself carried away. What power of will must the steady, unbroken elaboration of the *Divine Comedy* have required! And if we look at the matter of the poem we find that in the whole spiritual or physical world there is hardly an important subject which the poet has not fathomed, and on which his utterances—often only a few words—are not the most weighty of his time. For the plastic arts he is of the first importance, and this for better reasons than the few references to contemporary artists—he soon became himself the source of inspiration.

The fifteenth century is, above all, that of the many-sided men. There is no biography which does not, besides the chief work of its hero, speak of other pursuits all passing beyond the limits of dilettantism. The Florentine merchant and statesman was often learned in both the classical languages; the most famous humanists read the ethics and politics of Aristotle to him and his sons; even the daughters of the house were highly educated. It is in these circles that private education was first treated seriously. The humanist, on his side, was compelled to the most varied attainments, since his philological learning was not limited, as it now is, to the theoretical knowledge of classical antiquity, but had to serve the practical needs of daily life. While studying Pliny, he made collections of natural history; the geography of the ancients was his guide in treating of modern geography, their history was his pattern in writing contemporary chronicles, even when composed in Italian; he not only translated the comedies of Plautus, but acted as manager when they were put on the stage; every effective form of ancient literature down to the dialogues of Lucian he did his best to imitate; and besides all this he acted as magistrate, secretary, and diplomatist—not always to his own advantage.

But among these many-sided men some who may truly be called 'all-sided' tower above the rest. Before analysing the general phases of life and culture of this period we may here, on the threshold of the fifteenth century, consider for a moment the figure of one of these giants—Leon Battista Alberti (b. ? 1404, d. 1472). His biography, which is only a fragment, speaks of him but little as an artist, and makes no mention at all of his great significance in the history of architecture. We shall now see what he was apart from these special claims to distinction.

In all by which praise is won Leon Battista from his childhood excelled. Of his various gymnastic feats and exercises we read with astonishment how, with his feet together, he could spring over a man's head; how in the cathedral he threw a coin in the air till it was heard to ring against the distant roof; how the wildest horses trembled under him. In three things he desired to appear faultless to others, in walking, in riding, and in speaking. He learned music without a master, and yet his compositions were admired by professional judges. Under the pressure of poverty he studied both civil and canonical law for many years, till exhaustion brought on a severe illness. In his twenty-fourth year, finding his memory for words weakened, but his sense of facts unimpaired, he set to work at physics and mathematics. And all the while he acquired every sort of accomplishment and dexterity, cross-examining artists, scholars, and artisans of all descriptions down to the cobblers, about the secrets and peculiarities of their craft. Painting and modelling he practised by the way, and especially excelled in admirable likenesses from memory. Great admiration was excited by his mysterious *camera obscura,* in which he showed at one time the stars and the moon rising over rocky hills, at another wide landscapes with mountains and gulfs receding into dim perspective, and with fleets advancing on the waters in shade or sunshine. And that which others created he welcomed joyfully, and held every human achievement which followed the laws of beauty for something almost divine. To all this must be added his literary works, first of all those on art, which are landmarks and authorities of the first order for the Renaissance of Form, especially in architecture; then his Latin prose writings—novels and other works—of which some have been taken for productions of antiquity; his elegies, eclogues, and humorous dinner-speeches. He also wrote an Italian treatise on domestic life in four books; various moral, philosophical, and historical works; and many speeches and poems, including a funeral oration on his dog. Notwithstanding his admiration for the Latin language, he wrote in Italian, and encouraged others to do the same; himself a disciple of Greek science, he maintained the doctrine that without Christianity the world would wander in a labyrinth of error. His serious and witty sayings were thought worth collecting, and specimens of them, many columns long, are quoted in his biography. And all that he had and knew he imparted, as rich natures always do, without the least reserve, giving away his chief discoveries for nothing. But the deepest spring of his nature has yet to be spoken of—the sympathetic intensity with which he entered into the whole life around him. At the sight of noble trees and waving cornfields he shed tears; handsome and dignified old men he honoured as a "delight of nature," and could never look at them enough. Perfectly formed animals won his goodwill as being specially favoured by nature; and more than once, when he was ill, the sight of a beautiful landscape cured him. No wonder that those who saw him in this close and mysterious communion with the world ascribed to him the gift of prophecy. He was said to have foretold a bloody catastrophe in the family of Este, the fate of Florence, and the death of the Popes years before they happened, and to be able to read into the countenances and the hearts of men. It need not be added that an iron will pervaded and sustained his whole personality; like all the great men of the Renaissance, he said, "Men can do all things if they will."

And Leonardo da Vinci was to Alberti as the finisher to the beginner, as the master to the *dilettante*. Would only that Vasari's work were here supplemented by a description like that of Alberti! The colossal outlines of Leonardo's nature can never be more than dimly and distantly conceived. . . .

Now that this point in our historical view of Italian civilization has been reached it is time to speak of the influence of antiquity, the "new birth" of which has been one-sidedly chosen as the name to sum up the whole period. The conditions which have been hitherto described would have sufficed, apart from antiquity, to upturn and to mature the national mind; and most of the intellectual tendencies which yet remain to be noticed would be conceivable without it. But both what has gone before and what we have still to discuss are coloured in a thousand ways by the influence of the ancient world; and though the essence of the phenomena might still have been the same without the classical revival, it is only with and through this revival that they are actually manifested to us. The Renaissance would not have been the process of world-wide significance which it is if its elements could be so easily separated from one another. We must insist upon it, as one of the chief propositions of this book, that it was not the revival of antiquity alone, but its union with the genius of the Italian people, which achieved the conquest of the Western world. The amount of independence which the national spirit maintained in this union varied according to circumstances. In the modern Latin literature of the period it is very small, while in plastic art, as well as in other spheres, it is remarkably great; and hence the alliance between two distant epochs in the civilization of the same people, because concluded on equal terms, proved justifiable and fruitful. The rest of Europe was free either to repel or else partly or wholly to accept the mighty impulse which came forth from Italy. Where the latter was the case we may as well be spared the complaints over the early decay of medieval faith and civilization. Had these been strong enough to hold their ground they would be alive to this day. If those elegiac natures which long to see them return could pass but one hour in the midst of them they would gasp to be back in modern air. That in a great historical process of this kind flowers of exquisite beauty may perish without being made immortal in poetry or tradition is undoubtedly true; nevertheless, we cannot wish the process undone. The general result of it consists in this—that by the side of the Church, which had hitherto held the countries of the West together (though it was unable to do so much longer), there arose a new spiritual influence, which, spreading itself abroad from Italy, became the breath of life for all the more instructed minds in Europe. The worst that can be said of the movement is that it was anti-popular, that through it Europe became for the first time sharply divided into the cultivated and uncultivated classes. The reproach will appear groundless when we reflect that even now the fact, though clearly recognized, cannot be altered. The separation, too, is by no means as cruel and absolute in Italy as elsewhere. The most artistic of her poets, Tasso, is in the hands of even the poorest.

The civilization of Greece and Rome, which ever since the fourteenth century obtained so powerful a hold on Italian life, as the source and basis of culture, as the object and ideal of existence, partly also as an avowed reaction against preceding tendencies —this civilization had long been exerting a partial influence on medieval Europe, even beyond the boundaries of Italy. The culture of which Charles the Great was a representative was, in face of the barbarism of the seventh and eighth centuries, essentially a Renaissance, and could appear under no other form. Just as in the Romanesque architecture of the North, beside the general outlines inherited from antiquity, remarkable direct imitations of the antique also occur, so too monastic scholarship had not only gradually absorbed an immense mass of materials from Roman writers, but the style of it, from the days of Eginhard onward, shows traces of conscious imitations.

But the resuscitation of antiquity took a different form in Italy from that which it assumed in the North. The wave of barbarism had scarcely gone by before the people, in whom the former life was but half effaced, showed a consciousness of its past and a wish to reproduce it. Elsewhere in Europe men deliberately and with reflection borrowed this or the other element of classical civilization; in Italy the sympathies both of the learned and of the people were naturally engaged on the side of antiquity as a whole, which stood to them as a symbol of past greatness. The Latin language, too, was easy to an Italian, and the numerous monuments and documents in which the country abounded facilitated a return to the past. With this tendency other elements—the popular character, which time had now greatly modified, the political institutions imported by the Lombards from Germany, chivalry and other Northern forms of civilization, and the influence of religion and the Church—combined to produce the modern Italian spirit, which was destined to serve as the model and ideal for the whole Western world.

How antiquity began to work in plastic art, as soon as the flood of barbarism had subsided, is clearly shown in the Tuscan buildings of the twelfth and in the sculptures of the thirteenth centuries. In poetry too there will appear no want of similar analogies to those who hold that the greatest Latin poet of the twelfth century, the writer who struck the keynote of a whole class of Latin poems, was an Italian. We mean the author of the best pieces in the so-called *Carmina Burana*. A frank enjoyment of life and its pleasures, as whose patrons the gods of heathendom are invoked, while Catos and Scipios hold the place of the saints and heroes of Christianity, flows in full current through the rhymed verses. Reading them through at a stretch, we can scarcely help coming to the conclusion that an Italian, probably a Lombard, is speaking; in fact, there are positive grounds for thinking so. To a certain degree these Latin poems of the *clerici vagantes* of the twelfth century, with all their remarkable frivolity, are, doubtless, a product in which the whole of Europe had a share; but the writer of the song *De Phyllide et Flora* and the *Æstuans interius* can have been a Northerner as little as the polished Epicurean observer to whom we owe *Dum Dianæ vitrea sero lampas oritur*. Here, in truth, is a reproduction of the whole ancient view of life, which is all the more striking from the medieval form of the verse in which it is set forth. There are many works of this and the following centuries in which a careful imitation of the antique appears both in the hexameter and pentameter of the metre in the classical, often mythological, character of the subject, and which yet have not anything like the same spirit of antiquity about them. In the hexameter chronicles and other works of Gulielmus Apuliensis and his successors (from about 1100) we find frequent traces of a diligent study of Virgil, Ovid, Lucan, Statius, and Claudian; but this classical form is after all here a mere matter of archæology, as is the classical subject in collectors like Vincent of Beauvais, or in the mythological and allegorical writer, Alanus ab Insulis. The Renaissance is not a mere fragmentary imitation or compilation, but a new birth; and the signs of this are visible in the poems of the unknown "Clericus" of the twelfth century.

But the great and general enthusiasm of the Italians for classical antiquity did not display itself before the fourteenth century. For this a development of civic life was required, which took place only in Italy, and there not till then. It was needful that noble and burgher should first learn to dwell together on equal terms, and that a social world should arise which felt the want of culture, and had the leisure and the means to obtain it. But culture, as soon as it freed itself from the fantastic bonds of the Middle Ages, could not at once and without help find its way to the understanding of the physical and intellectual world. It needed a guide, and found one in the ancient civilization, with its wealth of truth and knowledge in every spiritual interest. Both the form and the substance of this civilization were adopted with admiring gratitude; it became the chief part of the culture of the age. The general condition of the country was favourable to this transformation. The medieval Empire, since the fall of the Hohenstaufen, had either renounced, or was unable to make good, its claims on Italy. The Popes had migrated to Avignon. Most of the political Powers actually in existence owed their origin to violent and illegitimate means. The spirit of the people, now awakened to self-consciousness, sought for some new and stable ideal on which to rest. And thus the vision of the world-wide empire of Italy and Rome so possessed the popular mind that Cola di Rienzi could actually attempt to put it into practice. The conception he formed of his task, particularly when tribune for the first time, could end only in some extravagant comedy; nevertheless, the memory of ancient Rome was no slight support to the national sentiment. Armed afresh with its culture, the Italian soon felt himself in truth citizen of the most advanced nation in the world.

It is now our task to sketch this spiritual movement, not, indeed, in all its fullness, but in its most salient features, and especially in its first beginnings.

EIGHTEEN

THE MYTH OF THE RENAISSANCE

Many historians have modified Burckhardt's thesis in an attempt to make a more sober evaluation of the Renaissance. In a brilliant chapter entitled "The Myth of the Renaissance," W. T. Waugh summarizes the main tendencies of revisionist research on the Renaissance era. Waugh correctly points out that the revival of civilization in the West began, not with the Renaissance after a millennium of darkness, but at about the year 1000, when medieval civilization began three centuries of spectacular flowering. Waugh also points out that Renaissance humanism (classical scholarship) had important medieval antecedents. In addition, he shows that humanism had prominent defects, in particular its adverse effect on vernacular literature. Further, he contends that where numerous classical models existed, for example in architecture and sculpture, Renaissance art was less worthy than it was in painting, which lacked direct classical prototypes. Finally, he concludes that the Renaissance spirit, so luminous in the arts, touched comparatively few people and had little effect on the next major phenomenon in Western history, the Protestant Reformation. His analysis suggests what many other scholars have come to believe, that the Renaissance as a distinct period has its main validity in literature and the arts rather than in the total experience of the Western world in the three centuries or so following 1300.

W. T. WAUGH

A HISTORY OF EUROPE FROM 1378 TO 1494*

It has been customary for historians to speak of "the Renaissance" as one of the great landmarks in the career of mankind. And, in view of the accredited conception of human history, the estimate was justified. For History fell into three clear-cut divisions. There was Ancient History, concerned with the fortunes of Greece from Homer to Alexander the Great and of Rome from Romulus to Marcus Aurelius or thereabouts, and thus dealing with communities which attained great material well-being, technical dexterity, intellectual power, and artistic taste. Then, with the decline of Rome, History entered its second phase—the Middle or Dark Ages,

* From *A History of Europe from 1378 to 1494*, pp. 486–501, by W. T. Waugh. Reprinted by permission of Methuen and Co. Ltd., London.

which lasted upwards of a thousand years. The regions comprised in the western half of the Roman Empire were submerged in barbarism. It was, in the words of a modern oracle, "a glacial age of the spirit." Its literature was dismissed as "monkish," its art as "Gothic," its thought, we were told, culminated in the man whose name gave us the word "dunce." Even after the Romantic Movement of the early nineteenth century had revived a sympathetic interest in the Middle Ages, they were admired because they were romantic, picturesque, or quaint. It was characteristic that medieval architecture was for long most highly appreciated when it was ruined. Even the great scholars who wrote on medieval history in the latter half of the nineteenth century, though they attributed many merits to medieval culture, usually assumed the existence of a great gulf between the Middle Ages and what were called Modern Times—the third Age of History.

There was a general agreement that what at length lightened the darkness of error and superstition in which Europe had been wandering was the Renaissance, the re-birth of learning and art, moribund if not dead since the barbarians had overwhelmed Rome. Ancient literature, especially that of Greece, was revealed to minds weary of the tyranny of monks and schoolmen. The result was miraculous. "Men opened their eyes and saw." And, looking at the world freely and directly, not through stained-glass windows, they saw that it was good. Scrutinizing the features and forms of their fellows, they found them worthy of admiration as creatures of flesh and blood, and not merely edifying as immortal souls destined probably for damnation. Their minds and imaginations emancipated, they turned from the trivialities of scholastic disputation to the great problems of life. Traditions, legends, superstitions crashed headlong. Beauty once more awoke. Literature recovered her form and comeliness. Grace and dignity unseen since the age of Pericles sprang into being under paint-brush and chisel. Man strode forth with head erect, ready not merely to endure but to master his fate. It was an inexhaustible theme, and much fine writing was provoked by it.

Here and there a voice protested that the darkness of medieval times was less intense, and the succeeding radiance less pure, than commonly depicted. A few remonstrances—from the pre-Raphaelite school, for instance—went further, actually denouncing the effects of the Renaissance as mainly evil, and bewailing the ruin of medieval art and the disruption of medieval society. But as the pre-Raphaelites and their kin were profoundly ignorant of the Middle Ages, they were easily refuted. The beliefs summarized above continued to be maintained by the most weighty authorities. The writer was brought up to accept them as beyond serious question.

Such views are still to be heard and read. Nevertheless, a distinguished American historian was able in 1929 to assert that they were now held only "by mechanical creatures of habit, by those who stopped thinking and reading twenty or thirty years ago, and who refuse to give up any catchword or prejudice that was instilled into their minds in childhood." Whatever we may think of this severe judgment, it is undeniable that within the last quarter of a century research into the Middle Ages and the times immediately following has fundamentally changed the old conception of the development of modern culture. It has become evident, nay obvious, that there was no suspension of intellectual life in medieval Europe. If there was a Revival of Learning, it occurred about the year A.D. 1000, since when human knowledge has never ceased to advance. It cannot even be said that the Humanists of the fourteenth and fifteenth centuries revived the study of the classics. Scholars had been nourished on the classics for centuries. Neither can it be maintained that the distinguishing feature of the Humanists was their acquaintance with Greek thought. In the first place, the classical writer most studied in the Middle Ages was a Greek, Aristotle, and though nearly all medieval students perforce read him in translation, the defects of the versions at their service were far less grave than most historians have asserted. Further, the early Humanists knew little or no Greek; indeed, even among the Italians passable Greek scholars were rare until late in the fifteenth century. It has often been alleged that what differentiated the Schoolman from the Humanist was the former's subservience to authority. But in this respect there was little to choose between the two. The Humanist usually kept the peace with the Church, and for the Schoolman's Aristotle he substituted other classical divinities, notably Cicero.

These considerations would not justify a denial that there was a very real difference between the Schoolman and the Italian Humanist of the fifteenth century. But it was a difference of standpoint rather than a difference in learning or originality. It has been judiciously pointed out that all extant manuscripts of the classics, apart from a few fragments of papyrus, are medieval. That is to say, the works they enshrine were known somewhere at some time during the Middle Ages. And actually the medieval scholars of western Europe were acquainted with most of the Latin authors familiar to us. In regard to the Greeks, their position was less fortunate, for the Greek dramatists, poets, and historians were hardly known at all, even in translation. Through becoming acquainted with them, the Humanists gained a great advantage, which few of them turned to the best account. It was not, however, in the Humanist's knowledge of the classics, but in his treatment of them that the difference between him and the Schoolman lies. The medieval scholar had read them for moral edification, or for the philosophical and scientific instruction which they were believed to supply; the Humanist read them for the light which they shed upon mankind and because of the beauty of their literary art. There had, it is true, been a Humanist school in the twelfth century, with its centre at Chartres, but its life had been short, and in the later enthusiasm of the Italian scholars for the classics as literature and as a revelation of man, there was a re-birth of something that had flourished in Ancient Times, but had scarcely existed in the Middle Ages.

At all events, it was with manifestly genuine zeal that the fifteenth-century scholars of Italy studied the writings of Greek and Roman antiquity. Every sentence, every phrase, every word, underwent meticulous scrutiny. Petrarch, who died just before the beginning of the time covered by this volume, has often been counted the first of the Humanists. But it was not long before he was far surpassed in depth of learning and elegance of style. Among his earlier successors, whose careers lie mainly in the first half of the fifteenth century, special notice may be given to Leonardo Bruni, Poggio Bracciolini, and Lorenzo Valla. The scholars of their generation were largely occupied with the discovery and collection of manuscripts, particularly of the works of authors who had long been neglected. All the while, however, a knowledge of Greek was steadily, if slowly, spreading. From the first years of the fifteenth century there was no lack of teachers of Greek in Italy. The contact of the West with Greek thought and culture became still closer during the negotiations for ecclesiastical union which culminated in the Council of Florence. Long before the fall of Constantinople every Italian scholar who wanted to learn Greek had ample opportunity of doing so, and there were in Italy countless manuscripts of the Greek classics. Yet modern historians, even though they betray a knowledge of these things, still repeat the myth that "the Renaissance" was caused by the capture of Constantinople and the imaginary stampede of learned men that followed.

In the second part of the century the Humanists applied themselves more thoroughly to the analysis and annotation of the literature at their disposal. Of course one may not draw a hard and fast line between the two phases of the Humanist movement; some long-lived scholars, such as the renowned Filelfo, belonged to both. Among the greater names of the second half of the century are Pomponius Laetus, Platina, and Politian. It must be understood that the strength of Humanism did not lie in the Universities, and that few of the great classical scholars of the century could have gained their renown, or indeed lived at all, but for the assistance of princely or ecclesiastical patrons. Among these the successive heads of the Medici family were pre-eminent. Alfonso of Naples was also a liberal friend of learning and art. Among the popes, as we have seen, the Humanists owed much to Nicolas V and Sixtus IV. And one might fill a page with the names of lesser princes and nobles who, whether from taste or from ostentation, patronized the "new learning." With such encouragement, the Humanist scholars were full of confidence in themselves. They wrote a good deal—grammars, commentaries, handbooks on rhetoric, a few histories (whether of ancient times or their own), imaginary dialogues, and controversial pamphlets. They emitted an immense torrent of talk in lectures and orations. They discerned and sometimes applied certain of the principles of historical criticism: perhaps, indeed, it was the earlier phase of Humanism, when the weight of erudition was less oppressive, that was most favourable to the rise of a critical spirit: at all events, it was Lorenzo Valla who performed the most notable feats of iconoclasm, demonstrating in 1440 that the document called the Donation of Constantine was a forgery and arguing also that the Apostles' Creed was not composed by the Apostles. Such achievements were naturally rare, and to most Humanists the paths of Higher Criticism seemed a little too dangerous. But in amending the texts of the classics, many of which had become grievously corrupt, they did very useful work. Further, their ability to read Aristotle in the original gave them a better comprehension of his philosophy than had been usual among medieval scholars. And a knowledge of Plato, whose works had for centuries been only in small part available and whose doctrines had seldom aroused much interest, was now widespread among the scholars of Italy. It must be admitted that the Humanists did not always discriminate intelligently between the teachings of Plato himself and the travesty of them known as neo-Platonism; but what were supposed to be Plato's doctrines became for a time the fashionable philosophy and furnished the Humanists with a useful weapon in their war against scholasticism.

Nevertheless, the fruit of all this learning and activity is woefully lacking in savour and nourishment. Not one of these fifteenth-century Humanists, so brilliant in their own eyes, produced a work which posterity has ranked among the masterpieces of literature. No one reads their writings now save a few historians who use them as sources just as they use the "monkish" chroniclers whom the Humanists so wittily decried. And of the fifteenth-century scholars, the one most prized as an historical authority is probably Aeneas Sylvius, whom his contemporaries deemed second-rate. Such of the speeches of the time as have been reported seem to modern taste intolerably windy. The polemics of the Humanists usually turned on trivialities, not infrequently personal. They may have understood ancient philosophy, but none was capable of making any advance upon it. The few who grasped the principles of historical criticism applied them timorously. And though Valla's exposure of the Donation of Constantine was the most convincing of the century, it should not be forgotten that his conclusions had been anticipated by Nicolas of Cusa—an amphibious scholar, partly Humanist, partly Schoolman—and that they were reached a few years later, quite independently, by the English bishop Reginald Pecock, who had been educated entirely in the atmosphere of the "old learning." The main cause of the barrenness of the Humanists was probably their lack of sincerity. Valla might question the authenticity of the Apostles' Creed, but when his doubts involved him in trouble with ecclesiastical authority he pretended that his argument had been only an academic exercise. Pomponius Laetus and Platina, whose tongues spared neither God nor man while the skies were clear, ate their words greedily as soon as Paul II clapped them in prison. And all the while these men and countless other scholars were conforming outwardly to a religion which everyone knew they derided. But nobody was quite certain which was a pose—the conformity or the derision.

If the Italian Humanists as a class were astonishingly sterile, in some respects they did positive harm. For a while—though not until after the end of the fifteenth century—they and their followers beyond the Alps dictated the opinions of educated Europe. They spread the contempt of their pedantic minds for the culture and art of the Middle Ages, and the distorted view of History thus created is only now being corrected. They destroyed the ascendancy of the scholastic philosophy and the dialectical method of education in the universities, replacing them by that regimen of the classics under the monstrous tyranny of which the youth of Europe suffered for centuries and in some places suffers still. And, paradoxical though it seems, in their exaltation of the Latin classics the Humanists ruined Latin as a living language. For medieval Latin, largely because it differed considerably from classical Latin, was an excellent medium of both written and oral expression. Having a much richer vocabulary, it could give voice to a much wider range of ideas than the Latin of the Augustan age. For the clergy and the educated laity it was an established vehicle of communication all over central and western Europe. Then came the Humanists damning it as barbarous because it was not identical with the Latin used by Cicero 1,500 years before. The Latin of Cicero came to be accepted as the only Latin a scholar might use. It was a speech quite inadequate to express many ideas familiar to the man of the sixteenth century. Indeed, it had never been spoken by anybody, even in Cicero's time, except in set orations. For a while it was used for works of erudition and academic discourses; but its employment for such purposes steadily declined, since a language forbidden to develop inevitably becomes ever more lifeless as time goes on. So bemused have later generations been by the self-praise of the Humanists that they have commonly lauded them for their overthrow of what has been foolishly called "monkish" Latin. How much the advance of knowledge has been retarded through the consequent necessity of spending time and energy on the study of foreign tongues it is impossible to compute.

This chapter has hitherto treated the Humanists as if they were exclusively Italians. So indeed they nearly all were during the years with which this volume is concerned. Though the Latin classics had been studied with increasing zest in France throughout the century, Greek was not taught in Paris until 1476; and the French literary movement, vigorous though it was, had different roots and a different spirit from those of the so-called classical Renaissance. Only in the ninth decade of the century was it possible to learn Greek in England, and English letters were but feebly affected by Humanism until about the same time. Into Germany, it is true, the influence of the Italian scholars penetrated somewhat sooner. As yet, however, their spirit seldom appeared there undiluted. This was largely because the great nursery of German classical scholars was the school of Deventer, the most notable of the numerous schools founded by the Brethren of the Common Life. Thus most of the earlier German Humanists were clergy, and they were usually versed and interested in theology as well as letters. They advocated the reform of educational method, preferring the reading of classical texts to the logic-chopping long in favour. But the unreasoning contempt of the Italians for everything later than the second century A.D. was not shared by the Germans. In their theology they were mostly conservative, though anxious for the remedy of ecclesiastical abuses. The nearest German approach to the Italian type was perhaps Rudolf Agricola (1442–85), who studied in Italy and acquired there the literary polish and empty verbosity then characteristic of that country's scholars. The man who did most to establish a thorough classical curriculum in German schools was Alexander Hegius (1433–98), the head of Deventer. But he used to declare that "all learning is harmful which is gained at the expense of piety," a dictum which reveals how wide a gulf separated him from such men as Poggio or Platina.

At the death of the Emperor Frederick III, however, the most brilliant phase of German Humanism was just opening, and in the next twenty-five years its temper became far more radical. To pursue it further, however, would mean trespassing on another's territory.

The term Renaissance, as we have seen, gives a very misleading notion of the development of learning in the fourteenth and fifteenth centuries. Nor does it serve much better to indicate the character of contemporary art. It is, in fact, only to Italian architecture that it can be justly applied. In architecture there was undoubtedly a classical revival, with very lamentable results. It is true that Gothic architecture had never flourished in Italy; and it is hard to say whether the early architects of the so-called Renaissance were continuing the Romanesque tradition or drawing inspiration from ancient Rome. And it was some time after Italian architects had unquestionably begun to imitate classical models that they became utterly subservient to classical authority. Further, there is no denying that the Italian architects of the later Middle Ages produced some magnificent work. Genius always manifests itself, however much it may be trammelled by pedantic principles; and such men as Brunelleschi and Alberti impressed on all their buildings the stamp of the true and original artist. But their successors—with but a handful of exceptions like Bramante, Giulio Romano, and the eccentric Michael Angelo—were dull. Their works are the productions not of artists but of scholars. Domestic architecture, it is true, suffered less than ecclesiastical; indeed, it derived some benefits from the Renaissance, though these were rather utilitarian than æsthetic. But the final result of the architectural Renaissance was the stifling of originality. Architects acquired the habit of conforming to recognized "styles," and they did not escape from it until the Americans began to build skyscrapers.

There is no need to add much about the "classical revival." It is often stated that it encouraged a growth of vernacular literature in several European countries. By discrediting the expressive and adaptable Latin which had been in current use, it probably did something to promote such a movement. But its influence in this respect was indirect and slow. Dante, who belongs essentially to the Middle Ages, wrote his greatest work in Italian; Petrarch, often praised as the first Humanist, forsook Italian for Latin. Vernacular writings in fifteenth-century Italy were usually trivial and ephemeral, for the literary leaders of the day disdained to write in anything but Latin. It was only towards the end of the century that, thanks largely to the encouragement and example of Lorenzo de' Medici, there were renewed tokens of a widespread interest in Italian as a means of literary expression, Pulci (1431–87) and Boiardo (1434–94) confirming what Dante and Boccaccio had proved long before—that it was an admirable tongue for poets. Machiavelli and Guicciardini were soon to illustrate its merits in prose. But their work belongs to the sixteenth century; and in France, England, and Germany, all through the fifteenth, the use of the vernacular for literary composition was spreading apace, though the impact of Italian Humanism was hardly felt in these lands until the century was far advanced.

This development of vernacular literature shows that the peoples of Europe were naturally and spontaneously outgrowing the ways of thought and action characteristic of the Middle Ages. There was no need for them to resort to the classics for incentives. They might and did learn much through the more intense and intelligent study of Roman and Greek literature which the Humanists introduced. But it is plain that many causes besides the so-called rediscovery of the Ancient World were at work to produce the great advances in thought and art which distinguished the fifteenth century. For, whatever we may call it, the epoch was one of widespread and rapid progress.

Take, for instance, the arts of sculpture and painting. The period covered by this book has justly been accepted as one of the most glorious in their history. But the sculptors and painters of those days have been sadly maligned by many of their professed admirers, who have written as though all their inspiration had been drawn from the ancient Greeks and Romans. The Humanists, to do them justice, knew better, their general neglect of contemporary artists being due to the belief that these men showed insufficient regard for antique authority.

It is of course false to say that the art of sculpture had been moribund during the Middle Ages. The famous Italian sculptors of the early fifteenth century—Ghiberti, Donatello, Luca della Robbia—learned much from the study of classical examples, they owed more to the promptings of their native genius, but they were also the heirs of a long and splendid tradition. It has often been said that the Italian sculptors of the period departed from medieval practice by treating secular as well as sacred subjects, by producing works significant in themselves and not merely accessory to architecture, and by following nature instead of arbitrary conventions. They were thus, it is urged, able to render due honour to the beauty of the human body, which medieval man is alleged to have despised. It is true that nearly, though not quite all, medieval sculpture was attached to or placed in a building, usually a sacred building. But it is a delusion to suppose that all the carving in a medieval church was necessarily concerned with religious subjects. On the other hand, the nooks and corners of a cathedral, the capitals of piers, the *misericordiæ* and canopies of choir-stalls, the jambs and tympana of doorways, pinnacles, corbels, water-spouts, provided excellent accommodation for representations of mere nature, of the comic, the grotesque, the horrible, the obscene, the devilish. It is also essential to grasp that in northern Europe a re-birth of sculpture, like the re-birth of learning, had taken place in the eleventh century. It occurred in France, whence the revival soon spread to other countries. The art progressed rapidly until the thirteenth century, after which it somewhat fell away, though remaining at a high level. All western, central, and southern Europe was influenced by it. Even in Italy, always slow to accept foreign teaching or example, its effects may be traced; the great sculptors Niccolo and Giovanni Pisano, and even Giotto, owed something to it. In the last years of the fourteenth century, and for long afterwards, the sculpture of northern Europe was dominated by the so-called Burgundian school, of which the most renowned masters were Jean de Marville and Claus Sluter; its works are notable for admirable composition and an astonishing vitality, though marred at times by a heaviness verging on grossness. Donatello himself did not scorn to learn from the Burgundians, who alone prove that there were in the last medieval century men capable of producing great sculpture by merely carrying on the tradition in which they were reared.

In architecture, where antique models were abundant, the achievements of the Renaissance were disappointing. In sculpture, where antique models (though available) were less readily accessible and not as numerous as they are today, it did far better. In painting, where antique models were altogether lacking, it reached its greatest heights.

Most extant examples of medieval painting are concerned with religious subjects. It must be remembered, however, that mural paintings in ecclesiastical buildings and pictures belonging to churches have had a better chance of survival than other products of the painter's art. And as a matter of fact we may often read in medieval records of frescoes and easel pictures which adorned secular buildings, and have disappeared. Nevertheless, we still possess a great many delightful miniatures illustrating secular books; nor must it be forgotten that, just as worldly topics appear in the carvings of churches, so do they figure in the pictures in religious books. It was, for example, common for books of devotion to contain calendars illustrated with miniatures of an entirely worldly character. Thus when Italian painters of the fifteenth century handled themes from classical mythology, they were not doing anything revolutionary; and, for that matter, all through this century, to say nothing of the next, religious subjects commanded most of their attention. Doubtless the growing interest in classical literature and the growing knowledge of Ancient Times had its effect on the spirit of their work. But the painting of the fourteenth and fifteenth centuries was essentially a development, though extraordinarily rapid and far-spreading, of what had gone before. That there was no need of classical influence to stimulate pictorial art is shown by the Flemish school of the early fifteenth century, with its leaders the brothers Hubert and Jan van Eyck and Roger van der Weyden, and by the French school of a somewhat later date, headed by Jean Fouquet. Fouquet, it is true, was acquainted with contemporary Italian work and slightly affected by it. But both he and the earlier Flemings are essentially medieval in method and spirit; and they display a mastery of their craft and a freedom of resource which was hardly excelled even in contemporary Italy. Nevertheless, while these northern schools are of the highest interest as showing what could come out of an environment that was in all important respects medieval, it is true that the greatest painting of our period was Italian.

The fifteenth-century Italian artists, sculptors as well as painters, merit the most comprehensive admiration. Many of them were men of the most charming simplicity and the most scrupulous uprightness. As artists, regarded collectively they are unsurpassed for enthusiasm, sincerity, power, and versatility. They stand in refreshing contrast to the scholars of the time, with their verbosity, conceit, and pedantry. One can judge them aright only by looking at their work. To read about them is worth little. No good purpose would be served by giving a long list of their names.

After the achievements of Giotto, early in the fourteenth century, Italian painting made little advance until the short but dazzling career of Tommaso, called Masaccio, a very close observer and faithful follower of nature, who, though he died at twenty-eight, inaugurated a series of great masters which far outlasted the century.

Historians and art critics are wont to distinguish between various local "schools" of Italian painters. The grounds for the accepted grouping are not always very clear, and some artists refuse to be captured and labelled. Such a one, for instance, is Fra Angelico (1387–1455), a manifest survival from a fast vanishing age, much admired by those who are touched by the rather insipid devoutness which is one of his main characteristics. Still, as the fashionable classification is commonly followed in picture-galleries, it would perhaps be captious to disregard it.

Masaccio was a Florentine, and of all the schools that of Florence was the most distinct and distinguished. It was remarkable for austerity, reserve, regard for form, and yet for its devotion to nature and freedom from convention. Its greatest figures were Fra

Filippo Lippi (1406–69), that ill-regulated genius, the first man to use his models' faces for the sacred characters he painted and obviously ill at ease in handling the religious subjects he was required to treat. Among his numerous pupils were Filippino Lippi (1457–1504), generally and, it seems, rightly believed to be his son, a painter conspicuous for charm and grace, and also Botticelli, admired by contemporaries, overshadowed by successors, and now exalted very high, perhaps too high—an artist tender rather than strong, and, though the first man to make extensive use of classical themes, open to the charge of extravagant religious emotionalism. Another eminent Florentine was Ghirlandajo (1449–94), very notable for his command over the technical resources of his art, but lacking insight and inspiration, and, in fact, a little dull. Fra Bartolommeo, a great colourist, who must also be termed a Florentine, illustrates the defects of this grouping into schools, for he was a disciple of Savonarola and extremely devout, his morality so dominating his art that nude humanity shocked him.

There is usually said to have been a Siennese school, which is not very clearly differentiated; it was notable for strong religious sentiment, not to say sentimentality. Its influence merged with that of Florence to produce what is called the Umbrian school, whose most illustrious master was Perugino (1446–1524), who had "a body belonging to the Renaissaince containing a soul belonging to the Middle Ages." His technique was of a very high standard; his work is marked by religious devotion of a rather inert type. Mention may be made of a Ferrarese and Bolognese school, whose leading representatives were Costa (1460–1536) and Francia (1450–1518), a very pious painter, much affected by Perugino; and the critics talk of a Lombard school, centred at Milan, though it hardly had a clear existence before the sixteenth century.

The north-east of Italy produced some of the finest work of our period. The Paduan school was more influenced by the study of the classics than any other, a characteristic which it owed largely to Francesco Squarcione (1394–1474), no great painter, but a most inspiring teacher and an enthusiastic admirer of ancient sculpture. His influence is very evident in the statuesque work of Mantegna (1431–1506), a master of composition and of light and shade, whose pictures, if rather stiff, are of remarkable dignity.

The Venetian school is in many ways very different from any other. It shows no deep religious feeling and no particular interest in the classics. It has been argued that the Venetians were hard-headed business men, who did not pretend to be artistic, but knew what they liked—namely, the pleasant things of life, in as rich profusion as possible, with of course "the best of everything." From the beginning, therefore, Venetian painting was inclined to be exuberant, and more remarkable for color than for form. The influence of the gorgeous East is manifest here, as it had been all through Venetian history. The earliest masters who truly represent the Venetian school were the Vivarini family of Murano, a Venetian dependency. They painted whatever in the natural world appealed to their love of colour. Of their successors before the end of the century, the Bellinis—Jacopo (1400–64), Gentile (1426–1507), and Giovanni (1428–1516)—are the most worthy to be remembered. The best of them was Giovanni, a splendid colourist, whose landscape backgrounds are particularly famous. But the greatest of the Venetian masters were to come later.

The highest peak of Italian painting was reached in the early years of the following century. In the year 1500 that prodigy of versatility, Leonardo da Vinci (1452–1519), scholar, painter, sculptor, architect, scientist, mechanic, engineer, was already renowned. Michael Angelo (1474–1564) and Raphael (1483–1520) were just rising to fame. Andrea del Sarto (1486–1531) and Correggio (1494–1534) were growing up.

There has never been a more astonishing outburst of creative originality than appeared among the Italian artists of the fifteenth century and the years immediately following. Its real nature has been obscured by the obsession which ascribed it all to the alleged re-birth of the classics and denied that anything good could evolve from the Middle Ages. It is true that the painters were increasingly disposed to select their themes from classical mythology. It is true that in their drawing many of them were much influenced by the study of classical sculpture. But their art had its roots in the earlier Middle Ages, they went to nature far more than to the classics for their inspiration, and what made them so magnificently great was not the teaching or example of the ancient Romans, or even of the ancient Greeks, but their own inborn genius.

The merits of the artists and the influence of the Humanist scholars must be acknowledged. But one must beware of exaggerating the practical results of their work. It is undeniable that very few people knew or cared anything about the sayings or doings of the Humanists. Even the educated classes were less influenced than one might think. The old learning was entrenched in the universities, and it took a long time to oust it. The Italian universities themselves devoted far more attention to law than to literature in the fifteenth century. The influence of the artists, many may urge, was wider. It may be true that the artistic taste of ordinary people was better in the Middle Ages than it is now. Perhaps, too, those are right who contend that the Italians have a unique capacity for the just appreciation of art, though, apart from the period which we are now considering, there is not much in history to lend colour to such a view. It is not incredible, furthermore, that in certain Italian cities, notably Florence, there was an amazingly widespread interest in art of every form during the fifteenth century. But, when every permissible concession has been made, the plain fact remains that the masterpieces of Renaissance sculpture can have been seen by few, those of Renaissance painting by fewer. And in those days, unless you actually saw them, you could not tell what they were like. North of the Alps of course the influence of both Humanists and artists was much less than it was in Italy. It is, in short, vain to pretend that the revival of the study of classical literature or the exuberant fruitfulness of Renaissance art had much to do with the rapid spread of the teachings of the ecclesiastical reformers of the next century.

NINETEEN

STATECRAFT

Despite objections about the concept of the Renaissance as a historical period with specific and related characteristics, little question can exist that its politics were violent and swift-moving. Among the highly gifted politicians of the period was Niccolo Machiavelli (1469–1527), who held high office in Florence until the seizure of the city by the Medici family in 1512. After arrest and torture Machiavelli was exiled to the countryside in 1513. It is scarcely an exaggeration to say that he knew intimately the political rewards and disasters of his day. In exile this brilliant and cynical opportunist, idealistic only in his love of politics and of the state, schemed tirelessly to regain political favor and to lead once again the life of political action which nourished his inner needs. His quest resulted mainly in frustration. But his frustration was the world's gain. In exile he wrote his most famous work, The Prince *(1513), addressed to Giuliano de Medici, ruler of Florence 1513–15, and addressed again to Giuliano's successor, Lorenzo II, who ruled 1515–19. Machiavelli did not set about to analyze government in typical theological terms of the Middle Ages, but attempted to describe successful governing in typical secular terms of the Renaissance. Success, then, replaced goodness as his main political goal. Machiavelli, inclined toward cynicism by his own experience, had low regard for human nature—an attitude in harmony not only with the classical tradition but also with the medieval concept of original sin. His proposed statecraft reflected this cynicism and has evoked much adverse criticism from successive generations of readers. His greatest contribution to political thought lay in separating politics from theology and in seeking political guidance in experience, particularly historical experience. Machiavelli's appeal to history rather than to theology reflected and accelerated the growing secularism of the Renaissance. His final chapter, an earnest plea for the political unification of Italy, foreshadowed the patriotism which, as it later ripened into full-blown nationalism, has become a major and often destructive force in the modern world.*

NICCOLO MACHIAVELLI

THE PRINCE*

CHAPTER III

OF MIXED PRINCEDOMS

But in new Princedoms difficulties abound. And, first, if the Princedom be not wholly new, but joined on to the ancient dominions of the Prince, so as to form with them what may be termed a mixed Princedom, changes will come from a cause common to all new States, namely, that men, thinking to better their condition, are always ready to change masters, and in this expectation will take up arms against any ruler; wherein they deceive themselves, and find afterwards by experience that they are worse off than before. This again results naturally and necessarily from the circumstance that the Prince cannot avoid giving offence to his new subjects, either in respect of the troops he quarters on them, or of some other of the numberless vexations attendant on a new acquisition. And in this way you may find that you have enemies in all those whom you have injured in seizing the Princedom, yet cannot keep the friendship of those who helped you to gain it; since you can neither reward them as they expect, nor yet, being under obligations to them, use violent remedies against them. For however strong you may be in respect of your army, it is essential that in entering a new Province you should have the goodwill of its inhabitants.

Hence it happened that Louis XII of France, speedily gaining possession of Milan, as speedily lost it; and that on the occasion of its first capture, Lodovico Sforza was able with his own forces only to take it from him. For the very people who had opened the gates to the French King, when they found themselves deceived in their expectations and hopes of future benefits, could not put up with the insolence of their new ruler. True it is that when a State rebels and is again got under, it will not afterwards be lost so easily. For the Prince, using the rebellion as a pretext, will not scruple to secure himself by punishing the guilty, bringing the suspected to trial, and otherwise strengthening his position in the points where it was weak. So that if to recover Milan from the French it was enough on the first occasion that a Duke Lodovico should raise alarms on the frontiers, to wrest it from them a second time the whole world had to be ranged against them, and their armies destroyed and driven out of Italy. And this for the reasons above assigned. And yet, for a second time, Milan was lost to the King. The general causes of its first loss have been shown. It remains to note the causes of the second, and to point out the remedies which the French King had, or which might have been used by another in like circumstances to maintain his conquest more successfully than he did.

I say, then, that those States which upon their acquisition are joined on to the ancient dominions of the Prince who acquires them, are either of the same Province and tongue as the people of these dominions, or they are

* Chapters 3, 17, 18, 25, and 26 of *The Prince* by Niccolo Machiavelli, in the English translation (1897) of J. H. Thompson.

not. When they are, there is great ease in retaining them, especially when they have not been accustomed to live in freedom. To hold them securely it is enough to have rooted out the line of the reigning Prince; because if in other respects the old condition of things be continued, and there be no discordance in their customs, men live peaceably with one another, as we see to have been the case in Brittany, Burgundy, Gascony, and Normandy, which have so long been united to France. For although there be some slight difference in their languages, their customs are similar, and they can easily get on together. He, therefore, who acquires such a State, if he mean to keep it, must see to two things; first, that the blood of the ancient line of Princes be destroyed; second, that no change be made in respect of laws or taxes; for in this way the newly acquired State speedily becomes incorporated with the hereditary.

But when States are acquired in a country differing in language, usages, and laws, difficulties multiply, and great good fortune, as well as address, is needed to overcome them. One of the best and most efficacious methods for dealing with such a State, is for the Prince who acquires it to go and dwell there in person, since this will tend to make his tenure more secure and lasting. This course has been followed by the Turk with regard to Greece, who, had he not, in addition to all his other precautions for securing that Province, himself come to live in it, could never have kept his hold of it. For when you are on the spot, disorders are detected in their beginnings and remedies can be readily applied; but when you are at a distance, they are not heard of until they have gathered strength and the case is past cure. Moreover, the Province in which you take up your abode is not pillaged by your officers; the people are pleased to have a ready recourse to their Prince; and have all the more reason if they are well disposed, to love, if disaffected, to fear him. A foreign enemy desiring to attack that State would be cautious how he did so. In short, where the Prince resides in person, it will be extremely difficult to oust him.

Another excellent expedient is to send colonies into one or two places, so that these may become, as it were, the keys of the Province; for you must either do this, or else keep up a numerous force of men-at-arms and foot soldiers. A Prince need not spend much on colonies. He can send them out and support them at little or no charge to himself, and the only persons to whom he gives offence are those whom he deprives of their fields and houses to bestow them on the new inhabitants. Those who are thus injured form but a small part of the community, and remaining scattered and poor can never become dangerous. All others being left unmolested, are in consequence easily quieted, and at the same time are afraid to make a false move, lest they share the fate of those who have been deprived of their possessions. In few words, these colonies cost less than soldiers, are more faithful, and give less offence, while those who are offended, being, as I have said, poor and dispersed, cannot hurt. And let it here be noted that men are either to be kindly treated, or utterly crushed, since they can revenge lighter injuries, but not graver. Wherefore the injury we do to a man should be of a sort to leave no fear of reprisals.

But if instead of colonies you send troops, the cost is vastly greater, and the whole revenues of the country are spent in guarding it; so that the gain becomes a loss, and much deeper offence is given; since in shifting the quarters of your soldiers from place to place the whole country suffers hardship, which as all feel, all are made enemies; and enemies who remaining, although vanquished, in their own homes, have power to hurt. In every way, therefore, this mode of defence is as disadvantageous as that by colonizing is useful.

The Prince who establishes himself in a Province whose laws and language differ from those of his own people, ought also to make himself the head and protector of his feebler neighbours, and endeavour to weaken the stronger, and must see that by no accident shall any other stranger as powerful as himself find an entrance there. For it will always happen that some such person will be called in by those of the Province who are discontented either through ambition or fear; as we see of old the Romans brought into Greece by the Aetolians, and in every other country that they entered, invited there by its inhabitants. And the usual course of things is that so soon as a formidable stranger enters a Province, all the weaker powers side with him, moved thereto by the ill-will they bear towards him who has hitherto kept them in subjection. So that in respect of these lesser powers, no trouble is needed to gain them over, for at once, together, and of their own accord, they throw in their lot with the government of the stranger. The new Prince, therefore, has only to see that they do not increase too much in strength, and with his own forces, aided by their good will, can easily subdue any who are powerful, so as to remain supreme in the Province. He who does not manage this matter well, will soon lose whatever he has gained, and while he retains it will find in it endless troubles and annoyances.

In dealing with the countries of which they took possession the Romans diligently followed the methods I have described. They planted colonies, conciliated weaker powers without adding to their strength, humbled the great, and never suffered a formidable stranger to acquire influence. A single example will suffice to show this. In Greece the Romans took the Achaians and Aetolians into their pay; the Macedonian monarchy was humbled; Antiochus was driven out. But the services of the Achaians and Aetolians never obtained for them any addition to their power; no persuasions on the part of Philip could induce the Romans to be his friends on the condition of sparing him humiliation; nor could all the power of Antiochus bring them to consent to his exercising any authority within that Province. And in thus acting the Romans did as all wise rulers should, who have to consider not only present difficulties but also future, against which they must use all diligence to provide; for these, if they be foreseen while yet remote, admit of easy remedy, but if their approach be awaited, are already past cure, the disorder having become hopeless; realizing what the physicians tell us of hectic fever, that in its beginning it is easy to cure, but hard to recognize; whereas, after a time, not having been detected and treated at the first, it becomes easy to recognize but impossible to cure.

And so it is with State affairs. For the distempers of a State being discovered while yet inchoate, which can only be done by a sagacious ruler, may easily be dealt with; but when, from not being observed, they are suffered to grow until they are obvious to every one, there is no longer any remedy. The Romans, therefore, foreseeing evils while they were yet far off, always provided against them, and never suffered them to take their course for the sake of avoiding war; since they knew that war is not so to be avoided, but is only postponed to the advantage of the other side. They chose, therefore, to make war with Philip and Antiochus in Greece, that they might not have to make it with them in Italy, although for a while they might have escaped both. This they did not desire, nor did the maxim *leave it to Time,* which the wise men of our own day have always on their lips, ever recommend itself to them. What they looked to enjoy were the fruits of their own valour and foresight. For Time, driving all things before it, may bring with it evil as well as good.

But let us now go back to France and examine whether she has followed any of those methods of which I have made mention. I shall speak of Louis and not of Charles, because from the former having held longer possession of Italy, his manner of acting is more plainly seen. You will find, then, that he has done the direct opposite of what he should have done in order to retain a foreign State.

King Louis was brought into Italy by the ambition of the Venetians, who hoped by his coming to gain for themselves a half of the State of Lombardy. I will not blame this coming, nor the part taken by the King, because, desiring to gain a footing in Italy, where he had no friends, but on the contrary, owing to the conduct of Charles, every door was shut against him, he was driven to accept such friendships as he could get. And his designs might easily have succeeded had he not made mistakes in other particulars of conduct.

By the recovery of Lombardy, Louis at once regained the credit which Charles had lost. Genoa made submission; the Florentines came to terms; the Marquis of Mantua, the Duke of Ferrara, the Bentivogli, the Countess of Forli, the Lords of Faenza, Pesaro, Rimini, Camerino, and Piombino, the citizens of Lucca, Pisa, and Siena, all came forward offering their friendship. The Venetians, who to obtain possession of a couple of towns in Lombardy had made the French King master of two-thirds of Italy, had now cause to repent the rash game they had played.

Let any one, therefore, consider how easily King Louis might have maintained his authority in Italy had he observed the rules which I have noted above, and secured and protected all those friends of his, who being weak, and fearful, some of the Church, some of the Venetians, were of necessity obliged to attach themselves to him, and with whose assistance, for they were many, he might readily have made himself safe against any other powerful State. But no sooner was he in Milan than he took a contrary course, in helping Pope Alexander to occupy Romagna; not perceiving that in seconding this enterprise he weakened himself by alienating friends and those who had thrown themselves into his arms, while he strengthened the Church by adding great temporal power to the spiritual power which of itself confers so mighty an authority. Making this first mistake, he was forced to follow it up, until at last, in order to curb the ambition of Pope Alexander, and prevent him becoming master of Tuscany, he was obliged to come himself into Italy.

And as though it were not enough for him to have aggrandized the Church and stripped himself of friends, he must needs in his desire to possess the Kingdom of Naples, divide it with the King of Spain; thus bringing into Italy, where before he had been supreme, a rival to whom the ambitious and discontented in that Province might have recourse. And whereas he might have left in Naples a King willing to hold as his tributary, he displaced him to make way for another strong enough to effect his expulsion. The wish to acquire is no doubt a natural and common sentiment, and when men attempt things within their power, they will always be praised rather than blamed. But when they persist in attempts that are beyond their power, mishaps and blame ensue. If France, therefore, with her own forces could have attacked Naples, she should have done so. If she could not, she ought not to have divided it. And if her partition of Lombardy with the Venetians may be excused as the means whereby a footing was gained in Italy, this other partition is to be condemned as not justified by the like necessity.

Louis, then, had made these five blunders. He had destroyed weaker States, he had strengthened a Prince already strong, he had brought into the country a very powerful stranger, he had not come to reside, and he had not sent colonies. And yet all these blunders might not have proved disastrous to him while he lived, had he not added to them a sixth in depriving the Venetians of their dominions. For had he neither aggrandized the Church, nor brought Spain into Italy, it might have been at once reasonable and necessary to humble the Venetians;

but after committing himself to these other courses, he should never have consented to the ruin of Venice. For while the Venetians were powerful they would always have kept others back from an attempt on Lombardy, as well because they never would have agreed to that enterprise on any terms save of themselves being made its masters, as because others would never have desired to take it from France in order to hand it over to them, nor would ever have ventured to defy both. And if it be said that King Louis ceded Romagna to Alexander, and Naples to Spain in order to avoid war, I answer that for the reasons already given, you ought never to suffer your designs to be crossed in order to avoid war, since war is not so to be avoided, but is only deferred to your disadvantage. And if others should allege the King's promise to the Pope to undertake that enterprise on his behalf, in return for the dissolution of his marriage, and for the Cardinal's hat conferred on d'Amboise, I answer by referring to what I say further on concerning the faith of Princes and how it is to be kept.

King Louis, therefore, lost Lombardy from not following any one of the methods pursued by others who have taken Provinces with the resolve to keep them. Nor is this anything strange, but only what might reasonably and naturally be looked for. And on this very subject I spoke to d'Amboise at Nantes, at the time when Duke Valentino, as Cesare Borgia, son to Pope Alexander, was vulgarly called, was occupying Romagna. For, on the Cardinal saying to me that the Italians did not understand war, I answered that the French did not understand statecraft, for had they done so, they never would have allowed the Church to grow so powerful. And the event shows that the aggrandizement of the Church and of Spain in Italy has been brought about by France, and that the ruin of France has been wrought by them. Whence we may draw the general axiom, which never or rarely errs, that *he who is the cause of another's greatness is himself undone,* since he must work either by address or force, each of which excites distrust in the person raised to power.

CHAPTER XVIII

Of Cruelty and Clemency, and Whether It Is Better to be Loved or Feared

Passing to the other qualities above referred to, I say that every Prince should desire to be accounted merciful and not cruel. Nevertheless, he should be on his guard against the abuse of this quality of mercy. Cesare Borgia was reputed cruel, yet his cruelty restored Romagna, united it, and brought it to order and obedience; so that if we look at things in their true light, it will be seen that he was in reality far more merciful than the people of Florence, who, to avoid the imputation of cruelty, suffered Pistoja to be torn to pieces by factions.

A Prince should therefore disregard the reproach of being thought cruel where it enables him to keep his subjects united and obedient. For he who quells disorder by a very few signal examples will in the end be more merciful than he who from too great leniency permits things to take their course and so to result in rapine and bloodshed; for these hurt the whole State, whereas the severities of the Prince injure individuals only.

And for a new Prince, of all others, it is impossible to escape a name for cruelty, since new States are full of dangers. Wherefore Virgil, by the mouth of Dido, excuses the harshness of her reign on the plea that it was new, saying:—

> 'A fate unkind, and newness in my reign
> Compel me thus to guard a wide domain.'

Nevertheless, the new Prince should not be too ready of belief, nor too easily set in motion; nor should he himself be the first to raise alarms; but should so temper prudence with kindliness that too great confidence in others shall not throw him off his guard, nor groundless distrust render him insupportable.

And here comes in the question whether it is better to be loved rather than feared, or feared rather than loved. It might perhaps be answered that we should wish to be both; but since love and fear can hardly exist together, if we must choose between them, it is far safer to be feared than loved. For of men it may generally be affirmed that they are thankless, fickle, false, studious to avoid danger, greedy of gain, devoted to you while you are able to confer benefits upon them, and ready, as I said before, while danger is distant, to shed their blood, and sacrifice their property, their lives, and their children for you; but in the hour of need they turn against you. The Prince, therefore, who without otherwise securing himself builds wholly on their professions is undone. For the friendships which we buy with a price, and do not gain by greatness and nobility of character, though they be fairly earned are not made good, but fail us when we have occasion to use them.

Moreover, men are less careful how they offend him who makes himself loved than him who makes himself feared. For love is held by the tie of obligation, which, because men are a sorry breed, is broken on every whisper of private interest; but fear is bound by the apprehension of punishment which never relaxes its grasp.

Nevertheless a Prince should inspire fear in such a fashion that if he do not win love he may escape hate. For a man may very well be feared and yet not hated, and this will be the case so long as he does not meddle with the property or with the women of his citizens and subjects. And if constrained to put any to death, he should do so only when there is manifest cause or reasonable justification. But, above all, he must abstain from the property of others. For men will sooner forget the death of their father than the loss of their patrimony. Moreover, pretexts for confiscation are never to seek, and he who has once begun to live by rapine always finds reasons for taking what is not his; whereas reasons for shedding blood are fewer, and sooner exhausted.

But when a Prince is with his army, and has many soldiers under his command, he must needs disregard the reproach of cruelty, for without such a reputation in its Captain, no army can be held together or kept under any kind of control. Among other things remarkable in Hannibal this has been noted, that having a very great army, made up of men of many different nations and brought to fight in a foreign country, no dissension ever arose among the soldiers themselves, nor any mutiny against their leader, either in his good or in his evil fortunes. This we can only ascribe to the transcendent cruelty, which, joined with numberless great qualities, rendered him at once venerable and terrible in the eyes of his soldiers; for without this reputation for cruelty these other virtues would not have produced the like results.

Unreflecting writers, indeed, while they praise his achievements, have condemned the chief cause of them; but that his other merits would not by themselves have been so efficacious we may see from the case of Scipio, one of the greatest Captains, not of his own time only but of all times of which we have record, whose armies rose against him in Spain from no other cause than his too great leniency in allowing them a freedom inconsistent with military strictness. With which weakness Fabius Maximus taxed him in the Senate House, calling him the corrupter of the Roman soldiery. Again, when the Locrians were shamefully outraged by one of his lieutenants, he neither avenged them, nor punished the insolence of his officer; and this from the natural easiness of his disposition. So that it was said in the Senate by one who sought to excuse him, that there were many who knew better how to refrain from doing wrong themselves than how to correct the wrong-doing of others. This temper, however, must in time have marred the name and fame even of Scipio, had he continued in it, and retained his command. But living as he did under the control of the Senate, this hurtful quality was not merely disguised, but came to be regarded as a glory.

Returning to the question of being loved or feared, I sum up by saying, that since his being loved depends upon his subjects, while his being feared depends upon himself, a wise Prince should build on what is his own, and not on what rests with others. Only, as I have said, he must do his utmost to escape hatred.

CHAPTER XVII

How Princes Should Keep Faith

Every one understands how praiseworthy it is in a Prince to keep faith, and to live uprightly and not craftily. Nevertheless, we see from what has taken place in our own days that Princes who have set little store by their word, but have known how to overreach men by their cunning, have accomplished great things, and in the end got the better of those who trusted to honest dealing.

Be it known, then, that there are two ways of contending, one in accordance with the laws, the other by force; the first of which is proper to men, the second to beasts. But since the first method is often ineffectual, it becomes necessary to resort to the second. A Prince should, therefore, understand how to use well both the man and the beast. And this lesson has been covertly taught by the ancient writers, who relate how Achilles and many others of these old Princes were given over to be brought up and trained by Chiron the Centaur; since the only meaning of their having for instructor one who was half man and half beast is, that it is necessary for a Prince to know how to use both natures, and that the one without the other has no stability.

But since a Prince should know how to use the beast's nature wisely, he ought of beasts to choose both the lion and the fox; for the lion cannot guard himself from the toils, nor the fox from wolves. He must therefore be a fox to discern toils, and a lion to drive off wolves.

To rely wholly on the lion is unwise; and for this reason a prudent Prince neither can nor ought to keep his word when to keep it is hurtful to him and the causes which led him to pledge it are removed. If all men were good, this would not be good advice, but since they are dishonest and do not keep faith with you, you, in return, need not keep faith with them; and no Prince was ever at a loss for plausible reasons to cloak a breach of faith. Of this numberless recent instances could be given, and it might be shown how many solemn treaties and engagements have been rendered inoperative and idle through want of faith in Princes, and that he who has best known to play the fox has had the best success.

It is necessary, indeed, to put a good colour on this nature, and to be skilful in simulating and dissembling. But men are so simple, and governed so absolutely by their present needs, that he who wishes to deceive will never fail in finding willing dupes. One recent example I will not omit. Pope Alexander VI had no care or thought but how to deceive, and always found material to work on. No man ever had a more effective manner of asseverating, or made promises with more solemn protestations, or observed them less. And yet, because he understood this side of human nature, his frauds always succeeded.

It is not essential, then, that a Prince should have all the good qualities which I have enumerated above, but it is most essential that he should seem to have them; I will even venture to affirm that if he has and invariably practises them all, they are hurtful, whereas the appearance of having them is useful. Thus, it is well to seem merciful, faithful, humane, religious, and upright, and also to be so; but the mind should remain so balanced that were it needful not to be so, you should be able and know how to change to the contrary.

And you are to understand that a Prince, and most of all a new Prince, cannot observe all those rules of conduct in respect whereof men are accounted good, being often forced, in order to preserve his Princedom, to act in opposition to good faith, charity, humanity, and religion. He must therefore keep his mind ready to shift as the winds and tides of Fortune turn, and, as I have already said, he ought not to quit good courses if he can help it, but should know how to follow evil courses if he must.

A Prince should therefore be very careful that nothing ever escapes his lips which is not replete with the five qualities above named, so that to see and hear him, one would think him the embodiment of mercy, good faith, integrity, humanity, and religion. And there is no virtue which it is more necessary for him to seem to possess than this last; because men in general judge rather by the eye than by the hand, for every one can see but few can touch. Every one sees what you seem, but few know what you are, and these few dare not oppose themselves to the opinion of the many who have the majesty of the State to back them up.

Moreover, in the actions of all men, and most of all of Princes, where there is no tribunal to which we can appeal, we look to results. Wherefore if a Prince succeeds in establishing and maintaining his authority, the means will always be judged honourable and be approved by every one. For the vulgar are always taken by appearances and by results, and the world is made up of the vulgar, the few only finding room when the many have no longer ground to stand on.

A certain Prince of our own days, whose name it is as well not to mention, is always preaching peace and good faith, although the mortal enemy of both; and both, had he practised them as he preaches them, would, oftener than once, have lost him his kingdom and authority.

CHAPTER XXV

What Fortune Can Effect in Human Affairs, and How She May Be Withstood

I am not ignorant that many have been and are of the opinion that human affairs are so governed by Fortune and by God, that men cannot alter them by any prudence of theirs, and indeed have no remedy against them; and for this reason have come to think that it is not worth while to labour much about anything, but that they must leave everything to be determined by chance.

Often when I turn the matter over, I am in part inclined to agree with this opinion, which has had the readier acceptance in our own times from the great changes in things which we have seen, and every day see happen contrary to all human expectation. Nevertheless, that our free will be not wholly set aside, I think it may be the case that Fortune is the mistress of one half our actions, and yet leaves the control of the other half, or a little less, to ourselves. And I would liken her to one of those wild torrents which, when angry, overflow the plains, sweep away trees and houses, and carry off soil from one bank to throw it down upon the other. Every one flees before them, and yields to their fury without the least power to resist. And yet, though this be their nature, it does not follow that in seasons of fair weather, men cannot, by constructing weirs and moles, take such precautions as will cause them when again in flood to pass off by some artificial channel, or at least prevent their course from being so uncontrolled and destructive. And so it is with Fortune, who displays her might where there is no organized strength to resist her, and directs her onset where she knows that there is neither barrier nor embankment to confine her.

And if you look at Italy, which has been at once the seat of these changes and their cause, you will perceive that it is a field without embankment or barrier. For if, like

Germany, France, and Spain, it had been guarded with sufficient skill, this inundation, if it ever came upon us, would never have wrought the violent changes which we have witnessed.

This I think enough to say generally touching resistance to Fortune. But confining myself more closely to the matter in hand, I note that one day we see a Prince prospering and the next day overthrown, without detecting any change in his nature or character. This, I believe, comes chiefly from a cause already dwelt upon, namely, that a Prince who rests wholly on Fortune is ruined when she changes. Moreover, I believe that he will prosper most whose mode of acting best adapts itself to the character of the times; and conversely that he will be unprosperous, with whose mode of acting the times do not accord. For we see that men in these matters which lead to the end that each has before him, namely, glory and wealth, proceed by different ways, one with caution, another with impetuosity, one with violence, another with subtlety, one with patience, another with its contrary; and that by one or other of these different courses each may succeed.

Again, of two who act cautiously, you shall find that one attains his end, the other not, and that two of different temperament, the one cautious, the other impetuous, are equally successful. All which happens from no other cause than that the character of the times accords or does not accord with their methods of acting. And hence it comes, as I have already said, that two operating differently arrive at the same result, and two operating similarly, the one succeeds and the other not. On this likewise depend the vicissitudes of Fortune. For if to one who conducts himself with caution and patience, time and circumstances are propitious, so that his method of acting is good, he goes on prospering; but if these change he is ruined, because he does not change his method of acting.

For no man is found so prudent as to know how to adapt himself to these changes, both because he cannot deviate from the course to which nature inclines him, and because, having always prospered while adhering to one path, he cannot be persuaded that it would be well for him to forsake it. And so when occasion requires the cautious man to act impetuously, he cannot do so and is undone: whereas, had he changed his nature with time and circumstances, his fortune would have been unchanged.

Pope Julius II proceeded with impetuosity in all his undertakings, and found time and circumstances in such harmony with his mode of acting that he always obtained a happy result. Witness his first expedition against Bologna, when Messer Giovanni Bentivogli was yet living. The Venetians were not favourable to the enterprise; nor was the King of Spain. Negotiations respecting it with the King of France were still open. Nevertheless, the Pope with his wonted hardihood and impetuosity marched in person on the expedition, and by this movement brought the King of Spain and the Venetians to a check, the latter through fear, the former from his eagerness to recover the entire Kingdom of Naples; at the same time, he dragged after him the King of France, who, desiring to have the Pope for an ally in humbling the Venetians, on finding him already in motion saw that he could not refuse him his soldiers without openly offending him. By the impetuosity of his movements, therefore, Julius effected what no other Pontiff endowed with the highest human prudence could. For had he, as any other Pope would have done, put off his departure from Rome until terms had been settled and everything duly arranged, he never would have succeeded. For the King of France would have found a thousand pretexts to delay him, and the others would have menaced him with a thousand alarms. I shall not touch upon his other actions, which were all of a like character, and all of which had a happy issue, since the shortness of his life did not allow him to experience reverses.

But if times had overtaken him, rendering a cautious line of conduct necessary, his ruin must have ensued, since he never could have departed from those methods to which nature inclined him.

To be brief, I say that since Fortune changes and men stand fixed in their old ways, they are prosperous so long as there is congruity between them, and the reverse when there is not. Of this, however, I am well persuaded, that it is better to be impetuous than cautious. For Fortune is a woman who to be kept under must be beaten and roughly handled; and we see that she suffers herself to be more readily mastered by those who so treat her than by those who are more timid in their approaches. And always, like a woman, she favours the young, because they are less scrupulous and fiercer, and command her with greater audacity.

CHAPTER XXVI

An Exhortation to Liberate Italy from the Barbarians

Turning over in my mind all the matters which have above been considered, and debating with myself whether in Italy at the present hour the times are such as might serve to confer honour on a new Prince, and whether a fit opportunity now offers for a prudent and valiant leader to bring about changes glorious for himself and beneficial to the whole Italian people, it seems to me that so many conditions combine to further such an enterprise, that I know of no time so favourable to it as the present. And if, as I have said, it was necessary in order to display the valour of Moses that the children of Israel should be slaves in Egypt, and to know the greatness and courage of Cyrus that the Persians should be oppressed by the Medes, and to illustrate the excellence of Theseus that the Athenians should be scattered and divided, so at this hour, to prove the worth of some Italian hero, it was required that Italy should be brought to her present abject condition, to be more a slave than the Hebrew, more oppressed than the Persian, more disunited than the Athenian, without a head, without order, beaten, spoiled, torn in pieces, over-run and abandoned to destruction in every shape.

But though, heretofore, glimmerings may have been discerned in this man or that, whence it might be conjectured that he was ordained by God for her redemption, nevertheless it has afterwards been seen in the further course of his actions that Fortune has disowned him; so that our country, left almost without life, still waits to know who it is that is to heal her bruises, to put an end to the devastation and plunder of Lombardy, to the exactions and imposts of Naples and Tuscany, and to stanch those wounds of hers which long neglect has changed into running sores.

We see how she prays God to send some one to rescue her from these barbarous cruelties and oppressions. We see too how ready and eager she is to follow any standard were there only some one to raise it. But at present we see no one except in your illustrious House (pre-eminent by its virtues and good fortune, and favoured by God and by the Church whose headship it now holds), who could undertake the part of a deliverer.

But for you this will not be too hard a task, if you keep before your eyes the lives and actions of those whom I have named above. For although these men were singular and extraordinary, after all they were but men, not one of whom had so great an opportunity as now presents itself to you. For their undertakings were not more just than this, nor more easy, nor was God more their friend than yours. The justice of the cause is conspicuous; for that war is just which is necessary, and those arms are sacred from which we derive our only hope. Everywhere there is the strongest disposition to engage in this cause; and where the disposition is strong the difficulty cannot be great, provided you follow the methods observed by those whom I have set before you as models.

But further, we see here extraordinary and unexampled proofs of Divine favour. The sea has been divided; the cloud has attended you on your way; the rock has flowed with water; the manna has rained from heaven; everything has concurred to promote your greatness. What remains to be done must be done by you; since in order not to deprive us of our free will and such share of glory as belongs to us, God will not do everything himself.

Nor is it to be marvelled at if none of those Italians I have named has been able to effect what we hope to see effected by your illustrious House; or that amid so many revolutions and so many warlike movements it should always appear as though the military virtues of Italy were spent; for this comes from her old system being defective, and from no one being found among us capable to strike out a new. Nothing confers such honour on the reformer of a State, as do the new laws and institutions which he devises; for these when they stand on a solid basis and have a greatness in their scope, make him admired and venerated. And in Italy material is not wanting for improvement in every form. If the head be weak the limbs are strong, and we see daily in single combats, or where few are engaged, how superior are the strength, dexterity, and intelligence of Italians. But when it comes to armies, they are nowhere, and this from no other reason than the defects of their leaders. For those who are skilful in arms will not obey, and every one thinks himself skilful, since hitherto we have had none among us so raised by merit or by fortune above his fellows that they should yield him the palm. And hence it happens that for the long period of twenty years, during which so many wars have taken place, whenever there has been an army purely Italian it has always been beaten. To this testify, first Taro, then Alessandria, Capua, Genoa, Vaila, Bologna, Mestri.

If then your illustrious House should seek to follow the example of those great men who have delivered their country in past ages, it is before all things necessary, as the true foundation of every such attempt, to be provided with national troops, since you can have no braver, truer, or more faithful soldiers; and although every single man of them be good, collectively they will be better, seeing themselves commanded by their own Prince, and honoured and esteemed by him. That you may be able, therefore, to defend yourself against the foreigner with Italian valour, the first step is to provide yourself with an army such as this.

And although the Swiss and the Spanish infantry are each esteemed formidable, there are yet defects in both, by reason of which troops trained on a different system might not merely withstand them, but be certain of defeating them. For the Spaniards cannot resist cavalry, and the Swiss will give way before infantry if they find them as resolute as themselves at close quarters. Whence it has been seen, and may be seen again, that the Spaniards cannot sustain the onset of the French men-at-arms, and that the Swiss are broken by the Spanish foot. And although of this last we have no complete instance, we have yet an indication of it in the battle of Ravenna, where the Spanish infantry confronted the German companies, who have the same discipline as the Swiss; on which occasion the Spaniards by their agility and with the aid of their bucklers forced their way under the pikes, and stood ready to close with the Germans, who were no longer in a position to defend themselves; and had they not been charged by cavalry, they must have put the Germans to utter rout. Knowing, then, the defects of each of these kinds of troops, you can train your men on some different system, to withstand cavalry and not to fear infantry. To effect this, will not require the creation of any new forces, but simply a change in the discipline of the old. And these are matters in reforming which the new Prince acquires reputation and importance.

This opportunity then, for Italy at last

to look on her deliverer, ought not to be allowed to pass away. With what love he would be received in all those Provinces which have suffered from the foreign inundation, with what thirst for vengeance, with what fixed fidelity, with what devotion, and what tears, no words of mine can declare. What gates would be closed against him? What people would refuse him obedience? What jealousy would stand in his way? What Italian but would yield him homage? This barbarian tyranny stinks in all nostrils.

Let your illustrious House therefore take upon itself this enterprise with all the courage and all the hopes with which a just cause is undertaken; so that under your standard this our country may be ennobled, and under your auspices be fulfilled the words of Petrarch:—

> Brief will be the strife
> When valour arms against barbaric rage;
> For the bold spirit of the bygone age
> Still warms Italian hearts with life.

TWENTY

ITALIAN POLITICAL DEVELOPMENT

In many respects the Italian peninsula was the most progressive part of Europe during the Renaissance, not only in art and trade but also in politics. In Italy a group of independent city-states arose, much like those of the Ancient World. Consequently, educated Italians could read ancient history with far greater understanding than scholars in northern Europe. In Italy the urban upper-middle class fused with the rural aristocracy, so that an urban governing class set the tone of Italian civilization, while in northern Europe the urban centers, less closely tied to the socially dominent feudal lords, had much less weight in determining patterns of taste and behavior. Indeed, some historians see Italy's urbanization as a prime ingredient in the creation of the Renaissance itself. In any case, Italy's political development in city-states such as Florence, Venice, and Milan achieved sophistication and specialized institutions hardly known in northern Europe until well into the sixteenth century. In this sense, Renaissance Italy anticipated and educated its northern neighbors, because Italian political ways in city-states later became standard procedure in the larger nation-states of the north. In his provocative volume on Renaissance diplomacy, Garrett Mattingly analyzes the many subtle and complex political institutions of Renaissance Italy which later entered the mainstream of national and international life in northern Europe.

GARRETT MATTINGLY

RENAISSANCE DIPLOMACY*

At the beginning of the fifteenth century Western society still lacked the resources to organize stable states on the national scale. On the scale of the Italian city state it could do so. Internally the smaller distances to be overcome brought the problems of transport and communication, and consequently the problems of collecting taxes and maintaining the central authority, within the range of practical solution. The capital wealth and per capita productivity of the Italian towns may not have been very much greater (it was certainly somewhat greater) than that of the more prosperous regions north of the Alps. But the relative concentration of population and the restricted area to be administered enabled the Italian city states to find the

* From *Renaissance Diplomacy* by Garrett Mattingly, pp. 59–70. Reprinted with permission of Houghton Mifflin Company, Boston. Copyright 1955 by Houghton Mifflin Company. Printed in England by Jonathan Cape Limited, London. Copyright 1955 by Jonathan Cape Limited.

means necessary for the ends of government to an extent long impossible to the sprawling, loose-jointed northern monarchies. In consequence, not only was the natural pull of each capital intensified by the regular activities of paid officials, but the whole state was able to mobilize its forces with rapidity and ease rarely possible beyond the Alps.

In external relations, scale had a double effect. The comparative efficiency of the new Italian states (in part a function of their limited areas) enabled them to pursue the objectives of their foreign policy with greater continuity and agility than Europe could show elsewhere. At the same time, the presence within the limited space of upper Italy of armed neighbours, equally efficient, agile and predatory, made continuous vigilance in foreign affairs a prime necessity.

North of the Alps the greater spaces to be overcome made the clash of foreign policies less continuous and less menacing. A Philippe le Bel, an Edward III, a Henry V might be just as aggressive, ambitious, and unscrupulous as any Italian tyrant, and such a king might be capable of summoning from his realm a spurt of energy comparable in intensity to the best Italian effort and, of course, enormously more formidable in size. But such bursts of energy proved sporadic. Because they had not yet succeeded in organizing their own internal space, the feudal monarchies were incapable of really sustained exertions, and the more they were driven towards it, the more likely they were to sink back into regional indifference and factional strife. Meanwhile, the relatively vast and unorganized spaces of transalpine Europe cushioned political conflicts.

'Vast spaces' is scarcely an exaggeration. We are accustomed to thinking of space as having shrunk in our day. We are vaguely aware that Moscow is nearer to Chicago now than London was to Paris in Napoleon's time. But we are not so aware that space has been shrinking, though at a slower rate, for a good many centuries, and that in terms of commercial intercourse, or military logistics, or even of diplomatic communication, European distances were perceptibly greater in the fourteenth century than in the sixteenth, and remained greater in the sixteenth than they were to become by the eighteenth. In the fourteenth and fifteenth centuries, the continental space of Western Europe still impeded any degree of political organization efficient enough to create a system of continuous diplomatic pressures. Rulers might indulge themselves in foreign adventures out of vainglory or greed or spite; they were not yet compelled to continuous vigilance and continuing action beyond their own frontiers by constant, unavoidable pressures.

It was otherwise in Italy. In upper Italy, by about 1400, space was becoming completely organized; political interstices were filling up; the margins and cushions were shrinking, and the states of the peninsula were being obliged by the resulting pressures to a continuous awareness of each other. Italy was beginning to become such a system of mutually balanced parts in unstable equilibrium as all Europe was to be three hundred years later, a small-scale model for experiments with the institutions of the new state.

For this model to work freely, one other condition was necessary: a relative isolation. For more than a century, from about 1378 to 1492, Italy did enjoy that condition. The schism of the papacy, the impotence of the Empire, the long misery of the Hundred Years War, the recurrent anarchy of the Iberian realms, produced all round Italy a series of crises and conflicts which diverted European pressures from the peninsula. Not that Italy was ever long free from the intrusion of some foreign adventurer in quest of a crown, a lordship or a subsidy. Not that there was ever a decade in which some Italian power was not intriguing to call in a foreigner in order to gain for itself some local advantage. But the foreign intrusions were all on what one may call an Italian scale. None of them threatened more than briefly to become unmanageable, or to alter radically the peninsular balance.

The final result of this long immunity from serious foreign threats was to make Italian statesmen insensitive to the difference in scale between their system and that of Europe, blind to the fact that the tallest giants among the Italian states were pigmies beside the monarchies beyond the Alps. They grew rashly confident of their ability to summon the barbarians when they might be useful and send them home if they became embarrassing. Thus, in the end they failed to understand the catastrophe that overwhelmed them. But the immediate result of the absence of severe outside pressures was to set the states of Italy free for their competitive struggle with one another, and so to intensify their awareness of the structure and tensions of their own peninsular system.

Mainly it was these tensions that produced the new style of diplomacy. Primarily it developed as one functional adaptation of the new type of self-conscious, uninhibited, power-seeking competitive organism. But relatively secondary factors had some influence: the character of Italian warfare and the trend of upper class Italian culture.

Warfare in Italy had changed as busy, pecuniary-minded citizens turned over more and more of the actual fighting to professional soldiers. These were recruited from the more backward regions of the peninsula and commanded by generals who were, in effect, large-scale contractors. Wars waged by mercenary troops under generals mainly zealous for their own professional reputation tended to be less bloody and less decisive than the earlier clashes of citizen militias, though still painfully expensive. War became more rational and, therefore, if less glorious, more civilized. But for this very reason, as campaigns became more and more a series of manœuvres for political advantage, conducted by relatively small bodies of not always trustworthy professionals, the management of wars made increasing demands upon statemanship. Success now depended less upon the brutal shock of massed force than upon vigilant and agile politics. The diplomat was needed to supplement the soldier.

At the same time the dominant elements in Italian society began to set a higher value on a form of contest in which their leading citizens, not mercenary strangers who might change sides for the next campaign, were the champions. Business men were delighted by the skills of the diplomat, the nimble anticipation of the next move on the chess board, the subtle gambit which could trip a stronger opponent, the conversion of an enemy into a partner against some common rival, the snatching of victory from defeat by bluff and persuasion and mental dexterity. These qualities were surely more admirable than the brute valour of the condottiere. Diplomacy was for rulers; war for hired men.

It was also natural for the ruling groups—merchants and professional men—most of them with some legal or notarial training (the practical basis of a humanistic education) and most of them experienced in the haggling of the forum and the market place—to believe that words might be as potent as swords. The faith of the merchants and the politicos in the efficacy of diplomatic and forensic persuasion as an auxiliary to or substitute for military force was probably heightened by the reviving interest in classical literature. In turn, no doubt, this faith strengthened the new humanism and helped to give it its prevailing bias towards public rhetoric. The real effectiveness of this form of psychological warfare no one can hope to estimate now. Certainly public opinion among the educated classes was more or less susceptible to propaganda, and certainly, from the time of Petrarch and Cola de Rienzi onward, there was an increasing tendency to try to manipulate this opinion by literary means.

One may be permitted to doubt that an oration by Coluccio Salutati really fell into the scales of political decision with the weight of a thousand horse, but the straight-faced ascription of such a remark to Salutati's most formidable antagonist reminds us of the norm of Renaissance judgment. In that judgment the importance to the state of the diplomat's power of public persuasion, of his ability to deliver a moving formal speech or compose an effectively argued state paper, was at least equal to his utility as an observer, reporter and manipulator of events. In both his aspects, as public orator and as secret negotiator, the fifteenth-century Italian tended to value the successful diplomat with or above the successful general. Not because 'the business of an ambassador is peace', but because the diplomat, like the general, was an agent for the preservation and aggrandizement of the state.

The pressures of the Italian system led to the invention of a new kind of diplomatic officer, the resident ambassador. Before the end of the fifteenth century, resident ambassadors, unknown elsewhere in Europe, were common throughout Italy. They had become the chief means by which Italian statecraft observed and continually readjusted the unstable equilibrium of power within the peninsula. They were at once the agents and the symbols of a continuous system of diplomatic pressures. And they had proved their worth as one of the most potent weapons of the new states in their unremitting struggle for survival and for the power on which they fed.

As weapons in the struggle for power, resident ambassadors began to be employed by the other states of Europe in about 1500. They have been the most characteristic officers of Western diplomacy ever since. They differentiate our system strikingly from any other we know about elsewhere. Naturally, therefore, scholars have inquired what prior suggestions could be found for this striking invention, and not unnaturally, the answers have been various.

Perhaps it would be as well to say here what is meant by a resident ambassador. He is, to put Wotton's wry epigram into English and disregard its English pun, 'a man sent to lie abroad for his country's good'. He is a regularly accredited envoy with full diplomatic status. But he is sent—this is the significant departure—not to discharge a specific piece of business and then return, as Bernard du Rosier assumed all ambassadors would be, but to remain at his post until recalled, in general charge of the interests of his principal. For the period before 1648 it is not sensible to impose any third requirement. Not all resident embassies were reciprocal. And not all residents were called 'ambassadors', though whenever there are enough documents it is easy to tell whether they enjoyed that status.

Most sixteenth-century writers about diplomacy were still puzzled and embarrassed by the mere fact of resident ambassadors. When, towards the end of the century, the humanists finally agreed on an account of their origins, the genealogy was fanciful. Some of the provisions of Roman law concerns those *legati* sent by the provinces to represent them at the capital. Some of these *legati* were obliged by their business to remain in Rome for years. 'Certainly,' said the humanists, who thought no institution respectable unless it had a classical ancestor, 'anyone can see what happened. When the empire fell, the barbarian kings of the succession states continued to maintain the *legati* of their provinces at the papal court. These were the first resident ambassadors.'

The explanation has not the slightest basis in historical fact, but it continued to survive in the textbooks for a long time. Even today most writers walk warily around it by excluding Rome from any generalization about the history of residents. In many respects, of course, the diplomatic relations of the papacy were quite unlike the relations of secular states with one another. But resident embassies are a secular institution, and the Roman curia played only a slight rôle in their development. There were no resident ambassadors at the Holy See before the 1430s, or at least there is no discernible trace of any. Their appearance at Rome in the fifteenth century was a consequence of the general development.

Two more recent suggestions connect the origin of the system with Rome. A nineteenth-century German canonist thought he had found the first resident ambassadors in the resident representatives maintained by the popes at Constantinople from the sixth to the middle of the eighth century. These officers, called *apokrisiarii* or *responsales,* were in charge of the business which the see of Rome still had with its then temporal overlords, the Eastern emperors. During the same period the patriarchs of Alexandria, Antioch and Jerusalem maintained similar representatives at Constantinople, also for ecclesiastical business. The popes stopped sending any before 750. Certainly nobody in the eighth century thought of such officers as ambassadors. Probably nobody in the fifteenth century remembered them at all.

In the early 1900s another German scholar pointed out that the procurators sent by James II of Aragon to Rome at the end of the thirteenth century actually discharged most of the duties later expected of resident ambassadors. This seems a more plausible precedent. Besides performing their normal legal function, the Aragonese procurators negotiated diplomatic business, and regularly reported to the king the latest developments in Italian politics. For at least a decade they constituted a continuous series. More recently a brilliant study has drawn attention to a whole line of procurators representing the kings of England at Paris in the early 1300s. It suggests that these procurators were prototypes of the resident ambassador, and that similar procurators at the papal court at Avignon, 'became the first permanent diplomatic representatives'.

These instances are interesting for their parallelism in certain respects to the first phase of the establishment of resident embassies, and for their differences in others. Both thirteenth-century examples show a prolonged period of negotiation between two powers with common interests, between the king of Aragon and Pope Boniface VIII, because of their alliance against Frederick of Sicily, and between the English and French kings because of their efforts to solve the problems of their feudal ties without resort to war. Both the Aragon of James II and the England of Edward I and Edward II displayed an unusual degree of diplomatic activity. Both left in their archives evidence of the precocious development of record-keeping and other foreign office techniques necessary for the conduct of continuous diplomacy. These are among the conditions which, nearly a century and a half later, seem to have favoured the development of resident embassies. Both England and Aragon, by maintaining procurators at the courts of their partners, did take what looks like the first step in such a direction.

The differences, however, are equally striking. In both countries the burst of diplomatic activity flagged and died away. After the transfer of the papacy of Avignon, the kings of Aragon were not always represented at the curia, and, when they were, their procurators rarely had any but the usual ecclesiastical business. After the 1330s England had no procurators in Paris, and a little later none at Avignon either. There is no evidence that the early experiment was remembered two hundred years afterwards, or that it had any influence as a precedent.

It scarcely could have had, since the very act of sending a legal procurator meant the acknowledgement of a superior legal jurisdiction. Legal procurators were officers attached to a court of law, representing the interests of clients with suits at its bar. If the king of England had not been, in his dignity as duke of Aquitaine, subject to the jurisdiction of the *Parlement de Paris,* he would have sent no legal procurators to France. Of course, not only kings but cities or corporations or individuals sometimes sent such procurators to the papal court. In the English and Aragonese instances confusion is easy because both groups of documents mention two kinds of procurators, legal ones, residing near a court of law, and envoys with powers to conclude diplomatic transactions. But the diplomatic procurators were not residents, and the resident ones were not diplomats.

This does not deny that resident legal procurators were sometimes useful to royal diplomacy. Apparently the Aragonese ones were in the 1290s, and later, after 1450, when most of the major powers were beginning to maintain permanent resident procurators at Rome, some of these church lawyers had occasion to report political news to their clients and even to meddle in diplomacy. In the 1480s England and Spain were represented at Rome by individuals who were accredited both as ambassadors and as procurators. So it is fair enough to say that their procurators at Rome gave transalpine powers their first experience of permanent diplomatic representation and, in a sense, their first resident ambassadors. But by the 1480s resident ambassadors were commonplace among the secular states of Italy. Whatever really influential precedents for the new institution there may have been, must have been available, therefore, in previous Italian experience.

One of the chief functions of the resident ambassador came to be to keep a continuous stream of foreign political news flowing to his home government. Long before 1400 the Italian city states had the opportunity to appreciate the value of such news to makers of policy. It came to them from two sources, from the consuls of their merchant communities abroad, and from the resident foreign agents of their bankers.

From the twelfth century onward Italian merchants began to cluster in colonies in the chief commercial cities of the Levant and to organize themselves under the jurisdiction of consuls. The consuls were often elected by the members of the community and were primarily judges or arbiters of disputes among its members and the official representatives of its interests before the local authorities. From the first, however, the home governments of the colonists participated in this colonial organization and sent out officers with various titles to supervise and direct it. Later the consuls themselves acquired a more official standing and were frequently appointed by the governments of their native cities and directly responsible to them. In a sense they represented not just the interests, say, of the Pisan merchants at Acre, the Genoese at Constantinople or the Venetians at Alexandria, but the whole power and dignity of the Pisan, Genoese and Venetian republics.

Strictly speaking, consuls were not diplomats. Their status depended not on the general principles of international law but on special treaties with the powers on whose territory they were. But they did in fact perform some of the services later performed by resident ambassadors. Although any really important message or negotiation would be entrusted to a special embassy, consuls did sometimes deliver messages on behalf of their governments to the local authorities, sometimes, therefore, to reigning princes. Sometimes they did negotiate on behalf of their governments. In some places they had positions assigned to them at public functions. And the consuls of some republics, those of Genoa and Venice, at least, were expected to report regularly news of political as well as of commercial interest.

For Venice, anyway, a case might be made for her consuls having been the precursors of her resident ambassadors. One Venetian representative abroad, the *bailo* at Constantinople, performed both consular and diplomatic functions in the fifteenth century. Other consuls were sometimes given special diplomatic credentials. And all the surviving evidence indicates that by the latter part of the fifteenth century regular consular reports to the Venetian Senate had become a long established custom. Apparently the Venetians themselves thought there was a close connection between the two institutions. When, in 1523, the Venetian ambassador was recalled from England, the

Senate voted that, until he could be replaced, the interests of the republic should be confided to the Venetian consul at London, according to the custom of former times'.

Even before Venetian consuls appeared in European cities, the merchant bankers of Lombardy and Tuscany had begun to maintain permanent resident representatives, the medieval equivalents of branch managers, at the courts or in the commercial centres where they did most business. Since much of that business was loans to sovereigns, the access of banking agents to the prince and his council could be as easy as that any diplomat enjoyed. In the correspondence of these agents the political news must often have been the most profitable part of the letter. When the bankers thus represented were members of the ruling oligarchy of their city, or the trusted clients of its tyrant, the reports of their agents could supply the basis for political action, and the conduct of the agents themselves might be guided, by political motives. When the banker reported to was himself the actual, if unofficial, ruler of his city—when, for example, he was Cosimo de'Medici—the diplomatic function of his foreign branch managers might become very considerable indeed. After 1434 it was progressively harder to distinguish between the resident representatives of the Medici bank and the political agents of the Florentine state. But this is a late instance.

Before 1400, the tyrants and oligarchs of northern Italy must already have learned all that experience with consuls and branch banks had to teach. The earliest Italian resident diplomatic agents are to be found well before that date. They were not called 'ambassadors' at first or entitled (as we shall see) to diplomatic honours and immunities. But they were received in the cities where they resided as the actual agents of their masters, and were charged with most of the duties later discharged by resident ambassadors. In northern and central Italy between 1380 and 1450 this kind of semi-official resident agent became increasingly common. Towards 1450 several of the earliest official residents of whom we have any certain notice began their careers as members of this ambiguous class, among them that Nicodemus of Pontremoli upon whom the consensus of recent writers has thrust, on somewhat slender grounds, the distinction of being the first resident ambassador.

We shall probably never be able to lay down with certainty every step in the period of transition before 1455. Many records have vanished. Those which survive are largely unpublished and inadequately explored. Nor is it likely that any number of documents would enable us to assign with confidence respective weights to the influence of such antecendents as procurators, consuls and banking agents on the invention of resident ambassadors. But the main outline of the story is clear. The new institution was Italian. It developed in the hundred years before 1454. And whatever suggestions, possible antecendents, and analogies may have offered, the development was, in the main, an empirical solution to an urgent practical problem. Italy first found the system of organizing interstate relationship which Europe later adopted, because Italy, towards the end of the Middle Ages, was already becoming what later all Europe became.

TWENTY-ONE

MICHELANGELO

The Renaissance made a number of important contributions to the growth of Western civilization. One was the development of a secular attitude, heavily reinforced by the Greek and Roman classics, which came to fruition in the Enlightenment of the eighteenth century. Another was its great achievement in the arts, particularly in painting. Not all critics have agreed about the relative merits of Renaissance painters. But the consensus has ranked Michelangelo Buonarroti (1475–1564) among the greatest painters of period. Some believe him to have been the greatest painter of the Renaissance, of higher stature even than Leonardo da Vinci. In a penetrating analysis, Sheldon Cheney has expressed his intense admiration for Michelangelo. Cheney has pointed out that Michelangelo went beyond the usual classical limits of humanism by making a profoundly moving synthesis of Biblical and Greek elements in the Christian tradition. Like other critics, Cheney has emphasized Michelangelo's gigantic achievement in painting superbly grouped and executed figures on the ceiling of the Sistine Chapel in Rome—a task which took over four years to complete. In addition, Michelangelo did work of first rank in sculpture, and he himself believed and stated on a number of occasions that he was primarily a sculptor and only secondarily a painter.

SHELDON CHENEY

A NEW WORLD HISTORY OF ART*

In coming to Michelangelo one meets the first overwhelming genius in painting since Giotto. Despite the extraordinary advance in the art, and the long procession of notable figures from Masaccio and Fra Angelico to Leonardo and Raphael, they are lesser men as compared with this unaccountable creative genius. Painting only under protest, insisting that he wanted only to practice his own art of sculpture, he yet outdid all his contemporaries in originality, vitality, and sheer compelling mastery in the mural art. A single figure by Michelangelo seems to today's modern artists and critics to have more plastic vigor than all that artists such as Perugino, Bronzino, and Fra Bartolommeo ever created.

For one thing, while everybody else was busy introducing Greek harmony and grace and idealization, and prettifying painting, here was an imagination that remembered that Christianity had a Hebrew-Biblical as well as a pagan inheritance; here was a man who could thunder like Jeremiah and praise mightily like the Psalmists, and be profoundly troubled by immediate life. In his re-creation of the Greeks, too, he saw

* From *A New World History of Art*, pp. 373–82, by Sheldon Cheney. Copyright 1937, © 1956 by Sheldon Cheney. Reprinted by permission of The Viking Press, Inc.

through the current sentimentalization and weakening of the classic heritage. The romantic sweetness of Raphael and the ecstatic eroticism of Correggio fade from memory when one meets Michelangelo's Greek Sibyls.

One may well ask which among the sixteenth-century artists is the truest symbol and voice of the age. The cultured circles had found refuge in the revival of learning and in visual arts that put on the face of a romanticized classicism. For more than a century the patrons, establishing academies and financing the uncovering of ancient monuments and the publication of treatises about them, had encouraged this neoclassic, reflective picturing. It progressed not without a new scientific acumen and a freshly reasoned understanding of optical law and of the structure of natural forms. But the classical was a refuge from all the larger realities of Italian life in that time. In the midst of murder, violence, and the shocks of war and overturned states, the current of "harmonizing" art flowed on.

Leonardo brought to a final expression the intellectualized attitude. Botticelli epitomized the pageant-like neo-pagan unrealities of the courtly classicism. Raphael equally avoided any but pleasing reality, while capping the procession toward facsimile statement. These painters expressed the spirit of the pedagogues and the aspirations of the rich patron-princes of their time. They were busy shaping a new Greece in a wish-formed likeness of the old. But may it not be that Michelangelo, thinking on Dante and Savonarola as well as on Plato and the Muses, giving up sweetened harmony and obvious charm for a passionate outpouring of emotion and a half-tamed cry of defiance, was the truest expression of that turbulent sixteenth century?

Personally Leonardo and Raphael had been cultured, graceful, not a little feminine —true courtiers, every inch. Michelangelo was rough in manner, troubled in mind, sharp-spoken. But his was no cramped, mean outlook. If his faculties refused to discount the miseries of the world and the immediate troubles of living, they nonetheless embraced a great passion for the joys of work and for the wonders of human aspiration. There is joyousness incarnate in the figures of the Sistine vault. The zest of living and the grandeur of human endeavor have never else been recorded with such relish—and with such galvanizing effect. As Michelangelo synthesized the Biblical and the Greek elements in Christianity, so he brought into one expression the world's woe and its joy, human tribulation and human glory. If he lived in tempestuous pain—and he recorded often that he did—he knew the other face of that experience: he emerged into a rapture and contemplation beyond the capacity of any of his neo-Greek contemporaries. In his own right he was philosopher, prophet, creator.

Michelangelo was born in 1475, in the mountains above Florence, of middle-class parentage. He early decided for himself that he would be an artist—against the wishes of his father, who, however, came to see the light when, in 1489, the lad's talent attracted the attention of the reigning Medici overlord in Florence and thus secured patronage for both himself and the family. In the Medici gardens he studied antique statues at first hand, and he was taken into the house of Lorenzo, where he met artists and scholars, poets and professional antiquarians. It was the time of Savonarola's fiery denunciation of worldly luxury and art, and the lad seems to have absorbed the evangelical influence with the courtly. He was himself silent, sensitive, and moody, and never came to proficiency in the politeness of the drawing-room. When Lorenzo de' Medici died and his son was driven from Florence, the young artist's exposure to the influences that shaped so many of his contemporaries was over. In 1496, at the age of twenty-one, he went to Rome. "Here," wrote Symonds, "while the Borgias were turning the Vatican into a den of thieves and harlots, he executed the purest of all his statues—a *Pietà* in marble."

It was thus that Michelangelo's first masterpiece was born, after perhaps a half-dozen trial statues. For many years thereafter he was destined to live in Rome, a paradoxically Christian temperament among pseudo-Greeks; a reserved, introspective contemplator of the historical comi-tragedy of man, among all the bright intelligences and the eager limners of the papal entourage.

Michelangelo stood his ground with popes and princes, pitting his dignity against their imperiousness, his solitary assurance against their whims. And yet it was a pope, Julius II, who overbore him in the matter of the decorations of the Sistine Chapel, forced him to take the commission for painting the ceiling vault, when what the artist solely wished was to be left to practice in peace the sculpture which he knew to be pre-eminently his art.

As Michelangelo was a superman, self-disciplined to the point of austere asceticism in an age of indulgence, broodingly mystical when everyone around him was trying to be bright and rational and open, so the figures he painted in the Vatican chapel are superhuman. The obvious largeness of aspect is matched by sublimity of conception and character. And—rarest of phenomena—the sheer plastic vitality of the paintings is similarly vast, inescapable.

Other artists had painted the side walls of the chapel. It was in 1508 that Pope Julius II decided that the ceiling, too, should be done and that Michelangelo was the man to paint it. At best the task would have seemed a thankless one, even to a practiced muralist. The vault is nearly a hundred feet above the floor—a curving surface, a half-cylinder in shape, 133 feet long. For this Michelangelo, gently setting aside the Pope's suggested scheme, devised a series of pictures and figures and architectural accessories which constitutes the greatest single exhibit of the painter's art in Europe—though difficult to see.

The conception is as audacious in the vast range of its subject-matter as in its organization. There are shown not only the creation and history of man, in the Christian interpretation, but the ancient prophets, Greek as well as Hebrew, who foretold Christ's world, and a host of supporting personages from legend and imagination. No observer could then or can today take in the full significance of the total work. Certain scenes, set off separately, may be studied as single pictorial entities, such as the *Creation of Man,* or the colossal figures of the *Sibyls* and *Prophets.* But the amazing thing is the sense of vigor and grandeur that runs through major and minor parts of the composition. There are 343 figures in the ceiling. After trying out assistants, Michelangelo painted the entire 10,000 square feet of surface himself. In a famous sonnet he complains of the discomfort he experienced in painting while lying on his back on the scaffolding.

It took him four and one-half years to complete the job. After the scaffolding was down and the work had been greatly admired, the Pope suggested that the artist enrich the composition with additions in bright colors and gold, to which Michelangelo replied that the prophets and the holy men pictured there were rich not by reason of that sort of wealth. Nor has the world since doubted that here a painter created richness that is without measure, beyond gold.

That Michelangelo the painter gained from the studies of Michelangelo the sculptor is not to be doubted. No other painter has accomplished figures so swelling with power, so statuesquely monumental. But the means he used are those legitimate to painting art. On the two-dimensional plane he created the space-volume impression by line, chiaroscuro, color, texture. Greater plastic mastery is not to be found in the whole range of painting. Powerful, rhythmic, profoundly animated is the impression. Each figure is living, abounding with life, and the throng of figures is gorgeously orchestrated, symphonically related. Never else has the human body been so sublimely utilized, so woven into poems epic and heroic.

It was twenty-one years after the completion of the Sistine ceiling—a period during which the artist did no painting—that Michelangelo was called by another Pope, Paul III, to paint an immense mural for the rear wall of the chapel, above the altar. For seven years more he labored, and then in 1541 *The Last Judgment* was unveiled, and a masterpiece of extraordinary vigor and originality was given to the world.

Again Michelangelo made his own rules. He had learned all that the Renaissance perfecting of the picturing medium made possible by way of clarity of statement and truth to light-and-shade appearance. But—stirred perhaps by the degradation and corruption of life around him, by the tragic decline of Italy and the crumbling of human character—he fixed a conception of the final judgment of man which is medieval in its uncompromising rectitude and somberness. It is no pretty picture, and perhaps too violently animated for achitectural "decoration." But it is surpassingly moving, plastically alive as a whole and in every part, and its allegory, its picturing of the divine judgment scene, stirs the mind. As the Chinese say, it has its own movement of life. As the Europeans say, it instructs and makes men better.

Unlike the ceiling decorations, *The Last Judgment* is laid out as one picture; but the surface is so vast—forty-three by fifty-four feet—and the troops of figures are so crowded, that ordinarily appreciation is directed to this or that part. One who has become adept at creating his own frames, picking an arbitrary section of the whole and mentally isolating it for study and enjoyment, will find a score of profoundly stirring pictures some of them subtly marked off by Michelangelo himself, though without disturbance of the total effectiveness.

Even in photographs one cannot fail to realize the power, the imaginativeness, and the superb draftsmanship of these detached fragments. Unfortunately the smoke and dust of four hundred years have almost obliterated the color. There has been also some damaging "restoration" attempted at times. It is said, moreover, that at the unveiling certain figures appeared too naked for the sensibilities of the Vatican ecclesiastics, and clothes were added by a minor artist who was known ever after as "the breeches-maker." Michelangelo himself was so incensed by the remarks of one of the prudish courtiers, a certain Biagio da Cesena, that he painted the man's portrait into the group of sinners in Hell.

Michelangelo the painter is known almost exclusively by the two works in the Sistine Chapel at the Vatican. He apparently had no interest in easel-pictures. In the only one that survives complete, the early *Holy Family* now in the Uffizi Gallery, he proves that he can pack into the smaller space a generous measure of that power so evident in his murals and his sculptures. The rhythms are strong and vital, and the drawing masterly. There is, however, concession to the fashion of sweet finish, which is not known in the more monumental works. Two or three unfinished pictures, with great virtues so far as they go, but still incomplete, are the only other paintings credited to him. There is, however, a portrait of the artist so fine, so rugged, and yet so sensitive, that it is difficult to avoid the inference that Michelangelo at least helped to paint it if he did not completely do so.

One of the main lines of Renaissance progress in art had been scientific, and one of the sciences perfected in this era was anatomy. Giotto had attempted no revelation of the human body beneath the voluminous garments of his figures. But Ghiberti and Donatello were already accomplished revealers of bone and muscle, and Masaccio individualized the anatomy of his nudes. Leonardo pursued the unusual aspects of the body, even to sketching the peculiar hunching and muscular sag of a corpse recently hanged. Thus was science in art pushed to an ultimate point.

But Michelangelo, evidently knowing

anatomy to the last physical detail, went on to that other half of the study of the human figure, learning as never did anyone else to fix the expressiveness of attitudes and movements. He used the body as an unsurpassed medium for the communication of emotion. Passion and heroism, despair and transfiguration, contemplation and exaltation, all are expressed by this one bodily means. It is said that toward the end of his life the beauty of the human form so obsessed him that he brooded continually over the ways in which the great truths of the life and aspiration (and tragedy) of mankind might be interpreted through it.

The little extras that Ghiberti and Donatello and the della Robbias had put into their sculptures—borrowing the perspective vistas of the theater designers and the landscapes of the painters to add variety to their reliefs—were here forgotten like toys gone out of fashion. In sculpture, as in painting, the body is Michelangelo's supreme material, the body set out free of all encumbering circumstance, the body alone speaking for the dignity and sorrows and triumphs of the human soul.

Where the eloquence of the body leaves off and pure sculptural eloquence begins, no one can say. Of the abstract values of the art on its own account—if it could be freed from subject matter—Michelangelo proved himself a master not only unrivaled in his age but unsurpassed by any artist in the whole history of Europe. Only the anonymous creators of the Parthenon figures had grasped so much of mountainous strength and exalted vigor. The sheer plastic vitality of his single figures is enormous. There is in them a hint of cosmic order and elemental power.

In that early work, the *Pietà,* done at twenty-four, so much more graceful and harmoniously rhythmic than Michelangelo's later things, there is already also an amplitude, a power, that heralds the arrival of a sculptural genius. Immediately the art is lifted out of the field of reproductive activity, of naturalism and sentimentality, to which the later sculptors of the *quattrocento* had degraded it. In the *Pietà* one does not have to look at the expression on Mary's face to feel the sentiment of the incident, and one does not remark the truth of the modeling or the marvelous exactitude of treatment of this or that part. The whole thing breathes the sentiment: the largeness of the enfolding feminine figure, the play and counterplay of mass and direction, the ample, sheltering completeness.

This largeness of conception, this powerful movement, is instinct throughout Michelangelo's sculpture. A few pieces sacrifice a little of it to more realistic statement of the observed figure and attitude, particularly the famous *David.* But almost always there is preserved the sense of the life of the stone block, the push of elemental energies, the poise of vast forces held in tension.

If, as some modern critics believe, every sculptural composition is an organization of volumes in space with relation to an indicated field or frame, Michelangelo is the supreme Western master, both in indication of the frame and in bold manipulation of the contained volumes for plastic vigor with repose. In the massive, voluminous ampleness of his works he rivals those world-masters the Egyptians and the Chinese.

Most of Michelangelo's statues are left to posterity as single figures, although planned originally as parts of great tomb compositions which never took more than fragmentary form. Long and bitter were the quarrels the artist waged with his patrons over these commissioned projects, and grievous was the loss of his time in balked effort. But even unfinished, with only seven of the score planned figures in place, the mausoleum room of the Medici family in San Lorenzo Church in Florence takes rank as a major shrine of the sculptural art in Europe. The four figures known as *Day, Night, Dawn,* and *Evening* are huge tomb guardians with an extraordinary appearance of confined movement. Here nudity lends itself to dignity and grandeur, and each single body is made to breathe the feeling of majestic power. The figures are not natural—heaven forbid! Rather they are superhuman conceptions, dramatized and superbly "artificial."

There are other celebrated works: the *Moses* in Rome; two slaves breaking their bonds planned for a grand tomb in St. Peter's, upon which the Moses, too, was to have been an item; a relief plaque of the Madonna and Child; and a bust known as the *Brutus*.

Michelangelo lived to be eighty-nine years old. In the end art itself failed to satisfy his longing to serve mankind. Having lived the most blameless of lives, as mortal standards go, he yet further denied worldly interests and gave his mind to God. His last statue was a *Deposition from the Cross* made for the cathedral in Florence. It pleased him to portray himself as Joseph of Arimathea, sorrowfully handing down Jesus' body to the Virgin Mother and the Magdalen below. The dejected yet dignified and loving figure was symbolic of what the world was to mean to him in the decade before his death in 1564.

TWENTY-TWO

THE EXPANSION OF EUROPE

The climax of the Renaissance came unexpectedly with the unprecedented expansion of Europe overseas—to the western hemisphere with the voyage of Columbus in 1492 and to India with the voyage of Da Gama in 1498. The progressive involvement of western Europe with the Americas, Asia, and Africa widened European horizons and in time brought about the worldwide interplay of historical forces usually associated with the modern world. But the beginnings were small. The original explorers, although filled with wonder at what they had accomplished, failed for the most part to understand the nature of their accomplishments. Christopher Columbus, on his first two voyages, believed that he had found a new westward route by sea to Asia. Only later did he conclude that he had found an unknown land, which he vaguely placed in the southeastern approaches to Asia. Nonetheless, his voyages to the New World opened the way to major historical changes. His reported discovery of America in his journal reveals enthusiasm mingled with bewilderment, and seen in later context reveals once again how often in human history great originators fail to understand what in fact they have accomplished.

CHRISTOPHER COLUMBUS

JOURNAL *

MONDAY, 1ST OF OCTOBER

Course west, and 25 leagues made good, counted for the crew as 20 leagues. There was a heavy shower of rain. At dawn the Admiral's pilot made the distance from Hierro 578 leagues to the west. The reduced reckoning which the Admiral showed to the crew made it 584 leagues; but the truth which the Admiral observed and kept secret was 707.

TUESDAY, 2ND OF OCTOBER

Course west, and during the day and night 39 leagues were made good, counted for the crew as 30. The sea always smooth. Many thanks be given to God, says the Admiral, that the weed is coming from east to west, contrary to its usual course. Many fish were seen, and one was killed. A white bird was also seen that appeared to be a gull.

WEDNESDAY, 3RD OF OCTOBER

They navigated on the usual course, and made good 47 leagues, counted as 40. Sandpipers appeared, and much weed, some of it very old and some quite fresh and having fruit. They saw no birds. The Admiral, therefore, thought that they had left the islands behind them which were depicted on the charts. The Admiral here says that he did not wish to keep the ships beating about

* Reprinted from the Journal of Christopher Columbus, pp. 31–38, edited by Clements R. Markham, London, The Hakluyt Society, 1893.

during the last week, and in the last few days when there were so many signs of land, although he had information of certain islands in this region. For he wished to avoid delay, his object being to reach the Indies. He says that to delay would not be wise.

THURSDAY, 4TH OF OCTOBER

Course west, and 63 leagues made good during the day and night, counted as 46. More than forty sandpipers came to the ship in a flock, and two boobies, and a ship's boy hit one with a stone. There also came a man-o'-war bird and a white bird like a gull.

FRIDAY, 5TH OF OCTOBER

The Admiral steered his course, going 11 miles an hour, and during the day and night they made good 57 leagues, as the wind increased somewhat during the night: 45 were counted. The sea was smooth and quiet. "To God", he says, "be many thanks given, the air being pleasant and temperate, with no weed, many sandpipers, and flying-fish coming on the deck in numbers."

SATURDAY, 6TH OF OCTOBER

The Admiral continued his west course, and during day and night they made good 40 leagues, 33 being counted. This night Martin Alonso said that it would be well to steer south of west, and it appeared to the Admiral that Martin Alonso did not say this with respect to the island of Cipango. He saw that if an error was made the land would not be reached so quickly, and that consequently it would be better to go at once to the continent and afterwards to the islands.

SUNDAY, 7TH OF OCTOBER

The west course was continued; for two hours they went at the rate of 12 miles an hour, and afterwards 8 miles an hour. They made good 23 leagues, counting 18 for the people. This day, at sunrise, the caravel *Niña,* which went ahead, being the best sailer, and pushed forward as much as possible to sight the land first, so as to enjoy the reward which the Sovereigns had promised to whoever should see it first, hoisted a flag at the mast-head and fired a gun, as a signal that she had sighted land, for such was the Admiral's order. He had also ordered that, at sunrise and sunset, all the ships should join him; because those two times are most proper for seeing the greatest distance, the haze clearing away. No land was seen during the afternoon, as reported by the caravel *Niña,* and they passed a great number of birds flying from N. to S.W. This gave rise to the belief that the birds were either going to sleep on land, or were flying from the winter which might be supposed to be near in the land whence they were coming. The Admiral was aware that most of the islands held by the Portuguese were discovered by the flight of birds. For this reason he resolved to give up the west course, and to shape a course W.S.W. for the two following days. He began the new course one hour before sunset. They made good, during the night, about 5 leagues, and 23 in the day, altogether 28 leagues.

MONDAY, 8TH OF OCTOBER

The course was W.S.W., and 11½ or 12 leagues were made good in the day and night; and at times it appears that they went at the rate of 15 miles an hour during the night (if the handwriting is not deceptive).[1] The sea was like the river at Seville. "Thanks be to God", says the Admiral, "the air is very soft like the April at Seville; and it is a pleasure to be here, so balmy are the breezes." The weed seemed to be very fresh. There were many land-birds, and they took one that was flying to the S.W. Terns, ducks, and a booby were also seen.

TUESDAY, 9TH OF OCTOBER

The course was S.W., and they made 5 leagues. The wind then changed, and the Admiral steered W. by N. 4 leagues. Altogether, in day and night, they made 11

[1] The parenthesis is by Las Casas.

leagues by day and 20½ leagues by night; counted as 17 leagues altogether. Throughout the night birds were heard passing.

WEDNESDAY, 10TH OF OCTOBER

The course was W.S.W., and they went at the rate of 10 miles an hour, occasionally 12 miles, and sometimes 7. During the day and night they made 59 leagues, counted as no more than 44. Here the people could endure no longer. They complained of the length of the voyage. But the Admiral cheered them up in the best way he could, giving them good hopes of the advantages they might gain from it. He added that, however much they might complain, he had to go to the Indies, and that he would go on until he found them, with the help of our Lord.

THURSDAY, 11TH OF OCTOBER

The course was W.S.W., and there was more sea than there had been during the whole of the voyage. They saw sandpipers, and a green reed near the ship. Those of the caravel *Pinta* saw a cane and a pole, and they took up another small pole which appeared to have been worked with iron; also another bit of cane, a land-plant, and a small board. The crew of the caravel *Niña* also saw signs of land, and a small branch covered with berries. Everyone breathed afresh and rejoiced at these signs. The run until sunset was 26 leagues.

After sunset the Admiral returned to his original west course, and they went along at the rate of 12 miles an hour. Up to two hours after midnight they had gone 90 miles, equal to 22½ leagues. As the caravel *Pinta* was a better sailer, and went ahead of the Admiral, she found the land, and made the signals ordered by the Admiral. The land was first seen by a sailor named Rodrigo de Triana. But the Admiral, at ten in the previous night, being on the castle of the poop, saw a light, though it was so uncertain that he could not affirm it was land. He called Pero Gutierrez, a gentleman of the King's bedchamber, and said that there seemed to be a light, and that he should look at it. He did so, and saw it. The Admiral said the same to Rodrigo Sanchez of Segovia, whom the King and Queen had sent with the fleet as inspector, but he could see nothing, because he was not in a place whence anything could be seen. After the Admiral had spoken he saw the light once or twice, and it was like a wax candle rising and falling. It seemed to few to be an indication of land; but the Admiral made certain that land was close. When they said the *Salve,* which all the sailors were accustomed to sing in their way, the Admiral asked and admonished the men to keep a good look-out on the forecastle, and to watch well for land; and to him who should first cry out that he saw land, he would give a silk doublet, besides the other rewards promised by the Sovereigns, which were 10,000 maravedis to him who should first see it. At two hours after midnight the land was sighted at a distance of two leagues. They shortened sail, and lay by under the mainsail without the bonnets. The vessels were hove to, waiting for daylight; and on Friday they arrived at a small island of the Lucayos, called, in the language of the Indians, *Guanahani.* Presently they saw naked people. The Admiral went on shore in the armed boat, and Martin Alonso Pinzon, and Vicente Yañez, his brother, who was captain of the *Niña.* The Admiral took the royal standard, and the captains went with two banners of the green cross, which the Admiral took in all the ships as a sign, with an F and a Y [2] and a crown over each letter, one on one side of the cross and the other on the other. Having landed, they saw trees very green, and much water, and fruits of diverse kinds. The Admiral called to the two captains, and to the others who leaped on shore, and to Rodrigo Escovedo, secretary of the whole fleet, and to Rodrigo Sanchez of Segovia, and said that they should bear faithful testimony that he, in presence of all, had taken, as he now took, possession of the

[2] Fernando and Ysabel.

said island for the King and for the Queen, his Lords making the declarations that are required, as is more largely set forth in the testimonies which were then made in writing.

Presently many inhabitants of the island assembled. What follows is in the actual words of the Admiral in his book of the first navigation and discovery of the Indies. "I," he says, "that we might form great friendship, for I knew that they were a people who could be more easily freed and converted to our holy faith by love than by force, gave to some of them red caps, and glass beads to put round their necks, and many other things of little value, which gave them great pleasure, and made them so much our friends that it was a marvel to see. They afterwards came to the ship's boats where we were, swimming and bring us parrots, cotton threads in skeins, darts, and many other things; and we exchanged them for other things that we gave them, such as glass beads and small bells. In fine, they took all, and gave what they had with good will. It appeared to me to be a race of people very poor in everything. They go as naked as when their mothers bore them, and so do the women, although I did not see more than one young girl. All I saw were youths, none more than thirty years of age. They are very well made, with very handsome bodies, and very good countenances. Their hair is short and coarse, almost like the hairs of a horse's tail. They wear the hairs brought down to the eyebrows, except a few locks behind, which they wear long and never cut. They paint themselves black, and they are the colour of the Canarians, neither black nor white. Some paint themselves white, others red, and others of what colour they find. Some paint their faces, others the whole body, some only round the eyes, others only on the nose. They neither carry nor know anything of arms, for I showed them swords, and they took them by the blade and cut themselves through ignorance. They have no iron, their darts being wands without iron, some of them having a fish's tooth at the end, and others being pointed in various ways. They are all of fair stature and size, with good faces, and well made. I saw some with marks of wounds on their bodies, and I made signs to ask what it was, and they gave me to understand that people from other adjacent islands came with the intention of seizing them, and that they defended themselves. I believed, and still believe, that they come here from the mainland to take them prisoners. They should be good servants and intelligent, for I observed that they quickly took in what was said to them, and I believe that they would easily be made Christians, as it appeared to me that they had no religion. I, our Lord being pleased, will take hence, at the time of my departure, six natives for your Highnesses, that they may learn to speak. I saw no beast of any kind except parrots, on this island." The above is in the words of the Admiral.

V

THE AGE OF THE REFORMATION

PART FIVE

⁂ THE AGE OF THE REFORMATION

In the Age of the Reformation, roughly from about 1500 to about 1650, religious controversy divided Europe and became the most central political issue. The Protestant Reformation, or Revolt, took the greater part of northern Europe out of the Church of Rome, and the breakup of the Western Church signalized the end of the Middle Ages. The Counter Reformation, or Catholic Reformation, attempted with limited success to regain these defected areas. But it had spent most of its force by the middle of the seventeenth century, when secular rivalries largely replaced religious divisions during and after the Thirty Years War (1618–48).

The causes of the Protestant Revolt were multiple and complex, and led to new situations which are by no means easy to delineate. Its immediate cause was the 95 Theses of Luther, which received widespread political support in the German states. Other religious reformers arose, among them Calvin, who brought conceptual depth and strength to a dissenting movement in danger of fragmentation. On the other hand, some of the intellectual elite, including Erasmus and the followers of Loyola in the Jesuit order, rallied to support the Church of Rome. Europe's religious controversies led to frightful civil disorder in many areas, among them France, the Netherlands, and some German states. But in England the statecraft of Elizabeth I preserved political peace. Other major phenomena entered the fast-shifting field of forces within Europe. During the sixteenth and early seventeenth centuries Europe made increasing contact with Asia, unlike the slight and transitory contact after the Mongol conquests of the thirteenth century. Increasingly the impact of Asiatic trade and institutions became a vital part of Western civilization.

TWENTY-THREE

CAUSES OF THE REFORMATION

Like other major historical movements, the Protestant Reformation, sometimes called the Protestant Revolt, has been the subject of heated controversy. Protestant and Catholic historians generally agree that considerable corruption existed in the late medieval Church. But they often disagree about the extent of the corruption and its effectiveness as a historical cause. In addition, disagreement exists about the nature of the Reformation itself. Some historians have insisted that it was primarily a religious movement. Others have emphasized its political aspect, for, with the exception of Scotland, it succeeded only in states where it received the support of the ruler. In analyzing the causes of the Reformation, Vivian H. H. Green has stressed corruption in the Church as an effective factor. But Green also insists that political forces were at work, mainly in the rise of the strong state, which finally ended its long medieval struggle with the Church by successful revolt. In addition, Green shows that certain phenomena associated with the Renaissance in northern Europe, among them Biblical scholarship and the printing press, were contributory factors, although in some respects, the Reformation, as a religious revival, ran counter to the secularism of the Renaissance. Green's summation represents the best of recent historical analysis of this complex and many-sided movement which has so strongly affected Western civilization that many scholars regard it as the proper beginning of the modern world.

VIVIAN H. H. GREEN

RENAISSANCE AND REFORMATION *

The Reformation occurred in the second and third decades of the sixteenth century because a certain set of circumstances created a situation which made its outbreak both possible and probable. Many of the factors which gave rise to the Reformation were not new nor was there any one cause which brought it into being. It was the particular correlation of events which produced a situation in which the teaching of the reformers met with an active response. But the reformers did not cause the Reformation; they were the instruments through which it was expressed. They were interpreting an obscurely-felt need in convincing popular terms. If there had been no necessity for their teaching, they would certainly have elicited a much less striking response. But the impact of men like Luther, Calvin and Zwingli cannot be properly measured; their particular cast of mind, profound emotions and established ideas all helped the Reformation as a movement to take the path it did, and to shatter the unity of Christendom. At the same time the reformers were responding to a widespread discontent with contemporary religion.

This dissatisfaction with the existing state of the Church had two aspects, firstly discontent with the Church as an institution and secondly a desire to return to a more satisfying personal religion, based more closely on the Gospel story than was that of the contemporary Church. Throughout the Middle Ages good churchmen had ventilated complaints about abuses and corruption. No one criticised the Church of his day more fiercely than did Erasmus but he died a Catholic. Dissatisfaction was in time to evoke the religious revival within the Roman Church which we call the Counter-Reformation. Similarly the desire to return to a simpler form of religion, in which there was less dependence on the mediatory powers of the priest and greater emphasis on the personal religion of the individual, had been a constant factor throughout Church history.[1] If, however, these two underlying issues had been present in the Middle Ages, the situation at the end of the fifteenth and the beginning of the sixteenth century was definitely propitious for a religious revolution.

What in fact made the situation in 1500 so different, say, from what it had been in 1400 and 1200? It is impossible to escape the conclusion that the Church was more corrupt, especially in respect of its higher officials, at that time than at any period of history since the tenth century (when circumstances being different there was no question of a Protestant Reformation, though there was Hildebrandine reform). It may be true that neither the nepotist Sixtus IV, the libertine Alexander VI, nor the soldier Julius II, were quite as bad as they have been made out to be by certain historians, but no one can deny that Sixtus IV showered benefices

* From *Renaissance and Reformation,* pp. 111–18, by Vivian H. H. Green. Reprinted by permission of Edward Arnold (Publishers) Ltd., London, 1952.

[1] Such is the theme of the two splendid volumes of Ernst Troeltsch, *The Social Teaching of the Christian Church.*

and offices on his family,[2] that Alexander VI had a mistress, Rosa Vanozza, and children whose careers he forwarded unscrupulously, or that Julius II was more interested in the expansion of the papal dominions than in the reform of the Church or that Leo X was at heart a charming, cultured but secular-minded gentleman. And none of these things should have characterised the *servus servorum,* the successor of St. Peter. The Pope had made himself into an Italian prince, much more concerned with the expansion of the temporal power of the Papacy than with the interests of the universal Church. 'Papal history', wrote the American historian H. C. Lea, 'after the Holy See had vindicated its supremacy over General Councils, becomes purely a political history of diplomatic intrigues, of alliances made and broken, of military enterprises. . . . No one could conclude that the Papacy represented interests higher than those of any other petty Italian Prince, save when—in a papal letter—an unctuous expression is used to shroud some peculiarly objectionable design.' To the fulfilment of such a policy as this the Popes devoted great ability—for these men were often intelligent and shrewd—and much money which they had amassed from the faithful throughout Europe. The pilgrim visiting Rome could not fail to be dismayed by the lack of spirituality, impressed as he might be by the magnificence of the papal court.

This rot had spread throughout the Church. Impartial evidence, much of it culled from episcopal visitations, is appallingly plentiful, as to simony, nepotism, plurality,[3] non-residence, immorality and neglect of duty. Although council after council had attacked these faults they were widespread throughout the fifteenth-century Church. The Conclave of the Sacred College of Cardinals which elected the Pope was as open to bribes as the Electoral College of the Empire. Moreover the unwillingness of the authorities to do anything to arrest the decay was another indication of how low the Curia had fallen. With the exception of some Spanish and English bishops, the European episcopate was gravely at fault. One small country provides an illustration the like of which could be found throughout Europe. There were six dioceses in Switzerland: Sion, Lausanne, Geneva, Constance, Chur and Basle. Cardinal Matthias Schinner, Bishop of Sion, an extremely able man who was nearly elected pope in 1521, was a statesman and warrior who delighted to lead the Swiss mercenaries into battle; political feuds had, however, made it impossible for him to live in his diocese in the Valais.[4] The Bishop of Geneva, John of Savoy, was a bastard of the ducal house placed in the see to serve his family's interests. The Bishop of Lausanne, Aymo of Montfaucon, was a servile tool of the French. Paul Ziegler, Bishop of Chur, 'chose his mistresses from the nunneries of his diocese' while his colleague of Constance, Hugo of Hohenlanden-

[2] Thus Sixtus was almost certainly aware of the plot engineered by his nephew Girolamo Riario in 1478 which resulted in the murder of Guiliano de' Medici and the wounding of his brother while at Mass. The Pope's support of the whole iniquitous business reveals the depth to which such nepotism could sink.

[3] There are innumerable illustrations, but note the following account (*Cambridge Modern History,* I, 659): 'Rodrigo Borgia (subsequently Cardinal) in his youth . . . accumulated benefices to the aggregate of 70,000 ducats a year. Guiliano della Rovere (Julius II) likewise owed his cardinalate to his uncle, Sixtus IV, who bestowed on him also the archbishopric of Avignon and the bishoprics of Bologna, Lausanne, Coutances, Viviers, Mende, Ostia, and Velletri, with the abbeys of Nonantola and Grottaferrate.' Cf. Jean of Lorraine who became coadjutor-bishop of Metz at the age of three (1501), was later Bishop of Toul (1517), of Terouanne (1518), Cardinal, of Valence and Die (1521), Verdun (1523), Archbishop of Narbonne (1524), Rheims (1533) and Lyons (1537), Bishop of Albi, Macon (1536), Agen (1541) and of Nantes (1542). This much-mitred prelate, who lived in such great state that he was always poor, also enjoyed the revenues of no less than nine abbeys.

[4] 'He was as cunning and as obstinate as a peasant', commented Gonzague de Reynold, 'Often he forgot those who had helped and served him; but he drove every slight into his memory, as one drives a rivet into steel plate. . . . He never let himself be beaten. He was ever for renown, and for profit; coming of a poor race, he knew the value of gold, and he was sustained until the day of his death by that one great thought.'

berg, 'derived a rich income from the concubinage practised by his priests, raising the penalty payable for every priest's child from four gulden to five'. Alone among the Swiss bishops, Christopher von Uttenheim, the Bishop of Basle, was genuinely trying to repair the abuses which rent church life in his diocese.[5] And this account may be regarded as a sample of the state of the Church throughout Europe. Such secularisation had also penetrated deeply into the lives of the lower clergy.

But perhaps these ranker and more dramatic vices were less dangerous to the Church than the apathy and indifference which characterised the lives of so many priests, both secular and religious. That a canon of Notre Dame should have turned his house into a gambling den was doubtless highly reprehensible, but that hundreds of men were being ordained or entering monasteries, which, like Erasmus, they often loathed, without any vocation, was a much more significant fact. The evidence certainly suggests that the number of monks was—proportionate to the population—less than it had once been. With certain exceptions, among them the Austrian abbey of Melk,[6] monasteries were too often affected by what medieval moralists called *acedia,* a boredom with religious duty; there were also a neglect of masses, an unauthorized use of private property, in fine an attitude to life which found expression in harmless (and not always so harmless) secular activity.

[5] Some idea of what he was trying to do may be gauged from the following warning to his clergy 'not to curl their hair with curling-tongs, nor to carry on trade in the churches, or to raise a disturbance there, not to keep drinking-booths or engage in horse-dealing, and not to buy stolen property'.

[6] It is perhaps important to point out that some monasteries had been reformed in the fifteenth century. Thus the Bursfeld Union or Congregation, so-called because it was initiated by Abbot Dederoth of Bursfeld near Gottingen, had led to a higher standard of life in the many monasteries which made up the Congregation, often in spite of opposition. The Windesheim Congregation did similar work in the Low Countries, and its example was followed by a number of French Benedictine houses.

Had there been a deterioration in the religious life of the laity as well as that of the clergy? This question is difficult to answer, simply because the quality of religious life in the Middle Ages was so different from that of the twentieth century. Certainly church-building showed little sign of diminution; England at least is rich with churches dating from the end of the fifteenth century. But there are a number of points which suggest cumulatively that religious life was lacking in balance. Adoration of the saints and of the Blessed Virgin had greatly increased. Masses, later abolished by the Church, had been instituted in honour of every detail of the Blessed Virgin's life, of her piety, of her seven sorrows, of her sisters and so on. The Mass had become for many a superstitious ceremony, a miracle without moral significance. In general, superstition increased rather than declined in the fifteenth century. Although the incomes of the great shrines, like those of St. Thomas of Canterbury and St. James of Compostella [7] grew less, relic-worship continued unabated. Louis XI, whose callous and cruel nature cannot be denied, was peculiarly superstitious. Frightened by the idea of dying, he had the world searched for the relics of saints who might yet save his life. 'He also', says the chronicler, 'sent for a great number of male and female bigots and devout people like hermits and saintly creatures, to pray God incessantly to allow that he should not die and that He might let him live longer'. Venice, careless of papal interdicts, was willing to offer ten thousand ducats for the so-called seamless coat of Christ in 1455 but the bid was insufficient. Cardinal Pierre d'Ailly criticised the increasing number of saints' days and the prolixity of church services. Pilgrimages continued but had more and more the appearance of a 'bank-holiday' outing; people went on them for 'folle plaisance'. The Burgundian, Chastellain, writing

[7] At Santiago in Spain, elevated by Pope Sixtus IV to the same rank as the Holy Places of Palestine.

in the fifteenth century, describes to what depths the once solemn procession, carrying the relics of St. Lievin from St. Bavon-le-Gand to the village of Houthem and back, had sunk. Where once there had been 'great and deep solemnity and reverence' there was now (in 1466) 'a mob of roughs, and boys of bad character', shouting and bawling 'and all are drunk'. Nearly eighty years later Charles V suppressed this pilgrimage which an anti-Lutheran cleric described as 'almost a mahometry and idolatry'. 'It was a pilgrimage', he wrote, 'rather of malediction than of devotion, wherein ten thousand mortal sins were yearly wrought, what with drunkenness and quarrels, homicides and lechery, blasphemies, execrable oaths, and other great and enormous sins and wickedness.' In some instances the sacraments of the Church could be bought for money. There was a growing interest in black magic, often a sign of a diseased society.[8]

In general, religion seems to have become more mechanistic and materialistic than it had once been. There was what may be called a 'penny-in-the-slot' attitude towards the Mass. Anecdotes and wills show clearly enough that many laymen believed that they could make their Eucharistic prayers more efficacious simply by multiplying them. To multiply candles or prayers was another way of increasing the soul's chance of salvation. Thus a layman was entitled to join a Cologne society by an annual subscription of 11,000 *Paternosters* and *Ave Marias*. The popularity of indulgences was yet another indication of the people's attitude towards religion. The indulgence system had originated at the time of the Crusades as a means by which a man could compensate for his inability to go on Crusade and yet gain the promised pardon for sin by a money payment to the Church. Theologically this rested, as the papal bull, *Unigenitus,* published in 1343, showed, on the belief that the merit represented by Christ's sacrifice exceeded what was needed for the redemption of the whole human race; as a result this superfluous merit [9] constituted a treasure placed in the hands of the Church. 'Now this treasure is not hidden in a napkin . . . but he entrusted it to be healthfully dispensed—through blessed Peter, bearer of heaven's keys, and his successors as vicars on earth—to the faithful, for fitting and reasonable causes, now for total, now for partial remission of punishment due for temporal sins, as well generally as specially (as they should understand it to be expedient with God), and to be applied in mercy to them that are truly penitent and have confessed.' Less and less emphasis was placed on the penitence involved in an indulgence and more and more on the mechanical pardon which the payment of money secured. Religion was thus pervaded by material and mechanical forms. There were, for instance, statuettes of the Virgin Mary which opened and disclosed the Trinity seated within.

All this represented a coarsening, often accompanied by anti-clericalism and profanation of religious things. People never seemed to weary of hearing attacks on dissolute monks and guzzling friars; the famous *Narrenschiff* (Ship of Fools) written by Sebastian Brandt was only one of many similar attacks on the monastic order. Resentment against the sacramental and jurisdictional powers of the clergy, exerted through a whole series of Church courts and unpopular officers as well as through the Mass and the Confessional, was very general throughout Europe. The Church had gained its mastery over the masses but seemed to have lost its mastery over its own soul. Some of these things, as many faithful Catholics recognised, could be, and later were, righted without a Reformation, but, and the point is significant, there was not much sign of this at the beginning of the sixteenth century.

[8] The extraordinary outbreak at Arras in 1460 is graphically described in Dr. Cartellieri's chapter 'La Vauderie d' Arras' in his *Court of Burgundy,* 194 ff.

[9] To which had been added 'the merits of the blessed Mother of God and of all the elect, from the first just man to the last . . . and no diminution or washing away of this treasure is in any way to be feared'.

This feeling had already led to some sort of return to a simpler and more personal religion. The popularity of the mystical writings of Tauler and Denis Ruysbroeck or of a simple devotional work like the *Imitation of Christ* reflected current dissatisfaction with the more formal side of religion and the desire to push behind the ceremonial façade to spiritual reality. Not every one could achieve, let alone pierce, the Dark Night of the Soul, but a more devotional teaching conveyed a more personal and simpler view of religion. But so far there was nothing to suggest that this might lead to a revolution in the actual teaching of the Church. That was why Luther's reaction was to be so epochal. He not only found the spiritual life of the Church inadequate but bull-like he blundered into the conclusion that the doctrine on which it was based was partly untrue.

Yet if the Reformation was primarily religious—and the contention is certainly controversial—it was assisted, indeed largely made possible, by secular developments. The rise of strong national monarchies made it certain that the State would do what it could to lessen the amount of papal interference in its internal affairs, to reduce papal control over church appointments, to break the Church's monopoly of education and to cut off the payment of money which was draining the country of its gold according to contemporary economic opinion. In particular the Papacy's intelligent exploitation of every possible source of revenue—annates, tithes, sales of dispensations and offices, indulgences, absolutions—aroused the jealous wrath of the national monarch. The Pope maintained his power in foreign countries by means of nuncios and legates who upheld his interests; he possessed a considerable appellate jurisdiction as well as immense patronage. A clash between the universal power of the Pope and the national authority of the monarch was clearly inevitable. For the past two centuries there had been a growing challenge to the Church's interpretation of her claim to universal dominion; as early as the fourteenth century the Roman lawyer, Bartolo of Sassoferrato, had remarked 'Rex in regno suo est imperator regni sui'. But whereas the Kings of France and Spain found that they could make arrangements with the Pope to suit their own interests, the Kings of Sweden and England found that a denial of papal authority was almost a corollary of the maintenance and extension of their regal power. In this step they were largely supported everywhere by a middle class, gaining in influence and confidence, individualistic enough to dislike the mediatory authority of the priest and avid of church property.

Finally the Renaissance had led to changes which favoured a Reformation. In Northern Europe it had a specifically Christian character. Through the detailed study of the Greek text of the New Testament, and the increasing availability of Bibles, brought about by the invention of printing, thoughtful men found that much that was typical of the contemporary Church had little support in the Gospels; there was, as one man put it, 'little about the Pope but much about Christ'. The study of the Greek text led to a more pronounced emphasis on the literal text of the Bible, as opposed to the allegorical and other methods of interpretation popular in the Middle Ages. Moreover the new translations of the Bible into the vernacular sometimes made significant alterations in the sense of the text; it is difficult to over-stress the importance of a translation which, for instance, replaced bishop (Gk. *episkopos*) and priest (Gk. *presbuteros*) by superintendent and elder, or church (*Gk. ekklesia* or Lat. *ecclesia*) by congregation, or to do penance (Gk. *metanoein* or Lat. *facere poenitentiam*) by to change one's attitude. Nor can the destructive criticism of Valla and Erasmus have passed unnoticed. The acid sarcasm which permeates Ulrich von Hutten's attack on the schoolmen, the *Epistolae Obscurorum Virorum* (1514), was a sign of the bitterness with which some of the humanists regarded the Church and its teaching. Although Luther was not himself a humanist, some of his followers, including the Greek scholar Melanchthon, were. Both Zwingli and Calvin owed much initially to the classical teaching of the Renaissance.

But the Reformation was as much a reaction from as a result of the Renaissance. In the reformers' philosophy of life, St. Paul and St. Augustine counted for more than Aristotle and Plato. The Puritan streak in medieval catholicism, which was so characteristic of Savonarola's bonfire of vanities,[10] reappeared more strongly than before in the teaching of the reformers, in their emphasis on sobriety and decency, on the strict observance of Sunday, in their attacks on Church finery and ceremonial. To some at least the Renaissance in Italy must have seemed paganism in disguise. In some ways the conservatism rather than the radicalism of the reformers' teaching is the more significant.

These factors taken together brought a religious and political revolution which shattered the unity of medieval Europe and helped to create the modern state and the modern Church. But there had to be a leader to act as the outward and visible expression of an inward and spiritual discontent. And the hour had such a man in Martin Luther.

[10] Many works of art and other treasures were piled on to this flaming pyre (last day of the Carnival at Florence, 1497). See Burckhardt, *Civilization of the Renaissance,* 252. Cf. Savonarola's opinion: 'An old woman knows more about the Faith than Plato.'

TWENTY-FOUR

MARTIN LUTHER

Martin Luther (1483–1546) was the pivotal figure in the early stages of the Protestant Revolt. The publication in 1517 of his 95 Theses, which attacked indulgences, led in short order to the breaking away of most north German states from the Church of Rome. Luther, an Augustinian friar and professor at the University of Wittenberg, was a devout and learned man. Once he had made his original dissenting step in 1517, his active and bold mind took him further and further from Catholic orthodoxy. In 1517 he was primarily concerned with reform of the Church. But particularly, as he developed his belief in justification by faith alone instead of by good works, he found himself in disagreement with much Catholic doctrine and practice. What began as reform within the Church ended as revolt against it. Luther remains a highly controversial figure, difficult to understand and to assess. Professor Harbison has analyzed with particularly clear insight the often complex development of Luther's thought.

E. HARRIS HARBISON

THE AGE OF THE REFORMATION*

The immediate origins of the Protestant Reformation lay in the religious experience of Martin Luther (1483–1546). We will never know precisely what happened to Luther in the years between his becoming a monk in 1505 and his dramatic attack on indulgences in 1517. But we know from his contemporary lecture notes and from his later writings and conversations with friends that he underwent years of harrowing emotional and intellectual tension which finally resulted in a "conversion" experience sometime during these years. The nature of this experience was to determine the main features of Protestant belief and the direction which the Protestant movement took. It is important, therefore—difficult as it is—to sketch briefly the inner struggles of this obscure Augustinian friar and their outcome.

SALVATION BY FAITH

Outwardly, young Martin Luther was one of the most pious and diligent monks in the friary at Erfurt. "If ever a monk got to heaven by his monkery," he wrote twenty years later, "I should certainly have got there." But he was haunted from the beginning by doubts about whether he, a mere man and a sinner, could ever satisfy a righteous God. In spite of fastings, scourgings, and prayer beyond the rule, he could gain no sense of being forgiven. Doubt aroused fear, and fear led to moments of panic and despair. Staupitz, the kindly vicar of the order, could not understand this sensi-

* Reprinted from *The Age of the Reformation*, pp. 47–55, by E. Harris Harbison. Copyright 1955 by Cornell University. Used by permission of Cornell University Press.

tive and intelligent younger brother who was constantly confessing his minor sins and yet could never quite rid himself of the sense of guilt.

Scholars differ in explaining Luther's predicament. Perhaps his conception of God as a stern and righteous Judge owed something to the character of his father, a hardworking peasant and miner, devoted to his son's welfare but strict and demanding. Perhaps it owed something to stern representations of God in either sculpture or story impressed upon him at an early age. He had taken the vow to become a monk in a moment of panic during a thunderstorm, and the fact that he immediately regretted it but went through with it may have contributed to his later tension. Luther was a high-strung person with keen sensibilities and a sensitive conscience, not the kind to persuade himself easily that he was doing the best he could and that the rest might be left to God (as his spiritual advisers urged). The theological school which dominated the teaching at the University of Erfurt where he had studied put strong emphasis on what were called "good works," a term which included sacramental and ceremonial acts (such as doing penance, fasting, going on a pilgrimage, entering a monastery) as well as acts of charity. The kernel of this teaching was that man through his own effort and will has a large share in determining his ultimate salvation or damnation. In effect, Luther was acting on this teaching, but failing miserably to gain any inner assurance of forgiveness and so of the promise of salvation.

Then something happened. In 1511 Staupitz had seen that Luther was appointed Professor of Bible at the new University of Wittenberg, and for a year or more the thirty-year-old professor had been soaking himself in Scripture. The influence of his friends and his reading began to suggest a solution to his soul's plight. As he remembered it later, it all happened suddenly (some scholars think in the winter of 1512–1513) in the tower room of the Augustinian friary at Wittenberg where he lived, perhaps while he was writing notes for his lectures on the Psalms (which scholars rediscovered only a half-century ago). Here is his own account, written 1545, of his attempt to probe St. Paul's meaning in Romans 1:17:

> After I had pondered the problem for days and nights, God took pity on me and I saw the inner connection between the two phrases, "The justice of God is revealed in the Gospel" and "The just shall live by faith." I began to understand that this "justice of God" is the righteousness by which the just man lives through the free gift of God, that is to say "by faith." . . . Thereupon I felt as if I had been born again and had entered Paradise through wide-open gates. Immediately the whole of Scripture took on a new meaning for me. I raced through the Scriptures, so far as my memory went, and found analogies in other expressions.[1]

Luther felt he had rediscovered the meaning of St. Paul's conviction that a Christian is saved not by moral or ceremonial "works," but by his faith in the loving and merciful Father who incarnated Himself in Jesus Christ in order to save men. This faith is a "free gift of God." Salvation cannot be deserved or merited, then; it cannot be bought or bargained for by the doing of good works —by fastings and prayer, penances and pilgrimages, or even by becoming a monk. No man can fulfill God's requirements and thus become righteous because all men are sinners, but God counts man's faith (which is His own free gift to man) as the equivalent of righteousness. Luther had tried and failed to merit forgiveness and salvation. At the moment of blackest despair he realized that in the saving of souls literally everything is God's work and nothing is man's. Salvation is the free gift of a loving God to undeserving man.

[1] Preface to Luther's Collected Works 1545, trans. by E. Harris Harbison in Kenneth M. Setton and Henry R. Winkler, eds., *Great Problems in European Civilization* (New York: Prentice-Hall, Inc., 1954), pp. 252–253.

Scripture and Conscience

Luther was not a systematic or logical thinker. Rather, his thinking was existential, that is, it developed out of his own personal experience and the decisions he had to make in living out his own life. If he had been more logically inclined, he might have concluded immediately that if a Christian is saved by his faith alone, then the whole mediaeval church, with its sacraments and ceremonies, its papacy and its priesthood, was really unnecessary. A man alone in his room with God and God's Word, the Bible, like Luther in his tower room—this would be the true picture of a Christian—not that of a man confessing his sins to a priest, traveling on a pilgrimage, or buying an indulgence to get his dead parents out of Purgatory. This was to be the heart of Protestant belief as it developed later: the Bible and a man's conscience are the channels through which God speaks to human beings, not the Roman Church and its sacraments. But it took personal contact with the practice of indulgences, and later the attacks of enemies, to make Luther realize the full implications of his own religious experience. And even to the end, he never broke with what he thought was the *true* Church of Christ and its sacraments.

The Mainz Indulgence of 1515 was a peculiarly lurid example of the connection between spiritual and financial abuses in the church. The pope proclaimed an indulgence ostensibly to raise money for the building of St. Peter's in Rome. Actually all but a very small percentage of the money raised found its way into the pockets of the Dominican monks who sold the coveted certificates to the people, of bankers who handled the receipts, and of a great ecclesiastical prince, Albert of Hohenzollern, who owed the pope a large bribe for the privilege of holding three bishoprics when the canon law said that no one might hold more than one. Luther, like the ordinary person, knew nothing of Albert's deal with the pope. He knew only that his students at the University of Wittenberg were flocking across the border of Saxony to buy indulgences in Magdeburg and returning to him convinced that their sins were forgiven. John Tetzel, a particularly unscrupulous Dominican, was preaching to the crowds that "so soon as coin in coffer rings, the soul from Purgatory springs." In indignation born of his own religious experience, Luther drafted 95 Theses attacking the current doctrine of indulgences. The most radical proposition was that "Any Christian whatever, who is truly repentant, enjoys full remission from penalty and guilt, and this is given him without letters of indulgence."

Luther probably had no intention of doing more than start an academic debate on his theses at the University of Wittenberg. But it became evident almost overnight that he had touched on the most sensitive nerve of the whole ecclesiastical organization of his day. The theses were published and devoured by Germans everywhere. The pent-up resentment against papal exactions and ecclesiastical abuses became polarized by his attack. The sale of indulgences fell off sharply, and the Dominicans demanded that Luther be curbed. Step by step, opponents who saw the doctrinal and financial dangers in Luther's criticisms forced him to work out the implications of his position. First he appealed to the pope, but the Medici Leo X was inclined to treat the whole matter as an unimportant quarrel between monks. When Leo's attitude became harder, he appealed from the pope to a general council. Finally a particularly skillful debater, Dr. John Eck, manoeuvred him into declaring that even a general council was fallible—which left him with Scripture and conscience as his only ultimate authorities. This became perfectly clear when he faced the emperor Charles V and the assembled Diet of the empire at Worms in 1521 and replied to the demand that he recant his views with words which were to become famous throughout Europe:

Unless I am convinced by the evidence of Scripture or by plain reason—for I do not accept the authority of the Pope or the councils alone, since it is established that they have often erred and contradicted themselves—I am bound by the Scriptures I have cited and my conscience is captive to the Word of God. I cannot and will not recant anything, for it is neither safe nor right to go against conscience. God help me. Amen.

Protestant Beliefs

Between 1520, when Luther wrote the tracts and pamphlets which are still the best expression of his religious ideas, and 1530, when the beliefs of the church he founded were summarized in the Augsburg Confession, the main lines of Protestant belief and practice were worked out by Luther himself and his lieutenants in Wittenberg, with some contributions from independent leaders of revolt against Rome such as Ulrich Zwingli in Zurich and Martin Bucer in Strasbourg.

The best general description of Protestantism [2] is still probably that of Ernst Troeltsch: "A modification of Catholicism, in which the Catholic formulation of problems was retained, while a different answer was given to them." In particular, Luther offered relatively new answers to four questions which go far back in Christian history. To the question how is a man to be saved, Luther answered: not by works but by faith. To the question where does religious authority lie, he answered: not in the visible institution known as the Roman Church, but in the "Word of God" contained in the Bible. To the question what is the church, he answered: the whole community of Christian believers, since all are really priests and since every man must be "a Christ to his neighbor." To the question what is the essence of Christian living, he replied: serving God in one's calling, whether secular or ecclesiastical, since all useful callings are equally sacred in the eyes of God. These were the four central Protestant beliefs, each closely related to the others: salvation by faith rather than by works, the authority of the Bible interpreted by the consecrated conscience, the priesthood of all believers, and the service of God in secular as well as clerical callings. All could be taken to follow from Luther's original experience of God's saving grace in the gift of faith.

To sixteenth-century followers of Luther, Protestantism was essentially a *restoration.* During the Middle Ages—so the theory ran—Christianity had become encrusted and overloaded with doctrines and practices which had nothing to do with its essence and which came close to obliterating the Gospel revealed to the early church. It was imperative to go back to Paul and the Gospels, back to the practices and insights of the Apostolic Age, in order to recapture Christian truth. The canon law and scholastic theology of recent centuries were satanic corruptions of the primitive Gospel. The bishop of Rome, far from representing Christ on earth, was the Anti-Christ prophesied in the Book of Revelation.

To sixteenth-century Catholics, Protestantism was essentially a *revolution.* To deny that Christ had founded his church on Peter and that the popes were Peter's successors, to question the divine institution of the seven sacraments, to say that all believers are equally priests, that all men are saved or damned by the arbitrary will of God with no respect to good works or merit—all this was either heresy or blasphemy to loyal sons of the mediaeval church. Luther, not Leo, was the Anti-Christ—the "wild boar" which was ravaging God's vineyards, in the words

[2] "Protestant" was a kind of nickname given to a group of Lutheran princes who presented a "protest" against repressive measures at an Imperial Diet in 1529. The name stuck and is generally applied today to all non-Catholic, non-Orthodox Christians, although it should perhaps be limited historically to the six major families of Protestant denominations: Lutheran, Anglican, Calvinist (Reformed or Presbyterian), Congregationalist, Baptist, and Methodist. This would exclude Unitarian groups. But it is impossible to be absolutely precise in use of the term. The quotation that follows is from *Protestantism and Progress* (New York, 1912), p. 59.

of the papal bull which excommunicated the heretic friar in 1520.

Today most historians refer to Protestantism as a *reformation.* In the ordinary sense of moral reform, Protestantism probably accomplished little. Nor did Luther think of his movement as aimed primarily at the improvement of clerical and lay morality. Protestantism is properly described, however, as a reforming or reformulating of the Christian tradition. In attempting to restore first-century Christianity, the early Protestants were inevitably revolutionists. In going back, they moved forward. And the result was that they gave a new shape to the Christian tradition in almost half of Europe.

TWENTY-FIVE

THE 95 THESES

The immediate cause of the Protestant Revolt came on October 31, 1517, when Martin Luther posted his famous 95 Theses, in Latin, on the door of the castle church in Wittenberg. The 95 Theses consist of vigorously stated theological propositions about indulgences. Posting of such propositions was a common medieval procedure, and by doing so Luther invited debate or comment from other scholars. But the results were uncommon. Within a few weeks his supporters had translated the Theses into German and had distributed printed copies of them throughout the German states. Luther objected to abuses connected with indulgences, papal remissions of penalties for sin, widely believed to be pardons. It was customary, and in practice obligatory, to make a "voluntary" contribution to get such remission, and peddlers of indulgences often made extravagant promises not sanctioned by canon law. Luther's central objection to indulgences was that they did not produce true repentance for sin. He also objected strongly to the financial corruption often associated with their distribution.

MARTIN LUTHER

THE 95 THESES *

Out of love and concern for the truth, and with the object of eliciting it, the following heads will be the subject of a public discussion at Wittenberg under the presidency of the reverend father, Martin Luther,[1] Augustinian, Master of Arts and Sacred Theology, and duly appointed Lecturer on these subjects in that place. He requests that whoever cannot be present personally to debate the matter orally will do so in absence in writing.[2]

* From *Reformation Writings of Martin Luther,* I, 32–43, translated by Bertram L. Woolf, by permission of Lutterworth Press, London. Copyright 1952 by Lutterworth Press.

[1] Luther spelled his name in various ways; the form used in the preamble to the *Theses* was Lutther.

1. When our Lord and Master, Jesus Christ, said "Repent",[3] He called for the entire life of believers to be one of penitence.

2. The word cannot be properly understood as referring to the sacrament of pen-

[2] Unfortunately, no one responded and there was no debate; but Luther preached that day in the Castle Church on the subject of Indulgences and Grace.

[3] This quotation from Matt. 4:17 was known throughout Europe in its Latin form: *poenitentiam agite.* Unfortunately, the phrase was capable of two meanings: repent; and, do penance. Although the two meanings were originally indistinguishable, the second became predominant, and, when taken alone, as only too frequently, opened the door to all the abuses against which Luther protested. The double meaning of the phrase is felt in many of the theses that follow, and sometimes occasions differences of translation.

ance, i.e., confession and satisfaction, as administered by the clergy.

3. Yet its meaning is not restricted to penitence in one's heart; for such penitence is null unless it produces outward signs in various mortifications of the flesh.

4. As long as hatred of self abides (i.e., true inward penitence) the penalty of sin abides, viz., until we enter the kingdom of heaven.

5. The pope has neither the will nor the power to remit any penalties beyond those imposed either at his own discretion or by canon law.

6. The pope himself cannot remit guilt, but only declare and confirm that it has been remitted by God; or, at most, he can remit it in cases reserved to his discretion. Except for these cases, the guilt remains untouched.

7. God never remits guilt to anyone without, at the same time, making him humbly submissive to the priest, His representative.

8. The penitential canons apply only to men who are still alive, and, according to the canons themselves, none applies to the dead.

9. Accordingly, the Holy Spirit, acting in the person of the pope, manifests grace to us, by the fact that the papal regulations always cease to apply at death, or in any hard case.

10. It is a wrongful act, due to ignorance, when priests retain the canonical penalties on the dead in purgatory.

11. When canonical penalties were changed and made to apply to purgatory, surely it would seem that tares were sown [4] while the bishops were asleep.

[4] Matt. 13:24ff.

12. In former days, the canonical penalties were imposed, not after, but before absolution was pronounced; and were intended to be tests of true contrition.

13. Death puts an end to all the claims of the church; even the dying are already dead to the canon laws, and are no longer bound by them.

14. Defective piety or love in a dying person is necessarily accompanied by great fear, which is greatest where the piety or love is least.

15. This fear or horror is sufficient in itself, whatever else might be said, to constitute the pain of purgatory, since it approaches very closely to the horror of despair.

16. There seems to be the same difference between hell, purgatory, and heaven as between despair, uncertainty, and assurance.

17. Of a truth, the pains of souls in purgatory ought to be abated, and charity ought to be proportionately increased.

18. Moreover, it does not seem proved, on any grounds of reason or Scripture, that these souls are outside the state of merit, or unable to grow in grace;

19. Nor does it seem proved to be always the case that they are certain and assured of salvation, even if we are very certain of it ourselves.

20. Therefore the pope, in speaking of the plenary remission of all penalties, does not mean "all" in the strict sense, but only those imposed by himself.

21. Hence those who preach indulgences are in error when they say that a man is absolved and saved from every penalty by the pope's indulgences;

22. Indeed, he cannot remit to souls in purgatory any penalty which canon law declares should be suffered in the present life.

23. If plenary remission could be granted to anyone at all, it would be only in the cases of the most perfect, i.e. to very few.

24. It must therefore be the case that the major part of the people are deceived by that indiscriminate and high-sounding promise of relief from penalty.

25. The same power as the pope exercises in general over purgatory is exercised in particular by every single bishop in his bishopric and priest in his parish.

(*The second series*)

1 (26). The pope does excellently when he grants remission to the souls in purgatory on account of intercessions made on their behalf, and not by the power of the keys (which he cannot exercise for them).

2 (27). There is no divine authority for preaching that the soul flies out of purgatory immediately the money clinks in the bottom of the chest.

3 (28). It is certainly possible that when the money clinks in the bottom of the chest avarice and greed increase; but when the church offers intercession, all depends on the will of God.

4 (29). Who knows whether all souls in purgatory wish to be redeemed in view of what is said of St. Severinus [5] and St. Paschal? [6]

5 (30). No one is sure of the reality of his own contrition, much less of receiving plenary forgiveness.

[5] Pope, 638–40, successor to Honorius I.

[6] Paschal I, pope 817–24. The legend is that he and Severinus were willing to endure the pains of purgatory for the benefit of the faithful.

6 (31). One who *bona fide* buys indulgences is as rare as a *bona fide* penitent man, i.e., very rare indeed.

7 (32). All those who believe themselves certain of their own salvation by means of letters of indulgence, will be eternally damned, together with their teachers.

8 (33). We should be most carefully on our guard against those who say that the papal indulgences are an inestimable divine gift, and that a man is reconciled to God by them.

9 (34). For the grace conveyed by these indulgences relates simply to the penalties of the sacramental "satisfactions" decreed merely by man.

10 (35). It is not in accordance with Christian doctrine to preach and teach that those who buy off souls, or purchase confessional licences, have no need to repent of their own sins.[7]

11 (36). Any Christian whatsoever, who is truly repentant, enjoys plenary remission from penalty and guilt, and this is given him without letters of indulgence.

12 (37). Any true Christian whatsoever, living or dead, participates in all the benefits of Christ and the Church; and this participation is granted to him by God without letters of indulgence.

13 (38). Yet the pope's remission and dispensation are in no way to be despised, for, as already said, they proclaim the divine remission.

14 (39). It is very difficult, even for the most learned theologians, to extol to the peo-

[7] This is what Tetzel appears to have preached; it appears also have had the support of Wimpina at the public debate on Indulgences at Frankfort-on-Oder, Jan. 20, 1518. It was not sound Roman doctrine according to Grisar, *Luther,* I, 344.

ple the great bounty contained in the indulgences, while, at the same time, praising contrition as a virtue.

15 (40). A truly contrite sinner seeks out, and loves to pay, the penalties of his sins; whereas the very multitude of indulgences dulls men's consciences, and tends to make them hate the penalties.

16 (41). Papal indulgences should only be preached with caution, lest people gain a wrong understanding, and think that they are preferable to other good works: those of love.

17 (42). Christians should be taught that the pope does not at all intend that the purchase of indulgences should be understood as at all comparable with works of mercy.

18 (43). Christians should be taught that one who gives to the poor, or lends to the needy, does a better action than if he purchases indulgences;

19 (44). Because, by works of love, love grows and a man becomes a better man; whereas, by indulgences, he does not become a better man, but only escapes certain penalties.

20 (45). Christians should be taught that he who sees a needy person, but passes him by although he gives money for indulgences, gains no benefit from the pope's pardon, but only incurs the wrath of God.

21 (46). Christians should be taught that, unless they have more than they need, they are bound to retain what is necessary for the upkeep of their home, and should in no way squander it on indulgences.

22 (47). Christians should be taught that they purchase indulgences voluntarily, and are not under obligation to do so.

23 (48). Christians should be taught that, in granting indulgences, the pope has more need, and more desire, for devout prayer on his own behalf than for ready money.

24 (49). Christians should be taught that the pope's indulgences are useful only if one does not rely on them, but most harmful if one loses the fear of God through them.

25 (50). Christians should be taught that, if the pope knew the exactions of the indulgence-preachers, he would rather the church of St. Peter were reduced to ashes than be built with the skin, flesh, and bones of his sheep.

(*The third series*)

1 (51). Christians should be taught that the pope would be willing, as he ought if necessity should arise, to sell the church of St. Peter, and give, too, his own money to many of those from whom the pardon-merchants conjure money.

2 (52). It is vain to rely on salvation by letters of indulgence, even if the commissary, or indeed the pope himself, were to pledge his own soul for their validity.

3 (53). Those are enemies of Christ and the pope who forbid the word of God to be preached at all in some churches, in order that indulgences may be preached in others.

4 (54). The word of God suffers injury if, in the same sermon, an equal or longer time is devoted to indulgences than to that word.

5 (55). The pope cannot help taking the view that if indulgences (very small matters) are celebrated by one bell, one pageant, or one ceremony, the gospel (a very great matter) should be preached to the accompaniment of a hundred bells, a hundred processions, a hundred ceremonies.

6 (56). The treasures of the church, out of which the pope dispenses indulgences, are not sufficiently spoken of or known among the people of Christ.

7 (57). That these treasures are not temporal is clear from the fact that many of the merchants do not grant them freely, but only collect them;

8 (58). Nor are they the merits of Christ and the saints, because, even apart from the pope, these merits are always working grace in the inner man, and working the cross, death, and hell in the outer man.

9 (59). St. Laurence said that the poor were the treasures of the church, but he used the term in accordance with the custom of his own time.

10 (60). We do not speak rashly in saying that the treasures of the church are the keys of the church, and are bestowed by the merits of Christ;

11 (61). For it is clear that the power of the pope suffices, by itself, for the remission of penalties and reserved cases.

12 (62). The true treasure of the church is the Holy Gospel of the glory and the grace of God.

13 (63). It is right to regard this treasure as most odious, for it makes the first to be the last.[8]

14 (64). On the other hand, the treasure of indulgences is most acceptable, for it makes the last to be the first.

15 (65). Therefore the treasures of the gospel are nets which, in former times, they used to fish for men of wealth.

16 (66). The treasures of the indulgences are the nets to-day which they use to fish for men of wealth.

17 (67). The indulgences, which the merchants extol as the greatest of favours, are seen to be, in fact, a favourite means for money-getting;

18 (68). Nevertheless, they are not to be compared with the grace of God and the compassion shown in the Cross.

19 (69). Bishops and curates, in duty bound, must receive the commissaries of the papal indulgences with all reverence;

20 (70). But they are under a much greater obligation to watch closely and attend carefully lest these men preach their own fancies instead of what the pope commissioned.

21 (71). Let him be anathema and accursed who denies the apostolic character of the indulgences;

22 (72). On the other hand, let him be blessed who is on his guard against the wantonness and licence of the pardon-merchants' words.

23 (73). In the same way, the pope rightly excommunicates those who make any plans to the detriment of the trade in indulgences.

24 (74). It is much more in keeping with his views to excommunicate those who use the pretext of indulgences to plot anything to the detriment of holy love and truth.

25 (75). It is foolish to think that papal indulgences have so much power that they can absolve a man even if he has done the impossible and violated the mother of God.

[8] Matt. 20:16.

(The fourth series)

1 (76). We assert the contrary, and say that the pope's pardons are not able to remove the least venial of sins as far as their guilt is concerned.

2 (77). When it is said that not even St. Peter, if he were now pope, could grant a greater grace, it is blasphemy against St. Peter and the pope.

3 (78). We assert the contrary, and say that he, and any pope whatever, possesses greater graces, viz., the gospel, spiritual powers, gifts of healing, etc., as is declared in I Corinthians 12.[9]

4 (79). It is blasphemy to say that the insignia of the cross with the papal arms are of equal value to the cross on which Christ died.

5 (80). The bishops, curates, and theologians, who permit assertions of that kind to be made to the people without let or hindrance, will have to answer for it.

6 (81). This unbridled preaching of indulgences makes it difficult for learned men to guard the respect due to the pope against false accusations, or at least from the keen criticisms of the laity;

7 (82). They ask, e.g.: Why does not the pope liberate everyone from purgatory for the sake of love (a most holy thing) and because of the supreme necessity of their souls? This would be morally the best of all reasons. Meanwhile he redeems innumerable souls for money, a most perishable thing, with which to build St. Peter's church, a very minor purpose.[10]

[9] 1 Cor. 12:28.

[10] Abelard made the point, *circa* A.D. 1140, that if the pope was willing to remit, on certain conditions, a third or a quarter of the due penance for money, he should be more willing to remit one half or even the whole, for *pietas*. Luther, therefore, in this thesis, is only making a point which had long become traditional.

8 (83). Again: why should funeral and anniversary masses for the dead continue to be said? And why does not the pope repay, or permit to be repaid, the benefactions instituted for these purposes, since it is wrong to pray for those souls who are now redeemed?

9 (84). Again: surely this is a new sort of compassion, on the part of God and the pope, when an impious man, an enemy of God, is allowed to pay money to redeem a devout soul, a friend of God; while yet that devout and beloved soul is not allowed to be redeemed without payment, for love's sake, and just because of its need of redemption.[11]

10 (85). Again: Why are the penitential canon laws, which in fact, if not in practice, have long been obsolete and dead in themselves,—why are they, to-day, still used in imposing fines in money, through the granting of indulgences, as if all the penitential canons were fully operative?

11 (86). Again: Since the pope's income to-day is larger than that of the wealthiest of wealthy men, why does he not build this one church[12] of St. Peter with his own money, rather than with the money of indigent believers?

12 (87). Again: What does the pope remit or dispense to people who, by their perfect penitence, have a right to plenary remission or dispensation?

13 (88). Again: Surely greater good could be done to the church if the pope were to bestow these remissions and dispensations, not once, as now, but a hundred times

[11] Innocent III issued a Bull after the Lateran Council of 1215, and promised indulgence for those taking part in the Crusade whether at their own or another's expense; and also for paying for someone to take part.

[12] As early as 1215, Innocent III had spoken against excess in issuing indulgences at the dedication of churches, and for similar causes, lest the power of the keys fell into disrepute.

a day, for the benefit of any believer whatever.

14 (89). What the pope seeks by indulgences is not money, but rather the salvation of souls; why then does he not suspend the letters and indulgences formerly conceded, and still as efficacious as ever?

15 (90). These questions are serious matters of conscience to the laity. To suppress them by force alone, and not to refute them by giving reasons, is to expose the church and the pope to the ridicule of their enemies, and to make Christian people unhappy.

16 (91). If, therefore, indulgences were preached in accordance with the spirit and mind of the pope, all these difficulties would be easily overcome, and, indeed, cease to exist.

17 (92). Away, then, with those prophets who say to Christ's people, "Peace, peace," where there is no peace.[13]

18 (93). Hail, hail to all those prophets who say to Christ's people, "The cross, the cross," where there is no cross.

19 (94). Christians should be exhorted to be zealous to follow Christ, their Head, through penalties, deaths, and hells;

20 (95). And let them thus be more confident of entering heaven through many tribulations [14] rather than through a false assurance of peace.

MDXVII.

[13] Jer. 6:14.
[14] Acts 14:22.

TWENTY-SIX

INSTITUTES OF THE CHRISTIAN RELIGION

The French Protestant theologian John Calvin (1509–64) was second only to Luther in influencing the course of the Reformation. Calvin, deeply indebted to Luther's thought, first published the Institutes of the Christian Religion *in 1536 in Latin. Subsequent expansions and revisions followed until the definitive edition of 1559, which was about five times as long as the first edition. Many translations and abridgements of the* Institutes *appeared in the sixteenth century and later. Calvin intended the* Institutes, *as he stated in the preface to the 1559 edition, "to prepare and qualify students of theology for the reading of the divine word." The* Institutes *succeeded in providing a soundly reasoned framework of Protestant theology at a time when dissent and controversy was rampant. The* Institutes, *written with both force and clarity, also appealed to the educated general reader. Calvin differed from Luther mainly in his more austere and intellectualized approach to theology and in weighty emphasis on predestination. The general outline of his work, as well as its specific arguments, reflect a penetrating and highly disciplined mind. The General Syllabus to the* Institutes, *from the Latin edition of Amsterdam, states, "He strictly follows the method of the Apostles' Creed, as being most familiar to all Christians. For as the Creed consists of four parts, the first relating to God the Father, the second to the Son, the third to the Holy Spirit, the fourth to the Church; so the Author distributes the whole of this work into Four Books, corresponding respectively to the four parts of the Creed."*

JOHN CALVIN

INSTITUTES OF THE CHRISTIAN RELIGION*

True and substantial wisdom principally consists of two parts, the knowledge of God, and the knowledge of ourselves. But, while these two branches of knowledge are so intimately connected, which of them precedes and produces the other, is not easy to discover. For, in the first place, no man can take a survey of himself but he must immediately turn to the contemplation of God, in whom he "lives and moves;"[1] since it is evident that the talents which we possess are

* From *Institutes of the Christian Religion,* I, 47–53, by John Calvin. Translated by John Allen and edited by Benjamin B. Warfield. Published 1936 by the Presbyterian Board of Christian Education, Philadelphia.

[1] Acts xvii, 2.

not from ourselves, and that our very existence is nothing but a subsistence in God alone. These bounties, distilling to us by drops from heaven, form, as it were, so many streams conducting us to the fountain-head. Our poverty conduces to a clearer display of the infinite fulness of God. Especially, the miserable ruin, into which we have been plunged by the defection of the first man, compels us to raise our eyes towards heaven, not only as hungry and famished, to seek thence a supply for our wants, but, aroused with fear, to learn humility. For, since man is subject to a world of miseries, and has been spoiled of his divine array, this melancholy exposure discovers an immense mass of deformity: every one, therefore, must be so impressed with a consciousness of his own infelicity, as to arrive at some knowledge of God. Thus a sense of our ignorance, vanity, poverty, infirmity, depravity, and corruption, leads us to perceive and acknowledge that in the Lord alone are to be found true wisdom, solid strength, perfect goodness, and unspotted righteousness; and so, by our imperfections, we are excited to a consideration of the perfections of God. Nor can we really aspire toward him, till we have begun to be displeased with ourselves. For who would not gladly rest satisfied with himself? where is the man not actually absorbed in self-complacency, while he remains unacquainted with his true situation, or content with his own endowments, and ignorant or forgetful of his own misery? The knowledge of ourselves therefore, is not only an incitement to seek after God, but likewise a considerable assistance towards finding him.

On the other hand, it is plain that no man can arrive at the true knowledge of himself, without having first contemplated the divine character, and then descended to the consideration of his own. For, such is the native pride of us all, we invariably esteem ourselves righteous, innocent, wise, and holy, till we are convinced, by clear proofs, of our unrighteousness, turpitude, folly, and impurity. But we are never thus convinced, while we confine our attention to ourselves, and regard not the Lord, who is the only standard by which this judgment ought to be formed. Because, from our natural proneness to hypocrisy, any vain appearance of righteousness abundantly contents us instead of the reality; and, every thing within and around us being exceedingly defiled, we are delighted with what is least so, as extremely pure, while we confine our reflections within the limits of human corruption. So the eye, accustomed to see nothing but black, judges that to be very white, which is but whitish, or perhaps brown. Indeed, the senses of our bodies may assist us in discovering how grossly we err in estimating the powers of the soul. For if at noon-day we look either on the ground, or at any surrounding objects, we conclude our vision to be very strong and piercing; but when we raise our eyes and steadily look at the sun, they are at once dazzled and confounded with such a blaze of brightness, and we are constrained to confess, that our sight, so piercing in viewing terrestrial things, when directed to the sun, is dimness itself. Thus also it happens in the consideration of our spiritual endowments. For as long as our views are bounded by the earth, perfectly content with our own righteousness, wisdom, and strength, we fondly flatter ourselves, and fancy we are little less than demigods. But, if we once elevate our thoughts to God, and consider his nature, and the consummate perfection of his righteousness, wisdom, and strength, to which we ought to be conformed,—what before charmed us in ourselves under the false pretext of righteousness, will soon be loathed as the greatest iniquity; what strangely deceived us under the title of wisdom, will be despised as extreme folly; and what wore the appearance of strength, will be proved to be most wretched impotence. So very remote from the divine purity is what seems in us the highest perfection.

Hence that horror and amazement with which the Scripture always represents the saints to have been impressed and disturbed, on every discovery of the presence of God. For when we see those, who before his appearance stood secure and firm, so astonished and affrighted at the manifestation of his glory, as to faint and almost expire through fear,—we must infer that man is never sufficiently affected with a knowledge of his own meanness, till he has compared himself with the Divine Majesty. Of this consternation we have frequent examples in the Judges and Prophets; so that it was a common expression among the Lord's people —"We shall die, because we have seen God."[2] Therefore the history of Job, to humble men with a consciousness of their pollution, impotence, and folly, derives its principal argument from a description of the Divine purity, power, and wisdom. And not without reason. For we see how Abraham, the nearer he approached to behold the glory of the Lord, the more fully acknowledged himself to be but "dust and ashes;"[3] and how Elias[4] could not bear his approach without covering his face, his appearance is so formidable. And what can man do, all vile and corrupt, when fear constrains even the cherubim themselves to veil their faces? This is what the prophet Isaiah speaks of—"the moon shall be confounded, and the sun ashamed, when the Lord of hosts shall reign:"[5] that is, when he shall make a fuller and nearer exhibition of his splendour, it shall eclipse the splendour of the brightest object besides. But, though the knowledge of God and the knowledge of ourselves be intimately connected, the proper order of instruction requires us first to treat of the former, and then to proceed to the discussion of the latter.

By the knowledge of God, I intend not merely a notion that there is such a Being, but also an acquaintance with whatever we ought to know concerning Him, conducting to his glory and our benefit. For we cannot with propriety say, there is any knowledge of God where there is no religion or piety. I have no reference here to that species of knowledge by which men, lost and condemned in themselves, apprehend God the Redeemer in Christ the Mediator; but only to that first and simple knowledge, to which the genuine order of nature would lead us, if Adam had retained his innocence. For though, in the present ruined state of human nature, no man will ever perceive God to be a Father, or the Author of salvation, or in any respect propitious, but as pacified by the mediation of Christ; yet it is one thing to understand, that God our Maker supports us by his power, governs us by his providence, nourishes us by his goodness, and follows us with blessings of every kind, and another to embrace the grace of reconciliation proposed to us in Christ. Therefore, since God is first manifested, both in the structure of the world and in the general tenor of Scripture, simply as the Creator, and afterwards reveals himself in the person of Christ as a Redeemer, hence arises a twofold knowledge of him; of which the former is first to be considered, and the other will follow in its proper place. For though our mind cannot conceive of God, without ascribing some worship to him, it will not be sufficient merely to apprehend that he is the only proper object of universal worship and adoration, unless we are also persuaded that he is the fountain of all good, and seek for none but in him. This I maintain, not only because he sustains the universe, as he once made it, by his infinite power, governs it by his wisdom, preserves it by his goodness, and especially reigns over the human race in righteousness and judgment, exercising a merciful forbearance, and defending them by his protection; but because there cannot be found the least particle of wisdom, light, righteousness, power, rectitude, or sincere truth which does not proceed from him, and claim him for its author: we should therefore learn to expect and supplicate all these things from him, and thankfully to acknowledge what he gives us. For this sense of the divine perfections is calculated to teach us

[2] Judg. xiii. 22.
[3] Gen. xviii. 27.
[4] 1 Kings xix. 13.
[5] Isaiah vi. 2; xxiv. 23.

piety, which produces religion. By piety, I mean a reverence and love of God arising from a knowledge of his benefits. For, till men are sensible that they owe every thing to God, that they are supported by his paternal care, that he is the Author of all the blessings they enjoy, and that nothing should be sought independently of him, they will never voluntarily submit to his authorit they will never truly and cordially devote themselves to his service, unless they rely upon him alone for true felicity.

Cold and frivolous, then, are the speculations of those who employ themselves in disquisitions on the essence of God, when it would be more interesting to us to become acquainted with his character, and to know what is agreeable to his nature. For what end is answered by professing, with Epicurus, that there is a God, who, discarding all concern about the world, indulges himself in perpetual inactivity? What benefit arises from the knowledge of a God with whom we have no concern? Our knowledge of God should rather tend, first, to teach us fear and reverence; and, secondly, to instruct us to implore all good at his hand, and to render him the praise of all that we receive. For how can you entertain a thought of God without immediately reflecting, that, being a creature of his formation, you must, by right of creation, be subject to his authority? that you are indebted to him for your life, and that all your actions should be done with reference to him? If this be true, it certainly follows that your life is miserably corrupt, unless it be regulated by a desire of obeying him, since his will ought to be the rule of our conduct. Nor can you have a clear view of him without discovering him to be the fountain and origin of all good. This would produce a desire of union to him, and confidence in him, if the human mind were not seduced by its own depravity from the right path of investigation. For, even at the first, the pious mind dreams not of any imaginary deity, but contemplates only the one true God; and, concerning him, indulges not the fictions of fancy, but, content with believing him to be such as he reveals himself, uses the most diligent and unremitting caution, lest it should fall into error by a rash and presumptuous transgression of his will. He who thus knows him, sensible that all things are subject to his control, confides in him as his Guardian and Protector, and unreservedly commits himself to his care. Assured that he is the author of all blessings, in distress or want he immediately flies to his protection, and expects his aid. Persuaded of his goodness and mercy, he relies on him with unlimited confidence, nor doubts of finding in his clemency a remedy provided for all his evils. Knowing him to be his Lord and Father, he concludes that he ought to mark his government in all things, revere his majesty, endeavour to promote his glory, and obey his commands. Perceiving him to be a just Judge, armed with severity for the punishment of crimes, he keeps his tribunal always in view, and is restrained by fear from provoking his wrath. Yet he is not so terrified at the apprehension of his justice, as to wish to evade it, even if escape were possible; but loves him as much in punishing the wicked as in blessing the pious, because he believes it as necessary to his glory to punish the impious and abandoned, as to reward the righteous with eternal life. Besides, he restrains himself from sin, not merely from a dread of vengeance, but because he loves and reveres God as his Father, honours and worships him as his Lord, and, even though there were no hell, would shudder at the thought of offending him. See, then, the nature of pure and genuine religion. It consists in faith, united with a serious fear of God, comprehending a voluntary reverence, and producing legitimate worship agreeable to the injunctions of the law. And this requires to be the more carefully remarked, because men in general render to God a formal worship, but very few truly reverence him; while great ostentation in ceremonies is universally displayed, but sincerity of heart is rarely to be found.

TWENTY-SEVEN

IGNATIUS OF LOYOLA

In the Counter Reformation, sometimes known as the Catholic Reformation, the Church of Rome responded vigorously to the Protestant challenge, and regained some areas, notably in south Germany, which had defected to Protestantism. The most vigorous agency in the Catholic revival was the Society of Jesus, more familiarly known as the Jesuit order, which was particularly active in education and in foreign missions, and less so (but significantly) in combating Protestantism in Europe. For 100 years or so after its formation, the Society of Jesus attracted some of Europe's ablest and most dedicated young men. Thereafter the Jesuits declined somewhat as a force in European life. The founder of the Jesuit order was Ignatius of Loyola (1491–1556), an aristocratic Spanish soldier who had a profound religious experience while recovering from a wound in 1521. After trying without success to make a pilgrimage to the Holy Land, Loyola attended universities in both Spain and France. In 1534 he gathered together a band of six religious enthusiasts who took vows to follow Christ. Six years later the papacy authorized the formation of the Jesuit order, and in 1541 Loyola became its first head. Loyola brought unswerving dedication to his work. In his autobiography, dictated between 1553 and 1555, Loyola vividly describes the events leading to his conversion and some of the incidents which followed.

THE AUTOBIOGRAPHY OF ST. IGNATIUS*

CHAPTER I

Up to his twenty-sixth year the heart of Ignatius was enthralled by the vanities of the world. His special delight was in the military life, and he seemed led by a strong and empty desire of gaining for himself a great name. The citadel of Pampeluna was held in siege by the French. All the other soldiers were unanimous in wishing to surrender on condition of freedom to leave, since it was impossible to hold out any longer; but Ignatius so persuaded the commander, that, against the views of all the other nobles, he decided to hold the citadel against the enemy.

When the day of assault came, Ignatius made his confession to one of the nobles, his companion in arms. The soldier also made his to Ignatius. After the walls were destroyed, Ignatius stood fighting bravely until

* From *The Autobiography of St. Ignatius,* chs. 1 and 2, edited by J. F. X. O'Connor, Benziger Brothers, New York, 1900.

a cannon ball of the enemy broke one of his legs and seriously injured the other.

When he fell, the citadel was surrendered. When the French took possession of the town, they showed great admiration for Ignatius. After twelve or fifteen days at Pampeluna, where he received the best care from the physicians of the French army, he was borne on a litter to Loyola. His recovery was very slow, and doctors and surgeons were summoned from all parts for a consultation. They decided that the leg should be broken again, that the bones, which had knit badly, might be properly reset; for they had not been properly set in the beginning, or else had been so jostled on the journey that a cure was impossible. He submitted to have his flesh cut again. During the operation, as in all he suffered before and after, he uttered no word and gave no sign of suffering save that of tightly clenching his fists.

In the meantime his strength was failing. He could take no food, and showed other symptoms of approaching death. On the feast of St. John the doctors gave up hope of his recovery, and he was advised to make his confession. Having received the sacraments on the eve of the feasts of Sts. Peter and Paul, toward evening the doctors said that if by the middle of the night there were no change for the better, he would surely die. He had great devotion to St. Peter, and it so happened by the goodness of God that in the middle of the night he began to grow better.

His recovery was so rapid that in a few days he was out of danger. As the bones of his leg settled and pressed upon each other, one bone protruded below the knee. The result was that one leg was shorter than the other, and the bone causing a lump there, made the leg seem quite deformed. As he could not bear this, since he intended to live a life at court, he asked the doctors whether the bone could be cut away. They replied that it could, but it would cause him more suffering than all that had preceded, as everything was healed, and they would need space in order to cut it. He determined, however, to undergo this torture.

His elder brother looked on with astonishment and admiration. He said he could never have had the fortitude to suffer the pain which the sick man bore with his usual patience. When the flesh and the bone that protruded were cut away, means were taken to prevent the leg from becoming shorter than the other. For this purpose, in spite of sharp and constant pain, the leg was kept stretched for many days. Finally the Lord gave him health. He came out of the danger safe and strong with the exception that he could not easily stand on his leg, but was forced to lie in bed.

As Ignatius had a love for fiction, when he found himself out of danger he asked for some romances to pass away the time. In that house there was no book of the kind. They gave him, instead, "The Life of Christ," by Rudolph, the Carthusian, and another book called the "Flowers of the Saints," both in Spanish. By frequent reading of these books he began to get some love for spiritual things. This reading led his mind to meditate on holy things, yet sometimes it wandered to thoughts which he had been accustomed to dwell upon before.

Among these there was one thought which, above the others, so filled his heart that he became, as it were, immersed and absorbed in it. Unconsciously, it engaged his attention for three and four hours at a time. He pictured to himself what he should do in honor of an illustrious lady, how he should journey to the city where she was, in what words he would address her, and what bright and pleasant sayings he would make use of, what manner of warlike exploits he should perform to please her. He was so carried away by this thought that he did not even perceive how far beyond his power it was to do what he proposed, for she was a lady exceedingly illustrious and of the highest nobility.

In the meantime the divine mercy was at work substituting for these thoughts others suggested by his recent readings. While perusing the life of Our Lord and the saints, he began to reflect, saying to himself: "What if I should do what St. Francis did?" "What if I should act like St. Dominic?" He pondered over these things in his mind, and kept continually proposing to himself serious and difficult things. He seemed to feel a certain readiness for doing them, with no other reason except this thought: "St. Dominic did this; I, too, will do it." "St. Francis did this; therefore I will do it." These heroic resolutions remained for a time, and then other vain and worldly thoughts followed. This succession of thoughts occupied him for a long while, those about God alternating with those about the world. But in these thoughts there was this difference. When he thought of worldly things it gave him great pleasure, but afterward he found himself dry and sad. But when he thought of journeying to Jerusalem, and of living only on herbs, and practising austerities, he found pleasure not only while thinking of them, but also when he had ceased.

This difference he did not notice or value, until one day the eyes of his soul were opened and he began to inquire the reason of the difference. He learned by experience that one train of thought left him sad, the other joyful. This was his first reasoning on spiritual matters. Afterward, when he began the Spiritual Exercises, he was enlightened, and understood what he afterward taught his children about the discernment of spirits. When gradually he recognized the different spirits by which he was moved, one, the spirit of God, the other, the devil, and when he had gained no little spiritual light from the reading of pious books, he began to think more seriously of his past life, and how much penance he should do to expiate his past sins.

Amid these thoughts the holy wish to imitate saintly men came to his mind; his resolve was not more definite than to promise with the help of divine grace that what they had done he also would do. After his recovery his one wish was to make a pilgrimage to Jerusalem. He fasted frequently and scourged himself to satisfy the desire of penance that ruled in a soul filled with the spirit of God.

The vain thoughts were gradually lessened by means of these desires—desires that were not a little strengthened by the following vision. While watching one night he plainly saw the image of the Blessed Mother of God with the Infant Jesus, at the sight of which, for a considerable time, he received abundant consolation, and felt such contrition for his past life that he thought of nothing else. From that time until August, 1555, when this was written, he never felt the least motion of concupiscence. This privilege we may suppose from this fact to have been a divine gift, although we dare not state it, nor say anything except confirm what has been already said. His brother and all in the house recognized from what appeared externally how great a change had taken place in his soul.

He continued his reading meanwhile, and kept the holy resolution he had made. At home his conversation was wholly devoted to divine things, and helped much to the spiritual advancement of others.

CHAPTER II

Ignatius, starting from his father's house, set out upon his journey on horseback. About this time he began his habit of taking the discipline every night. His brother desired to accompany him as far as Ogna, and during the journey was persuaded by the Saint to pass one night of watching at the shrine of Our Blessed Lady at Aruncuz. Having prayed some time at the shrine for new strength for his journey, leaving his brother at Ogna at the house of their sister, to whom he paid a short visit, he journeyed on to Navarre. Remembering that an official in the Duke's palace owed him some money, he collected it by sending in a written account to the treasurer, and distributed it among persons to whom he felt indebted. A portion of the money he devoted to the restoration of a picture of the Blessed Virgin. Then dismissing his two remaining servants, he rode forth alone from Navarre in the direction of Montserrat, a mountain town of Catalonia in the northern part of Spain.

It will not be amiss to recall an event that occurred during this journey, to show the manner in which God directed him. Although filled with an ardent desire of serving God, yet his knowledge of spiritual things was still very obscure. He had undertaken to perform extraordinary penances, not so much with a view to satisfy for his sins as with the intention of doing something pleasing to his Lord. He declared indeed that though filled with the liveliest abhorrence of his past sins, he could not assure himself that they were forgiven; yet in his austerities so intense was his desire to do great things for Christ that he did not think of his sins. When he recalled the penances practised by holy persons, his whole mind was bent on doing something to equal and even surpass them. In this holy ambition he found his consolation, for he had no interior motive for his penances, knowing as yet very little about humility or charity or patience, for to obtain these many holy men have led austere lives. He knew still less the value of discretion, which regulates the practice of these virtues. To do something great for the glory of his God, to emulate saintly men in all that they had done before him—this was the only object of Ignatius in his practices of external mortification.

While he journeyed on, a Saracen mounted on a horse came up with him. In the course of the conversation mention was made of the Blessed Virgin. The stranger remarked that though he admitted that the Mother of Christ had conceived without detriment to her virginal purity, yet he could not believe that after the conception of her divine Son she was still a virgin. He was so obstinate in holding this opinion, that no amount of reasoning on the part of Ignatius could force him to abandon it. Shortly afterward the Saracen rode on, leaving the pilgrim to his own reflections. These were not of the most peaceful nature. He was sorely troubled as he thought over the conduct of his recent fellow-traveler, and felt that he had but poorly acquitted himself of his duty of honoring the Mother of God. The longer his mind thought upon the matter, the more his soul was filled with indignation against himself for having allowed the Saracen to speak as he had done of the Blessed Virgin, and for the lack of courage he fancied he had shown in not at once resenting the insult. He consequently felt impelled by a strong impulse to hasten after him and slay the miscreant for the insulting language he had used. After much internal conflict with these thoughts, he still remained in doubt, nor could he decide what course to follow. The Saracen, who had ridden on, had mentioned to him that it was his intention to proceed to a town not far distant from the highroad. At length, Ignatius, wearied by his inward struggle and not arriving at any determination, decided to settle all his doubts in the following novel way: he would give free rein to his horse, and if, on coming to the cross-road, his horse should turn into the path that led to the destination of the Moor, he would pursue him and kill him; but if his horse kept to the highroad he would allow the wretch to escape. Having done as he had decided, it happened through the Providence of God that his horse kept to the highroad, though the place was distant only about thirty or forty yards, and the way leading to it was very wide and easy.

Arriving at a large village situated a short distance from Montserrat, he determined to procure a garment to wear on his journey to Jerusalem. He therefore bought a piece of sackcloth, poorly woven, and filled with prickly wooden fibres. Of this he made a garment that reached to his feet. He bought, also, a pair of shoes of coarse stuff that is often used in making brooms. He never wore but one shoe, and that not for the sake of the comfort to be derived from it, but because, as he was in the habit of wearing a cord tied below the knee by way of mortification, this leg would be very much swollen at night, though he rode all day on horseback. For this reason, he felt he ought to wear a shoe on that foot. He provided himself also with a pilgrim's staff and a gourd to drink from. All these he tied to his saddle.

Thus equipped, he continued on his way to Montserrat, pondering in his mind, as was his wont, on the great things he would do for the love of God. And as he had formerly read the stories of Amadeus of Gaul and other such writers, who told how the Christian knights of the past were accustomed to spend the entire night, preceding the day on which they were to receive knighthood, on guard before an altar of the Blessed Virgin, he was filled with these chivalric fancies, and resolved to prepare himself for a noble knighthood by passing a night in vigil before an altar of Our Lady at Montserrat. He would observe all the formalities of this ceremony, neither sitting nor lying down, but alternately standing and kneeling, and there he would lay aside his worldly dignities to assume the arms of Christ.

When he arrived at Montserrat, he passed a long time in prayer, and with the consent of his confessor he made in writing a general confession of his sins. Three whole days were employed in this undertaking. He begged and obtained leave of his confessor to give up his horse, and to hang up his sword and his dagger in the church, near the altar of the Blessed Virgin. This confessor was the first to whom he unfolded his interior, and disclosed his resolution of devoting himself to a spiritual life. Never before had he manifested his purpose to anybody.

The eve of the Annunciation of Our Blessed Lady in the year 1522 was the time he chose to carry out the project he had formed. At nightfall, unobserved by any one, he approached a beggar, and taking off his own costly garments gave them to the beggar. He then put on the pilgrim's dress he had previously bought, and hastened to the church, where he threw himself on his knees before the altar of the Blessed Mother of God, and there, now kneeling, now standing, with staff in hand, he passed the entire night.

After receiving the Blessed Sacrament, to avoid recognition he left the town at daybreak. He did not go by the direct route that leads to Barcelona, as he might have met those who knew him and would honor him, but he took a byway that led him to a town called Manresa. Here he determined to remain a few days in the hospital and write out some notes in his little book, which for his own consolation he carefully carried about with him. At about a league's distance from Montserrat, he was overtaken by a man who had ridden after him at a rapid pace. This man accosted him and inquired if he had given certain garments to a poor man, as the latter had declared. Ignatius answered that it was true that he had given them to a beggar. On learning that the latter had been ill-treated because he was suspected of having stolen the clothes, the eyes of Ignatius filled with tears, in pity for the poor man.

Although he had fled so anxiously from the praise of men, he did not remain long at Manresa before many marvellous things were narrated of him. This fame arose from what had occurred at Montserrat. His reputation increased day by day. Men vied with each other in adding some particulars about his sanctity, declaring that he had abandoned immense revenues, and other wonderful things without much regard to real facts.

At Manresa he lived on the alms that he daily begged. He never ate meat nor partook of wine, though they were offered him. On Sundays, however, he never fasted, and if wine were offered him, he drank of it sparingly. In former days he had been very careful of his hair, which he had worn, and, indeed, not unbecomingly, in the fashionable manner of the young men of his age; but now he determined to cease to care for it, neither to comb it nor to cut it, and to dispense with all covering for his head both day and night. To punish himself for the too great nicety which he had formerly had in the care of his hands and feet, he now resolved to neglect them.

It was while he was living at the hospital at Manresa that the following strange event took place. Very frequently on a clear moonlight night there appeared in the courtyard before him an indistinct shape which he could not see clearly enough to tell what it was. Yet it appeared so symmetrical and beautiful that his soul was filled with pleasure and joy as he gazed at it. It had something of the form of a serpent with glittering eyes, and yet they were not eyes. He felt an indescribable joy steal over him at the sight of this object. The oftener he saw it, the greater was the consolation he derived from it, and when the vision left him, his soul was filled with sorrow and sadness.

Up to this period he had remained in a constant state of tranquillity and consolation, without any interior knowledge of the trials that beset the spiritual life. But during the time that the vision lasted, sometimes for days, or a little previous to that time, his soul was violently agitated by a thought that brought him no little uneasiness. There flashed upon his mind the idea of the difficulty that attended the kind of life he had begun, and he felt as if he heard some one whispering to him, "How can you keep up for seventy years of your life these practices which you have begun?" Knowing that this thought was a temptation of the evil one, he expelled it by this answer: "Can you, wretched one, promise me one hour of life?" In this manner he overcame the temptation, and his soul was restored to peace. This was his first trial besides what has already been narrated, and it came upon him suddenly one day as he was entering the church. He was accustomed to hear Mass daily, and to assist at Vespers and Compline—devotions from which he derived much consolation. During Mass, he always read over the history of the Passion, and his soul was filled with a joyful feeling of uninterrupted calm.

Shortly after the temptation just spoken of, he began to experience great changes in his soul. At one time he was deprived of all consolation, so that he found no pleasure in vocal prayer, in hearing Mass, or in any spiritual exercise. At another, on the contrary, he suddenly felt as if all sorrow and desolation were taken from him, experiencing the relief of one from whose shoulders a heavy cloak had suddenly been lifted. On noticing all this, he was surprised, wondering what could be the import of these changes which he had never before experienced, and he said to himself, "What new kind of life is this upon which I am entering?"

At this time he became acquainted with some holy persons who manifested great confidence in him, and gladly conversed with him; for though he had, as yet, little knowledge of spiritual things, still he spoke with great fervor on religious subjects, and incited his hearers to make greater progress in the way of God's service. Among those holy persons who dwelt at Manresa, there was one lady well advanced in years who had long been given to the service of God, and who was so well known in many places in Spain that his Catholic Majesty, the King of Spain, had desired her presence on one occasion in order to take counsel with her about certain projects that he had in his mind. This lady, speaking one day to our new soldier of Christ, said to him, "Would that the Lord Jesus might appear to you some day!" Ignatius, wondering at her words, understood in a literal sense, and asked her, "What would He look like if He were to show Himself to me?"

He always persevered in his custom of approaching the Sacraments of Confession and Holy Communion every week. But herein he found a great source of anxiety on account of the scruples with which he was annoyed. For though he had written out his general confession at Montserrat, and with great diligence and care had tried to make it complete, yet he always felt that he had forgotten something in his confession, and this caused him much anxiety. Even though he should now confess it again, he received no consolation. He tried then to find a spiritual person, who could give him relief in his trouble, but he found no one. Finally, a certain doctor who had experience in spiritual things, and who was a preacher in the church, advised him to write down anything he remembered and feared that he had not confessed. He obeyed, and even after he had confessed these sins, his scruples still continued to fill his soul, and he was constantly recalling minor details that he had not confessed. In this way he was cruelly tormented. He knew well that these scruples caused no little harm to the spiritual life, and that it was most expedient to get rid of them, yet they continued to torture him. At times it occurred to him that it would be well if he could have his confessor command him in the name of the Lord Jesus not again to confess anything of his past sins; and he inwardly prayed that his confessor would give him some such command, but he could not bring himself to ask him to do so.

TWENTY-EIGHT

ELIZABETH I OF ENGLAND

The Protestant Reformation upset the medieval division of power between the Church and Europe's many states and created political turmoil of first magnitude. In the sixteenth century, religious issues dominated politics, diplomacy, and war. Everywhere in the West, rulers faced either the problem of finding an accommodation with the Church of Rome, as in France and Spain which remained Catholic, or the problem of establishing a national Protestant Church, as in England, the north German states, and the Scandinavian countries. Everywhere, also, religious minorities, such as the Huguenots in France, the Anabaptists in the German states, and the Puritans in England, demanded recognition in an atmosphere of self-righteousness which was often tinged with bigotry and fanaticism. Meanwhile, in religious wars, massacres, and riots thousands of Europeans lost their lives. Queen Elizabeth I of England, who ruled from 1558 to 1603, faced a particularly tangled and dangerous religious situation. After the mainly orthodox separation from Rome under Elizabeth's strong-willed father, Henry VIII, England experienced accelerated Protestantism under the boy-king Edward VI (1547–53), and a Catholic reaction under Bloody Mary (1553–8). By adroit silence and contrived ambiguity, Elizabeth I made a deliberately broad religious settlement with an Anglican Church which was largely Catholic in appearance and largely Protestant in substance. In so doing she achieved a near miracle—political peace at home broken only by occasional foreign wars. This triumph of statecraft sprang from her exceptional ability and courage. Elizabeth I, with deep-seated sense of situation, did not hesitate to play a role in ruling, and succeeded in evoking not only respect but adoration from her subjects. She became, in effect, a symbol of state in which English folk could take pride and through patriotism find identity as members of the realm. In his biography of Queen Elizabeth I, Professor Neale describes how she endeared herself to her subjects. Such endearment, rare in human annals, helped to bring greatness to Elizabeth I and contributed heavily to the greatness of England during her long reign.

JOHN E. NEALE

QUEEN ELIZABETH *

Parliament's fury against Mary Queen of Scots was partly an expression of Protestant feeling, but also a genuine tribute to the popularity of Elizabeth. No prince has been a greater courtier of the people, nor any actress known better how to move her audience to transports of love and admiration. Save for a fleeting crisis like that over Dudley, Elizabeth's mind was ever fixed on popular favour, at first as an art of government, and later as a profound emotional satisfaction.

The opportunities of showing herself to the people were numerous, for the Court was constantly on the move. Greenwich, Whitehall, Richmond, Hampton Court, Windsor: there was not a year but the Queen could often be seen, like some very human and approachable goddess with her train, going by river or road from one of these palaces to another, or visiting other royal houses or private homes in the near neighbourhood of London. The City was afforded an annual autumn spectacle on the return of the Court to Whitehall, where Christmas was ordinarily kept. It became a ceremonial occasion, when Mayor, Aldermen, and Citizens in their rich finery met the splendid royal procession, and to mutual greetings of "God save your Grace!," "God save my people!" welcomed their sovereign back to town. In 1570, after the Northern Rebellion, the anniversary of Elizabeth's accession, November 17th, which had before then been celebrated with ringing of bells, was made a day of national thanksgiving and festival, and continued throughout the reign to be one of the great days of the year It was revived in James I's reign, as Elizabeth's name came to connote the peak of national greatness, retained much of its emotional significance for a hundred years after that, and still left its traces during another century. On this day young courtiers displayed their manhood and wit before thousands of spectators, running at tilt in the tilt-yard at Westminster, with all the pageantry and extravagant devices, part of the romance between them and their Queen. After that, preparations were made for the plays and masks that marked the high season of festivity, the twelve days from Christmas on.

Londoners, naturally, had the lion's share of Elizabeth's favours. She kept them bewitched, for it was a secret of power to hold this key to the kingdom. But for those who could not come to City or Court, there were the annual royal progresses. These were the Queen's summer holidays, when, combining business with pleasure, she took the Court on a month's or two months' perambulation through the country, staying at some royal manor or claiming the ready hospitality of the gentry or towns. She loved them, as she had reason to do, for they satisfied her healthy desire for activity and change of air and surroundings, and offered supreme opportunities to her genius in winning the hearts of the people; and if they allowed little or no respite from the business of being Queen,

* Reprinted from *Queen Elizabeth,* ch. 13, by John E. Neale by permission of Macmillan and Co. Ltd., and St. Martin's Press, Inc. Published in England by Jonathan Cape Limited. Copyright 1934.

that was no disadvantage, for her work was the very breath of life, and she never seemed to lose her gusto for it.

Officials did not share the enthusiasm. Progresses involved tremendous preparations. Along with the personnel of the Household went hundreds of carts bearing the baggage, including furnishings for the bare houses which often had to be got ready; and it was the reverse of pleasure, in bad weather and on bad roads, to follow after an advance guard of this nature. Ten or twelve miles was as much as the stately procession travelled in a day. Moreover, it was often impossible to find reasonable accommodation for all the Queen's followers, and to add to their trials, Elizabeth had an increasing proclivity to change her mind and upset plans at the last minute. There were many complaints, and every excuse was exploited to stay a progress, though rarely with success. In 1571, in the midst of the unfolding of the Ridolfi Plot, the Council advised her for safety's sake to cancel her progress. She would not. Even in the last year of her life she kept the custom, and two years earlier, in her sixty-seventh year, when courtiers were grumbling at a "long progress," she bade "the old stay behind, and the young and able to go with her."

The Queen either rode on horseback or in an open litter to be seen by the people who flocked from the countryside and lined the roads. At the county boundary she was met by the sheriff and gentlemen who waited on her during her stay. On one progress into Suffolk and Norfolk the gentry of the former county bought up all the velvets and silks upon which they could lay their hands, no matter what the price, and when he met the Queen the sheriff had with him two hundred young gentlemen in white velvet, three hundred "of the graver sort" in black velvet coats and fair chains, with fifteen hundred serving men, all well and bravely mounted, "which surely was a comely troop and a noble sight to behold." Not to be outdone, the gentry of Norfolk "in most gallantest manner assembled and set forward with five and twenty hundred horsemen."

There was an extraordinary ease and informality about the slow procession, Elizabeth stopping from time to time as persons came to present petitions or say a word to her. "Stay thy cart, good fellow!" cried Serjeant Bendlowes of Huntingdonshire to the royal coachman, "stay thy cart, that I may speak to the Queen." "Whereat her Majesty laughed as she had been tickled . . . although very graciously, as her manner is, she gave him great thanks and her hand to kiss." The Spanish ambassador described the scene on progress in 1568: "She was received everywhere with great acclamations and signs of joy, as is customary in this country; whereat she was extremely pleased and told me so, giving me to understand how beloved she was by her subjects and how highly she esteemed this, together with the fact that they were peaceful and contented, whilst her neighbours on all sides are in such trouble. She attributed it all to God's miraculous goodness. She ordered her carriage sometimes to be taken where the crowd seemed thickest, and stood up and thanked the people."

Whenever a town was visited, there were great preparations:

> No sooner was pronounced the name,
> but babes in street gan leap;
> The youth, the age, the rich, the poor,
> came running all on heap,
> And, clapping hands, cried mainly out,
> "O blessed be the hour!
> Our Queen is coming to the Town,
> with princely train and power."

Rubbish was cleared, streets cleaned, houses gaily decked, speeches memorized, perhaps pageants prepared, and last, but not least, a silver-gilt cup purchased to present to the Queen, usually with money inside, varying from twenty to a hundred pounds according to the wealth of the town. Worcester's silver cup, with its cover double gilt, was worth £10 17*s.* 2*d.*, "the fairest that might be found in London," and in it was forty pounds in half sovereigns. Coventry put a hundred pounds in its cup, and Elizabeth "was pleased to say to her Lords, 'It was a good gift, £100 in gold; I have but few such gifts.' To which the Mayor answered boldly, 'If it please your Grace, there is a great deal more in it.' 'What is that?' said she. 'It is,' said he, 'the hearts of all your loving subjects.' 'We thank you, Mr. Mayor,' said she; 'it is a great deal more indeed.' "

At Warwick, after the Recorder had made his speech of welcome, "Come hither, little Recorder," said Elizabeth, offering her hand to be kissed. "It was told me that you would be afraid to look upon me or to speak boldly; but you were not so afraid of me as I was of you; and I now thank you for putting me in mind of my duty." At Norwich, the schoolmaster having to make a Latin speech and seeming nervous, she said graciously, "Be not afraid!"; and at the end purchased a loyal heart at the cost of a small lie, declaring, "It is the best that ever I heard; you shall have my hand." Moving on, she sent back to ask his name. There was as subtle flattery in her behaviour at Sandwich. Here the magistrates' wives made the Queen a banquet of one hundred and sixty dishes on a table twenty-eight feet long. Not only did she eat without the assay or preliminary tasting, employed as a precaution against poisoning, but also had certain of dishes reserved and sent to her lodging—unsurpassable compliments, both. Her farewell words to Norwich may be taken as typical of her partings: "I have laid up in my breast such good will, as I shall never forget Norwich"; and proceeding onward, she "did shake her riding-rod, and said, 'Farewell! Norwich,' with the water standing in her eyes."

Elizabeth visited both Universities, Oxford twice, Cambridge once, and listened to a heavy round of addresses, disputations, sermons, and plays, in Latin and Greek, which must have been insufferable boredom to less cultured courtiers, though she herself went through the routine with patience, nay, with pleasure, and let herself be prevailed upon to answer the Universities in their learned tongues. When one orator praised her many and singular virtues, she modestly shook her head, bit her lips and fingers, and interrupted with disclaimers; but when he turned to praise virginity, "God's blessing of thine heart," she called out; "there continue." There were rarely any unfortunate incidents, but after the Cambridge visit in 1564 some of the scholars pursued her to the next stage of her journey in order to present a farce for which there had been no time. It turned out to be a scandalous satire on Catholicism, one player representing Bishop Bonner, another being dressed as a dog with the Host in his mouth. Elizabeth rose and left the chamber, outraged, using strong language; and as the torch-bearers followed her, the farce met an ignominious end in darkness.

Elizabeth's descent on private houses was both coveted and feared; coveted for the honour, feared lest there might be some hitch, or the entertainment fall short of expectations. Apparently, there was no need to do more than surrender the house to the Queen's use: the cost of food, even the furnishings, would be provided by the Royal Household. But to do no more than this might be regarded as churlish behaviour, and in one instance certainly was so regarded, at least by courtiers. There are many little incidents to suggest that Elizabeth herself was reluctant that smaller folk should outreach themselves on her behalf, but the extravagant preparations made by wealthier hosts, or by courtiers trying to outdo one another, tended to set a standard that made royal visits an expensive honour. In 1577, a four-days' visit cost Sir Nicholas Bacon £577; a ten-days' visit to Burghley in 1591 cost rather over £1,000; a three-days' visit to Lord Keeper Egerton in 1602 cost as much as £2,000.

Apart from the problem of feeding and housing the Queen and her followers, the host had to have ready some gift or gifts and arrange entertainments. The gifts were often very costly. At a visit to Egerton in 1595, Elizabeth on alighting received a fine fan, the handle of which was set with diamonds. Before she reached the house, a man came running towards her, and with an appropriate speech gave her a nosegay in which was a rich jewel with diamond pendants, valued at £400. After dinner there was a present of a fair pair of virginals, and in her bed-chamber still another present—a fine gown and skirt. These were not all. "To grace his Lordship the more, she of herself took from him a salt, a spoon, and a fork of fair agate." Egerton could afford to be extravagant, the fees and perquisites of his office being notoriously great.

The entertainment *par excellence* of the reign was "The Princely Pleasures" at Kenilworth, where Leicester lavished his wealth and the imagination of professional versifiers in amusing the Queen during a three-weeks' stay in 1575. But other entertainments, if not so elaborate, were in the same vein. In 1591 the Earl of Hertford received the Queen at Elvetham. Though only a three-days' stay, three hundred men were set to work beforehand to enlarge the house, erect a host of out-buildings for the royal train, and dig a pond, half-moon shape, with three islands representing a ship, a fort, and a snail. At her arrival she was saluted in Latin verse by a poet clad in green to signify his joyful thoughts, with a laurel garland on his head and olive branch in his hand, and booted to betoken that he "was not a loose or low creeping prophet," as some ignorantly thought poets to be. While he spoke, six virgins removed blocks out of her Majesty's way, put there by Envy, and afterwards walked before her to the house, strewing the path with flowers and singing a sweet song of six parts. The next morning the pleasures were ordered, or rather, ruined by English weather: it rained. But in the afternoon the Queen came down to the pond, where Nereus, the prophet of the sea, was seen swimming ahead of five Tritons, "all with grisly heads and beards of divers colours and fashions," who waded, cheerfully sounding their trumpets. After the Tritons came Neptune and Oceanus drawing a pinnace, in which were three virgins playing cornets, a nymph named Neæra, and three singers—answered in the form of an echo from two other boats—and lastly, two jewels for the Queen. At a sign, Silvanus and his followers came forth out of a wood, to provide another oration and a diversion.

The next morning, when Elizabeth opened her casement window, she was greeted by three musicians, disguised in ancient country attire, singing the lovely lyric of Coridon and Phillida:

> In the merry month of May,
> In a morn by break of day,
> Forth I walked by the wood side,
> Where as May was in his pride.
> There I spied, all alone,
> Phillida and Coridon.
> Much ado there was, God wot!
> He would love, and she would not.

That evening there were fireworks from the three islands in the pond. "First, there was a peal of a hundred chambers discharged from the Snail-mount; in counter whereof, a like peal was discharged from the Ship-isle, and some great ordnance withal. Then there was a castle of fireworks of all sorts, which played in the fort. Answerable to that, there was in the Snail-mount a globe of all manner of fireworks, as big as a barrel. When these were spent on either side, there were many running rockets upon lines, which passed between the Snail-mount and the castle in the fort. On either side there were many fire-wheels, pikes of pleasure, and balls of wild fire, which burned in the water." During this display a banquet was served by two hundred gentlemen, the dishes numbering a thousand and being all in glass and silver.

On the last morning, the Fairy Queen and her maids saluted the Queen at her rising. And then came the departure, when the ditty of "Come again" was sung:

O come again, fair Nature's treasure,
Whose looks yield joys exceeding measure.

O come again, Heaven's chief delight,
Thine absence makes eternal night.

O come again, world's starbright eye,
Whose presence doth adorn the sky.

O come again, sweet beauty's sun:
When thou art gone, our joys are done.

Done their joys were! The Earl was left to foot the bill and count the silver and dishes and all manner of movables, for the passing of the Queen's followers was apt to resemble that of a plague of locusts.

The slow cumbersome character of a progress, together with constant political uncertainty, domestic and foreign, prevented Elizabeth from going very far afield. She visited Dover, Southampton, Bristol, Worcester, Stafford, Norwich, but a circle through these places represents the limits of her travels. There was a proposal to visit Shrewsbury: it came to nothing. In 1562 she was to have met Mary at York, and in 1575 was anxious to visit this city; but "the inly-working North" was never stirred by the emotions of an Elizabethan progress. It was left to its own loyalties and the romantic appeal of a rival, captive queen. It was a pity, but unavoidable. Accounts of these progresses, with their curious entertainments and equally curious verse, with their inimitable royal touches, and sometimes with unrehearsed incidents like that at Kenilworth, when a savage, tamed at sight of the Queen, in token of submission broke a tree that he carried and cast the top away, narrowly missing Elizabeth's horse and causing it to rear with fright: "No hurt, no hurt!" she cried—such accounts were printed as pamphlets, carrying to a wide audience the flavour of the occasion and the gratifying appeal of a Queen of whom Englishmen could be mightily proud and fond. The press and propaganda were powerful auxiliaries in this choice romance.

At Court there were regular spectacles to which it was easy for any gentleman to get access. Each Sunday there was a ceremonial procession through the rooms of the Palace to the Chapel, and the Presence Chamber was usually crowded with spectators to many of whom Elizabeth would say a few gracious words as she passed along. Lord Herbert of Cherbury, as a young man, came to Court on such an occasion, at the end of the reign. "As soon as she saw me," he tells, "she stopped, and swearing her usual oath, 'God's death!', demanded, 'Who is this?' Everybody there present looked upon me, but no man knew me until Sir James Croft, a Pensioner, finding the Queen stayed, returned back and told who I was, and that I had married Sir William Herbert of St. Julian's daughter. The Queen hereupon looked attentively upon me, and swearing again her ordinary oath, said, 'It is a pity he was married so young,' and thereupon gave her hand to kiss twice, both times gently clapping me on the cheek."

While the Queen was at service in the Chapel, the spectators could watch the ceremonial laying of dinner in the Presence Chamber, to the accompaniment of trumpets and kettledrums. The articles—table-cloth, salt-cellar, etc., as well as food—were brought in by attendants preceded by an usher with his rod, all of whom knelt three times before the Cloth of State, on entering and retiring. A lady-taster gave each attendant a morsel of the dish that he bore, this being the assay; and then, when everything was ready, a number of the Queen's maids appeared and solemnly carried the food into an inner, private apartment, for it was rarely, and only on great festival or state occasions, that Elizabeth actually fed in the Presence Chamber, before spectators. She was abstemious over food and drink.

In the Presence Chamber Elizabeth graced the general body of courtiers with her presence at various entertainments, including dancing, of which she was fond; in the Privy Chamber she talked or played cards or chess with councillors and the privileged great having access there; in her Withdrawing Chambers she became, so far as she could, a private person, and in addition to her ladies, passed the time with a very small intimate circle, who from one point of view were personal friends, but from the point of view of those without were "favourites." All monarchs had "favourites." How could it be otherwise? The anomaly in Elizabeth's reign was the difference in sex, and this was emphasized by the romantic note which the language of intimacy assumed. It betokened neither a lustful disposition, nor a callous heart; and though the amorous way in which men addressed her may seem highly suspicious, the staggering promiscuity of Elizabeth's "love" mocks at such fond credulity. Sir Thomas Heneage sent her a bodkin and pendant with the message, *Amat iste sine fine*—"This man loves you without end." She sent him answer that as these were his words to her, so hers to him were, "I love *sine fine,*" giving him "ten thousand millions of thanks" and promising to wear his pendant on that ear "that should not hearken to anything that should anyways hurt him that sent it." "Knowing that her Sanguine—presumably a nickname—was far in the cold north country where no butterflies were," she sent him a mother-of-pearl butterfly to play with. The quality of the "love" may be gauged by the fact that she told him to hasten back to his wife and bring her to Court.

All Elizabeth's close friends seem to have received nicknames. Leicester was her "Eyes," and ornamented his letters with a pair of eyes. Christopher Hatton, who was entering the fortunate circle of intimates in the late 'sixties, was her "Lids," and employed a cipher which may have been a crude representation of eyelids. "Adieu, most sweet Lady," he ended a letter. And then, with a play on the initials of *Elizabetha Regina,* went on "All and EveR yours, your most happy bondman, Lids." Later he became her "Mutton," or "Bell-wether." On one occasion, fearing that Sir Walter Raleigh, nicknamed "Water," was displacing him from Elizabeth's affections, he sent her what one imagines was a sweet, reproachful letter along with some "tokens," including a diminutive bucket, signifying Raleigh. She sent a verbal answer, "that if Princes were like Gods (as they should be) they would suffer no element so to abound as to breed confusion." The beasts of the field were "so dear unto her that she had bounded her banks so sure as no water or floods could be able ever to overthrow them"; and for better assurance unto him that he should fear no drowning, she sent him a bird—a dove—"that, together with the rainbow, brought the good tidings and the covenant that there should be no more destruction by water." Further, she willed him to remember she was a Shepherd, and then he might think "how dear her Sheep was unto her." The dark-featured Walsingham was her "Moor." Burghley was her "Spirit." "Sir Spirit," she wrote to him playfully, when he was in one of his blue moods, "I doubt I do nickname you, for those of your kind (they say) have no sense; but I have of late seen an *ecce signum,* that if an ass kick you, you feel it too soon. I will recant you from being my spirit, if ever I perceive that you disdain not such a feeling. Serve God, fear the King, and be a good fellow to the rest. Don't be "so silly a soul," she went on, "as not to regard her trust, who puts it in you. God bless you, and long may you last. *Omnino,* E.R."

It is difficult to convey a proper appreciation of this amazing Queen, so keenly intelligent, so effervescing, so intimate, so imperious and regal. She intoxicated Court and Country, keyed her realm to the intensity of her own spirit. No one but a woman could have done it, and no woman without her superlative gifts could have attempted it without disaster. In part instinctive, it was also conscious and deliberate. "Her mind," wrote her witty godson, Sir John Harington, "was oftime like the gentle air that cometh from the westerly point in a summer's morn; 'twas sweet and refreshing to all around. Her speech did win all affections, and her subjects did try to show all love to her commands; for she would say, 'Her state did require her to command, what she knew her people would willingly do from their own love to her' . . . Surely she did play well her tables to gain obedience thus, without constraint. Again, she could put forth such alterations, when obedience was lacking, as left no doubtings whose daughter she was." Harington tells how she would covertly search out the minds of her councillors, talking to Burghley till late at night, and then calling in another councillor, and so on; and afterwards compare their real thoughts with their utterances in council. "Sir Christopher Hatton was wont to say, 'The Queen did fish for men's souls, and had so sweet a bait that no one could escape her network' . . . I have seen her smile—sooth, with great semblance of good liking to all around—and cause everyone to open his most inward thought to her; when, on a sudden, she would ponder in private on what had passed, write down all their opinions, draw them out as occasion required, and sometimes disprove to their faces what had been delivered a month before. . . . She caught many poor fish, who little knew what snare was laid for them."

Elizabeth was exceedingly human, and was always letting impulse break through regal formality, which she regarded as made for her, not she for it. Glowing postscripts scribbled at the foot of formal letters to convey her gratitude or remind a distant servant of her affection: there were numerous touches of this kind, and we know their miraculous healing power. Or she might scribble a political letter, unbeknown to her officials, as she did to Sir Henry Sidney in Ireland in 1565. "Harry," it began; and went on in her most euphuistic style, like the utterance of some oracle, ending, "Let this memorial be only committed to Vulcan's base keeping, without any longer abode than the leisure of the reading thereof, yea, and with no mention made thereof to any other wight. I charge you, as I may command you. Seem not to have had but Secretary's letters from me. Your loving mistress, Elizabeth R." Fortunately, Penshurst and not Vulcan kept the letter. Or she might interrupt a speech or sermon. At the end of one parliament, when the Speaker had made a long-winded speech and Lord Keeper Bacon was rivalling him in the answer, Elizabeth told him to cease. In his text of the speech Bacon writes, "Hereafter followeth that I intended to have said if I had not been countermanded." In contrast, at the beginning of another parliament, after confirming the election of a new Speaker and listening to his happy and eloquent oration, as she passed she pulled off her glove and gave him her hand to kiss, and using a figure of archery, said, "You, sir, you are welcome to the butts, sir," and laid both her hands about his neck, and stayed a good space, and so most graciously departed; and in her Privy Chamber after, amongst her ladies, said, "she was sorry she knew him no sooner."

Preachers who overstepped discretion, sometimes found themselves sharply pulled up. Nowell, Dean of St. Paul's, preaching a Lenten sermon before a large congregation at Court in 1565, inveighed against a recent Catholic book dedicated to the Queen, and then went on to attack images and idolatry, an attack which in the circumstances was palpably meant for the crucifix in the royal Chapel. "Do not talk about that," Elizabeth called out; and as he went on, not hearing her, "Leave that," she cried, raising her voice, "it has nothing to do with your subject, and the matter is now threadbare." In 1596, when Elizabeth was in her sixty-third year—the grand climacteric, very much feared in those days—Bishop Rudd, encouraged by previous praise and Whitgift's report that "the Queen now is grown weary of the vanities of wit and eloquence wherewith her youth was formerly affected, and plain sermons which come home to her heart please her the best," chose for his Lenten sermon the text, "O teach us to number our days, that we may incline our hearts unto wisdom." Having spoken a while of some sacred and mystical numbers, as 3 for the Trinity, 3 times 3 for the heavenly Hierarchy, 7 for the Sabbath, and 7 times 7 for a Jubilee, he came to 7 times 9 for the grand climacterical year, and Elizabeth seeing the trend of his sermon grew troubled. The Bishop noticed this, and tried to save himself by treating of some more plausible numbers, as 666 making Latinus, "with which, he said, he could prove the Pope to be Antichrist," and also of the fatal number 88. But at the end of the service, the Queen opened the window of her closet and told him plainly that "he should have kept his arithmetic for himself." "I see," said she, "the greatest clerks are not the wisest men": a pertinent saying, for it was the height of folly to play on the fears that were entertained about her death.

In the sorrows of others the Queen was a woman. When the Earl of Huntingdon died she had the news kept from his wife and moved suddenly to Whitehall in order to break the blow by her own ministration of comfort. When Lady Norris lost a son in Ireland, "My own Crow," she wrote to her, "Harm not yourself for bootless help, but show a good example to comfort your dolorous yoke-fellow. . . ." And when two years later the same service took the lives of two more sons, she wrote to both father and mother: "We couple you together from desire that all the comfort we wish you may reach you both in this bitter accident. We were loth to write at all, lest we should give you fresh occasion of sorrow, but could not forbear, knowing your past resolution in like mishaps, and your religious obedience to Him whose strokes are unavoidable. We propose ourselves as an example, our loss being no less than yours." In 1595 when the Earl of Hertford took steps to set aside the declaration of invalidity against his marriage with Lady Catherine Grey, and was imprisoned in the Tower for his dangerous action, Elizabeth wrote to his second wife, who was distraught with anxiety. "Good Francke," she began, and bade her not to think the crime "more pernicious and malicious than an act of lewd and proud contempt against our own direct prohibition." "It is far from our desire to pick out faults in such as he. Being slow to rigour towards the meanest, we will use no more severity than is requisite for others' caution in like cases, and than shall stand with honour and necessity. . . . For a farewell, you are to observe this rule, that seeing griefs and troubles make haste enough, unsent for, to surprise us, there can be no folly greater than by fearing that which is not, or by over grieving for that which needs not, to overthrow the health of mind and body."

Another very human glimpse of the Queen is in a note which she sent to her godson Harington, then a boy, accompanying a copy of her speech to the Parliament of 1576: "Boy Jack, I have made a clerk write fair my poor words for thine use, as it cannot be such striplings have entrance into parliament assembly as yet. Ponder them in thy hours of leisure, and play with them till they enter thy understanding; so shalt thou hereafter, perchance, find some good fruits hereof when thy godmother is out of remembrance; and I do this, because thy father was ready to serve and love us in trouble and thrall"—a reference to the days of her sister, Mary.

Elizabeth's courtiers and advisers found her humours difficult. She had foibles: good health was one. Most of her life she enjoyed remarkable health and hated to be ill or even thought ill. In 1577 she several times commanded Leicester to write to Burghley, then at Buxton, asking him to send her some of the medicinal water from there. When it arrived, she mistrusted "it will not be of the goodness here it is there"; though the truth was that she had been told people were talking of it, "as though her Majesty had had some sore leg"; and she was half angry with Leicester now for writing to Burghley! In 1578 a tooth was giving her pain, and needed to come out, but because the Queen "doth not or will not so think," her physicians were afraid to tell her. In 1597 she had "a desperate ache" in her right thumb, but the gout it *could* not be, it *dare* not be; in fact, she had no ache, but she would not sign letters!

A person of such vivacity and wilfulness was in the nature of things trying at times. Her eyes were everywhere, faults were numerous, and she was exacting. Efficiency she would have, or know the reason why. And her very freedom with those around her, called for sharp tugs on the rein to remind them that she was mistress. When Lord Hunsdon, her cousin, took advantage—as others did—and overstayed his leave from his post at Berwick, his son wrote to him that Elizabeth "grew into a great rage, beginning with, 'God's wounds! that she would set you by the feet, and send another in your place if you dallied with her thus, for she would not be thus dallied withal!' " But when all is said of her passionate outbursts, they were usually little more than flashes of summer lightning. Sir John Harington, whose freshest memories were of her last years, when worry fretted her temper, says: "When she smiled, it was a pure sunshine that everyone did choose to bask in if they could; but anon came a storm from a sudden gathering of clouds, and the thunder fell in wondrous manner on all alike."

TWENTY-NINE

CHINA AND THE WEST

During the sixteenth century, as the Age of Discovery unfolded, traders and missionaries flocked to Asia. The East-West contact, first made tentatively in the thirteenth century by Marco Polo and others, became a continuing force in the life of both Asia and the West. An important stage in the increasing impact of Asia on the West came in 1615 with the publication in Latin of the journals of Matthew Ricci (1552–1610), a Jesuit missionary in China 1583–1610. Ricci's journals, many times reprinted, proved that China and Cathay were the same place, and stimulated a vogue for all things Chinese, which had mounting influence on Western civilization. In his description of China, Ricci gave prominence to the Chinese system of competitive civil service examinations which produced, by rigorously selective methods, scholar-administrators. This arrangement maintained an intellectual elite, drawn from all ranks of Chinese society, and provided a consistent way to attract men of ability, like Plato's Philosopher-Kings, into government. It influenced the later introduction of competitive civil service examinations in the West, probably as early as 1692 in Prussia and certainly in Britain in 1855, where Parliamentarians discussed at length the Chinese model for the proposed reforms. The examination system improved government administration in the West. But in China it centered exclusively on the Confucian classics so that Chinese officialdom found it difficult, in some cases impossible, to respond to powerful impulses from the West. In his book The Lore of Cathay, *published in 1901, W. A. P. Martin discusses the Chinese examination system, then still in operation in the Chinese Empire and at that time in fully developed form well over 1000 years old.*

WILLIAM A. P. MARTIN

THE LORE OF CATHAY*

In the arts which we have borrowed from the Chinese we have not been servile imitators. In every case we have made improvements that astonish the original inventors. We employ movable type, apply steam and electricity to printing, use the needle as a guide over seas which no junk would have ventured to traverse, and construct artillery such as the inventors of gunpowder never dreamed of. Would it be otherwise with a transplanted competitive system? Should we

* Reprinted from *The Lore of Cathay,* pp. 309–26, by William A. P. Martin by permission of Fleming H. Revell Company, Westwood, New Jersey. Copyright 1901, 1912.

not be able to purge it of certain defects which adhere to it in China, and so render it productive of better results than it yields in its native climate? I think, therefore, that I shall serve a better purpose than the simple gratification of curiosity if I devote a brief space to the consideration of the most admirable institution of the Chinese Empire.

Its primary object was to provide men of ability for the service of the State, and, whatever else it may have failed to accomplish, it is impossible to deny that it has fulfilled its specific end in a remarkable degree. The mandarins of China are almost without exception the choicest specimens of the educated classes. Alike in the capital and in the provinces, it is the mandarins that take the lead in every kind of literary enterprise. It is to them the Emperor looks to instruct as well as to govern his people; and it is to them that the publishers look for additions to the literature of the nation—nine-tenths of the new books being written by mandarins. In their social meetings, their conversation abounds in classical allusions; and instead of after-dinner speeches, they are accustomed to amuse themselves with the composition of impromptu verses, which they throw off with incredible facility. It is their duty to encourage the efforts of students, to preside at the public examinations, and to visit the public schools—to promote, in short, by example as well as precept, the interests of education. Scarcely anything is deemed a deeper disgrace than for a magistrate to be found incompetent for this department of his official duties. So identified, indeed, are the mandarins with all that constitutes the intellectual life of the Chinese people that foreigners have come to regard them as a favored caste, like the Brahmins of India, or as a distinct order enjoying a monopoly of learning, like the priesthood in Egypt.

Nothing could be further from the truth. Those stately officials, for whom the people make way with such awestruck deference, as they pass along the street with embroidered robes and imposing retinue, are not possessors of hereditary rank, neither do they owe their elevation to the favor of their sovereign, nor yet to the suffrages of their fellow-subjects. They are self-elected, and the people regard them with the deeper respect, because they know that they have earned their position by intellectual effort. What can be more truly democratic than (in the words of Anson Burlingame) to offer to all "the inspiration of fair opportunity?" In this genuine democracy China stands unapproached among the nations of the earth; for, whatever imperfections may attach to her social organization or to her political system, it must be acknowledged that she has devised the most effectual method for encouraging effort and rewarding merit. Here at least is one country where wealth is not allowed to raise its possessor to the seat of power; where the will even of an emperor cannot bestow its offices on uneducated favorites; and where the caprice of the multitude is not permitted to confer the honors of the State on incompetent demagogues.

The institution that accomplishes these results is not an innovation on the traditional policy of the Empire. It runs back in its essential features to the earliest period of recorded history. The adherence of the Chinese to it through so many ages well illustrates the conservative element in the national character; while the important changes it has undergone prove that this people is not by any means so fettered by tradition as to be incapable of welcoming improvements.

The germ from which it sprang was a maxim of the ancient sages, expressed in four syllables—*Chü hsien jên neng*—"Employ the able and promote the worthy;" and examinations were resorted to as affording the best test of ability and worth. Of the Great Shun, that model emperor of remote antiquity, who lived about B.C. 2200, it is recorded that he examined his officers every third year, and after these examinations either gave them promotion or dismissed them from the service. On what subjects he examined them at a time when letters were but newly invented, and when books had as yet no existence, we are not told; neither are we informed whether he subjected candidates to any test previous to appointment; yet the mere fact of such a periodical examination established a precedent which has continued to be observed to the present day. Every third year the government holds a great examination for the trial of candidates, and every fifth year makes a formal inquisition into the record of its civil functionaries. The latter is a poor substitute for the ordeal of public criticism to which officials are exposed in a country enjoying a free press; but the former, as we shall have occasion to show, is thorough of its kind, and severely impartial.

More than a thousand years after the above date, at the commencement of the Chou dynasty, B.C. 1115, the government was accustomed to examine candidates as well as officers; and this time we are not left in doubt as to the nature of the examination. The Chinese had become a cultivated people, and we are informed that all candidates for office were required to give proof of their acquaintance with the five arts—music, archery, horsemanship, writing, and arithmetic; and to be thoroughly versed in the rites and ceremonies of public and social life—an accomplishment that ranked as a sixth art. These "six arts," expressed in the concise formula *li, yüeh, shê, yü, shu, su,* comprehended the sum total of a liberal education at the period, and remind us of the *trivium* and *quadrivium* of the mediæval schools.

Under the dynasty of Han, after the lapse of another thousand years, we find the range of subjects for the civil-service examinations largely extended. The Confucian Ethics had become current, and a moral standard was regarded in the selection of the competitors—District magistrates were required to send up to the capital such men as had acquired a reputation for *hsiao* and *lien*—"filial piety" and "integrity"—the Chinese rightly considering that the faithful performance of domestic and social duties is the best guarantee for fidelity in public life. These *hsiao-lien,* "filial sons and honest subjects," whose moral character had been sufficiently attested, were now subjected to trial in respect to their intellectual qualifications. The trial was twofold—first, as to their skill in the "six arts" already mentioned; secondly, as to their familiarity with one or more of the following subjects: the civil law, military affairs, agriculture, the administration of the revenue, and the geography of the Empire with special reference to the state of the water communications. This was an immense advance on the meagre requirements of the more ancient dynasties.

Passing over another thousand years, we come to the era of the T'angs and the Sungs, when we find the standard of literary attainment greatly elevated, the graduates arranged in three classes, and officials in nine—a classification which is still retained.

Arriving at the close of the fourth millennium, under the sway of the Mings and of the Ch'ings of the present day, we find the simple trials instituted by Shun expanded into a colossal system, which may well claim to be the growth of four thousand years. It still exhibits the features that were prominent in its earlier stages—the "six arts," the "five studies," and the "three degrees" remaining as records of its progressive development. But the "six arts" are not what they once were; and the admirers of antiquity complain that examinations are sadly superficial as compared with those of the olden time, when competitors were required to ride a race, to shoot at a target, and to sing songs of their own composition to the accompaniment of their own guitars. In these degenerate days examiners are satisfied with odes in praise of music, and essays on the archery and horsemanship of the ancients.

Scholarship is a very different thing now from what it was in those ruder ages, when books were few, and the harp, the bow, and the saddle divided the student's time with the oral instructions of some famous master. Each century has added to the weight of his burden; and to the "heir of all the ages" each passing generation has bequeathed a legacy of toil. Doomed to live among the deposits of a buried world, and contending with millions of competitors, he can hardly hope for success without devoting himself to a life of unremitting study. True, he is not called upon to extend his researches beyond the limits of his own national literature; but that is all but infinite. It costs him at the outset years of labor to get possession of the key that unlocks it; for the learned language is totally distinct from his vernacular dialect, and justly regarded as the most difficult of the languages of man. Then he must commit to memory the whole circle of the recognized classics, and make himself familiar with the best writers of every age of a country which is no less prolific in books than in men. No doubt his course of study is too purely literary and too exclusively Chinese, but it is not superficial. In a popular "Student's Guide" we lately met with a course of reading drawn up for thirty years! We proposed putting it into the hands of a young American residing in China, who had asked advice as to what he should read. "Send it," he replied, "but don't tell my mother."

But it is time to take a closer view of these examinations as they are actually conducted. The candidates for office—those who are acknowledged as such in consequence of sustaining the initial trial—are divided into the three grades of *hsiu-ts'ai, chü-jen,* and *chin-shih*—"flowers of talent," "promoted scholars," and those who are "ready for office." The trials for the first are held in the chief city of each district or *hsien,* a territorial division which corresponds to our county or to an English shire. They are conducted by a chancellor, whose jurisdiction extends over an entire province containing, it may be, sixty or seventy such districts, each of which he is required to visit once a year, and each of which is provided with a resident sub-chancellor, whose duty it is to examine the scholars in the interval, and to have them in readiness on the chancellor's arrival.

About two thousand competitors enter the lists, ranging in age from the precocious youth just entering his teens up to the venerable grandsire of seventy winters. Shut up for a night and a day, each in his narrow cell, they produce each a poem and one or two essays on themes assigned by the chancellor, and then return to their homes to await the bulletin announcing their place in the scale of merit. The chancellor, assisted by his clerks, occupies several days in sifting the heap of manuscripts, from which he picks out some twenty or more that are distinguished by beauty of penmanship and grace of diction. The authors of these are honored with the degree of "Flower of Talent," and are entitled to wear the decorations of the lowest grade in the corporation of mandarins.

The successful student wins no purse of gold and obtains no office, but he has gained a prize which he deems a sufficient compensation for years of patient toil. He is the best of a hundred scholars, exempted from liability to corporal punishment, and raised above the vulgar herd. The social consideration to which he is now entitled makes it a grand day for him and his family.

Once in three years these "Flowers of Talent," these picked men of the districts, repair to the provincial capital to engage in competition for the second degree—that of *Chü Jên,* or "Promoted Scholar." The number of competitors amounts to ten thousand, more or less, and of these only one in every hundred can be admitted to the coveted degree. The trial is conducted by special examiners sent down from Peking; and this examination takes a wider range than the preceding. No fewer than three sessions of nearly three days each are occupied, instead of the single day for the first degree. Compositions in prose and verse are required, and themes are assigned with a special view to testing the extent of reading and depth of scholarship of the candidates. Penmanship is left out of the account—each production, marked with a cipher, being copied by an official scribe, that the examiners may have no clew to its author and no temptation to render a biassed judgment.

The victor still receives neither office nor emolument; but the honor he achieves is scarcely less than that which was won by the victors in the Olympic games. Again, he is one of a hundred, each of whom was a picked man; and as a result of this second victory he goes forth an acknowledged superior among ten thousand contending scholars. He adorns his cap with the gilded button of a higher grade, erects a pair of lofty flagstaves before the gate of his family residence, and places a tablet over his door to inform those who pass by that this is the abode of a literary prize-man. But our "Promoted Scholar" is not yet a mandarin in the proper sense of the term. The distinction already attained only stimulates his desire for higher honors—honors which bring at last the solid recompense of an income—travelling at the expense of the state.

In the spring of the following year he proceeds to Peking to seek the next higher degree, attainment of which will prove a passport to office. The contest is still with his peers; that is, with other "Promoted Scholars," who, like himself, have come up from all the provinces of the empire. But the chances are this time more in his favor, as the number of prizes is now tripled; and if the gods are propitious his fortune is made.

Though ordinarily not very devout, he now shows himself peculiarly solicitous to secure the favor of the divinities. He burns incense and gives alms. If he sees a fish floundering on the hook, he pays its price and restores it to its native element. He picks struggling ants out of the rivulet made by a recent shower, distributes moral tracts, or, better still, rescues chance bits of printed paper from being trodden in the mire of the streets.[1] If his name appears among the favored few, he not only wins himself a place in the front ranks of the lettered, but he plants his foot securely on the rounds of the official ladder by which, without the prestige of birth or the support of friends, it is possible to rise to a seat in the Grand Council of State or a place in the Imperial Cabinet. All this advancement presents itself in the distant prospect, while the office upon which he immediately enters is one of respectability, and it may be of profit. It is generally that of mayor or sub-mayor of a district city, or sub-chancellor in the district examinations—the vacant posts being distributed by lot, and therefore impartially, among those who have proved themselves to be "ready for office."

Before the drawing of lots, however, for the post of a magistrate among the people, our ambitious student has a chance of winning the more distinguished honor of a place in the Imperial Academy. With this view, the two or three hundred survivors of so many contests appear in the palace, where themes are assigned them by the Emperor himself, and the highest honor is paid to the pursuit of letters by the exercises being presided over by his Majesty in person. Penmanship reappears as an element in determining the result, and a score or more of those whose style is the most finished, whose scholarship the ripest, and whose handwriting the most elegant, are drafted into the college of Hanlin, the "forest of pencils," a kind of Imperial Institute the members of which are recognized as standing at the head of the literary profession. These are constituted poets and historians to the Celestial Court, or deputed to act as chancellors and examiners in the several provinces.

But the diminishing series in this ascending scale has not yet reached its final term. The long succession of contests culminates in the designation by the Emperor of some

[1] The bearing of good works of this kind on the result of the competition is copiously illustrated by collections of anecdotes which are widely circulated.

individual whom he regards as the *Chuang Yuan,* or Model Scholar of the Empire—the bright consummate flower of the season. This is not a common annual like the senior wranglership of Cambridge, nor the product of a private garden like the valedictory orator of our American colleges. It blooms but once in three years, and the whole Empire yields but a single blossom—a blossom that is culled by the hand of Majesty and esteemed among the brightest ornaments of his dominion. Talk of academic honors such as are bestowed by Western nations in comparison with those which this Oriental Empire heaps on her scholar laureate! Provinces contend for the shining prize, and the town that gives the victor birth becomes noted forever. Swift heralds bear the tidings of his triumph, and the hearts of the people leap at their approach. We have seen them enter a humble cottage, and amidst the flaunting of banners and the blare of trumpets announce to its startled inmates that one of their relations had been crowned by the Emperor as the laureate of the year. So high was the estimation in which the people held the success of their fellow-townsman that his wife was requested to visit the six gates of the city, and to scatter before each a handful of rice, that the whole population might share in the good-fortune of her household. A popular tale, represents a goddess as descending from heaven, that she might give birth to the scholar laureate of the Empire. So exalted is this dignity that in 1872 the daughter of a *Chuang Yuan* was deemed sufficiently noble to be chosen for Empress Consort.

All this has, we confess, an air of Oriental display and exaggeration. It suggests rather the dust and sweat of the great national games of antiquity than the mental toil and intellectual triumphs of the modern world. But it is obvious that a competition which excites so profoundly the interest of a whole nation must be productive of very decided results. That it leads to the selection of the best talent for the service of the public we have already seen; but beyond this—its primary object—it exercises a profound influence upon the education of the people and the stability of the government. It is all, in fact, that China has to show in the way of an educational system. She has few colleges and no universities in our Western sense,[2] and no national system of common-schools; yet it may be confidently asserted that China gives to learning a more effective patronage than she could have done if each of her emperors had been an Augustus and every premier a Mæcenas. She says to all her sons, "Prosecute your studies by such means as you may be able to command, whether in public or in private; and, when you are prepared, present yourselves in the examination-hall. The government will judge of your proficiency and reward your attainments."

Nothing can exceed the ardor which this standing offers infuses into the minds of all who have the remotest prospect of sharing in the prizes. They study not merely while they have teachers to incite them to diligence, but continue their studies with unabated zeal long after they have left the schools; they study in solitude and poverty; they study amidst the cares of a family and the turmoil of business; and the shining goal is kept steadily in view until the eye grows dim with age. Some of the aspirants impose on themselves the task of writing a fresh essay every day; and they do not hesitate to enter the lists as often as the public examinations recur, resolved, if they fail, to continue trying, believing that perseverance has power to command success, and encouraged by the legend of the man who, needing a sewing needle, made one by grinding a crowbar on a piece of granite.

We have met an old mandarin who related with evident pride how, on gaining the second degree, he had removed with his whole family to Peking, from the distant province

[2] This was written prior to the opening of the New University at Peking; and the North University at Tientsin—both closed suddenly, but not hopelessly, by the Boxer uprising.

of Yünnan, to compete for the third; and how at each triennial contest he had failed, until, after more than twenty years of patient waiting, at the seventh trial, and at the mature age of threescore he bore off the coveted prize. He had worn his honors for seven years, and was then mayor of the city of Tientsin. In a list now on our table of ninety-nine successful competitors for the second degree, sixteen are over forty years of age, one sixty-two, and one eighty-three. The average age of the whole number is above thirty; and for the third degree the average is of course proportionally higher.

So powerful are the motives addressed to them that the whole body of scholars who once enter the examination-hall are devoted to study as a life-long occupation. We thus have a class of men, numbering in the aggregate some two or three millions, who keep their faculties bright by constant exercise, and whom it would be difficult to parallel in any Western country for readiness with the pen and retentiveness of memory. If these men are not highly educated, it is the fault not of the competitive system, which proves its power to stimulate them to such prodigious exertions, but of the false standard of intellectual merit established in China. In that country letters are everything and science nothing. Men occupy themselves with words rather than with things; and the powers of acquisition are more cultivated than those of invention.

The type of Chinese education is not that of our modern schools; but when compared with the old curriculum of languages and philosophy it appears by no means contemptible. A single paper, intended for the last day of the examination for the second degree, may serve as a specimen. It covers five subjects—criticism, history, agriculture, military affairs, and finance. There are about twenty questions on each subject, and while they certainly do not deal with it in a scientific manner, it is something in their favor to say that they are such as cannot be answered without an extensive course of reading in Chinese literature. One question under each of the five heads is all that our space will allow us to introduce.

1. How do the rival schools of Wang and Ching differ in respect to the exposition of the meaning and the criticism of the text of the 'Book of Changes'?

2. The great historian Sze Ma Ch'ien prides himself on having gathered up much material that was neglected by other writers. What are the sources from which he derived his information?

3. From the earliest times great attention has been given to the improvement of agriculture. Will you indicate the arrangements adopted for that purpose by the several dynasties?

4. The art of war arose under Huang Ti, forty-four hundred years ago. Different dynasties have since that time adopted different regulations in regard to the use of militia or standing armies, the mode of raising supplies for the army, etc. Can you state these briefly?

5. Give an account of the circulating medium under different dynasties, and state how the currency of the Sung dynasty corresponded with our use of paper money at the present day.

In another paper, issued on a similar occasion, astronomy takes the place of agriculture; but the questions are confined to such allusions to the subject as are to be met with in the circle of their classical literature, and afford but little scope for the display of scientific attainments. Still, the fact that a place is found for this class of subjects is full of hope. It indicates that the door, if not fully open, is at least sufficiently ajar to admit the introduction of our Western sciences with all their progeny of arts, a band powerful enough to lift the Chinese out of the mists of their mediæval scholasticism, and to bring them into the full light of modern knowledge. If the examiners were scientific men, and if scientific subjects were made sufficiently prominent in these higher examinations, millions of aspiring students would soon become as earnest in the pursuit of modern science as they now are in the study of their ancient classics.[3] Thus reformed and renovated by the injection of fresh blood into the old arteries, this noble institution would be worthy of its dignity as a great national university—a university, not like those of Oxford and Cambridge, which train their own graduates, but—to compare great things with small—like the University of London, promoting the cause of learning by examining candidates and conferring degrees. The University of London admits to its initial examination annually about fourteen hundred candidates, and passes one half. The government examinations of China admit about two million candidates every year, and pass only two or three per cent.

The political bearings of this competitive system are too important to be passed over, and yet too numerous to be treated in detail. Its incidental advantages may be comprehended under three heads.

1. It serves the State as a safety-valve, providing a career for those ambitious spirits who might otherwise foment disturbances or excite revolutions. While in democratic countries the ambitious flatter the people, and in monarchies fawn on the great, in China, instead of resorting to dishonorable arts or to political agitation, they betake themselves to quiet study. They know that their mental calibre will be fairly gauged, and that if they are born to rule, the competitive examinations will open to them a career. The competitive system has not, indeed, proved sufficient to employ all the forces that tend to produce intestine commotion; but it is easy to perceive that without it the shocks must have been more frequent and serious.

2. It operates as a counterpoise to the power of an absolute monarch. Without it the great offices would be filled by hereditary nobles, and the minor offices be farmed out by thousands to imperial favorites.[4] With it a man of talent may raise himself from the humblest ranks to the dignity of viceroy or premier. *Chiang hsiang pên wu chung*—"The general and the prime-minister are not born in office"—is a line that every schoolboy is taught to repeat. Rising from the people, the mandarins understand the feelings and wants of the people, though it must be confessed that they are usually avaricious and oppressive in proportion to the length of time it has taken them to reach their elevation. Still, they have the support and sympathy of the people to a greater extent than they could have if they were creatures of arbitrary power. The system, therefore, introduces a popular element into the government that acts as a check on the prerogative of the Emperor as to the appointment of officers, and serves as a kind of constitution to his subjects, prescribing the conditions on which they shall obtain a share in the administration of the power of the State.

3. It gives the government a hold on the educated gentry, and binds them to the support of existing institutions. It renders the educated classes eminently conservative, because they know that in the event of a revolution civil office would be bestowed, not as the reward of learning, but for political or military services. The *literati,* the most influential portion of the population, are for this reason also the most loyal. It is their support that has upheld the reigning house, though of a foreign race, through these long years of civil commotion, while to the "revels" it has been a ground of

[3] As a sample of the practical bearing which it is possible to give to these examination exercises, we take a few questions from another paper:

"Fire-arms began with the use of rockets in the Chou dynasty (B.C. 1122–256); in what book do we first meet with the word for cannon? What is the difference in the two classes of engines to which it is applied (applied also to the catapult)? Is the defence of K'ai Fêng Fu its first recorded use? Kublai Khan, it is said, obtained cannon of a new kind; from whom did he obtain them? The Sungs had several varieties of small cannon, what were their advantages? When the Mings, in the reign of Yung Lo, invaded Cochin-China, they obtained a kind of cannon called the 'weapons of the gods;' can you give an account of their origin?"

[4] The Manchus in order to maintain their power have reserved to themselves an undue proportion of official posts.

reproach and a source of weakness that they have had but few literary men in their ranks.

In districts where the people have distinguished themselves by zeal in the Imperial cause, the only recompense they crave is a slight addition to the numbers on the competitive prize-list. Such additions the government has made very frequently of late years, in consideration of money supplies. It has also, to relieve its exhausted exchequer, put up for sale the decorations of the literary orders, and issued patents admitting contributors to the higher examinations without passing through the lower grades. But though the government thus debases the coin, it guards itself jealously against the issue of a spurious currency. Some years ago Pei Ching, first president of the Examining Board at Peking, was put to death for having fraudulently conferred two or three degrees. The fraud was limited in extent, but the damage it threatened was incalculable. It tended to shake the confidence of the people in the administration of that branch of the government which constituted their only avenue to honors and office. Even the Emperor cannot tamper with it without peril. He may lower its demands, in accordance with the wishes of a majority, but he could not set it aside without producing a revolution, for it is the ballot box of the people, the grand charter of their rights.

VI

THE ENLIGHTENMENT

PART SIX

◆§ THE ENLIGHTENMENT

The period in Western history extending from the second half of the seventeenth century through the French Revolution of 1789 is commonly known as the Enlightenment, or the Age of Reason. The main source of this momentous era is the so-called Scientific Revolution of the seventeenth century and the wider horizons which developed from increased knowledge of the non-Western world. In the seventeenth century, possibly stimulated by revolutionary impulses associated with the Protestant Revolt, scientists devised new methods, both rational and empirical, of investigating the physical world. Here was the articulated secularism of the Renaissance, with its classical roots, surpassing the best of classical science and venturing into new frontiers of inquiry. Indeed, some historians associate the modern Western world with the development of seventeenth-century science. In time, science left the laboratory and social philosophers such as Voltaire began to use scientific methods for criticism of and proposed reconstruction of Europe's political, economic, and social order. Generally they distrusted democracy, which they tended to dismiss as the tyranny of the many, and relied instead on enlightened (rational) despotism as the best means to social betterment. Other thinkers of the Enlightenment, such as Jefferson, used the English Natural Rights argument to justify the American Revolution. But not all thinkers in the Enlightenment were rationalists. Europe's governing classes were mainly traditionalist in attitude, and influential conservatives such as Burke bitterly attacked the French Revolution. This traditionalism prepared the way for the era of reaction which followed the final defeat of Napoleon in 1815.

THIRTY

SCIENCE AND THE MODERN WORLD

The increasing impact of science on world civilization over the past three centuries is a well-recognized historical phenomenon. Science, of course, is a basic ingredient in both the ideology and technology of the twentieth century. For historians, who seek coherence in past and present human experience by dealing with artificial time-spans such as "the Middle Ages" and "the Renaissance," modern science has presented a particularly hard problem. If science is such a dominant force in the present, in what part of the past did it appear? How did it influence and guide Western civilization to create the world of today? In a highly stimulating work, Professor Herbert Butterfield has set out to find answers to these and to other related questions. He has surveyed the traditional periodization of Western history from the Ancient World with its fusion of the Greco-Roman and Hebrew traditions through the Middle Ages and the Renaissance. He has concluded that the major turning point in the creation of the Western civilization of the present occurred with the many phenomenal scientific advances (often called the Scientific Revolution) of the seventeenth century.

HERBERT BUTTERFIELD

THE ORIGINS OF MODERN SCIENCE, 1300-1800 *

It was the passion of Ranke, whatever period or episode in history he might be studying, to seek to put it in its place in what he called "Universal History," which was the home you reached—the ocean you finally gazed upon—if you went far enough in your reflection upon a piece of narrative. To such a degree did he set his mind on this object that he could describe the quest for "the ocean of universal history" as the great purpose of his life, the ultimate goal of all his studies. It is strange that this—one of the most insistent parts of his message—should have been the one we have allowed to drop most completely out of sight in our usual studies of history, so that we tend to overlook it even when we are making an estimate of Ranke himself. Having examined many aspects of the seventeenth-century intellectual movement internally, however, it may be useful for us if we enlarge our perspective, standing some distance away from the story that we have been studying, and try to find the bearings of these events on the whole history of Western civilisation.

Until a comparatively recent date—that is to say, until the sixteenth or the seventeenth century—such civilisation as existed in our whole portion of the globe had been centred for thousands of years in the Mediterranean, and during the Christian era had been composed largely out of Græco-Roman and ancient Hebrew ingredients. Even at the Renaissance, Italy still held the intellectual leadership in Europe, and, even after this, Spanish culture had still to come to its climax, Spanish kings ruled over one of the great empires of history, and Spain had the ascendancy in the Counter-Reformation. Until a period not long before the Renaissance, the intellectual leadership of such civilisation as existed in this quarter of the globe had remained with the lands in the eastern half of the Mediterranean or in empires that stretched farther still into what we call the Middle East. While our Anglo-Saxon forefathers were semi-barbarian, Constantinople and Baghdad were fabulously wealthy cities, contemptuous of the backwardness of the Christian West.

In these circumstances it requires to be explained why the West should have come to hold the leadership in this part of the world; and, considering the Græco-Roman character of European culture in general, it is necessary to account for the division of the continent and to show why there should ever have arisen anything which we could call the civilisation of the West. Explanations are not difficult to find. Even when the Roman Empire surrounded the whole of the Mediterranean, there had been tension between East and West—a tension greatly increased when a second capital of the Empire had been founded and the oriental influences were able to gather themselves together and

* Reprinted from *The Origins of Modern Science, 1300–1800,* pp. 187–202, by Herbert Butterfield by permission of G. Bell & Sons, Ltd., London, 1949. Published in the United States by Collier Books.

focus their influence on the city of Constantinople. In the subsequent period—the age of the Barbarian Invasions—the differences were increased when Constantinople held out against attacks and preserved the continuity of classical culture, while, as we have seen, the West was so reduced that it had to spend centuries recapturing and reappropriating it—gathering the fragments together again and incorporating them into its own peculiar view of life. The religious cleavage between Rome and Byzantium in the middle ages (when differences of religion seemed to penetrate into every department of thought) accentuated the discrepancies between Latin and Greek and led to divergent lines of development—in the West, for example, the friction between Church and State gave a tremendous stimulus to the progress of society and the rise of political thought. The West developed independently, then, but, though it may have been more dynamic, it was still for a long time backward. Even in the fifteenth century—in the period of the high Renaissance—the Italians were ready to sit at the feet of exiled teachers from Constantinople and to welcome them as men like Einstein were welcomed not very long ago in England or America. By this time, however, visitors from the Byzantine Empire were expressing their wonder at the technological advances in the West.

An important factor in the decline of the East and the rise of Western leadership, however, was one which has been unduly overlooked in our historical teaching, for it has played a decisive part in the shaping of the map of Europe, as well as in the story of European civilisation itself. From the fourth to the twentieth century one of the most remarkable aspects of the story—the most impressive conflict that spans fifteen hundred years—is the conflict between Europe and Asia, a conflict in which down to the time of Newton's *Principia* it was the Asiatics who were on the aggressive. From the fourth to the seventeenth century—when they still expected to reach the Rhine—the greatest menace to any culture at all in Europe were the hordes of successive invaders from the heart of Asia, coming generally by a route to the north of the Black Sea (a region which remained therefore a sort of no-man's-land almost down to the time of the French Revolution), but coming later south of the Caspian Sea and into Asia Minor and the Mediterranean region. Beginning with the Huns, and continuing with the Avars, the Bulgars, the Magyars, the Petchenegs, the Cumans, etc., these hordes—generally Turkish or Mongol in character—sometimes succeeded one another so quickly that one group was thrust forward into Europe by the pressure of others in the rear, or a chain of them would be jostling one another in a westerly direction—all of which culminated in the Mongol invasions of the thirteenth century, and the conquests of the Ottoman Turks after that.

These Asiatic invaders had something to do with the downfall of Rome and the western empire over fifteen hundred years ago; they overthrew Constantinople, the second Rome, in 1453; and for centuries they virtually enslaved Russia and dominated Moscow, which later came to stand in the position of a third Rome. It was they who hung as a constant shadow over the East and eventually turned the eastern Mediterranean lands into desert; and they put an end to the glory of Baghdad. Because of their activity over so many centuries it was the western half of Europe that emerged into modern history as the effective heir and legatee of the Græco-Roman civilisation. From the tenth century A.D. these Asiatics—though for centuries they had tormented us and carried their depredations as far as the Atlantic coast—were never able to break into the West again or to do more than besiege Vienna. The tenth century represents something like a restoration of stability, therefore—the time from which Western civilisation makes its remarkable advance. One aspect of the period that comes to its culmination in the Renaissance is the emergence of western

Europe to a position of independence and, indeed, of conscious cultural leadership.

A primary aspect of the Renaissance, however, as we have seen, is the fact that it completes and brings to its climax the long process by which the thought of antiquity was being recovered and assimilated in the middle ages. It even carries to what at times is a ludicrous extreme the spirit of an exaggerated subservience to antiquity, the spirit that helped to turn Latin into a dead language. Ideas may have appeared in new combinations, but we cannot say that essentially new ingredients were introduced into our civilisation at the Renaissance. We cannot say that here were intellectual changes calculated to transform the character and structure of our society or civilisation. Even the secularisation of thought which was locally achieved in certain circles at this time was not unprecedented and was a hothouse growth, soon to be overwhelmed by the fanaticism of the Reformation and the Counter-Reformation. During much of the seventeenth century itself we can hardly fail to be struck, for example, by the power of religion both in thought and in politics.

People have talked sometimes as though nothing very new happened in the seventeenth century either, since natural science itself came to the modern world as a legacy from ancient Greece. More than once in the course of our survey we ourselves have even been left with the impression that the scientific revolution could not take place—that significant developments were held up for considerable periods—until a further draft had been made upon the thought of antiquity and a certain minimum of Greek science had been recovered. Against all this, however, it might be said that the course of the seventeenth century, as we have studied it, represents one of the great episodes in human experience, which ought to be placed—along with the exile of the ancient Jews or the building-up of the universal empires of Alexander the Great and of ancient Rome—amongst the epic adventures that have helped to make the human race what it is. It represents one of those periods when new things are brought into the world and into history out of men's own creative activity, and their own wrestlings with truth. There does not seem to be any sign that the ancient world, before its heritage had been dispersed, was moving towards anything like the scientific revolution, or that the Byzantine Empire, in spite of the continuity of its classical tradition, would ever have taken hold of ancient thought and so remoulded it by a great transforming power. The scientific revolution we must regard, therefore, as a creative product of the West—depending on a complicated set of conditions which existed only in western Europe, depending partly also perhaps on a certain dynamic quality in the life and the history of this half of the continent. And not only was a new factor introduced into history at this time amongst other factors, but it proved to be so capable of growth, and so many-sided in its operations, that it consciously assumed a directing rôle from the very first, and, so to speak, began to take control of the other factors—just as Christianity in the middle ages had come to preside over everything else, percolating into every corner of life and thought. And when we speak of Western civilisation being carried to an oriental country like Japan in recent generations, we do not mean Græco-Roman philosophy and humanist ideals, we do not mean the Christianising of Japan, we mean the science, the modes of thought and all that apparatus of civilisation which were beginning to change the face of the West in the latter half of the seventeenth century.

Now I think it would be true to say that, for the historian, as distinct perhaps from the student of pre-history, there are not in any absolute sense civilisations that rise and fall—there is just the unbroken web of history, the unceasing march of generations which themselves overlap with one another and interpenetrate, so that even the history of science is part of a continuous story of mankind going back to peoples far behind the ancient Greeks themselves. But we cannot hold our history in our minds without any landmarks, or as an ocean without fixed points, and we may talk about this civilisation and that as though they were ultimate units, provided we are not superstitious in our use of the word and we take care not to become the slaves of our terminology. Similarly, though everything comes by antecedents and mediations—and these may always be traced farther and farther back without the mind ever coming to rest—still, we can speak of certain epochs of crucial transition, when the subterranean movements come above ground, and new things are palpably born, and the very face of the earth can be seen to be changing. On this view we may say that in regard not merely to the history of science but to civilisation and society as a whole the transformation becomes obvious, and the changes become congested, in the latter part of the seventeenth century. We may take the line that here, for practical purposes, our modern civilisation is coming out in a perceptible manner into the daylight.

In this period the changes were not by any means confined to France, though what we have hitherto studied has drawn our attention to certain aspects of the transition in the case of that country in particular. The movement was localised, however, and it is connected with the humming activity which was taking place, say from 1660, not only in England, Holland and France, but also actually between these countries—the shuttle running to and fro and weaving what was to become a different kind of Western culture. At this moment the leadership of civilisation may be said to have moved in a definitive manner from the Mediterranean, which had held it for thousands of years, to the regions farther north. There had been a pull in this direction on the part of the university of Paris in the later middle ages, and a still stronger pull after the Renaissance, when Germany had revolted against Rome and the north had taken its own path at the Reformation. In any case the Mediterranean had become at times almost a Mohammedan lake, and the geographical discoveries had been transferring the economic predominance to the Atlantic seaboard for a number of generations. For a moment, then, the history of civilisation was focused on the English Channel, where things were weaving themselves into new patterns, and henceforward the Mediterranean was to appear to the moderns as a backward region. Not only did England and Holland hold a leading position, but that part of France which was most active in promoting the new order was the Huguenot or ex-Huguenot section, especially the Huguenots in exile, the nomads, who played an important part in the intellectual exchange that was taking place. After 1685—after the Revocation of the Edict of Nantes—the alliance between the French and the English Protestants became more close. Huguenots fled to England or became the intermediaries for the publication in Holland of journals written in French and communicating English ideas. As the eighteenth century proceeded, the balance in Europe shifted more definitely to the north, with the rise of the non-Catholic powers of Russia and Prussia. Even in the new world it was the northern half of the continent that came to the forefront, and it was soon decided that this northern part should be British not French, Protestant not Roman Catholic—an ally, therefore, of the new form of civilisation. The centre of gravity of the globe itself seemed to have changed and new areas of its surface found for a time their "place in the sun."

This new chapter in the history of civilisation really opened when in 1660, after a long period of internal upheaval and civil war, a comparative political stability was brought about not merely in France but in general throughout the continent, where on all sides the institution of monarchy had been gravely challenged but had managed to reassert itself and to re-establish a public order. In fact, what we have already noticed in the case of France was still more true in England and Holland in the seventeenth century—we see the power in intellectual matters of what, in spite of the objections to the term, we must call the middle class. And just as the Renaissance was particularly associated with city-states (or virtual city-states) in Italy, South Germany and the Netherlands, where the commerce and economic development had produced an exhilarating civic life, so in the last quarter of the seventeenth century the intellectual changes were centred on the English Channel, where commerce had been making so remarkable a rise and so much prosperity seemed to have been achieved. The city-state disappeared from history in the first half of the sixteenth century; but on the wider platform of the nation-state the future still belonged to what we call the middle classes.

If we have in mind merely the intellectual changes of the period we are considering, they have been described by one historian under the title, *La crise de la conscience européenne*—a title which itself gives some indication of the importance of the transition that was taking place. What was in question was a colossal secularisation of thought in every possible realm of ideas at the same time, after the extraordinarily strong religious character of much of the thinking of the seventeenth century. John Locke produces a transposition into secular terms of what had been a presbyterian tradition in political thought, and in doing so he is not a freak or a lonely prophet—he stands at the pivotal point in what is now a general transition. This secularisation came at the appropriate moment for combination with the work of the scientific revolution at the close of the seventeenth century; yet it would appear that it was not itself entirely the result of the scientific achievements—a certain decline of Christianity appears to have been taking place for independent reasons. One is tempted to say on quite separate grounds that this period emerges as one of the lowest points in the history of Western Christianity between the eleventh century and the twentieth. If we look at the general moral tone of Charles II's reign after the period of the Puritan ascendancy and compare it with the extraordinarily parallel case of the Regency in France after the religiosity of the closing years of Louis XIV's reign, it is difficult to resist the feeling that in both cases a general relaxation in religion and morals followed periods of too great tension—these things were not the straight results of the scientific revolution taken in isolation. In any case it lay perhaps in the dialectic of history itself that in the long conflicts between Protestant and Catholic the secular state should rise to independence and should secure an arbitral position over what now seemed to be mere religious parties within it. The whole story of the Renaissance shows within the limits of the city-state how the exhilarating rise of an urban civilisation is liable to issue in a process of secularisation—the priest as well as the noble loses the power that he was able to possess in a more conservative agrarian world. Something parallel has happened over and over again in the case of nation-states when not only have towns become really urban in character—which is late in the case of England, for example—but when a sort of leadership in society has passed to the towns, and literature itself comes to have a different character.

There is another reason why it would be wrong to impute all the changes in thought at this time to the effect of the scientific discoveries alone. It happened that just at this moment books of travel were beginning to have a remarkable effect on the general outlook of men—a postponed result of the geographical discoveries and of the growing acquaintance with distant lands. Western Europe was now coming to be familiar with the widespread existence of peoples who had never heard of ancient Greece or of Christianity. When these were taken into one's larger survey, the European outlook came to be envisaged not as universal, not necessarily even as central, but somewhat as a regional affair. It became possible to look upon it as only the local tradition of a comparatively small section of the globe. So one could begin to regard one's own culture, even one's own religion, with a great degree of relativity. It was possible to look on each local creed as embodying one essential truth, but covering that truth with its own local myths, perversions and accretions. What was common to all was the universal irreducible truth—the principles of natural religion—and in French books of travel, therefore, you find the essential ingredients of Deism before John Locke had shown the way. Furthermore, you could feel that in Western Europe Christianity had its basis in the same universal truth, but the principles had been covered (in Roman Catholicism, for example) by local accretions, revelations and miracles, from which it now required to be extricated. The results of all this harmonised with the operations of the new science, and strengthened the case for the kind of Deism which Newton's system seemed to encourage—a Deism which required a God only at the beginning of time to set the universe in motion.

From this period also there developed in a remarkable way and with extraordinary speed the tendency to a new type of Protestantism—the more liberal type which most of us have in mind when we are in controversy on this subject. It was a Protestantism married to the rationalising movement, and so different from the original Protestantism that it now requires an effort of historical imagination to discover what Martin Luther had in mind. Some remarkable developments in this rationalising tendency were only checked in England by the rise and the pervasive influence of John Wesley, who, however, also carries so many of the features of the Age of Reason in himself. On the other hand we have to note that if books of travel affected the attitude of western Europeans to their own traditions, the very attitude these people adopted (the kind of relativity they achieved) owed something to a certain scientific outlook which was now clearly becoming a more general habit of mind. Similarly, when in the 1660s a writer like Joseph Glanvill could produce a book on *The Vanity of Dogmatising,* insisting on the importance of scepticism in science and on the system of methodical doubt, it is impossible to deny that this critical outlook is an effect of the scientific movement. In general, we ought not to close our eyes to the extremely dislocating effects of that general overthrow of the authority of both the middle ages and antiquity which again had been produced by the scientific revolution. Either we may say, therefore, that a number of converging factors were moving the Western world in one prevailing direction, or we must say that there was one wind so overpowering that it could carry along with it anything else that happened—a wind so mighty that it gathered every other movement into its sweep, to strengthen the current in favour of secularisation at this time.

The changes which took place in the history of thought in this period, however, are not more remarkable than the changes in life and society. It has long been our tendency to push back the origins of both the industrial revolution and the so-called agrarian revolution of the eighteenth century, and though, as I have said, we can trace back the origin of anything as far as we like, it is towards the end of the seventeenth century that the changes are becoming palpable. The passion to extend the scientific method to every branch of thought was at least equalled by the passion to make science serve the cause of industry and agriculture, and it was accompanied by a sort of technological fervour. Francis Bacon had always laid stress on the immense utilitarian possibilities of science, the advantages beyond all dreams that would come from the control of nature; and it is difficult, even in the early history of the Royal Society, to separate the interest shown in the cause of pure scientilc truth from the curiosity in respect of useful inventions on the one part, or the inclination to dabble in fables and freakishness on the other. It has become a debatable question how far the direction of scientific interest was itself affected by technical needs or preoccupations in regard to shipbuilding and other industries; but the Royal Society followed Galileo in concerning itself, for example, with the important question of the mode of discovering longitude at sea. Those who wish to trace the development of the steam-engine will find that it is a story which really begins to be vivid and lively in this period. Apart from such developments, the possibilities of scientific experiment were likely themselves to be limited until certain forms of production and technique had been elaborated in society generally. Indeed, the scientific, the industrial and the agrarian revolutions form such a system of complex and interrelated changes, that in the lack of a microscopic examination we have to heap them all together as aspects of a general movement, which by the last quarter of the seventeenth century was palpably altering the face of the earth. The hazard consists not in putting all these things together and rolling them into one great bundle of complex change, but in thinking that we know how to disentangle them—what we see is the total intricate network of changes, and it is difficult to say that any one of these was the simple result of the scientific revolution itself.

Embraced in the same general movement is that growth of overseas trade which we have already noticed in the case of France—and once again we find a remarkable postponed result of the geographical discoveries of a much earlier period, reminding us that the New World represents one of the permanent changes in the conditioning circumstances of the modern age, one of the great standing differences between medieval and modern times, its results coming in relays and reproducing themselves at postponed periods. In the England of Charles II's reign we begin to see that we are an empire; the Board of Trade and Plantations comes to occupy a central position in the government; it is after 1660 that the East India Company reaps its colossal harvests. We begin to hear much less in the way of complaint about the excessive numbers of the clergy—henceforward what we begin to hear are complaints about the growing number of customs officials, Treasury men, colonial officers, contractors—all of them subject to corruption by the government. This is the epoch in which, as historians have long pointed out, wars of trade—especially amongst the Dutch, the French and the English—succeeded the long series of wars of religion. In a similar way we must take note of the foundation of such things as the Bank of England and the national debt—a new world of finance that alters not merely the government but the very fabric of the body politic. We have seen how in France and England there already existed signs of that speculative fever which culminated in the scheme of John Law on the one hand and the South Sea Bubble on the other; while in Holland there had been a parallel financial sensation earlier still.

For two thousand years the general appearance of the world and the activities of men had varied astonishingly little—the skyline for ever the same—so much so that men were not conscious of either progress or process in history, save as one city or state might rise by effort or good fortune while another fell. Their view of history had been essentially static because the world had been static so far as they could see—life in successive generations played out by human beings on a stage that remained essentially the same. Now, however, change became so quick as to be perceptible with the naked eye, and the face of the earth and the activities of men were to alter more in a century than they had previously done in a thousand years. We shall see later, in connection with the idea of progress, how in general—and for effective purposes—it was in this period that men's whole notion of the process of things in time was thrown into the melting-pot. And the publication of a host of journals in France, England and Holland speeded up the pace of intellectual change itself.

A curious feature of seventeenth-century English life illustrates the growing modernity of the world, and throws light not only on social change but on a certain different flavour that is becoming apparent in the prevailing mentality. There is a foretaste of it in the debates of James I's reign when we find that certain people called Projectors are being attacked in parliament—the sort of people whom we might call company-promoters, and who devised schemes for making money. They developed very greatly after the Restoration, becoming a considerable phenomenon in William III's reign, and they culminated in the period of the South Sea Bubble, when companies were founded to execute all kinds of fantastic schemes, including a method of procuring perpetual motion. Just before the end of the seventeenth century Daniel Defoe—who emerges as a remarkably modern mind—produced an *Essay on Projects* in which he commented on the whole phenomenon, satirised the Projectors, but then produced many schemes of his own to swell the flood. It is curious to note that these Projectors provided another of what we should call the "mediations" which assisted the passage to the *philosophe* movement; for though some of them had schemes for getting rich quickly—Defoe had a scheme for improving trade by settling the problem of the Barbary pirates, for example —some others had wider views: schemes of general amelioration, schemes for tackling the problem of the poor, plans for female education, devices for getting rid of the national debt. The famous socialistic system of Robert Owen was taken, as Owen himself explains, from John Bellairs, who produced the design of it in 1696 under the title of "a scheme by which the rich were to remain rich and the poor were to become independent, and children were to be educated." Bellairs had other proposals for general amelioration—for example in connection with prison-reform. Such things easily passed into projects for new forms of government, and curious mechanical schemes were put forward—the prelude to modern constitution-making and blue-prints for Utopia. They make it clear that the historical process is very complex; that while the scientific movement was taking place, other changes were occurring in society—other factors were ready to combine with it to create what we call the modern world.

It is always easy for a later generation to think that its predecessor was foolish, and it may seem shocking to state that even after the first World War good historians could write the history of the nineteenth century with hardly a hint of the importance of Socialism, hardly a mention of Karl Marx—a fact which we should misinterpret unless we took it as a reminder of the kind of faults to which all of us are prone. Because we have a fuller knowledge of after-events, we today can see the nineteenth century differently; and it is not we who are under an optical illusion—reading the twentieth century back unfairly into the nineteenth—when we say that the student of the last hundred years is missing a decisive factor if he overlooks the rise of Socialism. A man of insight could have recognised the importance of the phenomenon long before the end of the nineteenth century. But we, who have seen the implications worked out in the events of our time, need no insight to recognise the importance of this whole aspect of the story.

Something similar to this is true when we of the year 1957 take our perspective of the scientific revolution—we are in a position to see its implications at the present day much more clearly than the men who flourished fifty or even twenty years before us. And, once again, it is not we who are under an optical illusion—reading the present back into the past—for the things that have been revealed in the 1950s merely bring out more vividly the vast importance of the turn which the world took three hundred years ago, in the days of the scientific revolution. We can see why our predecessors were less conscious of the significance of the seventeenth century —why they talked so much more of the

Renaissance or the eighteenth-century Enlightenment, for example—because in this as in so many other cases we can now discern those surprising overlaps and time-lags which so often disguise the direction things are taking. Our Græco-Roman roots and our Christian heritage were so profound—so central to all our thinking—that it has required centuries of pulls and pressures, and almost a conflict of civilisations in our very midst, to make it clear that the centre had long ago shifted. At one time the effects of the scientific revolution, and the changes contemporary with it, would be masked by the persistence of our classical traditions and education, which still decided so much of the character of the eighteenth century in England and in France, for example. At another time these effects would be concealed through that popular attachment to religion which so helped to form the character of even the nineteenth century in this country. The very strength of our conviction that ours was a Græco-Roman civilisation—the very way in which we allowed the art-historians and the philologists to make us think that this thing which we call "the modern world" was the product of the Renaissance—the inelasticity of our historical concepts, in fact—helped to conceal the radical nature of the changes that had taken place and the colossal possibilities that lay in the seeds sown by the seventeenth century. The seventeenth century, indeed, did not merely bring a new factor into history, in the way we often assume—one that must just be added, so to speak, to the other permanent factors. The new factor immediately began to elbow the other ones away, pushing them from their central position. Indeed, it began immediately to seek control of the rest, as the apostles of the new movement had declared their intention of doing from the very start. The result was the emergence of a kind of Western civilisation which when transmitted to Japan operates on tradition there as it operates on tradition here—dissolving it and having eyes for nothing save a future of brave new worlds. It was a civilisation that could cut itself away from the Græco-Roman heritage in general, away from Christianity itself—only too confident in its power to exist independent of anything of the kind. We know now that what was emerging towards the end of the seventeenth century was a civilisation exhilaratingly new perhaps, but strange as Nineveh and Babylon. That is why, since the rise of Christianity, there is no landmark in history that is worthy to be compared with this.

THIRTY-ONE

THE SCIENTIFIC METHOD

Francis Bacon (1561–1626), English jurist, essayist, and philosopher of science, made an outstanding contribution to the development of the scientific method. In his Novum Organum *(New Instrument), published in 1620, he expounds at length his method of seeking scientific truth. His goal was exalted: humanity's control of nature through science. Bacon found four main obstacles to proper scientific investigation. He called these obstacles the Idols of the Tribe (human misunderstanding), Cave (human eccentricity), Marketplace (misuse of language), and Theater (misuse of philosophy). Bacon tried to find a balance between empirical and rational elements in scientific research. He states (Aphorism 95), "Those who have handled sciences have been either men of experiment or men of dogmas. The men of experiment are like the ant; they only collect and use: the reasoners resemble spiders, who make cobwebs out of their own substance. But the bee takes a middle course, it gathers its material from the flowers of the garden and of the field, but transforms and digests it by a power of its own. . . . Therefore from a closer and purer league between these two faculties, the experimental and the rational, (such as has never yet been made) much may be hoped." In addition, in his* New Atlantis, *published in 1627, Bacon describes in considerable detail an imaginary scientific society much like the Royal Society chartered 35 years later.*

FRANCIS BACON

NOVUM ORGANUM *

XXXIX

There are four classes of idols which beset men's minds. To these for distinction's sake I have assigned names,—calling the first class *Idols of the Tribe;* the second, *Idols of the Cave;* the third, *Idols of the Market-place;* the fourth, *Idols of the Theater*.

* From Francis Bacon, *Novum Organum,* pp. 85–99. First published in 1620.

XL

The formation of ideas and axioms by true induction is no doubt the proper remedy to be applied for the keeping off and clearing away of idols. To point them out, however, is of great use, for the doctrine of idols is to the interpretation of nature what the doctrine of the refutation of sophisms is to common logic.

XLI

The Idols of the Tribe have their foundation in human nature itself, and in the tribe or race of men. For it is a false assertion that the sense of man is the measure of things. On the contrary, all perceptions, as well of the sense as of the mind, are according to the measure of the individual and not according to the measure of the universe. And the human understanding is like a false mirror, which, receiving rays irregularly, distorts and discolors the nature of things by mingling its own nature with it.

XLII

The Idols of the Cave are the idols of the individual man. For everyone (besides the errors common to human nature in general) has a cave or den of his own, which refracts and discolors the light of nature; owing either to his own proper and peculiar nature or to his education and conversation with others; or to the reading of books, and the authority of those whom he esteems and admires; or to the differences of impressions, accordingly as they take place in a mind preoccupied and predisposed or in a mind indifferent and settled; or the like. So that the spirit of man (according as it is meted out to different individuals) is in fact a thing variable and full of perturbation, and governed as it were by chance. Whence it was well observed by Heraclitus that men look for sciences in their own lesser worlds, and not in the greater or common world.

XLIII

There are also idols formed by the intercourse and association of men with each other, which I call Idols of the Market-place, on account of the commerce and consort of men there. For it is by discourse that men associate; and words are imposed according to the apprehension of the vulgar. And therefore the ill and unfit choice of words wonderfully obstructs the understanding. Nor do the definitions or explanations wherewith in some things learned men are wont to guard and defend themselves, by any means set the matter right. But words plainly force and overrule the understanding, and throw all into confusion, and lead men away into numberless empty controversies and idle fancies.

XLIV

Lastly, there are idols which have immigrated into men's minds from the various dogmas of philosophies, and also from wrong laws of demonstration. These I call Idols of the Theater; because in my judgment all the received systems are but so many stage-plays, representing worlds of their own creation after an unreal and scenic fashion. Nor is it only of the systems now in vogue, or only of the ancient sects and philosophies, that I speak: for many more plays of the same kind may yet be composed and in like artificial manner set forth; seeing that errors the most widely different have nevertheless causes for the most part alike. Neither again do I mean this only of entire systems, but also of many principles and axioms in science, which by tradition, credulity, and negligence have come to be received.

But of these several kinds of idols I must speak more largely and exactly, that the understanding may be duly cautioned.

XLV

The human understanding is of its own nature prone to suppose the existence of more order and regularity in the world than it finds. And though there be many things in nature which are singular and unmatched, yet it devises for them parallels and conjugates and relatives which do not exist. Hence the fiction that all celestial bodies move in perfect circles; spirals and dragons being (except in name) utterly rejected. Hence too the element of fire with its orb is brought in, to make up the square with the other three which the sense perceives. Hence also the ratio of density of the so-called elements is arbitrarily fixed at ten to one. And so on of other dreams. And these fancies affect not dogmas only, but simple notions also.

XLVI

The human understanding when it has once adopted an opinion (either as being the received opinion or as being agreeable to itself) draws all things else to support and agree with it. And though there be a greater number and weight of instances to be found on the other side, yet these it either neglects and despises, or else by some distinction sets aside and rejects; in order that by this great and pernicious predetermination the authority of its former conclusions may remain inviolate. And therefore it was a good answer that was made by one who when they showed him hanging in a temple a picture of those who had paid their vows as having escaped shipwreck, and would have him say whether he did not now acknowledge the power of the gods,—"Aye," asked he again, "but where are they painted that were drowned after their vows?" And such is the way of all superstition, whether in astrology, dreams, omens, divine judgments, or the like; wherein men, having a delight in such vanities, mark the events where they are fulfilled, but where they fail, though this happen much oftener, neglect and pass them by. But with far more subtlety does this mischief insinuate itself into philosophy and the sciences; in which the first conclusion colors and brings into conformity with itself all that come after, though far sounder and better. Besides, independently of that delight and vanity which I have described, it is the peculiar and perpetual error of the human intellect to be more moved and excited by affirmatives than by negatives; whereas it ought properly to hold itself indifferently disposed towards both alike. Indeed in the establishment of any true axiom, the negative instance is the more forcible of the two.

XLVII

The human understanding is moved by those things most which strike and enter the mind simultaneously and suddenly, and so fill the imagination; and then it feigns and supposes all other things to be somehow, though it cannot see how, similar to those few things by which it is surrounded. But for that going to and fro to remote and heterogeneous instances, by which axioms are tried as in the fire, the intellect is altogether slow and unfit, unless it be forced thereto by severe laws and overruling authority.

XLVIII

The human understanding is unquiet; it cannot stop or rest, and still presses onward, but in vain. Therefore it is that we cannot conceive of any end or limit to the world; but always as of necessity it occurs to us that there is something beyond. Neither again can it be conceived how eternity has flowed down to the present day: for that distinction which is commonly received of infinity in time past and in time to come can by no means hold; for it would thence follow that one infinity is greater than another, and that infinity is wasting away and tending to become finite. The like subtlety arises touching the infinite divisibility of lines, from the same inability of thought to stop. But this inability interferes more mischievously in the discovery of causes: for although the most general principles in nature ought to be held merely positive, as they are discovered, and cannot with truth be referred to a cause; nevertheless the human understanding being unable to rest still seeks something prior in the order of nature. And then it is that in struggling towards that which is further off it falls back upon that which is more nigh at hand,—namely, on final causes; which have relation clearly to the nature of man rather than to the nature of the universe, and from this source have strangely defined philosophy. But he is no less an unskilled and shallow philosopher who seeks causes of that which is most general, than he who in things subordinate and subaltern omits to do so.

XLIX

The human understanding is no dry light, but receives an infusion from the will and affections; whence proceed sciences which may be called "sciences as one would." For what a man had rather were true he more readily believes. Therefore he rejects difficult things from impatience of research; sober things, because they narrow hope; the deeper things of nature, from superstition; the light of experience, from arrogance and pride, lest his mind should seem to be occupied with things mean and transitory; things not commonly believed, out of deference to the opinion of the vulgar. Numberless in short are the ways, and sometimes imperceptible, in which the affections color and infect the understanding.

L

But by far the greatest hindrance and aberration of the human understanding proceeds from the dullness, incompetency, and deceptions of the senses; in that things which strike the sense outweigh things which do not immediately strike it, though they be more important. Hence it is that speculation commonly ceases where sight ceases, insomuch that of things invisible there is little or no observation. Hence all the working of the spirits inclosed in tangible bodies lies hid and unobserved of men. So also all the more subtle changes of form in the parts of coarser substances (which they commonly call alteration, though it is in truth local motion through exceedingly small spaces) is in like manner unobserved. And yet unless these two things just mentioned be searched out and brought to light, nothing great can be achieved in nature, as far as the production of works is concerned. So again the essential nature of our common air, and of all bodies less dense than air (which are very many), is almost unknown. For the sense by itself is a thing infirm and erring; neither can instruments for enlarging or sharpening the senses do much: but all the truer kind of interpretation of nature is effected by instances and experiments fit and apposite; wherein the sense decides touching the experiment only, and the experiment touching the point in nature and the thing itself.

LI

The human understanding is of its own nature prone to abstractions and gives a substance and reality to things which are fleeting. But to resolve nature into abstractions is less to our purpose than to dissect her into parts; as did the school of Democritus, which went further into nature than the rest. Matter rather than forms should be the object of our attention, its configurations and changes of configuration, and simple action, and law of action or motion; for forms are figments of the human mind, unless you will call those laws of action forms.

LII

Such then are the idols which I call *Idols of the Tribe;* and which take their rise either from the homogeneity of the substance of the human spirit, or from its preoccupation, or from its narrowness, or from its restless motion, or from an infusion of the affections, or from the incompetency of the senses, or from the mode of impression.

LIII

The *Idols of the Cave* take their rise in the peculiar constitution, mental or bodily, of each individual; and also in education, habit, and accident. Of this kind there is a great number and variety; but I will instance those the pointing out of which contains the most important caution, and which have most effect in disturbing the clearness of the understanding.

LIV

Men become attached to certain particular sciences and speculations, either because they fancy themselves the authors and inventors thereof, or because they have bestowed the greatest pains upon them and become most habituated to them. But men of this kind, if they betake themselves to philosophy and contemplations of a general character, distort and color them in obedience to their former fancies; a thing especially to be noticed in Aristotle, who made his natural philosophy a mere bondservant to his logic, thereby rendering it contentious and well nigh useless. The race of chemists again out of a few experiments of the furnace have built up a fantastic philosophy, framed with reference to a few things; and Gilbert also, after he had employed himself most laboriously in the study and observation of the lodestone, proceeded at once to construct an entire system in accordance with his favorite subject.

LV

There is one principal and as it were radical distinction between different minds, in respect of philosophy and the sciences; which is this: that some minds are stronger and apter to mark the differences of things, others to mark their resemblances. The steady and acute mind can fix its contemplations and dwell and fasten on the subtlest distinctions; the lofty and discursive mind recognizes and puts together the finest and most general resemblances. Both kinds however easily err in excess, by catching the one at gradations the other at shadows.

LVI

There are found some minds given to an extreme admiration of antiquity, others to an extreme love and appetite for novelty; but few so duly tempered that they can hold the mean, neither carping at what has been well laid down by the ancients, nor despising what is well introduced by the moderns. This however turns to the great injury of the sciences and philosophy: since these affectations of antiquity and novelty are the humors of partisans rather than judgments; and truth is to be sought for not in the felicity of any age, which is an unstable thing, but in the light of nature and experience, which is eternal. These factions therefore must be abjured, and care must be taken that the intellect be not hurried by them into assent.

LVII

Contemplations of nature and of bodies in their simple form break up and distract the understanding, while contemplations of nature and bodies in their composition and configuration overpower and dissolve the understanding: a distinction well seen in the school of Leucippus and Democritus as compared with the other philosophies. For that school is so busied with the particles that it hardly attends to the structure; while the others are so lost in admiration of the structure that they do not penetrate to the simplicity of nature. These kinds of contemplation should therefore be alternated and taken by turns; that so the understanding may be rendered at once penetrating and comprehensive, and the inconveniences above mentioned, with the idols which proceed from them, may be avoided.

LVIII

Let such then be our provision and contemplative prudence for keeping off and dislodging the Idols of the Cave, which grow for the most part either out of the predominance of a favorite subject, or out of an excessive tendency to compare or to distinguish, or out of partiality for particular ages, or out of the largeness or minuteness of the objects contemplated. And generally let every student of nature take this as a rule,—that whatever his mind seizes and dwells upon with peculiar satisfaction is to be held in suspicion, and that so much the more care is to be taken in dealing with such questions to keep the understanding even and clear.

LIX

But the *Idols of the Market-place* are the most troublesome of all: idols which have crept into the understanding through the alliances of words and names. For men believe that their reason governs words; but it is also true that words react on the understanding; and this it is that has rendered philosophy and the sciences sophistical and inactive. Now words, being commonly framed and applied according to the capacity of the vulgar, follow those lines of division which are most obvious to the vulgar understanding. And whenever an understanding of greater acuteness or a more diligent observation would alter those lines to suit the true divisions of nature, words stand in the way and resist the change. Whence it comes to pass that the high and formal discussions of learned men end oftentimes in disputes about words and names; with which (according to the use and wisdom of the mathematicians) it would be more prudent to begin, and so by means of definitions reduce them to order. Yet even definitions cannot cure this evil in dealing with natural and material things; since the definitions themselves consist of words, and those words beget others: so that it is necessary to recur to individual instances, and those in due series and order; as I shall say presently when I come to the method and scheme for the formation of notions and axioms.

LX

The idols imposed by words on the understanding are of two kinds. They are either names of things which do not exist (for as there are things left unnamed through lack of observation, so likewise are there names which result from fantastic suppositions and to which nothing in reality corresponds), or they are names of things which exist, but yet confused and ill-defined, and hastily and irregularly derived from realities. Of the former kind are Fortune, the Prime Mover, Planetary Orbits, Elements of Fire, and like fictions which owe their origin to false and idle theories. And this class of idols is more easily expelled, because to get rid of them it is only necessary that all theories should be steadily rejected and dismissed as obsolete.

But the other class, which springs out of a faulty and unskillful abstraction, is intricate and deeply rooted. Let us take for example such a word as *humid,* and see how far the several things which the word is used to signify agree with each other; and we shall find the word *humid* to be nothing else than a mark loosely and confusedly applied to denote a variety of actions which will not bear to be reduced to any constant meaning. For it both signifies that which easily spreads itself round any other body; and that which in itself is indeterminate and cannot solidize; and that which readily yields in every direction; and that which easily divides and scatters itself; and that which easily unites and collects itself; and that which readily flows and is put in motion; and that which readily clings to another body and wets it; and that which is easily reduced to a liquid, or being solid easily melts. Accordingly when you come to apply the words,—if you take it in one sense, flame is humid; if in another, air is not humid; if in another, fine dust is humid; if in another, glass is humid. So that it is easy to see that the notion is taken by abstraction only from water and common and ordinary liquids, without any due verification.

There are however in words certain degrees of distortion and error. One of the least faulty kinds is that of names of substances, especially of lowest species and well-deduced (for the notion of *chalk* and of *mud* is good, of *earth* bad); a more faulty kind is that of actions, as *to generate, to corrupt, to alter;* the most faulty is of qualities (except such as are the immediate objects of the sense) as *heavy, light, rare, dense,* and the like. Yet in all these cases some notions are of necessity a little better than others, in proportion to the greater variety of subjects that fall within the range of the human sense.

LXI

But the *Idols of the Theater* are not innate, nor do they steal into the understanding secretly, but are plainly impressed and received into the mind from the play-books of philosophical systems and the perverted rules of demonstration. To attempt refutations in this case would be merely inconsistent with what I have already said: for since we agree neither upon principles nor upon demonstrations there is no place for argument. And this is so far well, inasmuch as it leaves the honor of the ancients untouched. For they are no wise disparaged—the question between them and me being only as to the way. For as the saying is, the lame man who keeps the right road outstrips the runner who takes a wrong one. Nay it is obvious that when a man runs the wrong way, the more active and swift he is the further he will go astray.

But the course I propose for the discovery of sciences is such as leaves but little to the acuteness and strength of wits, but places all wits and understandings nearly on a level. For as in the drawing of a straight line or a perfect circle, much depends on the steadiness and practice of the hand, if it be done by aim of hand only, but if with the aid of rule or compass, little or nothing; so is it exactly with my plan. But though particular confutations would be of no avail, yet touching the sects and general divisions of such systems I must say something; something also touching the external signs which show that they are unsound; and finally something touching the causes of such great infelicity and of such lasting and general agreement in error; that so the access to truth may be made less difficult, and the human understanding may the more willingly submit to its purgation and dismiss its idols.

LXII

Idols of the Theater, or of Systems, are many, and there can be and perhaps will be yet many more. For were it not that now for many ages men's minds have been busied with religion and theology; and were it not that civil governments, especially monarchies, have been averse to such novelties, even in matters speculative; so that men labor therein to the peril and harming of their fortunes,—not only unrewarded, but exposed also to contempt and envy: doubtless there would have arisen many other philosophical sects like to those which in great variety flourished once among the Greeks. For as on the phenomena of the heavens many hypotheses may be constructed, so likewise (and more also) many various dogmas may be set up and established on the phenomena of philosophy. And in the plays of this philosophical theater you may observe the same thing which is found in the theater of the poets, that stories invented for the stage are more compact and elegant, and more as one would wish them to be, than true stories out of history.

In general however there is taken for the material of philosophy either a great deal out of a few things, or a very little out of many things; so that on both sides philosophy is based on too narrow a foundation of experiment and natural history, and decides on the authority of too few cases. For the rational school of philosophers snatches from experience a variety of common instances, neither duly ascertained nor diligently examined and weighed, and leaves all the rest to meditation and agitation of wit.

There is also another class of philosophers, who having bestowed much diligent and careful labor on a few experiments, have thence made bold to educe and construct systems; wresting all other facts in a strange fashion to conformity therewith.

And there is yet a third class, consisting of those who out of faith and veneration mix their philosophy with theology and traditions; among whom the vanity of some has gone so far aside as to seek the origin of science among spirits and genii. So that this parent stock of errors—this false philosophy—is of three kinds; the *sophistical*, the *empirical*, and the *superstitious*.

LXIII

The most conspicuous example of the first class was Aristotle, who corrupted natural philosophy by his logic: fashioning the world out of categories; assigning to the human soul, the noblest of substances, a genus from words of the second intention; doing the business of density and rarity (which is to make bodies of greater or less dimensions, that is, occupy greater or less spaces), by the frigid distinction of act and power; asserting that single bodies have each a single and proper motion, and that if they participate in any other, then this results from an external cause; and imposing countless other arbitrary restrictions on the nature of things: being always more solicitous to provide an answer to the question and affirm something positive in words, than about the inner truth of things; a failing best shown when his philosophy is compared with other systems of note among the Greeks. For the *homœomera* of Anaxagoras; the atoms of Leucippus and Democritius; the Heaven and Earth of Parmenides; the Strife and Friendship of Empedocles; Heraclitus's doctrine how bodies are resolved into the indifferent nature of fire, and remolded into solids; have all of them some taste of the natural philosopher,—some savor of the nature of things, and experience, and bodies; whereas in the physics of Aristotle you hear hardly anything but the words of logic; which in his metaphysics also, under a more imposing name, and more forsooth as a realist than a nominalist, he has handled over again. Nor let any weight be given to the fact that in his books on animals, and his *Problems,* and other of his treatises, there is frequent dealing with experiments. For he had come to his conclusion before: he did not consult experience, as he should have done, in order to the framing of his decisions and axioms; but having first determined the question according to his will, he then resorts to experience, and bending her into conformity with his placets leads her about like a captive in a procession: so that even on this count he is more guilty than his modern followers, the school-men, who have abandoned experience altogether.

LXIV

But the empirical school of philosophy gives birth to dogmas more deformed and monstrous than the sophistical or rational school. For it has its foundations not in the light of common notions (which, though it be a faint and superficial light, is yet in a manner universal, and has reference to many things) but in the narrowness and darkness of a few experiments. To those therefore who are daily busied with these experiments, and have infected their imagination with them, such a philosophy seems probable and all but certain; to all men else incredible and vain. Of this there is a notable instance in the alchemists and their dogmas; though it is hardly to be found elsewhere in these times, except perhaps in the philosophy of Gilbert. Nevertheless with regard to philosophies of this kind there is one caution not to be omitted; for I foresee that if ever men are roused by my admonitions to betake themselves seriously to experiment and bid farewell to sophistical doctrines, then indeed through the premature hurry of the understanding to leap or fly to universals and principles of things, great danger may be apprehended from philosophies of this kind; against which evil we ought even now to prepare.

LXV

But the corruption of philosophy by superstition and an admixture of theology is far more widely spread, and does the greatest harm, whether to entire systems or to their parts. For the human understanding is obnoxious to the influence of the imagination no less than to the influence of common notions. For the contentious and sophistical kind of philosophy ensnares the understanding; but this kind, being fanciful and tumid and half poetical, misleads it more by flattery. For there is in man an ambition of the understanding, no less than of the will, especially in high and lofty spirits.

Of this kind we have among the Greeks a

striking example in Pythagoras, though he united with it a coarser and more cumbrous superstition; another in Plato and his school, more dangerous and subtle. It shows itself likewise in parts of other philosophies, in the introduction of abstract forms and final causes and first causes, with the omission in most cases of causes intermediate, and the like. Upon this point the greatest caution should be used. For nothing is so mischievous as the apotheosis of error; and it is a very plague of the understanding for vanity to become the object of veneration. Yet in this vanity some of the moderns have with extreme levity indulged so far as to attempt to found a system of natural philosophy on the first chapters of Genesis, on the book of Job, and other parts of the sacred writings; seeking for the dead among the living: which also makes the inhibition and repression of it the more important, because from this unwholesome mixture of things human and divine there arises not only a fantastic philosophy but also an heretical religion. Very meet it is therefore that we be sober-minded, and give to faith that only which is faith's.

THIRTY-TWO
SATIRE AND SOCIAL REFORM

With courage and often with acid satire the philosophes *(social philosophers) of the eighteenth century took up the huge task of reconstructing Western society. Their method was rational, as they dissected in detail what they regarded as the glaring social abuses inherited from the Middle Ages. But their motivation was humanitarian, and with full force of both mind and heart they urged a wide variety of social reforms. One of the greatest, if not the greatest, of the French* philosophes *was François Marie Arouet de Voltaire (1694–1778). Voltaire loved humanity and hated social evil with the ardor of a crusader. He brought to his self-imposed task of social reform tremendous energy and knowledge. His flowing style and dramatic irony found thousands of readers for his many literary productions, which ranged from letters and history to epics and satire, such as the incomparable* Candide. *Among his most engaging works is the* Philosophical Dictionary, *in which he exposes and scourges an extraordinarily wide variety of social abuses with consistent and masterful wit.*

VOLTAIRE
PHILOSOPHICAL DICTIONARY *

CERTAIN—CERTAINTY

I am certain; I have friends; my fortune is secure; my relations will never abandon me; I shall have justice done me; my work is good, it will be well received; what is owing to me will be paid; my friend will be faithful, he has sworn it; the minister will advance me —he has, by the way, promised it—all these are words which a man who has lived a short time in the world erases from his dictionary.

When the judges condemned L'Anglade, Le Brun, Calas, Sirven, Martin, Montbailli, and so many others, since acknowledged to have been innocent, they were certain, or they ought to have been certain, that all these unhappy men were guilty; yet they were deceived. There are two ways of being deceived; by false judgment and self-blindness—that of erring like a man of genius, and that of deciding like a fool.

The judges deceived themselves like men of genius in the affair of L'Anglade; they were blinded by dazzling appearances and did not sufficiently examine the probabilities on the other side. Their wisdom made them believe it certain that L'Anglade had com-

* From *Philosophical Dictionary,* pp. 49–55, 193–200, by François Marie Arouet de Voltaire. First published in 1769, and translated in 1901 by William F. Fleming.

mitted a theft, which he certainly had not committed; and on this miserable *uncertain* certainty of the human mind, a gentleman was put to the ordinary and extraordinary question; subsequent thrown, without succor, into a dungeon and condemned to the galleys, where he died. His wife was shut up in another dungeon, with her daughter, aged seven years, who afterwards married a counsellor of the same parliament which had condemned her father to the galleys and her mother to banishment.

It is clear that the judges would not have pronounced this sentence had they been really certain. However, even at the time this sentence was passed several persons knew that the theft had been committed by a priest named Gagnat, associated with a highwayman, and the innocence of L'Anglade was not recognized till after his death.

They were in the same manner certain when, by a sentence in the first instance, they condemned to the wheel the innocent Le Brun, who, by an arrêt pronounced on his appeal, was broken on the rack, and died under the torture.

The examples of Calas and Sirven are well known, that of Martin is less so. He was an honest agriculturist near Bar in Lorraine. A villain stole his dress and in this dress murdered a traveller whom he knew to have money and whose route he had watched. Martin was accused, his dress was a witness against him; the judges regarded this evidence as a certainty. Not the past conduct of the prisoner, a numerous family whom he had brought up virtuously, neither the little money found on him, nor the extreme probability of his innocence—nothing could save him. The subaltern judge made a merit of his rigor. He condemned the innocent victim to be broken on the wheel, and, by an unhappy fatality the sentence was executed to the full extent. The senior Martin is broken alive, calling God to witness his innocence to his last breath; his family is dispersed, his little property is confiscated, and scarcely are his broken members exposed on the great road when the assassin who had committed the murder and theft is put in prison for another crime, and confesses on the rack, to which he is condemned in his turn, that he only was guilty of the crime for which Martin had suffered torture and death.

Montbailli, who slept with his wife, was accused with having, in concert with her, killed his mother, who had evidently died of apoplexy. The council of Arras condemned Montbailli to expire on the rack, and his wife to be burnt. Their innocence was discovered, but not until Montbailli had been tortured. Let us cease advertence to these melancholy adventures, which make us groan at the human condition; but let us continue to lament the pretended certainty of judges, when they pass such sentences.

There is no certainty, except when it is physically or morally impossible that the thing can be otherwise. What! is a strict demonstration necessary to enable us to assert that the surface of a sphere is equal to four times the area of its great circle; and is not one required to warrant taking away the life of a citizen by a disgraceful punishment?

If such is the misfortune of humanity that judges must be contented with extreme probabilities, they should at least consult the age, the rank, the conduct of the accused—the interest which he could have in committing the crime, and the interest of his enemies to destroy him. Every judge should say to himself: Will not posterity, will not entire Europe condemn my sentence? Shall I sleep tranquilly with my hands tainted with innocent blood? Let us pass from this horrible picture to other examples of a certainty which leads directly to error.

Why art thou loaded with chains, fanatical and unhappy Santon? Why hast thou added a large iron ring on thy miserable scourge? It is because I am certain of being one day placed in the first heaven, by the side of our great prophet. Alas, my friend, come with me to the neighborhood of Mount Athos and thou wilt see three thousand mendicants who are as certain that thou wilt go to the gulf which is under the narrow bridge, as that they will all go to the first heaven!

Stop, miserable Malabar widow, believe not the fool who persuades you that you shall be reunited to your husband in all the delights of another world, if you burn yourself on his funeral pile! No, I persist in burning myself because I am certain of living in felicity with my husband; my brahmin told me so.

Let us attend to less frightful certainties, and which have a little more appearance of truth. What is the age of your friend Christopher? Twenty-eight years. I have seen his marriage contract, and his baptismal register; I knew him in his infancy; he is twenty-eight—I am certain of it.

Scarcely have I heard the answer of this man, so sure of what he said, and of twenty others who confirmed the same thing, when I learn that for secret reasons, and by a singular circumstance the baptismal register of Christopher has been antedated. Those to whom I had spoken as yet know nothing of it, yet they have still the same certainty of that which is not.

If you had asked the whole earth before the time of Copernicus: has the sun risen? has it set to-day? all men would have answered: We are quite certain of it. They were certain and they were in error.

Witchcraft, divinations, and possessions were for a long time the most certain things in the world in the eyes of society. What an innumerable crowd of people who have seen all these fine things and who have been certain of them! At present this certainty is a little shaken.

A young man who is beginning to study geometry comes to me; he is only at the definition of triangles. Are you not certain, said I to him, that the three angles of a triangle are equal to two right angles? He answered that not only was he not certain of it, but that he had not the slightest idea of the proposition. I demonstrated it to him. He then became very certain of it, and will remain so all his life. This is a certainty very different from the others; they were only probabilities and these probabilities, when examined, have turned out errors, but mathematical certainty is immutable and eternal.

I exist, I think, I feel grief—is all that as certain as a geometrical truth? Yes, skeptical as I am, I avow it. Why? It is that these truths are proved by the same principle that it is impossible for a thing to exist and not exist at the same time. I cannot at the same time feel and not feel. A triangle cannot at the same time contain a hundred and eighty degrees, which are the sum of two right angles, and not contain them. The physical certainty of my existence, of my identity, is of the same value as mathematical certainty, although it is of a different kind.

It is not the same with the certainty founded on appearances, or on the unanimous testimony of mankind.

But how, you will say to me, are you not certain that Pekin exists? Have you not merchandise from Pekin? People of different countries and different opinions have vehemently written against one another while preaching the truth at Pekin; then are you not assured of the existence of this town? I answer that it is extremely probable that there may be a city of Pekin but I would not wager my life that such a town exists, and I would at any time wager my life that the three angles of a triangle are equal to two right angles.

In the *"Dictionnaire Encyclopédique"* a very pleasant thing appears. It is there maintained that a man ought to be as certain that Marshal Saxe rose from the dead, if all Paris tells him so, as he is sure that Marshal Saxe gained the battle of Fontenoy, upon the same testimony. Pray observe the beauty of this reasoning: as I believe all Paris when it tells me a thing morally possible, I ought to believe all Paris when it tells me a thing morally and physically impossible. Apparently the author of this article has a disposition to be risible; as to ourselves who have only undertaken this little dictionary to ask a few questions, we are very far from possessing this very extensive certainty.

War

All animals are perpetually at war; every species is born to devour another. There are none, even to sheep and doves, who do not swallow a prodigious number of imperceptible animals. Males of the same species make war for the females, like Menelaus and Paris. Air, earth, and the waters, are fields of destruction.

It seems that God having given reason to men, this reason should teach them not to debase themselves by imitating animals, particularly when nature has given them neither arms to kill their fellow-creatures, nor instinct which leads them to suck their blood.

Yet murderous war is so much the dreadful lot of man, that except two or three nations, there are none but what their ancient histories represent as armed against one another. Towards Canada, man and warrior are synonymous; and we have seen, in our hemisphere, that thief and soldier were the same thing. Manichæans! behold your excuse.

The most determined of flatterers will easily agree, that war always brings pestilence and famine in its train, from the little that he may have seen in the hospitals of the armies of Germany, or the few villages he may have passed through in which some great exploit of war has been performed.

This is doubtless a very fine art which desolates countries, destroys habitations, and in a common year causes the death of from forty to a hundred thousand men. This invention was first cultivated by nations assembled for their common good; for instance, the diet of the Greeks declared to the diet of Phrygia and neighboring nations, that they intended to depart on a thousand fishers' barks, to exterminate them if they could.

The assembled Roman people judged that it was to their interest to go and fight, before harvest, against the people of Veii or the Volscians. And some year after, all the Romans, being exasperated against all the Carthaginians, fought them a long time on sea and land. It is not exactly the same at present.

A genealogist proves to a prince that he descends in a right line from a count, whose parents made a family compact, three or four hundred years ago, with a house the recollection of which does not even exist. This house had distant pretensions to a province, of which the last possessor died of apoplexy. The prince and his council see his right at once. This province, which is some hundred leagues distant from him, in vain protests that it knows him not; that it has no desire to be governed by him; that to give laws to its people, he must at least have their consent; these discourses only reach as far as the ears of the prince, whose right is incontestable. He immediately assembles a great number of men who have nothing to lose, dresses them in coarse blue cloth, borders their hats with broad white binding, makes them turn to the right and left, and marches to glory.

Other princes who hear of this equipment, take part in it, each according to his power, and cover a small extent of country with more mercenary murderers than Genghis Khan, Tamerlane, and Bajazet employed in their train. Distant people hear that they are going to fight, and that they may gain five or six sous a day, if they will be of the party; they divide themselves into two bands, like reapers, and offer their services to whoever will employ them.

These multitudes fall upon one another, not only without having any interest in the affair, but without knowing the reason of it. We see at once five or six belligerent powers, sometimes three against three, sometimes two against four, and sometimes one against five; all equally detesting one another, uniting with and attacking by turns; all agree in a single point, that of doing all the harm possible.

The most wonderful part of this infernal enterprise is that each chief of the murderers causes his colors to be blessed, and solemnly invokes God before he goes to exterminate his neighbors. If a chief has only the fortune to kill two or three thousand men, he does not thank God for it; but when he has exterminated about ten thousand by fire and sword, and, to complete the work, some town has been levelled with the ground, they then sing a long song in four parts, composed in a language unknown to all who have fought, and moreover replete with barbarism. The same song serves for marriages and births, as well as for murders; which is unpardonable, particularly in a nation the most famous for new songs.

Natural religion has a thousand times prevented citizens from committing crimes. A well-trained mind has not the inclination for it; a tender one is alarmed at it, representing to itself a just and avenging God; but artificial religion encourages all cruelties which are exercised by troops—conspiracies, seditions, pillages, ambuscades, surprises of towns, robberies, and murder. Each marches gaily to crime, under the banner of his saint.

A certain number of orators are everywhere paid to celebrate these murderous days; some are dressed in a long black close coat, with a short cloak; others have a shirt above a gown; some wear two variegated stuff streamers over their shirts. All of them speak for a long time, and quote that which was done of old in Palestine, as applicable to a combat in Veteravia.

The rest of the year these people declaim against vices. They prove, in three points and by antitheses, that ladies who lay a little carmine upon their cheeks, will be the eternal objects of the eternal vengeances of the Eternal; that Polyeuctus and Athalia are works of the demon; that a man who, for two hundred crowns a day, causes his table to be furnished with fresh sea-fish during Lent, infallibly works his salvation; and that a poor man who eats two sous and a half worth of mutton, will go forever to all the devils.

Of five or six thousand declamations of this kind, there are three or four at most, composed by a Gaul named Massillon, which an honest man may read without disgust; but in all these discourses, you will scarcely find two in which the orator dares to say a word against the scourge and crime of war, which contains all other scourges and crimes. The unfortunate orators speak incessantly against love, which is the only consolation of mankind, and the only mode of making amends for it; they say nothing of the abominable efforts which we make to destroy it.

You have made a very bad sermon on impurity—oh, Bourdaloue!—but none on these murders, varied in so many ways; on these rapines and robberies; on this universal rage which devours the world. All the united vices of all ages and places will never equal the evils produced by a single campaign.

Miserable physicians of souls! you exclaim, for five quarters of an hour, on some pricks of a pin, and say nothing on the malady which tears us into a thousand pieces! Philosophers! moralists! burn all your books. While the caprice of a few men makes that part of mankind consecrated to heroism, to murder loyally millions of our brethren, can there be anything more horrible throughout nature?

What becomes of, and what signifies to me, humanity, beneficence, modesty, temperance, mildness, wisdom, and piety, while half a pound of lead, sent from the distance of a hundred steps, pierces my body, and I die at twenty years of age, in inexpressible torments, in the midst of five or six thousand dying men, while my eyes which open for the last time, see the town in which I was born destroyed by fire and sword, and the last sounds which reach my ears are the cries of women and children expiring under the ruins, all for the pretended interests of a man whom I know not?

What is worse, war is an inevitable

scourge. If we take notice, all men have worshipped Mars. Sabaoth, among the Jews, signifies the god of arms; but Minerva, in Homer, calls Mars a furious, mad, and infernal god.

The celebrated Montesquieu, who was called humane, has said, however, that it is just to bear fire and sword against our neighbors, when we fear that they are doing too well. If this is the spirit of laws, it is also that of Borgia and of Machiavelli. If unfortunately he says true, we must write against this truth, though it may be proved by facts.

This is what Montesquieu says: "Between societies, the right of natural defence sometimes induces the necessity of attacking, when one people sees that a longer peace puts another in a situation to destroy it, and that attack at the given moment is the only way of preventing this destruction."

How can attack in peace be the only means of preventing this destruction? You must be sure that this neighbor will destroy you, if he become powerful. To be sure of it, he must already have made preparations for your overthrow. In this case, it is he who commences the war; it is not you: your supposition is false and contradictory.

If ever war is evidently unjust, it is that which you propose: it is going to kill your neighbor, who does not attack you, lest he should ever be in a state to do so. To hazard the ruin of your country, in the hope of ruining without reason that of another, is assuredly neither honest nor useful; for we are never sure of success, as you well know.

If your neighbor becomes too powerful during peace, what prevents you from rendering yourself equally powerful? If he has made alliances, make them on your side. If, having fewer monks, he has more soldiers and manufacturers, imitate him in this wise economy. If he employs his sailors better, employ yours in the same manner: all that is very just. But to expose your people to the most horrible misery, in the so often false idea of overturning your dear brother, the most serene neighboring prince!—it was not for the honorary president of a pacific society to give you such advice.

THIRTY-THREE
ENLIGHTENED DESPOTISM

The philosophes *generally distrusted democracy as an instrument of social reform. Instead they emphasized reform through wide authoritarian rule, a system of government known as Enlightened Despotism. These thinkers generally distrusted the people and put their faith in a strong, rational monarch, an eighteenth-century version of Plato's Philosopher-King. Of the various monarchs of the Enlightenment, Frederick II the Great (1713–86), of Prussia, clearly exemplifies Enlightened Despotism. An energetic, self-confident, and strong-minded ruler, Frederick the Great called himself the "first servant of the state." He tried through hard and imaginative work to improve the efficiency of the Prussian state, in part through sound administration and in part through positive reforms; for example, in farming, public works, and canal construction. His highly centralized government worked well by contemporary standards. But he centered so much responsibility on the crown and so consistently refused to delegate responsibility that he prepared the way for political decline in the reigns of his less capable successors. Sidney B. Fay has analyzed the methods, merits, and shortcomings of Enlightened Despotism as it functioned in Prussia under Frederick the Great.*

SIDNEY B. FAY

THE RISE OF BRANDENBURG-PRUSSIA *

Frederick II, whom other monarchs and their ministers of the latter eighteenth century sought to emulate, was the most distinguished representative of what is called Enlightened Despotism. This was based on the idea that the king, having studied the enlightened doctrines of the *philosophes,* knew better than his subjects what was for their good, and that he had, or should have, the despotic power to carry out reforms, not for his own glory, but for the well-being of his people and the advantage of his State.

"I am the first servant of the State," was Frederick's oft-repeated motto. When a delegation of townspeople came to thank him for a generous donation of money which he had made to enable them to rebuild their houses destroyed by fire, Frederick, "visibly moved," replied characteristically: "You have no need to thank me; it was my duty; that is what I am here for." The justification of his absolute authority, he believed, did not rest upon the Grace of God, Divine

* From *The Rise of Brandenburg-Prussia,* pp. 132–42, by Sidney Fay, copyright 1937, Henry Holt and Company, Inc. Revised by Klaus Epstein, © 1964 by Holt, Rinehart and Winston, Inc.

Right, or dynastic inheritance, but upon the Natural Law theory of the Social Contract—upon his ability to serve his people better than they could serve themselves.

The Enlightened Despotism of the latter eighteenth century thus stands as a transition between the seventeenth century Absolutism as typified by Louis XIV and the nineteenth century Democracy which was introduced on the Continent by the French Revolution. Louis XIV exalted his own personal glory, considering himself the source of all radiance and light, and choosing as his symbol the Rising Sun like that of a modern stove polish advertisement. He constituted the whole State according to the maxim which Voltaire put into his mouth: *L'état, c'est moi*. His will was law: *Si veut le Roi, si veut la Loi*. In the well-being of his subjects, whom he exhausted by long wars and oppressed with heavy taxation, he took relatively little interest. His government was neither *by* the people nor *for* the people.

Frederick the Great, on the other hand, as Enlightened Despot, marked a great step forward. He distinguished between himself as the servant of the State and the Prussian State itself. "The Ruler is the first servant of the State; he is well paid so that he may uphold the dignity of his position." Like Montesquieu, he believed that the monarch was subject to the law. In his *Political Testament* of 1752 he wrote: "I have resolved never to interfere with the course of legal procedure; for in the halls of justice the laws shall speak and the monarch shall keep silence." In the famous Miller Arnold case, where he broke this resolution, he did so because he believed—incorrectly—that a noble, backed by unjust judges, had done a great wrong to a poor peasant. If he exacted oppressive taxes, he did not spend them on costly robes to replace his simple blue uniform, soiled with dust and snuff, but returned a large part of them, even amounting to a quarter of his revenues in the years following the Seven Years' War, in free gifts for the amelioration and well-being of his subjects. His reforms, imposed with moderation from above, served in some sort as a lightning-rod which drew off discontent and averted in Prussia violent reform by the masses from below, such as took place in France soon after his death. His was a government *for* the people, if not *by* the people. He was nearer than Louis XIV to the nineteenth century and to Lincoln's conception of a "government of the people, by the people, for the people."

Frederick was a man of action rather than an organizer. He did not greatly change the framework of centralized institutions which he inherited from his father. He did, however, in actual practice gather much more power directly into his own hands, and left less freedom of action to his ministers. The members of the General Directory rarely reported to him in person, or even saw him, except once a year when the budget was drawn up. The reports of the various boards sitting in Berlin were sent to him at Sans Souci in Potsdam in writing, and he gave his decisions by dictating to his cabinet secretaries or by jotting down marginal notes from which they prepared his "Cabinet Orders." The amount and variety of the business which he thus dealt with is almost incredible. A fraction of it which has been published fills forty-four volumes of his *Politische Korrespondenz* and a score of volumes of the *Acta Borussica*. His working day began at 6 A.M. In the evenings he sought recreation in music, playing the flute to the Round Table of select friends; or in reading, in discussing philosophy, or in catching up on his literary writings and correspondence which comprise the thirty-three volumes of his *Oeuvres*.

In addition to this daily routine at Sans Souci and to commanding his troops in the Silesian Wars, Frederick made frequent journeys of inspection through his provinces. He talked with nobles, burghers, peasants and local officials, noting down with neat precision all sorts of statistics in the little red leather notebooks which he always carried with him. This information gathered on the spot enabled him to check up on the reports of his ministers, spend money where he was convinced it was needed, and inspire everywhere his own sense of duty and hard work. If his sharp eye detected corruption, incompetence or insubordination, instant dismissal and a year's imprisonment at Spandau were likely to be the offender's fate.

Frederick II's minute personal direction of every branch of the government had its advantages. Decisions by the king were far more speedy than by majority votes after long discussions by boards of ministers. Secrecy, where desirable, could more easily be maintained. All responsibility was centered in himself. As in his campaigns he never called a council of war, so in administration in general he saw no need for similar assemblies for discussion and advice. By his example, by his extraordinarily wide knowledge and mastery of detail, and by the fear of disapprobation which he inspired he carried further his father's work of educating Prussian military officials and civil servants to severe standards of duty, honesty, efficiency and impartial justice which for a century and a half were to make the army and the bureaucracy the two solid pillars of the Prussian State. His system, however, had also its disadvantages. It could be completely successful in the long run only if his successors equaled him in genius—which was not the case. Like Bismarck, he expected obedience, not initiative and independent responsibility, in his officials. He did not develop ministers of outstanding ability who could take over his autocratic machinery of government when his guiding hand was removed, nor did he try to provide a machine which would run itself, as a representative democracy is supposed to do.

With the disappearance at the Reformation of the clergy as one of the "three estates" of the Middle Ages, the nobles, burghers, and peasants came to form the three-fold division of society in Brandenburg-Prussia. This division was retained by Frederick II, and even sharpened by his social measures and by the provisions of his Prussian Law Code.

The nobility, instead of offering a narrow-minded local opposition to the Hohenzollern centralized monarchy, had now become its main and loyal support. No longer fearing the selfish political ambitions of the Junkers, Frederick extended their powers and privileges. In his name they exercised wide police powers on their landed estates. They were appointed more exclusively to officer positions in the army, for Frederick believed that they had a higher sense of honor than the middle and lower classes, and in any case they were used to commanding the peasants on their estates who formed the bulk of the recruits for the army.

The burghers were expected to serve the State, not by fighting, but by increasing its wealth through industry and trade. Consequently, after the Seven Years' War, they were not appointed officers and were exempted from being recruited as soldiers under the cantonal system. To promote internal trade and industry, Frederick II followed the usual mercantilist methods of excluding foreign manufacturers by tariffs and by restricting the exportation of raw materials. He also swept away many internal tolls, especially those on the Oder which with the acquisition of Silesia had now become a water highway wholly within the Prussian boundaries. He established new monopolies for tobacco, porcelain, silk and other manufactures. He stimulated other industries by generous subventions from his *Dispositionskasse*. With the assistance of his able Minister of Mines, Heinitz, he began to develop the mineral resources of Upper Silesia. Shipbuilding began to flourish at Stettin; in a single year twenty ships were launched, some of which were sold abroad. In 1765, with the advice of an Italian, Calzabigi, he founded a Prussian Bank with a capital of 400,000 talers to aid recovery after the Seven Years' War. It received deposits, made loans, discounted paper bills, and later issued paper money. By 1786 it was making an annual profit of 22,000 talers.

According to statistics furnished by Heinitz in 1783, Prussia's annual exports amounted to 14,800,000 talers and her imports to 11,800,000, making a favorable balance of 3,000,000. Her manufactures had a total annual value of 29,000,000 talers, as follows:

Manufactures (not including Silesia)	*Workers*	*Home Consumption* (*value in talers*)	*Exported*
Silk	5,055	1,356,702	531,026
Woolens	39,367	3,344,166	1,691,305
Linen	22,523	373,506	897,757
Leather	3,595	996,614	399,986
Cotton	4,503	540,056	106,765
Iron and glass	8,373	2,126,675	1,053,844
Totals	83,416	8,737,719	4,606,683

Total home consumption and exports, approximately	13,500,000
Paper, tobacco, sugar, porcelain, tallow, soap	4,500,000
Silesian woolens, linen, iron, steel, lead, etc.	11,000,000
Total Prussian manufactures	29,000,000

In spite of this considerable industrialization under Frederick the Great, which raised Prussia to be the fourth manufacturing country of the world, Prussia still remained essentially an agrarian state, and the peasantry still bore the chief burden of the political and social order. Their sons were recruited for the rank and file of the army, which had increased to 200,000 in 1786. The heavy military land-tax was assessed exclusively on peasant land-holdings, except in East Prussia and Silesia where the land of the nobles also bore a part. In addition, the peasants had to perform labor services of three or four days a week for their overlords, not to mention services to the State such as building roads, transporting troops, and doing errands for officials and army officers. The peasant was, as Frederick the Great said, "the beast of burden of human society."

Frederick II attempted to do something to ameliorate the peasants' hard lot. On his own domain lands, which constituted about a third of the kingdom, he succeeded in assuring them heredity of tenure, in limiting in writing the nature and amount of their labor services, and in some cases in abolishing the obligation of menial service on the part of the peasants' sons and daughters. On the private estates of the nobles, however, he found that traditional custom and bitter opposition on the part of the Junker landlords were too strong for him to accomplish much. The only important reform he was able to achieve here was the prevention of *Bauernlegung,* i.e., the prying of the peasant off of his tenement so that the lord might add the peasant's acre strips to his own demesne lands.

To improve agriculture Frederick sent agents to England to study the better methods coming into use there. As a result he taught his own subjects to make greater use of fodder crops and of clover which enriched the soil instead of impoverishing it. It also made possible more feeding of cattle in the stalls instead of in the fields, improved the quality and amount of milk, and produced more stable manure which could be used further to enrich the fields. He persuaded his people to make greater use of such cheap forms of food as potatoes and turnips. He adopted better methods of cattle breeding, so that the number of sheep was increased from 5,500,000 in 1765 to 8,000,000 in 1786, making possible a considerable export of wool.

Frederick II began the systematic planting and care of pines and firs which gave Germany a leading place in modern forestry methods. To increase available agricultural land, he carried out extensive drainage projects, especially in the regions of the lower Oder and Vistula. These two rivers were connected by the Bromberg canal, thus making a direct east-west cheap water transportation between East Prussia and the central provinces. Like the Great Elector who settled 20,000 French Huguenots, and like Frederick William I who provided traveling expenses, land and live-stock for an equal number of exiled Salzburg Protestants, Frederick the Great was very active in colonization work. Not having at hand any such convenient bands of religious exiles, he sought his colonists in little groups from all over Germany and from neighboring foreign lands. In the course of his whole reign he far exceeded the work of his predecessors by settling a total of 300,000 colonists.

Frederick's grain policy was much the same as that of the Great Elector, but was pursued on a much larger scale. Generally the exportation and importation of grain was forbidden, though he sometimes allowed his own grain officials to import under cover from Poland. With the frontiers generally closed to grain, Frederick bought up and stored in government warehouses wheat, barley and rye in plentiful years when the price was low, and sold it again in years of bad harvest when prices tended to rise and would otherwise have caused great hardship to consumers. In this way he succeeded in his aim of keeping a fairly stable price level for grain and at the same time made a handsome profit.

In the intervals between his wars, and partly to aid recovery by public works, Frederick built many of the public buildings which have a prominent place in central Berlin today. The Opera House in 1743 was one of the first. Near it, on the same side of the Unter den Linden promenade, he constructed a library to house the growing collection of books which the Great Elector had started, and, a little to the rear, the Church of St. Hedwig for his Roman Catholic subjects. Across the Linden from the Opera House he erected a large palace for his brother, Prince Henry, which is now occupied by the University of Berlin.

One of Frederick's most important achievements was the reform and codification of the law. His father had made efforts at legal reform, but he had been too impatient, too ignorant of the fundamental difficulties, and too strongly opposed by the Junker justices to accomplish much. Frederick's success was largely due to Samuel von Cocceji. This able lawyer and skillful organizer had been dismissed by Frederick William I, but was restored to office by Frederick the Great. He raised the quality of the judges by giving them better pay, instead of having them largely dependent on gifts from the litigants. He simplified the long and costly Roman written procedure by restricting appeals and by making greater use of the Germanic oral procedure. He made use of the period of his enforced idleness, after his dismissal by Frederick William I, in drafting a code of simplified law to harmonize the practice in the different provinces. In 1751 he translated his Latin draft into German. During the next forty years other eminent lawyers and judges worked on it, and it was the basis of the Prussian Code finally put into practice in 1794.

Frederick the Great's reign is the culmination of a century and a half of extraordinary development of the Brandenburg-Prussian State. From a weak Electorate it had risen to be the strongest military state in Europe, with a population little smaller than that of England. A glance at four of the factors which the eighteenth century regarded as decisive for state strength will show the striking progress in this century and a half from the end of the Thirty Years' War to the death of Frederick the Great:

	1648	*1740*	*1786*
Population	750,000	2,500,000	5,000,000
Army	8,000	83,000	200,000
Annual revenues, in talers	?	7,000,000	19,000,000
Stored treasure, in talers	0	8,000,000	51,000,000

Under Frederick the Great Prussia had become the powerful rival of Austria, and, by accentuating the dualism in the Holy Roman Empire had, in spite of Frederick's efforts at conservation, actually hastened the disruption of that decaying medieval structure.

The Great Elector and Frederick William I had been fertile in creating new institutions and in organizing the resources of their lands. Frederick the Great added valuable new lands, but created little that was new in the way of institutions, being content to use and develop those which he inherited. However, by his demonic energy, his shrewd estimate of Prussia's interests, and his successful opportunism, he did more than either of his predecessors to raise Prussia high in importance as a European State. But Prussia still remained a despotic State, such as was characteristic of the eighteenth century. Unfortunately Frederick's genius as an Enlightened Despot was not a heritable quality to be transmitted to his immediate successors. It required the shock of the Napoleonic conquest and the genius of Freiherr vom Stein to bring about a new creative period of institutional changes which were to regenerate and further strengthen Prussia in the nineteenth century.

THIRTY-FOUR

NATURAL RIGHTS AND REVOLUTION

The Declaration of Independence, passed by the American Continental Congress on July 4, 1776, is one of the most stirring and influential expressions of the entire Enlightenment. It really did not "declare" independence. Congress had done the actual declaring by a resolution passed two days previously. Instead, the Declaration was intended, as indeed it states plainly, to explain to the "candid world" why the American colonists had rebelled against the mother country. Thomas Jefferson was the Declaration's main author, helped in committee by Benjamin Franklin, John Adams, and others. Congress then reviewed the Declaration with care appropriate to such a solemn occasion, and made a number of changes. But by far the greater part of the work was Jefferson's. The body of the Declaration consists of a long list of specific American complaints against the government of George III. Not all of the grievances stand up under impartial historical scrutiny. Yet it is well to remember that Jefferson and his colleagues were not writing history. They were making a strong case, much like a legal brief, in support of the American position. At any event, the most interesting part of the Declaration is its philosophy, as expressed in its opening two paragraphs. Here Jefferson forcefully restated the familiar Natural Rights argument, which Locke and others had used to justify the English Revolution of 1688. In essence, the Declaration asserted that government is, by mutual contract, designed to protect the natural rights of each citizen, in particular, his right to life, liberty, and the pursuit of happiness. Should the government fail to preserve these innate rights, so the argument ran, the citizenry have a natural right, even a duty, to overthrow the government and regain what is rightfully theirs. It is ironic that the American colonists should justify their rebellion by using one of England's most venerable and cherished political arguments.

THE DECLARATION OF INDEPENDENCE

When, in the Course of human events, it becomes necessary for one people to dissolve the political bands which have connected them with another, and to assume among the powers of the earth, the separate and equal station to which the Laws of Nature and of Nature's God entitle them, a decent respect to the opinions of mankind requires that they should declare the causes which impel them to the separation.

We hold these truths to be self-evident, that all men are created equal, that they are endowed by their Creator with certain unalienable Rights, that among these are Life, Liberty and the pursuit of Happiness. That to secure these rights, Governments are instituted among Men, deriving their just powers from the consent of the governed. That whenever any Form of Government becomes destructive of these ends, it is the Right of the People to alter or to abolish it, and to institute new Government, laying its foundation on such principles and organizing its powers in such form, as to them shall seem most likely to effect their Safety and Happiness. Prudence, indeed, will dictate that Governments long established should not be changed for light and transient causes; and accordingly all experience hath shewn, that mankind are more disposed to suffer, while evils are sufferable, than to right themselves by abolishing the forms to which they are accustomed. But when a long train of abuses and usurpations, pursuing invariably the same object, evidence a design to reduce them under absolute Despotism, it is their right, it is their duty, to throw off such Government, and to provide new Guards for their future security. Such has been the patient sufferance of these Colonies; and such is now the necessity which constrains them to alter their former Systems of Government. The history of the present King of Great Britain is a history of repeated injuries and usurpations, all having in direct object the establishment of an absolute Tyranny over these States. To prove this, let Facts be submitted to a candid world.

He has refused his Assent to Laws, the most wholesome and necessary for the public good.

He has forbidden his Governors to pass Laws of immediate and pressing importance, unless suspended in their operation till his Assent should be obtained, and when so suspended, he has utterly neglected to attend to them.

He has refused to pass other Laws for the accommodation of large districts of people, unless those people would relinquish the right of Representation in the Legislature, a right inestimable to them and formidable to tyrants only.

He has called together legislative bodies at places, unusual, uncomfortable, and distant from the depository of their public Records, for the sole purpose of fatiguing them into compliance with his measures.

He has dissolved Representative Houses repeatedly, for opposing with manly firmness his invasions on the rights of the people.

He has refused for a long time, after such dissolutions, to cause others to be elected; whereby the Legislative powers, incapable of Annihilation, have returned to the People at large for their exercise; the State remaining in the meantime exposed to all the dangers of invasion from without, and convulsions within.

He has endeavored to prevent the population of these States; for that purpose obstructing the Laws for Naturalization of Foreigners; refusing to pass others to encourage their migrations hither, and raising the conditions of new Appropriations of Lands.

He has obstructed the Administration of Justice, by refusing his Assent to Laws for establishing Judiciary powers.

He has made Judges dependent on his Will alone, for the tenure of their offices, and the amount and payment of their salaries.

He has erected a multitude of New Offices, and sent hither swarms of Officers to harass our people, and eat out their substance.

He has kept among us, in times of peace, Standing Armies, without the Consent of our legislatures.

He has affected to render the Military independent of and superior to the Civil power.

He has combined with others to subject us to a jurisdiction foreign to our constitution and unacknowledged by our laws; giving his Assent to their Acts of pretended Legislation: For quartering large bodies of armed troops among us: For protecting them by a mock Trial from punishment for any Murders which they should commit on the Inhabitants of these States: For cutting off our Trade with all parts of the world: For imposing Taxes on us without our Consent: For depriving us in many cases of the benefits of Trial by Jury: For transporting us beyond Seas to be tried for pretended offenses: For abolishing the free System of English Laws in a neighbouring Province, establishing therein an Arbitrary government, and enlarging its Boundaries so as to render it at once an example and fit instrument for introducing the same absolute rule into these Colonies: For taking away our Charters, abolishing our most valuable Laws and altering fundamentally the Forms of our Governments: For suspending our own Legislatures and declaring themselves invested with power to legislate for us in all cases whatsoever.

He has abdicated Government here by declaring us out of his Protection and waging War against us.

He has plundered our seas, ravished our Coasts, burnt our towns, and destroyed the lives of our people.

He is at this time transporting large Armies of foreign Mercenaries to complete the works of death, desolation and tyranny, already begun with circumstances of cruelty and perfidy scarcely paralleled in the most barbarous ages, and totally unworthy the Head of a civilized nation.

He has constrained our fellow Citizens taken Captive on the high Seas to bear Arms against their Country, to become the executioners of their friends and Brethren, or to fall themselves by their Hands.

He has excited domestic insurrections amongst us, and has endeavoured to bring on the inhabitants of our frontiers, the merciless Indian Savages, whose known rule of warfare is an undistinguished destruction of all ages, sexes and conditions. In every stage of these Oppressions We have Petitioned for Redress in the most humble terms. Our repeated Petitions have been answered only by repeated injury. A Prince, whose character is thus marked by every act which may define a Tyrant, is unfit to be the ruler of a free people. Nor have We been wanting in attention to our British brethren. We have warned them from time to time of attempts by their legislature to extend an unwarrantable jurisdiction over us. We have reminded them of the circumstances of our emigration and settlement here. We have appealed to their native justice and magnanimity, and we have conjured them by the ties of our common kindred to disavow these usurpations, which would inevitably interrupt our connections and correspondence. They too have been deaf to the voice of justice and of consanguinity. We must, therefore, acquiesce in the necessity, which denounces our Separation, and hold them, as we hold the rest of mankind, Enemies in War, in Peace Friends.

WE, THEREFORE, the Representatives of the United States of America, in General Congress, Assembled, appealing to the Supreme Judge of the world for the rectitude of our intentions do, in the Name, and by authority of the good People of these Colonies, solemnly publish and declare, That these United Colonies are, and of Right ought to be, Free and Independent States: that they are Absolved from all Allegiance to the British Crown, and that all political connection between them and the State of Great Britain is and ought to be totally dissolved: and that as Free and Independent States, they have full Power to levy War, conclude Peace, contract Alliances, establish Commerce, and to do all other Acts and Things which Independent States may of right do. And for the support of this Declaration, with a firm reliance on the protection of Divine Providence, we mutually pledge to each other our Lives, our Fortunes, and our sacred Honor.

THIRTY-FIVE

TRADITIONALISM: THE GOVERNING CLASSES

Despite the intellectual ferment of the Enlightenment, the forces of traditionalism dominated Western civilization during the greater part of the eighteenth century. Even in France, convulsed by revolution in the decade after 1789, much traditionalism reappeared under Napoleon as a prelude to the frankly reactionary regimes of Napoleon's Bourbon successors. In England, the most progressive major European state in the eighteenth century, traditionalism was deeply rooted in the classically educated governing class, which dominated both Houses of Parliament. Thus the influence of the crown was restricted. This self-assured aristocracy, titled and untitled, with broad economic interests in both land and trade, set the social and intellectual tone of the age. For all practical purposes, the aristocracy's history was England's history from the Glorious Revolution of 1688 to at least a generation after the passage of the Reform Act of 1832. Even after the governing class lost its almost complete monopoly of political power, its values and code of conduct, reinforced by a strong sense of inherited status, persisted in the inner circle of England's leaders, a group that later became known as the Establishment. In his biography of Lord Melbourne (1779–1848), prime minister 1835–41 and mentor to Queen Victoria in the opening years of her long reign, David Cecil has described with deft insight the characteristics, pretensions, strengths, and weaknesses of England's governing class in the late eighteenth century.

DAVID CECIL

MELBOURNE *

The great Whig country houses of the eighteenth and early nineteenth centuries are among the most conspicuous monuments of English history. Ornate and massive, with their pedimented porticoes, their spreading balustraded wings, they dominate the landscape round them with a magnificent self-assurance. Nor are their interiors less imposing. Their colonnaded entrance halls, whence the Adam staircase sweeps up beneath a fluted dome; their cream and gilt libraries piled with sumptuous editions of the classics; their orangeries peopled with casts from the antique; their saloons hung with yellow silk, and with ceiling and doorways painted in delicate arabesque by An-

* From *Melbourne,* pp. 15–25, copyright 1939, 1954, by David Cecil. Reprinted by permission of the publishers, The Bobbs-Merrill Company, Inc. Published in England by Constable and Company Limited.

gelica Kauffmann—all combine to produce an extraordinary impression of culture and elegance and established power.

Yet, they are not palaces. There is something easy-going and unofficial about them. Between library and saloon one comes on little rooms, full of sporting prints and comfortable untidiness; the bedrooms upstairs are friendly with chintz and flowered wallpaper. Even the great rooms themselves, with their roomy writing-tables, their armchairs, their tables piled with albums and commonplace books, seem designed less for state occasions than for private life—for leisure and lounging, for intimate talk and desultory reading. And the portraits that glow down from the walls exhibit a similar character. The gentlemen lean back in their hunting coats, the ladies stroll in their parks with spaniels snapping at the ribbons that dangle from the garden hats slung on their arms. In big and in detail these houses convey an effect of splendid naturalness. In this they are typical of the society which was their creator.

The Whig aristocracy was a unique product of English civilization. It was before all things a governing class. At a time when economic power was concentrated in the landed interest, the Whigs were among the biggest landowners: their party was in office for the greater part of the eighteenth century; during this period they possessed a large proportion of the seats in the House of Commons; they produced more ambassadors and officers of state than the rest of England put together. And they lived on a scale appropriate to their power. "A man," said one of their latest representatives, "can jog along on £40,000 a year." And jog very well they did. They possessed, most of them, a mansion in London and two or three in the country; they moved through the world attended by a vast retinue of servants, of secretaries and chaplains, of companions, librarians and general hangers-on; they never travelled but in their own carriages; they kept open house to a continuous stream of guests, whom they entertained in the baroque and lavish style approved by their contemporaries.

For the elaboration of their life was increased by the period they lived in. The eighteenth century, that accomplished age, did not believe in the artless and the austere. In its view the good man, or, as they would have phrased it, "the man of sense and taste," was he whose every activity was regulated in the light of a trained judgment and the experience of the wise in his own and former ages. From his earliest years the Whig nobleman was subjected to a careful education. He was grounded in the classics first by a tutor, then at Eton, then at the University. After this he went abroad for two years' grand tour to learn French and good manners in the best society of the Continent. His sisters learnt French and manners equally thoroughly at home; and their demeanour was further improved by a course of deportment. The Whigs' taste was in harmony with the ideal that guided their education. They learnt to admire the grand style in painting, the "correct" in letters, the Latin tradition in oratory. And in everything they paid strict attention to form. Since life to them was so secure and so pleasant, the Whig aristocrats tended to take its fundamental values very much for granted; they concentrated rather on how to live. And here again their ideal was not an artless one. Their customs, their mode of speech, their taste in decoration, their stylish stiff clothes, are alike marked by a character at once polished and precise, disciplined and florid. If one of them writes a note, it is rounded with a graceful phrase, their most extempore speeches are turned with a flourish of rotund rhetoric.

Yet—and here it is that it differs from those of similar societies on the Continent—theirs was not an unreal life, no Watteau-like paradise of exquisite trifling and fastidious idleness. For one thing it had its roots in the earth. Founded as their position was on landed property, the Whig aristocracy was never urban. They passed at least half the year in their country seats, and there they occupied themselves in the ordinary avocations of country life. The ladies interested themselves in their children and visited the poor; the gentlemen looked after their estates, rode to hounds and administered from the local bench justice to poachers and pilferers. Their days went by, active out-of-door, unceremonious; they wore riding-boots as often as silk stockings. Moreover, they were always in touch with the central and serious current of contemporary life. The fact that they were a governing class meant that they had to govern. The Whig lord was as often as not a minister, his eldest son an M.P., his second attached to a foreign embassy, so that their houses were alive with the effort and hurry of politics. Red Foreign Office boxes strewed the library tables; at any time of day or night a courier might come galloping up with critical news, and the minister must post off to London to attend a Cabinet meeting. He had his work in the country too. He was a landlord and magistrate, often a lord lieutenant, while every few years would come a general election when his sons, if not himself, might have to sally forth to stand on the hustings and be pelted with eggs and dead cats by the free and independent electors of the neighbouring borough. Indeed his was not a protected existence. The eighteenth century was the age of clubs; and Whig society itself was a sort of club, exclusive, but in which those who managed to achieve membership lived on equal terms—a rowdy, rough-and-tumble club, full of conflict and plain speaking, where people were expected to stand up for themselves and take and give hard knocks. At Eton the little dukes and earls cuffed and bullied one another like street urchins. As mature persons in their country homes, or in the pillared rooms of Brooks's Club, their intercourse continued more politely, yet with equal familiarity, while their House of Commons life passed in a robust atmosphere of combat and crisis and defeat. The Whigs despised the royal family; and there was certainly none of the hush and punctilio of court existence about them. Within the narrow limits of their world they were equalitarians.

Their life, in fact, was essentially a normal life, compounded of the same elements as those of general humanity, astir with the same clamour and clash and aspiration and competition as filled the streets round their august dwellings. Only, it was normal life played out on a colossal stage and with magnificent scenery and costumes. Their houses were homes, but homes with sixty bedrooms, set in grounds five miles round; they fought to keep their jobs, but the jobs were embassies and prime ministerships; their sons went to the same universities as humbler students, but were distinguished from them there by a nobleman's gold-tasselled mortarboard. When the Duke of Devonshire took up botany, he sent out a special expedition to the East Indies to search for rare plants; Lord Egremont liked pictures, so he filled a gallery with Claudes and Correggios; young Lord Palmerston was offered the Chancellorship of the Exchequer a year or two after entering Parliament.

This curiously blended life produced a curiously blended type of character. With so many opportunities for action, its interests were predominantly active. Most of the men were engaged in politics. And the women—for they lived to please the men—were political too. They listened, they sympathized, they advised; through them two statesmen might make overtures to each other, or effect a reconciliation. But politics then were not the life sentence to hard labour that in our iron age they have become. Parliament sat for only a few months in the year; and even during the session, debates did not start till the late afternoon. The Whigs had the rest of their time to devote to other things. If they were sporting, they raced and hunted; if interested in agriculture, they farmed on an ambitious scale; if artistic, they collected marbles and medals; if intellectual, they read history and philosophy; if literary, they composed compliments in verse and sonorous, platitudinous orations. But the chief of their spare time was given up to social life. They gave balls, they founded clubs, they played cards, they got up private theatricals; they cultivated friendship and every variety, platonic and less platonic, of the art of love. Their ideal was the Renaissance ideal of the whole man, whose aspiration it is to make the most of every advantage, intellectual and sensual, that life has to offer.

In practice, of course, this ideal was not so broad as it sounds. The Whigs could not escape the limitations imposed by the splendour of their circumstances. Like all aristocrats they tended to be amateurs. When life is so free and so pleasant, a man is not likely to endure the drudgery necessary to make himself really expert in any one thing. Even in those affairs of state which took up most of the Whigs' time, they troubled little with the dry details of economic theory or administrative practice. Politics to them meant, first of all, personalities and, secondly, general principles. And general principles to them were an occasion for expression rather than thought. They did not dream of questioning the fundamental canons of Whig orthodoxy. All believed in ordered liberty, low taxation and the enclosure of lands; all disbelieved in despotism and democracy. Their only concern was to restate these indisputable truths in a fresh and effective fashion.

Again, their taste was a little philistine. Aristocratic taste nearly always is. Those whose ordinary course of life is splendid and satisfying find it hard to recognize the deeper value of the exercises of the solitary imagination; art to them is not the fulfilment of the soul, but an ornamental appendage to existence. Moreover, the English nobility were too much occupied with practical affairs to achieve the fullest intellectual life. They admired what was elegant, sumptuous and easy to understand: portraits that were good likenesses and pleasing decorations, architecture which appropriately housed a stately life. In books, they appreciated acute, wittily phrased observation of human nature, or noble sentiments expressed in flowing periods: Cicero, Pope, Horace, Burke. The strange and the harsh they dismissed immediately. Among contemporary authors they appreciated Jane Austen, condemned Crabbe, for the most part, as sordid and low, and neglected Blake almost entirely. If they had read him, they would not have liked him. For—it is another of their limitations—they were not spiritual. Their education did not encourage them to be; and, anyway, they found this world too absorbing to concern themselves much with the next. The bolder spirits among them were atheists. The average person accepted Christianity, but in a straightforward spirit, innocent alike of mysticism and theological exactitude.

Further, their circumstances did not encourage the virtues of self-control. Good living gave them zest; wealth gave them opportunity; and they threw themselves into their pleasures with an animal recklessness at once terrifying and exhilarating to a modern reader. The most respectable people often drank themselves under the table without shocking anyone. "Colonel Napier came in to-night as drunk as an owl," remarks Lady Sarah Napier of the staid middle-aged gentleman who was her husband. And their drinking was nothing to their gambling. Night after night they played loo and faro from early evening till the candles guttered pale in the light of the risen sun. Lord Stavordale lamented he had not been playing higher, on a night when he won £11,000 in a single hand at hazard. Georgiana, Duchess of Devonshire, cost her husband nearly £1,000,000 in card debts. Rich as they were, they often ruined themselves. The letters of the time are loud with lamentations about the duns coming in and the furniture going out. Nor was their sexual life of a kind to commend them to an austere morality. "I was afraid I was going to have the gout the other day," writes Lord Carlisle to a friend. "I believe I live too chaste: it is not a common fault with me." It was not a common fault with any of them. In fact, an unmarried man was thought unpleasantly queer if he did not keep under his protection some sprightly full-bosomed Kitty Clive or Mrs. Bellamy, whose embraces he repaid with a house in Montpelier Square, a box at the opera and a smart cabriolet in which to drive her down to Brighthelmstone for a week's amorous relaxation. Nor did he confine himself to professional ladies of pleasure. Even unmarried girls like Lady Hester Stanhope were suspected of having lovers; among married women the practice was too common to stir comment. The historian grows quite giddy as he tries to disentangle the complications of heredity consequent on the free and easy habits of the English aristocracy. The Harley family, children of the Countess of Oxford, were known as the Harleian Miscellany on account of the variety of fathers alleged to be responsible for their existence. The Duke of Devonshire had three children by the Duchess and two by Lady Elizabeth Foster, the Duchess one by Lord Grey; and most of them were brought up together in Devonshire House, each set of children with a surname of its own. "Emily, does it never strike you," writes Miss Pamela Fitzgerald in 1816, "the vices are wonderfully prolific among Whigs? There are such countless illegitimates, such a tribe of children of the mist." It is noteworthy that the author of this lively comment was a carefully brought-up young lady of the highest breeding. The free habits of these days encouraged free speech. "Comfortable girls," remarks a middle-aged lady of her growing nieces, "who like a dirty joke." And the men, as can be imagined, were a great deal freer than the women. For all their polish the Whigs were not refined people in the Victorian sense of the word.

It appears in other aspects of their lives. They could be extremely arrogant, treating their inferiors with a patrician insolence which seems to us the reverse of good breeding. Lady Catherine de Bourgh was not the caricature that an ignorant person might suppose. Fashionable young men of refined upbringing amused themselves by watching fights where the Game Chicken battered the Tutbury Pet into unconsciousness with bare and blood-stained fists. And the pamphlets, the squibs, the appalling political cartoons that lay open in the most elegant drawing-rooms show that the ladies of the day were not squeamish either.

Still, unseemly as some of its manifestations were, one must admit that there is something extremely attractive in this earthy exuberance. And, as a matter of fact, it was the inevitable corollary of their virtues. English society had the merits of its defects. Its wide scope, its strong root in the earth, gave it an astounding, an irresistible vitality. For all their dissipation there was nothing decadent about these eighteenth-century aristocrats. Their excesses came from too much life, not too little. And it was the same vitality that gave them their predominance in public life. They took on the task of directing England's destinies with the same self-confident vigour that they drank and diced. It was this vigour that made Pitt Prime Minister at twenty-four years old,* that enabled the Foxites to keep the flag of liberty flying against the united public opinion of a panic-stricken nation. Nor did they let their pleasures interfere with these more serious activities. After eighteen hours of uninterrupted gambling, Charles Fox would arrive at the House of Commons to electrify his fellow members by a brilliant discourse on American taxation. Rakes and ladies of fashion intersperse their narratives of intrigue with discussions on politics, on literature, even on morals. For they were not unmoral. Their lapses came from passion, not from principle; and they are liable at any time to break out in contrite acknowledgements of guilt and artless resolutions for future improvement. Indeed it was one of the paradoxes created by their mixed composition that, though they were worldly, they were not sophisticated. Their elaborate manners masked simple reactions. Like their mode of life

* Pitt diverged from the Whigs in later life, but he was brought up among them and is, so far, representative of the Whig tradition.

their characters were essentially natural: spontaneous, unintrospective, brimming over with normal feelings, love of home and family, loyalty, convivality, desire for fame, hero-worship, patriotism. And they showed their feelings too. Happy creatures! They lived before the days of the stiff upper lip and the inhibited public-school Englishman. A manly tear stood in their eye at the story of a heroic deed; they declared their loves in a strain of flowery hyperbole. They were the more expressive from their very unselfconsciousness. It never struck them that they needed to be inarticulate to appear sincere. They were equally frank about their less elevated sentiments. Eighteenth-century rationalism combined with rural common sense to make them robustly ready to face unedifying facts. And they declared their impressions with a brusque honesty, outstandingly characteristic of them. From Sir Robert Walpole, who encouraged coarse conversation on the ground that it was the only form of talk which everyone enjoyed, down to the Duke of Wellington, who described the army of his triumphs as composed of "the scum of the earth, enlisted for drink," the Augustan aristocracy, Whig and Tory alike, said what they thought with a superb disregard for public opinion. For if they were not original they were independent-minded. The conventions which bounded their lives were conventions of form only. Since they had been kings of their world from birth, they were free from the tiresome inhibitions that are induced by a sense of inferiority. Within the locked garden of their society, individuality flowered riotous and rampant. Their typical figures show up beside the muted introverts of to-day as clear-cut and idiosyncratic as characters in Dickens. They took for granted that you spoke your mind and followed your impulses. If these were odd, they were amused but not disapproving. They enjoyed eccentrics: George Selwyn, who never missed an execution, Beau Brummell, who took three hours to tie his cravat. The firm English soil in which they were rooted, the spacious freedom afforded by their place in the world, allowed personality to flourish in as many bold and fantastic shapes as it pleased.

But it was always a garden plant, a civilized growth. Whatever their eccentricities, the Whig nobles were never provincial and never uncouth. They had that effortless knowledge of the world that comes only to those who from childhood have been accustomed to move in a complex society, that delightful unassertive confidence possible only to people who have never had cause to doubt their social position. And they carried to the finest degree of cultivation those social arts which engaged so much of their time. Here we come to their outstanding distinction. They were the most agreeable society England has ever known. The character of their agreeability was of a piece with the rest of them: mundane, straightforward, a trifle philistine, largely concerned with gossip, not given to subtle analyses or flights of fancy. But it had all their vitality and all their sense of style. It was incomparably racy and spontaneous and accomplished, based solidly on a wide culture and experience, yet free to express itself in bursts of high spirits, in impulses of appreciation, in delicate movements of sentiment, in graceful compliments. For it had its grace—a virile classical grace like that of the Chippendale furniture which adorned its rooms, lending a glittering finish to its shrewd humour, its sharp-eyed observation, its vigorous disquisitions on men and things. Educated without pedantry, informal but not slipshod, polished but not precious, brilliant without fatigue, it combined in an easy perfection the charms of civilization and nature. Indeed the whole social life of the period shines down the perspective of history like some masterpiece of natural art—a prize bloom, nurtured in shelter and sunshine and the richest soil, the result of generations of breeding and blending, that spreads itself to the open sky in strength and beauty.

It was at its most characteristic in the middle of the century; it was at its most dazzling towards its close. By 1780 a new spirit was rising in the world. Ossian had taught people to admire ruins and ravines, Rousseau to examine the processes of the heart; with unpowdered heads and the ladies in simple muslin dresses, they paced the woods meditating, in Cowper-like mood, on the tender influences of nature. Though they kept the style and good sense of their fathers, their sympathies were wider. At the same time their feelings grew more refined. The hardness which had marred the previous age dwindled. Gainsborough, not Hogarth, mirrored the taste of the time; "sensibility" became a fashionable word. For a fleeting moment Whig society had a foot in two worlds and made the best of both of them. The lucid outline of eighteenth-century civilization was softened by the glow of the romantic dawn.

Dawn—but for them it was sunset. The same spirit that tinged them with their culminating glory was also an omen of their dissolution. For the days of aristocratic supremacy were numbered. By the iron laws which condition the social structure of man's existence, it could last only as long as it maintained an economic predominance. With the coming of the Industrial Revolution this predominance began to pass from the landlords to other ranks of the community. Already by the close of the century go-ahead manufacturers in the north were talking of Parliamentary reform; already, in the upper rooms of obscure London alleys, workingmen met together to clamour for liberty, equality and fraternity. Within forty years of its zenith the Whig world was completely swept away. Only a few survivors lingered on to illustrate to an uncomprehending generation the charm of the past. Of these the most distinguished was William Lamb, second Viscount Melbourne.

THIRTY-SIX

ENLIGHTENED CONSERVATISM

The traditionalism of the eighteenth century is strongly revealed in Edmund Burke (1729–97), the celebrated British orator, member of Parliament, and political philosopher. Burke's position was eminently and persuasively conservative. Thoroughly alarmed at the mounting radicalism of the French Revolution, in 1790 Burke wrote one of his most popular works, Reflections on the Revolution in France. *This long tract, somewhat uneven in tone and argument, contains the gist of Burke's political philosophy. Burke disliked change and distrusted reason. Instead he put his trust in human experience, that is, the accumulated wisdom of many generations, and he regarded human society, including government, as a religious rather than a rational entity. His conservatism, better suited to slowly changing preindustrial society than to more mobile, later times, appealed strongly to the established governing classes of his generation in Britain and in continental Europe. In all probability, his greatest contribution to the development of political thought was his insistence on the organic nature of society and government, as opposed to the often shallow and glib belief that society and government often operated according to rationally based mechanical principles.*

EDMUND BURKE

REFLECTIONS ON THE REVOLUTION IN FRANCE *

The ceremony of cashiering kings, of which these gentlemen talk so much at their ease, can rarely, if ever, be performed without force. It then becomes a case of war, and not of consitution. Laws are commanded to hold their tongues amongst arms; and tribunals fall to the ground with the peace they are no longer able to uphold. The Revolution of 1688 was obtained by a just war, in the only case in which any war, and much more a civil war, can be just. 'Justa bella quibus *necessaria.*' The question of dethroning, or if these gentlemen like the phrase better, 'cashiering kings,' will always be, as it has always been, an extraordinary question of state, and wholly out of the law; a question (like all other questions of state) of dispositions, and of means, and of probable consequences, rather than of positive rights.

* From Edmund Burke, *Reflections on the Revolution in France,* pp. 34–37, 44–50, 54–58, 82–84. First published in London in 1790.

As it was not made for common abuses, so it is not to be agitated by common minds. The speculative line of demarcation, where obedience ought to end, and resistance must begin, is faint, obscure, and not easily definable. It is not a single act, or a single event, which determines it. Governments must be abused and deranged indeed, before it can be thought of; and the prospect of the future must be as bad as the experience of the past. When things are in that lamentable condition, the nature of the disease is to indicate the remedy to those whom nature has qualified to administer in extremities this critical, ambiguous, bitter potion to a distempered state. Times, and occasions, and provocations, will teach their own lessons. The wise will determine from the gravity of the case; the irritable from sensibility to oppression; the high-minded from disdain and indignation at abusive power in unworthy hands; the brave and bold from the love of honourable danger in a generous cause: but, with or without right, a revolution will be the very last resource of the thinking and the good. . . .

The Revolution was made to preserve our *ancient*, indisputable laws and liberties, and that *ancient* constitution of government which is our only security for law and liberty. If you are desirous of knowing the spirit of our constitution, and the policy which predominated in that great period which has secured it to this hour, pray look for both in our histories, in our records, in our Acts of Parliament, and journals of Parliament, and not in the sermons of the Old Jewry, and the after-dinner toasts of the Revolution Society. In the former you will find other ideas and another language. Such a claim is as ill-suited to our temper and wishes as it is unsupported by any appearance of authority. The very idea of the fabrication of a new government is enough to fill us with disgust and horror. We wished at the period of the Revolution, and do now wish, to derive all we possess as *an inheritance from our forefathers.* Upon that body and stock of inheritance we have taken care not to inoculate any scion alien to the nature of the original plant. All the reformations we have hitherto made have proceeded upon the principle of reference to antiquity; and I hope, nay I am persuaded, that all those which possibly may be made hereafter, will be carefully formed upon analogical precedent, authority, and example.

Our oldest reformation is that of Magna Charta. You will see that Sir Edward Coke, that great oracle of our law, and indeed all the great men who follow him, to Blackstone, are industrious to prove the pedigree of our liberties. They endeavour to prove, that the ancient charter, the Magna Charta of King John, was connected with another positive charter from Henry I., and that both the one and the other were nothing more than a re-affirmance of the still more ancient standing law of the kingdom. In the matter of fact, for the greater part, these authors appear to be in the right; perhaps not always; but if the lawyers mistake in some particulars, it proves my position still the more strongly; because it demonstrates the powerful prepossession towards antiquity, with which the minds of all our lawyers and legislators, and of all the people whom they wish to influence, have been always filled; and the stationary policy of this kingdom in considering their most sacred rights and franchises as an *inheritance*.

In the famous law of the 3rd of Charles I., called the *Petition of Right,* the Parliament says to the King, 'Your subjects have *inherited* this freedom,' claiming their franchises not on abstract principles 'as the rights of men,' but as the rights of Englishmen, and as a patrimony derived from their forefathers. Selden, and the other profoundly learned men, who drew this Petition of Right, were as well acquainted, at least, with all the general theories concerning the 'rights of men,' as any of the discoursers in our pulpits, or on your tribune; full as well as Dr. Price, or as the Abbé Sieyes. But, for reasons worthy of that practical wisdom which superseded their theoretic science, they preferred this positive, recorded, *hereditary* title to all which can be dear to the man and the citizen, to that vague speculative right, which exposed their sure inheritance to be scrambled for and torn to pieces by every wild, litigious spirit.

The same policy pervades all the laws which have since been made for the preservation of our liberties. In the 1st of William and Mary, in the famous statute, called the Declaration of Right, the two Houses utter not a syllable of 'a right to frame a government for themselves.' You will see, that their whole care was to secure the religion, laws, and liberties, that had been long possessed, and had been lately endangered. 'Taking into their most serious consideration the *best* means for making such an establishment, that their religion, laws, and liberties, might not be in danger of being again subverted,' they auspicate all their proceedings, by stating as some of those *best* means, 'in the *first place'* to do 'as their *ancestors in like cases have usually* done for vindicating their *ancient* rights and liberties, to *declare;'*—and then they pray the King and Queen, 'that it may be *declared* and enacted, that *all and singular* the rights and liberties *asserted and declared,* are the true *ancient* and indubitable rights and liberties of the people of this kingdom.'

You will observe, that from Magna Charta to the Declaration of Right, it has been the uniform policy of our constitution to claim and assert our liberties, as an *entailed inheritance* derived to us from our forefathers, and to be transmitted to our posterity; as an estate especially belonging to the people of this kingdom, without any reference whatever to any other more general or prior right. By this means our constitution preserves an unity in so great a diversity of its parts. We have an inheritable Crown; an inheritable peerage; and a House of Commons and a people inheriting privileges, franchises, and liberties, from a long line of ancestors.

The policy appears to me to be the result of profound reflection; or rather the happy effect of following nature, which is wisdom without reflection, and above it. A spirit of innovation is generally the result of a selfish temper, and confined views. People will not look forward to posterity, who never look backward to their ancestors. Besides, the people of England well know, that the idea of inheritance furnishes a sure principle of conservation, and a sure principle of transmission; without at all excluding a principle of improvement. It leaves acquisition free; but it secures what it acquires. Whatever advantages are obtained by a state proceeding on these maxims, are locked fast as in a sort of family settlement; grasped as in a kind of mortmain for ever. By a constitutional policy working after the pattern of nature, we receive, we hold, we transmit our government and our privileges, in the same manner in which we enjoy and transmit our property and our lives. The institutions of policy, the goods of fortune, the gifts of providence, are handed down to us, and from us, in the same course and order. Our political system is placed in a just correspondence and symmetry with the order of the world, and with the mode of existence decreed to a permanent body composed of transitory parts; wherein, by the disposition of a stupendous wisdom, moulding together the great mysterious incorporation of the human race, the whole, at one time, is never old, or middle-aged, or young, but, in a condition of unchangeable constancy, moves on through the varied tenor of perpetual decay, fall, renovation, and progression. Thus, by preserving the method of nature in the conduct of the state, in what we improve, we are never wholly new; in what we retain, we are never wholly obsolete. By adhering in this manner and on those principles to our forefathers, we are guided not by the superstition of antiquarians, but by the spirit of philosophic analogy. In this choice of inheritance we have given to our frame of polity the image of a relation in blood; binding up the constitution of our country with our dearest domestic ties; adopting our fundamental laws into the bosom of our family affections; keeping inseparable, and cherishing with the warmth of all their combined and mutually reflected charities, our state, our hearths, our sepulchres, and our altars.

Through the same plan of a conformity to nature in our artificial institutions, and by calling in the aid of her unerring and powerful instincts, to fortify the fallible and feeble contrivances of our reason, we have derived several other, and those no small benefits, from considering our liberties in the light of an inheritance. Always acting as if in the presence of canonised forefathers, the spirit of freedom, leading in itself to misrule and excess, is tempered with an awful gravity. This idea of a liberal descent inspires us with a sense of habitual native dignity, which prevents that upstart insolence almost inevitably adhering to and disgracing those who are the first acquirers of any distinction. By this means our liberty becomes a noble freedom. It carries an imposing and majestic aspect. It has a pedigree and illustrating ancestors. It has its bearings and its ensigns armorial. It has its gallery of portraits; its monumental inscriptions; its records, evidences, and titles. We procure reverence to our civil institutions on the principle upon which nature teaches us to revere individual men; on account of their age, and on account of those from whom they are descended. All your sophisters cannot produce anything better adapted to preserve a rational and manly freedom than the course that we have pursued, who have chosen our nature rather than our speculations, our breasts rather than our inventions, for the great conservatories and magazines of our rights and privileges. . . .

We know that the British House of Commons, without shutting its doors to any merit in any class, is, by the sure operation of adequate causes, filled with everything illustrious in rank, in descent, in hereditary and acquired opulence, in cultivated talents, in military, civil, naval, and politic distinction, that the country can afford. But supposing, what hardly can be supposed as a case, that the House of Commons should be composed in the same manner with the *Tiers Etat* in France, would this dominion of chicane be borne with patience, or even conceived without horror? God forbid I should insinuate anything derogatory to that profession, which is another priesthood, administering the rights of sacred justice. But whilst I revere men in the functions which belong to them, and would do as much as one man can do to prevent their exclusion from any, I cannot, to flatter them, give the lie to nature. They are good and useful in the composition; they must be mischievous if they preponderate so as virtually to become the whole. Their very excellence in their peculiar functions may be far from a qualification for others. It cannot escape observation, that when men are too much confined to professional and faculty habits, and as it were inveterate in the recurrent employment of that narrow circle, they are rather disabled than qualified for whatever depends on the knowledge of mankind, on experience in mixed affairs, on a comprehensive, connected view of the various, complicated, external, and internal interests, which go to the formation of that multifarious thing called a state.

After all, if the House of Commons were to have an wholly professional and faculty composition, what is the power of the House of Commons, circumscribed and shut in by the immovable barriers of law, usages, positive rules of doctrine and practice, counterpoised by the House of Lords, and every moment of its existence at the discretion of the Crown to continue, prorogue, or dissolve us? The power of the House of Commons, direct, or indirect, is indeed great; and long may it be able to preserve its greatness, and the spirit belonging to true greatness, at the full; and it will do so, as long as it can keep the breakers of law in India from becoming the makers of law for England. The power, however, of the House of Commons, when least diminished, is as a drop of water in the

ocean, compared to that residing in a settled majority of your National Assembly. That Assembly, since the destruction of the orders, has no fundamental law, no strict convention, no respected usage to restrain it. Instead of finding themselves obliged to conform to a fixed constitution, they have a power to make a constitution which shall conform to their designs. Nothing in heaven or upon earth can serve as a control on them. What ought to be the heads, the hearts, the dispositions, that are qualified, or that dare, not only to make laws under a fixed constitution, but at one heat to strike out a totally new constitution for a great kingdom, and in every part of it, from the monarch on the throne to the vestry of a parish? But—*'fools rush in where angels fear to tread.'* In such a state of unbounded power, for undefined and undefinable purposes, the evil of a moral and almost physical inaptitude of the man to the function, must be the greatest we can conceive to happen in the management of human affairs.

Having considered the composition of the Third Estate as it stood in its original frame, I took a view of the representatives of the clergy. There too it appeared, that full as little regard was had to the general security of property, or to the aptitude of the deputies for their public purposes, in the principles of their election. That election was so contrived, as to send a very large proportion of mere country curates to the great and arduous work of new-modelling a state; men who never had seen the state so much as in a picture; men who knew nothing of the world beyond the bounds of an obscure village; who, immersed in hopeless poverty, could regard all property, whether secular or ecclesiastial, with no other eye than that of envy; among whom must be many who, for the smallest hope of the meanest dividend in plunder, would readily join in any attempts upon a body of wealth, in which they could hardly look to have any share, except in a general scramble. Instead of balancing the power of the active chicaners in the other Assembly, these curates must necessarily become the active coadjutors, or at best the passive instruments, of those by whom they had been habitually guided in their petty village concerns. They too could hardly be the most conscientious of their kind, who, presuming upon their incompetent understanding, could intrigue for a trust which led them from their natural relation to their flocks, and their natural spheres of action, to undertake the regeneration of kingdoms. This preponderating weight, being added to the force of the body of chicane in the *Tiers Etat,* completed that momentum of ignorance, rashness, presumption, and lust of plunder, which nothing has been able to resist.

To observing men it must have appeared from the beginning, that the majority of the Third Estate, in conjunction with such a deputation from the clergy as I have described, whilst it pursued the destruction of the nobility, would inevitably become subservient to the worst designs of individuals in that class. In the spoil and humiliation of their own order these individuals would possess a sure fund for the pay of their new followers. To squander away the objects which made the happiness of their fellows, would be to them no sacrifice at all. Turbulent, discontented men of quality, in proportion as they are puffed up with personal pride and arrogance, generally despise their own order. One of the first symptoms they discover of a selfish and mischievous ambition, is a profligate disregard of a dignity which they partake with others. To be attached to the subdivision, to love the little platoon we belong to in society, is the first principle (the germ as it were) of public affections. It is the first link in the series by which we proceed towards a love to our country, and to mankind. The interest of that portion of social arrangement is a trust in the hands of all those who compose it; and as none but bad men would justify it in abuse, none but traitors would barter it away for their own personal advantage.

There were, in the time of our civil troubles in England, (I do not know whether you have any such in your Assembly in France,) several persons, like the then Earl of Holland, who by themselves or their families had brought an odium on the throne, by the prodigal dispensation of its bounties towards them, who afterwards joined in the rebellions arising from the discontents of which they were themselves the cause; men who helped to subvert that throne to which they owed, some of them, their existence, others all that power which they employed to ruin their benefactor. If any bounds are set to the rapacious demands of that sort of people, or that others are permitted to partake in the objects they would engross, revenge and envy soon fill up the craving void that is left in their avarice. Confounded by the complication of distempered passions, their reason is disturbed; their views become vast and perplexed; to others inexplicable; to themselves uncertain. They find, on all sides, bounds to their unprincipled ambition in any fixed order of things. But in the fog and haze of confusion all is enlarged, and appears without any limit.

When men of rank sacrifice all ideas of dignity to an ambition without a distinct object, and work with low instruments and for low ends, the whole composition becomes low and base. Does not something like this now appear in France? Does it not produce something ignoble and inglorious? a kind of meanness in all the prevalent policy? a tendency in all that is done to lower along with individuals all the dignity and importance of the state? Other revolutions have been conducted by persons, who, whilst they attempted or affected changes in the commonwealth, sanctified their ambition by advancing the dignity of the people whose peace they troubled. They had long views. They aimed at the rule, not at the destruction, of their country. They were men of great civil and great military talents, and if the terror, the ornament of their age. . . . The compliment made to one of the great bad men of the old stamp (Cromwell) by his kinsman, a favourite poet of that time, shows what it was he proposed, and what indeed to a great degree he accomplished, in the success of his ambition:

> 'Still as *you* rise, the *state* exalted too,
> Finds no distemper whilst 'tis chang'd by *you;*
> Chang'd like the world's great scene, when without noise
> The rising sun night's *vulgar* lights destroys'

These disturbers were not so much like men usurping power, as asserting their natural place in society. Their rising was to illuminate and beautify the world. Their conquest over their competitors was by outshining them. The hand that, like a destroying angel, smote the country, communicated to it the force and energy under which it suffered. I do not say, (God forbid,) I do not say, that the virtues of such men were to be taken as a balance to their crimes: but they were some corrective to their effects. Such was, as I said, our Cromwell. Such were your whole race of Guises, Condés, and Colignis. Such the Richelieus, who in more quiet times acted in the spirit of a civil war. Such, as better men, and in a less dubious cause, were your Henry IV. and your Sully, though nursed in civil confusions, and not wholly without some of their taint. It is a thing to be wondered at, to see how very soon France, when she had a moment to respire, recovered and emerged from the longest and most dreadful civil war that ever was known in any nation. Why? Because, among all their massacres, they had not slain the *mind* in their country. A conscious dignity, a noble pride, a generous sense of glory and emulation, was not extinguished. On the contrary, it was kindled and enflamed. The organs also of the state, however shattered, existed. All the prizes of honour and virtue, all the rewards, all the distinctions, remained. But your present confusion, like a palsy, has attacked the fountain of life itself. Every person in your country, in a situation to be actuated by a principle of honour, is disgraced and degraded, and can entertain no sensation of life, except in a mortified and humiliated indignation. But this generation will quickly pass away. . . . Believe me, Sir, those who attempt to level, never equalise. In all societies, consisting of various descriptions of citizens, some description must be uppermost. The levellers therefore only change and pervert the natural order of things; they load the edifice of society, by setting up in the air what the solidity of the structure requires to be on the ground. The associations of tailors and carpenters, of which the republic (of Paris, for instance) is composed, cannot be equal to the situation, into which, by the worst of usurpations, an usurpation on the prerogatives of nature, you attempt to force them.

The Chancellor of France at the opening of the states, said, in a tone of oratorical flourish, that all occupations were honourable. If he meant only, that no honest employment was disgraceful, he would not have gone beyond the truth. But in asserting, that anything is honourable, we imply some distinction in its favour. The occupation of a hair-dresser, or of a working tallow-chandler, cannot be a matter of honour to any person—to say nothing of a number of other more servile employments. Such descriptions of men ought not to suffer oppression from the state; but the state suffers oppression, if such as they, either individually or collectively, are permitted to rule. In this you think you are combating prejudice, but you are at war with nature.

I do not, my dear Sir, conceive you to be of that sophistical, captious spirit, or of that uncandid dullness, as to require, for every general observation or sentiment, an explicit detail of the correctives and exceptions, which reason will presume to be included in all the general propositions which come from reasonable men. You do not imagine, that I wish to confine power, authority, and distinction to blood, and names, and titles. No, Sir. There is no qualification for government but virtue and wisdom, actual or presumptive. Wherever they are actually found, they have, in whatever state, condition, profession, or trade, the passport of Heaven to human place and honour. Woe to the country which would madly and impiously reject the service of the talents and virtues, civil, military, or religious, that are given to grace and to serve it; and would condemn to obscurity everything formed to diffuse lustre and glory around a state. Woe to that country too, that, passing into the opposite extreme, considers a low education, a mean contracted view of things, a sordid, mercenary occupation, as a preferable title to command. Everything ought to be open; but not indifferently to every man. No rotation; no appointment by lot; no mode of election operating in the spirit of sortition, or rotation, can be generally good in a Government conversant in extensive objects. Because they have no tendency, direct or indirect, to select the man with a view to the duty, or to accommodate the one to the other. I do not hesitate to say, that the road to eminence and power, from obscure condition, ought not to be made too easy, nor a thing too much of course. If rare merit be the rarest of all rare things, it ought to pass through some sort of probation. The temple of honour ought to be seated on an eminence. If it be opened through virtue, let it be remembered too, that virtue is never tried but by some difficulty and some struggle.

Nothing is a due and adequate representation of a state, that does not represent its ability, as well as its property. But as ability is a vigorous and active principle, and as property is sluggish, inert, and timid, it never can be safe from the invasions of ability, unless it be, out of all proportion, predominant in the representation. It must be represented too in great masses of accumulation, or it is not rightly protected. The characteristic essence of property, formed out of the combined principles of its acquisition and conservation, is to be *unequal*. The great masses therefore which excite envy, and tempt rapacity, must be put out of the possibility of danger. Then they form a natural rampart about the lesser properties in all their gradations. The same quantity of property, which is by the natural course of things divided among many, has not the same operation. Its defensive power is weakened as it is diffused. In this diffusion each man's portion is less than what, in the eagerness of his desires, he may flatter himself to obtain by dissipating the accumulations of others. The plunder of the few would indeed give but a share inconceivably small in the distribution to the many. But the many are not capable of making this calculation; and those who lead them to rapine never intend this distribution.

The power of perpetuating our property in our families is one of the most valuable and interesting circumstances belonging to it, and that which tends the most to the perpetuation of society itself. It makes our weakness subservient to our virtue; it grafts benevolence even upon avarice. The possessors of family wealth, and of the distinction which attends hereditary possession, (as most concerned in it,) are the natural securities for this transmission. With us the House of Peers is formed upon this principle. It is wholly composed of hereditary property and hereditary distinction; and made therefore the third of the legislature; and, in the last event, the sole judge of all property in all its subdivisions. The House of Commons too, though not necessarily, yet in fact, is always so composed, in the far greater part. Let those large proprietors be what they will, and they have their chance of being among the best, they are, at the very worst, the ballast in the vessel of the commonwealth. For though hereditary wealth, and the rank which goes with it, are too much idolised by creeping sycophants, and the blind, abject admirers of power, they are too rashly slighted in shallow speculations of the petulant, assuming, short-sighted coxcombs of philosophy. Some decent, regulated pre-eminence, some preference (not exclusive appropriation) given to birth, is neither unnatural, nor unjust, nor impolitic. . . .

These gentlemen value themselves on being systematic; and not without reason. They must therefore look on this gross and palpable defect of representation, this fundamental grievance, (so they call it,) as a thing not only vicious in itself, but as rendering our whole government absolutely *illegitimate,* and not at all better than a downright *usurpation.* Another revolution, to get rid of this illegitimate and usurped government, would of course be perfectly justifiable, if not absolutely necessary. Indeed their principle, if you observe it with any attention, goes much further than to an alteration in the election of the House of Commons; for, if popular representation, or choice, is necessary to the *legitimacy* of all government, the House of Lords is, at one stroke, bastardised and corrupted in blood. That House is no representative of the people at all, even in 'semblance or in form.' The case of the Crown is altogether as bad. In vain the Crown may endeavour to screen itself against these gentlemen by the authority of the establishment made on the Revolution. The Revolution which is resorted to for a title, on their system, wants a title itself. The Revolution is built, according to their theory, upon a basis not more solid than our present formalities, as it was made by a House of Lords, not representing any one but themselves; and by a House of Commons exactly such as the present, that is, as they term it, by a mere 'shadow and mockery' of representation.

Something they must destroy, or they seem to themselves to exist for no purpose. One set is for destroying the civil power through the ecclesiastical; another for demolishing the ecclesiastic through the civil. They are aware that the worst consequences might happen to the public in accomplishing this double ruin of Church and State; but they are so heated with their theories, that they give more than hints, that this ruin, with all the mischiefs that must lead to it and attend it, and which to themselves appear quite certain, would not be unacceptable to them, or very remote from their wishes. A man amongst them of great authority, and certainly of great talents, speaking of a supposed alliance between Church and State, says, 'perhaps *we must wait for the fall of the civil powers* before this most unnatural alliance be broken. Calamitous no doubt will that time be. But what convulsion in the political world ought to be a subject of lamentation, if it be attended with so desirable an effect?' You see with what a steady eye these gentlemen are prepared to view the greatest calamities which can befall their country.

It is no wonder therefore, that with these ideas of everything in their constitution and government at home, either in Church or State, as illegitimate and usurped, or at best as a vain mockery, they look abroad with an eager and passionate enthusiasm. Whilst they are possessed by these notions, it is vain to talk to them of the practice of their ancestors, the fundamental laws of their country, the fixed form of a constitution, whose merits are confirmed by the solid test of long experience, and an increasing public strength and national prosperity. They despise experience as the wisdom of unlettered men; and as for the rest, they have wrought underground a mine that will blow up, at one grand explosion, all examples of antiquity, all precedents, charters, and Acts of Parliament. They have 'the rights of men.' Against these there can be no prescription; against these no argument is binding: these admit no temperament, and no compromise: anything withheld from their full demand is so much of fraud and injustice. Against these their rights of men let no Government look for security in the length of its continuance, or in the justice and lenity of its administration. The objections of these speculatists, if its forms do not quadrate with their theories, are as valid against such an old and beneficent Government as against the most violent tyranny, or the greenest usurpation. They are always at issue with Governments, not on a question of abuse, but a question of competency, and a question of title. I have nothing to say to the clumsy subtilty of their political metaphysics. Let them be their amusement in the schools.—'Illa *se jactat in aula—Æolus, et clauso ventorum carcere regnet.'*—But let them not break prison to burst like a *Levanter,* to sweep the earth with their hurricane, and to break up the fountains of the great deep to overwhelm us.

Far am I from denying in theory, full as far is my heart from withholding in practice, (if I were of power to give or to withhold,) the *real* rights of men. In denying their false claims of right, I do not mean to injure those which are real, and are such as their pretended rights would totally destroy. If civil society be made for the advantage of man, all the advantages for which it is made become his right. It is an institution of beneficence; and law itself is only beneficence acting by a rule. Men have a right to live by that rule; they have a right to do justice; as between their fellows, whether their fellows are in politic function or in ordinary occupation. They have a right to the fruits of their industry; and to the means of making their industry fruitful. They have a right to the acquisitions of their parents; to the nourishment and improvement of their offspring; to instruction in life, and to consolation in death. Whatever each man can separately do, without trespassing upon others, he has a right to do for himself; and he has a right to a fair portion of all which society, with all its combinations of skill and force, can do in his favour. In this partnership all men have equal rights; but not to equal things. He that has but five shillings in the partnership, has as good a right to it, as he that has five hundred pounds has to his larger proportion. But he has not a right to an equal dividend in the product of the joint stock; and as to the share of power, authority, and direction which each individual ought to have in the management of the state, that I must deny to be amongst the direct original rights of man in civil society; for I have in my contemplation the civil social man, and no other. It is a thing to be settled by convention.

If civil society be the offspring of convention, that convention must be its law. That convention must limit and modify all the descriptions of constitution which are formed under it. Every sort of legislature, judicial, or executory power, are its creatures. They can have no being in any other state of things; and how can any man claim, under the conventions of civil society, rights which do not so much as suppose its existence? Rights which are absolutely repugnant to it? One of the first motives to civil society, and which becomes one of its fundamental rules, is, *that no man should be judge in his own cause.* By this each person has at once divested himself of the first fundamental right of uncovenanted man, that is, to judge for himself, and to assert his own cause. He abdicates all right to be his own governor. He inclusively, in a great measure, abandons the right of self-defence, the first law of nature. Men cannot enjoy the rights of an uncivil and of a civil state together. That he may obtain justice, he gives up his right of determining, what it is in points the most essential to him. That he may secure some liberty, he makes a surrender in trust of the whole of it.

Government is not made in virtue of natural rights, which may and do exist in total independence of it; and exist in much greater clearness, and in a much greater degree of abstract perfection: but their abstract perfection is their practical defect. By having a right to everything they want everything. Government is a contrivance of human wisdom to provide for human *wants.* Men have a right that these wants should be provided for by this wisdom. Among these wants is to be reckoned the want, out of civil society, of a sufficient restraint upon their passions. Society requires not only that the passions of individuals should be subjected, but that even in the mass and body, as well as in the individuals, the inclinations of men should frequently be thwarted, their will controlled, and their passions brought into subjection. This can only be done *by a power out of themselves;* and not, in the exercise of its function, subject to that will and to those passions which it is its office to bridle and subdue. In this sense the restraints on men, as well as their liberties, are to be reckoned among their rights. But as the liberties and the restrictions vary with times and circumstances, and admit of infinite modifications, they cannot be settled upon any abstract rule; and nothing is so foolish as to discuss them upon that principle.

The moment you abate anything from the full rights of men, each to govern himself, and suffer any artificial, positive limitation upon those rights, from that moment the whole organisation of government becomes a consideration of convenience. This it is which makes the constitution of a state, and the due distribution of its powers, a matter of the most delicate and complicated skill. It requires a deep knowledge of human nature and human necessities, and of the things which facilitate or obstruct the various ends, which are to be pursued by the mechanism of civil institutions. The state is to have recruits to its strength, and remedies to its distempers. What is the use of discussing a man's abstract right to food or medicine? The question is upon the method of procuring and administering them. In that deliberation I shall always advise to call in the aid of the farmer and the physician, rather than the professor of metaphysics.

The science of constructing a commonwealth, or renovating it, or reforming it, is, like every other experimental science, not to be taught *à priori.* Nor is it a short experience that can instruct us in that practical science; because the real effects of moral causes are not always immediate; but that which in the first instance is prejudicial may be excellent in its remoter operation; and its excellence may arise even from the ill effects it produces in the beginning. The reverse also happens; and very plausible schemes, with very pleasing commencements, have often shameful and lamentable conclusions. In states there are often some obscure and almost latent causes, things which appear at first view of little moment, on which a very great part of its prosperity or adversity may most essentially depend. The science of government being therefore so practical in itself, and intended for such practical purposes, a matter which requires experience, and even more experience than any person can gain in his whole life, however sagacious and observing he may be, it is with infinite caution that any man ought to venture upon pulling down an edifice, which has answered in any tolerable degree for ages the common purposes of society, or on building it up again, without having models and patterns of approved utility before his eyes.

These metaphysic rights entering into common life, like rays of light which pierce into a dense medium, are, by the laws of nature, refracted from their straight line. Indeed in the gross and complicated mass of human passions and concerns, the primitive rights of men undergo such a variety of refractions and reflections, that it becomes absurd to talk of them as if they continued in the simplicity of their original direction. The nature of man is intricate; the objects of society are of the greatest possible complexity: and therefore no simple disposition or direction of power can be suitable either to man's nature, or to the quality of his affairs. When I hear the simplicity of contrivance aimed at and boasted of in any new political constitutions, I am at no loss to decide that the artificers are grossly ignorant of their trade, or totally negligent of their duty. The simple governments are fundamentally defective, to say no worse of them. If you were to contemplate society in but one point of view, all these simple modes of polity are infinitely captivating. In effect each would answer its single end much more perfectly than the more complex is able to attain all its complex purposes. But it is better that the whole should be imperfectly and anomalously answered, than that, while some parts are provided for with great exactness, others might be totally neglected, or perhaps materially injured, by the over-care of a favourite member.

The pretended rights of these theorists are all extremes: and in proportion as they are metaphysically true, they are morally and politically false. The rights of men are in a sort of *middle,* incapable of definition, but not impossible to be discerned. The rights of men in governments are their advantages; and these are often in balances between differences of good; in compromises sometimes between good and evil, and sometimes between evil and evil. Political reason is a computing principle; adding, subtracting, multiplying, and dividing, morally and not metaphysically or mathematically, true moral denominations. . . .

When the people have emptied themselves of all the lust of selfish will, which without religion it is utterly impossible they ever should, when they are conscious that they exercise, and exercise perhaps in a higher link of the order of delegation, the power, which to be legitimate must be according to that eternal, immutable law, in which will and reason are the same, they will be more careful how they place power in base and incapable hands. In their nomination to office, they will not appoint to the exercise of authority, as to a pitiful job, but as to a holy function; not according to their sordid, selfish interest, nor to their wanton caprice, nor to their arbitrary will; but they will confer that power (which any man may well tremble to give or to receive) on those only, in whom they may discern that predominant proportion of active virtue and wisdom, taken together and fitted to the charge, such, as in the great and inevitable mixed mass of human imperfections and infirmities, is to be found.

When they are habitually convinced that no evil can be acceptable, either in the act or the permission, to him whose essence is good, they will be better able to extirpate out of the minds of all magistrates, civil, ecclesiastical, or military, anything that bears the least resemblance to a proud and lawless domination.

But one of the first and most leading principles on which the commonwealth and the laws are consecrated, is lest the temporary possessors and life-renters in it, unmindful of what they have received from their ancestors, or of what is due to their posterity, should act as if they were the entire masters; that they should not think it amongst their rights to cut off the entail, or commit waste on the inheritance, by destroying at their pleasure the whole original fabric of their society; hazarding to leave to those who come after them a ruin instead of an habitation—and teaching these successors as little to respect their contrivances, as they had themselves respected the institutions of their forefathers. By this unprincipled facility of changing the state as often, and as much, and in as many ways, as there are floating fancies of fashions, the whole chain and continuity of the commonwealth would be broken. No one generation could link with the other. Men would become little better than the flies of a summer.

And first of all, the science of jurisprudence, the pride of the human intellect, which, with all its defects, redundancies, and errors, is the collected reason of ages, combining the principles of original justice with the infinite variety of human concerns, as a heap of old exploded errors, would be no longer studied. Personal self-sufficiency and arrogance (the certain attendants upon all those who have never experienced a wisdom greater than their own) would usurp the tribunal. Of course no certain laws, establishing invariable grounds of hope and fear, would keep the actions of men in a certain course, or direct them to a certain end. Nothing stable in the modes of holding property, or exercising function, could form a solid ground on which any parent could speculate in the education of his offspring, or in a choice for their future establishment in the world. No principles would be early worked into the habits. As soon as the most able instructor had completed his laborious course of institution, instead of sending forth his pupil, accomplished in a virtuous discipline, fitted to procure him attention and respect, in his place in society, he would find everything altered; and that he had turned out a poor creature to the contempt and derision of the world, ignorant of the true grounds of estimation. Who would insure a tender and delicate sense of honour to beat almost with the first pulses of the heart, when no man could know what would be the test of honour in a nation, continually varying the standard of its coin? No part of life would retain its acquisitions. Barbarism with regard to science and literature, unskilfulness with regard to arts and manufactures, would infallibly succeed to the want of a steady education and settled principle; and thus the commonwealth itself would, in a few generations, crumble away, be disconnected into the dust and powder of individuality, and at length dispersed to all the winds of heaven.

To avoid therefore the evils of inconstancy and versatility, ten thousand times worse than those of obstinacy and the blindest prejudice, we have consecrated the state, that no man should approach to look into its defects or corruptions but with due caution; that he should never dream of beginning its reformation by its subversion; that he should approach to the faults of the state as to the wounds of a father, with pious awe, and trembling solicitude. By this wise prejudice we are taught to look with horror on those children of their country, who are prompt rashly to hack that aged parent in pieces, and put him into the kettle of magicians, in hopes that by their poisonous weeds, and wild incantations, they may regenerate the paternal constitution, and renovate their father's life.

Society is indeed a contract. Subordinate contracts for objects of mere occasional interest may be dissolved at pleasure—but the state ought not to be considered nothing better than a partnership agreement in a trade of pepper and coffee, calico or tobacco, or some other such low concern, to be taken up for a little temporary interest, and to be dissolved by the fancy of the parties. It is to be looked on with other reverence; because it is not a partnership in things subservient only to the gross animal existence of a temporary and perishable nature. It is a partnership in all science; a partnership in all art; a partnership in every virtue, and in all perfection. As the ends of such a partnership cannot be obtained in many generations, it becomes a partnership not only between those who are living, but between those who are living, those who are dead, and those who are to be born. Each contract of each particular state is but a clause in the great primæval contract of eternal society, linking the lower with the higher natures, connecting the visible and invisible world, according to a fixed compact sanctioned by the inviolable oath which holds all physical and all moral natures, each in their appointed place. This law is not subject to the will of those, who by an obligation above them, and infinitely superior, are bound to submit their will to that law. The municipal corporations of that universal kingdom are not morally at liberty at their pleasure, and on their speculations of a contingent improvement, wholly to separate and tear asunder the bands of their subordinate community, and to dissolve it into an unsocial, uncivil, unconnected chaos of elementary principles. It is the first and supreme necessity only, a necessity that is not chosen, but chooses, a necessity paramount to deliberation, that admits no discussion, and demands no evidence, which alone can justify a resort to anarchy. This necessity is no exception to the rule; because this necessity itself is a part too of that moral and physical disposition of things, to which man must be obedient by consent of force: but if that which is only submission to necessity should be made the object of choice, the law is broken, nature is disobeyed, and the rebellious are outlawed, cast forth, and exiled, from this world of reason, and order, and peace, and virtue, and fruitful penitence, into the antagonist world of madness, discord, vice, confusion, and unavailing sorrow.

VII

MODERN CIVILIZATION, 1815-71

PART SEVEN

Two basic revolutions convulsed the nineteenth century: the French Revolution of 1789, which created continuing bitter controversy in politics, and the Industrial Revolution, which created a totally new economic order. The era of reaction after 1815 could not extinguish the rational elements in the Enlightenment which had come to a climax in France's revolutionary decade after 1789. Liberalism, cast in a bourgeois frame of property-conscious values, persisted and grew strong. Economic liberalism, persuasively argued by Adam Smith and his followers, taught that the economic process should be free from traditional government controls. Political liberalism, of which John Stuart Mill was a leading exponent, taught that government, responsive to the popular will, should remain weak and in that way free the individual to make his maximum contribution to society. Meanwhile, nationalism, nourished by romanticism and often in harmony with liberal aspirations, accentuated ethnic differences and further convulsed the fast-flowing historical tides in Western life. While the West was attempting to adjust to both liberalism and nationalism, the Industrial Revolution brought to the West unprecedented material change. Industrialism produced a greatly expanded urban proletariat in urgent need of social protection which the almost totally free economy of the liberals failed either to recognize or to provide. Abuses in the factory system led to social protest, for example in the novels of Disraeli, and in time also produced platforms of social reorganization, varying from Marxism, with emphasis on violent revolution, to Fabian Socialism, with emphasis on scholarly analysis and gradual reform through the democratic process. In view of the magnitude and complexity of the new historical forces at work, along with the urgent necessity of creating new ideologies to contain and channel them, it seems remarkable not that the West produced imperfect solutions to its problems but that in this fast-moving era it managed to survive at all.

THIRTY-SEVEN

REACTION: FRENCH SOCIETY IN 1815

After a generation of warfare and the ideological and institutional upsets which accompanied the French Revolution, France emerged shaken and profoundly changed as Napoleon went into final exile in 1815. Some conservative elements, prominent among them the higher clergy and both the new and the restored aristocracy, persisted in a way of life and attitude that approximated but did not quite recapture the prevailing mood of the ancien régime *of the halcyon days before 1789. New social elements appeared, modifying France's social structure: a stronger than ever bourgeoisie groping for liberalism in an era of reaction, and a larger urban proletariat groping for economic and psychological security in an era of fast industrial change. Meanwhile Paris, which had played a prominent role in the French Revolution, remained the focal point of French creativity. Paris, with its impressive buildings, parks, restaurants, and theaters, seemed outwardly calm. Yet the calm was deceptive, for the whirlwinds of change were already on their way. In his survey of the France of 1815, Professor Artz has sketched France's social structure, with particular—and welcome—descriptions of Parisian life.*

FREDERICK B. ARTZ

FRANCE UNDER THE BOURBON RESTORATION, 1814-1830 *

The social life of the Restoration presents those interesting contrasts which always mark any society in a state of change. In such a transition some classes are little affected by new forces, while other groups owe their very existence to the new conditions.

After 1815 the life of the aristocracy and of the clergy retained much of the atmosphere and flavor of the Ancien Régime. Although they were forced to recognize parvenu groups which shouldered in beside them,—the nobility of the Empire and the newer industrial bourgeoisie of the cities,—they tried to hold themselves aloof, and would have maintained the older life had it been possible. During the period of the Restoration the life of the peasants was least affected; their daily round continued much as it had been before the Revolution. Their lot was perhaps somewhat easier, but not essentially changed.

The new economic forces were developing two new classes—the rising bourgeoisie of the towns, and, in sharp contrast, the working classes of the cities. Among the workers the abuses of the Industrial Revolution caused much misery and wretchedness. The new proletariat, however, was almost without class consciousness. Trade-unionism was just beginning to develop, in spite of laws against it, and isolated groups like the Saint-Simonians conceived the first programs of social action for the workers. As in England before the Reform Bill of 1832, the workers, so far as they envisaged reform, joined forces with the bourgeois Liberals in working for the extension of the franchise and for the freedom of the press. All over Western Europe the ballot box was at this time regarded as the new Ark of the Covenant. Mill owner and mill hand had hardly begun to realize their divergent economic and political interests.

In the large towns there was an inevitable fusion of the new and the old. The old nobility, the nobility of the Empire, and the new industrial plutocracy were more or less thrown together by common interests; in effect they were the ruling classes, though some of them looked to the future while others looked to the past. The industrial bourgeoisie were proud of their newly acquired wealth and social position as well as of the political power which they had gained through the Revolution. Moreover, they preserved from the Revolutionary period a marked distrust of hereditary kings, of nobles, and of priests. It is true that the women of the middle class still went to church and looked upon the priest as their truest guide, but the men leaned more and more to Liberalism in politics and to anticlericalism and free-thought in all that pertained to religion. Much of this was in direct opposition to the traditional position of the

* Reprinted from *France under the Bourbon Restoration, 1814–1830,* pp. 234–53, by Frederick B. Artz by permission of Harvard University Press.

old aristocracy, and to a lesser extent to the interests of the Napoleonic nobility, but as a whole the old nobility and the new plutocracy were opposed to the peasants and the working classes, and they had common interests in social life, in art and literature, and to some measure in politics.

This newer, composite society appeared in the larger towns and in the cities. The older social forms, and distinctions, and ways of thinking persisted in the country districts. As always in France, the cities, with the capital at their head, were the foci of reorganization.

In the life and activity of the nation Paris dominated everything. This concentration of the forces of French society in the capital had become more marked with every stage of French history since the Middle Ages. The Revolution had accelerated this age-long process by destroying the old provinces, and the Napoleonic regime had completed this centralization with a thoroughness that could be equaled in no country of the Western World.

After 1815 the Court lived in Paris, not at Versailles. Economically Paris dominated France as never before, while the Chambers focused all political attention on the capital. Paris, moreover, drew to herself most of the talent of the country, and after 1815 was the artistic capital of the whole of Europe. The gaiety and charm of its society, its intense artistic and intellectual activity, its unrivaled theaters and cafés, made it the favorite resort of every people in Europe. Paris was especially popular, after 1815, with the English. There were so many English in the city that an English newspaper, Galignani's *Messenger,* was established. After the reactionary settlement at Vienna in 1815, the city was also full of political refugees, and as Vienna was to all European Liberals the City of Darkness, Paris from 1815 to 1848 seemed the City of Light.

The Paris of the Restoration was still, by present standards, a small city. According to the census of 1817, the population was about 715,000. By 1830 it had increased to 800,000. The city remained in many ways quite mediæval in appearance, in spite of the improvements that had been made by Louis XIV, Louis XV, and Napoleon—modern Paris, in fact, is largely the work of Baron Haussmann, and dates only from the Second Empire. At this period most of the streets were narrow, ill paved, and dirty, and the houses were crowded together. The congestion was worst on the Ile de la Cité and in the central part of the old city on both the Right and Left Banks of the Seine. The occasional Gothic doorways, the many dark passages, and the jumbled masses of old buildings were greatly admired by the rising Romantic generation, but they were looked upon as a disgrace by the new industrialists.

In the period of the later Middle Ages the city had begun to spread rapidly on to the Right Bank. Here was the enormous pile of the Louvre and the Tuileries, the sixteenth-century Hôtel de Ville, the old noble Quartier du Marais, the wholesale and trading district of Saint-Antoine, and finally, bounding this solidly built mass, a ring of boulevards built under the last Bourbon kings before the Revolution. Beyond this half-circle to the west, along the Seine, lay the Champs Elysées and the Cours La Reine. These formed a sort of ill-kept and open forest through which were scattered a number of out-of-door summer restaurants. At the end of the Champs Elysées rose the half-finished Arc de Triomphe, which Charles X proposed to complete in honor of the Duc d'Angoulême and the Spanish Campaign of 1823. This absurd project was not carried out, and it rose above the trees a strange, unfinished mass of masonry until its completion during the July Monarchy. The present fashionable quarter about the Arc de Triomphe was at this time occupied by a few small houses and truck gardens.

The Place Louis XV (after 1815 the Place de la Concorde), between the Tuileries Gardens and the lower end of the Champs

Elysées, was a huge ill-paved square, impressive for its size, but not much frequented except on Sundays and holidays. The Tuileries Gardens were then, as they are now, a favorite promenade. On the river side of the Place Louis XV a bridge led across to the Palais Bourbon. During the Restoration this belonged to the Condé family, who rented it to the government as a meeting place for the Chamber of Deputies. On the fourth side of the Place stood the two beautiful pavilions built by Gabriel during the reign of Louis XV. Between them ran a wide street which revealed the incomplete façade of the Madeleine. The obelisk, the fountains, and the statues of French cities which now decorate the square had not yet been set up.

From a corner of the Place Louis XV Napoleon had constructed the rue de Rivoli, which led down the side of the Tuileries Gardens to the square in front of the Palais Royal. This fine street, with its arcaded walk, is one of the great building achievements of the Empire. It was a favorite promenade during the Restoration, but its shops were considered much inferior to those of the Palais Royal. Behind the Madeleine, and beyond it to the west in the direction of the Champs Elysées, there were a few scattered houses. The district was quite open, and most of the better houses had fine gardens. Here was the Faubourg Saint-Honoré, where lived many of the Napoleonic nobility and a group of wealthy bourgeois families. In the opposite direction, to the east of the Madeleine, the city was more closely built, especially in the old part between the circle of boulevards—built in the seventeenth century on the site of the old fortifications—and the Seine. Besides the Louvre, the Hôtel de Ville, and a number of large churches, this section included the Place Vendôme and the Palais Royal. Here were many of the most fashionable shops. In one part of the quarter, the Chaussée d'Antin, lived a group of very wealthy bourgeois families. Further to the east, following the river, was the Marais, once the home of the old nobility where the fine eighteenth-century houses of the Rohans and the Soubises are still to be found. After 1815 this quarter was largely occupied by the lesser bourgeoisie. Finally, at the extreme east of the city, near the site of the old Bastille, was the poorest quarter of Paris, the Quartier Saint-Antoine, famous for its rôle in the Revolution.

Crossing to the Left Bank, one found there was less differentiation of classes and districts. At the west end of this bank, across the river from the Place de la Concorde and the Tuileries Gardens, was the Faubourg Saint-Germain, where after 1815 the old aristocracy lived in indignant seclusion. The principal buildings on the Left Bank were the Luxembourg Palace, where the Chamber of Peers had its sessions, and the Panthéon, reconsecrated in 1815 as the Church of Sainte-Geneviève—an amusing anomaly when one remembers that Mirabeau, Voltaire, and Rousseau lie buried in the crypt. In the center of this part of the city on the Left Bank was the Latin Quarter, with its old traditions and its new Romantic Bohemia. Here, as elsewhere in Paris, were many old gardens belonging to private individuals and to religious houses, some of them quite extensive. There are remnants of these still in Paris. One knows of their existence only by the tall chestnut trees that hang over high forbidding walls, or by an occasional glimpse through an open doorway.

Paris was still very much as it was in the eighteenth century. The Restoration made fewer changes than had been made during the Empire. Some of the street names were changed after 1815. The rue d'Arcole, for example, became the rue de Beaujolais, while the rue Napoléon was renamed the rue de la Paix. Very little public building was done between 1815 and 1830. A bronze equestrian statue of Henry IV was set up on the Pont Neuf in 1818. It was cast by a Napoleonic sympathizer, who is said to have put a statuette of his hero into the arm of the figure of Henry, and a box full of anti-Bourbon pamphlets inside the body of the horse. In 1821 a figure of Louis XIII was set up in the Place des Vosges, and in 1824 Louis XIV again appeared in the center of the Place des Victoires. All these monuments are still in place. An expiatory chapel was built on the spot where Louis XVI and Marie Antoinette were first buried. In 1821 a new opera house, which has since disappeared, was inaugurated. The Bourse, a huge building still in use, was finished in 1826. The only important church erected was the basilica of Saint-Vincent-de-Paul, begun in 1824, but not completed until after 1830.

Although the government did almost no building, the city was extended through private enterprise. Sixty-five new streets were opened up, and in the fifteen years from 1815 to 1830 about 21,000 houses were built. Among these were many apartment houses, Paris being the first city in Europe to house a large part of its population in apartments. Great improvements in means of getting about in the city were made by building the first sidewalks, and by the establishment of public omnibuses. Both were considered startling innovations. Vast crowds gathered to see the first sidewalk built along one side of the rue de l'Odéon. The first public bus line was opened up in 1826. It ran from the Place de la Bastille down the Boulevard to the Madeleine. The passengers paid twenty-five to thirty centimes, depending on the distance traveled. The buses carried from eighteen to twenty people each. Their popularity was immediate, and by 1829 there were fifteen bus lines in Paris. All these improvements were of especial benefit to the new bourgeoisie and to the working class. Another improvement, much commented upon in the newspapers of the period, was the introduction of gas lighting, which was first used in 1825, on the Place Vendôme. Three years later there were 10,000 gas outlets and 1500 subscribers in Paris.

The parks, the cafés and restaurants, and the theaters in Paris outranked all others in Europe. Among her parks, the Tuileries Garden and the Palais Royal held first place. The Tuileries was merely a place to promenade, but it was frequented at different times of the day by all the classes of Parisian society. Here on pleasant Sundays and holidays were to be seen bourgeois and workingmen with their families dressed in their best. They strolled about or sat on chairs which could be rented for a few sous. The children fed the fish in the ponds and rolled their hoops. In the evening the family foregathered at some restaurant. The Palais Royal was much more lively. Here one saw with their nursemaids children sitting on the benches under the trees, shoppers, grisettes, tourists studying their guidebooks and Napoleonic officers retired on half pay and with plenty of time to waste in loafing. Mornings and evenings great crowds of clerks and workingmen poured through the long galleries. At lunch time the cafés were filled with lawyers, shop-owners, and brokers on their way to the Bourse, which opened at two. At night it was enlivened with foreign visitors, adventurers, gamblers, and prostitutes, who visited its restaurants and cafés.

On Sundays and holidays when the weather was good great crowds streamed out along the Champs Elysées as far as Longchamp, where they might watch the rich ride by in their fine turnouts. Nearer the center of the city were a number of privately owned amusement parks. Here for a small admission fee one could dance or see a puppet show or sit in a pleasant open-air restaurant. The greatest thrill was offered by a kind of scenic railroad called the Montagnes russes. This had a great vogue. Soon there were "montagnes suisses," "montagnes françaises," and even "montagnes égyptiennes." Special holidays were celebrated in these parks by fireworks and balloon ascensions. These paying parks were beyond the range of the poorer classes from the Faubourg Saint-Denis and the Quartier

Saint-Antoine, who on Sundays and fête days were to be seen at Enghien and Montmorency.

Restaurants were among the first attractions of the city. The most famous cuisinier in Europe was Brillat-Savarin, a Parisian, who in 1825 published his famous *Physiologie de goût*. The restaurant that was also a café was just coming in. Each class—aristocrats, bourgeois, and workingmen, writers and painters, Liberals and Ultras—had its own favorite rendezvous, which served it as a kind of clubhouse. Certain restaurants in the Palais Royal—among them were Chez les Frères Provençaux, Chez Véry, and Chez Véfour—were the finest in Europe. The rendezvous of the dandies of the day was the Maison d'Or on the Boulevard. Each section of the city had its own cafés and restaurants famous for some special dish or drink. The queen of coffee-houses in the Palais Royal was the Café Corozza. In the same gardens was the famous Café Lemblin, a great place for foreigners to go to see the local types, and the favorite gathering place of Napoleonic officers. These officers were often picturesque characters. They wore absurd uniforms, and were always boasting or quarreling. No type was more often seen in the cafés, either in Paris or in the provinces. The cafés were then, as they still are, popular places for spending the evening. They were also frequented by those who wished to read the newspapers, which in these days were expensive and had few private subscribers. For those who cared to smoke—smoking was far less common then than it is now, and was not allowed in most cafés—there were the estaminets. For the women of the well-to-do classes the favorite afternoon rendezvous was Tortoni's on the Boulevard. There were some picturesque restaurants in the Latin Quarter—as Thicoteau's, which furnished a fair meal for twelve sous and was very popular with the students of the law and medical faculties. Other restaurants served meals to students for as low a price as two sous. Tourists usually included a visit to these Latin Quarter restaurants and cafés during their stay in the capital.

The theaters furnish an interesting reflection of the life of the Restoration. It was an age of theatergoing. The censorship was less severe than under the Empire, and many of the public and private weaknesses of the period were freely lampooned on the stage. Party passions ran high in the theater, and there were frequent clashes between Ultras and Liberals to enliven the entr'actes. These fights—such as a famous one that took place in 1817 at the first performance of *Germanicus,* where a number of prominent people were more or less battered—were responsible for the introduction of a checkroom in French theaters where the management insisted that all canes and umbrellas be left.

The state subsidized, as it had earlier, a number of important theaters, chief of which was the Comédie-Française. Here the reigning favorites were Talma and Mademoiselle Mars, two of the most remarkable actors of the nineteenth century. The new plays put on at the Comédie-Française from 1815 to 1830 are usually less interesting reflections of the life of the time than the pieces given at some of the other theaters. Many of the plays given at the Comédie were written in stilted verse in strict imitation of the great dramatists of the seventeenth and eighteenth centuries. Full of stock characters and situations, these plays were created to please actors who found it easier and surer to play in rôles whose effects had been carefully worked out. Mademoiselle Mars was almost the only first-rate actor who would try anything in a new style. She played the Duchesse de Guise in Dumas' *Henri III et sa cour,* and Doña Sol in Hugo's *Hernani*. It was the fashion then, as now, to poke fun at the Comédie-Française, though the theater was usually crowded in spite of it.

At the state opera the company was good. It was less frequented, however, than the Théatre des Italiens, which received state aid after 1827, and where the presiding deity was Rossini, the greatest showman of his time. Here one heard the most popular songbirds of the day, Mademoiselle Sontag and her rival, Malibran. Public concerts were rare except at Easter time, when a series of Concerts Spirituels were given. In 1828 Chérubini and Habeneck founded what is still the best symphony orchestra in Paris, the Société des Concerts, which held its performances in the Conservatory of Music. The first concert in 1828 was devoted entirely to the works of Beethoven. Some of the first performances of Liszt were given under its auspices.

In much greater favor with the public than the state theatres were the playhouses on the Boulevard. Here were Franconi's; the Folies-Dramatiques; the Variétés-Amusantes—very popular with the lower classes; the Vaudeville; the Cirque Olympique, which specialized in showing such historical pieces as the entry of Henry IV into Paris and Condé at the Victory of Rocroy; the Porte Saint-Martin; and, most popular of all, the Ambigu-Comique and the Gymnase. In these theaters one saw comedies, farces, and melodramas of all sorts, which, if far from being literature, were close enough to life. Plays, often only one-act sketches, were written for every kind of occasion. Many were suppressed by the police for their Bonapartism or their anti-clerical tone. Hundreds of these occasional pieces have survived, and they deal with every passing matter, from the murder of the Duc de Berri to a new giraffe in the Jardin des Plantes.

Of the fortunes of these boulevard theaters, those of the Théatre du Gymnase on the Boulevard Bonne-Nouvelle are the most interesting to follow. It was opened in 1820, and in 1824 was renamed the Théatre de Madame, in honor of the Duchesse de Berri, who became its special patron. It became popular with the old aristocracy, though it was chiefly frequented by the wealthy bourgeois. The house was always sold out long in advance. In one month its receipts were 77,000 francs, while those at the state opera house were only 18,000 francs. The management after 1824 received a subsidy from the government, and the theater became a sort of training school for the Comédie-Française and the Odéon. Here one saw clever comedies ridiculing—though usually gently enough—the National Guard, the artist Bohemian, the porter, the peasant, the new rich, and the old aristocracy.

It was at this theater that Scribe, the most popular French playwright of the nineteenth century, began a career that lasted down into the Second Empire. Whatever may be their literary merit, his little comedies of manners are still among the best sources for French social history during this long period from 1815 to 1870. His earlier plays written during the Restoration, especially his comédies-vaudevilles, were popular with the bourgeoisie, whose prosaic and common-sense views he upheld against the morbid and extravagant ideas of the Romanticists and the Saint-Simonians. He defends the authority of parents, the sanctity of marriage, and the virtues of the home. He attacks the Romantic's idea that a marriage can be happy only when based on love. According to Scribe, the foundations of a happy marriage are a good dowry, emotional steadiness, and equality of social position. After marriage it is order, economy, and children that make a happy home. No wonder Alexandre Dumas and Gautier heaped scorn upon him as a smug bourgeois. Scribe does, however, criticize the hypocrisies and meanness of parents and of children, of place hunters, and of charlatans. He stands for order, industry, and economy, and the happiness that comes to those who earn their living through honest effort. His plays are full of genuine wit, and, though often superficial, they represent the life of the period with surprising accuracy.

Besides Scribe, there were a number of other playwrights who devoted their attention to the comedy of manners. Some of these authors are far more radical than Scribe, though none were so popular. All sorts of abuses were attacked—abuses of money, the tyrannies of family life, the prejudices against the illegitimate child, against manual labor, and against prostitutes. It is interesting to trace in these minor playwrights the growth of the modern social idea that many of the ills and misfortunes that beset individuals are due chiefly to a badly organized society.

Besides the parks, the theaters, and the restaurants and cafés, other characteristic places of Parisian amusement were the public reading rooms and lending libraries. These libraries were privately owned, but their benefits might be secured for a small sum. The Restoration seems to have been a period more given to reading than any time that preceded it. In some of these reading rooms popular lectures were given on social, literary, and scientific subjects. Through the lending libraries books of all sorts circulated, though the first place was always held by novels. After 1824 the great interest in political and religious questions increased the circulation of books and newspapers. Visitors from other countries were amazed at the number of readers they saw in the reading rooms and in the parks of Paris.

A book written in 1830 gives an interesting and detailed description of a typical day in Paris at the time of the Restoration.[1] Before daybreak the quarter about the Halles, the city markets, was alive with activity. Carts filled with green cabbages and foodstuffs of all sorts, driven by heavy, overclothed, moustached peasants, their wives fast asleep on top of the greens, filled the streets of the quarter from midnight on. Early in the morning, peasants and food dealers with eggs, butter, vegetables, and meat—quarreling and bickering as they do today—arranged their products for sale. By nine the wholesale dealing was over and the Halles were turned over to the host of housemaids and housewives who came there to shop.

In the meantime the streets in the working quarters had been filled from as early as six o'clock with men, women, and children on their way to various places of employment. At nine the workers in the trades stopped for breakfast. Dinner was at two. Work continued until six in the building trades, and often until eight in the factories. Retail stores of all sorts usually opened at six in the summer and seven in the winter. The schools opened at eight, some of them closing again at ten to reopen for several hours at two. Museums and libraries opened at ten. Doctors and lawyers were usually in their offices by eight, though many business offices did not open before nine. The Bourse did not open until two. Most offices, all the banks, and the Bourse closed at four. Retail stores often remained open until nine at night. It is interesting to note that in the past hundred years there has been little change in the length of the working day, except in the case of the manual worker, where a revolution has been brought about.

The Paris of the Restoration, if one may judge from the memoirs and from the prints and caricatures of the period, was a city of much ease and elegance, quieter and more prosperous than in the days of the Revolution and the Empire, and, at the same time, largely untouched by the Industrial Revolution, with both its sordidness and its lavish display of wealth. The bourgeoisie, who formed the majority of the population, were contented and fairly prosperous; the worst sufferings for the proletariat lay in the future. No period in over a century of the history of Paris since 1789 seems so calm in retrospect.

Since the time of Louis XIV the larger provincial cities had tried to imitate Paris in their public buildings and in their shops, cafés, and parks. Great changes in the provincial cities, however, did not come until after 1850. It was the railroad which really ended the fascinating provincial differences of old France and made most of the provincial towns seem insipid imitations of Paris. The churches and some of the old houses were mediæval; the public buildings and the better houses belonged to the seventeenth

[1] Ch. Simond, *Paris de 1800 à 1900* (1900), I, 54.

and eighteenth centuries. The poorer houses would be harder to date, for the type of construction—rubble and plaster—had not been much affected by the various changes of style. The provincial cities, even the larger ones, had few suburbs. The houses stopped with the town wall. The Parisians made fun of the provincial cities, which they looked upon as vassal states. In turn, the provincials loved to tell stories of Parisian ignorance. Stendhal tells a story of a Parisian stopping at Mâcon, who was told that the city was on the Saône; whereupon the Parisian replied, "In Paris we call it the Seine!"

In 1826 there were only two provincial cities having more than 100,000 inhabitants: Lyons, which with its suburbs had 170,000, and Marseilles, which had 115,000. There were five cities with a population between 50,000 and 100,000, and twenty-two with between 20,000 and 50,000. There are no accurate statistics, but it is estimated that only about one-seventh of the population lived in towns of 20,000 or over.[2] Even the largest cities were so small that the city dweller could still go easily into the country, and the division between city and country was less marked than it is today. Until the reign of Charles X the provinces were little interested in politics, though at election times one sometimes heard lively political discussions in the cafés. Between elections, the Liberals worked for the extension of primary education and for compulsory vaccination, while the Ultras prepared for visits of the Missionaries.

Judging from the novels of the time, life in the provincial cities was simple and monotonous. The greatest excitement was furnished by some sensational crime. In the South the traveler noted the lazy good humor of the people, and their love of fêtes of all sorts. In the northern towns the population seemed less demonstrative and more industrious. The capitalist had in some places become the lord of the town, replacing a feudal seigneur. The schools were better in the North, and more books were read. The chief amusement consisted in passing the evening in a café; and sometimes there were plays in the local theater. The family dominated everything. A few of the larger cities had a sort of learned society, an Académie or a Socéité des Sciences, des Lettres et d'Agriculture, which went back in its origin to the eighteenth century. Usually they were social in nature, and fell into the hands of a coterie, which turned them into self-admiration societies. Traveling was almost unheard of in the provinces. Such traveling as there was was done chiefly by British tourists, who found living in France much cheaper than in England. Classes were sharply divided one from another. The nobility lived apart. Next to them stood the lawyers, doctors, and the more important government officials, then the bourgeoisie, and finally the workers and domestic servants. The break-up of society during the Revolution had been in many places a serious blow to the economic life of the larger communities. After 1815 the growth of industry and commerce helped to restore their life and prosperity.

Between Paris and the departments the chief connection was through the government officials. The government official, the fonctionnaire, as he exists in modern France, was a creation of Napoleon and his highly centralized regime. Under the Ancien Régime the provinces were largely governed by men of local origin and interests. Napoleon changed all this and made all appointments depend on the capital. The Restoration inherited this evil system. Soon after 1815 it was estimated that, exclusive of the army, half a million persons were in the employment of the state. Place hunting for positions in the provinces became a major occupation. Talleyrand said that fifty thousand people had come to him asking for government positions, each with the claim that he had followed Louis XVIII to Ghent in 1815, whereas less than eight hundred had actually done so. The French have always had a mania for safe positions with

[2] Charléty, p. 315.

fixed incomes, and the innumerable positions at the disposal of the government seemed insufficient to satisfy the demand.[3] Through all the French departments, from the Rhine to the Pyrenees, the fonctionnaire—a symbol of laziness, stupidity, and obsequiousness—was one of the most characteristic figures of provincial society.

[3] Cf. Scribe's *Le solliciteur* (1817) and *La manie des places* (1828) for two brilliant satires of this place hunting.

THIRTY-EIGHT

ECONOMIC LIBERALISM

In 1776 Adam Smith (1723–90), a Scottish professor, published in two volumes An Inquiry into the Nature and Causes of the Wealth of Nations. *This long and somewhat rambling work, with its forbidding title, has become a classic in economics, many times reprinted and widely translated. Smith divided his work into five parts: (1) a discussion of labor, value, and price; (2) an analysis of stock; (3) a discourse on economic history; (4) an attack on mercantilism; (5) a treatise on state finances. In the* Wealth of Nations *Smith formulates many basic concepts of modern economic analysis. He believes that the natural self-interest of individuals promotes the welfare of the community, and he concludes that the state should therefore not interfere with the economic process. His argument delighted those businessmen who chafed at mercantilist restrictions and it later formed the basis for arguments in favor of economic liberalism* (laissez-faire). *Ironically, socialist and Communist writers, among them Karl Marx, also used some of Smith's concepts, such as the labor theory of value, for their economic arguments.*

ADAM SMITH

INQUIRY INTO THE NATURE AND CAUSES OF THE WEALTH OF NATIONS*

The greatest improvement in the productive powers of labour, and the greater part of the skill, dexterity, and judgment with which it is any where directed, or applied, seem to have been the effects of the division of labour.

The effects of the division of labour, in the general business of society, will be more easily understood, by considering in what manner it operates in some particular manufactures. It is commonly supposed to be carried furthest in some very trifling ones; not perhaps that it really is carried further in them than in others of more importance: but in those trifling manufactures which are destined to supply the small wants of but a small number of people, the whole number of workmen must necessarily be small; and those employed in every different branch of the work can often be collected into the same workhouse, and placed at once under the

* From *Inquiry into the Nature and Causes of the Wealth of Nations,* extracts from Book I, ch. 1, 2, 6, and 10, by Adam Smith. Fifth edition, 1789.

view of the spectator. In those great manufactures, on the contrary, which are destined to supply the great wants of the great body of the people, every different branch of the work employs so great a number of workmen, that it is impossible to collect them all into the same workhouse. We can seldom see more, at one time, than those employed in one single branch. Though in such manufactures, therefore, the work may really be divided into a much greater number of parts, than in those of a more trifling nature, the division is not near so obvious, and has accordingly been much less observed.

To take an example, therefore, from a very trifling manufacture; but one in which the division of labour has been very often taken notice of, the trade of the pin-maker; a workman not educated to this business (which the division of labour has rendered a distinct trade), nor acquainted with the use of the machinery employed in it (to the invention of which the same division of labour has probably given occasion), could scarce, perhaps, with his utmost industry, make one pin in a day, and certainly could not make twenty. But in the way in which this business is now carried on, not only the whole work is a peculiar trade, but it is divided into a number of branches, of which the greater part are likewise peculiar trades. One man draws out the wire, another straights it, a third cuts it, a fourth points it, a fifth grinds it at the top for receiving the head; to make the head requires two or three distinct operations; to put it on, is a peculiar business, to whiten the pins is another; it is even a trade by itself to put them into the paper; and the important business of making a pin is, in this manner, divided into about eighteen distinct operations, which, in some manufactories, are all performed by distinct hands, though in others the same man will sometimes perform two or three of them. I have seen a small manufactory of this kind where ten men only were employed, and where some of them consequently performed two or three distinct operations. But though they were very poor, and therefore but indifferently accommodated with the necessary machinery, they could, when they exerted themselves, make among them about twelve pounds of pins in a day. There are in a pound upwards of four thousand pins of a middling size. Those ten persons, therefore, could make among them upwards of forty-eight thousand pins in a day. Each person, therefore, making a tenth part of forty-eight thousand pins, might be considered as making four thousand eight hundred pins in a day. But if they had all wrought separately and independently, and without any of them having been educated to this peculiar business, they certainly could not each of them have made twenty, perhaps not one pin in a day; that is, certainly, not the two hundred and fortieth, perhaps not the four thousand eight hundredth part of what they are at present capable of performing, in consequence of a proper division and combination of their different operations. . . .

This division of labour, from which so many advantages are derived, is not originally the effect of any human wisdom, which foresees and intends that general opulence to which it gives occasion. It is the necessary, though very slow and gradual, consequence of a certain propensity in human nature which has in view no such extensive utility; the propensity to truck, barter, and exchange one thing for another.

Whether this propensity be one of those original principles in human nature, of which no further account can be given; or whether, as seems more probable, it be the necessary consequence of the faculties of reason and speech, it belongs not to our present subject to enquire. It is common to all men, and to be found in no other race of animals, which seem to know neither this nor any other species of contracts. Two greyhounds, in running down the same hare, have sometimes the appearance of acting in some sort of concert. Each turns her towards his companion, or endeavours to intercept her when his companion turns her towards himself. This, however, is not the effect of any contract, but of the accidental concurrence of their passions in the same object at that particular time. Nobody ever saw a dog make a fair and deliberate exchange of one bone for another with another dog. Nobody ever saw one animal by its gestures and natural cries signify to another, this is mine, that yours; I am willing to give this for that. When an animal wants to obtain something either of a man or of another animal, it has no other means of persuasion but to gain the favour of those whose service it requires. A puppy fawns upon its dam, and a spaniel endeavours by a thousand attractions to engage the attention of its master who is at dinner, when it wants to be fed by him. Man sometimes uses the same arts with his brethren, and when he has no other means of engaging them to act according to his inclinations, endeavours by every servile and fawning attention to obtain their good will. He has not time, however, to do this upon every occasion. In civilized society he stands at all times in need of the co-operation and assistance of great multitudes, while his whole life is scarce sufficient to gain the friendship of a few persons. In almost every other race of animals each individual, when it is grown up to maturity, is entirely independent, and in its natural state has occasion for the assistance of no other living creature. But man has almost constant occasion for the help of his brethren, and it is in vain for him to expect it from their benevolence only. He will be more likely to prevail if he can interest their self-love in his favour, and shew them that it is for their own advantage to do for him what he requires of them. Whoever offers to another a bargain of any kind, proposes to do this. Give me that which I want, and you shall have this which you want, is the meaning of every such offer; and it is in this manner that we obtain from one another the far greater part of those good offices which we stand in need of. It is not from the benevolence of the butcher, the brewer, or the baker, that we expect our dinner, but from their regard to their own interest. We address ourselves, not to their humanity but to their self-love, and never talk to them of our own necessities but of their advantages. Nobody but a beggar chuses to depend chiefly upon the benevolence of his fellow-citizens. Even a beggar does not depend upon it entirely. The charity of well-disposed people, indeed, supplies him with the whole fund of his subsistence. But though this principle ultimately provides him with all the necessaries of life which he has occasion for, it neither does nor can provide him with them as he has occasion for them. The greater part of his occasional wants are supplied in the same manner as those of other people, by treaty, by barter, and by purchase. With the money which one man gives him he purchases food. The old cloaths which another bestows upon him he exchanges for other old cloaths which suit him better, or for lodging, or for food, or for money, with which he can buy either food, cloaths, or lodging, as he has occasion.

As it is by treaty, by barter, and by purchase, that we obtain from one another the greater part of those mutual good offices which we stand in need of, so it is this same trucking disposition which originally gives occasion to the division of labour. In a tribe of hunters or shepherds a particular person makes bows and arrows, for example, with more readiness and dexterity than any other. He frequently exchanges them for cattle or for venison with his companions; and he finds at last that he can in this manner get more cattle and venison, than if he himself went to the field to catch them. From a regard to his own interest, therefore, the making of bows and arrows grows to be his chief business, and he becomes a sort of armourer. Another excels in making the frames and covers of their little huts or moveable houses. He is accustomed to be of use in this way to his neighbours, who reward him in the same manner with cattle and with venison, till at last he finds it his interest to dedicate himself entirely to this employment, and to become a sort of house-carpenter. In the same manner a third becomes a smith or a brazier; a fourth a tanner or dresser of hides or skins, the principal part of the clothing of savages. And thus the certainty of being able to exchange all that surplus part of the produce of his own labour, which is over and above his own consumption, for such parts of the produce of other men's labour as he may have occasion for, encourages every man to apply himself to a particular occupation, and to cultivate and bring to perfection whatever talent or genius he may possess for that particular species of business. . . .

In that early and rude state of society which precedes both the accumulation of stock and the appropriation of land, the proportion between the quantities of labour necessary for acquiring different objects seems to be the only circumstance which can afford any rule for exchanging them for one another. If among a nation of hunters, for example, it usually costs twice the labour to kill a beaver which it does to kill a deer, one beaver should naturally exchange for or be worth two deer. It is natural that what is usually the produce of two days or two hours labour, should be worth double of what is usually the produce of one day's or one hour's labour.

If the one species of labour should be more severe than the other, some allowance will naturally be made for this superior hardship; and the produce of one hour's labour in the one way may frequently exchange for that of two hours labour in the other.

Or if the one species of labour requires an uncommon degree of dexterity and ingenuity, the esteem which men have for such talents, will naturally give a value to their produce, superior to what would be due to the time employed about it. Such talents can seldom be acquired but in consequence of long application, and the superior value of their produce may frequently be no more than a reasonable compensation for the time and labour which must be spent in acquiring them. In the advanced state of society, allowances of this kind, for superior hardship and superior skill, are commonly made in the wages of labour; and something of the same kind must probably have taken place in its earliest and rudest period.

In this state of things, the whole produce of labour belongs to the labourer; and the quantity of labour commonly employed in acquiring or producing any commodity, is the only circumstance which can regulate the quantity of labour which it ought commonly to purchase, command, or exchange for.

As soon as stock has accumulated in the hands of particular persons, some of them will naturally employ it in setting to work industrious people, whom they will supply with materials and subsistence, in order to make a profit by the sale of their work, or by what their labour adds to the value of the materials. In exchanging the complete manufacture either for money, for labour, or for other goods, over and above what may be sufficient to pay the price of the materials, and the wages of the workmen, something must be given for the profits of the undertaker of the work who hazards his stock in this adventure. The value which the workmen add to the materials, therefore, resolves itself in this case into two parts, of which the one pays their wages, the other the profits of their employer upon the whole stock of materials and wages which he advanced. He could have no interest to employ them, unless he expected from the sale of their work something more than what was sufficient to replace his stock to him; and he could have no interest to employ a great stock rather than a small one, unless his profits were to bear some proportion to the extent of his stock.

The profits of stock, it may perhaps be thought, are only a different name for the wages of a particular sort of labour, the labour of inspection and direction. They are, however, altogether different, are regulated by quite sufficient principles, and bear no proportion to the quantity, the hardship, or the ingenuity of this supposed labour of inspection and direction. They are regulated altogether by the value of the stock employed, and are greater or smaller in proportion to the extent of this stock. Let us suppose, for example, that in some particular place, where the common annual profits of manufacturing stock are ten per cent. there are two different manufactures, in each of which twenty workmen are employed at the rate of fifteen pounds a year each, or at the expence of three hundred a year in each manufactory. Let us suppose too, that the coarse materials annually wrought up in the one cost only seven hundred pounds, while the finer materials in the other cost seven thousand. The capital annually employed in the one will in this case amount only to one thousand pounds; whereas that employed in the other will amount to seven thousand three hundred pounds. At the rate of ten per cent. therefore, the undertaker of the one will expect an yearly profit of about one hundred pounds only; while that of the other will expect about seven hundred and thirty pounds. But though their profits are so very different, their labour of inspection and direction may be either altogether or very nearly the same. In many great works, almost the whole labour of this kind is committed to some principal clerk. His wages properly express the value of this labour of inspection and direction. Though in settling them some regard is had commonly, not only to his labour and skill, but to the trust which is reposed in him, yet they never bear any regular proportion to the capital of which he oversees the management; and the owner of this capital, though he is thus discharged of almost all labour, still expects that his profits should bear a regular proportion to his capital. In the price of commodities, therefore, the profits of stock constitute a component part altogether different from the wages of labour, and regulated by quite different principles.

In this state of things, the whole produce of labour does not always belong to the labourer. He must in most cases share it with the owner of the stock which employs him. Neither is the quantity of labour commonly employed in acquiring or producing any commodity, the only circumstance which can regulate the quantity which it ought commonly to purchase, command, or exchange for. An additional quantity, it is evident, must be due for the profits of the stock which advanced the wages and furnished the materials of that labour.

As soon as the land of any country has all become private property, the landlords, like all other men, love to reap where they never sowed, and demand a rent even for its natural produce. The wood of the forest, the grass of the field, and all the natural fruits of the earth, which, when land was in common, cost the labourer only the trouble of gathering them, come, even to him, to have an additional price fixed upon them. He must give up to the landlord a portion of what his labour either collects or produces. This portion, or, what comes to the same thing, the price of this portion, constitutes the rent of land, and in the price of the greater part of commodities makes a third component part.

The real value of all the different component parts of price, it must be observed, is measured by the quantity of labour which they can, each of them, purchase or command. Labour measures the value not only of that part of price which resolves itself into labour, but of that which resolves itself into rent, and of that which resolves itself into profit.

In every society the price of every commodity finally resolves itself into some one or other, or all of those three parts; and in every improved society, all the three enter more or less, as component parts, into the price of the far greater part of commodities. . . .

The whole of the advantages and disadvantages of the different employments of labour and stock must, in the same neighbourhood, be either perfectly equal or continually tending to equality. If in the same neighbourhood, there was any employment evidently either more or less advantageous than the rest, so many people would crowd into it in the one case, and so many would desert it in the other, that its advantages would soon return to the level of other employments. This at least would be the case in a society where things were left to follow their natural course, where there was perfect liberty, and where every man was perfectly free both to chuse what occupation he thought proper, and to change it as often as he thought proper. Every man's interest would prompt him to seek the advantageous, and to shun the disadvantageous employment.

Pecuniary wages and profit, indeed, are every-where in Europe extremely different according to the different employments of labour and stock. But this difference arises partly from certain circumstances in the employments themselves, which, either really, or at least in the imaginations of men, make up for a small pecuniary gain in some, and counter-balance a great one in others; and partly from the policy of Europe, which nowhere leaves things at perfect liberty.

The particular consideration of those circumstances and of that policy will divide this chapter into two parts.

The five following are the principal circumstances which, so far as I have been able to observe, make up for a small pecuniary gain in some employments, and counter-balance a great one in others: first, the agreeableness or disagreeableness of the employments themselves; secondly, the easiness and cheapness, or the difficulty and expence of learning them; thirdly, the constancy or inconstancy of employment in them; fourthly, the small or great trust which must be reposed in those who exercise them; and fifthly, the probability or improbability of success in them. . . .

Such are the inequalities in the whole of the advantages and disadvantages of the different employments of labour and stock, which the defect of any of the three requisites above-mentioned must occasion, even where there is the most perfect liberty. But the policy of Europe, by not leaving things at perfect liberty, occasions other inequalities of much greater importance.

It does this chiefly in the three following ways. First, by restraining the competition in some employments to a smaller number than would otherwise be disposed to enter into them; secondly, by increasing it in others beyond what it naturally would be; and, thirdly, by obstructing the free circulation of labour and stock, both from employment to employment and from place to place.

THIRTY-NINE

POLITICAL LIBERALISM

Political liberalism, with deep roots in the Enlightenment, arose after 1815 as a consistent body of protest against the reactionary principles of Metternich and other traditionalists. Political liberalism sought to free the individual from excessive government restraints. It emphasized freedom of thought and speech, religious toleration, and a parliamentary system of government. In general, liberals wished to keep government powers at a minimum. At the same time, liberals maintained middle-class values, especially the sanctity of private property and property qualifications for voting and holding office. In Britain an important branch of the liberal movement consisted of Utilitarians, headed by Jeremy Bentham, who urged rational reform of government in the interest of greater political efficiency. After Bentham the most distinguished of the Utilitarians was the humanitarian philosopher and economist John Stuart Mill (1806–73). In his most popular work, the essay On Liberty, *Mill argued persuasively for individual liberty, so long as that liberty did no social harm. In liberty Mill saw the means for the individual to make his greatest contribution to society, so that in effect liberty promoted utility. Like Adam Smith, but with a number of significant reservations, Mill advocated free trade. Mill also recognized the growth of government power in Britain during his lifetime. He deplored and opposed strong government on the ground that it was inefficient and harmful to the development of individual citizens.*

JOHN STUART MILL

ON LIBERTY*

The principles asserted in these pages must be more generally admitted as the basis for discussion of details, before a consistent application of them to all the various departments of government and morals can be attempted with any prospect of advantage. The few observations I propose to make on questions of detail, are designed to illustrate the principles, rather than to follow them out to their consequences. I offer, not so much applications, as specimens of application; which may serve to bring into greater clearness the meaning and limits of the two maxims which together form the entire doctrine of this Essay, and to assist the judgment in holding the balance between them, in the cases where it appears doubtful which of them is applicable to the case.

* From *On Liberty,* ch. 5, by John Stuart Mill. First published in 1859.

The maxims are, first, that the individual is not accountable to society for his actions, in so far as these concern the interests of no person but himself. Advice, instruction, persuasion, and avoidance by other people if thought necessary by them for their own good, are the only measures by which society can justifiably express its dislike or disapprobation of his conduct. Secondly, that for such actions as are prejudicial to the interests of others, the individual is accountable, and may be subjected either to social or to legal punishment, if society is of opinion that the one or the other is requisite for its protection.

In the first place, it must by no means be supposed, because damage, or probability of damage, to the interests of others, can alone justify the interference of society, that therefore it always does justify such interference. In many cases, an individual, in pursuing a legitimate object, necessarily and therefore legitimately causes pain or loss to others, or intercepts a good which they had a reasonable hope of obtaining. Such oppositions of interest between individuals often arise from bad social institutions, but are unavoidable while those institutions last; and some would be unavoidable under any institutions. Whoever succeeds in an overcrowded profession, or in a competitive examination; whoever is preferred to another in any contest for an object which both desire, reaps benefit from the loss of others, from their wasted exertion and their disappointment. But it is, by common admission, better for the general interest of mankind, that persons should pursue their objects undeterred by this sort of consequences. In other words, society admits no right, either legal or moral, in the disappointed competitors, to immunity from this kind of suffering; and feels called on to interfere, only when means of success have been employed which it is contrary to the general interest to permit—namely, fraud or treachery, and force.

Again, trade is a social act. Whoever undertakes to sell any description of goods to the public, does what affects the interest of other persons, and of society in general; and thus his conduct, in principle, comes within the jurisdiction of society: accordingly, it was once held to be the duty of governments, in all cases which were considered of importance, to fix prices, and regulate the processes of manufacture. But it is now recognized, though not till after a long struggle, that both the cheapness and the good quality of commodities are most effectually provided for by leaving the producers and sellers perfectly free, under the sole check of equal freedom to the buyers for supplying themselves elsewhere. This is the so-called doctrine of Free Trade, which rests on grounds different from, though equally solid with, the principle of individual liberty asserted in this Essay. Restrictions on trade, or on production for purposes of trade, are indeed restraints; and all restraint, *quâ* restraint, is an evil: but the restraints in question affect only that part of conduct which society is competent to restrain, and are wrong solely because they do not really produce the results which it is desired to produce by them. As the principle of individual liberty is not involved in the doctrine of Free Trade, so neither is it in most of the questions which arise respecting the limits of that doctrine; as for example, what amount of public control is admissible for the prevention of fraud by adulteration; how far sanitary precautions, or arrangements to protect workpeople employed in dangerous occupations, should be enforced on employers. Such questions involve considerations of liberty, only in so far as leaving people to themselves is always better, *caeteris paribus,* than controlling them: but that they may be legitimately controlled for these ends, is in principle undeniable. On the other hand, there are questions relating to interference with trade, which are essentially questions of liberty; such as the Maine Law, already touched upon; the prohibition of the importation of opium into China; the restriction of the sale of poisons; all cases, in short, where the object of the interference is to make it impossible or difficult to obtain a particular commodity. These interferences are objectionable, not as infringements on the liberty of the producer or seller, but on that of the buyer.

One of these examples, that of the sale of poisons, opens a new question; the proper limits of what may be called the functions of police; how far liberty may legitimately be invaded for the prevention of crime, or of accident. It is one of the undisputed functions of government to take precautions against crime before it has been committed, as well as to detect and punish it afterwards. The preventive function of government, however, is far more liable to be abused, to the prejudice of liberty, than the punitory function; for there is hardly any part of the legitimate freedom of action of a human being which would not admit of being represented, and fairly too, as increasing the facilities for some form or other of delinquency. Nevertheless, if a public authority, or even a private person, sees any one evidently preparing to commit a crime, they are not bound to look on inactive until the crime is committed, but may interfere to prevent it. If poisons were never bought or used for any purpose except the commission of murder, it would be right to prohibit their manufacture and sale. They may, however, be wanted not only for innocent but for useful purposes, and restrictions cannot be imposed in the one case without operating in the other. Again, it is a proper office of public authority to guard against accidents. If either a public officer or any one else saw a person attempting to cross a bridge which had been ascertained to be unsafe, and there were no time to warn him of his danger, they might seize him and turn him back, without any real infringement of his liberty; for liberty consists in doing what one desires, and he does not desire to fall into the river. Nevertheless, when there is not a certainty, but only a danger of mischief, no one but the person himself can judge of the sufficiency of the motive which may prompt him to incur the risk: in this case, therefore (unless he is a child, or delirious, or in some state of excitement or absorption incompatible with the full use of the reflecting faculty), he ought, I conceive, to be only warned of the danger; not forcibly prevented from exposing himself to it. Similar considerations, applied to such a question as the sale of poisons, may enable us to decide which among the possible modes of regulation are or are not contrary to principle. Such a precaution, for example, as that of labeling the drug with some word expressive of its dangerous character, may be enforced without violation of liberty: the buyer cannot wish not to know that the thing he possesses has poisonous qualities. But to require in all cases the certificate of a medical practitioner, would make it sometimes impossible, always expensive, to obtain the article for legitimate uses. The only mode apparent to me, in which difficulties may be thrown in the way of crime committed through this means, without any infringement, worth taking into account, upon the liberty of those who desire the poisonous substance for other purposes, consists in providing what, in the apt language of Bentham, is called "preappointed evidence." This provision is familiar to every one in the case of contracts. It is usual and right that the law, when a contract is entered into, should require as the condition of its enforcing performance, that certain formalities should be observed, such as signatures, attestation of witnesses, and the like, in order that in case of subsequent dispute, there may be evidence to prove that the contract was really entered into, and that there was nothing in the circumstances to render it legally invalid: the effect being, to throw great obstacles in the way of fictitious contracts, or contracts made in circumstances which, if known, would destroy their validity. Precautions of a similar nature might be enforced in the sale of articles adapted to be instruments of crime. The seller, for example, might be required to enter in a register the exact time of the transaction, the name and address of the buyer, the precise quality and quantity sold; to ask the purpose for which it was wanted, and record the answer he received. When there was no medical prescription, the presence of some third person might be required, to bring home the fact to the purchaser, in case there should afterwards be reason to believe that the article had been applied to criminal purposes. Such regulations would in general be no material impediment to obtaining the article, but a very considerable one to making an improper use of it without detection.

The right inherent in society, to ward off crimes against itself by antecedent precautions, suggests the obvious limitations to the maxim, that purely self-regarding misconduct cannot properly be meddled with in the way of prevention or punishment. Drunkenness, for example, in ordinary cases, is not a fit subject for legislative interference; but I should deem it prefectly legitimate that a person, who had once been convicted of any act of violence to others under the influence of drink, should be placed under a special legal restriction, personal to himself; that if he were afterwards found drunk, he should be liable to a penalty, and that if when in that state he committed another offense, the punishment to which he would be liable for that other offense should be increased in severity. The making himself drunk, in a person whom drunkenness excites to do harm to others, is a crime against others. So, again, idleness, except in a person receiving support from the public, or except when it constitutes a breach of contract, cannot without tyranny be made a subject of legal punishment; but if, either from idleness or from any other avoidable cause, a man fails to perform his legal duties to others, as for instance to support his children, it is no tyranny to force him to fulfill that obligation, by compulsory labor, if no other means are available.

Again, there are many acts which, being directly injurious only to the agents themselves, ought not to be legally interdicted, but which, if done publicly, are a violation of good manners, and coming thus within the category of offenses against others, may rightfully be prohibited. Of this kind are offenses against decency; on which it is unnecessary to dwell, the rather as they are only connected indirectly with our subject, the objection to publicity being equally strong in the case of many actions not in themselves condemnable, nor supposed to be so.

There is another question to which an answer must be found, consistent with the principles which have been laid down. In cases of personal conduct supposed to be blameable, but which respect for liberty precludes society from preventing or punishing, because the evil directly resulting falls wholly on the agent; what the agent is free to do, ought other persons to be equally free to counsel or instigate? This question is not free from difficulty. The case of a person who solicits another to do an act, is not strictly a case of self-regarding conduct. To give advice or offer inducements to any one, is a social act, and may, therefore, like actions in general which affect others, be supposed amenable to social control. But a little reflection corrects the first impression, by showing that if the case is not strictly within the definition of individual liberty, yet the reasons on which the principle of individual liberty is grounded, are applicable to it. If people must be allowed, in whatever concerns only themselves, to act as seems best to themselves at their own peril, they must equally be free to consult with one another about what is fit to be so done; to exchange opinions, and give and receive suggestions. Whatever it is permitted to do, it must be permitted to advise to do. The question is doubtful, only when the instigator derives a personal benefit from his advice; when he makes it his occupation, for subsistence or pecuniary gain, to promote what society and the State consider to be an evil. Then, indeed, a new element of complication is introduced; namely, the existence of classes of persons with an interest opposed to what is considered as the public weal, and whose mode of living is grounded on the counteraction of it. Ought this to be interfered with, or not? Fornication, for example, must be tolerated, and so must gambling; but should a person be free to be a pimp, or to keep a gambling-house? The case is one of those which lie on the exact boundary line between two principles, and it is not at once apparent to which of the two it properly belongs. There are arguments on both sides. On the side of toleration it may be said, that the fact of following anything as an occupation, and living or profiting by the practice of it, cannot make that criminal which would otherwise be admissible; that the act should either be consistently permitted or consistently prohibited; that if the principles which we have hitherto defended are true, society has no business, *as* society, to decide anything to be wrong which concerns only the individual; that it cannot go beyond dissuasion, and that one person should be as free to persuade, as another to dissuade. In opposition to this it may be contended, that although the public, or the State, are not warranted in authoritatively deciding, for purposes of repression or punishment, that such or such conduct affecting only the interests of the individual is good or bad, they are fully justified in assuming, if they regard it as bad, that its being so or not is at least a disputable question: That, this being supposed, they cannot be acting wrongly in endeavoring to exclude the influence of solicitations which are not disinterested, of instigators who cannot possibly be impartial—who have a direct personal interest on one side, and that side the one which the State believes to be wrong, and who confessedly promote it for personal objects only. There can surely, it may be urged, be nothing lost, no sacrifice of good, by so ordering matters that persons shall make their election, either wisely or foolishly, on their own prompting, as free as possible from the arts of persons who stimulate their inclinations for interested purposes of their own. Thus (it may be said) though the statutes respecting unlawful games are utterly indefensible—though all persons should be free to gamble in their own or each other's houses, or in any place of meeting established by their own subscriptions, and open only to the members and their visitors—yet public gambling-houses should not be permitted. It is true that the prohibition is never effectual, and that, whatever amount of tyrannical power may be given to the police, gambling-houses can always be maintained under other pretenses; but they may be compelled to conduct their operations with a certain degree of secrecy and mystery, so that nobody knows anything about them but those who seek them; and more than this, society ought not to aim at. There is considerable force in these arguments. I will not venture to decide whether they are sufficient to justify the moral anomaly of punishing the accessary, when the principal is (and must be) allowed to go free; of fining or imprisoning the procurer, but not the fornicator, the gambling-house keeper, but not the gambler. Still less ought the common operations of buying and selling to be interfered with on analogous grounds. Almost every article which is bought and sold may be used in excess, and the sellers have a pecuniary interest in encouraging that excess; but no argument can be founded on this, in favor, for instance, of the Maine Law; because the class of dealers in strong drinks, though interested in their abuse, are indispensably required for the sake of their legitimate use. The interest, however, of these dealers in promoting intemperance is a real evil, and justifies the State in imposing restrictions and requiring guarantees which, but for that justification, would be infringements of legitimate liberty.

A further question is, whether the State, while it permits, should nevertheless indirectly discourage conduct which it deems contrary to the best interests of the agent; whether, for example, it should take measures to render the means of drunkenness more costly, or add to the difficulty of procuring them by limiting the number of the places of sale. On this as on most other practical questions, many distinctions require to be made. To tax stimulants for the sole purpose of making them more difficult to be obtained, is a measure differing only in degree from their entire prohibition; and would be justifiable only if that were justifiable. Every increase of cost is a prohibition, to those whose means do not come up to the augmented price; and to those who do, it is a penalty laid on them for gratifying a particular taste. Their choice of pleasures, and their mode of expending their income, after satisfying their legal and moral obligations to the State and to individuals, are their own concern, and must rest with their own judgment. These considerations may seem at first sight to condemn the selection of stimulants as special subjects of taxation for purposes of revenue. But it must be remembered that taxation for fiscal purposes is absolutely inevitable; that in most countries it is necessary that a considerable part of that taxation should be indirect; that the State, therefore, cannot help imposing penalties, which to some persons may be prohibitory, on the use of some articles of consumption. It is hence the duty of the State to consider, in the imposition of taxes, what commodities the consumers can best spare; and *a fortiori,* to select in preference those of which it deems the use, beyond a very moderate quantity, to be positively injurious. Taxation, therefore, of stimulants, up to the point which produces the largest amount of revenue (supposing that the State needs all the revenue which it yields) is not only admissible, but to be approved of.

The question of making the sale of these commodities a more or less exclusive privilege, must be answered differently, according to the purposes to which the restriction is intended to be subservient. All places of public resort require the restraint of a police, and places of this kind peculiarly, because offenses against society are especially apt to originate there. It is, therefore, fit to confine the power of selling these commodities (at least for consumption on the spot) to persons of known or vouched-for respectability of conduct; to make such regulations respecting hours of opening and closing as may be requisite for public surveillance, and to withdraw the license if breaches of the peace repeatedly take place through the connivance or incapacity of the keeper of the house, or if it becomes a rendezvous for concocting and preparing offenses against the law. Any further restriction I do not conceive to be, in principle, justifiable. The limitation in number, for instance, of beer and spirit houses, for the express purpose of rendering them more difficult of access, and diminishing the occasions of temptation, not only exposes all to an inconvenience because there are some by whom the facility would be abused, but is suited only to a state of society in which the laboring classes are avowedly treated as children or savages, and placed under an education of restraint, to fit them for future admission to the privileges of freedom. This is not the principle on which the laboring classes are professedly governed in any free country; and no person who sets due value on freedom will give his adhesion to their being so governed, unless after all efforts have been exhausted to educate them for freedom and govern them as freemen, and it has been definitely proved that they can only be governed as children. The bare statement of the alternative shows the absurdity of supposing that such efforts have been made in any case which needs be considered here. It is only because the institutions of this country are a mass of inconsistencies, that things find admittance into our practice which belong to the system of despotic, or what is called paternal, government, while the general freedom of our institutions precludes the exercise of the amount of control necessary to render the restraint of any real efficacy as a moral education.

It was pointed out in an early part of this

Essay, that the liberty of the individual, in things wherein the individual is alone concerned, implies a corresponding liberty in any number of individuals to regulate by mutual agreement such things as regard them jointly, and regard no persons but themselves. This question presents no difficulty, so long as the will of all the persons implicated remains unaltered; but since that will may change, it is often necessary, even in things in which they alone are concerned, that they should enter into engagements with one another; and when they do, it is fit, as a general rule, that those engagements should be kept. Yet, in the laws, probably, of every country, this general rule has some exceptions. Not only persons are not held to engagements which violate the rights of third parties, but it is sometimes considered a sufficient reason for releasing them from an engagement, that it is injurious to themselves. In this and most other civilized countries, for example, an engagement by which a person should sell himself, or allow himself to be sold, as a slave, would be null and void; neither enforced by law nor by opinion. The ground for thus limiting his power of voluntarily disposing of his own lot in life, is apparent, and is very clearly seen in this extreme case. The reason for not interfering, unless for the sake of others, with a person's voluntary acts, is consideration for his liberty. His voluntary choice is evidence that what he so chooses is desirable, or at the least endurable, to him, and his good is on the whole best provided for by allowing him to take his own means of pursuing it. But by selling himself for a slave, he abdicates his liberty; he forgoes any future use of it beyond that single act. He therefore defeats, in his own case, the very purpose which is the justification of allowing him to dispose of himself. He is no longer free; but is thenceforth in a position which has no longer the presumption in its favor, that would be afforded by his voluntarily remaining in it. The principle of freedom cannot require that he should be free not to be free. It is not freedom, to be allowed to alienate his freedom. These reasons, the force of which is so conspicuous in this peculiar case, are evidently of far wider application; yet a limit is everywhere set to them by the necessities of life, which continually require, not indeed that we should resign our freedom, but that we should consent to this and the other limitation of it. The principle, however, which demands uncontrolled freedom of action in all that concerns only the agents themselves, requires that those who have become bound to one another, in things which concern no third party, should be able to release one another from the engagement: and even without such voluntary release, there are perhaps no contracts or engagements, except those that relate to money or money's worth, of which one can venture to say that there ought to be no liberty whatever of retractation. Baron Wilhelm von Humboldt, in the excellent essay from which I have already quoted, states it as his conviction, that engagements which involve personal relations or services, should never be legally binding beyond a limited duration of time; and that the most important of these engagements, marriage, having the peculiarity that its objects are frustrated unless the feelings of both the parties are in harmony with it, should require nothing more than the declared will of either party to dissolve it. This subject is too important, and too complicated, to be discussed in a parenthesis, and I touch on it only so far as is necessary for purposes of illustration. If the conciseness and generality of Baron Humboldt's dissertation had not obliged him in this instance to content himself with enunciating his conclusion without discussing the premises, he would doubtless have recognized that the question cannot be decided on grounds so simple as those to which he confines himself. When a person, either by express promise or by conduct, has encouraged another to rely upon his continuing to act in a certain way —to build expectations and calculations, and stake any part of his plan of life upon that supposition—a new series of moral obligations arises on his part towards that person, which may possibly be overruled, but cannot be ignored. And again, if the relation between two contracting parties has been folloyed by consequences to others; if it has placed third parties in any peculiar position, or, as in the case of marriage, has even called third parties into existence, obligations arise on the part of both the contracting parties towards those third persons, the fulfillment of which, or at all events the mode of fulfillment, must be greatly affected by the continuance or disruption of the relation between the original parties to the contract. It does not follow, nor can I admit, that these obligations extend to requiring the fulfillment of the contract at all costs to the happiness of the reluctant party; but they are a necessary element in the question; and even if, as Von Humboldt maintains, they ought to make no difference in the *legal* freedom of the parties to release themselves from the engagement (and I also hold that they ought not to make *much* difference), they necessarily make a great difference in the *moral* freedom. A person is bound to take all these circumstances into account, before resolving on a step which may affect such important interests of others; and if he does not allow proper weight to those interests, he is morally responsible for the wrong. I have made these obvious remarks for the better illustration of the general principle of liberty, and not because they are at all needed on the particular question, which, on the contrary, is usually discussed as if the interest of children was everything, and that of grown persons nothing.

I have already observed that, owing to the absence of any recognized general principles, liberty is often granted where it should be withheld, as well as withheld where it should be granted; and one of the cases in which, in the modern European world, the sentiment of liberty is the strongest, is a case where, in my view, it is altogether misplaced. A person should be free to do as he likes in his own concerns; but he ought not to be free to do as he likes in acting for another, under the pretext that the affairs of the other are his own affairs. The State, while it respects the liberty of each in what specially regards himself, is bound to maintain a vigilant control over his exercise of any power which it allows him to possess over others. This obligation is almost entirely disregarded in the case of the family relations, a case, in its direct influence on human happiness, more important than all others taken together. The almost despotic power of husbands over wives needs not be enlarged upon here, because nothing more is needed for the complete removal of the evil, than that wives should have the same rights, and should receive the protection of law in the same manner, as all other persons; and because, on this subject, the defenders of established injustice do not avail themselves of the plea of liberty, but stand forth openly as the champions of power. It is in the case of children, that misapplied notions of liberty are a real obstacle to the fulfillment by the State of its duties. One would almost think that a man's children were supposed to be literally, and not metaphorically, a part of himself, so jealous is opinion of the smallest interference of law with his absolute and exclusive control over them; more jealous than of almost any interference with his own freedom of action: so much less do the generality of mankind value liberty than power. Consider, for example, the case of education. Is it not almost a self-evident axiom, that the State should require and compel the education, up to a certain standard, of every human being who is born its citizen? Yet who is there that is not afraid to recognize and assert this truth? Hardly any one indeed will deny that it is one of the most sacred duties of the parents (or, as law and usage now stand, the father), after summoning a human being into the world, to give to that being an education fitting him to perform his part well in life towards others and towards himself. But while this is unanimously declared to be the father's duty, scarcely anybody, in this country, will bear to hear of obliging him to perform it. Instead of his being required to make any exertion or sacrifice for securing education to the child, it is left to his choice to accept it or not when it is provided gratis! It still remains unrecognized, that to bring a child into existence without a fair prospect of being able, not only to provide food for its body, but instruction and training for its mind, is a moral crime, both against the unfortunate offspring and against society; and that if the parent does not fulfill this obligation, the State ought to see it fulfilled, at the charge, as far as possible, of the parent.

Were the duty of enforcing universal education once admitted, there would be an end to the difficulties about what the State should teach, and how it should teach, which now convert the subject into a mere battlefield for sects and parties, causing the time and labor which should have been spent in educating, to be wasted in quarreling about education. If the government would make up its mind to *require* for every child a good education, it might save itself the trouble of *providing* one. It might leave to parents to obtain the education where and how they pleased, and content itself with helping to pay the school fees of the poorer classes of children, and defraying the entire school expenses of those who have no one else to pay for them. The objections which are urged with reason against State education, do not apply to the enforcement of education by the State, but to the State's taking upon itself to direct that education: which is a totally different thing. That the whole or any large part of the education of the people should be in State hands, I go as far as any one in deprecating. All that has been said of the importance of individuality of character, and diversity in opinions and modes of conduct, involves, as of the same unspeakable importance, diversity of education. A general State education is a mere contrivance for molding people to be exactly like one another: and as the mold in which it casts them is that which pleases the predominant power in the government, whether this be a monarch, a priesthood, an aristocracy, or the majority of the existing generation in proportion as it is efficient and successful, it establishes a despotism over the mind, leading by natural tendency to one over the body. An education established and controlled by the State should only exist, if it exist at all, as one among many competing experiments, carried on for the purpose of example and stimulus, to keep the others up to a certain standard of excellence. Unless, indeed, when society in general is in so backward a state that it could not or would not provide for itself any proper institutions of education, unless the government undertook the task: then, indeed, the government may as the less of two great evils, take upon itself the business of schools and universities, as it may that of joint-stock companies, when private enterprise, in a shape fitted for undertaking great works of industry, does not exist in the country. But in general, if the country contains a sufficient number of persons qualified to provide education under government auspices, the same persons would be able and willing to give an equally good education on the voluntary principle, under the assurance of remuneration afforded by a law rendering education compulsory, combined with the State aid to those unable to defray the expense.

The instrument for enforcing the law could be no other than public examinations, extending to all children, and beginning at an early age. An age might be fixed at which every child must be examined, to ascertain if he (or she) is able to read. If a child proves unable, the father, unless he has some sufficient ground of excuse, might be subjected to a moderate fine, to be worked out, if necessary, by his labor, and the child might be put to school at his expense. Once in every year the examination should be renewed, with a gradually extending range of subjects, so as to make the universal acquisition, and what is more, retention, of a certain minimum of general knowledge, virtually compulsory. Beyond that minimum, there should be voluntary examinations on all subjects, at which all who come up to a certain standard of proficiency might claim a certificate. To prevent the State from exercising, through these arrangements, an improper influence over opinion, the knowledge required for passing an examination (beyond the merely instrumental parts of knowledge, such as languages and their use) should, even in the higher classes of examinations, be confined to facts and positive science exclusively. The examinations on religion, politics, or other disputed topics, should not turn on the truth or falsehood of opinions, but on the matter of fact that such and such an opinion is held, on such grounds, by such authors, or schools, or churches. Under this system, the rising generation would be no worse off in regard to all disputed truths, than they are at present; they would be brought up either churchmen or dissenters as they now are, the State merely taking care that they should be instructed churchmen, or instructed dissenters. There would be nothing to hinder them from being taught religion, if their parents chose, at the same schools where they were taught other things. All attempts by the State to bias the conclusions of its citizens on disputed subjects, are evil; but it may very properly offer to ascertain and certify that a person possesses the knowledge, requisite to make his conclusions, on any given subject, worth attending to. A student of philosophy would be the better for being able to stand an examination both in Locke and in Kant, whichever of the two he takes up with, or even if with neither: and there is no reasonable objection to examining an atheist in the evidences of Christianity, provided he is not required to profess a belief in them. The examinations, however, in the higher branches of knowledge should, I conceive, be entirely voluntary. It would be giving too dangerous a power to governments, were they allowed to exclude any one from professions, even from the profession of teacher, for alleged deficiency of qualifications: and I think, with Wilhelm von Humboldt, that degrees, or other public certificates of scientific or professional acquirements, should be given to all who present themselves for examination, and stand the test; but that such certificates should confer no advantage over competitors, other than the weight which may be attached to their testimony by public opinion.

It is not in the matter of education only, that misplaced notions of liberty prevent moral obligations on the part of parents from being recognized, and legal obligations from being imposed, where there are the strongest grounds for the former always, and in many cases for the latter also. The fact itself, of causing the existence of a human being, is one of the most responsible actions in the range of human life. To undertake this responsibility—to bestow a life which may be either a curse or a blessing—unless the being on whom it is to be bestowed will have at least the ordinary chances of a desirable existence, is a crime against that being. And in a country either overpeopled, or threatened with being so, to produce children, beyond a very small number, with the effect of reducing the reward of labor by their competition, is a serious offense against all who live by the remuneration of their labor. The laws which, in many countries on the Continent, forbid marriage unless the parties can show that they have the means of supporting a family, do not exceed the legitimate powers of the State: and whether such laws be expedient or not (a question mainly dependent on local circumstances and feelings), they are not objectionable as violations of liberty. Such laws are interferences of the State to prohibit a mischievous act—an act injurious to others, which ought to be a subject of reprobation, and social stigma, even when it is not deemed expedient to superadd legal punishment. Yet the current ideas of liberty, which bend so easily to real infringements of the freedom of the individual in things which concern only himself, would repel the attempt to put any restraint upon his inclinations when the consequence of their indulgence is a life or lives of wretchedness and depravity to the offspring, with manifold evils to those sufficiently within reach to be in any way affected by their actions. When we compare the strange respect of mankind for liberty, with their strange want of respect for it, we might imagine that a man had an indispensable right to do harm to others, and no right at all to please himself without giving pain to any one.

I have reserved for the last place a large class of questions respecting the limits of government interference, which, though closely connected with the subject of this Essay, do not, in strictness, belong to it. These are cases in which the reasons against interference do not turn upon the principle of liberty: the question is not about restraining the actions of individuals, but about helping them: it is asked whether the government should do, or cause to be done, something for their benefit, instead of leaving it to be done by themselves, individually, or in voluntary combination.

The objections to government interference, when it is not such as to involve infringement of liberty, may be of three kinds.

The first is, when the thing to be done is likely to be better done by individuals than by the government. Speaking generally, there is no one so fit to conduct any business, or to determine how or by whom it shall be conducted, as those who are personally interested in it. This principle condemns the interferences, once so common, of the legislature, or the officers of government, with the ordinary processes of industry. But this part of the subject has been sufficiently enlarged upon by political economists, and is not particularly related to the principles of this Essay.

The second objection is more nearly allied to our subject. In many cases, though individuals may not do the particular thing so well, on the average, as the officers of government, it is nevertheless desirable that it should be done by them, rather than by the government, as a means to their own mental education—a mode of strengthening their active faculties, exercising their judgment, and giving them a familiar knowledge of the subjects with which they are thus left to deal. This is a principal, though not the sole, recommendation of jury trial (in cases not political); of free and popular and local municipal institutions; of the conduct of industrial and philanthropic enterprises by voluntary associations. These are not questions of liberty, and are connected with that subject only by remote tendencies; but they are questions of development. It belongs to a different occasion from the present to dwell on these things as parts of national education; as being, in truth, the peculiar training of a citizen, the practical part of the political education of a free people, taking them out of the narrow circle of personal and family selfishness, and accustoming them to the comprehension of joint interests, the management of joint concerns—habituating them to act from public or semi-public motives, and guide their conduct by aims which unite instead of isolating them from one another. Without these habits and powers, a free constitution can neither be worked nor preserved; as is exemplified by the too-often transitory nature of political freedom in countries where it does not rest upon a sufficient basis of local liberties. The management of purely local business by the localities, and of the great enterprises of industry by the union of those who voluntarily supply the pecuniary means, is further recommended by all the advantages which have been set forth in this Essay as belonging to individuality of development, and diversity of modes of action. Government operations tend to be everywhere alike. With individuals and voluntary associations, on the contrary, there are varied experiments, and endless diversity of experience. What the State can usefully do, is to make itself a central depository, and active circulator and diffuser, of the experience resulting from many trials. Its business is to enable each experimentalist to benefit by the experiments of others; instead of tolerating no experiments but its own.

The third, and most cogent reason for restricting the interference of government, is the great evil of adding unnecessarily to its power. Every function superadded to those already exercised by the government, causes its influence over hopes and fears to be more widely diffused, and converts, more and more, the active and ambitious part of the public into hangers-on of the government, or of some party which aims at becoming the government. If the roads, the railways, the banks, the insurance offices, the great joint-stock companies, the universities, and the public charities, were all of them branches of the government; if, in addition, the municipal corporations and local boards, with all that now devolves on them, became departments of the central administration; if the employés of all these different enterprises were appointed and paid by the government, and looked to the government for every rise in life; not all the freedom of the press and popular constitution of the legislature would make this or any other country free otherwise than in name. And the evil would be greater, the more efficiently and scientifically the administrative machinery was constructed—the more skillful the arrangements for obtaining the best qualified hands and heads with which to work it. In England it has of late been proposed that all the members of the civil service of government should be selected by competitive examination, to obtain for those employments the most intelligent and instructed persons procurable; and much has been said and written for and against this proposal. One of the arguments most insisted on by its opponents, is that the occupation of a permanent official servant of the State does not hold out sufficient prospects of emolument and importance to attract the highest talents, which will always be able to find a more inviting career in the professions, or in the service of companies and other public bodies. One would not have been surprised if this argument had been used by the friends of the proposition, as an answer to its principal difficulty. Coming from the opponents it is strange enough. What is urged as an objection is the safety-valve of the proposed system. If indeed all the high talent of the country *could* be drawn into the service of the government, a proposal tending to bring about that result might well inspire uneasiness. If every part of the business of society which required organized concert, or large and comprehensive views, were in the hands of the government, and if government offices were universally filled by the ablest men, all the enlarged culture and practiced intelligence in the country, except the purely speculative, would be concentrated in a numerous bureaucracy, to whom alone the rest of the community would look for all things: the multitude for direction and dictation in all they had to do; the able and aspiring for personal advancement. To be admitted into the ranks of this bureaucracy, and when admitted, to rise therein, would be the sole objects of ambition. Under this régime, not only is the outside public ill-qualified, for want of practical experience, to criticize or check the mode of operation of the bureaucracy, but even if the accidents of despotic or the natural working of popular institutions occasionally raise to the summit a ruler or rulers of reforming inclinations, no reform can be effected which is contrary to the interest of the bureaucracy. Such is the melancholy condition of the Russian empire, as shown in the accounts of those who have had sufficient opportunity of observation. The Czar himself is powerless against the bureaucratic body; he can send any one of them to Siberia, but he cannot govern without them, or against their will. On every decree of his they have a tacit veto, by merely refraining from carrying it into effect. In countries of more advanced civilization and of a more insurrectionary spirit, the public, accustomed to expect everything to be done for them by the State, or at least to do nothing for themselves without asking from the State not only leave to do it, but even how it is to be done, naturally hold the State responsible for all evil which befalls them, and when the evil exceeds their amount of patience, they rise against the government and make what is called a revolution; whereupon somebody else, with or without legitimate authority from the nation, vaults into the seat, issues his orders to the bureaucracy, and everything goes on much as it did before; the bureaucracy being unchanged, and nobody else being capable of taking their place.

A very different spectacle is exhibited among a people accustomed to transact their own business. In France, a large part of the people having been engaged in military service, many of whom have held at least the rank of non-commissioned officers, there are in every popular insurrection several persons competent to take the lead, and improvise some tolerable plan of action. What the French are in military affairs, the Americans are in every kind of civil business; let them be left without a government, every body of Americans is able to improvise one, and to carry on that or any other public business with a sufficient amount of intelligence, order, and decision. This is what every free people ought to be: and a people capable of this is certain to be free; it will never let itself be enslaved by any man or body of men because these are able to seize and pull the reins of the central administration. No bureaucracy can hope to make such a people as this do or undergo anything that they do not like. But where everything is done through the bureaucracy, nothing to which the bureaucracy is really adverse can be done at all. The constitution of such countries is an organization of the experience and practical ability of the nation, into a disciplined body for the purpose of governing the rest; and the more perfect that organization is in itself, the more successful in drawing to itself and educating for itself the persons of greater capacity from all ranks of the community, the more complete is the bondage of all, the members of the bureaucracy included. For the governors are as much the slaves of their organization and discipline, as the governed are of the governors. A Chinese mandarin is as much the tool and creature of a despotism as the humblest cultivator. An individual Jesuit is to the utmost degree of abasement the slave of his order, though the order itself exists for the collective power and importance of its members.

It is not, also, to be forgotten, that the absorption of all the principal ability of the country into the governing body is fatal, sooner or later, to the mental activity and progressiveness of the body itself. Banded together as they are—working a system which, like all systems, necessarily proceeds in a great measure by fixed rules—the official body are under the constant temptation of sinking into indolent routine, or, if they now and then desert that mill-horse round, of rushing into some half-examined crudity which has struck the fancy of some leading member of the corps: and the sole check to these closely allied, though seemingly opposite, tendencies, the only stimulus which can keep the ability of the body itself up to a high standard, is liability to the watchful criticism of equal ability outside the body. It is indispensable, therefore, that the means should exist, independently of the government, of forming such ability, and furnishing it with the opportunities and experience necessary for a correct judgment of great practical affairs. If we would possess permanently a skillful and efficient body of functionaries—above all, a body able to originate and willing to adopt improvements; if we would not have our bureaucracy degenerate into a pedantocracy, this body must not engross all the occupations which form and cultivate the faculties required for the government of mankind.

To determine the point at which evils, so formidable to human freedom and advancement, begin, or rather at which they begin to predominate over the benefits attending the collective application of the force of society, under its recognized chiefs, for the removal of the obstacles which stand in the way of its well-being; to secure as much of the advantages of centralized power and intelligence, as can be had without turning into governmental channels too great a proportion of the general activity—is one of the most difficult and complicated questions in the art of government. It is, in a great measure, a question of detail, in which many and various considerations must be kept in view, and no absolute rule can be laid down. But I believe that the practical principle in which safety resides, the ideal to be kept in view, the standard by which to test all arrangements intended for overcoming the difficulty, may be conveyed in these words: the greatest dissemination of power consistent with efficiency; but the greatest possible centralization of information, and diffusion of it from the center. Thus, in municipal administration, there would be, as in the New England States, a very minute division among separate officers, chosen by the localities, of all business which is not better left to the persons directly interested; but besides this, there would be, in each department of local affairs, a central superintendence, forming a branch of the general government. The organ of this superintendence would concentrate, as in a focus, the variety of information and experience derived from the conduct of that branch of public business in all the localities, from everything analogous which is done in foreign countries, and from the general principles of political science. This central organ should have a right to know all that is done, and its special duty should be that of making the knowledge acquired in one place available for others. Emancipated from the petty prejudices and narrow views of a locality by its elevated position and comprehensive sphere of observation, its advice would naturally carry much authority; but its actual power, as a permanent institution, should, I conceive, be limited to compelling the local officers to obey the laws laid down for their guidance. In all things not provided for by general rules, those officers should be left to their own judgment, under responsibility to their constituents. For the violation of rules, they should be responsible to law, and the rules themselves should be laid down by the legislature; the central administrative authority only watching over their execution, and if they were not properly carried into effect, appealing, according to the nature of the case, to the tribunals to enforce the law, or to the constituencies to dismiss the functionaries who had not executed it according to its spirit. Such, in its general conception, is the central superintendence which the Poor Law Board is intended to exercise over the administrators of the Poor Rate throughout the country. Whatever powers the Board exercises beyond this limit, were right and necessary in that peculiar case, for the cure of rooted habits of maladministration in matters deeply affecting not the localities merely, but the whole community; since no locality has a moral right to make itself by mismanagement a nest of pauperism, necessarily overflowing into other localities, and impairing the moral and physical condition of the whole laboring community. The powers of administrative coercion and subordinate legislation possessed by the Poor Law Board (but which, owing to the state of opinion on the subject, are very scantily exercised by them), though perfectly justifiable in a case of first-rate national interest, would be wholly out of place in the superintendence of interests purely local. But a central organ of information and instruction for all the localities, would be equally valuable in all departments of administration. A government cannot have too much of the kind of activity which does not impede, but aids and stimulates, individual exertion and development. The mischief begins when, instead of calling forth the activity and powers of individuals and bodies, it substitutes its own activity for theirs; when, instead of informing, advising, and, upon occasion, denouncing, it makes them work in fetters, or bids them stand aside and does their work instead of them. The worth of a State, in the long run, is the worth of the individuals composing it; and a State which postpones the interests of *their* mental expansion and elevation, to a little more of administrative skill, or of that semblance of it which practice gives, in the details of business; a State which dwarfs its men, in order that they may be more docile instruments in its hands even for beneficial purposes—will find that with small men no great thing can really be accomplished; and that the perfection of machinery to which it has sacrificed everything, will in the end avail it nothing, for want of the vital power which, in order that the machine might work more smoothly, it has preferred to banish.

FORTY

NATIONALISM

Nationalism was one of the basic forces of the nineteenth century in the West. In the twentieth century, nationalism in Western civilization has declined somewhat, in part because the great alliances of two World Wars created larger-than-national loyalties, in part because ideological conflicts (especially democracy versus communism) have added new allegiances, and in part because many men of good will have seen in internationalism the only sure road to world peace. Nonetheless, nationalism has been one of the West's most vital exports in the twentieth century to the underdeveloped areas of Africa and Asia, where its future development is a matter of speculation. In any case, nationalism was and remains an active force in the modern world. In a thoughtful work, Boyd C. Shafer has defined nationalism as "that sentiment unifying a group of people who have a real or imagined common historical experience and a common aspiration to live together as a separate group in the future." Shafer has also pointed out the complexity in the development of modern nationalism, and its relation to the "historical, political, eonomic, and social forces" of the modern world.

BOYD C. SHAFER

NATIONALISM: MYTH AND REALITY *

A century of study of the group loyalty that has most powerfully motivated men in our time, nationalism, has produced no precise and acceptable definition. Many French, British, German, Italian, Russian, and American students have tried their hand with varying but never complete success. Other students have found flaws and omissions, and for the purposes of their own studies or influenced by their own political philosophies have proceeded to form their own definitions. Clarity has seldom been achieved, scientific study has thus been hindered.

A short, scholarly definition of a sentence or two, a precise definition which includes everything nationalism contains and excludes all that is irrelevant, may be impossible. Yet if nationalism is to be understood, clearer general understanding of what the word means must be achieved. Here an attempt is made to identify some of the elements commonly embodied in the idea, and to eliminate some of the semantic confusion that has grown up around it.

The confusion in meaning has not been unnatural. While the period between 1789 and 1955 saw intensification, especially in

* From *Nationalism: Myth and Reality*, pp. 3–11, copyright, 1955, by Boyd C. Shafer. Reprinted by permission of Harcourt, Brace & World, Inc.

wartime, of the sentiment everywhere, different historical factors have been involved in the making of each nation, nationality, and nationalism. Differing political, economic, social, and geographic conditions have influenced their development. The etymology of the basic word, nation, helps little, for it comes from the Latin *natio* which has the same stem as *natus,* and both come from *nascor,* meaning simply, "I am born." The nationalism of each people has hence expressed itself differently and altered with time. The American nationalisms, lacking deep roots in history and evolving under different material conditions, are not exactly synonymous with those of Europe and Asia. The lateness of German and Italian unification, as well as their different earlier histories, has made their nationalisms somewhat dissimilar to those of older Britain and France. A moat of twenty miles has helped to differentiate British nationalism from that of the French, who have been little protected by river and mountain. The revolutionary national patriotism of France in 1789–1790, influenced by eighteenth-century rationalism, was more humanitarian than that of the French in a year of war and terror, 1793, while the nationalism of Bismarck's Germany of 1871 was mild compared to that of Hitler's totalitarian Reich in 1939. The national spirit of rich, industrial, liberal nineteenth-century Britain was not the same as that of poor, agricultural, autocratic Tsarist Russia, though both experienced a messianic zeal toward imperial expansion. The nationalism of contemporary China with its masses of illiterate people, its poverty, its communism, differs in many ways from that of the richer and better educated Western nations. Consequently, because the thing itself has differed and changed, the meaning given the word has varied with each language, each nationalist, and with each period of time. Quite understandably, students, looking at it from different nations, at different times, and for different reasons, have defined it differently.

This understandable confusion does not excuse anachronistic and faulty usage of the word nor does it preclude description of common elements in contemporary nationalisms. An often committed error of students of ideas is to tear generic words like nation and nationalism from their historical context, to read their contemporary substance back into the past, and thus to see in the past the generalities and universals evident actually and only in contemporary life. The result is not only false history but further misunderstanding.

Any use of the word nationalism to describe historical happenings before the eighteenth century is probably anachronistic. Loyalty to family and tribe appeared in prehistoric societies. Patriotism toward city-state and empire existed in ancient Greece and Rome. Consciousness of nationality and some forms of national patriotism can be traced back to the late medieval period in France and England. That patriotism identifiable with devotion to the nation spread widely and became popular in western Europe only toward the end of the eighteenth century during the era of the French Revolution. It is with reference to this era that the term nationalism can accurately be used for the first time. Not until the first half of the twentieth century did this patriotism become for most (not all) men so intense and active a devotion to the national group and to the nation-state that it can rightly be called nationalism in the fullest modern sense. The careful scholar must be aware not only of the danger of this fairly obvious anachronism; it is equally erroneous to say that the sentiment was always incipient and to trace it in contrived chronological sequence from origins in primitive and early historical societies. Loyalty, patriotism, and national consciousness are ingredients in nationalism and preceded it in time. Out of them as well as other ideas and conditions the sentiment developed, but when *only they* existed, modern nationalism did not. Unless one assumes an unjustifiable historical determinism they might never have combined and developed into nationalism.

If nationalism has been falsely seen long before it came into being, the word has also been used much too narrowly. Scholars like to categorize and nationalists are eager to make a case for their own brand of nationalism. By nationalism today may be meant (1) the love of a common soil, race, language, or historical culture, (2) a desire for the political independence, security, and prestige of the nation, (3) a mystical devotion to a vague, sometimes even supernatural, social organism which, known as the nation or *Volk,* is more than the sum of its parts, (4) the dogma that the individual lives exclusively for the nation with the corollary that the nation is an end in itself, or (5) the doctrine that the nation (the nationalist's own) is or should be dominant if not supreme among other nations and should take aggressive action to this end.

None of these definitions is wrong, but all are too narrow, too exclusive. Taken alone each describes only one aspect of nationalism. Modern nationalism is compounded of all of them and more.

A discussion of two extreme conceptions of what constitutes a nation will illustrate the inadequacy of any narrow definition. To some nationalists, otherwise of widely different views, like Renan, Treitschke, Barrès, and Zangwill, the nation was a kind of Hegelian organism, a soul or a spiritual principle arising out of the history and the nature of man. To a modern social scientist this may seem either nonsense or pure mysticism, in any case a myth to be ignored or refuted. Yet the historical and contemporary significance of this "myth" cannot be denied. Nationalists everywhere have worshiped the nation, if not as supernatural creation, then as something beyond the individuals and institutions which compose it. As this worship is part of the substance of contemporary nationalism it must, whatever the basis of fact behind it, be included in descriptions of it, and yet it is only part of it. Likewise the more realistic though too clever definition of Huxley and Haddon cannot be cavalierly dismissed. To them a nation was a "society united by a common error as to its origins and a common aversion to its neighbors." It may be rightly objected that nation and nationalism are more than compounded error and aversion, that as institution and idea they have developed historically into concrete realities quite apart from their origins. It is true, owing to the almost exclusive study of perverted national history, that nations are misinformed about their own origins and development, and that they are often partly united, particularly in times of crisis and war, by hostility to their neighbors. But false history and aversion are by no means all of nationalism. They are two reasons for it but they remain only part of it.

Nationalism is what the nationalists have made it; it is not a neat, fixed concept but a varying combination of beliefs and conditions. It may be in part founded on myth but myths like other errors have a way of perpetuating themselves and of becoming not true but real. The fact is that myth and actuality and truth and error are inextricably intermixed in modern nationalism. The only reasonable way to get at the nature of nationalism is to determine what beliefs—however true or false—and what conditions—however misinterpreted—are commonly—present. The following ten are here hypothetically advanced. No claim is laid for their infallibility or finality.

1. A certain defined (often vaguely) unit of territory (whether possessed or coveted).

2. Some common cultural characteristics such as language (or widely understood languages), customs, manners, and literature (folk tales and lore are a beginning). If an individual believes he shares these, and wishes to continue sharing them, he is usually said to be a member of the nationality.

3. Some common dominant social (as Christian) and economic (as capitalistic or recently communistic) institutions.

4. A common independent or sovereign

government (type does not matter) or the desire for one. The "principle" that each nationality should be separate and independent is involved here.

5. A belief in a common history (it can be invented) and in a common origin (often mistakenly conceived to be racial in nature).

6. A love or esteem for fellow nationals (not necessarily as individuals).

7. A devotion to the entity (however little comprehended) called the nation, which embodies the common territory, culture, social and economic institutions, government, and the fellow nationals, and which is at the same time (whether organism or not) more than their sum.

8. A common pride in the achievements (often the military more than the cultural) of this nation and a common sorrow in its tragedies (particularly its defeats).

9. A disregard for or hostility to other (not necessarily all) like groups, especially if these prevent or seem to threaten the separate national existence.

10. A hope that the nation will have a great and glorious future (usually in territorial expansion) and become supreme in some way (in world power if the nation is already large).

To almost any generalization about nationalism, and obviously to the above ten, exceptions can be raised. Few nationals know intimately their own "rocks and rills" and the national states' desire for territory often seems to have no real bounds. As everyone knows, the Swiss use four languages. In the United States the dominant group is white and of western European origin but over 10 per cent are colored, chiefly from Africa. These exceptions do not invalidate the generalizations as these are qualified above. It is not necessary to know a territory to love it or want it. The Swiss have overcome their language barriers by being able to speak and understand more than one of their languages. A common race is not essential but rather a belief in a common history of the dominant group or a willingness to assimilate (or crush) the minority groups for national actions. Further, all of the beliefs and conditions need not always be present in the same degree and combination. The Swiss may stress their common history and their common defense so much that they do not need the fiction of a common race or the tie of one language. Nationalism, however, is developed and strong in proportion as these beliefs and conditions are present, and the presence of all of them in some degree is essential before nationalism fully materializes.

A weightier objection may be that most of these ten beliefs and conditions could be and often have been the basis of unity and devotion in other human institutions such as church or empire. The answer is not that they could not apply to other institutions but that today for historical reasons they do apply peculiarly to the nation, that group of like-minded people living together (or hoping to) within the same political boundaries.

The historical factors in the formation of the nation and nationalism are numerous and extremely complex. They are described in Chapters II to XI. Disraeli approximated part of the truth when he, following Montesquieu and Burke, wrote in 1836 that nations were "gradually created by a variety of influences—the influence of original organization, of climate, soil, religion, laws, customs, manners, extraordinary accidents and incidents in their history, and the individual character of their illustrious citizens." But Disraeli made the process too simple. A conservative politician, he here overlooked, for example, the politico-economic influences in the formation of the nation, those forces which led to the nation-state rather than to a city-state or empire and which in turn helped shape the nation. What he ignored is of as much import as what he mentioned.

The nation-state, or the political organization of the nation, came into being and became dominant in part because that form of institution fitted the economic organization and the state of transportation and communication of modern times. Nation-states did not develop earlier because feudal, agricultural Europe did not need or foster them. The middle and working classes were not strong enough to demand them or did not desire them. The local nature and low level of industry, the trickle of trade and the bad roads did not demand or permit them. And the slow communication of ideas and the illiteracy of the bulk of the people prevented the rise of that national consciousness essential to their rise and growth. Conversely the nation-state and nationalism are possibly beginning to decline today because modern technology, the volume of industrial production and commerce, the speed of communication, and perhaps the enlightenment of many people are making national boundaries obsolete.

This is to say nothing more than that as a result of a multitude of historical, political, economic, and social forces a sentiment of unity grew within groups of people which expressed itself in devotion to what was called the nation. Nationalism, then, becomes a concept so complex and changing that it defies short, logical definition. At present by the word may be denoted that sentiment unifying a group of people who have a real or imagined common historical experience and a common aspiration to live together as a separate group in the future. This unifying sentiment expresses itself in loyalty to the nation-state whatever the government, in love of native land however little known, in pride in common culture and economic and social institutions though these may not be understood, in preference for fellow nationals in contrast to disregard for members of other groups, and in zeal not only for group security but for glory and expansion. In its most modern form it requires, as Rousseau advocated as early as the eighteenth century, almost absolute devotion to and conformity with the will of the nation-state as this is expressed by the ruler or rulers (autocratic or democratic), and it demands the supremacy (in watchmaking or military might) of the nation to which the nationalist belongs.

Nationalism may not yet have reached its final stage. Even Hitler's totalitarian Germany did not completely submerge all individuals and all other loyalties. Nationalism may be transformed into some larger sentiment by the creation of world institutions and consciousness. It may disappear through the destructive conquests of a super nation or in class warfare. One thing is certain. It is complex and dynamic. Like all human phenomena it has several dimensions, its structure constantly varies, and it moves with time. As it changes so must scholarly descriptions of it. Tidy formulas do not fit a sentiment which is itself in the process of becoming.

FORTY-ONE

THE FACTORY SYSTEM

The Industrial Revolution, which began in England about 1760, soon spread to the continent of Europe. By 1900, it had caused more material change in the West than had occurred in the preceding 50 centuries of civilization. An unprecedented volume of mass-produced commodities accompanied a revolution in transportation. The railroad and the steamship were able to bring raw materials swiftly and cheaply to industrial centers and to send finished products to worldwide markets where they could compete successfully with local handmade goods. Central to the Industrial Revolution were the steam engine and the dynamo, the providers of the huge amounts of cheap power necessary to operate industrial machinery. In addition, the new industrialists developed, and in some cases adapted from former times, the factory system, which concentrated production in one place. The results were both revolutionary and catastrophic. The leaders of the West, schooled in values of farming and trade, had only dim awareness of the huge social problems which the fast-moving revolution in industry was creating. Workers who were used to the slower rhythms of small shops and country life entered the new factories by the thousands, where they encountered strict discipline foreign to their former habits. Preindustrial conditions, with heavy labor and excessively long hours, left much to be desired, and whether the Industrial Revolution worsened these working conditions is a much debated and possibly unanswerable question. But in any case, the factory system aggravated and expanded previous social abuses and led ultimately to a considerable number of basic social reforms. In a widely read and much discussed work, the Hammonds have described the appalling working conditions in the new factory system, with particular emphasis on the grueling discipline which the newly recruited urban workers found all but intolerable.

J. L. AND BARBARA HAMMOND

THE TOWN LABOURER, 1760-1832 *

In 1831 the Society for the Diffusion of Useful Knowledge published a volume called *The Results of Machinery,* addressed to the working men of the United Kingdom. The

* Reprinted from *The Town Labourer, 1760–1832,* pp. 17–36, by J. L. and Barbara Hammond by permission of Longmans, Green & Co. Limited, London, 1918.

little book gives a glowing picture of the glories of invention, of the permanent blessings of machinery, of the triumphant step that man takes in comfort and civilisation every time that he transfers one of the meaner drudgeries of the world's work from human backs to wheels and pistons. The argument is developed with great animation and vigour, and the writer, as he skirmishes with the workman's prejudices, travels over one industry and one country after another. Almost every page offers a graphic illustration of Macaulay's proud verdict on English industrial life, "Nowhere does man exercise such dominion over matter."

If we study the speeches and writings that represent working-class feeling we shall notice very specially one aspect of the new system. The system threatened the employment and livelihood of a large number of people, and complaints to that effect are, of course, constant and general. The fear of this fate or its actual experience was the cause of violence against machinery and of violence against persons. But there appears in the protests and remonstrances of the time a spirit that was quite independent of these anxieties and resentments, a feeling of hatred and terror that no magician among economists could have dispelled by the most convincing demonstration that machinery could not hurt the poor.[1] This spirit finds its most articulate expression, after our period, in the Chartist movement and the passionate response of the working men and the working women of the north of England to the mobilising rhetoric of Stephens and Oastler. The men and women of Lancashire and Yorkshire felt of this new power that it was inhuman, that it disregarded all their instincts and sensibilities, that it brought into their lives an inexorable force, destroying and scattering their customs, their traditions, their freedom, their ties of family and home, their dignity and character as men and women. If one sentence can sum up this impression, we might say, transposing Macaulay's words, "Nowhere does matter exercise such dominion over man." [2]

Scarcely any evil associated with the factory system was entirely a new evil in kind. In many domestic industries the hours were long, the pay was poor, children worked from a tender age, there was overcrowding, and both home and workshop were rendered less desirable from the combination of the two under a single roof. In many, not in all, for there were home workers who were very prosperous, and in his halcyon days the hand-loom weaver was in the enviable position of a man who had something valuable to sell and could make very comfortable terms for himself. But the home worker at the worst, even in cases where to those who examine the economic forces on which his livelihood depended, he seems to have been at the end of a shorter chain than he realised, was in many respects his own master. He worked long hours, but they were his own hours; his wife and children worked, but they worked beside him, and there was no alien power over their lives; his house was stifling, but he could slip into his garden; he had spells of unemployment, but he could use them sometimes for cultivating his cabbages. The forces that ruled his fate were in a sense outside his daily life; they did not overshadow and envelop his home, his family, his movements and habits, his hours for work and his hours for food.

What the new order did in all these respects was to turn the discomforts of the life of the poor into a rigid system. Hours were not shortened, the atmosphere in which they worked was not made fresher or cleaner,

[1] See, for example, *The Voice of the People,* which expressly repudiates hostility to machinery, but lays great stress on the servitude to which the working classes had been reduced by its means from their want of power. "Every successive improvement which is introduced tends only to deteriorate their condition" (Jan. 22, 1831). At a meeting at Ashton it was declared that the negroes were slaves in name, but the factory employees were slaves in reality.

[2] "A steam engine in the hands of an interested or avaricious master is a relentless power to which old and young are equally bound to submit" (a factory inspector, quoted by Fielden, *Curse of Factory System,* p. 43).

child labour was not abolished. In none of these respects was the early factory better than the home, in some it was worse. But to all the evils from which the domestic worker had suffered, the Industrial Revolution added discipline, and the discipline of a power driven by a competition that seemed as inhuman as the machines that thundered in factory and shed. The workman was summoned by the factory bell; his daily life was arranged by factory hours; he worked under an overseer imposing a method and precision for which the overseer had in turn to answer to some higher authority; if he broke one of a long series of minute regulations he was fined, and behind all this scheme of supervision and control there loomed the great impersonal system. Let anybody think of the life of Bamford's uncle at Middleton, who used to retire into his house every morning and every afternoon to enjoy a pipe,[3] or of the account of his early days given by a Nottingham stocking maker, mentioned by Felkin, where every other Saturday was taken off for gardening,[4] and then let him enter into the feelings of a spinner at Tyldesley, near Manchester, who worked in a temperature of 80 to 84 degrees, and was subject to the following penalties:—[5]

	s.	*d.*
Any spinner found with his window open	1	0
Any spinner found dirty at his work	1	0
Any spinner found washing himself	1	0
Any spinner leaving his oil can out of its place	1	0
Any spinner repairing his drum banding with his gas lighted	2	0
Any spinner slipping with his gas lighted	2	0
Any spinner putting his gas out too soon	1	0
Any spinner spinning with gas light too long in the morning	2	0
Any spinner having his lights too large for each light	1	0
Any spinner heard whistling	1	0
Any spinner having hard ends hanging on his weights	0	6
Any spinner having hard ends on carriage band	1	0
Any spinner being five minutes after last bell rings	1	0
Any spinner having roller laps, no more than two draws for each roller lap	0	6
Any spinner going further than the roving-room door when fetching rovings	1	0
Any spinner being sick and cannot find another spinner to give satisfaction must pay for steam per day	6	0
Any spinner found in another's wheel gate	1	0
Any spinner neglecting to send his sweepings three mornings in the week	1	0
Any spinner having a little waste on his spindles	1	0

[3] Bamford, *Early Days,* p. 103.
[4] Felkin, *History of Machine-Wrought Hosiery and Lace Manufactures,* p. 451.
[5] *Political Register,* August 30, 1823.

This list of fines was given by the spinners during a strike, in a pamphlet published at Manchester. The pamphlet adds, "At Tyldesley they work fourteen hours per day, including the nominal hour for dinner; the door is locked in working hours, except half an hour at tea time; the workpeople are not allowed to send for water to drink, in the hot factory; and even the rain water is locked up, by the master's order, otherwise they would be happy to drink even that."

In the modern world most people have to adapt themselves to some kind of discipline, and to observe other people's time-tables, to do other people's sums, or work under other people's orders, but we have to remember that the population that was flung into the brutal rhythm of the factory had earned its living in relative freedom, and that the discipline of the early factory was particularly savage. To understand what this discipline meant to men, women, and children, we have to remember too that poor people rarely had a clock in the house. Sadler said that you could hear the feet of children pattering along the dark streets long before the time for the mills to open.[6] No economist of the day, in estimating the gains and the losses of factory employment, ever allowed for the strain and violence that a man suffered in his feelings when he passed from a life in which he could smoke or eat, or dig or sleep as he pleased, to one in which somebody turned the key on him, and for fourteen hours he had not even the right to whistle.[7] It was like entering the airless and laughterless life of a prison. Unless we keep this moral sacrifice in mind, we shall not understand why the hand-loom weavers refused to go into the power-loom factories, where they would have earned much higher wages: a refusal that is an important fact in the history of the cotton industry.[8] Moreover, although to the authors of the books on the advantages of machinery, invention seemed to have lightened the drudgery of men and women, it had introduced a wearing tension: the nervous strain of watching machinery and working with machinery aged men and women faster than the heaviest physical exertions. The machinery never tired. "Whilst the engine runs the people must work—men, women, and children are yoked together with iron and steam. The animal machine—breakable in the best case, subject to a thousand sources of suffering—is chained fast to the iron machine, which knows no suffering and no weariness." [9]

[6] *Memoirs of Life and Writings of Sadler,* p. 374.

[7] An Englishman went to Rouen to superintend a factory there, and when he tried to establish the English discipline among workmen who were accustomed to leave their work as they pleased, there was a strike, and the soldiers had to be called in. See Evidence of Mr. Wm. Smith before Sadler's Committee.

[8] See Chapman, p. 46: "Only the direst necessity, however, could drive the typical hand-loom weaver into a steam factory, and not infrequently he preferred to fight famine at close quarters rather than surrender his liberty."

[9] *Moral and Physical Conditions of the Operatives employed in the Cotton Manufacture in Manchester,* by James Philip Kay, 1832, p. 24, quoted by Hutchins and Harrison, *History of Factory Legislation,* p. 50. Greg said that the work of a spinner was almost the most laborious work known (Fielden, p. 35).

The hours at Tyldesley were exceptionally long, but the normal working day in Manchester and the neighbourhood in 1825 varied from twelve and a half to fourteen hours,[10] and mills, like mines, sometimes worked day and night. Moreover, under the system there was a strong pressure for a longer day. A master spinner, who was a member of an association formed at Manchester in 1831 for the purpose of securing the observance of the earlier Factory Acts, gave it as his opinion that if there were no Factory Acts, the tremendous competition in the industry would make masters work their mills for the whole twenty-four hours with no relief except for meals.[11]

In 1824 the Macclesfield masters tried to lengthen the working day in the silk mills. The story was told by a silk spinner before the Committee on Artisans and Machinery.[12] The hours were from 6 A.M. to 6 P.M., and the masters published a paper signed by forty-five firms, stating that in future the hours in Macclesfield would be the same as those in the neighbouring towns, namely, from 6 A.M. to 7 P.M. The men refused to agree to this, and after several ineffectual meetings the masters withdrew their proposed rule. Each side appealed to the public. "It is a well-known fact," said the men, "that children very young are employed in the above branch; and can we as men submit to a proposition so highly indecorous, as to increase the hours of labour, knowing that it would not only greatly affect the present age, but ages yet unborn? You are well aware that we have of late obliged them, by working night and day for their peculiar interest." The masters, in announcing their decision not to press their demand, told the public "that it is deeply to be regretted, that the orderly, quiet, and peaceable working classes of this town and neighbourhood should so far have lost sight of their true interest, and given way to the representation of the vicious

[10] Hutchins and Harrison, *op. cit.,* p. 30.

[11] Factory Commission, Second Report, 1833, Mr. Tufnell, p. 50.

[12] Pp. 582–6.

and designing amongst them, as to reject the proposition of the masters, for working twelve hours to the day, with a proportionate addition to their wages." The witness told the Committee that the increase of wages was an afterthought, and that the men knew well enough that if it were granted, it would soon be withdrawn, on the pretence of trade stagnation. Moreover, there were children in the Macclesfield mills who were under five years of age. "We told them they had made cripples enough already in Macclesfield." [13]

It was not only the life of the men that was swallowed up in the factory. Women and children were shut out from the daylight as well.[14] The home life of Lancashire is described as follows [15] at the end of our time. The factory woman has had no time, no means, no opportunities of learning the common duties of domestic life. "Even if she had acquired the knowledge, she has still no time to practise them. In addition to the twelve hours' labour is an additional absence from home in the going and the returning. Here is the young mother absent from her child about twelve hours daily. And who has the charge of the infant in her absence? Usually some little girl or aged woman, who is hired for a trifle and whose services are equivalent to the reward. Too often the dwelling of the factory family is no home; it sometimes is a cellar, which includes no cookery, no washing, no making, no mending, no decencies of life, no invitations to the fireside." This point had been put in a letter to the Home Office from a Manchester correspondent as early as 1800.[16] "The people employed in the different manufactures are early introduced into them, many at five and six years old, both girls and boys, so that when the former become Women they have not had any opportunity of acquiring any habits of Domestic economy or the management of a family. . . . The greater part of the Working and lower class of people have not wives that can dress a joint of meat if they were to have it given them. The consequence is that such articles become their food that are the most easily acquired, consequently their general food now consists of bread and cheese." The writer goes on to mention that in a family known to him, 24s. out of 26s. or 28s. a week earned by its members are spent on bread.

The same sense of an inexorable and inhuman power overshadowed the mining population. Their living was gained in the midst of dangers and hardships of the most terrifying kind, for the age of great accidents and deeper mines had begun, and there was nothing in the administration of the system that seemed to take any account of their feelings.[17] The most brutal and direct illustration of the light in which they were regarded was the policy of intimidation and concealment practised by the coalowners when lives were lost in the mines. "As so many deplorable accidents have lately happened in collieries," said the *Newcastle Journal* in 1767, "it certainly claims the attention of coal owners to make a provision for the distressed widows and fatherless children occasioned by these

[13] It is interesting to note that in 1833 the manager of some silk mills in Macclesfield referred to this incident, dating it 1825, representing the proposal of the masters as a proposal to reduce the working day, and the men as standing out for thirteen hours. See Factory Commission, Second Report, 1833, Mr. Tufnell, p. 31. The witness wished to confirm his argument that a shorter working day would be unpopular.

[14] It was calculated in 1833 that the cotton mills employed 60,000 adult males, 65,000 adult females, 43,000 boys under eighteen, and 41,000 girls under eighteen. About half of those under eighteen were less than fourteen years old (Factory Commission, Supplementary Report, 1834, part i. p. 138). Of the factory operatives in 1839 rather less than a quarter were men over eighteen (Engels, *Condition of the Working Class in England in* 1844, quoting Ashley, p. 142). A manufacturer gave statistics to show that there were 10,721 married women employed in Lancashire factories; of the husbands of these women half were also employed in the factories, 3927 were otherwise employed, 821 were unemployed, and information was not forthcoming as to 659 (Engels, p. 147).

[15] Factory Commission, Second Report, 1833, Dr. Hawkins, p. 5.

[16] H. O., 42. 53.

[17] In one mine men were paid an extra allowance of 6d. a day for working in a temperature of 130 degrees, but 2d. was deducted for every hour lost (*A Voice from the Coal Mines*, 1825).

mines, as the catastrophes, from foul air, become more common than ever; yet as we are requested to take no particular notice of these things, which, in fact, could have very little good tendency, we drop the further mentioning of it." [18] Down to 1815 it was not the custom to hold inquests on the victims of accidents in the mines of Northumberland and Durham.[19] That public attention was drawn to the facts was due to two men, a judge and a parson. The judge was Sir John Bayley, who made very strong representations at the Assizes at Newcastle in 1814 on the scandal of omitting all inquiry into the circumstances under which hundreds of persons had lost their lives, and the parson was John Hodgson, Vicar of Jarrow, who, "braving the displeasure of the affluent Brandlings," wrote and published an account of the accident at Felling, in which ninety-two of his parishioners had perished. Hodgson's action led to the establishment of a Society at Sunderland for preventing accidents,[20] and it was in answer to an appeal from this Society that Sir Humphry Davy visited Newcastle and gave his mind to the problem.[21] Unfortunately even the alleviations of science were turned to the miner's disadvantage. The Davy lamp, for which the inventor refused to take out a patent, renouncing an income of £5000 or £10,000 a year, "his sole object to serve the cause of humanity," was used in many cases to serve the cause of profits. Deeper and more dangerous seams were worked, and accidents actually increased in number.[22] The writer of *A Voice from the Coal Mines,* a pamphlet published by the Northumberland miners in 1825, stated that since the introduction of the lamp the miner had had to work in still higher temperatures, under conditions that caused him physical agony. The Children's Employment Commission [23] reported in 1842 that in the West Riding the lamp was often made a substitute for ventilation, that in South Staffordshire accidents were so common that the people talked as if the whole population was engaged in a campaign, and that in Northumberland and Durham the mining population had become absolutely indifferent to its danger. The indifference of the coalowners scandalised this Commission, and commenting on the accidents that had occurred from negligence in the pits belonging to Curwen and Lord Lonsdale, they observed "when such management is allowed in the mines of two of the most opulent coal proprietors in the kingdom, we cease to wonder at anything that may take place in mines worked by men equally without capital and science." The Commission were severe on the conduct of coalowners and their agents, in throwing all the blame on their workpeople and making them responsible for chains and tackle, but they were most severe about the tasks on which children were employed. In Derbyshire, and some parts of Lancanshire and Cheshire, especially around Oldham, it was the custom to employ children to let down and draw up the workpeople. The Chief Constable of Oldham mentioned a case in which three or four boys were killed because the attention of the child of nine years who was in charge of the engine for drawing up the cage was distracted by a mouse. But in all mines children were employed on most responsible work, and the Commission concluded that it was astonishing that accidents were not more frequent, seeing that all expedients for safety might be counteracted by allowing a single trap door to remain open,[24] "and yet in all the coal

[18] *Newcastle Journal,* March 14, 1767.
[19] Boyd, *Coal Pits and Pitmen,* p. 67.
[20] Galloway, *History of Coal Mining,* pp. 157 and 179.
[21] Evidence of Founder of Society (Wilkinson) before Select Committee on Accidents in Mines, 1835.
[22] The Select Committee on Accidents in 1835 reported that there were 447 death in Northumberland and Durham in the eighteen years before 1816, and 538 in the eighteen years following.
[23] See First Report of Commission for inquiring into employment of children in mines and manufactures, 1842.
[24] The whole system of ventilation in mines depended on the shutting of the trap doors.

mines, in all the districts of the United Kingdom, the care of these trap doors is entrusted to children of from five to seven or eight years of age, who for the most part sit, excepting at the moments when persons pass through these doors, for twelve hours consecutively in solitude, silence and darkness." [25] Sir J. C. Hippisley, a Somerset magistrate, wrote to the Home Office in 1817: "At the great colliery of Clan Down . . . from 100 to 150 men are employed in the veins at a perpendicular depth of above 1200 feet, and it is in the power of an idle or mischievous Engine Boy to drown the whole of them without destroying or injuring the Fire Engine." [26] The magistrate noted this as an argument, not for prohibiting the employment of boys in such responsible work, but for making the punishment for damaging collieries more drastic.

The population that lived thus on the brink of the mines and the brink of the next world became an hereditary race. In some parts of England the women worked as well as the men. Women were employed in Durham at the beginning of the eighteenth century, for there were women killed in explosions in Gateshead (1705) and Chester-le-Street (1708), but the practice died out there before the end of the century.[27] Women were also said to have been killed in an explosion in Whitehaven. When the Children's Employment Commission reported in 1842, women were working in the pits in the West Riding, in Cheshire, in some parts of Lancashire, and in South Wales. The custom had strict local frontiers, as a miner found when he went from Wigan, where women were so employed, to Oldham, where the feeling was strong against it. Women were apparently not employed down the Lancashire mines east of Manchester. They were generally employed as "drawers," *i.e.* in carrying or pushing the corves containing the coal "won" by the hewers, for the men liked women in this capacity, finding them easy to manage, and yet too spirited to let others pass them. Also, though women coal-getters were not unknown, they were rare, and therefore the danger of competition for employment was diminished by using women for "drawing." [28] A witness told the Commission of 1842 that a married woman miner worked day and night, the day being spent in the mine and the night in washing, cooking, and cleaning her house. Children were employed from earliest years, some so young that they were put to bed when they got home. The working day varied; for men it was often twelve hours, for women and children it was longer. At the Felling Pit at the beginning of the nineteenth century boys' hours were from eighteen to twenty. There was thus little daylight for father or children out of the mine. The race lived underground like the refugees in *Les Misérables,* who lived in the sewers of Paris. One miner described how he used to put his child in its cradle in the seam where he worked, to keep the rats off his dinner. Children who were going to work in the mines were often brought to the pit on their fathers' backs.[29]

If the treatment of the miners gave the new society the look of a civilisation in which human life seemed a good deal less important than the profits of capital, the same impression was made, not on the working classes only, by the behaviour of the ship-owners on the Tyne and Wear. In 1815 there

[25] Mr. Buddle told the Lords Committee on the Coal Trade in 1829 that there was no provision for the victims of accidents except parochial relief and the generosity of the employers. He had never known an employer turn out a widow after an accident, and often if she had a boy he was "indulged with some employment at advanced wages."

[26] H. O., 42. 161.

[27] Galloway (*Annals of Coal Mining,* 1st series, p. 305) says employment of women and girls underground in Tyne and Wear district ceased about 1780.

[28] Boyd, *op. cit.,* says women hewed in Yorkshire, and in most districts only "hurried" (p. 84).

[29] According to census of 1841, there were 83,408 men over twenty, 32,475 under twenty, 1185 women over twenty, and 1165 under twenty (Engels, p. 241).

For documents on the subject, see H. O., 42. 146.

was a seamen's strike in the north-eastern ports, which was suppressed after a long struggle by the use of troops. The cause of the strike was the conduct of the shipowners, who made a practice of undermanning their ships and refused, in spite of the appeals of the magistrates, to bind themselves to any fixed scale. Local opinion was largely on the side of the seamen, and the behaviour of the owners was stigmatised in severe language by the general commanding the troops, by several of the magistrates, including the Vicar of Bishops Wearmouth, and by a Home Office envoy who, going down to the scene of the dispute with the strongest bias against the men, gradually learned that the seamen who had upset the entire industry of the ports, forbidding any boat to leave without their sanction and taking over the discipline of the towns, had been driven to these measures by the masters' wanton disregard of life. "Ships from these ports," he wrote to Sidmouth, "have gone to sea shamefully deficient in strength to navigate them, and should ever the subject excite the attention of the legislature, hundreds of cases may be produced in which avarice has risked at sea a helpless insufficient crew in a crazy but highly insured ship." After a good deal of bickering between the Home Office and the Admiralty a twenty-gun ship was sent to Shields. The sentiments of the bluejackets were so strong that the officers doubted whether they would act against the men, and the officers themselves were scarcely less warm in their sympathy with the cause of the seamen or their admiration of their bearing and discipline. They tried to act as mediators, but found that the seamen would not accept any undertakings that did not formally bind the masters. The men's suspicions were soon justified. Cartwright, the Home Office envoy, described in a letter to Sidmouth how he found himself at a public table among shipowners, and "heard a full discussion of the subject. They openly, to my deep disgust, avowed the base dissimulation with which they are acting, and that they intend to observe any terms they may *agree to* only till the present compact association and the consequent danger are dispersed." General Riall describes a characteristic incident after the men had been overcome by military force. "At Sunderland, where a compromise had been made with the Ship Owners and an agreement entered into with the Seamen that a certain number were to be taken into each Ship according to her size or Tonnage, they have broken their faith, in a very shameful manner, the numbers were actually taken on board *eight* ships, but after the ships had got a certain distance from the Harbour the extra men they had promised to take were relanded." In this case, although the men's demand commended itself as fundamentally just to persons who were shocked by their way of presenting it, no influence could prevent the masters from taking complete advantage of the victory they owed to the intervention of the forces of the Crown, and magistrates continued to urge the Home Office in vain for measures to enforce some respect for human life on this formidable interest.

The new power of capital seemed all the more crushing and overwhelming because even the efforts of leading employers could not soften its incidence. Brotherton, when he was sent to the Reformed Parliament by the electors of Salford, put this truth about the agitation against the long hours of children. Parents had petitioned in their tens of thousands, and forty of the largest manufacturers in Manchester had signed a manifesto, but unless the law intervened, no force could shake a system that was defended, in some quarters as essential to manufacturers, in others as essential to parents. John Fielden, according to Cobbett, worked up one-hundredth part of all the cotton imported into England, and he employed two thousand persons, but neither he nor any other employer believed it possible to abate the evils of the system under which they grew rich, without the help of Parliament and the successful coercion of the entire class of employers.[30] It happened more than once in the course of agitations for better wages that the workmen were able to enlist the support and sympathy of a considerable body of masters, but sympathy and support were valueless, because Parliament would not ratify their wishes. Men might work astonishing miracles in acquiring mastery and guidance over the forces of fire and water, but the industrial system itself was so contrived as to make the public spirit, or the human sympathy, or the generous commonsense of the best employers, dependent on the selfishness or indifference or the blind greed of the worst. A good man who built a mill gave a hostage to the man who wanted to work the longest hours at the lowest wages. The history of the cotton industry, of the framework knitters, and of the ribbon weavers shows that there were many employers who understood that low wages were bad for industry and bad for the nation. With the economic notions then in power, the workmen had to convince either the most unenlightened employer or Parliament before they could obtain a remedy. Even Robert Owen's successful experiment in the economy of good wages and shorter hours made no impression on his competitors. The fierce struggle that is the subject of this book looks from one point of view like a class conflict of a most cruel and exhausting kind. So it was: but it was none the less a conflict in which there were employers as eager for the victory of the men as the men themselves. In the old days the workmen were dealing with a comparatively small circle of masters; they were now pitted against a system, and not only they, but every good employer and every good citizen as well. At Leicester on one occasion the men were supported by the Lord Lieutenant, Mayor, Aldermen, and the churches and chapels. The Industrial Revolution had delivered society from its primitive dependence on the forces of nature, but in return it had taken society prisoner.

The spectacle of this new power as a profane and brutal system that spared neither soul nor body, and denied to men and women the right to human treatment, was impressed upon the imagination with special force by its ruthless violation of all the ties and affections of the family. These ties were particularly strong in a community where the rich would not have expected to find them. All observers agreed that among the miners the women had great influence over their husbands, and that they were invariably consulted on all questions of strikes and combinations. "The females exercise or are destined early to exercise an unusual and unlimited influence over the miners: and nearly the whole of the arrangements and duties of upper ground life are by common consent deputed to them." [31] The idea of the family wage as the economic unit, though not of course explicitly formulated, governed men's thinking about the industrial system, and thus the factories seemed to offer special advantages to the poor by providing employment for their children. A manifesto from the Female Political Union of Newcastle, in 1839, put just the opposite view that it was a special grievance that men's wages were so low that the mother and her small children were driven to work at a labour that degraded soul and body.[32]

When the revolt against the barbarities began, it was a common retort that if this system was bad the parents were to blame, for they sent their children into the factory. This argument disregarded history. The system began with serf labour from the workhouses, and it was not until the weavers had been reduced to want that they took their children to the hated mill.[33] In many par-

[30] In Fielden's mill the hours were at first ten a day. His father, competing with men using the same machinery and working for 77 to 84 hours in the week, raised the hours to 12 a day and 11 on Saturday. After 1819 (under Peel's Act) the hours for children were reduced to 72 (*Curse of the Factory System,* p. 34).

[31] Children's Employment Commission, Report of 1842.

[32] Dolléans, *Le Chartisme,* vol. i. p. 241.

[33] The first children were the sons of Irish weavers (Fielden, p. 12).

ishes the overseers refused relief unless the children went out to work.[34] A family could not live on an income of five or six shillings a week. Cobbett described how women took their children to the mill through the snow; the child was crying, but the mother too was crying.[35] It is true, again, that a great deal of the beating in the factories was done by the workpeople without orders, or even against orders, but that only emphasized the brutality of the system. Fathers beat their own children to save them from a worse beating by some one else; overseers and spinners beat children, sometimes no doubt from sheer brutality, but often because they had to get so much work out of them or go. In 1833 nearly two-thirds of the boys in mills, and one-third of the girls, were directly employed by men workers,[36] but the men workers did not prescribe the hours or the volume of work to be done. The system imposed on children more work and longer hours than human nature could bear, and somebody had to wring it out of them. Everywhere this cruel necessity hemmed in the life of the new society, and the new system wore a more inexorable face just because it made workmen, or even parents, the agents of its iron rule. In some cases, of course, not involuntary agents, for there have always been parents ready to exploit their children, and the factory system offered a powerful incentive to that spirit. One witness before a Lords Committee boasted that he had broken his child's arm for disobedience in the mill. A system such as this was bound to find parents, and bound to make parents, callous to their children's sufferings, and no charge more bitter could be brought against it.

That system further aggravated the horrors of industrial life by setting up a class of small contractors for child labour. The piecers were generally provided and paid by the wheelmen or spinners out of the wages per lb. weight they received from the millowner.[37] One of the witnesses, Mr. George Gould, before Peel's Committee in 1816, said that spinning men and women were allowed to employ children of their own selecting, and if they could get a child to do their business for a shilling, or one and six, "they would take that child before they would give four, five, six, or seven shillings to an older one." [38] In the mines, again, the women and children who dragged the tubs were sometimes engaged and employed by the hewers. Thus the avarice of men and women of their own class was made another scourge for the backs of the children. The vested interest thus established has been at all times a serious obstacle to reforms, and the industrial life of the nation has not yet been freed from it.

The miners were a better paid class than the weavers during the last part of the period discussed in this book, but if their earnings were higher, the nature of their work made a higher expenditure on food necessary. A pamphlet was published by the Northumberland miners in 1825, with the title *A Voice from the Coal Mines*. The writer takes a man with wife and three children and puts his gross earnings at £2 a fortnight. This, he

[34] See, *e.g.*, the evidence of William Osburn, ex-overseer of Leeds, before Sadler's Committee as to the practice of the Leeds overseers; also of assistant overseer of Keighley (G. Sharpe).

[35] Oastler was asked by Sadler's Committee whether he knew instances in which parents lived entirely on the earnings of their children, and he replied: "Yes, I met with a case, a little while ago, of a man who lives a short distance from my house, and who said to me, 'I hope you will get this Ten Hours Bill passed; I have two children, one seven and the other thirteen, at work at the factories, and I have not had the least stroke for' —I think he said—'the last thirteen months.' He told me that they were earning seven or eight shillings a week, and he said, 'That little girl has to go a mile and a half very early, to her work, and she comes home at half-past eight, and all that I see of her is to call her up in the morning, and send her to bed, and it almost makes my heart break. We cannot get any work, and I know that I am living by the death of that child'; and he cried when he told me. In fact, they weep when they tell their tales, and the poor children weep too."—Quoted, Wing, *Evils of the Factory System,* p. 100.

[36] Factory Commission, Supplementary Report, 1834, part i. p. 138.

[37] See Colonel Fletcher of Bolton's letter about the Factories, H. O., 52. 3.

[38] Quoted Hutchins and Harrison, *op. cit.*, p. 25.

says, is a high figure. Deductions for fines, rent, and candles will bring it down to thirty shillings, or fifteen shillings a week. How far will this go?

	s.	*d.*
Bread, 2½ stone at 2s. 6d. per stone	6	3
1 lb. of butcher's meat a day, 7d. per lb.	4	1
2 pecks of potatoes at 1s. a peck	2	0
Oatmeal and milk for seven breakfasts at 4½d each morning	2	8
	15	0
The family need as well to produce comfort—		
2 oz. of tea at 6d. per oz.	1	0
2 lbs. sugar at 8d. per lb.	1	4
1 lb. salt butter	1	2
1 lb. cheese	0	9
Pepper, salt, mustard, vinegar	0	4
Soap, starch, blue, etc.	1	6
Tobacco, 1½ oz.	0	5¼
1 pint of ale a day	1	9
Clothing for five persons	3	0
£1	6	3¼

Is this too much? the writer asks, and he replies that many colliers would die of want if they did not take their children to work fourteen hours a day as soon as they could speak and walk.

The Oldham miners issued a handbill in 1818 addressed to the gentlemen of Oldham and Manchester.[39] "It is well known to the greatest part of you that when you come to the side of a Coal Pit for to look down, that sight will make many of you to tremble; but was you to go down to the bottom of the Pit, and there see the dangers that Colliers are exposed to, you would never think the wages too much was they to get a Pound per day. . . . We think it very hard that we must be confined in the bowels of the Earth from 9 to 10 and from that to an 11 and 12 hours or more to the day, for 10 to 12, and from that to 14 shillings per week." One of the Factory Commissioners took evidence from miners in 1833, and the answers to his questions showed that in Lancashire men got 15s. a week when in full employment, but often they did not receive more than 10s. in the week, and out of that they had to pay for tools and candles. It was stated that colliers were short lived, and that if they lived to fifty they were unable to work and came upon the parish.[40]

The depreciation of human life was thus the leading fact about the new system for the working classes. The human material was used up rapidly; workmen were called old at forty; [41] the arrangements of society ensured an infinite supply; women and children were drawn in, and at the end the working class, which was now contributing not only the men but the entire family, seemed to be what it was at the beginning, a mere part of the machinery without share in the increased wealth or the increased power over life that machinery had brought. For the revolution that had raised the standard of comfort for the rich had depressed the standard of life for the poor; [42] it had given to the capitalist a new importance, while it had degraded the workpeople to be the mere muscles of industry. Men, women, and children were in the grasp of a great machine that threatened to destroy all sense of the dignity of human life. We have now to see what inspirations were to be found in the towns where they lived, or in the character and aspect of government, justice, law, and order, to keep that struggling sense alive.

[39] H. O., 42. 179.

[40] The Commission of 1842 reported that in Lancashire, Derbyshire, and Yorkshire "each generation of this class of the population is commonly extinct soon after fifty."

[41] Engels, *op. cit.*, p. 160. Sadler said that spinners rarely lived beyond forty.

[42] Compare Knight's letter to Sidmouth, July 17, 1817 (H. O., 42. 168): "MY LORD,—I have always been intimately acquainted with the circumstances of the labouring class in the vicinity of Manchester, and I can assure your Lordship that they have seen very few good days since the year 1792, compared with those they experienced before that period; notwithstanding the vast improvements which have during that time been made in their Manufactures."

FORTY-TWO
SOCIAL PROTEST

Benjamin Disraeli (1804–81), one of Britain's most distinguished prime ministers, led a major movement for social reform in the Victorian period. Disraeli, a humanitarian and romantic, had genuine sympathy for industrial workers. Disraeli also hoped that by sponsoring social reform he might give the Conservative (Tory) Party a positive program to replace its former do-nothing reaction. He accordingly formulated Tory Democracy, in which the crown and aristocracy would protect the masses against middle-class Liberal (Whig) industrialists. In his many novels, among them Sybil, *as well as in many speeches, Disraeli described the horrors of working conditions in British industry. One of the characters in* Sybil *states, "There is more serfdom in England now than at any time since the Conquest [A.D. 1066]. I speak of what passes under my daily eyes when I say, that those who labour can as little choose or change their masters now, as when they were born thralls. There are great bodies of the working classes of this country nearer the condition of brutes than they have been at any time since the Conquest. Indeed, I see nothing to distinguish them from brutes, except that their morals are inferior." He hardly exaggerated. Parliamentary and other investigations generally corroborated this sweeping indictment. Disraeli was among the earliest of British statesmen to contend that Liberalism, with its central concern for political and economic freedoms, ignored a central domestic problem of the West during the nineteenth century, that is, the just distribution of wealth within the new industrial order. Because he prodded Britain's social conscience and helped to put community problems in economic instead of political terms, Disraeli has assumed a position of first prominence in the long history of modern society's adjustment to the Industrial Revolution. His contribution in this respect alone entitles him to greatness.*

BENJAMIN DISRAELI
SYBIL OR THE TWO NATIONS*

Wodgate, or Wogate, as it was called on the map, was a district that in old days had been consecrated to Woden, and which appeared destined through successive ages to retain its heathen character. At the beginning of the Revolutionary War, Wodgate was a sort of squatting district of the great mining region to which it was contiguous, a place

* From Benjamin Disraeli, *Sybil, or The Two Nations,* Book 3, chs. 4, 7. First published in 1845.

where adventurers in the industry which was rapidly developing, settled themselves; for though the great veins of coal and ironstone cropped up, as they phrase it, before they reached this bare and barren land, and it was thus deficient in those mineral and metallic treasures which had enriched its neighbourhood, Wodgate had advantages of its own, and of a kind which touch the fancy of the lawless. It was land without an owner; no one claimed any manorial right over it; they could build cottages without paying rent. It was a district recognized by no parish; so there were no tithes, and no meddlesome supervision. It abounded in fuel which cost nothing, for though the veins were not worth working as a source of mining profit, the soil of Wodgate was similar in its superficial character to that of the country around. So a population gathered, and rapidly increased, in the ugliest spot in England, to which neither Nature nor Art had contributed a single charm; where a tree could not be seen, a flower was unknown, where there was neither belfry nor steeple, nor a single sight or sound that could soften the heart or humanize the mind.

Whatever may have been the cause, whether, as not unlikely, the original squatters brought with them some traditionary skill, or whether their isolated and unchequered existence concentrated their energies on their craft, the fact is certain, that the inhabitants of Wodgate early acquired a celebrity as skilful workmen. This reputation so much increased, and in time spread so far, that, for more than a quarter of a century, both in their skill and the economy of their labour, they have been unmatched throughout the country. As manufacturers of ironmongery, they carry the palm from the whole district; as founders of brass and workers of steel, they fear none; while, as nailers and locksmiths, their fame has spread even to the European markets, whither their most skilful workmen have frequently been invited.

Invited in vain! No wages can tempt the Wodgate man from his native home, that squatters' seat which soon assumed the form of a large village, and then in turn soon expanded into a town, and at the present moment numbers its population by swarming thousands, lodged in the most miserable tenements in the most hideous borough in the ugliest country in the world.

But it has its enduring spell. Notwithstanding the spread of its civic prosperity, it has lost none of the characteristics of its original society; on the contrary, it has zealously preserved them. There are no landlords, head-lessees, main-masters, or butties in Wodgate. No church there has yet raised its spire; and, as if the jealous spirit of Woden still haunted his ancient temple, even the conventicle scarcely dares show its humble front in some obscure corner. There is no municipality, no magistrate; there are no local acts, no vestries, no schools of any kind. The streets are never cleaned; every man lights his own house; nor does any one know anything except his business.

More than this, at Wodgate a factory or large establishment of any kind is unknown. Here Labour reigns supreme. Its division indeed is favoured by their manners, but the interference or influence of mere capital is instantly resisted. The business of Wodgate is carried on by master workmen in their own houses, each of whom possesses an unlimited number of what they call apprentices, by whom their affairs are principally conducted, and whom they treat as the Mamelukes treated the Egyptians.

These master workmen indeed form a powerful aristocracy, nor is it possible to conceive one apparently more oppressive. They are ruthless tyrants; they habitually inflict upon their subjects punishments more grievous than the slave population of our colonies were ever visited with; not content with beating them with sticks or flogging them with knotted ropes, they are in the habit of felling them with hammers, or cutting their heads open with a file or lock. The most usual punishment, however, or rather stimulus to increase exertion, is to pull an apprentice's ears till they run with blood. These youths, too, are worked for sixteen and even twenty hours a day; they are often sold by one master to another; they are fed on carrion, and they sleep in lofts or cellars: yet, whether it be that they are hardened by brutality, and really unconscious of their degradation and unusual sufferings, or whether they are supported by the belief that their day to be masters and oppressors will surely arrive, the aristocracy of Wodgate is by no means so unpopular as the aristocracy of most other places.

In the first place, it is a real aristocracy; it is privileged, but it does something for its privileges. It is distinguished from the main body not merely by name. It is the most knowing class at Wodgate; it possesses indeed in its way complete knowledge; and it imparts in its manner a certain quantity of it to those whom it guides. Thus it is an aristocracy that leads, and therefore a fact. Moreover the social system of Wodgate is not an unvarying course of infinite toil. Their plan is to work hard, but not always. They seldom exceed four days of labour in the week. On Sunday the masters begin to drink; for the apprentices there is dog-fighting without any stint. On Monday and Tuesday the whole population of Wodgate is drunk; of all stations, ages, and sexes, even babes who should be at the breast; for they are drammed with Godfrey's cordial. Here is relaxation, excitement; if less vice otherwise than might be at first anticipated, we must remember that excesses are checked by poverty of blood and constant exhaustion. Scanty food and hard labour are in their way, if not exactly moralists, a tolerably good police.

There are no others at Wodgate to preach or to control. It is not that the people are immoral, for immorality implies some forethought; or ignorant, for ignorance is relative; but they are animals; unconscious; their minds a blank; and their worst actions only the impulse of a gross or savage instinct. There are many in this town who are ignorant of their very names; very few who can spell them. It is rare that you meet with a young person who knows his own age; rarer to find the boy who has seen a book, or the girl who has seen a flower. Ask them the name of their sovereign, and they will give you an unmeaning stare; ask them the name of their religion, and they will laugh: who rules them on earth, or who can save them in heaven, are alike mysteries to them.

Such was the population with whom Morley was about to mingle. Wodgate had the appearance of a vast squalid suburb. As you advanced, leaving behind you long lines of little dingy tenements, with infants lying about the road, you expected every moment to emerge into some streets, and encounter buildings bearing some correspondence, in their size and comfort, to the considerable population swarming and busied around you. Nothing of the kind. There were no public buildings of any sort; no churches, chapels, town-hall, institute, theatre; and the principal streets in the heart of the town in which were situate the coarse and grimy shops, though formed by houses of a greater elevation than the preceding, were equally narrow, and if possible more dirty. At every fourth or fifth house, alleys seldom above a yard wide, and streaming with filth, opened out of the street. These were crowded with dwellings of various size, while from the principal court often branched out a number of smaller alleys, or rather narrow passages, than which nothing can be conceived more close and squalid and obscure. Here, during the days of business, the sound of the hammer and the file never ceased, amid gutters of abomination, and piles of foulness, and stagnant pools of filth; reservoirs of leprosy and plague, whose exhalations were sufficient to taint the atmosphere of the whole kingdom, and fill the country with fever and pestilence.

A lank and haggard youth, rickety and smoke-dried, and black with his craft, was sitting on the threshold of a miserable hovel, and working at the file. Behind him stood a stunted and meagre girl, with a back like a grasshopper; a deformity occasioned by the displacement of the bladebone, and prevalent among the girls of Wodgate from the cramping posture of their usual toil. Her long melancholy visage and vacant stare at Morley as he passed, attracted his notice, and it occurring to him that the opportunity was convenient to inquire something of the individual of whom he was in search, he stopped and addressed the workman:

'Do you happen to know, friend, a person here or hereabouts by name Hatton?'

'Hatton!' said the youth, looking up with a grin, yet still continuing his labour, 'I should think I did!'

'Well, that's fortunate; you can tell me something about him?'

'Do you see this here?' said the youth, still grinning, and, letting the file drop from his distorted and knotty hand, he pointed to a deep scar that crossed his forehead, 'he did that.'

'An accident?'

'Very like. An accident that often happened. I should like to have a crown for every time he has cut my head open. He cut it open once with a key, and twice with a lock; he knocked the corner of a lock into my head twice, once with a bolt, and once with a shut; you know what that is; the thing what runs into the staple. He hit me on the head with a hammer once. That was a blow! I fell away that time. When I came to, master had stopped the blood with some fur off his hat. I had to go on with my work immediately; master said I should do my stint if I worked till twelve o'clock at night. Many's the ash stick he has broken on my body; sometimes the weals remained on me for a week; he cut my eyelid open once with a nutstick; cut a regular hole in it, and it bled all over the files I was working at. He has pulled my ears sometimes that I thought they must come off in his hand. But all this was a mere nothin' to this here cut; that was serious; and if I hadn't got thro' that, they do say there must have been a crowner's quest; though I think that gammon, for old Tugsford did for one of his prentices, and the body was never found. And now you ask me if I know Hatton? I should think I did!' And the lank, haggard youth laughed merrily, as if he had been recounting a series of the happiest adventures.

'But is there no redress for such iniquitous oppression?' said Morley, who had listened with astonishment to this complacent statement. 'Is there no magistrate to apply to?'

'No, no,' said the filer with an air of obvious pride, 'we don't have no magistrates at Wodgate. We've got a constable, and there was a prentice who, coz his master laid it on only with a heat rod, went over to Ramborough and got a warrant. He fetched the summons himself, and giv it to the constable, but he never served it. That's why they has a constable here.'

'I am sorry,' said Morley, 'that I have affairs with such a wretch as this Hatton.'

'You'll find him a wery hearty sort of man,' said the filer, 'if he don't hap to be in drink. He's a little robustious then, but take him all in all for a master, you may go further and fare worse.'

'What! this monster!'

'Lord bless you, it's his way, that's all; we be a queer set here; but he has his pints. Give him a lock to make, and you won't have your box picked; he's wery lib'ral too in the wittals. Never had horse-flesh the whole time I was with him; they has nothin' else at Tugsford's; never had no sick cow except when meat was very dear. He always put his face agin still-born calves; he used to say he liked his boys to have meat what was born alive, and killed alive. By which token there never was any sheep what had bust in the head sold in our court. And then sometimes he would give us a treat of fish, when it had been four or five days in town, and not sold. No, give the devil his due, say I. There never was no want for anything at meals with the bishop, except time to eat them in.'

'And why do you call him the bishop?'

'That's his name and authority; for he's the governor here over all of us. And it has always been so that Wodgate has been governed by a bishop; because as we have no church, we will have as good. And by this token that this day se'nnight, the day my time was up, he married me to this here young lady. She is of the Baptist school religion, and wanted us to be tied by her clergyman, but all the lads that served their time with me were married by the bishop, and many a more, and I saw no call to do no otherwise. So he sprinkled some salt over a gridiron, read "Our Father" backward, and wrote our name in a book: and we were spliced; but I didn't do it rashly, did I, Suky, by the token that we had kept company for two years, and there isn't a gal in all Wodgate what handles a file like Sue.'

'And what is your name, my good fellow?"

'They call me Tumma, but I ain't got no second name; but now I am married I mean to take my wife's, for she has been baptized, and so has got two.'

'Yes, sir,' said the girl with the vacant face and the back like a grasshopper; 'I be a reg'lar born Christian and my mother afore me, and that's what few gals in the Yard can say. Thomas will take to it himself when work is slack; and he believes now in our Lord and Saviour Pontius Pilate, who was crucified to save our sins; and in Moses, Goliath, and the rest of the Apostles.'

'Ah! me,' thought Morley, 'and could not they spare one Missionary from Tahiti for their fellow-countrymen at Wodgate!'. . .

At the end of a court in Wodgate, of rather larger dimensions than usual in that town, was a high and many-windowed house, of several stories in height, which had been added to it at intervals. It was in a most dilapidated state; the principal part occupied as a nail-workshop, where a great number of heavy iron machines were working in every room on each floor; the building itself in so shattered a condition that every part of it creaked and vibrated with their motion. The flooring was so broken that in many places one could look down through the gaping and rotten planks, while the upper floors from time to time had been shored up with props.

This was the Palace of the Bishop of Wodgate, and here, with his arms bare and black, he worked at those locks, which defied any skeleton key that was not made by himself. He was a short, thickset man, powerfully made, with brawny arms disproportionately short even for his height, and with a countenance, as far as one could judge of a face so disfigured by his grimy toil, rather brutal than savage. His choice apprentices, full of admiration and terror, worked about him; lank and haggard youths, who never for an instant dared to raise their dingy faces and lack-lustre eyes from their ceaseless labour. On each side of their master, seated on a stool higher than the rest, was an urchin of not more than four or five years of age, serious and demure, and as if proud of his eminent position, and working incessantly at his little file:—these were two sons of the bishop.

'Now, boys,' said the bishop, in a hoarse, harsh voice, 'steady there; steady. There's a file what don't sing; can't deceive my ear; I know all their voices. Don't let me find that 'un out, or I won't walk into him, won't I? Ain't you lucky, boys, to have reg'lar work like this, and the best of prog! It worn't my lot, I can tell you that. Give me that shut, you there, Scrubbynose, can't you move? Look sharp, or I won't move you, won't I? Steady, steady! All right! That's music. Where will you hear music like twenty files all working at once! You ought to be happy, boys, oughtn't you? Won't there be a treat of fish after this, that's all! Hulloa, there, you red-haired varmint, what are you looking after? Three boys looking about them; what's all this? won't I be among you?' and he sprang forward and seized the luckless ears of the first apprentice he could get hold of, and wrung them till the blood spouted forth.

'Please, bishop,' sang out the boy, 'it worn't my fault. Here's a man what wants you.'

'Who wants me?' said the bishop, looking round, and he caught the figure of Morley, who had just entered the shop.

'Well, what's your will? Locks or nails?'

'Neither,' said Morley; 'I wish to see a man named Hatton.'

'Well, you see a man named Hatton,' said the bishop; 'and now what do you want of him?'

'I should like to say a word to you alone,' said Morley.

'Hem! I should like to know who is to finish this lock, and to look after my boys! If it's an order, let's have it at once.'

'It is not an order,' said Morley.

'Then I don't want to hear nothing about it,' said the bishop.

'It's about family matters,' said Morley.

'Ah!' said Hatton, eagerly, 'what, do you come from him?'

'It may be,' said Morley.

Upon this the bishop, looking up to the ceiling of the room in which there were several large chinks, began calling out lustily to some unseen person above, and immediately was replied to in a shrill voice of objurgation, demanding in peremptory words, interlarded with many oaths, what he wanted. His reply called down his unseen correspondent, who soon entered his workshop. It was the awful presence of Mrs Hatton; a tall, bearded virago, with a file in her hand, for that seemed the distinctive arm of the house, and eyes flashing with unbridled power.

'Look after the boys,' said Hatton, 'for I have business.'

'Won't I?' said Mrs Hatton; and a thrill of terror pervaded the assembly. All the files moved in regular melody; no one dared to raise his face; even her two young children looked still more serious and demure. Not that any being present flattered himself for an instant that the most sedulous attention on his part could prevent an outbreak; all that each aspired to, and wildly hoped, was that he might not be the victim singled out to have his head cut open, or his eye knocked out, or his ears half pulled off by the being who was the terror not only of the workshop, but of Wodgate itself,—their bishop's gentle wife.

FORTY-THREE
MARXISM

Marxism, a violent reaction against the social abuses of the Industrial Revolution, originated early in 1848 when Karl Marx (1818–83) and his friend Friedrich Engels (1820–95) published the Manifesto of the Communist Party, *commonly known as the* Communist Manifesto. *Marx believed that economic forces determined the historic process in a dialectic (adapted from Hegel) in which dominant economic interests (social classes) oppressed weaker economic interests (social classes), only to meet inevitable overthrow. In sum, as he stated succinctly in the* Communist Manifesto, *"The history of all hitherto existing society is the history of class struggles." In particular, Marx believed that the dominant bourgeois (capitalist) class of industrial society would increasingly oppress factory workers (proletarians) and in so doing would provoke unavoidable revolution. The result, he believed, would be a classless society. Marx developed his ideas fully in* Das Capital, *a turgid and tedious work, the first volume of which appeared in 1867. But the* Communist Manifesto *presents the gist of his long and complicated argument in such simple and dramatic prose that it still ranks as an outstanding piece of modern propaganda.*

KARL MARX AND FRIEDRICH ENGELS
MANIFESTO OF THE COMMUNIST PARTY *

A spectre is haunting Europe—the spectre of Communism. All the powers of old Europe have entered into a holy alliance to exorcise this spectre: Pope and Czar, Metternich and Guizot, French Radicals and German police-spies.

Where is the party in opposition that has not been decried as communistic by its opponents in power? Where the Opposition that has not hurled back the branding reproach of Communism, against the more advanced opposition parties, as well as against its reactionary adversaries?

Two things result from this fact:

I. Communism is already acknowledged by all European powers to be itself a power.

II. It is high time that Communists should openly, in the face of the whole world, publish their views, their aims, their tendencies, and meet this nursery tale of the spectre of Communism with a manifesto of the party itself.

To this end, Communists of various nationalities have assembled in London, and sketched the following manifesto, to be

* Karl Marx and Friedrich Engels, *Manifesto of the Communist Party,* pp. 8–21, 43–44. Authorized English translation by Samuel F. Moore, ed., Engels, New York, 1888.

published in the English, French, German, Italian, Flemish and Danish languages.

The history of all hitherto existing society is the history of class struggles.

Freeman and slave, patrician and plebeian, lord and serf, guildmaster and journeyman, in a word, oppressor and oppressed, stood in constant opposition to one another, carried on an uninterrupted, now hidden, now open fight, a fight that each time ended, either in a revolutionary reconstitution of society at large, or in the common ruin of the contending classes.

In the earlier epochs of history, we find almost everywhere a complicated arrangement of society into various orders, a manifold gradation of social rank. In ancient Rome we have patricians, knights, plebians, slaves; in the Middle Ages, feudal lords, vassals, guild-masters, journeymen, apprentices, serfs; in almost all of these classes, again, subordinate gradations.

The modern bourgeois society that has sprouted from the ruins of feudal society, has not done away with class antagonisms. It has but established new classes, new conditions of oppression, new forms of struggle in place of the old ones.

Our epoch, the epoch of the bourgeoisie, possesses, however, this distinctive feature: It has simplified the class antagonisms. Society as a whole is more and more splitting up into two great hostile camps, into two great classes directly facing each other—bourgeoisie and proletariat.

From the serfs of the Middle Ages sprang the chartered burghers of the earliest towns. From these burgesses the first elements of the bourgeoisie were developed.

The discovery of America, the rounding of the Cape, opened up fresh ground for the rising bourgeoisie. The East-Indian and Chinese markets, the colonisation of America, trade with the colonies, the increase in the means of exchange and in commodities generally, gave to commerce, to navigation, to industry, an impulse never before known, and thereby, to the revolutionary element in the tottering feudal society, a rapid development.

The feudal system of industry, in which industrial production was monopolised by closed guilds, now no longer sufficed for the growing wants of the new markets. The manufacturing system took its place. The guild-masters were pushed aside by the manufacturing middle class; division of labour between the different corporate guilds vanished in the face of division of labour in each single workshop.

Meantime the markets kept ever growing, the demand ever rising. Even manufacture no longer sufficed. Thereupon, steam and machinery revolutionised industrial production. The place of manufacture was taken by the giant, modern industry, the place of the industrial middle class, by industrial millionaires—the leaders of whole industrial armies, the modern bourgeois.

Modern industry has established the world market, for which the discovery of America paved the way. This market has given an immense development to commerce, to navigation, to communication by land. This development has, in its turn, reacted on the extension of industry; and in proportion as industry, commerce, navigation, railways extended, in the same proportion the bourgeoisie developed, increased its capital, and pushed into the background every class handed down from the Middle Ages.

We see, therefore, how the modern bourgeoisie is itself the product of a long course of development, of a series of revolutions in the modes of production and of exchange.

Each step in the development of the bourgeoisie was accompanied by a corresponding political advance of that class. An oppressed class under the sway of the feudal nobility, it became an armed and self-governing association in the mediæval commune; here independent urban republic (as in Italy and Germany), there taxable "third estate" of the monarchy (as in France); afterwards, in the period of manufacture proper, serving either the semi-feudal or the absolute monarchy as a counterpoise against the nobility, and, in fact, corner-stone of the great monarchies in general—the bourgeoisie has at last, since the establishment of modern industry and of the world market, conquered for itself, in the modern representative state, exclusive political sway. The executive of the modern state is but a committee for managing the common affairs of the whole bourgeoisie.

The bourgeoisie has played a most revolutionary rôle in history.

The bourgeoisie, wherever it has got the upper hand, has put an end to all feudal, patriarchal, idyllic relations. It has pitilessly torn asunder the motley feudal ties that bound man to his "natural superiors," and has left no other bond between man and man than naked self-interest, than callous "cash payment." It has drowned the most heavenly ecstasies of religious fervour, of chivalrous enthusiasm, of philistine sentimentalism, in the icy water of egotistical calculation. It has resolved personal worth into exchange value, and in place of the numberless indefeasible chartered freedoms, has set up that single, unconscionable freedom—Free Trade. In one word, for exploitation, veiled by religious and political illusions, it has substituted naked, shameless, direct, brutal exploitation.

The bourgeoisie has stripped of its halo every occupation hitherto honoured and looked up to with reverent awe. It has converted the physician, the lawyer, the priest, the poet, the man of science, into its paid wage-labourers.

The bourgeoisie has torn away from the family its sentimental veil, and has reduced the family relation to a mere money relation.

The bourgeoisie has disclosed how it came to pass that the brutal display of vigour in the Middle Ages, which reactionaries so much admire, found its fitting complement in the most slothful indolence. It has been the first to show what man's activity can bring about. It has accomplished wonders far surpassing Egyptian pyramids, Roman aqueducts, and Gothic cathedrals; it has conducted expeditions that put in the shade all former migrations of nations and crusades.

The bourgeoisie cannot exist without constantly revolutionising the instruments of production, and thereby the relations of production, and with them the whole relations of society. Conservation of the old modes of production in unaltered form, was, on the contrary, the first condition of existence for all earlier industrial classes. Constant revolutionising of production, uninterrupted disturbance of all social conditions, everlasting uncertainty and agitation distinguish the bourgeois epoch from all earlier ones. All fixed, fast-frozen relations, with their train of ancient and venerable prejudices and opinions, are swept away, all new-formed ones become antiquated before they can ossify. All that is solid melts into air, all that is holy is profaned, and man is at last compelled to face with sober senses his real conditions of life and his relations with his kind.

The need of a constantly expanding market for its products chases the bourgeoisie over the whole surface of the globe. It must nestle everywhere, settle everywhere, establish connections everywhere.

The bourgeoisie has through its exploitation of the world market given a cosmopolitan character to production and consumption in every country. To the great chagrin of reactionaries, it has drawn from under the feet of industry the national ground on which it stood. All old-established national industries have been destroyed or are daily being destroyed. They are dislodged by new industries, whose introduction becomes a life and death question for all civilised nations, by industries that no longer work up indigenous raw material, but raw material drawn from the remotest zones; industries whose products are consumed, not only at home, but in every quarter of the globe. In place of the old wants, satisfied by the production of the country, we find new wants, requiring for their satisfaction the products of distant lands and climes. In place of the old local and national seclusion and self-sufficiency, we have intercourse in every direction, universal interdependence of nations. And as in material, so also in intellectual production. The intellectual creations of individual nations become common property. National one-sidedness and narrow-mindedness become more and more impossible, and from the numerous national and local literatures there arises a world literature.

The bourgeoisie, by the rapid improvement of all instruments of production, by the immensely facilitated means of communication, draws all nations, even the most barbarian, into civilisation. The cheap prices of its commodities are the heavy artillery with which it batters down all Chinese walls, with which it forces the barbarians' intensely obstinate hatred of foreigners to capitulate. It compels all nations, on pain of extinction, to adopt the bourgeois mode of production; it compels them to introduce what it calls civilisation into their midst, *i.e.,* to become bourgeois themselves. In a word, it creates a world after its own image.

The bourgeoisie has subjected the country to the rule of the towns. It has created enormous cities, has greatly increased the urban population as compared with the rural, and has thus rescued a considerable part of the population from the idiocy of rural life. Just as it has made the country dependent on the towns, so it has made barbarian and semi-barbarian countries dependent on the civilised ones, nations of peasants on nations of bourgeois, the East on the West.

More and more the bourgeoisie keeps doing away with the scattered state of the population, of the means of production, and of property. It has agglomerated population, centralised means of production, and has concentrated property in a few hands. The necessary consequence of this was political centralisation. Independent, or but loosely connected provinces, with separate interests, laws, governments and systems of taxation, became lumped together into one nation, with one government, one code of laws, one national class interest, one frontier and one customs tariff.

The bourgeoisie, during its rule of scarce one hundred years, has created more massive and more colossal productive forces than have all preceding generations together. Subjection of nature's forces to man, machinery, application of chemistry to industry and agriculture, steam-navigation, railways, electric telegraphs, clearing of whole continents for cultivation, canalisation of rivers, whole populations conjured out of the ground—what earlier century had even a presentiment that such productive forces slumbered in the lap of social labour?

We see then that the means of production and of exchange, which served as the foundation for the growth of the bourgeoisie, were generated in feudal society. At a certain stage in the development of these means of production and of exchange, the conditions under which feudal society produced and exchanged, the feudal organisation of agriculture and manufacturing industry, in a world, the feudal relations of property became no longer compatible with the already developed productive forces; they became so many fetters. They had to be burst asunder; they were burst asunder.

Into their place stepped free competition, accompanied by a social and political constitution adapted to it, and by the economic and political sway of the bourgeois class.

A similar movement is going on before our own eyes. Modern bourgeois society with its relations of production, of exchange and of property, a society that has conjured up such gigantic means of production and of exchange, is like the sorcerer who is no longer able to control the powers of the nether world whom he has called up by his spells. For many a decade past the history of industry and commerce is but the history of the revolt of modern productive forces against modern conditions of production, against the property relations that are the conditions for the existence of the bourgeoisie and of its rule. It is enough to mention the commercial crises that by their periodical return put the existence of the entire bourgeois society on trial, each time more threateningly. In these crises a great part not only of the existing products, but also of the previously created productive forces, are periodically destroyed. In these crises there breaks out an epidemic that, in all earlier epochs, would have seemed an absurdity—the epidemic of over-production. Society suddenly finds itself put back into a state of momentary barbarism; it appears as if a famine, a universal war of devastation had cut off the supply of every means of subsistence; industry and commerce seem to be destroyed. And why? Because there is too much civilisation, too much means of subsistence, too much industry, too much commerce. The productive forces at the disposal of society no longer tend to further the development of the conditions of bourgeois property; on the contrary, they have become too powerful for these conditions, by which they are fettered, and no sooner do they overcome these fetters than they bring disorder into the whole of bourgeois society, endanger the existence of bourgeois property. The conditions of bourgeois society are too narrow to comprise the wealth created by them. And how does the bourgeoisie get over these crises? On the one hand by enforced destruction of a mass of productive forces; on the other, by the conquest of new markets, and by the more thorough exploitation of the old ones. That is to say, by paving the way for more extensive and more destructive crises, and by diminishing the means whereby crises are prevented.

The weapons with which the bourgeoisie felled feudalism to the ground are now turned against the bourgeoisie itself.

But not only has the bourgeoisie forged the weapons that bring death to itself; it has also called into existence the men who are to wield those weapons—the modern working class—the proletarians.

In proportion as the bourgeoisie, *i.e.*, capital, is developed, in the same proportion is the proletariat, the modern working class, developed—a class of labourers, who live only so long as they find work, and who find work only so long as their labour increases capital. These labourers, who must sell themselves piecemeal, are a commodity, like every other article of commerce, and are consequently exposed to all the vicissitudes of competition, to all the fluctuations of the market.

Owing to the extensive use of machinery and to division of labour, the work of the proletarians has lost all individual character, and, consequently, all charm for the workman. He becomes an appendage of the machine, and it is only the most simple, most monotonous, and most easily acquired knack, that is required of him. Hence, the cost of production of a workman is restricted, almost entirely, to the means of subsistence that he requires for his maintenance, and for the propagation of his race. But the price of a commodity, and therefore also of labour, is equal to its cost of production. In proportion, therefore, as the repulsiveness of the work increases, the wage decreases. Nay more, in proportion as the use of machinery and division of labour increases, in the same proportion the burden of toil also increases, whether by prolongation of the working hours, by increase of the work exacted in a given time, or by increased speed of the machinery, etc.

Modern industry has converted the little workshop of the patriarchal master into the great factory of the industrial capitalist. Masses of labourers, crowded into the factory, are organised like soldiers. As privates of the industrial army they are placed under the command of a perfect hierarchy of officers and sergeants. Not only are they slaves of the bourgeois class, and of the bourgeois state; they are daily and hourly enslaved by the machine, by the over-looker, and, above all, by the individual bourgeois manufacturer himself. The more openly this despotism proclaims gain to be its end and aim, the more petty, the more hateful and the more embittering it is.

The less the skill and exertion of strength implied in manual labour, in other words, the more modern industry develops, the more is the labour of men superseded by that of women. Differences of age and sex have no longer any distinctive social validity for the working class. All are instruments of labour, more or less expensive to use, according to their age and sex.

No sooner has the labourer received his wages in cash, for the moment escaping exploitation by the manufacturer, than he is set upon by the other portions of the bourgeoisie, the landlord, the shopkeeper, the pawnbroker, etc.

The lower strata of the middle class—the small tradespeople, shopkeepers, and retired tradesmen generally, the handicraftsmen and peasants—all these sink gradually into the proletariat, partly because their diminutive capital does not suffice for the scale on which modern industry is carried on, and is swamped in the competition with the large capitalists, partly because their specialised skill is rendered worthless by new methods of production. Thus the proletariat is recruited from all classes of the population.

The proletariat goes through various stages of development. With its birth begins its struggle with the bourgeoisie. At first the contest is carried on by individual labourers, then by the work people of a factory, then by the operatives of one trade, in one locality, against the individual bourgeois who directly exploits them. They direct their attacks not against the bourgeois conditions of production, but against the instruments of production themselves; they destroy imported wares that compete with their labour, they smash machinery to pieces, they set factories ablaze, they seek to restore by force the vanished status of the workman of the Middle Ages.

At this stage the labourers still form an incoherent mass scattered over the whole country, and broken up by their mutual competition. If anywhere they unite to form more compact bodies, this is not yet the consequence of their own active union, but of the union of the bourgeoisie, which class, in order to attain its own political ends, is compelled to set the whole proletariat in motion, and is moreover still able to do so for a time. At this stage, therefore, the proletarians do not fight their enemies, but the enemies of their enemies, the remnants of absolute monarchy, the landowners, the non-industrial bourgeois, the petty bourgeoisie. Thus the whole historical movement is concentrated in the hands of the bourgeoisie; every victory so obtained is a victory for the bourgeoisie.

But with the development of industry the proletariat not only increases in number; it becomes concentrated in greater masses, its strength grows, and it feels that strength more. The various interests and conditions of life within the ranks of the proletariat are more and more equalised, in proportion as machinery obliterates all distinctions of labour and nearly everywhere reduces wages to the same low level. The growing competition among the bourgeois, and the resulting commercial crises, make the wages of the workers ever more fluctuating. The unceasing improvement of machinery, ever more rapidly developing, makes their livelihood more and more precarious; the collisions between individual workmen and individual bourgeois take more and more the character of collisions between two classes. Thereupon the workers begin to form combinations (trade unions) against the bourgeoisie; they club together in order to keep up the rate of wages; they found permanent associations in order to make provision beforehand for these occasional revolts. Here and there the contest breaks out into riots.

Now and then the workers are victorious, but only for a time. The real fruit of their battles lies, not in the immediate result, but in the ever expanding union of the workers. This union is furthered by the improved means of communication which are created by modern industry, and which place the workers of different localities in contact with one another. It was just this contact that was needed to centralise the numerous local struggles, all of the same character, into one national struggle between classes. But every class struggle is a political struggle. And that union, to attain which the burghers of the Middle Ages, with their miserable highways, required centuries, the modern proletarians, thanks to railways, achieve in a few years.

This organisation of the proletarians into a class, and consequently into a political party, is continually being upset again by the competition between the workers themselves. But it ever rises up again, stronger, firmer, mightier. It compels legislative recognition of particular interests of the workers, by taking advantage of the divisions among the bourgeoisie itself. Thus the ten-hour bill in England was carried.

Altogether, collisions between the classes of the old society further the course of development of the proletariat in many ways. The bourgeoisie finds itself involved in a constant battle. At first with the aristocracy; later on, with those portions of the bourgeoisie itself whose interests have become antagonistic to the progress of industry; at all times with the bourgeoisie of foreign countries. In all these battles it sees itself compelled to appeal to the proletariat, to ask for its help, and thus, to drag it into the political arena. The bourgeoisie itself, therefore, supplies the proletariat with its own elements of political and general education, in other words, it furnishes the proletariat with weapons for fighting the bourgeoisie.

Further, as we have already seen, entire sections of the ruling classes are, by the advance of industry, precipitated into the proletariat, or are at least threatened in their conditions of existence. These also supply the proletariat with fresh elements of enlightenment and progress.

Finally, in times when the class struggle nears the decisive hour, the process of dissolution going on within the ruling class, in fact within the whole range of old society, assumes such a violent, glaring character, that a small section of the ruling class cuts itself adrift, and joins the revolutionary class, the class that holds the future in its hands. Just as, therefore, at an earlier period, a section of the nobility went over to the bourgeoisie, so now a portion of the bourgeoisie goes over to the proletariat, and in particular, a portion of the bourgeois ideologists, who have raised themselves to the level of comprehending theoretically the historical movement as a whole.

Of all the classes that stand face to face with the bourgeoisie today, the proletariat alone is a really revolutionary class. The other classes decay and finally disappear in the face of modern industry; the proletariat is its special and essential product.

The lower middle class, the small manufacturer, the shopkeeper, the artisan, the peasant, all these fight against the bourgeoisie, to save from extinction their existence as fractions of the middle class. They are therefore not revolutionary, but conservative. Nay more, they are reactionary, for they try to roll back the wheel of history. If by chance they are revolutionary, they are so only in view of their impending transfer into the proletariat; they thus defend not their present, but their future interests; they desert their own standpoint to adopt that of the proletariat.

The "dangerous class," the social scum *(Lumpenproletariat),* that passively rotting mass thrown off by the lowest layers of old society, may, here and there, be swept into the movement by a proletarian revolution; its conditions of life, however, prepare it far more for the part of a bribed tool of reactionary intrigue.

The social conditions of the old society no longer exist for the proletariat. The proletarian is without property; his relation to his wife and children has no longer anything in common with bourgeois family relations; modern industrial labour, modern subjection to capital, the same in England as in France, in America as in Germany, has stripped him of every trace of national character. Law, morality, religion, are to him so many bourgeois prejudices, behind which lurk in ambush just as many bourgeois interests.

All the preceding classes that got the upper hand, sought to fortify their already acquired status by subjecting society at large to their conditions of appropriation. The proletarians cannot become masters of the productive forces of society, except by abolishing their own previous mode of appropriation, and thereby also every other previous mode of appropriation. They have nothing of their own to secure and to fortify; their mission is to destroy all previous securities for, and insurances of, individual property.

All previous historical movements were movements of minorities, or in the interest of minorities. The proletarian movement is the self-conscious, independent movement of the immense majority, in the interest of the immense majority. The proletariat, the lowest stratum of our present society, cannot stir, cannot raise itself up, without the whole superincumbent strata of official society being sprung into the air.

Though not in substance, yet in form, the struggle of the proletariat with the bourgeoisie is at first a national struggle. The proletariat of each country must, of course, first of all settle matters with its own bourgeoisie.

In depicting the most general phases of the development of the proletariat, we traced the more or less veiled civil war, raging within existing society, up to the point where that war breaks out into open revolution, and where the violent overthrow of the bourgeoisie lays the foundation for the sway of the proletariat.

Hitherto, every form of society has been based, as we have already seen, on the antagonism of oppressing and oppressed classes. But in order to oppress a class, certain conditions must be assured to it under which it can, at least, continue its slavish existence. The serf, in the period of serfdom, raised himself to membership in the commune, just as the petty bourgeois, under the yoke of feudal absolutism, managed to develop into a bourgeois. The modern labourer, on the contrary, instead of rising with the progress of industry, sinks deeper and deeper below the conditions of existence of his own class. He becomes a pauper, and pauperism develops more rapidly than population and wealth. And here it becomes evident, that the bourgeoisie is unfit any longer to be the ruling class in society, and to impose its conditions of existence upon society as an overriding law. It is unfit to rule because it is incompetent to assure an existence to its slave within his slavery, because it cannot help letting him sink into such a state, that it has to feed him, instead of being fed by him. Society can no longer live under this bourgeoisie, in other words, its existence is no longer compatible with society.

The essential condition for the existence and sway of the bourgeois class, is the formation and augmentation of capital; the condition for capital is wage-labour. Wage-labour rests exclusively on competition between the labourers. The advance of industry, whose involuntary promoter is the bourgeoisie, replaces the isolation of the labourers, due to competition, by their revolutionary combination, due to association. The development of modern industry, therefore, cuts from under its feet the very foundation on which the bourgeoisie produces and appropriates products. What the bourgeoisie therefore produces, above all, are its own grave-diggers. Its fall and the victory of the proletariat are equally inevitable. . . .

The Communists fight for the attainment of the immediate aims, for the enforcement of the momentary interests of the working class; but in the movement of the present, they also represent and take care of the future of that movement. In France the Communists ally themselves with the Social-Democrats, against the conservative and radical bourgeoisie, reserving, however, the right to take up a critical position in regard to phrases and illusions traditionally handed down from the great Revolution.

In Switzerland they support the Radicals, without losing sight of the fact that this party consists of antagonistic elements, partly of Democratic Socialists, in the French sense, partly of radical bourgeois.

In Poland they support the party that insists on an agrarian revolution as the prime condition for national emancipation, that party which fomented the insurrection of Cracow in 1846.

In Germany they fight with the bourgeoisie whenever it acts in a revolutionary war, against the absolute monarchy, the feudal squire archy, and the petty bourgeoisie.

But they never cease, for a single instant, to instil into the working class the clearest possible recognition of the hostile antagonism between bourgeoisie and proletariat, in order that the German workers may straightway use, as so many weapons against the bourgeoisie, the social and political conditions that the bourgeoisie must necessarily introduce along with its supremacy, and in order that, after the fall of the reactionary classes in Germany, the fight against the bourgeoisie itself may immediately begin.

The Communists turn their attention chiefly to Germany, because that country is on the eve of a bourgeois revolution that is bound to be carried out under more advanced conditions of European civilisation and with a much more developed proletariat than what existed in England in the 17th and in France in the 18th century, and because the bourgeois revolution in Germany will be but the prelude to an immediately following proletarian revolution.

In short, the Communists everywhere support every revolutionary movement against the existing social and political order of things.

In all these movements they bring to the front, as the leading question in each case, the property question, no matter what its degree of development at the time.

Finally, they labour everywhere for the union and agreement of the democratic parties of all countries.

The Communists disdain to conceal their views and aims. They openly declare that their ends can be attained only by the forcible overthrow of all existing social conditions. Let the ruling classes tremble at a Communist revolution. The proletarians have nothing to lose but their chains. They have a world to win.

Workingmen of all countries, unite!

VIII

MODERN CIVILIZATION, 1871-1929

PART EIGHT

◆ MODERN CIVILIZATION, 1871–1929

While the West was making an incomplete adjustment to the Industrial Revolution, for example in Fabian Socialism, diverse forces and events of gigantic magnitude brought both swift change and catastrophe. The historical process accelerated, in part because of the revolution in science and technology—and therefore in industry and in society—and in part because of the population explosion which accompanied and made possible the other changes. As a further and in many ways tragic complication, these revolutions in the Western way of life occurred within a social framework mainly inherited from preindustrial times. In the last three decades of the nineteenth century the major Western powers became involved in a headlong scramble for imperial possessions overseas, especially in Africa and Asia but also in Oceania. Imperialism, with abrupt beginnings and mixed motivation, paralleled the westward expansion of the United States and the eastward expansion of Russia in Central Asia. In East Asia the impact of the West produced violent effects, among them the rising movement for national independence in India and the westernization of Japan in both politics and industry. In the West, imperialism sharpened national rivalries and increased international tension. Imperialism was a major factor in precipitating the World War of 1914–18, which arose from complex and unenlightened diplomacy, and lasted far longer than Europe's leaders had anticipated. The First World War caused unprecedented devastation. In retrospect it seems to be among the central forces, possibly *the* central force, in the troubled experience of the twentieth century. Peace-making at Versailles solved few problems, and thereafter the democracies maintained a mainly defensive posture. Meanwhile, Fascism arose in Italy, and Russia became totalitarian when the first Five-Year Plan went into effect after the Second Revolution of 1928. The depression of 1929 set the stage for further conflict in the years to follow.

FORTY-FOUR

FABIAN SOCIALISM

Whereas the Marxists predicted and advocated social reform through revolution, a group of English socialists founded the Fabian Society in 1884 to achieve similar ends through peaceful means. The Fabians, among them George Bernard Shaw (1856–1950), later famous as a dramatist, Graham Wallas, and Sidney and Beatrice Webb, insisted on gradual reform based on scholarly studies of society and on endorsement in popular elections. The Fabians earnestly supported the British Labor Party, which in later years enacted many of their reforms. In 1889 seven members of the Fabian Society, including Shaw, Wallas, and Sidney Webb, published the Fabian Essays, *a collection of articles adapted from lectures on various aspects of socialism. This modest volume, many times reprinted and translated, had enormous influence in spreading the Fabian message. Its preface states, with characteristic clarity and humility, "The writers are all Social-Democrats, with a common conviction of the necessity of vesting the organization of industry and the material production in a State identified with the whole people by complete Democracy. . . . There are at present no authoritative teachers of Socialism. The essayists make no claim to be more than communicative learners." Shaw wrote the first article in the* Fabian Essays, *an economic analysis which balanced moral indignation with optimism and cutting wit.*

GEORGE BERNARD SHAW

FABIAN ESSAYS *

All economic analyses begin with the cultivation of the earth. To the mind's eye of the astronomer, the earth is a ball spinning in space without ulterior motives. To the bodily eye of the primitive cultivator it is a vast green plain, from which, by sticking a spade into it, wheat and other edible matters can be made to spring. To the eye of the sophisticated city man, this vast green plain appears rather as a great gaming-table, your chances in the game depending chiefly on the place where you deposit your stakes. To the economist, again, the green plain is a sort of burial-place of hidden treasure, where all the forethought and industry of man are set at naught by the caprice of the power which hid the treasure. The wise and patient workman strikes his spade in here, and with heavy toil can discover nothing but a poor quality of barley, some potatoes and plentiful nettles, with a few dock leaves to cure his stings. The foolish spendthrift on the other side of the hedge, gazing idly at the sand glittering in the sun, suddenly realizes that the earth is offering him gold—is dancing it before his listless eyes lest it

* From *Fabian Essays,* pp. 1–25, by the Fabian Society. First published in 1889.

should escape him. Another man, searching for some more of this tempting gold, comes upon a great hoard of coal, or taps a jet of petroleum. Thus is Man mocked by Earth, his step-mother, and never knows as he tugs at her closed hand whether it contains diamonds or flints, good red wheat or a few clayey and blighted cabbages. Thus, too, he becomes a gambler, and scoffs at the theorists who prate of industry and honesty and equality. Yet against this fate he eternally rebels. For since in gambling the many must lose in order that the few may win; since dishonesty is mere shadow-grasping where every one is dishonest; and since inequality is bitter to all except the highest, and miserably lonely for him, men come greatly to desire that these capricious gifts of Nature might be intercepted by some agency having the power and the good-will to distribute them justly according to the labor done by each in the collective search for them. This desire is Socialism; and, as a means to its fulfilment, Socialists have devised communes, kingdoms, principalities, churches, manors, and finally, when all these had succumbed to the old gambling spirits, the Social Democratic State, which yet remains to be tried. As against Socialism, the gambling spirit urges man to allow no rival to come between his private individual powers and Step-mother Earth, but rather to secure some acres of her and take his chance of getting diamonds instead of cabbages. This is Private Property, or Unsocialism. Our own choice is shewn by our continual aspiration to possess property, our common hailing of it as sacred, our setting apart of the word Respectable for those who have attained it, our ascription of pre-eminent religiousness to commandments forbidding its violation, and our identification of law and order among men with its protection. Therefore is it vital to a living knowledge of our society that Private Property should be known in every step of its progress from its source in cupidity to its end in confusion.

Let us, in the manner of the Political Economist, trace the effects of settling a country by private property with undisturbed law and order. Figure to yourself the vast green plain of a country virgin to the spade, awaiting the advent of man. Imagine then the arrival of the first colonist, the original Adam, developed by centuries of civilization into an Adam Smith, prospecting for an suitable patch of Private Property. Adam is, as Political Economy fundamentally assumes him to be, "on the make"; therefore he drives his spade into, and sets up his stockade around, the most fertile and favorably situated patch he can find. When he has tilled it, Political Economy inspired to prophesy by the spectacle, metaphorically exhibits Adam's little patch of cultivation as a pool that will yet rise and submerge the whole land. Let us not forget this trope: it is the key to the ever-recurring phrase, "margin of cultivation," in which, as may now be perceived, there lurks a little unsuspected poetry. And truly the pool soon spreads. Other Adams come, all on the make, and therefore all sure to pre-empt patches as near as may be to that of the first Adam's, partly because he has chosen the best situation, partly for the pleasure of his society and conversation, and partly because where two men are assembled together there is a two-man power that is far more than double one-man power, being indeed in some instances a quite new force, totally destructive of the idiotic general hypothesis that society is no more than the sum of the units which compose it. These Adams, too, bring their Cains and Abels, who do not murder one another, but merely pre-empt adjacent patches. And so the pool rises, and the margin spreads more and more remote from the centre, until the pool becomes a lake, and the lake an inland sea.

Rent

But in the course of this inundation the caprices of Nature begin to operate. That specially fertile region upon which Adam pitched is sooner or later all pre-empted;

and there is nothing for the new-comer to pre-empt save soil of the second quality. Again, division of labor sets in among Adam's neighbors; and with it, of course, comes the establishment of a market for the exchange of the products of their divided labor. Now it is not well to be far afield from that market, because distance from it involves extra cost for roads, beasts of burden, time consumed in travelling thither and back again. All this will be saved to Adam at the centre of cultivation, and incurred by the new-comer at the margin of cultivation. Let us estimate the annual value of Adam's produce at £1,000, and the annual produce of the new-comer's land on the margin of cultivation at £500, assuming that Adam and the new-comer are equally industrious. Here is a clear advantage of £500 a year to the first comer. This £500 is economic rent. It matters not at all that it is merely a difference of income, and not an overt payment from a tenant to a landlord. The two men labor equally; and yet one gets £500 a year more than the other through the superior fertility of his land and convenience of its situation. The excess due to that fertility is rent; and before long we shall find it recognized as such and paid in the fashion with which we are familiar. For why should not Adam let his patch to the new-comer at a rent of £500 a year? Since the produce will be £1,000, the new-comer will have £500 left for himself, or as much as he could obtain by cultivating a patch of his own at the margin; and it is pleasanter, besides, to be in the centre of society than on the outskirts of it. The new-comer will himself propose the arrangement; and Adam may retire as an idle landlord with a perpetual pension of £500 rent. The excess of fertility in Adam's land is thenceforth recognized as rent and paid, as it is to-day, regularly by a worker to a drone. A few samples of the way in which this simple and intelligible transaction is stated by our economists may now, I hope, be quoted without any danger of their proving so difficult as they appear in the text-books from which I have copied them.

Stuart Mill [1] says that "the rent of land consists of the excess of its return above the return to the worst land in cultivation." Fawcett [2] says that "the rent of land represents the pecuniary value of the advantages which such land possesses over the worst land in cultivation." Professor Marshall [3] says that "the rent of a piece of land is the excess of its produce over the produce of an adjacent piece of land which would not be cultivated at all if rent were paid for it." Professor Sidgwick [4] cautiously puts it that "the normal rent *per acre* of any piece" [of land] "is the surplus of the value of its produce over the value of the net produce per acre of the least advantageous land that it is profitable to cultivate." General Walker [5] declares that "specifically, the rent of any piece of land is determined by the difference between its annual yield and that of the least productive land acutally cultivated for the supply of the same market, it being assumed that the quality of the land as a productive agent is, in neither case, impaired or improved by such cultivation." All these definitions are offered by the authors as elaborations of that given by their master Ricardo,[6] who says, "Rent is that portion of the produce of the earth which is paid to the landlord for the use of the original and indestructible powers of the soil."

The County Family

Let us return to our ideal country. Adam is retiring from productive industry on £500 a year; and his neighbors are hastening to imitate him as fresh tenants present themselves. The first result is the beginning of a

[1] "Principles of Political Economy," Vol. I, Index to chap. xvi (1865).
[2] "Manual of Political Economy," Book II, chap. iii, p. 116 (1876).
[3] "Economics of Industry," Book II, chap. iii, sec. 3, p. 84 (1879).
[4] "Principles of Political Economy," Book II, chap. vii, p. 301 (1883).
[5] "Brief Text-book of Political Economy," chap. ii, sec. 216, p. 173 (1885).
[6] "Principles of Political Economy and Taxation," chap. ii. p. 34 (1817).

tradition that the oldest families in the country enjoy a superior position to the rest, and that the main advantage of their superior position is that they enjoy incomes without working. Nevertheless, since they still depend on their tenants' labor for their subsistence, they continue to pay Labor, with a capital L, a certain meed of mouth honor; and the resultant association of prosperity with idleness, and praise with industry, practically destroys morality by setting up that incompatibility between conduct and principle which is the secret of the ingrained cynicism of our own time, and which produces the curious Ricardian phenomenon of the man of business who goes on Sunday to the church with the regularity of the village blacksmith, there to renounce and abjure before his God the line of conduct which he intends to pursue with all his might during the following week.

According to our hypothesis, the inland sea of cultivation has now spread into the wilderness so far that at its margin the return to a man's labor for a year is only £500. But as there is always a flood-tide in that sea, caused by the incessant increase of population, the margin will not stop there; it will at last encroach upon every acre of cultivable land, rising to the snow line on the mountains and falling to the coast of the actual salt water sea, but always reaching the barrenest places last of all, because the cultivators are still, as ever, on the make, and will not break bad land when better is to be had. But suppose that now, at last, the uttermost belt of free land is reached, and that upon it the yield to a man's year's labor is only £100. Clearly now the rent of Adam's primeval patch has risen to £900, since that is the excess of its produce over what is by this time all that is to be had rent free. But Adam has yielded up his land for £500 a year to a tenant. It is this tenant accordingly who now lets Adam's patch for £900 a year to the new comer, who of course loses nothing by the bargain, since it leaves him the £100 a year with which he must be content anyhow. Accordingly he labors on Adam's land; raises £1,000 a year from it; keeps £100 and pays £900 to Adam's tenant, who pays £500 to Adam, keeping £400 for himself, and thus also becoming an idle gentleman, though with a somewhat smaller income than the man of older family. It has, in fact, come to this, that the private property in Adam's land is divided between three men, the first doing none of the work and getting half the produce; the second doing none of the work and getting two-fifths of the produce; and the third doing all the work and getting only one-tenth of the produce. Incidentally also, the moralist who is sure to have been prating somewhere about private property leading to the encouragement of industry, the establishment of a healthy incentive, and the distribution of wealth according to exertion, is exposed as a futile purblind person, starting *a priori* from blank ignorance, and proceeding deductively to mere contradiction and patent folly.

All this, however, is a mere trifle compared to the sequel. When the inland sea has risen to its confines—when there is nothing but a strip of sand round the coast between the furrow and the wave—when the very waves themselves are cultivated by fisherfolk—when the pastures and timber forests have touched the snow line—when, in short, the land is all private property, yet every man is a proprietor, though it may be only of a tenant right. He enjoys fixity of tenure at what is called a fair rent; that is, he fares as well as he could on land wholly his own. All the rent is economic rent; the landlord cannot raise it nor the tenant lower it; it is fixed naturally by the difference between the fertility of the land for which it is paid and that of the worst land in the country. Compared with the world as we know it, such a state of things is freedom and happiness.

The Proletariat

But at this point there appears in the land a man in a strange plight—one who wanders from snow line to sea coast in search of land, and finds none that is not the property of some one else. Private property had forgotten this man. On the roads he is a vagrant; off them he is a trespasser; he is the first disinherited son of Adam, the first proletarian, one in whose seed all the generations of the earth shall yet be blest, but who is himself for the present foodless, homeless, shiftless, superfluous, and everything that turns a man into a tramp or a thrall. Yet he is still a man with brain and muscle, able to devise and execute, able to deal puissantly with land if he only could get access to it. But how to get that access! Necessity is the mother of Invention. It may be that this second Adam, the first father of the great proletariat, has one of those scarce brains which are not the least of Nature's capricious gifts. If the fertile field yields rent, why not the fertile brain? Here is the first Adam's patch still yielding its £1,000 a year to the labor of the tenant who, as we have seen, has to pay £900 away in rent. How if the proletarian were boldly to bid £1,000 a year to that man for the property? Apparently the result would be the starvation of the proletarian, since he would have to part with all the produce. But what if the proletarian can contrive—invent—anticipate a new want—turn the land to some hitherto undreamt-of use—wrest £1,500 a year from the soil and site that only yielded £1,000 before? If he can do this, he can pay the full £1,000 rent, and have an income of £500 left for himself. This is his profit—the rent of his ability—the excess of its produce over that of ordinary stupidity. Here then is the opportunity of the cunning proletarian, the hero of that modern Plutarch, Mr. Samuel Smiles. Truly, as Napoleon said, the career is open to the talented. But alas! the social question is no more a question of the fate of the talented than of the idiotic. In due replenishment of the earth there comes another proletarian who is no cleverer than other men, and can do as much, but not more than they. For him there is no rent of ability. How then is he to get a tenant right? Let us see. It is certain that by this time not only will the new devices of the renter of ability have been copied by people incapable of inventing them; but division of labor, the use of tools and money, and the economies of civilization will have greatly increased man's power of extracting wealth from Nature. All this increase will be so much gain to the holder of a tenant right, since his rent is a fixed payment out of the produce of his holding, and the balance is his own. Therefore an addition to the produce not foreseen by the landlord enriches the tenant. So that it may well be that the produce of land on the margin of cultivation, which, as we have seen, fixes the produce left to the cultivators throughout the whole area, may rise considerably. Suppose the yield to have doubled; then our old friends who paid £900 rent, and kept £100 for themselves, have now, though they still pay £900 rent, £1,100 for themselves, the total produce having risen to £2,000. Now here is an opportunity for our proletarian who is not clever. He can very well offer to cultivate the land subject to a payment of, for instance, £1,600 a year, leaving £400 a year. This will enable the last holder of the tenant right to retire as an idle gentleman receiving a net income of £700 a year, and a gross income of £1,600, out of which he pays £900 a year rent to a landlord who again pays to the head landlord £500. But it is to be marked that this £700 a year net is not economic rent. It is not the difference between the best and the worst land. It has nothing to do with the margin of cultivation. It is a payment for the priviledge of using land at all—for access to that which is now a close monopoly; and its amount is regulated, not by what the purchaser could do for himself on land of his own at the margin, but simply by the landholder's eagerness to be idle on the one hand, and the proletarian's need of subsistence on the other. In current economic terms the price is regulated by supply and demand. As the demand for land intensifies by the advent of fresh proletarians, the price goes up; and the bargains are made more stringent. Tenant rights, instead of being granted in perpetuity, and so securing for ever to the tenant the increase due to unforeseen improvements in production, are granted on leases for finite terms, at the expiration of which the landlord can revise the terms or eject the tenant. The payments rise until the original head rents and quit rents appear insignificant in comparison with the incomes reaped by the intermediate tenant right holders or middlemen. Sooner or later the price of tenant right will rise so high that the actual cultivator will get no more of the produce than suffices him for subsistence. At that point there is an end of sub-letting tenant rights. The land's absorption of the proletarians as tenants paying more than the economic rent stops.

And now what is the next proletarian to do? For all his forerunners we have found a way of escape: for him there seems none. The board is at the door, inscribed "Only standing room left"; and it might well bear the more poetic legend, *Lasciate ogni speranza, voi ch' entrate*. This man, born a proletarian, must die a proletarian, and leave his destitution as an only inheritance to his son. It is not yet clear that there is ten days' life in him; for whence is his subsistence to come if he cannot get at the land? Food he must have, and clothing; and both promptly. There is food in the market, and clothing also; but not for nothing: hard money must be paid for it, and paid on the nail too; for he who has no property gets no credit. Money then is a necessity of life; and money can only be procured by selling commodities. This presents no difficulty to the cultivators of the land, who can raise commodities by their labor; but the proletarian, being landless, has neither commodities nor means of producing them. Sell something he must. Yet he has nothing to sell—except himself. The idea seems a desperate one; but it proves quite easy to carry out. The tenant cultivators of the land have not strength enough or time enough to exhaust the productive capacity of their holdings. If they could buy men in the market for less than these men's labor would add to the produce, then the purchase of such men would be a sheer gain. It would indeed be only a purchase in form: the men would literally cost nothing, since they would produce their own price, with a surplus for the buyer. Never in the history of buying and selling was there so splendid a bargain for buyers as this. Aladdin's uncle's offer of new lamps for old ones, was in comparison a catch-penny. Accordingly, the proletarian no sooner offers himself for sale than he finds a rush of bidders for him, each striving to get the better of the others by offering to give him more and more of the produce of his labor, and to content themselves with less and less surplus. But even the highest bidder must have some surplus, or he will not buy. The proletarian, in accepting the highest bid, sells himself openly into bondage. He is not the first man who has done so; for it is evident that his forerunners, the purchasers of tenant right, had been enslaved by the proprietors who lived on the rents paid by them. But now all the disguise falls off; the proletarian renounces not only the fruit of his labor, but also his right to think for himself and to direct his industry as he pleases. The economic change is merely formal; the moral change is enormous. Soon the new direct traffic in men overspreads the whole market, and takes the place formerly held by the traffic in tenant rights. In order to understand the consequences, it is necessary to undertake an analysis of the exchange of commodities in general, since labor power is now in the market on the same footing as any other ware exposed there for sale.

Exchange Value

It is evident that the custom of exchange will arise in the first instance as soon as men give up providing each for his own needs by his own labor. A man who makes his own tables and chairs, his own poker and kettle, his own bread and butter, and his own house and clothes, is jack-of-all-trades and master of none. He finds that he would get on much faster if he stuck to making tables and chairs, and exchanged them with the smith for a poker and kettle, with bakers and dairymen for bread and butter, and with builders and tailors for a house and clothes. In doing this, he finds that his tables and chairs are worth so much—that they have an exchange value, as it is called. As a matter of general convenience, some suitable commodity is set up to measure this value. We set up gold, which in this particular use of it, is called money. The chairmaker finds how much money his chairs are worth, and exchanges them for it. The blacksmith finds out how much money his pokers are worth, and exchanges them for it. Thus, by employing money as a go-between, chairmakers can get pokers in exchange for their chairs, and blacksmiths chairs for their pokers. This is the mechanism of exchange; and once the values of the commodities are ascertained it works simply enough. But it is a mere mechanism, and does not fix the values or explain them. And the attempt to discover what does fix them is beset with apparent contradictions which block up the right path, and with seductive coincidences which make the wrong seem the more promising.

The apparent contradictions soon shew themselves. It is evident that the exchange value of anything depends on its utility, since no mortal exertion can make a useless thing exchangeable. And yet fresh air and sunlight, which are so useful as to be quite indispensable, have no exchange value; whilst a meteoric stone, shot free of charge from the firmament into the back garden, has a considerable exchange value, although it is an eminently dispensable curiosity. We soon find that this somehow depends on the fact that fresh air is plenty and meteoric stones scarce. If by any means the supply of fresh air could be steadily diminished, and the supply of meteoric stones, by celestial cannonade or otherwise, steadily increased, the fresh air would presently acquire an exchange value which would gradually rise, whilst the exchange value of meteoric stones would gradually fall, until at last fresh air would be supplied through a meter and charged for like gas, and meteoric stones would be as unsaleable as ordinary pebbles. The exchange value, in fact, decreases with the supply. This is due to the fact that the supply decreases in utility as it goes on, because when people have had some of a commodity, they are partly satisfied, and do not value the rest so much. The usefulness of a pound of bread to a man depends on whether he has already eaten some. Every man wants a certain number of pounds of bread per week, no man wants much more; and if more is offered he will not give much for it —perhaps not anything. One umbrella is very useful: a second umbrella is a luxury: a third is mere lumber. Similarly, the curators of our museums want a moderate collection of meteroic stones; but they do not want a cartload apiece of them. Now the exchange value is fixed by the utility, not of the most useful, but of the least useful part of the stock. Why this is so can readily be made obvious by an illustration. If the stock of umbrellas in the market were sufficiently large to provide two for each umbrella carrier in the community, then, since a second umbrella is not so useful as the first, the doctrinaire course would be to ticket half the umbrellas at, say, fifteen shillings, and the other half at eight and sixpence. Unfortunately, no man will give fifteen shillings for an article which he can get for eight and sixpence; and when the public came to buy, they would buy up all the eight and sixpenny umbrellas. Each person being thus supplied with an umbrella, the remainder of the stock, though marked fifteen shillings, would be in the position of second umbrellas, only worth eight and sixpence. This is how the exchange value of the least useful part of the supply fixes the exchange value of all the rest. Technically, it occurs by "the law of indifference." And since the least useful unit of the supply is generally that which is last produced, its utility is called the final utility of the commodity. The utility of the first or most useful unit is called the total utility of the commodity. If there were but one umbrella in the world, the exchange value of its total utility would be what the most delicate person would pay for it on a very wet day sooner than go without it. But practically, thanks to the law of indifference, the most delicate person pays no more than the most robust: that is, both pay alike the exchange value of the utility of the last umbrella produced—or of the final utility of the whole stock of umbrellas. These terms—law of indifference, total utility, and final utility—though admirably expressive and intelligible when you know beforehand exactly what they mean, are, taken by themselves, failures in point of lucidity and suggestiveness. Some economists, transferring from cultivation to utility our old metaphor of the spreading pool, call final utility "marginal utility." Either will serve our present purpose, as I do not intend to use the terms again. The main point to be grasped is, that however useful any commodity may be, its exchange value can be run down to nothing by increasing the supply until there is more of it than is wanted. The excess, being useless and valueless, is to be had for nothing; and nobody will pay anything for a commodity as long as plenty of it is to be had for nothing. This is why air and other indispensable things have no exchange value, whilst scarce gewgaws fetch immense prices.

These, then, are the conditions which confront man as a producer and exchanger. If he produces a useless thing, his labor will be wholly in vain: he will get nothing for it. If he produces a useful thing, the price he will get for it will depend on how much of it there is for sale already. If he increases the supply by producing more than is sufficient to replace the current consumption, he inevitably lowers the value of the whole. It therefore behooves him to be wary in choosing his occupation, as well as industrious in pursuing it. His choice will naturally fall on the production of those commodities whose value stands highest relatively to the labor required to produce them—which fetch the highest price in proportion to their cost, in fact. Suppose, for example, that a maker of musical instruments found that it cost him exactly as much to make a harp as to make a pianoforte, but that harps were going out of fashion and pianofortes coming in. Soon there would be more harps than were wanted, and fewer pianofortes: consequently the value of harps would fall, and that of pianofortes rise. Since the labor cost of both would be the same, he would immediately devote all his labor to pianoforte-making; and other manufacturers would do the same, until the increase of supply brought down the value of pianofortes to the value of harps. Possibly fashion then might veer from pianofortes to American organs, in which case he would make less pianofortes and more American organs. When these, too, had increased sufficiently, the exertions of the Salvation Army might create such a demand for tambourines as to make them worth four times their cost of production, whereupon there would instantly be a furious concentration of the instrument-making energy on the manufacture of tambourines; and this concentration would last until the supply had brought down the profit [7] to less than might be gained by gratifying the public craving for trombones. At last, as pianofortes were cheapened until they were no more profitable than harps; then American organs until they were no more profitable than pianos; and then tambourines until they were level with American organs; so eventually trombones will pay no better than tambourines; and a general level of profit will be attained, indicating the proportion in which the instruments are wanted by the public. But to skim off even this level of profit, more of the instruments may be produced in the ascertained proportion until their prices fall

[7] Profit is here used colloquially to denote the excess of the value of an article over its cost.

to their costs of production, when there will be no profit. Here the production will be decisively checked, since a further supply would cause only a loss; and men can lose money, without the trouble of producing commodities, by the simple process of throwing it out of a window.

What occurred with the musical instruments in this illustration occurs in practice with the whole mass of manufactured commodities. Those which are scarce, and therefore relatively high in value, tempt us to produce them until the increase of the supply reduces their value to a point at which there is no more profit to be made out of them than out of other commodities. The general level of profit thus attained is further exploited until the general increase brings down the price of all commodities to their cost of production, the equivalent of which is sometimes called their normal value. And here a glance back to our analysis of the spread of cultivation, and its result in the phenomenon of rent, suggests the question: What does the cost of production of a commodity mean? We have seen that, owing to the differences in fertility and advantage of situation between one piece of land and another, cost of production varies from district to district, being highest at the margin of cultivation. But we have also seen how the landlord skims off as economic rent all the advantages gained by the cultivators of superior soils and sites. Consequently, the addition of the landlord's rent to the expenses of production brings them up even on the best land to the level of those incurred on the worst. Cost of production, then, means cost of production on the margin of cultivation, and is equalized to all producers, since what they may save in labor per commodity is counterbalanced by the greater mass of commodities they must produce in order to bring in the rent. It is only by a thorough grasp of this levelling-down action that we can detect the trick by which the ordinary economist tries to cheat us into accepting the private property system as practically just. He first shews that economic rent does not enter into cost of production on the margin of cultivation. Then he shews that the cost of production on the margin of cultivation determines the price of a commodity. Therefore, he argues, first, that rent does not enter into price; and second, that the value of commodities is fixed by their cost of production, the implication being that the landlords cost the community nothing, and that commodities exchange in exact proportion to the labor they cost. This trivially ingenious way of being disengenuous is officially taught as political economy in our schools to this day. It will be seen at once that it is mere thimblerig. So far from commodities exchanging, or tending to exchange, according to the labor expended in their production, commodities produced well within the margin of cultivation will fetch as high a price as commodities produced at the margin with much greater labor. So far from the landlord costing nothing, he costs all the difference between the two.

This, however, is not the goal of our analysis of value. We now see how Man's control over the value of commodities consists solely in his power of regulating their supply. Individuals are constantly trying to decrease supply for their own advantage. Gigantic conspiracies have been entered into to forestall the world's wheat and cotton harvests, so as to force their value to the highest possible point. Cargoes of East Indian spices have been destroyed by the Dutch as cargoes of fish are now destroyed in the Thames, to maintain prices by limiting supply. All rings, trusts, corners, combinations, monopolies and trade secrets have the same object. Production and the development of the social instincts are alike hindered by each man's consciousness that the more he stints the community the more he benefits himself, the justification, of course, being that when every man has benefited himself at the expense of the community, the community will benefit by every man in it being benefited. From one thing the community is safe. There will be no permanent conspiracies to reduce values by increasing supply. All men will cease producing when the value of their product falls below its cost of production, whether in labor or in labor *plus* rent. No man will keep on producing bread until it will fetch nothing, like the sunlight, or until it becomes a nuisance, like the rain in the summer of 1888. So far, our minds are at ease as to the excessive increase of commodities voluntarily produced by the labor of man.

Wages

I now ask you to pick up the dropped subject of the spread of cultivation. We had got as far as the appearance in the market of a new commodity—of the proletarian man compelled to live by the sale of himself! In order to realize at once the latent horror of this, you have only to apply our investigation of value, with its inevitable law that only by restricting the supply of a commodity can its value be kept from descending finally to zero. The commodity which the proletarian sells is one over the production of which he has practically no control. He is himself driven to produce it by an irresistible impulse. It was the increase of population that spread cultivation and civilization from the centre to the snowline, and at last forced men to sell themselves to the lords of the soil: it is the same force that continues to multiply men so that their exchange falls slowly and surely until it disappears altogether—until even black chattel slaves are released as not worth keeping in a land where men of all colors are to be had for nothing. This is the condition of our English laborers to-day: they are no longer even dirt cheap: they are valueless, and can be had for nothing. The proof is the existence of the unemployed, who can find no purchasers. By the law of indifference, nobody will buy men at a price when he can obtain equally serviceable men for nothing. What, then, is the explanation of the wages given to those who are in employment, and who certainly do not work for nothing? The matter is deplorably simple. Suppose that horses multiplied in England in such quantities that they were to be had for the asking, like kittens condemned to the bucket. You would still have to feed your horse—feed him and lodge him well if you used him as a smart hunter—feed him and lodge him wretchedly if you used him only as a drudge. But the cost of keeping would not mean that the horse had an exchange value. If you got him for nothing in the first instance—if no one would give you anything for him when you were done with him, he would be worth nothing, in spite of the cost of his keep. That is just the case of every member of the proletariat who could be replaced by one of the unemployed to-day. Their wage is not the price of themselves; for they are worth nothing: it is only their keep. For bare subsistence wages you can get as much common labor as you want, and do what you please with it within the limits of a criminal code which is sure to be interpreted by a proprietary-class judge in your favor. If you have to give your footman a better allowance than your wretched hewer of match wood, it is for the same reason that you have to give your hunter beans and a clean stall instead of chopped straw and a sty.[8]

Capitalism

At this stage the acquisition of labor becomes a mere question of provender. If a railway is required, all that is necessary is to provide subsistence for a sufficient number of laborers to construct it. If, for example, the railway requires the labor of a thousand men for five years, the cost to the proprietors of the site is the subsistence of a thousand men for five years. This subsis-

[8] When one of the conditions of earning a wage is the keeping up of a certain state, subsistence wages may reach a figure to which the terms seems ludicrously inappropriate. For example, a fashionable physician in London cannot save out of £1,000 a year; and the post of Lord Lieutenant of Ireland can only be filled by a man who brings considerable private means to the aid of his official salary of £20,000.

tence is technically called capital. It is provided for by the proprietors not consuming the whole excess over wages of the produce of the labor of their other wage workers, but setting aside enough for the subsistence of the railway makers. In this way capital can claim to be the result of saving, or, as one ingenious apologist neatly put it, the reward of abstinence, a gleam of humor which still enlivens treatises on capital. The savers, it need hardly be said, are those who have more money than they want to spend: the abstainers are those who have less. At the end of the five years, the completed railway is the property of the capitalists; and the railway makers fall back into the labor market as helpless as they were before. Sometimes the proprietors call the completed railway their capital; but, strictly, this is only a figure of speech. Capital is simply spare subsistence. Its market value, indicated by the current rate of interest, falls with the increase of population, whereas the market value of established stock rises with it.[9] If Mr. Goschen, encouraged by his success in reducing Consols, were to ask the proprietors of the London and North Western Railways to accept as full compensation for their complete expropriation capital just sufficient to make the railway anew, their amazement at his audacity would at once make him feel the difference between a railway and capital. Colloquially, one property with a farm on it is said to be land yielding rent; whilst another, with a railway on it, is called capital yielding interest. But economically there is no distinction between them when they once become sources of revenue. This would be quite clearly seen if costly enterprises like railways could be undertaken by a single landlord on his own land out of his own surplus wealth. It is the necessity of combining a number of possessors of surplus wealth, and devising a financial machinery for apportioning their shares in the produce to their shares in the capital contributed, that modifies the terminology and external aspect of the exploitation. But the modification is not an alteration: shareholder and landlord live alike on the produce extracted from their property by the labor of the proletariat.

"Overpopulation"

The introduction of the capitalistic system is a sign that the exploitation of the laborer toiling for a bare subsistence wage has become one of the chief arts of life among the holders of tenant rights. It also produces a delusive promise of endless employment which blinds the proletariat to those disastrous consequences of rapid multiplication which are obvious to the small cultivator and peasant proprietor. But indeed the more you degrade the workers, robbing them of all artistic enjoyment, and all chance of respect and admiration from their fellows, the more you throw them back, reckless, on the one pleasure and the one human tie left to them—the gratification of their instinct for producing fresh supplies of men. You will applaud this instinct as divine until at last the excessive supply becomes a nuisance: there comes a plague of men; and you suddenly discover that the instinct is diabolic, and set up a cry of "overpopulation." But your slaves are beyond caring for your cries; they breed like rabbits; and their poverty breeds filth, ugliness, dishonesty, disease, obscenity, drunkenness, and murder. In the midst of the riches which their labor piles up for you, their misery rises up too and stifles you. You withdraw in disgust to the other end of the town from them; you appoint special carriages on your railways and special seats in your churches and theatres for them; you set your life apart from theirs by every class barrier you can devise; and yet they swarm about you still: your face gets stamped with

[9] The current rate must, under present conditions, eventually fall to zero, and even become "negative." By that time shares which now bring in a dividend of 100 per cent, may very possibly bring in 200 or more. Yet the fall of the rate has been mistaken for a tendency of interest to disappear. It really indicates a tendency of interest to increase.

your habitual loathing and suspicion of them; your ears get so filled with the language of the vilest of them that you break into it when you lose your self-control; they poison your life as remorselessly as you have sacrificed theirs heartlessly. You begin to believe intensely in the devil. Then comes the terror of their revolting; the drilling and arming of bodies of them to keep down the rest; the prison, the hospital, paroxysms of frantic coercion, followed by paroxysms of frantic charity. And in the meantime, the population continues to increase!

"Illth"

It is sometimes said that during this grotesquely hideous march of civilization from bad to worse, wealth is increasing side by side with misery. Such a thing is eternally impossible; wealth is steadily decreasing with the spread of poverty. But riches are increasing, which is quite another thing. The total of the exchange values produced in the country annually is mounting perhaps by leaps and bounds. But the accumulation of riches, and consequently of an excessive purchasing power, in the hands of a class, soon satiates that class with socially useful wealth, and sets them offering a price for luxuries. The moment a price is to be had for a luxury, it acquires exchange value, and labor is employed to produce it. A New York lady, for instance, having a nature of exquisite sensibility, orders an elegant rosewood and silver coffin, upholstered in pink satin, for her dead dog. It is made; and meanwhile a live child is prowling barefooted and hunger-stunted in the frozen gutter outside. The exchange-value of the coffin is counted as part of the national wealth; but a nation which cannot afford food and clothing for its children cannot be allowed to pass as wealthy because it has provided a pretty coffin for a dead dog. Exchange value itself, in fact, has become bedevilled like everything else, and represents, no longer utility, but the cravings of lust, folly, vanity, gluttony, and madness, technically described by genteel economists as "effective demand." Luxuries are not social wealth; the machinery for producing them is not social wealth; labor skilled only to manufacture them is not socially useful labor; the men, women, and children who make a living by producing them are no more self-supporting than the idle rich for whose amusement they are kept at work. It is the habit of counting as wealth the exchange values involved in these transactions that makes us fancy that the poor are starving in the midst of plenty. They are starving in the midst of plenty of jewels, velvets, laces, equipages, and racehorses; but not in the midst of plenty of food. In the things that are wanted for the welfare of the people we are abjectly poor; and England's social policy to-day may be likened to the domestic policy of those adventuresses who leave their children half-clothed and half-fed in order to keep a carriage and deal with a fashionable dressmaker. But it is quite true that whilst wealth and welfare are decreasing, productive power is increasing; and nothing but the perversion of this power to the production of socially useless commodities prevents the apparent wealth from becoming real. The purchasing power that commands luxuries in the hands of the rich, would command true wealth in the hands of all. Yet private property must still heap the purchasing power upon the few rich and withdraw it from the many poor. So that, in the end, the subject of the one boast that private property can make—the great accumulation of so-called "wealth" which it points so proudly to as the result of its power to scourge men and women daily to prolonged and intense toil, turns out to be a simulacrum. With all its energy, its Smilesian "self-help," its merchant-princely enterprise, its ferocious sweating and slave-driving, its prodigality of blood, sweat and tears, what has it heaped up, over and above the pittance of its slaves? Only a monstrous pile of frippery, some tainted class literature and class art, and not a little poison and mischief.

This, then, is the economic analysis which convicts Private Property of being unjust even from the beginning, and utterly impossible as a final solution of even the individualist aspect of the problem of adjusting the share of the worker in the distribution of wealth to the labor incurred by him in its production. All attempts yet made to construct true societies upon it have failed; the nearest things to societies so achieved have been civilizations, which have rotted into centres of vice and luxury, and eventually been swept away by uncivilized races. That our own civilization is already in an advanced stage of rottenness may be taken as statistically proved. That further decay instead of improvement must ensure if the institution of private property be maintained, is economically certain. Fortunately, private property in its integrity is not now practicable. Although the safety-valve of emigration has been furiously at work during this century, yet the pressure of population has forced us to begin the restitution to the people of the sums taken from them for the ground landlords, holders of tenant right, and capitalists, by the imposition of an income tax, and by compelling them to establish out of their revenues a national system of education, besides imposing restrictions—as yet only of the forcible-feeble sort—on their terrible power of abusing the wage contract. These, however, are dealt with by Mr. Sidney Webb in the historic essay which follows. I should not touch upon them at all, were it not that experience has lately convinced all economists that no exercise in abstract economics, however closely deduced, is to be trusted unless it can be experimentally verified by tracing its expression in history. It is true that the process which I have presented as a direct development of private property between free exchangers had to work itself out in the Old World indirectly and tortuously through a struggle with political and religious institutions and survivals quite antagonistic to it. It is true that cultivation did not begin in Western Europe with the solitary emigrant pre-empting his private property, but with the tribal communes in which arose subsequently the assertion of the right of the individual to private judgment and private action against the tyranny of primitive society. It is true that cultivation has not proceeded by logical steps from good land to less good; from less good to bad; and from bad to worse: the exploration of new countries and new regions, and the discovery of new uses for old products, has often made the margin of cultivation more fruitful than the centre, and, for the moment (whilst the centre was shifting to the margin), turned the whole movement of rent and wages directly counter to the economic theory. Nor is it true that, taking the world as one country, cultivation has yet spread from the snowline to the water's edge. There is free land still for the poorest East End match-box maker if she could get there, reclaim the wilderness there, speak the language there, stand the climate there, and be fed, clothed, and housed there whilst she cleared her farm; learned how to cultivate it; and waited for the harvest. Economists have been ingenious enough to prove that this alternative really secures her independence; but I shall not waste time in dealing with that. Practically, if there is no free land in England, the economic analysis holds good of England, in spite of Siberia, Central Africa, and the Wild West. Again, it is not immediately true that men are governed in production solely by a determination to realize the maximum of exchange value. The impulse to production often takes specific direction in the first instance; and a man will insist on producing pictures or plays although he might gain more money by producing boots or bonnets. But, his specific impulse once gratified, he will make as much money as he can. He will sell his picture or play for a hundred pounds rather than for fifty. In short, though there is no such person as the celebrated "economic man," man being wilful rather than rational, yet when the wilful man has had his way he will take what else he can get; and so he always does appear, finally if not primarily, as the economic man. On the whole, history, even in the Old World, goes the way traced by the economist. In the New World the correspondence is exact. The United States and the Colonies have been peopled by fugitives from the full-blown individualism of Western Europe, pre-empting private property precisely as assumed in this investigation of the conditions of cultivation. The economic relations of these cultivators have not since put on any of the old political disguises. Yet among them, in confirmation of the validity of our analysis, we see all the evils of our old civilizations growing up; and though with them the end is not yet, still it is from them to us that the great recent revival of the cry for nationalization of the land has come, articulated by a man who had seen the whole tragedy of private property hurried through its acts with unprecedented speed in the mushroom cities of America.

On Socialism the analysis of the economic action of Individualism bears as a discovery, in the private appropriation of land, of the source of those unjust privileges against which Socialism is aimed. It is practically a demonstration that public property in land is the basic economic condition of Socialism. But this does not involve at present a literal restoration of the land to the people. The land is at present in the hands of the people: its proprietors are for the most part absentees. The modern form of private property is simply a legal claim to take a share of the produce of the national industry year by year without working for it. It refers to no special part or form of that product; and in process of consumption its revenue cannot be distinguished from earnings, so that the majority of persons, accustomed to call the commodities which form the income of the proprietor his private property, and seeing no difference between them and the commodities which form the income of a worker, extend the term private property to the worker's subsistence also, and can only conceive an attack on private property as an attempt to empower everybody to rob everybody else all round. But the income of a private proprietor can be distinguished by the fact that he obtains it unconditionally and gratuitously by private right against the public weal, which is incompatible with the existence of consumers who do not produce. Socialism involves discontinuance of the payment of these incomes, and addition of the wealth so saved to incomes derived from labor. As we have seen, incomes derived from private property consist partly of economic rent; partly of pensions, also called rent, obtained by the subletting of tenant rights; and partly of a form of rent called interest, obtained by special adaptations of land to production by the application of capital: all these being finally paid out of the difference between the produce of the worker's labor and the price of that labor sold in the open market for wages, salary, fees, or profits.[10] The whole, except economic rent, can be added directly to the incomes of the workers by simply discontinuing its exaction from them. Economic rent, arising as it does from variations of fertility or advantages of situation, must always be held as common or social wealth, and used, as the revenues raised by taxation are now used, for public purposes, among which Socialism would make national insurance and the provision of capital matters of the first importance.

The economic problem of Socialism is thus solved; and the political question of how the economic solution is to be practically applied does not come within the scope of this essay. But if we have got as far as an intellectual conviction that the source of our social misery is no eternal well-spring of confusion and evil, but only an artificial system susceptible of almost infinite modification and readjustment—nay, of practical demolition and substitution at the will of Man,

[10] This excess of the product of labor over its price is treated as a single category with impressive effect by Karl Marx, who called it "surplus value" (*mehrwerth*).

then a terrible weight will be lifted from the minds of all except those who are, whether avowedly to themselves or not, clinging to the present state of things from base motives. We have had in this century a stern series of lessons on the folly of believing anything for no better reason than that it is pleasant to believe it. It was pleasant to look round with a consciousness of possessing a thousand a year, and say, with Browning's David, "All's love; and all's law." It was pleasant to believe that the chance we were too lazy to take in this world would come back to us in another. It was pleasant to believe that a benevolent hand was guiding the steps of society; overruling all evil appearances for good; and making poverty here the earnest of a great blessedness and reward hereafter. It was pleasant to lose the sense of worldly inequality in the contemplation of our equality before God. But utilitarian questioning and scientific answering turned all this tranquil optimism into the blackest pessimism. Nature was shewn to us as "red in tooth and claw": if the guiding hand were indeed benevolent, then it could not be omnipotent; so that our trust in it was broken: if it were omnipotent, it could not be benevolent; so that our love of it turned to fear and hatred. We had never admitted that the other world, which was to compensate for the sorrows of this, was open to horses and apes (though we had not on that account been any the more merciful to our horses); and now came Science to shew us the corner of the pointed ear of the horse on our own heads, and present the ape to us as our blood relation. No proof came to the existence of that other world and that benevolent power to which we had left the remedy of the atrocious wrongs of the poor; proof after proof came that what we called Nature knew and cared no more about our pains and pleasures than we know or care about the tiny creatures we crush underfoot as we walk through the fields. Instead of at once perceiving that this meant no more than that Nature was unmoral and indifferent, we relapsed into a gross form of devil worship, and conceived Nature as a remorselessly malignant power. This was no better than the old optimism, and infinitely gloomier. It kept our eyes still shut to the truth that there is no cruelty and selfishness outside Man himself; and that his own active benevolence can combat and vanquish both. When the Socialist came forward as a meliorist on these lines, the old school of political economists, who could see no alternative to private property, put forward in proof of the powerlessness of benevolent action to arrest the deadly automatic production of poverty by the increase of population, the very analysis I have just presented. Their conclusions exactly fitted in with the new ideas. It was Nature at it again—the struggle for existence—the remorseless extirpation of the weak—the survival of the fittest—in short, natural selection of work. Socialism seemed too good to be true: it was passed by as merely the old optimism foolishly running its head against the stone wall of modern science. But Socialism now challenges individualism, scepticism, pessimism, worship of Nature personified as a devil, on their own ground of science. The science of the production and distribution of wealth is Political Economy. Socialism appeals to that science, and, turning on Individualism its own guns, routs it in incurable disaster. Henceforth the bitter cynic who still finds the world an eternal and unimprovable doghole, with the placid person of means who repeats the familiar misquotation, "The poor ye shall have always with you," lose their usurped place among the cultured, and pass over to the ranks of the ignorant, the shallow, and the superstitious. As for the rest of us, since we were taught to revere proprietary respectability in our unfortunate childhood, and since we found our childish hearts so hard and unregenerate that they secretly hated and rebelled against respectability in spite of that teaching, it is impossible to express the relief with which we discover that our hearts were all along right, and that the current respectability of to-day is nothing but a huge inversion of righteous and scientific social order weltering in dishonesty, uselessness, selfishness, wanton misery, and idiotic waste of magnificent opportunities for noble and happy living. It was terrible to feel this, and yet to fear that it could not be helped—that the poor must starve and make you ashamed of your dinner—that they must shiver and make you ashamed of your warm overcoat. It is to economic science—once the Dismal, now the Hopeful—that we are indebted for the discovery that though the evil is enormously worse than we knew, yet it is not eternal—not even very long lived, if we only bestir ourselves to make an end of it.

FORTY-FIVE

INDIA AND THE WEST

During the nineteenth century, Britain gradually gained direct control of the major part of India and indirect control of the remaining native states. British rule in India was generally efficient and of far greater benefit to Indians than anti-imperialists have realized. For the most part, India enjoyed peace under the British raj, broken by the Great Mutiny of 1857 and by recurrent border warfare. But many critical problems arose because Britain brought to this disunited and underdeveloped subcontinent a number of Western institutions and attitudes unfamiliar to the Indian population, among them liberalism, with its reliance on self-government and freedom of speech, and nationalism, with its reliance on civic responsibility. Among Britain's most distinguished rulers in India was Field Marshal Earl Roberts (1832–1914), the son of a British general in India and himself born there. Lord Roberts was commissioned in the Bengal artillery in 1851, fought gallantly in the Mutiny and in numerous frontier campaigns, and returned to England in 1893. Four years later he published his long and thoughtful autobiography Forty-One Years in India. *Lord Roberts knew India well. In his autobiography he pointed out what he believed to be errors in Britain's administration there, mainly overcentralized government and the tendency to force British ways on the native population. Instead he urged caution in forcing Western institutions on the Indian way of life. His formula for British rule was simple: benevolent despotism. In many ways he represented what was best in Victorian imperialism. But at the same time he was a typical Victorian in his calm assumption that British institutions were far superior to those of the natives. He deplored agitation by Indian patriots, and saw in Indian nationalism, already well started when he left India, little more than a regrettable nuisance which disturbed British rule. He, like most of his self-satisfied Victorian contemporaries, failed to understand that India was reacting swiftly and vigorously to British domination, and that in time the very liberalism and nationalism which Britain had brought to India would put an end to British rule there.*

LORD ROBERTS OF KANDAHAR

FORTY-ONE YEARS IN INDIA *

The India of to-day is altogether a different country from the India of 1857. Much has been done since then to improve the civil administration, and to meet the legitimate demands of the Native races. India is more tranquil, more prosperous, and more civilized than it was before the Mutiny, and the discipline, efficiency, and mobility of the Native army have been greatly improved. Much, however, still remains to be done, and a good deal might with advantage be undone, to secure the contentment of the Natives with our rule.

Our position has been materially strengthened by the provision of main and subsidiary lines of communication by road and railway; by the great network of telegraphs which now intersects the country; and by the construction of canals. These great public works have largely increased the area of land under cultivation, minimized the risk of famine, equalized the prices of agricultural produce, and developed a large and lucrative export trade. Above all, while our troops can now be assembled easily and rapidly at any centre of disturbance, the number of British soldiers has been more than doubled and the number of Native soldiers has been materially reduced. Moreover, as regards the Native equally with the British army of India, I believe that a better feeling never existed throughout all ranks than exists at present.

Nevertheless, there are signs that the spirit of unrest and discontent which sowed the seeds of the Mutiny is being revived. To some extent this state of things is the natural result of our position in India, and is so far unavoidable, but it is also due to old faults reappearing—faults which require to be carefully watched and guarded against, for it is certain that, however well disposed as soldiers the men in our ranks may be, their attitude will inevitably be influenced by the feelings of the people generally, more especially should their hostility be aroused by any question connected with religion.

For a considerable time after the Mutiny we became more cautious and conciliatory in administrative and legislative matters, more intent on doing what would keep the Chiefs and Rulers satisfied, the masses contented, and the country, quiet, than on carrying out our own ideas. Gradually this wholesome caution is being disregarded. The Government has become more and more centralized, and the departmental spirit very strong. Each department, in its laudable wish for progress and advancement, is apt to push on measures which are obnoxious to the Natives, either from their not being properly understood, or from their being opposed to their traditions and habits of life, thus entailing the sacrifice of many cherished customs and privileges. Each department admits in theory the necessity for caution, but in practice presses for liberty of action to further its own particular schemes.

Of late years, too, the tendency has been to increase the number of departments and of secretariat offices under the supreme Gov-

* From *Forty-One Years in India,* pp. 245–51, by Lord Roberts of Kandahar. New York, Longmans, Green and Co., 1904.

ernment, and this tendency, while causing more work to devolve on the supreme Government than it can efficiently perform, results in lessening the responsibility of provincial Governments by interference in the management of local concerns. It is obvious that in a country like India, composed as it is of great provinces and various races differing from one another in interests, customs, and religions, each with its own peculiar and distinct necessities, administrative details ought to be left to the people on the spot. The Government of India would then be free to exercise a firm and impartial control over the Empire and Imperial interests, while guiding into safe channels, without unduly restraining, intelligent progress.

In times of peace the administration is apt to fall too exclusively into the hands of officials whose ability is of the doctrinaire type; they work hard, and can give logical and statistical reasons for the measures they propose, and are thus able to make them attractive to, and believed in by, the authorities. But they lack the more perfect knowledge of human nature, and the deeper insight into, and greater sympathy with, the feelings and prejudices of Asiatics, which those possessed in a remarkable degree who proved by their success that they had mastered the problem of the best form of government for India. I allude to men like Thomas Munro, Mountstuart Elphinstone, John Malcolm, Charles Metcalfe, George Clerk, Henry and John Lawrence, William Sleeman, James Outram, Herbert Edwardes, John Nicholson, and many others. These administrators, while fully recognizing the need for a gradual reform, understood the peculiarities of our position in the east, the necessity for extreme caution and toleration, and a 'live and let live' policy between us and the Natives. The sound and broad views of this class of public servant are not always appreciated either in India or England, and are too often put aside as unpractical, obstructive, and old-fashioned.

Amongst the causes which have produced discontent of late years, I would mention our forest laws and sanitary regulations, our legislative and fiscal systems—measures so necessary that no one interested in the prosperity of India could cavil at their introduction, but which are so absolutely foreign to Native ideas, that it is essential should be applied with the utmost gentleness and circumspection.

I think, also, that the official idea of converting the young Princes and Nobles of India into English gentlemen by means of English tutors and English studies should be carried out with great care and caution. It has not hitherto invariably succeeded, and the feeling in many States is strongly opposed to it. The danger of failure lies in the wholesome restraint of the tutor being suddenly removed, and in the young Prince being left at too early an age to select his advisers and companions. The former, perhaps not unnaturally, are interested in proving that the training of their young Ruler by his European governor or tutor has not resulted in good either to himself or his people, while the latter are too often of the lowest class of European adventurers.

The proceedings and regulations of the Forest Department, desirable as they may be from a financial and agricultural point of view, have provoked very great irritation in many parts of India. People who have been accustomed from time immemorial to pick up sticks and graze their cattle on forest lands, cannot understand why they should now be forbidden to do so, nor can they realize the necessity for preserving the trees from the chance of being destroyed by fire, a risk to which they were frequently exposed from the Native custom of making use of their shelter while cooking, and of burning the undergrowth to enrich the grazing.

The action taken by the Government in sanitary matters has also aroused much ill-feeling and apprehension. Sanitary precautions are entirely ignored in eastern countries. The great majority of the people can see no good in them, and no harm in using the same tank for drinking purposes and for bathing and washing their clothes. The immediate surroundings of their towns and villages are most offensive, being used as the general receptacles for dead animals and all kinds of filth. Cholera, fever, and other diseases, which carry off hundreds of thousands every year, are looked upon as the visitation of God, from which it is impossible, even were it not impious to try, to escape; and the precautionary measures insisted upon by us in our cantonments, and at the fairs and places of pilgrimage, are viewed with aversion and indignation. Only those who have witnessed the personal discomfort and fatigue to which Natives of all ages and both sexes willingly submit in their struggle to reach some holy shrine on the occasion of a religious festival, while dragging their weary limbs for many hundreds of miles along a hot, dusty road, or being huddled for hours together in a crammed and stifling railway carriage, can have any idea of the bitter disappointment to the pilgrims caused by their being ordered to disperse when cholera breaks out at such gatherings, without being given the opportunity of performing their vows or bathing in the sacred waters.[1]

Further, our legislative system is based on western ideas, its object being to mete out equal justice to the rich and poor, to the Prince and peasant. But our methods of procedure do not commend themselves to the Indian peoples. Eastern races are accustomed to a paternal despotism, and they conceive it to be the proper function of the local representatives of the supreme Power to investigate and determine on the spot the various criminal and civil cases which come under the cognizance of the district officials. Legal technicalities and references to distant tribunals confuse and harass a population which, with comparatively few exceptions, is illiterate, credulous, and suspicious of underhand influence. An almost unlimited right of appeal from one court to another, in matters of even the most trivial importance, not only tends to impair the authority of the local magistrate, but gives an unfair advantage to the wealthy litigant whose means enable him to secure the services of the ablest pleader, and to purchase the most conclusive evidence in support of his claims. For it must be remembered that in India evidence on almost any subject can be had for the buying, and the difficulty, in the administration of justice, of discriminating between truth and falsehood is thereby greatly increased. Under our system a horde of unscrupulous pleaders has sprung up, and these men encourage useless litigation, thereby impoverishing their clients, and creating much ill-feeling against our laws and administration.

Another point worthy of consideration is the extent to which, under the protection of our legal system, the peasant proprietors of India are being oppressed and ruined by village shop-keepers and money-lenders. These men advance money at a most exorbitant rate of interest, taking as security the crops and occupancy rights of the cultivators of the soil. The latter are ignorant, improvident, and in some matters, such as the marriage ceremonies of their families, inordinately extravagant. The result is that a small debt soon swells into a big one, and eventually the aid of the law courts is invoked to oust the cultivator from a holding which, in many cases, has been in the possession of his ancestors for hundreds of years. The money-lender has his accounts to produce,

[1] Few acts have been more keenly resented than the closing of the great Hurdwar Fair in the autumn of 1892, on account of a serious outbreak of cholera. It was looked upon by the Natives as a direct blow aimed at their religion, and as a distinct departure from the religious tolerance promised in Her Majesty's proclamation of 1858. The mysterious mud marks on mango-trees in Behar have been attributed by some to a self-interested motive on the part of certain priests to draw the attention of Hindus to the sanctity of some temple outside the limits of British jurisdiction, where the devotees would be at liberty to assemble in any numbers without being troubled by officious inspectors, and where they could remain as long as they pleased, irrespective of the victims daily claimed by cholera, that unfailing avenger of the neglect of sanitary laws in the east.

and these can hardly be disputed, the debtor as a rule being unable to keep accounts of his own, or, indeed, to read or write. Before the British dominion was established in India, the usurer no doubt existed, but his opportunities were fewer, his position more precarious, and his operations more under control than they are at present. The money-lender then knew that his life would not be safe if he exacted too high interest for the loans with which he accommodated his customers, and that if he became too rich, some charge or other would be trumped up against him, which would force him to surrender a large share of his wealth to the officials of the State in which he was living. I do not say that the rough-and-ready methods of Native justice in dealing with money-lenders were excusable or tolerable, but at the same time I am inclined to think that, in granting these men every legal facility for enforcing their demands and carrying on their traffic, we may have neglected the interests of the agriculturists, and that it might be desirable to establish some agency under the control of Government, which would enable the poorer landholders to obtain, at a moderate rate of interest, advances proportionate to the security they had to offer.[2]

Another danger to our supremacy in India is the license allowed to the Native press in vilifying the Government and its officials, and persistently misrepresenting the motives and policy of the ruling Power. In a free country, where the mass of the population is well educated, independent, and self-reliant, a free press is a most valuable institution, representing as it does the requirements and aspirations of important sections of the community, and bringing to light defects and abuses in the social and political system. In a country such as Great Britain, which is well advanced in the art of self-government, intolerant and indiscriminate abuse of public men defeats its own object, and misstatements of matters of fact can be at once exposed and refuted. Like most of the developments of civilization which are worth anything, the English press is a plant of indigenous growth, whereas in India the Native press is an exotic which, under existing conditions, supplies no general want, does nothing to refine, elevate, or instruct the people, and is used by its supporters and promoters—an infinitesimal part of the population—as a means of gaining its selfish ends, and of fostering sedition, and racial and religious animosities. There are, I am afraid, very few Native newspapers actuated by a friendly or impartial spirit towards the Government of India, and to Asiatics it seems incredible that we should permit such hostile publications to be scattered broadcast over the country, unless the assertions were too true to be disputed, or unless we were too weak to suppress them. We gain neither credit nor gratitude for our tolerant attitude towards the Native press—our forbearance is misunderstood; and while the well-disposed are amazed at our inaction, the disaffected rejoice at being allowed to promulgate baseless insinuations and misstatements which undermine our authority, and thwart our efforts to gain the goodwill and confidence of the Native population.

Yet another danger to the permanence of our rule in India lies in the endeavours of well-intentioned faddists to regulate the customs and institutions of eastern races in accordance with their own ideas. The United Kingdom is a highly civilized country, and our habits and convictions have been gradually developed under the influences of our religion and our national surroundings. Fortunately for themselves, the people of Great Britain possess qualities which have made them masters of a vast and still expanding Empire. But these qualities have their defects as well as their merits, and one of the defects is a certain insularity of thought, or narrow-mindedness—a slowness to recognize

[2] The proposal would seem to be quite a practical one, for I read in the *Times* of the 28th November, 1894, that the Government of New Zealand invited applications for Consols in connexion with the scheme for granting loans at a reasonable rate of interest to farmers on the security of their holdings.

that institutions which are perfectly suitable and right for us may be quite unsuited, if not injurious, to other races, and that what may not be right for us to do is not necessarily wrong for people of a different belief, and with absolutely different traditions and customs.

Gradually the form of Government in the United Kingdom has become representative and democratic, and it is therefore assumed by some people, who have little, if any, experience of the east, that the Government of India should be guided by the utterances of self-appointed agitators who pose as the mouth-pieces of an oppressed population. Some of these men are almost as much aliens [3] as ourselves, while others are representatives of a class which, though intellectually advanced, has no influence amongst the races in whom lies the real strength of India. Municipal self-government has been found to answer well in the United Kingdom, and it is held, therefore, that a similar system must be equally successful in India. We in England consume animal food and alcoholic liquors, but have no liking for opium; an effort has accordingly been made to deprive our Asiatic fellow-subjects, who, as a rule, are vegetarians, and either total abstainers or singularly abstemious in the matter of drink, of a small and inexpensive stimulant, which they find necessary to their health and comfort. British institutions and ideas are the embodiment of what long experience has proved to us to be best for ourselves; but suddenly to establish these institutions and enforce these ideas on a community which is not prepared for them, does not want them, and cannot understand them, must only lead to suspicion and discontent. The Government of India should, no doubt, be progressive in its policy, and in all things be guided by the immutable principles of right, truth, and justice; but these principles ought to be applied, not necessarily as we should apply them in England, but with due regard to the social peculiarities and religious prejudices of the people whom it ought to be our aim to make better and happier.

It will be gathered from what I have written that our administration, in my opinion, suffers from two main defects. First, it is internally too bureaucratic and centralizing in its tendencies; and, secondly, it is liable to be forced by the external pressure of well-meaning but irresponsible politicians and philanthropists to adopt measures which may be disapproved of by the authorities on the spot, and opposed to the wishes, requirements, and interests of the people. It seems to me that for many years to come the best form of government for India will be the intelligent and benevolent despotism which at present rules the country. On a small scale, and in matters of secondary importance, representative institutions cannot perhaps do much harm, though I am afraid they will effect but little good. On a large scale, however, such a system of government would be quite out of place in view of the fact that ninety-nine out of every hundred of the population are absolutely devoid of any idea of civil responsibility, and that the various races and religious sects possess no bond of national union.

In reply, then, to the question, 'Is there any chance of a Mutiny occurring again?' I would say that the best way of guarding against such a calamity is—

By never allowing the present proportion of British to Native soldiers to be diminished or the discipline and efficiency of the Native army to become slack.

By taking care that men are selected for the higher civil and military posts whose self-reliance, activity, and resolution are not impaired by age, and who possess a knowledge of the country and the habits of the peoples.

By recognizing and guarding against the dogmatism of theorists and the dangers of centralization.

By rendering our administration on the one hand firm and strong, on the other hand

[3] I allude to the Parsis, who came from Persia, and whose religion and customs are as distinct from those of the Natives of India as are our own.

tolerant and sympathetic; and last, but not least, by doing all in our power to gain the confidence of the various races, and by convincing them that we have not only the determination, but the ability to maintain our supremacy in India against all assailants.

If these cardinal points are never lost sight of, there is, I believe, little chance of any fresh outbreak disturbing the stability of our rule in India, or neutralizing our efforts to render that country prosperous, contented, and thoroughly loyal to the British Crown.

FORTY-SIX

THE SCHLIEFFEN PLAN AND THE OUTBREAK OF WORLD WAR I

The tangled diplomacy of the great powers in the 30 years preceding and the six weeks following the assassination of the Austrian archduke Francis Ferdinand, on June 28, 1914, has been the subject of minute historical analysis. Obviously the diplomacy, along with factors immediately conditioning it, was the main channel for the forces leading to the outbreak of the first World War. The war and its aftermath dealt a grievous blow to Western civilization, and led directly to other catastrophes: the rise of totalitarianism in Russia, Italy, and Germany. Analysis of the war's causes, therefore, has far more than academic interest. Some scholars think that an understanding of how the war came about might help us to avoid future wars. Other scholars have expressed reservations on this point and have cast doubt on the whole process of research in depth—that is, a day-to-day and hour-to-hour analysis of the diplomacy. In any case, Luigi Albertini has written a monumental and lucid account of the war's diplomacy, based on exhaustive study of thousands of documents in various archives, along with more easily accessible printed accounts. Probably his three volumes will become the standard work on the subject. One of Albertini's most brilliant chapters concerns the Schlieffen Plan, the German blueprint for mobilization combined with an immediate attack on France. Albertini points out that Germany had only one plan of mobilization, and that once that plan went into effect Germany had to attack France, while other nations could mobilize without immediately going to war. Albertini accordingly found in the Schlieffen Plan a pivotal cause for the outbreak of hostilities.

LUIGI ALBERTINI

THE ORIGINS OF THE WAR OF 1914 *

1. The Mistakenness of Both the Russian and the German Mobilization

Now that we have seen how the great tragedy began which brought affliction to the whole human race and from whose consequences we still suffer and our children's children will go on suffering, we must ask ourselves the question whether there was any justification for the way Germany acted from 30 July onwards. In other words, was it inevitable that the Russian mobilization should let slip the dogs of war in Berlin and cause the abandonment of all attempt to compose the conflict?

There is not the slightest doubt that the Russian partial mobilization, decided in principle as early as 24 July and ordered on the evening of the 29th, was a blunder of the first magnitude, and that in the circumstances and for the reasons we have examined, it led on to her general mobilization which Germany made the reason for carrying out a predetermined procedure of ultimatum, general mobilization, war. This partial mobilization was a very serious mistake, and one without justification, because so long as Austria mobilized only eight army corps for operations against Serbia, Russia had no reason to arm. On the contrary, it would have been from the military point of view of great advantage to her to let Austria send those eight army corps against Serbia, intervening herself, if needful, when the Dual Monarchy had thus diverted part of its forces to a minor field of operations. This had not escaped the attention of Moltke, who in his memorandum of 28 July had written that Austria would not be able to wage war on Serbia

> without making Russian intervention certain. That means she will have to mobilize the other half of her army, for she cannot possibly put herself at the mercy of a Russia ready for war.

Thus the mere threat of Russian partial mobilization, or rather the bare possibility of it, would oblige Austria to protect herself by mobilizing her whole army. And then it would not be Russia who gave the bad example and bore the responsibility for mobilizing. She could say, as Moltke foresaw: 'You, Austria, are mobilizing against us; that means you intend to make war on us.' [1] On the other hand, by mobilizing first against Austria, Russia was forcing Austria to take similar measures in self-defence, the fault lying with Russia, and it also meant bringing Germany on to the scene. Sazonov did not perceive the danger. At the beginning he wanted the partial mobilization, not in order to take active measures, but to frighten Austria and obtain diplomatic satisfaction. But such weapons cannot rashly be resorted to with impunity. By transferring the con-

* From *The Origins of the War of 1914,* III, 230–53, by Luigi Albertini by permission of Oxford University Press, London, 1957.

[1] DD. II, 349. See Vol. II, pp. 488–9.

duct of affairs from the hands of the politicians to those of the generals, they produce the very opposite effect to the one intended, that is they cause the failure of diplomatic action. And, as events showed, once partial mobilization had been decided, unobjectionable as it was held to be even by Jagow, the Russian generals showed that it was impossible of execution and that general mobilization was required. Unfortunately, Sazonov was talked over by their arguments, instead of giving up the idea of even partial mobilization.

Nevertheless, having agreed that Sazonov was mistaken about the consequences which would follow from partial mobilization and that, instead of suspending it, he took the fatal step of ordering general mobilization, for which he bears the entire blame, one is faced with the question whether this measure was such a menace to Germany that she was constrained forthwith to throw up all attempts to achieve the peaceful solution which was already in sight. The pro-German writers avoid touching on this aspect of the situation which presented itself to Berlin at noon on 31 July. They prefer to attack the standpoint of those who maintain that Germany could have confined herself to mobilizing without going to war, on the lines suggested by Sazonov and the Tsar, namely, that the mobilized armies should stand at ease so long as negotiations went on. The thesis of these writers is that 'static' mobilization is a chimera, because all mobilization is necessarily bound up with a plan of offensive operations beyond the frontiers of the State in question. This point has been examined in an earlier chapter.[2] Here it is sufficient to repeat that, in all countries except Germany, mobilization was a proceeding which required a certain amount of time, and the plan of war only came into operation when mobilization was completed. This meant that between mobilization and war there was a considerable interval of time during which, if it were so desired, there was the possibility of carrying on and concluding a train of negotiations, without attaching too great importance to such frontier incidents as might occur. A sufficient proof hereof is the case of Austria, where Conrad, to the disapproval of Berlin, decided that, although war was declared on Serbia on 28 July, operations were not to begin until 12 August. Germany, however, was not in that category. As has repeatedly been stated, she had given herself a plan of campaign which laid down that the act of mobilization was immediately followed by an advance beyond the frontiers. Thus the pro-German writers are correct in maintaining that Germany could not mobilize and then await the outcome of negotiations in progress, even if of short duration. The opposite view is taken by Kautsky, who writes:

> That Germany should mobilize in her turn after the Russian mobilization was quite understandable. If Germany had regarded mobilization simply as a precautionary measure, as did all other nations—even France—there would be nothing to condemn in this step. . . . If Germany had accompanied her mobilization with similar assurances [to those given by Russia], negotiations could have really gone on and finally ended peacefully. Had not Russia and Austria mobilized in 1913 without coming to blows? . . . Mobilization, therefore, did not necessarily mean war. Demobilization could still follow it at the last moment without this bloody result, if people came to an understanding meanwhile.[3]

In theory this was true, but in practice the German plan of mobilization ruled out the possibility.

2. Germany Could Have Saved the Peace by the Halt in Belgrade Formula

In spite of this it cannot be proved that after the Russian general mobilization the German leaders had no other resource than

[2] See Vol. II, pp. 479–82.

[3] Kautsky, pp. 202–3.

to send St. Petersburg and Paris the ultimatums which set Europe ablaze. If on the evening of 30 July the Chancellor had not let the situation get 'out of hand', if he had not capitulated to Moltke's will to war, a way of escape could still have been found. Let it not be objected that Moltke was justified in maintaining that every hour lost endangered the success of the German plan, based as it was on speed and surprise. Moltke was doubtless induced to maintain this chiefly by the fear that, if the negotiations lasted on, the conflict might be composed. However, from the military point of view the fact remains that the German plan did not provide for an offensive against Russia, but only for one against France through Belgium. Now, so long as France did not mobilize—and France would not have mobilized if both she and Russia had not received an ultimatum on 31 July—the success of the German plan would not have been directly jeopardized. It would have been so indirectly in as far as Russia could have taken advantage of any delay on the part of Germany to push forward her own mobilization and put herself into a position to take the initiative in East Prussia. As Bethmann telegraphed to Lichnowsky at 1:50 a.m. on 1 August:

> A mobilized Russian army on our frontier, without our having mobilized, is a mortal danger to us even without 'provocative action'.

And Stumm's original draft had continued:

> For instance, our East Prussian province and perhaps also Posen and Silesia would be abandoned beyond recall to Russian conquest.[4]

But it is not the case that a start of twenty-four or even forty-eight hours would definitely have tipped the scales in favour of Russia, whose mobilization was an exceedingly slow affair. This was admitted even by Falkenhayn when on 29 July he wrote in his diary that there was no need for haste in ordering mobilization,

> for it was to be assumed that our mobilization, even if two or three days later than that of Russia and Austria, would be more rapid than theirs.[5]

What he thought ought to be done first was to proclaim the *Kriegsgefahrzustand,* which would enable preparations to be begun without actual mobilization and the opening of hostilities. Here is the proof that, in view of the immense issue at stake, Germany could well have afforded to wait a moment. If this was not realized by Moltke, who was soon to prove himself altogether unfitted for his task, it was intuitively felt by both Wilhelm and the Chancellor, who had been counting on the neutrality of England and the intervention of Italy and Roumania, and now saw these essential preconditions of their venture failing them.

We have seen that on 31 July there still existed a basis of negotiation: the *Halt in Belgrade*. Knowing what the position was and that the *Halt in Belgrade* was a suggestion of Grey's and would therefore have his backing, Berlin could have taken advantage of the silence of Vienna (whence at noon on the 31st no answer had yet been received to the appeal sent on the evening of the 28th) to take a decisive step which Germany, as the country on whom would fall the brunt of the war, had a perfect right to do, namely, to give a promise to St. Petersburg that she would recommend at Vienna the *Halt in Belgrade,* which had also the backing of London, in return for a suspension of mobilization. The *Halt in Belgrade* would not of course be satisfactory to Sazonov if it implied the unconditional acceptance by Serbia of all the demands of the ultimatum. Wilhelm showed appreciation of this when he wrote to Jagow:

> The few reservations made by Serbia on single points can in my opinion well be cleared up by negotiation.[6]

[4] DD. III, 529.

[5] See Vol. II, p. 502.

[6] DD. II. 293. See Vol. II, pp. 468–9.

The Chancellor, it is true, in sending on the Kaiser's suggestion to Tschirschky had added that 'the temporary occupation of Belgrade and other definite points on Serbian territory' would serve 'to force the Serbian Government to integral fulfilment of Austrian demands'.[7]

The difference between the two formulas was serious, and that of Bethmann would certainly never have been accepted by Sazonov, who was determined to have guarantees against any infringement of Serbian independence, guarantees which were to be fixed by negotiation. However, by the 30th Bethmann had shown himself prepared to take a long step towards meeting Sazonov's wishes when, to a telegram from Pourtalès communicating Sazonov's last peace formula, he appended the minute:

> What points of the Austrian ultimatum has Serbia rejected? As far as I know only the participation of Austrian officials in law-court trials. Austria could dispense with this participation on condition that she occupies parts of Serbia with her troops until the end of the negotiations.[8]

Only one more step forward, even at the risk of somewhat forcing the hand of Vienna, and conciliation would have been achieved.

Grey would certainly have lent his aid. It must not be forgotten that on the evening of the 30th he had telegraphed to Buchanan proposing a variant of Sazonov's formula:

> If Austrian advance were stopped after occupation of Belgrade, I think Russian Minister for Foreign Affairs' formula might be changed to read that the Powers would examine how Serbia could fully satisfy Austria without impairing Serbian sovereign rights or independence.[9]

And Sazonov himself in that last formula of his had, as Pourtalès commented, asked no more than that Austria should refrain from entering Serbia. On receiving Grey's variant, Sazonov had merged his proposal with Grey's to form the formula which has already been quoted and elucidated above.

> If Austria agrees to stop the march of her troops into Serbian territory and if . . . she agrees that the Great Powers shall inquire into the satisfaction which Serbia might give to the Austro-Hungarian Government without infringement of her rights as a sovereign state and her independence, Russia engages to maintain her waiting attitude.[10]

But this was still not what the situation demanded. What was needed was that Russia should undertake to revoke the mobilization order. This would not have been beyond the bounds of possibility, as can be perceived from the optimistic language in which Sazonov thanked the English Government through Buchanan for what it had done in the cause of peace,[11] and in the similar message sent to Benckendorff:

> Be so good as to express to Sir Edward Grey our lively gratitude for his friendly attitude and the firmness and clarity of the views which it has expressed and communicated to the German and Austro-Hungarian Governments. Thanks to the point of view put forward by Sir Edward Grey all hope of a peaceful solution is not ruled out.[12]

The goal was in sight. To reach it, all that would have been necessary was that Grey, as he said to Mensdorff on the 30th, had something to offer St. Petersburg, and that something was the *Halt in Belgrade*.[13] Nay more, to Lichnowsky on the morning of 31 July Grey had gone so far as to say that

> if Germany could get any reasonable proposal put forward which made it clear that Germany and Austria were striving to preserve European peace and that Russia and France would be unreasonable if they rejected it, I would support it at St Petersburg and Paris and go to the length of saying that if Russia and France would not

[7] DD. II, 323. See Vol. II, pp. 476–7.
[8] D.D. II, 421. See p. 18.
[9] BD. XI, 309. See Vol. II, p. 635.
[10] *Int. Bez.* i. V, 343. See p. 57.
[11] BD. XI, 393. See p. 58.
[12] *Int. Bez.* i. V, 346; BD. XI, 409.
[13] Oe-U VIII, 11064. See Vol. II, pp. 633–4.

> accept it, His Majesty's Government would have nothing more to do with the consequences.[14]

What proposal could be more reasonable than this of Grey? Only, in order to result in peace, it ought to have been presented at St. Petersburg by Berlin in place of the ultimatum in a supreme effort to avert German mobilization and war.

This was not done. And—be it noted—the reason why it was not done was not the proclamation of general mobilization at St. Petersburg. As early as the evening of the 30th, when the mobilization was not yet known, Berlin, as we have seen, decided to give Russia no other choice than to accept the demand that she should cease her military preparations, which then were thought to be directed only against Austria.[15] And this came about because, as the Chancellor himself confessed on the 30th to the Prussian Cabinet, 'the situation had got out of hand and the stone had started rolling',[16] or rather, as Tirpitz puts it, because of the 'stupidity of our political leadership. . . . Since the Russian mobilization the Chancellor gave one the impression of a drowning man'.[17] Had Bethmann not lost his nerve, he would not have ceased putting pressure on Vienna at the very moment when a formula had been found on which Germany and England could agree, and when Grey had promised that he would leave Russia and France to their fate if they did not accept it. Armed with such a series of powerful arguments Bethmann could have firmly resisted the pressure from the generals to drop all further negotiation, instead of which he either made no use of them or used them lamely and belatedly.

3. The Arguments Brought Forward by Moltke; the Schlieffen Plan

Before discussing these arguments, let us first take a look at those used by Moltke. He, as has already been said, thought that Germany ought to crush the enemy coalition before it grew stronger.[18] However, he did not go so far as to say so on the afternoon of the 30th. In fact, on the 29th he had raised no strong objection to the Chancellor's view that the Russian partial mobilization did not call for mobilization on the part of Germany, and on the morning of the 30th had spoken in this sense to the Austrian Major Fleischmann, to Conrad's great dismay.[19] This may have been either because his temperament did not incline to undertaking responsibilities to which he did not feel equal—in 1906 he had begged the Kaiser not to appoint him to his post—or because he did not venture to oppose the Kaiser's pacific intentions. But about midday on the 30th an unexpected change took place in his attitude in circumstances explained above.[20] Once bent on war, however, he naturally wanted to speed up the pace of action. Not only was Russia mobilizing against Austria and was Germany taking the measures prescribed for the 'period preparatory to war',[21] but France, too, was arming. This was the worst, because the French preparations boded no good for the success of the Schlieffen plan whereon hung the fate of the war on two fronts about which it is necessary to say a few words.

Schlieffen, the German Chief of General Staff from 1891 to 1905, was undoubtedly a remarkable general who never had the chance to display his notable gifts of intelligence, force of will and daring which were the marvel of his subordinates. His admirers regard him as a mighty figure and deplore that he was removed from the supreme command when he might still have rendered signal service.[22] However, after he vacated his post the spirit of Schlieffen still reigned in

[14] BD. XI, 340. See Vol. II, p. 642.
[15] See pp. 22–3.
[16] DD. II, 456. See p. 16.
[17] Tirpitz, *Memoirs,* I, p. 279.

[18] See Vol. II, p. 487.
[19] See Vol. II, p. 671.
[20] See pp. 6–13.
[21] See Vol. II, pp. 304–6.
[22] Among these admirers one of the foremost is Lieutenant-Colonel Wolfgang Foerster, the Director of the Imperial Archives, who is the author of an important work, *Graf Schlieffen und der Weltkrieg* (Berlin, 1925). It is the source of the technical details here given.

the German General Staff through his writings, which were regarded as gospel up to 1913, the year of his death.

Like Bismarck, he thought that 'War with France was unavoidable; sometime or other accounts must be settled between the two nations'.[23] He had made a close study of the battle of Cannae, which he regarded as the model of a decisive battle, and he meant to inflict a 'Cannae' on France. Hannibal, though weaker than Terentius Varro, had attacked the latter on both flanks and in the rear and destroyed him.

> Weapons and military methods—wrote Schlieffen—have entirely changed in two thousand years. The basic conditions of battle remain unchanged. . . . The target of the main attack is not the enemy front. . . . The essential is to crush in the flanks. . . . Annihilation is completed by an attack on the enemy rear.[24]

Placing no reliance on the co-operation of Italy, which he regarded as an 'illusion',[25] Schlieffen saw

> Germany and Austria-Hungary exposed alone to the concentric attack of a world of enemies simultaneously on several fronts. 'At the given moment the gates were to be opened, the drawbridge let down, and armies of millions, devastating and annihilating, were to surge across the Meuse, the Königsau, the Niemen, the Bug, even across the Isonzo and the Tirolese Alps'.[26]

But since the combined forces of the Central Powers were inferior to those of their enemies, they could not wage war at the same time on Russia and France. They must beat them one by one and do so quickly, since time was not on their side.

Which should they attack first? The great Moltke and his successor, Waldersee, had thought the decision should be sought first in Russia, leaving the defence on the French front based on the fortresses of Metz and Strasbourg and the fortified line of the Rhine. In case of need Waldersee was even prepared to sacrifice this line and withdraw eastwards behind the Main.[27] But Schlieffen took a different view. For one thing, the strategic premises from which the older Moltke started had undergone a change. The Russian plan now, if attacked by Austria and Germany, was to deploy in the interior and this would render an early, decisive battle impossible. Moreover, if Germany were to allow the French to reach the Rhine it would mean sacrificing the Saar coal-basin and the rich mineral and industrial region of Lorraine. Finally there was the danger that France might violate the neutrality of Belgium by crossing her territory to invade the Rhineland. The first need therefore was to put France out of action before she could muster her full strength and receive the reinforcement of the English Expeditionary Force.

> The whole of Germany must hurl itself against one opponent, the one who is the strongest, most powerful, most dangerous; this cannot but be France-England. Austria need feel no anxiety. The Russian army, destined to serve against Germany, will not march on Galicia before the die has been cast in the west, and the fate of Austria will be decided, not on the Bug, but on the Seine.[28]

While the attack on France was proceeding, East Prussia was to be protected by a weak strategic defence based on the Masurian Lakes, at the worst even by the evacuation of the territory east of the Vistula and a withdrawal behind that river. For, as Schlieffen wrote shortly before his death:

> Better sacrifice a province than divide an army with which one is determined and destined to win victory.[29]

To deal France a knock-out blow the assault must be made, not against the powerfully fortified, impregnable Verdun-Belfort

[23] Foerster, p. 5.
[24] Foerster, p. 10.
[25] Foerster, p. 17.
[26] Foerster, p. 18.
[27] General H. von Kuhl, *Ost- oder Westaufmarsch* 1914?, KSF., 1923, pp. 73–6.
[28] Foerster, p. 27.
[29] Foerster, p. 24.

line, but against the weak, probably ill-defended, more northerly line of Dunkirk-Lille-Maubeuge, wheeling then southwards and encircling the French forces. This entailed the violation of Belgian neutrality, and it was well understood that such violation would in all probability call England on to the scene. The German General Staff therefore gave serious attention to devising ways and means of avoiding this, but came to the conclusion that without violating Belgian neutrality it would not be possible to destroy the enemy quickly, and that if the Germans did not violate Belgian neutrality the French would probably do so in order to reach the Rhineland.

In 1905, shortly before Schlieffen ceased to be Chief of Staff and when plans were being drawn up for a war against France and England alone, the attack was entrusted to a powerful right wing:

> The mass of the western force—seven armies with 69 divisions, counting front line and reserve, 8 cavalry divisions, 22 *Landwehr* brigades—was to concentrate in the Rhine Province, with sections also in Lorraine on the Saar. For the decisive offensive they were to advance first against the Dunkirk-Verdun line in a vast leftward wheel with Metz as its pivot, the 8 *Ersatz* army corps were to follow as soon as they were available. In Lorraine only one army was to be retained with 10 divisions, counting front line and reserve, 3 cavalry divisions, 1 *Landwehr* brigade, apart from the war-time garrisons of Metz and Strasbourg. On the Upper Rhine only 3½ *Landwehr* brigades were to remain. Upper Alsace was to be left undefended. The relative strengths of the right and left wings of the army in front line and reserve divisions was approximately 7:1.[30]

4. Moltke Opposed to the Violation of Dutch Neutrality; Modifications of the Schlieffen Plan

Holland, also, was not spared by the Schlieffen plan. The Dutch province of Limburg forms a salient jutting forty miles southward, and thus covers part of the Belgian frontier against Germany, constituting an obstacle to the direct westward advance of the German right wing. To avoid it, the German right wing would be obliged to strike south before turning west through the Liége defile.

> Operational expediency gave rise to the idea of letting the extreme right wing pass through this Dutch territory. Count Schlieffen accordingly contemplated this possibility—but only on condition that German diplomacy succeeded in persuading Holland at the beginning of the war to attach herself to the Central Powers. He started from the assumption that England was as dangerous an enemy to the Dutch colonial empire as to Germany and that awareness of this would perhaps bring the the Dutch Government over to our side.[31]

On becoming Schlieffen's successor, Moltke adopted the strategic concept carrying the sanction of his predecessor's authority and prestige, although he was not entirely convinced of its merits. In his memoirs he writes that he was in agreement with Schlieffen about the necessity of circumventing the French belt of fortifications and that this could only be achieved by using Belgian territory. He differed profoundly, however, over the methods to be pursued.

> My predecessor's plan of deployment was so conceived that the German right wing would have to advance via Roermond, thus crossing not only Belgian but also Dutch territory. Count Schlieffen took the view that Holland would confine herself to a protest and would otherwise allow the violation of her territory to take place unhindered. I had the gravest doubts about this opinion. I did not believe that Holland would quietly tolerate violation, and on the other hand I anticipated that a hostile Holland would mean a loss to the German right wing of such considerable forces that it would no longer have the necessary strik-

[30] Foerster, p. 30.

[31] Foerster, p. 30.

ing power against the west. The advance through Belgium could, in my view, only be carried out under the assumption of a strictly neutral Holland.

Though I did not know what attitude England would take in a war of Germany against Russia and France, I regarded it as more than likely that she would side with our foes as soon as we violated Belgian neutrality. . . . It was clear to me that on this ground alone respect of Dutch neutrality was an essential demand, and I allowed for all the difficulties which must necessarily attend our deployment and advance if we meant not to touch Dutch soil. . . . I think that circumstances have proved me to be in the right. One need only think how they would have shaped themselves if we had found ourselves faced with a hostile Holland, whose coasts stood open to an English landing, what would have become of the expedition against Antwerp if the Schelde had not been neutral, how many troops would have been needed to cover our rear when we advanced westward. I was and still am convinced that the campaign in the west would have failed if we had not spared Holland. Moreover, I saw that it must at all costs be preserved as an airpipe for our economic life. Moreover, if we spared Holland, England, having declared war on us allegedly for the defence of small neutrals, could not possibly violate Dutch neutrality on her own account.[32]

This apologia on the part of Moltke elicits from Schlieffen's champion the footnote:

If Moltke rather boasts of having eliminated the operational possibility of crossing Dutch territory from his plans, it must be pointed out that this rests on a different political basic concept, namely that our diplomacy would not be successful in attracting Holland to our side. The thought of doing violence to Holland by infringing her neutrality was as remote from Count Schlieffen as from Colonel General von Moltke.[33]

[32] Moltke, pp. 428–32.
[33] Foerster, p. 30, note 1.

But supposing Holland did not join with Germany? In a letter to Lutz, Foerster writes:

Count Schlieffen planned the deployment of the German right wing in such a manner that the advance could take place either by crossing or by avoiding Dutch territory. March routes were provided for both eventualities. The plan taking in Holland was to come into force if Germany diplomacy were successful in persuading Holland at the outbreak of war to come to an amicable settlement with Germany. Failing that, the advance was to proceed leaving Dutch neutrality intact exactly as actually took place in 1914.

Lutz adds the comment:

This categoric affirmation stands in contrast to the equally categoric written statements of Moltke. . . . Foerster's evidence has not been regarded as convincing in Dutch military circles.[34]

Moltke realized that the violation of Belgian neutrality would have serious consequences and he was disquieted by the idea that the enormous right wing of the German deployment, having crossed Belgium, would plunge into the unknown. The French might put up strong opposition in the north, or they might carry out a counter-offensive and penetrate into Lorraine. This latter possibility perturbed Moltke more than Schlieffen, who felt confident of retaining the initiative and was prepared, if need be, to withdraw his left wing as far as the right bank of the Rhine. Moltke, moreover, had to plan for a war not merely against France, with or without English help, but against France and Russia acting in concert. The case might, it is true, arise that Germany would have to act against Russia alone, if France and England at the beginning remained neutral, leaving open the possibility that they might intervene later. To meet this contingency Moltke prepared the so-called Plan No. 2.

On 30 January 1910, in a long letter to

[34] Lutz, pp. 531–2.

Conrad discussing what was to be done if, in the event of a war against Russia, Italy and France at the beginning assumed a waiting attitude without the Central Powers having any assurance that their neutrality would be permanently maintained (as in fact happened with Italy in 1914–15), he wrote:

> The only radical means of clarifying this critical situation would be an immediate declaration of war on the untrustworthy neutrals. Such a means is, however, not applicable on legal, political, and general human grounds. I have therefore proposed that if war between the allies and Russia comes to be regarded as unavoidable and impending, the German Government should demand an immediate, full, and unambiguous declaration from the French Government as to the attitude it intends to take on the outbreak of war [as was actually done on 31 July 1914]. . . . If France promises to maintain strict neutrality . . . the entire army will be mobilized but the forces not destined for immediate service against Russia will for the time being remain at their stations. In accordance with these considerations the military arrangements made by the General Staff are such that in the event of a satisfactory declaration of neutrality by France the troops destined for the east will be dispatched immediately, while the rest of the army for the time being remains mobilized on home territory and can at need be sent to the east later or used immediately against France if her neutrality proved doubtful. This procedure has, no doubt, the disadvantage for Germany that she may be obliged for a considerable time to send only inferior forces against her most dangerous foe.[35]

However, before the war Moltke came to the conclusion that there was no probability of France's remaining neutral and dropped Plan No. 2. He thus came to the same conclusion as Schlieffen, namely, that France must be put out of action before the attack on Russia was begun.

[35] Conrad, II, pp. 57–60.

> If Colonel-General von Moltke destined only 9 infantry divisions, 1 cavalry division, 1 *Landwehr* corps and 3 *Landwehr* brigades for the eastern front he was going down to the lowest permissible limit. It clearly shows how convinced he was of the need to concentrate all available forces in the first place on the great decisive battle in the west. . . . At the opening of the war the German forces in the west consisted of 72 front-line and reserve divisions, 10 cavalry divisions, 6½ *Ersatz* divisions and 19½ *Landwehr* brigades. . . . The relative strengths of the two wings, the right for the main offensive via Belgium and Luxemburg, and the left for a subsidiary task in Alsace-Lorraine, shows a profound departure from Schlieffen's plan. In Alsace-Lorraine and Baden were concentrated two armies, the 6th and 7th, with a total of 16 front line and reserve divisions,[36]

thus reducing the relative strength of the right wing from the 7:1 ratio planned by Schlieffen to one of 3:1, a fundamental change.

A modification of the 1905 plan had been worked out by Schlieffen in December 1912, shortly before his death, leaving Holland uninvaded as cover for the Rhineland industrial area and meeting the case where neutral frontiers at both ends of the enemy's territory rendered the enveloping movement on his extreme left impracticable. In this case the attack was to be launched along the entire length of the enemy front, leading to a tactical breakthrough in breadth at a suitable point from which the several portions of the enemy line could be rolled up and enveloped from the rear. The most suitable area for the breakthrough, in Schlieffen's opinion, was in Belgium, and to the Abbeville-St. Quentin section of the line his plan assigned twenty-one army corps. And the last words he murmured as he lay dying were: 'Be sure and make the right wing strong.' This plan was substantially the one put into operation by Moltke in August-September 1914, but with a lowered ratio of

[36] Foerster, pp. 35–6.

right to left wing, a factor profoundly altering the character of the plan.[37] Moreover, as events were to show, Moltke was prepared in certain circumstances to allow himself to be enveloped, and this proved his undoing.

But the weakening of his right wing made Moltke think it all the more necessary not to waste any time. The week of political negotiations had been precious not only to France and Russia. It had enabled Belgium and England also to take vital military measures. Such negotiations must be brought to an end. Too much precious time had already been lost.[38]

5. The Chancellor Under Pressure from Moltke

If this was the line of reasoning of the military, it should have been the right and duty of the civil authorities to counter it with their own arguments, which were strong. Why was it, indeed, that the Great General Staff had prepared only one strategic plan, as if there were no other possibility than that of a war on two great fronts and that France would necessarily make common cause with Russia? Supposing that in France a Government had come or returned to power of other views than those of Poincaré, Delcassé, Millerand, a Government determined not to be dragged into a conflagration caused by the Balkan interests of Russia? Was France to be attacked all the same because that was laid down in the Schlieffen plan? One may reply that Russia would never have shown herself so unbending had she not known she could count on France. But this assumption was not something to be depended on, since it might unexpectedly be proved wrong by the facts. It should have been the General Staff's duty to provide for several alternatives, and prepare the relevant plans of mobilization and concentration, so that the political authorities would be free in whatever international crisis to choose the solution most in accordance with the interests of the Reich.

Among the various possible alternatives there was one not provided for in the Schlieffen plan, not even in Plan No. 2, which Moltke threw aside. As has just been mentioned, it was designed to meet the case in which France would declare neutrality, but a neutrality on which too much reliance could not be placed. It might have served Germany—indeed, would have served her in 1914 to prevent English intervention and not give Italy the right to declare herself neutral—to operate the plan of the elder Moltke and Waldersee, maintaining the defensive towards France while taking the offensive against Russia, even though the outcome of the eastern offensive might appear much more doubtful and less decisive than the Schlieffen manœuvre. The sound basis of this assumption was demonstrated in 1936 when the Germans militarily reoccupied the Rhineland, which they had pledged themselves to leave demilitarized, and began to fortify it for the purpose of remaining on the defensive towards France and Belgium so as to have a free hand in the south and east. Had some such plans been prepared and the necessary fortifications executed, it would have been possible for Germany to ask for English neutrality in return for a promise to refrain from attack not only on the French coast and navy, as was actually proposed in 1914, but also on the French army, only reserving the right of self-defence in case an attack were made by France. There is likelihood that Grey would have given a different reception to a request for English neutrality on such a basis than he did to the

[37] Foerster, pp. 41–3.

[38] Tirpitz writes: 'The subject of the conversation between Bethmann and Goschen was certainly known in Brussels the same day. . . . Thus Belgium gained precious time to organize resistance against us. This resistance had an extraordinarily unfavourable influence on the whole course of the war. England also learnt of our plans earlier than was strictly necessary. This enabled her to take military and naval measures which had bad consequences for us. . . . A delay of even only a few days in the preparation of the English expeditionary force and its transport to France might have been of the greatest importance to us' (Tirpitz, *Dokumente,* II, p. 13.)

disgraceful suggestion made by Bethmann to Goschen on the evening of 29 July. Nor can it be objected that it was impossible to remain on the defensive towards France. A Metz-Strasbourg line could have been rendered no less impregnable than was actually the Verdun-Belfort line. Moreover, the danger that France might invade the Rhineland by way of Belgium could have been averted by suitable fortification works, and was, in fact, purely imaginary, since it would never have been tolerated by England. The Germans knew this perfectly well. They merely used it as a pretext to cover up the invasion they themselves had planned.

Besides compelling Germany, in the event of a conflict with Russia, to throw her full weight against France and to that end violate the neutrality of Belgium even though it were inadvisable to do so, the Great General Staff, by preparing a plan of war under which hostilities began with the act of mobilization, placed the German Government in the painful position of being unable to order a measure of mobilization corresponding to that of Russia without unleashing a European war. In other words, the Government had only the choice between leaving Germany disarmed or plunging her headlong into the mortal perils of a general war. Historians have failed to dwell sufficiently on this aspect of the tragedy. Taking for granted that the German principle was a universal practice and basing themselves on utterances of French and Russian generals which were never meant to be taken in this rigid sense, they have drawn the conclusion that mobilization was in every case the equivalent of going to war. It has been shown above that nothing is further from the truth, save in the one case of Germany herself.[39] Mobilization was an affair of more than a few days during which frontier incidents might well occur, but there was no need to pay much attention to them unless they were wanted to serve as a pretext for war. If on 1 August the Berlin Government had been able to order general mobilization in reply to that of Russia without implying the occupation of Luxemburg and the sending of an ultimatum to Belgium, the probabilities are that the Kaiser and the Chancellor, fearing English intervention no less than Italian and Roumanian neutrality, would have authorized mobilization but not war and the Anglo-German formula of conciliation would have had time to bear fruit.

[39] See Vol. II, pp. 479–82.

At the worst the Germans would have avoided appearing as the aggressors, to their own great advantage, material and moral, a fact which was realized at the moment when hostilities opened not only by Tirpitz but also by Falkenhayn and Moltke. Schlieffen's apologist, Foerster, could not but perceive how seriously the great general's plan handicapped the German Government, compelling it to declare war on Russia and France and thus to take on its shoulders the responsibility of causing the European conflagration. On this point he writes:

> It is a completely mistaken opinion, though widespread both at home and abroad and much exploited by propaganda, that the Schlieffen plan of marching through Belgium forced Germany to assume the role of aggressor. But the declaration of war on Russia of 1 August was not the result of any strategic necessity. The correctness of Bethmann Hollweg's assertion that General von Moltke advised it on military grounds is highly questionable. In agreement with the War Minister von Falkenhayn, Moltke in the early hours of 2 August attempted, alas in vain, to prevent the declaration of war on Russia. The German Supreme Command would have been satisfied as regards Russia with the mobilization which had been ordered on 1 August. And even the declaration of war on France of 3 August did not stand in any causal connexion with the planned move in Belgium. As late as 2 August, in a memorandum to the Imperial Chancellor, Moltke explicitly stated: 'Our eventual declaration of war [on France] is entirely independent of the *démarche* made in Belgium. The one does not entail the other. I do not regard it as needful to serve the

declaration of war on France yet, on the contrary I calculate that, if we for the moment refrain, France will be forced by popular opinion to order military operations against Germany without war being formally declared.'[40] If, therefore, the political leaders of the Reich acted otherwise during those days and by declaring war brought upon Germany the odium of being the aggressor in the eyes of the outside world, it was not by the Schlieffen plan that they were forced to do so.[41]

This is the opposite of the truth. It was precisely the Schlieffen plan which dictated their action and it is childish to imagine that, simply by omitting the declaration of war, the odium would have been avoided. What caused the odium was the act of aggression, and this would have made an even worse impression than it did, had it taken place without being preceded by a declaration of war.

6. Reasons Alleged in Defence of the Schlieffen Plan; How It Limited Germany's Choice of Action

Germany could not act otherwise, reply the politicians, military experts, and historians in Germany who have made a study of the question, and they find strong support in those scholars of other countries who are determined to absolve Germany from all guilt.[42] The words of Wegerer will serve as an illustration of their line of argument:

> Surveying the military situation which faced Germany early in August 1914 . . . we understand why Germany could not afford to await inactively the outbreak of hostilities. She had to utilize her slight remaining advantage of operation on the inner line and defend herself as best she could. Accordingly, the struggle of the Central Powers against the expected coalition of Russia, Serbia, France, Belgium and England required not only the speediest mobilization and marshalling of the German and Austrian forces but also an immediate attack for the purpose of making the effectual co-operation of the enemies impossible. . . . For the purpose of defence . . . the German General Staff had since the beginning of the century adopted the plan outlined by General von Schlieffen, namely, of defeating by means of an offensive that opponent who was strongest and who could most readily be attacked—France. If neutral territory were not to be invaded, Germany's offensive against France could be executed only along the short line between Switzerland and Luxemburg. But the territory facing this line could not be rapidly invaded on account of the concrete construction of the forts and barriers at the frontier. The accuracy of this assumption was later proved by the struggles at Verdun which alone cost Germany several hundred thousand men. At the beginning of the campaign, therefore, the hopeless struggles for the French Thermopylean passes had to be avoided and the attempt made to invade northern France by strategically circling round the left flank of the enemy. But the protection of the German industrial region made it necessary also to create a *glacis,* which could be obtained by carrying the war into the enemy's country. Thus we see that the Russian general mobilization forced Germany to resort to an offensive against France, and that this offensive had to be conducted in Belgium.[43]

In these terms Wegerer seeks to defend both the Schlieffen plan and the necessity contained in it of beginning operations with

[40] DD. III, 662. See p. 198.
[41] Foerster, p. 28.
[42] Among these foreign scholars one of the foremost is G. Demartial who writes: 'The Russian Government was the first to know that the mobilization of the Russian army would provoke not only German mobilization, but war, since Germany, for strategic reasons which a baby could understand, could not mobilize without attacking' (G. Demartial, 'L'état de la question des responsabilités de la guerre en France', in *Évolution,* 15 March, 1926, p. 40). Demartial's assumption is baseless. Russia had no knowledge of the fact that for Germany mobilization meant going to war (See Vol. II. pp. 579–81.) Germany might have mobilized without attacking if, beside the Schlieffen plan, there had existed other less dangerous and ambitious plans of war, which without inflicting a Cannæ on the French army, might have not led Germany to the total defeat which was in store for her notwithstanding the Schlieffen plan.

[43] Wegerer, *Refutation,* pp. 309–10.

the act of mobilization. But he says nothing which disproves the basis of the objections that can be raised against the plan itself and the necessities it takes for granted. He makes assumptions but brings no proofs. Nor can he do so, in view of the fact that Germany's experiences with the plan were, to say the least of it, anything but happy. Let us leave aside the moral aspect of the violation of Belgian neutrality to which the Germans in general attach no importance, arguing with the utmost candour that if, in order to crush France, who had been guilty of the indelicacy of erecting impregnable defences along her frontier, Germany had no other way open than to pass through Belgium, it was quite natural that she should do so in breach of the pledge she had given.[44] Let us rather ask Wegerer whether in the conjuncture presenting itself in July 1914, when it was a matter of putting Serbia in her place and restoring Austrian prestige, influence, and security in the Balkans, it was necessary for Germany to regard the crushing of the French army as the principle underlying her military action.

Wars, it will be replied, are waged by the methods which ensure maximum military success. That may be so. But one sets about them in such a manner as not to add to the number of one's enemies and diminish the number of one's friends; in other words, one does not endanger the final result because of an attachment to a risky plan of operations, however brilliant. Designed to inflict a mortal blow on the Dual Alliance in a war in which Italy and Roumania would march with the Central Powers and England would remain neutral, the Schlieffen plan, especially after the modifications introduced by Moltke, was not sufficient to assure victory in a war of aggression, i.e. one in which Italy would take no part while England would range herself in the opposite camp. As events were to show, the larger forces available to France on the Marne as a result of Italian neutrality and the presence there of the British Expeditionary Force brought about the failure of all the high hopes placed on the grand manœuvre of the German right wing. Even had these hopes been realized, there is no certainty that they would have led to final victory. Victory on land was not enough. There must also be victory at sea.

In this connexion Tirpitz writes:

> On 6 August I was visited by Jagow. . . . I remonstrated with him on the subject of the complete *déroute* of the political leaders, who ought to have given the event of war a certain amount of preliminary consideration. . . . In reply to my question what would happen if we beat France and Russia but not England, Jagow shrugged his shoulders. The conflict of opinion came to the surface when I said: 'Couldn't you promise Russia the passage of the Dardanelles and anything they like, to prevent the war?' Jagow replied: 'If you had only brought us a little naval agreement with England, the war would not have been necessary.'[45]

They were both right. Precisely because Tirpitz had opposed the naval agreement offered by London the German Government should have been doubly careful to avoid giving England any pretext or reason for going to war with Germany. To propose not only to invade France and take her colonies but also to invade Belgium, in other words

[44] A sample of the cool effrontery with which the question is treated and regarded in Germany is provided by the following words of Tirpitz: 'The General Staff had for decades considered the possibility of an invasion through Belgium all the more seriously since the French policy of *revanche* began to support itself on the Russian armies. There could not exist a doubt in the whole world that the French were at least morally the aggressors in a Franco-German war. In warding off a French war of *revanche,* which threatened us on the Vistula just as much as on the Meuse and the Moselle, our march through neutral Belgium could only be justified in the eyes of the world if the political offensive of France against us was made as clear as day' (Tirpitz, *My Memoirs,* I, p. 281). He goes on to say: 'Those who were specially engaged on this question on the General Staff . . . had been led to the conviction by many symptoms during the few years before the war, that the French and the English would march through Belgium to attack the Rhineland.' This assumption does not attenuate the cynicism of the words just quoted.

[45] Tirpitz, *My Memoirs,* I, pp. 283–4; *Dokumente,* II, p. 27.

to carry out the Schlieffen plan, was to offer this very pretext or reason. It would never have been necessary to do this if, alongside of that plan, Germany had had another, less ambitious but better suited to the end proposed, which was neither to crush France nor to go to Moscow, but to save the existence of Austria. On all sides it has been agreed that Germany had nothing to gain from war. In peace she was every year increasing in strength and influence, expanding and becoming ever more feared and respected. Far from wanting to attack her, England had actually come to an agreement with her over the Bagdad railway. Thus even if Germany was obliged to take up arms in defence of her ally and of the latter's Balkan interests, she would have done so at smaller cost and with less risk, even though sacrificing the possibility of inflicting a colossal Cannae on the French and Russians. Wars can, moreover, be won without victories like that of Cannae. It is often wiser to be victorious only up to a certain point. Furthermore, the enemy's power of resistance has to be measured not only by military but also by political standards. Theoretically, it might be right to crush the French army first. Practically, it was doubtful, because Russia at the opening of the struggle was politically and morally in such a state that she would have quickly collapsed under the combined attack of the Central Powers. These would then have found themselves in 1915 in a position to negotiate a peace similar to the one they negotiated at Brest Litowsk in 1917.

7. Lack of Co-ordination Between the Army and Navy General Staffs

But for that to happen the military authority would have had to be subordinated to the political. It would have been for the political authorities to weigh the various possibilities of conflict that might arise and expect the General Staff to supply different plans to suit the different cases. In Germany, however, the military caste, represented by the Chiefs of Staff, who ranked as equal to the Chancellor, would never have allowed the latter to interfere in such problems. And at the decisive moment the military took over the direction of affairs and imposed their law. Nor was Bethmann the man to change a state of things to which his predecessors had submitted and which he could not have altered without entering into conflict with his Sovereign. Moltke on 30 July outstepped his powers and invaded those of the Chancellor, who might quite well have resisted. But to do so he would have had to be endowed with the requisite powers of mind and of will.

What, above all, Bethmann should have done in the terrible emergency was to measure the handicap which the Schlieffen plan constituted for Germany in preventing her from mobilizing without going to war, making her appear as responsible for the war in the eyes of the world, rendering English intervention inevitable and justifying the neutrality of Italy and Roumania. It was too late to change the plan and, create another, but it was not too late to make a supreme effort to save peace. Just because in going to war Germany would have to entrust her fate to the Schlieffen plan it was to her supreme interest to act with the utmost caution and to refrain from mobilization as long as there was any possibility of negotiating and while there still existed a prospect of reaching agreement on a peace formula. Thus it was on 30 July, not on 1 August, that the Chancellor should have considered this problem of the declarations of war and discussed it with the military chiefs, in order that if it proved intractable, in other words, if the declarations could not be foregone but would make the German Government appear as the aggressor, everything should be done to compose a conflict presenting itself in conditions so overwhelmingly unfavourable to Germany.

The fact is that Bethmann, who had made every effort to cast the blame on Russia, failed to see that his endeavours would be defeated by the very demands of the Schlieffen plan. Had he but realized this and resisted the pressure from Moltke and Falkenhayn, he would certainly have had the support of the Kaiser, who was temperamentally disinclined for war, and still more of Tirpitz, who had fully grasped the madness of what was being done not only by the declarations of war but also by the violation of Belgian neutrality and the challenge to England. It was a real disaster that, because of his jealousy of the Grand Admiral, Bethmann never took counsel with him and sought to keep him away from Berlin during the days of crisis on the pretext that his return would make things more difficult. If in 1912 there had been a difference of opinion between the two men about the naval agreement, desired by London, Bethmann being willing to agree to it and Tirpitz unwisely opposing it. Tirpitz was nevertheless more alive to the need for saving the peace than was Bethmann. He would have thrown his weight on the side of conciliation if for no other reason than that he had no high opinion of the political leadership of the Reich any more than of its military leadership. In his memoirs he writes:

> I was troubled by the feeling that the General Staff was not correctly estimating the meaning of a war against England and was heedlessly going on with the war against France because this apparently meant only a short war. The decisions of the hour were never guided by previously considered politico-strategical plans of mobilization for the whole war.[46]

Just so! There had been no collaboration between the army and navy General Staffs. Germany had acquired a powerful navy worthy to measure swords with that of England. But the navy chiefs were not asked for their opinion on the problems raised by a possible European war. And yet the invasion of Belgium created a situation which concerned the navy no less than the army. As Tirpitz asked Jagow on 6 August:

> What would happen if we beat France and Russia and found ourselves alone in face of England? [47]

In truth, Tirpitz frames a very serious accusation against the highest authorities of the Reich when he writes:

> In his fear of clearness, the Chancellor was so little prepared for the war that collective consultations between the political and military leaders never took place, either on the politico-strategical problems of the conduct of the war or even on the prospects of a world war at all. I was never even informed of the invasion of Belgium, which immediately raised naval questions when it took place. The question might here be raised whether in time of peace I on my side would not have been in a position to urge the preparation of a mobilization of the collective leadership of the Reich. Anyone knowing the conditions existing in our Government at that time would not ask such a question.[48]

This is an accusation directed against Tirpitz himself, who never explains what obstacle prevented co-operation between the political and military authorities. In the very interests of the powerful navy which he had created, he should have insisted on the absolute necessity of such co-operation. He writes:

> If the Chancellor had consulted me, as was his duty—he ought to have explored the military possibilities in every direction before taking such a course—then I should have had to tell him that from the standpoint of the navy the danger of war, in itself undesirable, would be presenting itself at a strategically unfavourable moment. Dreadnought construction, by the introduction of which England automatically doubled the fighting force of our navy, had only been going on for four years. The Kiel Canal was not yet ready. The navy would not reach its maximum until 1920.[49]

[46] Tirpitz, *My Memoirs,* I, p. 280.

[47] Tirpitz, *Dokumente,* II, p. 27.

[48] Tirpitz, *Erinnerungen,* p. 228; *My Memoirs,* I, pp. 263–4.

[49] Tirpitz, *My Memoirs,* I, pp. 262–3.

Why, when he realized the gravity of the situation, did not Tirpitz write at once on these lines to the Chancellor?

The German navy, it is true, was a recent growth to which no doubt the spiritual heirs of Frederick the Great and of the illustrious Moltke, who had beaten first Austria and then France and on these victories had reared the edifice of the Reich, would have refused to pay deference. But the Grand Admiral had perhaps more influence with the Kaiser than anyone else, as his own narrative shows:

> On Monday, 3 August at 8.30 a.m. I received the following missive from the Kaiser:
>
> 'In my opinion this position is absolutely untenable under international law; England, while claiming to be neutral and prepared to remain so stands guards over the French coast and ties down my fleet, although I am at war with France and France has already committed acts of hostility against us. England must at once be reminded by Ambassador that this attitude would have to be regarded by us as an act of war against us. . . . Ambassador must tell England to make up her mind whether she means to be at war with us or neutral. Any concentration against us to cover France would be regarded as an act of war. My fleet must have freedom of movement.'

Tirpitz perceived the folly of this attitude and wrote to the Kaiser and Bethmann:

> Urgently recommend Chancellor to telegraph to Lichnowsky:
>
> No action against French coast intended as long as England remains neutral.

And to the Chancellor's proposed statement to the Reichstag on 4 August Tirpitz obtained the addition of the words:

> And I may add that as long as England remains neutral we should be prepared, in the event of reciprocity, to refrain from taking hostile measures against French mercantile shipping.[50]

[50] Tirpitz, *Dokumente,* II, pp. 25–6.

8. Consequences of the Personal Rivalries Between the German Leaders

The conclusion to be drawn is that it was personal rivalries and jealousies between the various authorities which prevented their taking timely counsel together about the problems raised by the possibility of a European war. Bethmann, Moltke, Tirpitz each went his own way without seeking contact with the others until noon on 30 July when Moltke declared that the fate of Germany would be irreparably jeopardized if his opinion was not heeded.[51]

The Chancellor yielded, but after the die was cast the discussion on the question of French neutrality, hopes of which had been raised by Grey, and on whether or not it was necessary to send declarations of war brought to light a difference of opinion which, if it had been known before the dispatch of the ultimatum to Russia, would have prevented the taking of this fatal step. But coming to light after things had gone too far it brought about that moral and nervous collapse of the Kaiser, the Chancellor and Moltke which is copiously displayed in the Kaiser's marginalia and in the memoirs of Tirpitz, Falkenhayn and Moltke, and had an adverse influence on the course of operations. Moltke was visibly not master of himself when he telegraphed to Conrad: 'Will Austria leave her [Germany] in the lurch?'[52]

Foerster writes of Moltke:

> His nature inclined to introspection (*Grübeln*) and was not inaccessible to attacks of pessimism. . . . Severe struggles in the days immediately before and during the outbreak of war had shaken the equilibrium of his sensitive soul. . . . Moltke emerged from these struggles in the end as victor. But their after-effects had not been completely effaced when operations began.[53]

[51] See pp. 7–13.
[52] See p. 47.
[53] Foerster, pp. 27–8.

These were the men whom the world regarded with awe and reverence, reverence for them personally and for their main instrument, the German army, the perfect expression of the incomparable German genius for organization unbeaten in all fields of human activity. The world did not perceive that the marvellous machine that Germany was, was in the hands of men who were unequal to their task. Sovereign, Chancellor, Chief of Staff were launching the country on a hazardous, all but desperate venture, the two former well knowing, the third not realizing, what the consequences would be if Italy and Roumania were to refuse their co-operation, England were to aid the enemy with her navy and her small but dauntless army, and Belgium were to offer resistance. Nor can Tirpitz be absolved of all responsibility however much more clearly than the others he saw the danger. To his action more than to anyone else's was due the 'encirclement' in which Germany found herself caught at the outbreak of the war. Creator of a fine navy, which performed prodigies in the battle of Jutland, Tirpitz never comprehended, never wanted to comprehend, that by refusing all understanding with the Power which could not yield up the command of the seas without imperilling its very existence, he was preparing the most calamitous end for his country's defeat. He was to live long enough to see this come to pass.[54]

The most unrivalled qualities of discipline and organization are not in themselves sufficient to assure the welfare of a great and powerful nation. It is undeniable that in 1914 neither the Kaiser nor his Chancellor wanted a European war, any more than it was wanted by Berchtold, Sazonov and Grey. All of them would willingly have continued to negotiate for the peaceful solution of the conflict. It is a source of amazement to historians that notwithstanding this, the war did break out. There is no doubt that the mediocrity of all the personages just mentioned played an important part in bringing about the disaster. But if one seeks to specify how and why Germany—since it was she who set fire to the powder-cask—was led to this grievous action, one must draw the conclusion from what has been said above that she was led to it by the requirements of the Schlieffen plan, which no doubt was a masterpiece of military science, but also a monument of that utter lack of political horse-sense which is the main cause of European disorders and upheavals.

[54] Tirpitz's efforts at self-defence and his Anglophobia involve him in much self contradiction. Perceiving that his vast plans of naval construction and his opposition to any agreement on the pace of construction had driven England towards France and Russia, he exculpates himself, as we have seen (see pp. 187–9), by maintaining that England had let the right moment slip for defeating the German navy which had passed the 'danger zone.' England, in fact, showed every consideration for Germany and made colonial concessions which by the irony of fate were sent by Lichnowsky to Berlin for signature on the very day war was declared. Two more years of peace and Germany would have had nothing more to fear. These two years she might have had—since, as Tirpitz writes, it was untrue 'that in view of the enemy's malevolence the world war could not have been arrested', were it not that 'the fatal mediocrity of the men in office' gave the Triple *Entente* a reason for making war on Germany. 'So the old pirate State, England, has again succeeded in letting Europe tear herself to pieces' (Tirpitz, *My Memoirs,* I, p. 287). More illogical than this it would be difficult to be. England had her faults, as has been shown. But if she had let the right moment slip for defeating the German navy, if 'the inclination for an understanding, which was rising in England in spite of everything, reposed . . . on a sober estimate of the decreasing profitableness of a war' (Tirpitz, *My Memoirs,* I, p. 255), if war was avoidable provided the German statesmen refrained from provoking it or furnishing a pretext for it, it is self evident that it was not 'the old pirate State' which sought the European war. On the contrary it had allowed the German navy to attain proportions which would have rendered it unassailable had the German rulers not declared war on Russia and France and perpetrated the violation of Belgian neutrality which inevitably brought England into the arena.

FORTY-SEVEN

THE VERSAILLES TREATY IN RETROSPECT

The Versailles Treaty of 1919 has had few defenders. Its many critics have pointed out that it violated all but the most transient of President Wilson's Fourteen Points, which had been the basis of the German surrender in November 1918. Some critics have also pointed out that, unlike the Treaty of Vienna in 1815, which, with exceptions, preserved peace for 100 years, the Versailles Treaty led to the Second World War in 1939, 20 years after its signing. But other critics, although fully aware of the deficiencies of the Versailles Treaty, have ascribed World War II to other causes, and have asked the pointed, if unanswerable, question whether any treaty, however skillfully drawn, could have kept peace in Europe after 1919. Nonetheless, whatever the final verdict of historians, the Versailles Treaty contributed to the dislocation of the postwar world. Harold Nicolson, who attended the peace conference as a junior member of the British delegation in 1919, published, 14 years later, a penetrating and at times scathing analysis of the treaty making. He ascribes a large share of the responsibility for its failure to President Wilson. Not all historians agree with his analysis, but it reflects a prevailing attitude of the interwar years, and in its indictment represents the sadness and disillusion of a generation which had fought a ruinous war "to end all wars" only to realize that a second world war was in the making.

HAROLD NICOLSON

PEACEMAKING 1919 *

1

Those writers who have ventured upon complete records of the Paris Peace Conference have tended to adopt one or other of three methods of treatment, striving thereby to find, through all that inchoate confusion, some clue to continuity, some consecutive thread of narrative. A few of them have chosen the chronological system and have sought to tell their story in terms of time. Others have divided their account under the headings of subjects, and have discussed each particular issue as a problem in itself. Others again have dramatised the whole negotiations in the form of a conflict of wills, and have achieved thereby a readable, yet essentially inaccurate, representation. Each of these three methods of treatment entails a certain falsification of values. The chronological method is apt to give an

* From *Peacemaking 1919*, pp. 157–84, by Harold Nicolson. Reprinted by permission of Harcourt, Brace & World, Inc., and by Constable and Company Limited, London. Copyright 1933.

erroneous impression of continuity, and to omit the element of synchronisation as well as the element of fits and starts. The piecemeal treatment, though valuable for purposes of lucidity, ignores the interrelation of subjects and gives no account of the effect of obstruction in one area upon concession in another. The 'conflict of wills' system errs on the side of over-simplification, and attributes to Wilson, Lloyd George and Clemenceau antagonistic as well as protagonistic positions which are often exaggerated.

There is, however, one quite central problem of the Peace Conference which lends itself readily enough to all three methods. That problem is the problem of the Adriatic, or, in its wider sense, the position of Italy at the Peace Conference. Here is a subject which is fairly continuous in time, which is comparatively self-contained within its own limits, and which certainly does reflect, in its crudest form, the opposition between the hopes of the New World, and the desires of the Old. I propose in this chapter to take the Italian question as an isolated whole, and to indicate the corrosive influence of that problem upon the moral and diplomatic basis of the Conference of Paris. It furnishes a convenient, and comparatively simple illustration of the type of complexity in which the Conference became involved. The same sort of difficulty (the conflict, that is, between the intensive egoism of one member of a coalition and the extensive egoism of other members) is certain to occur again at future Congresses.

The essential factors, precedent to the Italian controversy in Paris, can be stated in summary form.

Italy, on the outbreak of the European War, was the ally of Germany and Austria. She refused from the first moment to fulfil her obligations under the Triple Alliance, contending, and rightly, that with her exposed seaboard she would be at the mercy of the British Fleet. She went further. Early in January 1915 she made overtures at Vienna to ascertain what price Austria would pay her for maintaining her 'neutrality.' She asked for Trieste and the Trentino. The Austrian Government refused this concession. Baron Sonnino, the Italian Foreign Minister, then enquired in London and Paris what price the enemies of Austria would offer to induce Italy to desert her allies. He at the same time continued his negotiations at Vienna and obtained a grudging offer of some territory in the region of Trent. On May 3, 1915, he informed the Austrian Government that 'Italy must renounce the hope of coming to an agreement and proclaim from this moment her complete liberty of action.' The expression 'from this moment' was an euphemism: for five weeks already had Italy been engaged in negotiation with Austria's enemies: and the Treaty of London, which was the price which France, Great Britain and Russia had agreed to pay Italy, had actually been signed on April 26, a week before Baron Sonnino discontinued his overtures at Viensa.

The sentimentalists of the British Foreign Office had not entered upon this negotiation with any exuberance of heart. In the first place they had a feeling that Italy, as an ally, might be even more trouble than she was worth. In the second place they did not relish promising so huge a price for Italy's act of betrayal and at the expense of the very people whom she was about to betray. These old-world emotions had, however, to be suppressed in favour of 'war necessity.' Yet the Foreign Office took unkindly to the task. Sir Edward Grey was so disconcerted by Italy's conduct and demands that he retired to the country on a plea of illness. The Permanent Under-Secretary, in his first conversation with the Italian Ambassador, allowed himself an expression which savoured of somewhat contemptuous realism. 'You speak,' said the Ambassador, 'as if you were purchasing our support.' 'Well,' said the Under-Secretary, 'and so we are.' Marchese Imperiali was much offended by this remark and sought sympathy elsewhere. The details of the Treaty were negotiated by minor officials under the vaguely penitent supervision of Mr. Asquith.

The main provisions of the Secret Treaty of London can be tabulated as follows:

(1) Italy was promised, not only the Trentino, but the whole southern Tyrol as far as the Brenner Pass. This entailed placing 229,261 pure Austrians under Italian rule.

(2) Italy was promised further territories and islands such as Trieste, Goricia, Gradisca, Lussin, Istria, Cherso, and portions of Carniola and Carinthia which would place under her rule 477,387 Jugoslavs.

(3) Italy was promised Northern Dalmatia and most of the Dalmation Islands which entailed placing under her rule a further 751,571 Jugoslavs.

(4) She was promised full sovereignty over the Albanian town and naval base of Valona, plus a protectorate over the future State of Albania. The northern and southern portions of that State were to be annexed by Serbia and Greece respectively.

(5) She was promised complete sovereignty over Rhodes and the other eleven Islands of the Dodecanese which contained a purely Greek population, and which she had 'provisionally' occupied at the time of the Tripoli war.

(6) In the event of the partition of Turkey, she was promised 'a just share' in the region of Adalia.

(7) In the event of Great Britain or France increasing their colonial possessions in Africa at the expense of Germany she was promised 'equitable compensation.'

In other words, Italy was by the Treaty of London promised territories which would place under her domination some 1,300,000 Jugoslavs, some 230,000 Germans, the whole Greek population of the Dodecanese, the Turks and Greeks of Adalia, all that was left of the Albanians, and vague areas in Africa. It was not, therefore, a Treaty which was in any consonance with the principle of self-determination or the doctrine of the Fourteen Points.

In return for these vast and wholly indefensible concessions Italy, on her part, undertook two obligations only. The first was to accord the port of Fiume to the Jugoslavs. The second was to declare war upon all our enemies. She evaded both these obligations. The former obligation will be considered later, the latter obligation was also not fulfilled. Italy did, it is true, declare war upon Austria in May 1915, upon Turkey in August of that year, and upon Bulgaria a few weeks later. She did not, however, declare war upon Germany until August 27, 1916. Signor Salandra actually boasted of this evasion as 'an important service rendered to my country.' An attempt was made, in Paris, to get Mr. Balfour to adduce this act of sacred egoism as an omission sufficiently serious to invalidate the whole Treaty of London. He lolled patrician and dissentient. 'That,' he said, 'is a lawyer's argument.' It was only half-heartedly, and at a much later stage of the negotiations, that Mr. Lloyd George raised this point. The Italians, with their wonted irreverence, their unfailing irrelevance, muttered something about a 'scrap of paper.'

So much for the Treaty of London in its prearmistice stage. Between its conclusion and the collapse of Austria-Hungary certain other events occurred which must be briefly mentioned. The Bolsheviks, in the first place, published the Treaty of London. It was at once assailed, not only in Great Britain, America and France, but also in the Italian Chamber. It was described as a document of shameless imperialism. Upon the Jugoslav portions of the Austrian army it had a galvanic effect. They became more hostile to Italy than ever before. Caporetto taught the Italians that something must be done to conciliate these Jugoslav belligerents. Signor Orlando, who had by then become Prime Minister, encouraged certain deputies to form a committee of conciliation. Under the calm Scotch aegis of Dr. Seton Watson, under the persistent Europeanism of Mr. Wickham Steed, contact was established in

London between Signor Torre of the Italian Chamber, and M. Trumbic, the spokesman of the Jugoslav Committee. On April 10, 1918, the 'Pact of Rome' was concluded between these two authorised although unofficial representatives. Under this pact Italo-Jugoslav differences were to be solved on the principle of nationality. The Italian Government, on September 8, 1918, issued a pronouncement expressing deep sympathy with the desires of the Jugoslavs to form an independent and united kingdom. This, as Vittorio Veneto proved, was a remunerative pronouncement. It was universally felt, at that date, that the Treaty of London had been superseded by these unofficial and yet approved pronouncements and accords. This feeling was increased when Italy enthusiastically accepted the Fourteen Points of President Wilson. Point Nine provided that the Italian frontiers should be defined 'upon clearly recognisable lines of nationality.' It is true that on November 1 Signor Orlando mumbled something about a reservation. When asked to repeat himself he merely mumbled further. It was then suggested to him that Point Nine of the Fourteen Points had no bearing upon the armistice with Germany which was then under discussion. He gladly accepted that suggestion. He did not publish the fact that he had made any reservation until May 1, 1919. This is a classic instance of the dangers of affable imprecision in international negotiation. Signor Orlando was left under the impression that he had accepted the Fourteen Points subject to a reservation upon Point Nine. President Wilson and the rest of the world were left under the impression that he had accepted the Fourteen Points without any reservation. It was this misunderstanding which added a further complication to the ensuing controversy.

2

It must be admitted that the Italian Representatives, on reaching Paris, were in a position of great difficulty. Italy had been brought into the war against her allies, and on the side of their enemies, on the principle of 'sacred selfishness': that principle implied that she would receive material, rather than moral, satisfaction in return. Great Britain and France had pledged themselves to deliver this material satisfaction in the currency of the old imperialism, in the form, that is, of annexations and protectorates. By no human ingenuity, by no statistical or other juggling, could it be made to appear that this debt could ever be liquidated in the new currency of the Fourteen Points. Nothing could disguise the central fact that the fulfilment of the pledges of the Secret Treaty would violate the principle of self-determination to the extent of placing some two million unwilling and very self-determined people under Italian rule. The battle was thus unescapably joined between a Secret Treaty and the Fourteen Points, between imperialism and self-determination, between the old order and the new, between diplomatic convention and the Sermon on the Mount. France and Great Britain were bound by the letter of their bond: the hands of President Wilson were fettered only by his own principles. Here, if ever, was an opportunity for the Prophet of the New World to enforce his message upon the old. The Italian problem thus became, for them that knew, the test case of the whole Conference. It was on Woodrow Wilson's handling of the Treaty of London that we decided to judge his essential value. He was tested: and he compromised. We may have taken an unfair issue on which to test him: yet there was the issue that we chose. He failed us. We were shocked by this failure. We ceased, from that moment, to believe that President Wilson was the Prophet whom we had followed. From that moment we saw in him no more than a presbyterian dominie.

I relate these emotions as they arose at the time. I quite see that it was easy for us to choose so vicarious an operation wherewith to test Mr. Wilson's surgical skill. I do not say that we were right, unselfish, clear headed, or even honest in so doing. I say only that that is what we did.

The claims of Italy were weakened by other considerations. SS. Orlando and Sonnino might have surmised that the principle of self-determination would not be applied with any academic rigour in favour of Germany or even Hungary. It was awkward for the Italians that their claims extended over just those sections of enemy territory which aroused warm feelings in the hearts of both associates and allies. Everybody liked the Tyrolese. Mr. Lloyd George was reported even to have a deep veneration, a fellow-feeling, for the memory of Andreas Hofer. And then there were the Jugoslavs. In Italian eyes, the Croats and the Slovenes were the most pestilential of all our late enemies. It was distressing for Baron Sonnino to discover on reaching Paris that the Americans, the British and the French, regarded these liberated Slavs as the lost sheep over whom there was much rejoicing. The Greeks, again, could claim with justice that the Dodecanese were wholly Greek in population and desire. Moreover, the state of public opinion at home was not very healthy: there were murmurs of socialism, or even worse: these murmurs could only be stilled by large slices of successful imperialism. Yet how, with Woodrow Wilson smiling his evangelical Princeton smile, could those slices be produced?

One is forced, in common humanity, to have a certain sympathy for the Italians. Behind all these perplexities, were preoccupations of a more compelling character. The complete collapse of Austria had taken Italy by surprise. What they would have preferred was some 'combinazione' which would have left a chain of weak and separated states upon their northern and eastern borders. Instead of this they saw themselves faced with the Germans as their neighbours in the north, and on the east a strong new nation of over thirteen million Jugoslavs. I shall refer later to this important aspect. For the moment it is necessary to record how inevitable it was that their thought should have concentrated on the Brenner and the Monte Nevoso.

It diverts me to find in my diary so much naïve and confident indignation with the diplomatic tactics of SS. Orlando and Sonnino. Now that I realise their immense difficulties, the abysmal futility of those to whom they were opposed, I am not certain that they were wholly incompetent. Externally and internally they were in a very weak position; they knew that their political, military and naval strength entitled them to scant esteem in allied quarters: they knew that everything they desired was in opposition to the principles of President Wilson: they knew that those principles would in other areas be strained beyond bearing under the pressure of France, Belgium, the New States, and other elements stronger than themselves: they knew that their own public opinion, still fervent with war propaganda, expected glories which they could not possibly produce: and they thus manœuvred for both time and position with a subtlety and a consistency which to-day compels both my indignation and my unwilling respect for technique. I should like to feel that Italy would have done better by throwing herself, virginal and sobbing, upon the neck of President Wilson and espousing in one rapturous gesture the good, the beautiful and the true. I question, however, whether any such gesture would have given birth to the Treaty of Rapallo of November 12, 1920. It would have given birth to communism in Italy and at a stage when Mussolini was no more than a journalist of Milan. To a certain extent Italy was an anachronism in our counsels: yet she was an injured and ill-treated anachronism. I do not, to-day, consider that Sonnino and Orlado were absolutely unjustified in their conduct. I regret merely that this inevitable combination of evils should in effect have destroyed Wilsonism at the Conference of Paris. The attempt to combine the fifteenth with the thirtieth century would, in the best of circumstances, be liable to lead to some misconception of motive. And Paris of 1919 was not the best of circumstances.

The stages by which President Wilson surrendered to Italy, the spasmodic gestures which he made to recover his original position, have not been clearly divulged. It is evident, I think, that Orlando and Sonnino, who did not in everything see eye to eye, divided their functions. Orlando, who was a liberal at heart, concentrated on winning the approval of Colonel House. In this he amply succeeded. He knew that there were two points of weakness in the American armour, two points which they ardently desired. The first was to obtain a moral victory over Europe such as would, once and for all, satisfy their passion for rescue-work and allay their own illusions of cultural and historic inferiority. The second was to obtain that victory without the slightest effort of personal abnegation. These two purposes were admirably combined in a Covenant of the League of Nations which would include the Monroe doctrine. Signor Orlando, being a clever if slightly unbelieving man, was the first to realise that President Wilson would shut one eye to countless inconsistencies if only a Covenant, thus emasculated, could be inextricably entwined within the fabric of the Treaties. He was quick to see, when the President returned from his interim visit to Washington, that the opposition of the American Senate had placed their delegation in Paris in a highly illogical situation.

Readily did he offer Colonel House the support of Italy in the League Committee: readily did he assure the President that there could be nothing easier, or more just, than to exclude the American continent both from the sanctions and the responsibilities of the League Machinery; to accord it the pleasures of uplift, with none of the pain of action or interference. Signor Orlando, with the utmost affability, backed the clause under which the Monroe Doctine should remain unaffected by the Covenant of the League. Yet he made one mistake. He failed to observe that since the President's return from Washington—since that ghastly dinner-party at which Senator Lodge had been so silent —Colonel House was no longer in favour. Colonel House had taken Clemenceau aside. There were henceforward two parties in the Hotel Crillon. The first, which might be called the party of conciliation, was represented by Colonel House and Mr. Henry White. The second was the party of Wilsonism, represented by the American experts. Nobody, least of all Mr. Wilson himself, had any consistent idea to which of these two parties the President belonged. It was Signor Orlando's assumption that the President and Colonel House were still at one which led him to assume an attitude which, without American backing, was a very silly attitude to assume.

The Italian Foreign Minister, Baron Sonnino, stood for, and was detached for, other purposes. He represented 'rugged honesty'—a reputation which he had acquired owing to one chance (and one deliberate) circumstance. His mother was of Scottish nationality. That made us all feel that Signor Sonnino was clean of heart. Upon his mantelpiece at home he had inscribed the motto: *'aliis licet, tibi non licet':* the knowledge of this inscription filled us with the certainty that Baron Sonnino possessed independence, high-mindedness, a nimble wit and the humanities. These are immortal assets. They enabled Baron Sonnino to be protractedly unreliable before we found him out.

In spite, however, of these initial advantages of a dual personality and a dual approach, it remains a complete mystery how the Italian Delegation managed to induce President Wilson to consent to Italy being accorded the Brenner frontier and the South Tyrol. It seems that this vitally damaging concession was accorded by Mr. Wilson as early as January of 1919. It has been suggested that the President was still under the emotional excitement of his Roman triumph. It has been suggested that the Italians threatened, unless he consented, to oppose the inclusion of the Covenant in the Treaty of Peace. It has been suggested that they promised, were this concession granted, to be Wilsonian and amenable in all other matters such as those which affected the Jugoslavs, the Albanians, the Greeks and the Turks. Not one of these suggestions is based on any wholly convincing authority. There is nothing to explain how the President could, at the very outset of the Conference, have agreed to place 230,000 Tyrolese under Italian rule in flagrant violation of the most central of all his principles. I prefer to accept the simple explanation that Woodrow Wilson was quite unaware at the time what his concession really implied. He confessed subsequently to Dr. Charles Seymour that his surrender on this point had been due to 'insufficient study.' Professor Coolidge has left the following record: 'The well founded belief among our people was that he gave his consent without due consideration and frankly regretted it afterwards, but felt bound by his word.'

Whatever may have been the motives which led the President to hand the Tyrolese over to Italy, the consequences of this concession were disastrous. They worked out as follows. From the very first days of the Conference it was widely realised that the President had already sacrificed the principle of nationality in a case where no arguments existed for such abandonment beyond the argument of strategic necessity. He had apparently made this concession gratuitously, and without demanding any assurances in return. By so doing, he had, at the same time, implied approval of the Treaty of London. He had thus compromised his own moral position and the authority of his delegation from the very outset. If Wilson could swallow the Brenner, he would swallow anything. The moral effect of this discovery can scarcely be exaggerated. Even on practical, as distinct from moral, grounds, his concession was an appalling blunder. When he came to deal with the ensuing Adriatic question he found that he had already discarded his ace of trumps. In his desire to rectify this ill-considered gesture he became obstinate and professorial in matters of far less vital importance. He played his hand with a pernickety gesture and provocatively. And as a result the Adriatic problem emerged from the lower regions of a difference of opinion into the nervous peaks of a world crisis.

3

It may be observed that in this vital matter also Mr. Wilson suffered much from his prim and thoughtless rejection of the Jusserand programme of November 29. Had that programme been accepted and imposed, not only would the Treaty of London have been automatically cancelled, but it would have been possible to avoid the dislocation of time and energy by all these Italian impositions. Even had the Conference, at its first sitting, laid down that the first objective was the conclusion of peace with our main enemy, then these Adriatic differences would not with such inevitable insistence have arisen until a later and less crucial stage. Here again it was their lack of scientific planning which landed the Supreme Council in all these complexities from the outset. In their desire to placate the smaller Powers they had gratuitously invited those Powers to state their claims. It was these statements of claim which, in the case of Jugoslavia, Greece and Albania, imposed upon the Supreme Council the necessity of considering as early as February how far these claims were in conflict with the claims of Italy. It is true, of course, that the Italians would, in any case, have striven hard to postpone the signature of the Covenant and of the Treaty with Germany until their own claims against Austria, Jugoslavia, Greece and even Turkey had, at least in principle, been accepted. Yet the lack of any rigid programme enabled them to achieve this object with a minimum of effort. What should have been an arduous and costly manœuvre was rendered, owing to the amateurishness of the Supreme Council, an easy walk-over.

The main issue of the Italian question, once the Brenner had been disposed of, was what is known generally as the 'Adriatic Problem.' In other words it centred around the dispute between Italy and Jugoslavia as to their joint frontier, and more particularly as to the ownership of Fiume, Dalmatia, and the Islands. The Adriatic problem is too congested with detail to lend itself readily to any practical examination: I shall consider it later in terms of the principles and methods involved. Yet it is impossible to convey any impression of the effect upon the Peace Conference of this incessant controversy with Italy, unless some indication be given of the constant flux and reflux between fact and principle, principle and fact. I shall therefore choose as my 'exhibits' of these difficulties of detail, not the central problem of Fiume and the Adriatic, but two secondary and far more manageable products of the Secret Treaty of London. I shall choose the problems of Albania and the Dodecanese.

Until the Balkan wars of 1912–1913 Albania, although possessing a distinct Illyrian nationality of her own, had been a province of the Turkish Empire. With the collapse of Turkish rule in Macedonia and Thrace Albania found herself independent but somewhat in the air. Her future status and frontiers were considered by the Conference of Ambassadors then sitting in London under the chairmanship of Sir Edward Grey. On July 29, 1913, the Ambassadors agreed, after much benevolence and some wrangling, upon the northern frontiers of the future Albanian Principality. These frontiers placed Scutari within Albanian territory, but allocated the Albanian towns of Ipek and Djakova to Montenegro. The delimitation of the southern frontier between Albania and Greece was to be decided after it had been examined by a Commission on the spot. The recommendations of that Commission had not fully been approved at the outbreak of the European War. Meanwhile the crown of Albania had been offered to Prince William of Wied who landed at Durazzo on May 7, 1914, and who was turned out of the country on September 4 following by Essad Pasha, his own Minister of War. On November 25 Italy, although a neutral at the time, seized the naval base of Valona, while Austrian troops garrisoned the north and centre. The Treaty of London in the following April promised to Italy Valona and the protectorate of a small central Albanian State, whereas the rest of Albania was to be partitioned between Serbia and Greece. On June 3, 1917, Italy, without consulting her Allies, proclaimed the independence of Albania under Italian protection. The French replied to this by establishing an Independent Republic at Koritza in Southern Albania, thus commanding the important strategic road from Santi Quaranta into Greece. They obstinately, and to my mind nobly, maintained forces in that remote district until May 1920. The Serbians for their part crossed the northern frontier and occupied Scutari and the line of the Drin. They were subsequently obliged to surrender Scutari to an interallied force, but still remained in occupation of the rest of Northern Albania. The position of Albania at the opening of the Conference of Paris was thus anomalous and confused.

The situation was further deteriorated by the fact that each of Albania's neighbours and protectors cherished designs upon her integrity and frontiers, and that, in the south at least, the populations were closely intermingled and the statistics involved. The Greeks claimed the whole of Southern Albania including Koritza, on the grounds that it constituted 'Northern Epirus' and was mainly inhabited by Greeks. The Serbs claimed the whole of Northern Albania partly on strategic and partly on ethnical grounds. Their main argument, however, was that the Grand Trunk Railway which was to connect Jugoslavia with the lower Adriatic could only find its outlet at Scutari and along the Drin Valley.

The attitude of the Great Powers towards

this intricate problem was illustrative and diverse. The Americans and the British were pro-Albanian in sympathy, although in the south our own enthusiasm was clouded by a doubt whether it was wise, if Italy were to obtain a foothold in Albania, to give her the strategic advantage of Koritza and the Santi Quaranta road, which was in fact the only line of communication between Janina and Salonika. The French tended to adopt our attitude, and it was they who finally persuaded us that Koritza should be given to Greece. The attitude of Italy towards this problem was illogical, irritating, and strange.

The Italians, since April 1915, had come to dislike the Albanian section of the Treaty of London. They still wanted their naval base at Valona in full sovereignty: they still wanted a protectorate over the future Albanian State. They still, as always, wanted the Treaty of London. They were no longer prepared, however, to fulfil the remaining conditions of that section of the Treaty, and to hand over to Serbia and Greece the northern and southern portions of Albania. The former cession would represent an accession of territory to Jugoslavia. The latter cession would place Greece in strategic command of the Corfu channel. And in any case, if Italy were to be given a protectorate over Albania, it seemed fitting to her that Albania should be as large, both north and south, as possible.

The result was that, although on all other matters (except Fiume) the Italians clamoured, on the basis of the 'Sanctity of Treaties,' for the integral fulfilment of the Treaty of London, they argued that in respect of Albania this Treaty was not fully in accord with the principle of self-determination. When it was pointed out to them that the retention of Valona might also be regarded as a violation of that principle, they contended that in such retention 'the honour of Italy' was involved.

Day after day were we obliged to listen patiently to this exegesis of our Italian colleagues upon the doctrine of Wilsonism, without being permitted to express the distaste, and indeed the blind fury, which such sophistry evoked. Upon myself the tolerance displayed by the Americans and the Conference generally in face of such distortion of doctrine had a most demoralising effect. The courtesy of international conduct forbade us to express our righteous indignation by anything but a pained silence. Yet at any moment it would have been open to the United States Representatives to explode as follows: 'You have just appealed in this matter to the doctrine of self-determination as overriding the Treaty of London. May I inform my President that Italy will apply this principle to every question in which Italian interests are involved?' There would have been no answer to such a question. Yet it was never asked. We endured in silence. And day by day our confidence in Wilsonism as an applicable and self-assertive doctrine was destroyed.

It is necessary to add that the Albanian question was never finally settled by the Paris Conference. The Italians remained in military occupation of that country until August of 1920 when the Albanians rose against them and drove them into the sea. An armistice was hurriedly negotiated and the Italians, with small appearance of dignity, withdrew. A policy of financial penetration was thereafter adopted. It was extremely successful. Long after the Paris Conference, the frontiers of Albania and the position of Italy in that country were regularised by diplomatic agreement.

The question of Rhodes and the eleven other Greek Islands of the Dodecanese can be dealt with shortly. The Italians possessed no moral, and small juridical, right to these Islands. Baron Sonnino kept on trying to negotiate with M. Venizelos a direct agreement for the settlement of Graeco-Italian difficulties. The Americans and British were constantly put off by assurances that a settlement agreeable to both parties was about to be arranged. Such a settlement was, in fact, concluded between M. Venizelos and Signor

Tittoni, the successor of Baron Sonnino. But when the Greeks fell upon evil days, this arrangement was repudiated by a subsequent Government, and to this day the Italian flag flaunts unrighteously (but I admit hygienically) above the Dodecanese.

I have cited these two problems, not merely as an illustration of the shifts, hypocrisies and pretences which we were obliged to endure in courtly silence, but as an example of the unfortunate extent to which President Wilson and his assistants fluctuated between principle and detail. To that extent, I admit, their professorial training was a misfortune. Our own hands were tied by the Treaty of London and we could say nothing. We longed for the Americans to call down fire from heaven and to proclaim their principles against any array of detail. They hesitated, partly from an exaggerated fear of 'breaking up the Peace Conference' and partly from a too scrupulous diffidence. Yet once they had abandoned the unassailable fortress of their own principles for the surrounding marshes of detail, they were immediately surrounded, outnumbered and disarmed. The tragedy of the Peace Conference was that the New World consented to meet the Old World on ground of the latter's choosing.

4

It is easy, and not very historical, to depict the Italians as the villains of the whole drama. Objectively, I now realise that there was much, that there is much, to be said in their defence. I admit (I have already admitted) their difficulties. The emotions of the Italian Chamber were even more disordered than those of the House of Commons. It drove them mad to feel that the Fourteen Points were being relaxed in favour of France and Great Britain, while being rigidly enforced as against Italy. The temper of the country was even more hysterical than that of the *Daily Mail*. The labour situation was even more menacing than that at Glasgow. The appetite of Italy was greater, her digestive capacity far less, than that of any other country. She was determined to become a Great Power without the internal force to justify such an ambition. Italy, in January 1919, was obviously at her very worst.

There were other considerations which rendered the issues facing Orlando and Sonnino peculiarly baffling. I have already stated that the complete collapse of Austria-Hungary took the Italians by surprise. It is only fair to elaborate that statement in terms of Italian necessity. The Treaty of London had been devised on the assumption that something, at least, would remain of the old Austro-Hungarian Empire, that some balance of power, as between the Teuton and the Slav, would persist upon Italy's northern and eastern frontiers. This assumption had been falsified by events. Against the German menace they were, it is true, protected by the Brenner line. Yet on the east they were exposed, not (as they had anticipated) to a purely naval or polynesian danger, but to the military menace of a land frontier to be defended against thirteen million Jugoslavs. In other words, the Treaty of London had been devised in terms of Austria-Hungary. Those terms no longer applied. It was essential for a weak country such as Italy to obtain strategic and economic safeguards against this new menace. These safeguards expressed themselves in terms of two objectives. (1) The Monte Nevoso as a strategical defence against the Jugoslav army. (2) Fiume, as a guarantee of, and a victim to, the economic prosperity of Trieste. Neither of these two objectives had been promised to Italy by the Treaty of London. Both of them violated the principle of President Wilson.

It is only in terms of essential Italian necessity that we can hope to comprehend the apparent mistake of Signor Orlando (once he had obtained the Brenner) in thus selecting as his main objectives the only two points (Fiume and the Monte Nevoso) on which the signatories of the Treaty of

London were free to unite with President Wilson. It is frequently stated (by Mr. Lansing among others) that Signor Orlando unloosed upon the Fiume question a public opinion which he was unable subsequently to control. There is a certain truth in this thesis. I question, however, whether the Italian Delegation were to any serious extent the victims of their own propaganda. They knew of course that the Treaty of London promised them Dalmatia and denied them Fiume. They also knew that under the Fourteen Points, Dalmatia was unattainable and that Fiume might, with a little statistical juggling, be obtained. They may have felt that if the Great Voice of the Italian People were incited to yell for Fiume, then the great heart of the Italian people would accept the ensuing surrender of Dalmatia. To a certain extent this may have been their intention and their misfortune. Yet, essentially, they felt that circumstances had changed; and that the possession of Fiume and the Monte Nevoso was an Italian necessity far more compelling than any flourishes in Dalmatia or the Islands.

I deal in this summary way with the central core of the Adriatic problem. I make no mention of the Armistice of the Villa Giusti of November 3, 1918, of the Italian refusal in Paris to sit at the same table as the Croats and the Slovenes, of the Jugoslav attempt to secure the arbitral decision of President Wilson, of all the notes and negotiations which took place between April 13 and April 23, of the dissensions between the House-group and the Bowman-group within the American delegation, of the ensuing 'Wilson line,' of our own 'pound of flesh' attitude towards the Treaty of London, or of Mr. Lloyd George's wholly disinterested flitting between the Hotel Crillon and the Hotel Edouard VII. The main issue can be boiled down to the following formula:

(1) The Treaty of London promised Italy Dalmatia and some Adriatic Islands. It did *not* assign to them either Fiume or the Monte Nevoso.

(2) France and Great Britain were bound by the Treaty of London. President Wilson refused even to take it into consideration.

(3) The collapse of Austria-Hungary and the unexpected emergence of a compact and powerful Jugoslav State rendered it essential that Italy should obtain Fiume for economic reasons; the Monte Nevoso for strategical reasons.

(4) If they abandoned the Treaty of London they would release Great Britain and France from any contractual obligation at all. If they insisted upon the application of the Treaty of London, they would be frustrated by the veto of President Wilson.

(5) Their policy was, therefore, with one hand to hold Great Britain and France down to the Treaty of London, while negotiating with President Wilson regarding Fiume and the Monte Nevoso. Once these had been obtained, a new Treaty could be negotiated with France and Great Britain which, while releasing them from the European clauses of the Treaty of London, would bind them to the execution of the Asiatic and African clauses.

It is not surprising that the Italian Delegation should have endeavoured in this manner to hunt with the hounds and run with the hare. What is so disheartening is that President Wilson (who held every card except the Brenner ace within his hand) should have adopted a precisely similar method of chase and scurry. He first (on April 14) indicated to Signor Orlando that he was prepared to compromise on Fiume. And he then (on April 23) issued to the Press a statement in which he appealed to the Italian People over the head of their elected Representative. He thus combined the secrecy of the old diplomacy with the most flagrant indiscretions of the new.

It may be surmised that this duality of action on the part of the President was due to the conflicting influences of Colonel House and the group of American experts who ranged themselves behind Mr. Isaiah Bowman. The former was rightly obsessed by the terror of delay and believed that any Treaty, if rapidly concluded, would be better than any Treaty postponed. Colonel House, let it be remembered, was a very wise, though somewhat inarticulate, man. The experts felt that the President must, in this last resounding ditch, make a stand for his own principles. They thus addressed to him the sort of appeal which would be most likely to awake afresh his theocratic feelings. 'Never,' they wrote, 'did the President have such an opportunity to strike a death-blow to the discredited methods of the old diplomacy. . . . To the President is given the rare privilege of going down in history as the statesman who destroyed, by a clean-cut decision against an infamous arrangement, the last vestige of the old order.'

It was not, as a matter of fact, the last vestige. Shantung remained as a final humiliation. It was certainly not a clean-cut decision. Yet by these revivalist words the President was revived. On April 23 he issued to the Press a statement of his own views on the Fiume problem, in which he appealed, not without his old eloquence, to the heart of Italy against the brain of the Italian Delegation in Paris. The next day Signor Orlando left Paris in dramatic, although somewhat prearranged, indignation. And the emotions of the Italian people founted in passionate abuse of President Wilson. 'Either Fiume,' they yelled, 'or death.' The President had appealed both to his principles and to The People. And the latter gnashed their teeth at him in rage. He was much discouraged. From that moment he seems to have abandoned all hope of imposing his doctrines on the false democracies of Europe.

The details of the ensuing imbroglio are less important than this defeat of principle. On May 5 the Italians returned to Paris. Mr. Lloyd George thereafter endeavoured (and as I now feel, rightly) to effect a settlement on the basis of vast compensations in Asia Minor. M. Tardieu on May 30 produced his own compromise. In June and July there were troubles in Fiume and some French soldiers were killed. On September 12 D'Annunzio occupied the city. In December Signor Nitti evolved an attempt at compromise. In January of 1920 that compromise was succeeded by another. Both Trumbic and President Wilson (by that time ailing in aloof Washington) refused that compromise. The latter suggested direct negotiations between the two disputants. The problem was thus further negotiated at San Remo in May of 1920, as between Trumbic and Nitti. An agreement was almost reached, when Nitti fell. By November of 1920 the Jugoslavs had lost heart. President Wilson was by then a stricken man: there was no hope of his assistance: the Allied Powers were wearied of the controversy: the Jugoslavs were obliged to surrender to Count Sforza at Rapallo and to accord to Italy what in effect meant Fiume and the Monte Nevoso. It was in this manner, eighteen months after the Conference of Paris, that, while Wilson was dying in Washington, Italy obtained her desires.

I am not concerned with the ultimate solution of the Adriatic problem. I am concerned only with what happened in Paris between January 18, 1919 and June 28. How came it that President Wilson, having surrendered on the Brenner frontier, was unable to impose upon Italy an equitable solution of the Adriatic and Dodecanese questions? It might be contended that the President, until the day of his death, never actually consented to any concessions on these points, and that his attitude was, in regard to this controversy at least, less illogical than was his attitude regarding Shantung, Poland, the Mandates or the inclusion of War Pensions in Reparation. In the cold light of history it may seem even that, in his dealings with Italy, Woodrow Wilson, except for that error about South Tyrol, did in truth maintain his principles intact. Such was not, however, the impression which spread through the hot saloons of Paris. We recognised, in the methods rather than in the purposes of the Italian Delegation, all that was most odious in the old diplomacy. We trusted that the President would also recognise the danger and confront the Italians with the strong weapons which he held. The spectacle of Woodrow Wilson billing and cooing with Orlando filled us with a blank despair. It was not that he negotiated unskilfully; it was that he consented to negotiate at all. Had he taken a strong line from the very start as against Italian claims he might have triumphed later against Great Britain, France and Japan. It was his early shambling over the Italian question that convinced us that Woodrow Wilson was not a great or potent man. That conviction was a profound disappointment: on its heels demoralisation spread through Paris like a disease.

FORTY-EIGHT

THE DEMOCRACIES ON THE DEFENSIVE

In the democracies the postwar years were far from heroic. The United States retreated into isolationism. Britain sought valiantly for prewar normalcy, and refused to take drastic, if unorthodox, steps to end unemployment. France, which carried more or less alone the immense burden of maintaining international order on the continent, drifted through the 1920's and 1930's in an atmosphere of protracted apathy. The depression of 1929 added fresh tension to the already tense mood of the victors of 1918. Meanwhile, as the democracies slumbered, Italy followed Mussolini into Fascism in 1922, Russia began its first Five-Year Plan in 1928, Japan began a campaign of naked aggression in Manchuria in 1931, and Hitler became chancellor of the infamous Third Reich in 1933. The stage was already set for the decline and fall of the League of Nations, abandoned by the major democratic powers, and for the Nazi war of nerves which flamed into real war in 1939. Professor Mowat has charted Britain's wavering course in the postwar, more properly called interwar, years. His clear and penetrating analysis presents a case study of indecision and wishful thinking, as Great Britain, like the other democracies, took a mainly defensive attitude and awoke to firm action when already it was almost too late to stop the dictators.

CHARLES L. MOWAT

BRITAIN BETWEEN THE WARS, 1918-1940 *

1. THE NATIONAL GOVERNMENT

The history of the National government was one long diminuendo. From its triumph in 1931 it shambled its unimaginative way to its fall in 1940, when the failure of the campaign in Norway and the Nazi invasion of the Low Countries brought Great Britain to the crisis of the new world war. Its origin was an emergency which was financial and domestic; its tasks were to overcome a series of catastrophes which were international and military. Its responses were not bold. It retreated before aggression; it rearmed, but at first too slowly. In fact it was not unsuccessful in its economic policies but fatally narrow in its political conduct. Failure in the

* Reprinted from *Britain Between the Wars, 1918–1940,* pp. 413–26, by Charles L. Mowat by permission of The University of Chicago Press, copyright 1955 by The University of Chicago Press. Published in England by Methuen & Co. Ltd.

latter sphere darkened its reputation in the former; in retrospect it has been blamed for all the misfortunes of the time, partly because its opponents rose to power by reiterating their version of its history and its period.

The mood of the early thirties was not heroic. Gone was the hopeful internationalism of the twenties, the return to the gold standard, the restoration of world trade. Britain, beset by depression, turned inward, like every other country, and concentrated on internal problems and domestic solutions. In time the mood changed, but the government remained the same; 1935 was the year of decision. Other countries might have new and adventurous governments: Germany the Third Reich, France the Popular Front, the United States the New Deal, Russia another Five-Year Plan. Only in Britain did the Conservatives remain in power; hence the Second World War, restoring conservatism in other countries, could only dethrone it in Great Britain.

That the National government was in harmony with the national mood could not be doubted. MacDonald and Baldwin, having alternated in office in the twenties, shared it in the thirties, and combined their talents for calming the passions and rubbing the sharp edges off awkward questions. MacDonald should not be judged by these last years as Prime Minister. Prisoner of the Conservatives, he could have given a lead to the government only if he had been a stronger and younger man than he was. His health was failing; his speeches, never crystal-clear, became more and more difficult to follow; only his courage, sternly tested by trouble with his eyes, remained with him to the last. He had the misfortune, it has been said, to outlive himself not in retirement but in office.[1]

The one strong man in the government was not of the sort to endear it with the people: Neville Chamberlain, the Chancellor of the Exchequer. It was he who largely directed its domestic policies and more and more dominated the Cabinet. In the day of the lesser men he was outstanding, with his clear, civil-service mind, high principles, narrow but progressive views, great energy and self-confidence. What he lacked was warmth. He repelled Labour men by his scorn, Conservatives by the discipline he demanded of them.[2] 'Weaned on a pickle', a normally generous Labour observer called him; [3] the rasping voice seemed symbolic of the man.

Of the other members of the government little need be said. The Cabinet, unlike the emergency Cabinet of August 1931, was of normal size—twenty members. It contained at first eleven Conservatives, four Labour members, and five Liberals (three from the official party, two from Sir John Simon's group). Of the Labour members MacDonald, Thomas and Lord Sankey retained their former positions: Snowden became Lord Privy Seal, and went to the Lords with a viscountcy. Sir Herbert Samuel was Home Secretary, Sir John Simon Foreign Secretary—an unexpected and unfortunate choice. Another Simonite, Walter Runciman, went to the Board of Trade at Snowden's insistence that it and the Treasury should not both be in the charge of protectionists. Seldom was Snowden so mistaken. The Conservative ministers included hardworking men, such as Sir Samuel Hoare, Cunliffe-Lister, Lord Hailsham, Lord Londonderry (1878–1949). They were not men to inspire others. It was the omissions which were conspicuous; Winston Churchill, Leopold Amery, Austen Chamberlain (who stood down in favour of younger men).

To oppose this government of all the talents the Labour remnant elected George

[1] See Pierre Maillaud, *The English Way* (Oxford, 1945), pp. 145, 155–68 (the acute observations of a Frenchman resident in England since 1932).

[2] K. Feiling, *N. Chamberlain,* brings out the best in him and also shows his weaknesses; see pp. 81–3, 104, 118–24, 130, 135, 142.

[3] Lord Snell, *Men, movements and myself* (London, 1936), p. 248.

Lansbury as chairman; his unorthodox but effective discharge of the duties of leader of the Opposition received the praise of Baldwin.[4] Clement Attlee was vice-chairman of the party. On occasion, after his recovery, Lloyd George was also to be found on the front Opposition bench.

2. The Triumph of the Tariff: The End of the Honeymoon

The first important measures of the government were those taken to promote recovery by fiscal means. In November 1931, Runciman introduced the Abnormal Importations bill to give the Board of Trade power for six months to impose duties up to 100 per cent *ad valorem* on manufactured articles which were entering the country in 'abnormal' quantities. There had been no inquiry, such as had been promised during the election campaign; no justification for the measure was made save that the country was suffering from the 'dumping' of foreign goods in 'abnormal' amounts—words of undefined but pejorative meaning; and even the fact of 'dumping' was not proved. Such a bill was a stern trial of the patriotism of the Liberal free traders; but they accepted it, and despite Labour opposition it was quickly passed. Duties of 50 per cent were at once imposed on imported pottery, cutlery, typewriters, woollen goods, paper, gloves, followed soon by others on bottles, cameras, cotton goods, electric lamps and radio parts. The Horticultural Products (Emergency Duties) Act, passed soon afterwards, gave the Minister of Agriculture similar powers to hamper the importation of fresh fruits, flowers and vegetables.[5]

With these new precedents in their hands, the Conservatives advanced towards a general tariff. The Cabinet appointed a Balance of Trade Committee under Neville Chamberlain's chairmanship; Snowden and Samuel were members, but the protectionists, among whom Runciman was now included, were in a majority. Again, despite all promises, there was no exhaustive, impartial enquiry. All the Board of Trade's evidence, under Runciman's leadership, was directed to the support of a tariff; no other expert opinion was sought; Samuel later described the whole inquiry as 'merely perfunctory'.[6]

Before the committee's recommendation of a general tariff was accepted a Cabinet crisis occurred. The Liberal ministers, Samuel, Maclean, Sir Archibald Sinclair, threatened to resign, and so did Snowden. Following a lengthy Cabinet meeting on January 21, 1932, MacDonald reasoned with the dissentients at Snowden's flat during the evening, though more concerned with his personal position in the government than with its principles. Next day a solution was announced: the 'agreement to differ', first proposed by Chamberlain and pressed by other Conservatives. 'Because of the paramount importance of maintaining national unity in the presence of the grave problems that now confront the country and the whole world', the dissenters would remain in the Cabinet, bowing to the majority's decision in favour of a tariff but free to express their opposition to it. This breach with constitutional practice, incompatible with the party system and the collective responsibility of the Cabinet, was greeted by some with ridicule and by most with indifference. It did not last long.[7]

This settled, the Import Duties bill was introduced on February 4, by Neville Chamberlain, speaking in the presence of Joseph Chamberlain's widow and children, and claiming, with a show of emotion hitherto rare with him in public, that the measure vindicated his father's work and would have been a consolation for 'the bitterness of his disappointment'. The main provisions of the

[4] G. M. Young, *Baldwin,* pp. 202–3.

[5] D. Abel, *History of British Tariffs,* pp. 87–91; *Annual Register, 1931,* pp. 94–8, 103.

[6] P. Snowden, *Autobiography,* II, 1007–8; Viscount Samuel, *Grooves of Change,* p. 260.

[7] P. Snowden, *Autobiography,* II, 1010–12; D. Abel, *History of British Tariffs,* pp. 92–5.

Act, which went into operation on March 1, were (1) the imposition of a general customs duty of 10 per cent on almost all imports, those already dutiable being exempt from the new duty; (2) the exemption from the duty of goods from within the Empire, pending the Imperial Economic Conference to be held in Ottawa in the summer; (3) the exemption of certain other goods, which were placed on a free list; (4) the creation of a committee, the Import Duties Advisory Committee, on whose recommendation the Treasury could order the imposition of additional duties. The free list included wheat and maize, meat and animals (but not all foodstuffs), iron and tin ores, scrap steel, zinc, lead, rubber, pulp and newsprint, pitprops, cotton, wool, flax, hides and skins. Despite vigorous opposition from Samuel in the Commons and Snowden in the Lords, the bill passed: in the Commons the vote was 454 to 78, the opposition comprising all the Labour members and 32 Liberals.[8]

The Import Duties Advisory Committee was at once constituted: it consisted of Sir George May, as chairman, and two other members. Its first work was a report, published on April 21, 1932 (Cmd. 4066), recommending as a general policy that duties on manufactured goods should be raised to 20 per cent *ad valorem,* on luxury goods to 25 per cent or 30 per cent, and on bicycles, bicycle parts and some chemicals to 33⅓ per cent. Certain goods used in British manufactures were put under a duty of 15 per cent. These recommendations were at once adopted. During the next three years the Committee considered some 300 applications concerning duties, and about 100 orders were issued, some raising, others lowering duties on particular imports. A tariff which was nearly all-embracing but also generally moderate was thus constructed. Its most tangible results were in the iron and steel industry, as will be seen later. Its effect, coupled with the Ottawa agreements, was to leave about a quarter of Britain's exports free of duty, and half paying duties of 10–20 per cent.[9]

There followed the Imperial Economic Conference, held at Ottawa from July 21 to August 20, 1932. It was not the love-feast for which Conservative imperialists and protectionists had hoped. The British delegation, headed by Baldwin and including Chamberlain, Thomas and four other ministers, was made up of protectionists; accompanying it was a large body of civil servants, industrialists and journalists. The hope was that mutually advantageous means for increasing trade within the Empire might be found. Britain now had a tariff, and could offer more imperial preferences in return for concessions by the Dominions for British manufactures. On the other hand, the ministers' freedom in negotiation was limited by the policy of protecting the British farmer, and the desire not to damage Britain's trade with foreign countries. The Dominions could offer little in the way of real help to British manufacturers without hurting their own carefully-nursed 'infant industries', however much they desired concessions from Great Britain for their own primary products. 'Empire free trade' suited them only as a one-way proposition.[10]

Hence from the start the British and Dominion delegates were at cross-purposes. The British ministers found themselves amateurs at the game of bargaining over tariffs. The fighting, haggling and snubbing to which they were subjected even threatened their own unity. They were exposed to sharp attacks in the Canadian press. Even civil servants such as Sir Horace Wilson, adept at the production of mollifying 'formulas', were not spared from criticism. At the end, the conference almost broken down at an all-

[8] D. Abel, *History of British Tariffs,* pp. 95–103; J. H. Richardson, *British Economic Foreign Policy* (London, 1936), pp. 93–5.

[9] J. H. Richardson, pp. 96–9, 127; F. C. Benham, *Great Britain under Protection* (New York, 1941), pp. 25–8.

[10] See W. K. Hancock, *Survey of British Commonwealth Affairs,* II, part i (Oxford, 1940), pp. 214–20.

night session which Chamberlain left in disgust (August 19–20).[11]

Twelve agreements were signed, of which seven were between Britain and the other Dominions, the Irish Free State excepted. Britain promised to continue and in some cases to increase the imperial preference already given to foodstuffs and other products coming from the Dominions. In return, British imports into the Dominions were to receive preference, but chiefly by increasing the tariff against foreign goods, leaving untouched the rate against British goods, already impossibly high in many cases. British traders and the British government were given the right to make representations to the tariff boards in the Dominions about particular duties.[12]

The news of these agreements was too much for the free traders in the Cabinet. Snowden and Samuel exchanged letters at the end of August; both of them, and also the other Liberal ministers, were ready to resign in protest. MacDonald, alarmed at the threat to the unity of the National government, attempted to dissuade them. 'He was disturbed about his personal position,' wrote Snowden, 'and kept on repeating, "I do not know what to do".' To Samuel he argued that Britain's strong position in the world was due to 'our present political combination'; were the Liberals to end it, his own influence as head of such a combination would be destroyed ('I should be regarded as a limpet in office'), and with the ending of the 'national effort in co-operation' the country would be 'grievously damaged'. Action was delayed until the Cabinet could meet. Samuel made a counter-proposal; that 'further progress' with the Ottawa agreements should be suspended until after the World Economic Conference. This received short shrift from the Tories. Snowden, in a letter to MacDonald on the 15th, protesting against the appeal to personal loyalty, asked why the Tories should not be asked 'to subordinate personal views on principle' in the national interest. Too late he was tasting the bitter fruits of his own conduct:

> They have sacrificed nothing, but have used the enormous Tory majority we gave them at the Election to carry out a Tory policy and to identify us with it. We have sacrificed our Party and ruined the political careers of a score of young Labour M.P.'s.

When the Cabinet met on September 28, Snowden resigned, as did the Liberal ministers (Samuel and Sinclair) and Lord Lothian and Isaac Foot among the under-secretaries. MacDonald, Thomas and Sankey stayed on.[13]

Precious little National flavour was left in the government. Sir William Jowitt, the Attorney-General and a Labour member, had resigned in January (lacking a seat) and was replaced by Inskip, a Conservative. A Liberal, Sir Donald Maclean, had died in June and been replaced at the Board of Education by Lord Irwin, the ex-viceroy, who was a Conservative. Snowden's cherished land valuation had been suspended as early as December 1931, by Neville Chamberlain, though the *coup de grâce* was not given to the elusive land tax until 1934. Of course, the Prime Minister was left, and his two colleagues. And Simon and his loyal band of Liberal Nationals were still on hand.

3. The Paralysis of Foreign Policy

In the event, the most important decisions which the National government had to take were those of foreign policy. The first large violation of the peace of the world since the war of 1914–18 occurred in Manchuria on September 18, 1931. It came at the worst possible moment for stern action by Great Britain. The National government was not a month old, and was fully occupied in

[11] D. Abel, *History of British Tariffs,* pp. 104–8; K. Feiling, *N. Chamberlain,* pp. 213–15.

[12] The terms of the agreements are to be found in J. H. Richardson, *British Economic Foreign Policy,* pp. 138–56; D. Abel, *History of British Tariffs,* pp. 108–10; W. K. Hancock, *Survey,* II, i, pp. 222–30.

[13] P. Snowden, *Autobiography,* II, 1020–30, 1081–5; Viscount Samuel, *Grooves of Change,* pp. 273–80; *Annual Register, 1932,* pp. 82–5.

balancing the budget, saving—and then abandoning—the gold standard, and caballing about a general election. When Japanese soldiers suddenly occupied Mukden, following a well-timed explosion on a length of railway track, and gave the signal for the Japanese army rapidly to take over the whole of Manchuria, the Chinese government appealed to the League of Nations under Article 11 of the Covenant and to the United States as a signatory of the Nine-Power Pact and the Kellogg Treaty. The matter was debated in the Council of the League on September 22. The Japanese representative was conciliatory. Lord Cecil, for Great Britain, proposed an inquiry, and persuaded the Council to appeal to both Japan and China to stop fighting and to return their forces to their own frontiers. No one seemed to be very much worried. There was a good deal of sympathy in Great Britain for the Japanese, whose economic rights in Manchuria had been impaired by Chinese anarchy and the recurrence of incidents involving Japanese troops stationed in the country. The *Spectator,* for example, hardly alluded to the Manchurian crisis until October 3, when its tone was reassuring: Japan was complying with the League's appeal. In the contest which followed, the League and the ideas of collective security and the rule of law were defeated; partly because of indifference and of sympathy with the aggressor, but partly because the League powers were unprepared, preoccupied with other matters, and too slow to perceive the scale of Japanese ambitions.

Already the League had lost the first round. The proposed inquiry was abandoned by the Council on September 25, when H. L. Stimson, the United States Secretary of State, published a note which, though warmly supporting the the League's appeal, advised against holding an inquiry contrary to the wishes of Japan. Hope of co-operation between the League and the United States over the crisis perhaps faded as early as this, encouraging the Japanese government—or rather the army—to go ahead in Manchuria. By the time the Council met again in mid-October, with the American consul at Geneva present, not much could be done. Japan was asked to evacuate the territory she had occupied by November 16. When that day came, she had not done so, and the Council then accepted a Japanese proposal of a commission of inquiry (November 21), and on December 10 postponed indefinitely any coercive measures against Japan. This was the critical decision, and its significance was not unnoticed at the time. On October 31, the *Spectator* had declared that the League was 'facing the most critical moment of its career'; on November 14, when urging Sir John Simon to propose strong action at Geneva, it said that if the appeal to Japan was in vain 'that is an end of any pretence that war as an instrument of national policy has been renounced . . . war is re-enthroned . . . a straight road back to 1914 lies open'.

Early in 1932 the pace quickened. On January 29 China invoked Articles 10 and 15 of the Covenant, which would normally lead to the application of sanctions against Japan by members of the League. At the same time fighting between Chinese and Japanese broke out in Shanghai, Japanese reinforcements were landed and the Chapei area bombed. A month's fighting followed, as the Chinese forces in Shanghai made a strong resistance to the Japanese. The Asiatic squadron of the United States navy was despatched to Shanghai. The British and American consuls worked together to secure a truce, which was arranged on May 5. The Japanese withdrew from the parts of Shanghai which they had occupied.

If the interest of the public was then centred on Shanghai, the interest of students later was centred on the Anglo-American diplomatic exchanges of the time. On January 7, 1932, Stimson published a note enunciating the doctrine of 'non-recognition', which would apply to Japanese conquests in Manchuria and to any territorial changes effected by force. He hoped for the support of other powers in this policy; instead he received the frigid reply on January 9 that since Japan had promised to maintain the 'open door' in Manchuria, the British government 'have not considered it necessary to address any formal note to the Japanese Government . . .' Both then [14] and later it was argued that Simon, by this communiqué, squashed a proposal for joint British-American action which would have brought the Japanese to heel, restored the strength of the League and reversed the fatal courses which led to 1939. Neither country, however, then contemplated economic or military action. What Simon's rebuff to Stimson accomplished was the stiffening of Japanese contempt for the League and the great powers, and the frustration of co-operation between Britain and the United States, which might have led, however unintentionally, to strong measures against Japan. On February 8 a second episode of the same sort occurred. The United States proposed that the Nine-Power Pact be invoked against Japan. Transatlantic telephone conversations followed. The Foreign Office drafted a statement on 'non-recognition' which, on February 16, the Council of the League adopted; but the British reply, urging that other League powers should join in invoking the Pact, chilled Stimson's resolution even though it involved a difference of method and not of end.

In any case, what was the invoking of the Pact to mean? Nothing, the Japanese decided. Being now sure of Manchuria, they inaugurated their puppet state of Manchukuo on March 9 and recognised it on September 15, 1932. The League, waiting for the report of its commission of inquiry under Lord Lytton, did nothing. The Lytton report, published on October 2, was sympathetic with Japanese grievances in Manchuria, but condemned the Japanese invasion, refused to accept Manchukuo's independence as genuine and proposed for Manchuria an autonomous regime under Chinese sovereignty. More delay followed while the report was considered. In February 1933, when the League adopted the report, Japan gave notice of its resignation from the League and launched its attack on Jehol, part of China proper. The League did nothing. Japan's war against China was to drag on for years of nominal peace, until it became part of the greater world war of the forties. The League was to blame, the National government was to blame, Sir John Simon was to blame. 'The British representatives at Geneva seem intent on consulting Tokyo's convenience in all things', complained the *Spectator* (April 30, 1932). There was no strong body of opinion in the country which wanted anything very different.[15]

In 1932 and 1933 pacifist sentiment, a vague belief in the League as the guardian of peace, a disbelief in the possibility of a European war were still dominant among the British people—indeed, they remained so until 1935. The Peace Society was strong, and held large meetings addressed by men of eminence. The famous resolution in the Oxford Union, that 'this House will in no circumstance fight for its King and Country', was passed by 275 votes to 153 on February 9, 1933, and received world-wide notice out of all proportion to its importance, as a sign of Britain's pacifism and de-

[14] See an article by Alfred Zimmern on 'The United States and Manchuria' in *Spectator,* January 16, 1932. Cf. ibid., March 5, 1932: 'It is by no means a question today of whether the United States would be willing to keep pace with the League, but whether the League is prepared to take steps sufficiently decisive to satisfy the United States.'

[15] W. N. Medlicott, *British Foreign Policy since Versailles,* pp. 145–57; G. M. Gathorne-Hardy, *Short History of International Affairs,* pp. 303–20. For a summary of the controversy over the parts of Stimson and Simon in the Manchurian crisis see Sara R. Smith, *The Manchurian Crisis, 1931–1932* (New York, 1948). R. Bassett, *Democracy and Foreign Policy: a case history: the Sino-Japanese Dispute, 1931–33* (London, 1952), exhaustively examines the Manchurian crisis in the light of contemporary and later opinion in Great Britain (for critical comment, see Salvador de Madariaga in *Manchester Guardian Weekly,* September 3 and 11, 1952).

cadence which was an encouragement to dictators abroad. More potent in influencing policy was the by-election in East Fulham in October 1933. The Conservative candidate, advocating an increase in the strength of the army, navy and air force, was defeated by the Labour candidate who accused him of preparing for war; a Conservative majority of 14,521 was replaced by a Labour majority of 4,840.

Despite the portent of Manchuria, hopes for peace in Europe persisted. The postwar occupation of the Rhineland had been ended, reparations were finally abandoned at a conference at Lausanne in June 1932, after having been suspended for a year by the Hoover moratorium. After token payments in 1933, Britain in 1934 ceased to make payments on her war debt to the United States; the other European debtors, saving only Finland, were already in default. It remained only to complete the pacification of Europe by holding the long-awaited Disarmament Conference and carrying out in all countries a programme of disarmament already imposed upon Germany.

The Disarmament Conference opened at Geneva, under the presidency of Arthur Henderson, on February 2, 1932—just after the Japanese attack on Chapei. It soon ran into familiar difficulties. The fact of German rearmament beyond the limits prescribed in the Treaty of Versailles was already well known. Hence the French demand for security clashed with the British instinct for conciliation. Germany was demanding in armaments the equality with the other powers which she had already won at all other points; either the powers must disarm to her level or she must be allowed to rearm to theirs. The British were prepared to concede this, the French were not. For the British public had long been ashamed of the Treaty of Versailles, had long been ready to treat the Germans as equals.

> Sir John Simon could have said in three sentences what the country, if it had been consulted, would have required him to say—that Great Britain admits in principle, without cavil or reserve, the justice of the German claim to equality status; that equality must be achieved not by the rearmament of Germany, but by the reduction of the armaments of other countries.[16]

The conference soon came to a standstill. To disagreement over principle was added disagreement over detail—British experts being as stubborn as those of other countries in refusing to give up their favourite weapons, especially on the sea. The moderate Chancellor in Germany, Bruening, having failed to win concessions from the powers, fell from office in May 1932, to be replaced by the wily von Papen, who in turn gave place to General Schleicher in November. It was von Papen's government which announced Germany's withdrawal from the conference on September 16; but Germany returned later, after a Five-Power conference at Geneva in December (Britain, France, Italy, Germany, the United States) had found a formula which ingeniously combined the incompatible; Germany was conceded 'equality of rights in a system which would provide security for all nations'.

It was too late. On January 30, 1933, Hitler became Chancellor in Germany, von Papen having persuaded President von Hindenburg that office would either tame or discredit him. The strength of the Nazis had apparently been waning. In the elections of November 1932 their number had fallen from 230 to 196 among the 584 members. The Nazis prepared for new elections on March 5, particularly by exploiting (if not arranging) the firing of the Reichstag building on the night of February 27 as a Communist conspiracy. Even so, the Nazis won

[16] *Spectator,* September 24, 1932, 'Sophistry and statesmanship'. Cf. ibid.: 'the mind of the vast majority of the British people is made up [that] Germany cannot be held down by force; she cannot be treated thirteen years after the War as a conquered nation; she cannot be tied hand and foot in the matter of armaments while other countries are left free.' For the evolution of British sentiment towards Germany see R. B. McCallum, *British Opinion and the Last Peace,* 'The retreat from Versailles.'

only 288 seats, and with their allies, the Nationalists, had a majority of 33 in the Reichstag—enough, however, to seize dictatorial powers by a bill passed on March 23. The *gleichschaltung* of the states, the liquidation of opposition, the persecution of the Jews followed without delay.

Despite these unfavourable events, a new start was made in the Disarmament Conference. On March 16 Ramsay MacDonald brought to the conference a plan (the work of Anthony Eden, Under-secretary for Foreign Affairs, and of civil servants) which included, along with several proposals made previously, actual figures for the armed forces of the various countries, and limits on the size and type of armaments. The proposals would have reduced the size of the French army, and permitted Germany to attain parity with it; which led Winston Churchill to condemn them in the House of Commons (March 23) as 'somewhat unseasonable' while he exclaimed, to the annoyance of many, 'Thank God for the French Army.'[17] None the less, in spite of some obstruction by Germany, the proposals were approved in principle before the conference adjourned in June and Henderson set off on a pilgrimage of the capitals on behalf of disarmament.

Meanwhile, the powers had made an attempt, on the initiative of Mussolini, to appease Germany by an agreed revision of the peace treaties. Mussolini proposed to MacDonald and Simon, when they were at Rome on March 18, a Four-Power Pact (Britain, France, Italy, Germany) for this purpose. Its method was hardly admirable since it involved, in effect, circumventing the League and reducing the influence of the smaller powers (and especially Poland, the principal intended victim of revision) at the expense of the great ones, among which Mussolini was anxiously ranging Italy. France, with her all-important association with the Little Entente, was only lukewarm in her support, and the plan was so modified as to come to nothing. Hitler, however, had taken notice, and on May 17 soothed the apprehensions of the powers by the first of the conciliatory speeches which marked his path of terror down to 1940: a European war would be 'madness'; Germany would do her part for international security, and was ready to dissolve all her military forces and destroy her weapons if other nations would do the same; but if the others did not disarm, 'Germany must at least maintain her claim to equality'. What could be more reasonable than that?

Hopes were high, therefore, when the Disarmament Conference resumed on October 14, 1933. Sir John Simon offered a plan, concerted with France, that for five years there should be international supervision of arms, without disarmament or rearmament; after this probationary period there would be disarmament, bringing all to an equality with Germany. Germany, it seemed, might accept—and was even committed to doing so by Hitler's speech of May 17. In the nick of time Hitler slipped out of the trap, summoned his cabinet, telegraphed his representative at Geneva, and on the afternoon of October 14 gave notice of Germany's withdrawal from the conference and of her intended resignation from the League of Nations. This was a 'momentous date in world history'; the Locarno period was over, and 'the world entered upon an uneasy progress towards a new conflict'. It was the first of Hitler's gambles; he expected dire consequences: a French invasion of the Ruhr, a Polish invasion of East Prussia. Nothing happened. He had won his first diplomatic victory, and could expect several more such easy triumphs.[18]

The Disarmament Conference was dead, though not formally pronounced so until May 1934, when it adjourned *sine die*. Rearmament was beginning. The necessary efforts for peace, whether in Europe or the

[17] W. S. Churchill, *The Gathering Storm* (new ed.; London, 1949), p. 68.

[18] J. W. Wheeler-Bennett, *Munich: Prologue to Tragedy* (London, 1948), pp. 213–14.

Far East, were inhibited by the depression, by the lack of harmony between Great Britain and France, by apathy and by pacifism among the British people, by the opportunism of Sir John Simon at the Foreign Office.[19] From early in 1933 the tone of articles in periodicals like the *Contemporary Review* was more and more pessimistic: it was an age of disintegration; international co-operation was gone; Britain lacked any policy; war lay not far ahead. The *Spectator* had bidden farewell to 1932 'unmourned and unregretted, with its memories of inconclusive disarmament discussions, nerveless Manchurian discussions, its currency crisis, its tariff increases . . .'[20] Yet 1933 had been far worse. What hope was there for 1934?[21]

[19] M. D. Stocks, *Eleanor Rathbone* (London, 1949), pp. 227–9.

[20] *Spectator,* December 30, 1932.

[21] For general accounts of international affairs see G. M. Gathorne-Hardy, *Short History,* pp. 342–64; R. W. Seton-Watson, *Britain and the Dictators* (Cambridge, 1938), pp. 68–101.

FORTY-NINE

AGGRESSIVE COMMUNISM IN RUSSIA

Eleven years after the Revolution of 1917, the Communist Party in Russia, headed by Stalin, began what is sometimes called (in B. H. Sumner's phrase) the "Second Revolution" with the first Five-Year Plan of 1928–32. Russia had passed through a massive civil war, and, for the sake of sheer survival, had returned temporarily in 1921–7 to modified capitalism under Lenin's famous New Economic Policy (NEP). Meanwhile the Communist Party gained control of the secret police, the labor unions, and the army. With these means of coercion, the Communist Party launched the first Five-Year Plan. Its ostensible goals were to increase production and to socialize the Russian economy in both industry and agriculture. Its main effect was to extend the control of the Communist regime in unprecedented degree over every aspect of Russian life. The net result was the creation of a totalitarian state. Professor Treadgold traces the successive stages in this huge economic and political transformation and emphasizes the appalling human cost which accompanied it.

DONALD W. TREADGOLD

TWENTIETH CENTURY RUSSIA *

AIMS OF THE FIRST FIVE-YEAR PLAN

Why did the "Second Revolution" occur? Partly because Stalin found it expedient to launch it, but the deeper reason was, as one well-known economist says, that without such an effort it would have been "impossible to solve those ideological problems for the sake of which the Revolution had been made." [1] An attempt was to be made to transform the economy and to increase the production of capital goods and other items. But that was not the chief purpose of the First Five-Year Plan. The essential point was to convert the entire labor force, rural as well as urban, into employees of state-controlled enterprise.

The assumption was that once the economic "foundation" was changed, the non-economic "superstructure" would change correspondingly. Once the economy was put into a state socialist mold, men's minds would come to accept that mold. No longer would the regime be troubled by the attachment of the peasantry to its land, the ambivalence on the part of the workers as to what their "real" interests were, the persistence of religious belief, the survival of

* From *Twentieth Century Russia,* pp. 263–72, by Donald W. Treadgold. Reprinted by permission of Rand McNally & Company. Copyright 1959.

[1] Alexander Baykov, *The Development of the Soviet Economic System* (Cambridge: Cambridge University Press, 1946), p. 158.

prerevolutionary values in the family, and in general mass indifference or hostility to the aims of the materialist and socialist Soviet state. Stalin and the Russian Communists expected some resistance and were ready for it, repeating to each other that "one cannot make an omelet without breaking eggs." Nevertheless, it is doubtful that anyone realized in 1928 quite what the human cost would be, since the human factor was left out of the oversimplified ideological equation.

The First Five-Year Plan was not an inflexible blueprint prepared in advance and inaugurated at a given moment. Soviet economic planning—though the planning was never exclusively economic—has always been characterized by a periodic revision of goals. Such revision might have scaled down targets as unforeseen obstacles were encountered; instead, more often the targets have been revised upward. It has been argued that in the strict sense the USSR has never employed "planning" at all: overfulfillment of goals has always been praised, underfulfillment criticized or punished, yet the former is no more reconcilable with the original "plan" than the latter and may lead to serious distortion in resource allocation. In this light Soviet "planning" appears not as a rationalized method of the satisfaction of human wants, or even of the demands of the regime (which intentionally subordinates the welfare of the consumer to the task of strengthening its own military strength and potential), but as a means of universal and permanent intimidation of the labor force.

In 1926 the State Planning Commission, headed by Professor Strumilin, was first entrusted with the task of preparing an over-all plan. The plan as actually instituted is known as the "August version," presented in August 1928 and covering the period through August 1933. It was predicated on four assumptions: that there would be no serious crop failure, that world trade would increase (since the USSR could, it was hoped, export more and obtain more foreign loans), that "qualitative indices" (cost of production and individual laborer productivity) would show improvement, and that the proportion of expenditure for national defense would fall.

These expectations were all disappointed, in part because of the Soviets' own mistakes. The Great Depression, beginning in 1929, which brought on a catastrophic decline in world trade, was not the Soviets' fault, nor was the Japanese invasion of Manchuria in 1931, which occasioned an increase in Soviet military spending. But the famine of 1932–1933 was largely man-made, and the failure of costs to decline and of productivity to rise as expected was the result of a combination of the managers' inexperience and ignorance with the regime's disregard of human welfare and the incentives for which men may be induced to work. It was planned that productivity would rise twice as fast as wages; instead the wage rise was over twice the rise in productivity. In consequence many more workers were taken on than intended and the urban demand vastly increased, pushing up prices and forcing the regime to introduce rationing once more, as in the time of the Civil War. The real miscalculation was not in any of these specific respects. It lay in the attempt to use political fanaticism as a substitute for rational principles of management, and in the failure to grasp the limits of what brute force could achieve when inspiration and persuasion failed.

The Five-year Plan in Industry

The First Five-Year Plan was formally adopted in April 1929 by the Sixteenth Party Conference. The XV Congress had merely considered a draft plan, and one generally much more modest in its goals than the "August version" finally instituted. The objectives were stunning: total industrial output was to increase by 250%, that of heavy industry by 330%; output of pig iron was to be nearly tripled, that of coal more than doubled, that of electric power to increase more than four times. Agricultural production was scheduled to increase 150%, and 20% of the peasant farms were to be collectivized.

Bukharin and the Right were at that time still resisting such targets. Stalin repeatedly accused Bukharin of wanting to "put the brake on the revolution . . . surrender the position to the capitalist elements." There was a grain of truth in what he said. Of course Bukharin was a Communist and not a defender of "capitalism" at all; but his voice was the last raised in open defense of at least the economic freedom of the Russian people, against which large-scale violence was about to be used. When he called for "normalized" conditions of trade, when he cited Lenin as urging caution in regard to the peasantry, when he spoke of "military-feudal" exploitation of the villagers, he was to be sure not speaking for the "kulak," as Stalin charged, but he was expressing for the last time in the USSR doubts about the advisability of crushing the independent peasantry which still made up the bulk of the Russian population.

Far from paying any attention to Bukharin's insistence that the targets of the "August version" were too high, the Party Central Committee in the summer of 1929 raised them still higher. In November Bukharin was removed from the Politburo and was no longer in a position to protest; in fact, he joined the other Rightist leaders in a public recantation of error. No one was left to urge putting on the "brakes." By the end of the year the pace of industrial construction and especially of collectivization had reached breakneck speed. In November 1929 Stalin declared, "We are advancing full steam ahead along the path of industrialization to socialism, leaving behind the age-long 'Russian' backwardness . . . when we have put the USSR in a motor car and the muzhik upon a tractor . . . we shall see which countries may then be classified as backward and which as advanced."

Optimism surpassed all limits. The XVI Congress, held in June and July 1930, adopted the slogan, "the Five-Year Plan in four years"—although five years had seemed a short enough time for the realization of Stalin's announced objectives. The Congress also approved a revision of the plan for agriculture so as to bring about wholesale collectivization of peasant farms within the next few years. A further decision was taken to create a "Ural-Kuznetsk Combine," based on the exchange of Ural iron for Kuznetsk Basin coal, which would place an especially heavy strain on the whole transportation system.

In 1930 signs of trouble were beginning to appear. Factories were erected for which no machines were available; machines were delivered to plants unable to house them; hastily recruited and untrained workers ruined shiny new machines in one place, while skilled workers elsewhere sat idle for want of equipment. In the last quarter of 1930 there was an attempt to overcome all difficulties at once in connection with a statistical change-over from the agricultural (autumn to autumn) to the calendar year: October, November, and December were proclaimed a special "shock quarter." (This was one of many cases in which Stalin borrowed Trotsky's device of using military terminology in nonmilitary situations for propaganda purposes.)

The "shock quarter," Stalin's efforts to wheedle and frighten workers and technicians into greater exertions . . . , and all other expedients were not enough. In 1931 something went wrong, and from that year onward the USSR ceased to publish price indices. At the end of 1932, when four and a quarter years had elapsed, the First Five-Year Plan was declared to have been fulfilled, but the claim had a hollow ring. Stalin contended that production of machinery and electrical equipment had risen 157%, but it was admitted that output in heavy metallurgy (iron and steel) had increased only 67%, coal output 89%, and consumer goods 73%, and even these figures are questionable.

No doubt in the First Plan great industrial expansion occurred, and in subsequent plans has continued to occur, whether or not goals are precisely fulfilled. That the Communists can get "results" from their methods is not in doubt; but the "results" are designed not to build a healthy economy, but to strengthen the totalitarian system, to which end the physical and moral well-being of the Soviet worker and consumer is ruthlessly sacrificed.

The underlying assumption of certain students of the Five-Year Plans, and of many influential persons in the so-called "underdeveloped areas" in recent years, has been that the chief Soviet objective is "economic development." Yet the Communists have never contended that their main aim was to increase output, nor does the evidence indicate that it has been such in fact. Their aim has been rather to achieve a transformation of society in which industrial growth is only one aspect, related to a much broader and more fundamental set of changes in men's way of life, attitudes, and allegiances.

By 1931 the headlong rush of the "Second Revolution" had evoked alarm among the technicians who were accustomed to operate on the basis of costs and rational calculations in general. Addressing a group of industrial managers in February of that year, Stalin admitted, "It is sometimes asked whether it is not possible to slow down a bit . . . ," but he declared that on the contrary a still swifter pace was dictated by the Party's "obligations to the workers and peasants" of the USSR and its "still higher" obligations to the world proletariat. He continued, "We are fifty to a hundred years behind the advanced countries. We must cover this distance in ten years. Either we do this or they will crush us." [2]

Thus Stalin stated the doctrine of no respite which thereafter was not only to govern the effort to increase industrial production, but was to become the keynote of all sides of life under Soviet totalitarianism. A Communist is always at war. There may be periods of calm on the front, but the battle is still waiting—for the millions of unwilling fighters who make up the Soviet citizenry as well as for the Party leadership.

The Five-year Plan in Agriculture

The aspect of the "Second Revolution" which was the most dramatic and sweeping—indeed it was laden with sheer horror—was the collectivization of agriculture. The problem of the "alliance between the proletariat and the peasantry," which Lenin considered so crucial to the Russian Communists, was to be solved by the elimination of the peasantry in its hitherto familiar form. The class struggle which Lenin had in 1918–1919 tried in vain to foment within the village was to be carried into the village, if necessary, from without. The kulaks or rich peasants would be destroyed; the "poor peasants," carrying with them a portion of the "middle peasants," would emerge victors from the struggle. They would then establish collective farms in token of their achievement of the attitude proper to a proletariat.

Who were the kulaks? By the 1927 census estimates, the peasantry was divided into "proletarian" peasants (without land or livestock), who made up about 4% of the total, and "independent" peasant smallholders, who constituted the remaining 96%. Of the "independent" group, about 5% were classified as "kulaks"—defined as those who owned property worth roughly $800 and who hired labor for fifty days out of the year. By the Marxist definition, exploiters are those who own the means of production but do not work it themselves; Stalin's census-takers had used criteria bearing only the feeblest and most distant relationship to those of Marxism. Stalin could not be entirely blamed, however, for such ideological

[2] This statement has been interpreted as a prophecy of Hitler's invasion in 1941. However, it should be noted that in 1931 Soviet relations with the Germans were better than with either the British or French. As far as Hitler was concerned, moreover, Moscow and the German Communists were for their own purposes co-operating with his Nazis against the forces supporting the Weimar Republic. See pp. 309 ff.

dubiousness. Long ago Lenin had also used a distinction resting on wealth rather than on economic function in trying to discover classes within the peasantry when he calculated "rich" and "poor" peasants on the basis of number of horses owned. As for Marx and Engels, they were fortunate enough not to be writing about countries in which the peasants made up the majority of the people. Although they did not embarrass themselves with attempts to divide the rural masses into "exploiters" and "exploited," they provided justification for collectivization by holding that the peasantry as a whole represented a survival of feudalism and would disappear in the modern world. Engels had indeed advised giving the small peasant plenty of time to ponder whether he was ready to enter a co-operative farm, but the assumption was that he ought to and would be ready sooner or later.

In December 1929 Stalin quoted those very lines of Engels but asserted that they were inapplicable in the situation existing in the Soviet Union. Although in May 1928 he had declared that the "expropriation of the kulaks would be folly," in the summer of 1929 he had ordered Party workers to "liquidate the kulaks as a class." In December he went still further. It was ridiculous, he said, to suggest that after being expropriated the kulaks should be allowed to join the collectives. That was unequivocal language, and the result in the winter and spring of 1929–1930 was bloodshed and chaos.

When traveling with Rykov in the Volga region in the mid-1920's, William Reswick, a foreign correspondent, heard the peasants question Rykov anxiously: "What is a kulak? Can it be a muzhik who owns a horse, a cow, and some poultry?" Rykov replied that a kulak was simply a village usurer—which was indeed the original meaning of the word, but was not the meaning employed by Lenin and the Communist Party. The Communists meant by "kulak" a peasant who had more property than his neighbors and therefore might exploit them in some way. It is doubtful that the criteria of the 1927 census were ever taken very seriously in determining who a kulak was, and in many cases no economic criteria were applied at all. It is reported, for example, the Uzbek peasants were catechized: "What is socialism?" and "When was Darwin born?" If a recalcitrant peasant failed to give a satisfactory answer, he might be branded a kulak.

It remained for Tito, many years later, to confess that Communists defined a kulak to mean any peasant opposed to "socialism," but Soviet collectivization had already put that definition into practice. Peasants who resisted inclusion in collective farms were uprooted and transported away from their homes, often to the far north in unheated freight cars. Many times whole villages were simply surrounded and attacked. During this period an OGPU colonel confided to a foreign journalist, "I am an old Bolshevik. I worked in the underground against the Tsar and then I fought in the Civil War. Did I do all that in order that I should now surround villages with machine-guns and order my men to fire indiscriminately into crowds of peasants? Oh, no, no!" [3] The peasants who could not fight openly resorted to passive resistance by killing their own livestock and burning their own crops. They were able to do grave economic damage to the regime as well as to themselves, but they could not halt the pursuit of the political objective of creating collectives.

On January 20, 1930, there were slightly over four million peasant families in collective farms, most of them having been taken in during the previous year or two. By March 1 of the same year the number had risen to over fourteen million—fifty-five per cent of all peasant families. There were supposed to be over a hundred and ten thousand collective farms, but it would be more accurate to say that fourteen million peasants had surrendered and were awaiting the orders of the terrible and incomprehensible invaders of their countryside. Then, abruptly,

[3] Deutscher, *Stalin,* p. 325, n. 1.

on March 2 Stalin published an article in *Pravda* entitled "Dizziness from Success." In it he contended that "the fundamental turn of the village toward socialism may be already considered secured," but he warned, "It is impossible to establish collective farms by force. To do so would be stupid and reactionary."

The peasants who were heard later saying that things improved when Stalin got over *his* dizziness from success were quite right. Stalin in the *Pravda* article tried to blame the chaos in the village on Party underlings, but for the most part they had merely tried to obey his orders. At any rate the Communists who were carrying on the virtual civil war in the countryside responded at once. By May 1, 1930, it was reported that the number of peasant families on collective farms had fallen below six million. However, Stalin had made it clear that the objective was unaltered. By the end of 1932 sixty per cent of peasant families were reported collectivized. One can only conjecture what brutality, suffering, and bewilderment lay behind the fantastic fluctuation in these statistics.

The political victory was substantially won, but the economic consequences were disastrous. In 1933 the number of horses in the Soviet Union was less than half the 1928 figure; during the period from 1929 to 1931 alone, the number of cattle fell by one-third, the number of sheep and goats by one-half. It was intended that the horses, which had been used as draft animals, should be replaced by tractors, but they could not be supplied in anything like the quantity needed. Nothing could replace the other animals. Tractors do not give milk, furnish meat, or produce manure. Politically, however, the introduction of tractors had great significance. They and other agricultural machines were pooled in Machine-Tractor Stations (MTS's), each of which served several collective farms. The MTS became the political headquarters of the victorious Communists in the defeated countryside, where records were kept and orders were received from above and transmitted to the collectives.

The new collective enterprises were of two basic types: the state farm (*sovkhoz,* short for *sovetskoe khoziaistvo*) and the collective farm (*kolkhoz,* short for *kollektivnoe khoziaistvo*). The state farm was (and is) the full property of the Soviet government; its manager operated it with hired labor, in accordance with the directives of the Ministry of State Farms or any other ministry to which the farm in question was allotted. The state farm, as a "factory in the field," was and remains the Communist objective for agriculture; there the peasant is truly a proletarian with no property of his own.

In contrast, the collective farm was supposed to be a self-governing co-operative made up of peasants who voluntarily pooled their means of production and divided the proceeds. The first collectives were of various kinds of which three were the best known. The "commune" (not to be confused with the prerevolutionary village commune) was the closest to the state farm; all implements and livestock were owned in common by the members, who lived in communal buildings. The *toz* (or "society for joint land cultivation") was the loosest type of collective; it was a production co-operative, in which each peasant family kept title to its own plot of land, livestock, and implements, and joined with others to work the land and buy machinery. Intermediate between the "commune" and the *toz* was the *artel* (not to be confused with the prerevolutionary craft association). Under the *artel* the peasant retained possession of his own livestock and a small garden plot, on which he might raise crops either for his own use or for sale on the market.[4]

The resistance of the peasants to collectivization was not entirely in vain, for it

[4] It should be noted that none of these types of collective resembled the prerevolutionary commune, wherein each peasant family had its own house and land, which it worked by its own labor even when the land lay in widely scattered strips.

forced the Communists to accept the *artel* as the prevalent, in fact, almost universal, type of collective. At the beginning of the plan Stalin, although he did not expect *state* farms to be set up everywhere immediately, continually referred to "state and collective farms" as the goal of the collectivization campaign. After the disastrous first quarter of 1930, however, he reversed the order of priority, and began to speak of the goal as "collective and state farms." A considerable number of state farms were actually dissolved and their holdings turned over to collective farms. The type of collective farm to which Stalin gave his support in the "Dizziness from Success" article and which the XVI Congress approved two months later was the *artel.*

The Communists viewed the *artel* as a temporary compromise. The XVI Congress's resolution declared that the *artel* "*does not complete, but is only the beginning* of the creation of a new social discipline, of the task of teaching the peasants socialist construction." In the continuing struggle on the agricultural "front," it might be said that the state had won the "commanding heights"—to borrow a phrase from the NEP period. Most of the land was held by the *artel,* and that "collective sector" of the land was tilled in common. The *artel* was clearly dependent on the state: the state agency, the MTS, dealt with the *artel,* not the individual peasant, furnishing the machinery required to sow and harvest. In the apportionment of the proceeds, the compulsory grain deliveries had first to be made to the state—this was called the collective farm's "First Commandment." Next the MTS had to be paid for the machinery the farm had used, and only then was the residual share divided among the individual households. However, the peasant retained his own tiny garden plot and his livestock, and thus every day he was able, even compelled, to compare the advantages of individual and collective farming, since he engaged in both. The *artel,* wholly satisfying the aims of neither the Communists nor the peasants, thus contained a built-in contradiction. Since by 1933 over ninety-six per cent of all collective farms were of the *artel* type, and the state farms included only a very small proportion of the tilled land, the contradiction within the *artel* affected most of Soviet agriculture.

The economic and human costs of collectivization had to be set alongside the substantial, if incomplete, political victory which the regime had gained. By 1937, it has been computed, the over-all pre-1928 per capita level of all agricultural production was barely regained, but in food production alone, it is doubtful that the pre-1928 per capita level has ever been exceeded since. The human losses were colossal. At least five million peasants died in the process of collectivization and the resultant famine of 1932–1933 (the figure Stalin revealed to Churchill at Yalta was ten million). No wonder that there were Russians who survived the horrors of World War II who could not talk of their experiences years before, during collectivization, without losing their composure.

It is difficult to compute the economic results or the human casualties with precision. More fundamental than such computation is the question of what possible moral and political justification could be found for completely overturning the lives of a hundred million people, in peacetime, in the name of a goal which was anathema to them. Stalin admitted that collectivization entailed a "revolution from above," although he insisted that it was supported "from below" by the "poor peasants." Certainly it involved a struggle—but chiefly one between urban Communists and the villagers; the "poor peasants" proved as much of a will-o'-the-wisp as they had in 1918. . . . Although the victory of the Party over the peasantry was incomplete, it was decisive enough that a battle of such dimensions did not need to be fought again. The collectivization of agriculture had vast economic consequences in that it enabled the regime to obtain much of the capital desired for industrialization from the defeated village (largely by selling the compulsory grain deliveries, received at a nominal valuation, at high prices). The political consequences were still greater. Collectivization was the decisive step in the building of Soviet totalitarianism, for it imposed on the majority of the people a subjection which only force could maintain.

IX

CONTEMPORARY CIVILIZATION, 1929 AND AFTER

PART NINE

☙ CONTEMPORARY CIVILIZATION, 1929 AND AFTER

The world faced its next major crisis in the years after 1929. The dislocations and psychological strains resulting from World War I, the numbing depression of 1929, and the Japanese militarism in the Far East combined with the apathy of the democracies to create an atmosphere that made possible the rise of the totalitarian state (probably the most harmful result of World War I), first in Italy (1922), then in Russia (1928), and then in Germany (1933). In 1939 Hitler's invasion of Poland began World War II, longer and much more devastating than the war of 1914–18. Britain's lonely stand against Nazi Germany in 1940–1 rallied the democracies. Persuaded by the example of Churchill's magnificent leadership in England, the conscience of the West, which had slumbered during the interwar years, revived and grew strong. In the postwar era the West once again faced economic and social devastation. Bitter tensions in domestic politics and equally bitter tensions on the international scene set the stage for the Cold War in which the democracies, led by the United States, confronted Russia. The postwar era also saw fast and sweeping changes in the world's underdeveloped areas as they reacted to dynamic forces from the West, forces both material and ideological. Western-inspired nationalism led to the independence of India, Pakistan, and almost all the colonies in Southeast Asia and Africa. Marxism, another Western ideology, triumphed in China with the seizure of power by the Chinese Communists in 1949. Meanwhile, with the explosion of the first atomic bomb by the United States in 1945 the world entered the Nuclear Age. Twelve years later, as a possible prelude to an Interstellar Age, Russia launched the first man-made earth satellite Sputnik I.

FIFTY

JAPAN AND THE WEST

Perry's forcible opening of Japan to the West in 1854 led to Japan's rapid westernization. By 1900 Japan had adopted Western nationalism and industrialism. Japan's defeat of Russia in 1904–5, which astonished the world, proved that Japan had become a major power. In the 1920's liberalism grew in Japan, although almost entirely in urban areas. But in the 1930's, largely as a result of the depression, militarism reasserted itself, as fully evidenced by Japanese aggression in Manchuria in 1931. In sum, Japan responded to the Western impact without a major and abrupt political revolution, such as had occurred in China. But Japan's overall response to the West was nevertheless violent indeed. The fanaticism of Japanese militarists led to war with China in 1937 and to the attack on Pearl Harbor four years later, which plunged Japan into World War II. In his book Nationalism in Japan, *Delmer M. Brown has described the murder of Premier Inukai on May 15, 1932, by a group of young officers. This act of violence, widely condoned in Japan and lightly punished, ended party government and vastly strengthened the power of the military in the state.*

DELMER M. BROWN

NATIONALISM IN JAPAN *

But as the world depression began to press in upon Japan, conditions became even more favorable for the growth of the National Reconstruction movement. The young officers, since most of them had come from rural families, were well aware of the economic distress that prevailed in agricultural communities. After 1929 they were therefore more ready than ever to listen to condemnations directed at party politicians, and more inclined to support proposals of direct-action tactics that would place the affairs of state directly in the hands of the military. However, as aroused as they were by economic distress, they were probably concerned more about the tendency of the government to cut down on military expenditures.

The Hamaguchi cabinet not only attempted to pare down military and naval estimates but obviously made a resolute effort to bring about an administrative reform that would weaken military control over nonmilitary affairs. The attitude of the cabinet was made clear at the time of the London Naval Conference in March, 1930, when it decided to accept a compromise that was not acceptable to the Navy. Furthermore, in the face of Navy opposition the government ratified the treaty. The implications of this development were well understood by all military leaders, and thenceforth they tended to be even more irked by the political-party activities, which they considered to be arbitrary, selfish, and unpatriotic.

The effects of economic depression, the entrenchment policy, and finally the government's attack on the political power of the military combined to make Hamaguchi and his party extremely unpopular, not only among military men but among many civilians of various classes and occupations. The young officers who backed National Reconstruction programs were therefore encouraged to organize themselves for action, rather than for propaganda. And the civilian leaders, such as Ōkawa Shūmei, toured the country making lectures in support of their programs, demanding a "people's movement" that would oust the capitalists and the politicians and place political affairs in the hands of soldiers. The assassination of Hamaguchi in November, 1930, was indicative of the growing opposition to political-party government.

In order to assume leadership of a movement which it was felt the times demanded, Lieutenant Colonel Hashimoto Kingorō and two other army officers organized a secret society in September, 1930, called the *Sakura Kai* (Cherry Blossom Society). The officers of the society were prepared to resort to the use of force, if necessary, to bring about the reconstruction of the Japanese state. The society's prospectus declared that the members could not stand the immoral behavior of the upperclass statesmen, the deterioration of the political parties, the capitalists' lack of understanding of the masses, the tendency of the press to confuse

* From *Nationalism in Japan,* pp. 189–99, by Delmer M. Brown. Reprinted by permission of the University of California Press. Copyright 1955 by the Regents of the University of California.

the minds of the people with no thought of the future of the state, the distress of the rural communities, unemployment, depression, the radicalism of various intellectual groups, the lack of patriotism among students, and the concentration of bureaucrats on protecting their positions. For all these unfortunate conditions the greedy politicians were assigned most of the blame, since, according to the same prospectus, they were not merely deceiving the people but were disregarding the wishes of the Emperor and were turning against the armed forces of the nation. Unlike earlier national reconstruction societies, the Cherry Blossom Society turned immediately to devising plans for seizing control of the government by direct action. With the coöperation of Ōkawa Shūmei and others, in March, 1931, it plotted to assassinate key men in the government, force the resignation of the cabinet, and dictate the appointment of military men who would initiate the reconstruction of Japan. But at the last minute, high-level military officials who had been counted on to coöperate backed out, and the plot had to be called off.

Having failed in this initial attempt to place the army in control of the government, the young officers of the Cherry Blossom Society, aware now that Japan's relations with China were causing widespread concern, decided to direct their efforts toward a basic "solution of the Manchurian problem." The Chinese had become determined to exercise sovereign rights over the area, and the Japanese Kwantung Army was determined to protect the interests and rights of Japanese subjects. The diplomats, according to Shigemitsu, who was in China at the time, were making substantial progress toward a diplomatic solution of major issues; but members of the Cherry Blossom Society and a large part of the officers in the Kwantung Army—and of those in the War Department in Tokyo—were apparently convinced that the situation had reached a point where diplomacy was useless. Furthermore, there was a tendency in these circles to class diplomats with the greedy politicians, the *zaibatsu* (financial cliques), and the bureaucrats, whom they blamed for bringing Japan to its sorry state. It was therefore the Cherry Blossom Society type of "solution" that prevailed. A plot was hatched, with Hashimoto in a leading part, which was designed to give the Kwantung Army an excuse to seize direct control of Manchuria. The moves were opposed by most of the leading civilian officials in the government, and by the Emperor; but once the deed was committed, the civilian officials found themselves carried along in a current which they could not control.

With the extension of Japanese army control over most of Manchuria and the outbreak of hostilities in Shanghai in January, 1932, the League of Nations and the United States resorted to a series of diplomatic steps which gradually created the impression in Japan that the Western nations, as well as China, were resisting Japan's "righteous mission" on the continent of Asia. There was once more a stirring of the type of nationalist sentiment that had prevailed in the years preceding and during the Russo-Japanese War. Farmers, laborers, and even socialists, were more enthusiastic about performing military service. The attitude was reflected in various aspects of Japanese life, but particularly in politics.

The decisive, spectacular activities of the army in Manchuria seemed to capture the imagination and sympathy of most of the Japanese people. The political-party government, which was valiantly trying to bring the army into line, lost more of its prestige by revealing its ineffectiveness and by giving the impression of dragging its feet in this great national venture. Two months after the Incident, the Wakatsuki cabinet (with Shidehara still serving as Foreign Minister) resigned. If it had not been for the pressure exerted by Prince Saionji, political-party government probably would have come to an end then, rather than a few months later.

The new upsurge of nationalist fervor led the proletarian parties to take a more definitely national position. One writer estimates that the two major proletarian parties lost one-third of their membership, after the Manchurian Incident, to the National Socialist movement. One faction of the most conservative of the parties, the *Shakai Minshu Tō,* broke off from the party and set up the Japan National Socialist party (*Nihon Kokka Shakai Tō*) under the leadership of a former socialist, Akamatsu Katsumaro. The platform carried the declaration that the party would work toward the establishment of a new Japan which would be founded in a spirit of unity among the people under the Emperor, and would be free of exploitation. More specifically, the members, by means of a people's movement, were to destroy money-power rule and perfect a government based upon the principles of the Imperial Way (*Kōdō*). Also, the party would attempt to bring about the destruction of capitalism by legal means and would guarantee adequate standards of living for the people by instituting a state-controlled economy. Finally, efforts would be made to bring about a "liberation of the Asian peoples in accordance with the principle of equal human rights and the principle of the equal distribution of natural resources."

In spite of the efforts of political parties to take advantage of the rising tide of national sentiment, it was the various nationalist societies, working with or under the Army, that exercised the most influence in the political developments of the period. Many men who had formerly belonged to political parties now joined such societies, because they preferred direct-action tactics and "positive" programs to democratic processes. Thus, after the Manchurian Incident there was a new crop of nationalist societies, mostly with national reconstruction programs, and a whole new series of plots and assassinations; for in spite of the successes in Manchuria, military government devoted to the reconstruction had not yet been established at home.

One of the most prominent and active societies after the Manchurian Incident was the *Jimmu Kai* (Emperor Jimmu Society), headed by Ōkawa Shūmei. Although the society was considered to be the successor to the earlier *Gyōchi Sha* (also organized by Ōkawa), it assigned a more prominent position to militarists and received more generous financial support from businessmen. The *Jimmu Kai* soon claimed a membership of 30,000 and was engaged in a wide range of activities, including nation-wide lecture campaigns in support of National Socialist candidates seeking election to the Diet. But its part in the coup d'état of May 15, 1932 (called the May Fifteenth Incident) was more important—members of the society assassinated Premier Inukai. Inukai had opposed the Army's policy of occupying Manchuria, and he still felt that representative institutions had real value. One week before the assassination, he made a speech at Yokohama in which he berated Fascism and praised democratic principles. After his death a nonparty Premier was appointed—a step that marked the beginning of military dominance in the internal affairs of Japan. The men who participated in the plot were arrested and tried, but in the public eye they were considered brave patriots, doing their bit to bring about the reconstruction of Japan in accordance with the Imperial Way. Government officials are said to have received, in the course of the trial, more than 300,000 petitions for clemency. War Minister Araki, who was gaining the reputation for being the outstanding exponent of the Imperial Way movement, reported the receipt of a parcel which contained nine fingers and a petition stating that the nine donors were willing to give their lives if that would save the conspirators from punishment. After prolonged trials, in both military and civilian courts, the verdicts were finally announced. No death sentences were imposed. Ōkawa received the longest sentence, and after an appeal in 1935, it was reduced to five years.

Although the young officers did not succeed in establishing the kind of regime they had envisaged, the Army itself was placed in a much stronger political position, and the government thereafter tended to adopt an even more uncompromising attitude in the management of foreign affairs. As a result of the Manchurian Incident and the outbreak of hostilities in Shanghai, the anti-Japanese feelings in China took on a very disturbing character; and experts in Chinese affairs, such as Shigemitsu, who was currently the Japanese minister to China, were helpless in the face of pressure for positive action.

The anti-Japanese sentiment in China, however, had relatively little effect upon the development of a more intense form of nationalism in Japan, for the Japanese did not fear Chinese opposition. There was merely a sense of national pride in the military victories against the "bandits" in Manchuria. But when the Western nations began to take a stiffer attitude toward Japan's advances, fears were aroused that the Western powers might join forces against Japan. This development presented an entirely different situation, and consequently, as Japan's relations with the West worsened, nationalism became more intense and began once more to take on a "fearful" character.

Even by the time of the May Fifteenth Incident in 1932, the Japanese were beginning to be disturbed by Secretary Stimson's notes and by the dispatch of the Lytton mission to investigate the Manchurian disturbance. Then, when the Lytton Report was made public and the Japanese government issued a statement to the effect that the report had passages that were "marked by omissions, inconsistencies and misapprehensions," public sentiment was stirred to a higher pitch of resentment against the unreasonableness and injustice of Western powers. Finally, when, on March 27, 1933, notice was given of Japan's decision to withdraw from the League, a strong nationalist wave swept over the country. Matsuoka Yōsuke, the Japanese representative to the League, was hailed as a great national hero because of his courageous stand against the selfish Western powers. It was at this time, too, that Japanese businessmen became excited about the tariff barriers that were being thrown up against Japanese goods. These moves were considered to be nearsighted and to be convincing evidence that the Western nations were bent on preventing Japan from obtaining her just due, in trade as well as in land and resources.

Relations between Japan and Russia were also more alarming, for the military campaigns in northern Manchuria definitely threatened Soviet interests in that area. Both the Japanese and the Russians, however, wished then to avoid an actual outbreak of hostilities. The Japanese promised to protect Soviet interests, and the Russians were extremely careful to remain neutral. But the Manchurian Incident had a powerful effect upon Russian estimates of the world situation, leading Molotov in December, 1931, to report to the Central Executive Committee that the Far Eastern conflict was "the most important problem of our foreign policy." Not being in a position, militarily or economically, to resist the Japanese, the Russians showed a very conciliatory attitude. But at the same time, Soviet leaders began to prepare for the defense of their Siberian territory by stationing more troops in border areas and by adopting a new Five-Year Plan, which was focused upon the development of Far Eastern areas. Also, diplomatic relations with Nationalist China were resumed. On the Japanese side, too, actions were taken and thoughts were expressed which tended to aggravate the unfriendly relations between the two countries. After the May Fifteenth Incident of 1932, a new cabinet was formed in which General Araki Sadao, who only one month before had publicly advocated war with Russia, was appointed Minister of War. Thenceforth, border disputes, railway incidents, and White Russian problems multiplied and became more difficult to handle.

By the summer of 1933, Japanese-Soviet relations had become so explosive that American military attachés in Tokyo predicted that war would break out between the two countries within two years. In the midst of negotiations for the sale of the Chinese Eastern Railway to Manchukuo (the new name for the puppet state of Manchuria) seven Soviet officials of the railway were arrested in Harbin. The Union of Soviet Socialist Republics claimed to have reliable information that the orders for the arrests had come from the Kwantung Army, and so broke off the railway negotiations. By this time the Tangku Truce had brought an end to Japanese army advances in China, and more officers were demanding a stronger policy toward Russia. One of Japan's leading diplomats, Shigemitsu, is said to have remarked, in October, 1933, that the Japanese Army seemed determined to attack Russia in 1935. The lines were even more sharply drawn in November, 1933, when the U.S.S.R. and the United States opened up diplomatic relations with each other.

But toward the end of 1933, after the bellicose General Araki was replaced by General Hayashi as War Minister, Russo-Japanese relations quieted down. Negotiations for the sale of the Chinese Eastern Railway were continued, and finally an agreement was reached in March, 1935. Also, after the spring of 1933 the United States, under the new Roosevelt administration, had taken a calmer attitude toward Japan's activities in Manchuria. There continued to be considerable anxiety about the possibility of Japanese isolation in a tempestous world; but Japan's relations with foreign nations were sufficiently calm to permit the leading national activists to turn their attention once more to the work of bringing about the reconstruction of the Japanese state.

Until about 1933 the direct-action tactics of army officers had been serving the interests of all the militarists, for such activities were gradually strengthening the hand of the Army in the internal and external affairs of the country. But thereafter, the radical aspects of the Young Officer movement caused increasing concern among the older, more conservative officers of both services. There arose, therefore, a rather clear-cut cleavage within both the Army and the Navy. The so-called Young Officer group wanted to carry out a reorganization of society that would eliminate the power of the financial, political-party, and bureaucratic cliques so that Japan would have greater power for fulfilling her national mission. But the Control Group (*Tōseiha*) did not recognize the desirability of a drastic internal social-reform program, although it was in complete agreement with the Young Officers concerning the importance of giving the Army a more responsible role in the affairs of state. The Control Group held most of the high-level positions, nominally at least; but after 1933, men influenced by Imperial Way (*Kōdō*) principles were beginning to work their way into positions of greater influence and responsibility.

In 1934 the War Ministry undertook to issue a series of pamphlets designed to gain greater popular support for the military position, and although most of the points of view expressed in the pamphlets were acceptable to all elements of the Army, one of the pamphlets reflected the views of the Young Officer group and therefore became a source of considerable controversy in both Army and civilian circles. The pamphlet, entitled *Kokubō no Hongi to Sono Kyōka no Teishō* (Principles of National Defense and Proposals for Strengthening Them), first emphasized the dangers inherent in the international situation and underlined the urgency of giving greater attention to national defense, but it did not adhere to the orthodox line in its discussion of the internal economic and political conditions. It took up the position that effective national defense was possible only with the elimination of poverty. Consequently, the pamphlet undertook to analyze the causes of poverty and to suggest concrete measures for improving the situation. Greater restrictions upon free competition and more government attention to measures that would "stabilize the people's livelihood" were suggested. It was argued that with more effective state control of production and distribution, not only could the living conditions of the people be improved but industrial production could be more easily adjusted to defense needs. These radical thoughts, appearing in pamphlets published by the Army, were very disturbing, not only to the business world but to the Control Group within the Army. About the time this pamphlet appeared, and due in part to it, the ideological struggle within the Army became more intense, and it soon developed into a complex political interplay which broke out into the open in the Aizawa Incident in July, 1935.

The Control Group in the spring of 1935 began to reshuffle army posts in an effort to weaken the influence of the more radical Young Officers. The most important change was the removal of General Mazaki, a recognized leader of the Young Officer group (*Kōdōha*), from the position of inspector general of military education. The appointment of General Watanabe to the position gave the conservatives a stronger hold over the Army, and the Young Officers were furious. The reshuffle aroused the radicals to train their guns upon the conservative militarists, as well as upon the civilian financiers, bureaucrats, and politicians. A pamphlet was issued condemning the arbitrary action of the conservative generals. General Nagata, head of the Bureau of Military Affairs, was singled out for most of the criticism, for his office was considered to be the real center of military administration. In view of the heated invective that was thrown at him by the young nationalists, the news of his assassination did not greatly surprise those who were familiar with the situation. A Lieutenant Colonel Aizawa Saburo, an officer in the Young Officer group, became convinced that the cause of Reconstruction could not be advanced without the elimination of the hated Nagata. Aizawa felt, according to his own testimony, that conservative officers of the Army were allied with politicians, financiers, and bureaucrats in a concerted attempt to head off the Reconstruction movement. Thus, on August 11, 1935, Aizawa went to Tokyo to discuss the matter with like-minded patriots. He then went personally to Nagata to advise him to resign. General Nagata refused to comply with the "advice" and, furthermore, ordered Aizawa transferred to a post in Formosa. Before leaving for Formosa, however, Aizawa walked calmly into the War Ministry and murdered General Nagata. At the trial, the Colonel showed no signs of regret. He was merely humiliated that he had not been sufficiently adept with the sword to kill his victim instantly, and that he had not been sufficiently composed to pick up his hat before leaving the murder room.

The incident created a tremendous sensation. The War Minister, General Hayashi, resigned; and other changes were made in a desperate attempt to quiet the Young Officer group, which, to a man, considered Colonel Aizawa a dedicated patriot. The conservative senior generals decided to proceed cautiously with the court-martial hearings, for they were aware that the occasion might serve to arouse even deeper and more widespread resentment against the senior officers of the army and their alleged allies. They decided to open the court-martial proceedings to the public and to give Aizawa complete freedom to present his case, apparently because they felt that to act quickly, or secretly, would create an even more explosive situation. Aizawa was permitted to criticize not only politicians, financiers, and bureaucrats but generals of the army who, he said, did not fully understand the critical conditions which prevailed in Japan. He spoke at great length about scandals and corruption in high places. The defense lawyer admitted the seriousness of murdering a senior officer but insisted that the "sincerity" of Aizawa's motives should be weighed carefully. The defense also made much of the thousands of letters and telegrams of sympathy that were coming in—many were read in court. It looked as though Aizawa was certain to come off with a light sentence. About all that conservative generals could do at the moment was to order the First Division at Tokyo—the division most deeply affected by Young Officer sentiment—to Manchuria.

But the Young Officers apparently overplayed their hand. They decided upon another plot against those who were opposed to their reform program, and they felt they had to carry it out before the First Division left Tokyo. The result was the February Twenty-sixth Incident of 1936, the most ambitious of the conspiracies and the one that almost accomplished the kind of coup d'état Kita Ikki had outlined some seventeen years earlier. Martial law was declared, and General Mazaki was given an opportunity to state the case of the rebels. For a time the official army announcements reflected a certain sympathy for the ideas of the Young Officers. But in jockeying for position, the Young Officers gradually lost ground. In a few days the rebel noncommissioned officers surrendered, and all the major civilian conspirators were arrested. Eventually the Young Officer leaders either committed suicide or surrendered.

The conservative senior officers were now in no mood to put up with such coddling as had taken place at the time of the Aizawa Incident. There were no public trials, which would have given the assassins a chance to gain public acclaim. Thirteen officers and four civilians were sentenced to death, and five officers were given life imprisonment. Kita Ikki and Nishida Zei, after a somewhat longer trial, received the death sentence and were executed on August 19, 1937. A new court-martial was convened for Colonel Aizawa, and he too was executed. By positive measures such as these the Control Group reëstablished its control over the Army. The entire National Reconstruction movement was severely damaged. Not only were many of its leaders lost, but many of the civilian reformers tended to lose confidence in military men as the natural leaders of the Reconstruction movement.

The period between 1919 and 1936 seems to constitute a distinctly different stage in the development of Japanese nationalism—one in which nationalist energy was no longer directed primarily toward taking advantage of foreign opportunities but rather toward strengthening the nation from within, and one in which Japanese nationalism, once more, began to take on a "fearful" character. In this period there were two distinct phases, the one before 1931 and the one after that year. In both, the emphasis was upon internal reform that would strengthen the nation; but before 1931 the movement was propelled for the most part by civilians, and after 1931 by militarists.

During the civilian phase of National Reconstructionism, probably nationalism was at its lowest ebb in modern Japanese history, for internationalist interests tended to overshadow nationalist concerns. But as the economic situation began to deteriorate and social tensions to increase, intellectuals and patriots became more energetic in their search for ways to restore social harmony and economic prosperity. The story of nationalist development before 1931, then, is chiefly one of the formulation and support of various programs to save the nation from poverty and social strife. They ranged all the way from the simple use of force against undesirable changes to reforms which involved radical changes in the Japanese social structure. However, in each effort—by those who wished to serve the nation, rather than a class—the Imperial institution and the peculiar relationships embodied in *kokutai* were upheld.

In the militarist phase after 1931, reconstruction programs were altered, not only because the militarists were in power but because the crisis facing the nation was becoming a foreign, as well as an internal, crisis. The nationalist societies began to resort to direct-action tactics, both at home and abroad—tactics which accelerated the rise of the militarists to power and put further strain on the relations with foreign powers. Japanese nationalism began to revert to its classical form: that is to be something guided and stimulated primarily from above, and to be focused more upon foreign danger than upon internal growth. Thus, the years of National Reconstruction were a transitional period in which nationalism was losing its "confident" character and was reverting once more to a "fearful" type.

FIFTY-ONE

BRITAIN DEFIES HITLER

In the fall of 1939 and early spring of 1940, Hitler's mechanized armies overran Poland and prepared for new campaigns. Meanwhile the Western front was quiet, almost as if no war existed. Observers called this weird inactivity the Phony War or the Sitzkrieg, in contrast to the Blitzkrieg (Lightning War) which had crushed Poland. Then, without warning, Hitler struck north at Denmark and Norway. On May 10, 1940, he sent his panzer (armored) divisions into France in one of the most brilliantly planned and executed campaigns in the history of warfare. Between May 26 and June 4 British naval forces with the help of civilian craft rescued 338 thousand trapped troops at Dunkirk. France asked for an armistice on June 17 and surrendered five days later. At this point and for the next year, Britain faced Hitler's victorious armies alone, until Hitler began his ill-starred invasion of Russia in June 1941. In the Battle of Britain, German aircraft battered Britain's cities, and Britain's Royal Air Force struck back with skill and fury. In those dark days of disaster and defiance, Winston Churchill rallied his people with incomparable oratory. He took office as Prime Minister on May 10, the day the Germans attacked France. In the House of Commons and on the radio he voiced Britain's will to stand firm. He became a strong symbol of national unity and of the higher values of the West which Hitler's armies threatened to destroy. No one who heard his speeches can ever forget them. Unforgettable also are the numerous and often-photographed street scenes of Churchill, cigar in hand, standing in the ruins of bombed areas offering courage and comfort to gathering crowds.

WINSTON CHURCHILL

WAR SPEECHES *

June 4, 1940

From the moment that the French defences at Sedan and on the Meuse were broken at the end of the second week of May, only a rapid retreat to Amiens and the south could have saved the British and French Armies who had entered Belgium at the appeal of the Belgian King, but this strategic fact was not immediately realised. The French High Command hoped they would be able to close the gap, and the Armies of the north were under their orders.

* Reprinted from *Hansard*, pp. 787–96, 56–61, June 1940, by permission of The Hansard Society for Parliamentary Government and Her Majesty's Stationery Office.

Moreover, a retirement of this kind would have involved almost certainly the destruction of the fine Belgian Army of over 20 divisions and the abandonment of the whole of Belgium. Therefore, when the force and scope of the German penetration were realised and when a new French Generalissimo, General Weygand, assumed command in place of General Gamelin, an effort was made by the French and British Armies in Belgium to keep on holding the right hand of the Belgians and to give their own right hand to a newly created French Army which was to have advanced across the Somme in great strength to grasp it.

However, the German eruption swept like a sharp scythe around the right and rear of the Armies of the north. Eight or nine armoured divisions, each of about 400 armoured vehicles of different kinds, but carefully assorted to be complementary and divisible into small self-contained units, cut off all communications between us and the main French Armies. It severed our own communications for food and ammunition, which ran first to Amiens and afterwards through Abbeville, and it shore its way up the coast to Boulogne and Calais, and almost to Dunkirk. Behind this armoured and mechanised onslaught came a number of German divisions in lorries, and behind them again there plodded comparatively slowly the dull brute mass of the ordinary German Army and German people, always so ready to be led to the trampling down in other lands of liberties and comforts which they have never known in their own.

I have said this armoured scythe-stroke almost reached Dunkirk—almost but not quite. Boulogne and Calais were the scenes of desperate fighting. The Guards defended Boulogne for a while and were then withdrawn by orders from this country. The Rifle Brigade, the 60th Rifles, and the Queen Victoria's Rifles, with a battalion of British tanks and 1,000 Frenchmen, in all about 4,000 strong, defended Calais to the last. The British Brigadier was given an hour to surrender. He spurned the offer, and four days of intense street fighting passed before silence reigned over Calais, which marked the end of a memorable resistance. Only 30 unwounded survivors were brought off by the Navy and we do not know the fate of their comrades. Their sacrifice, however, was not in vain. At least two armoured divisions, which otherwise would have been turned against the British Expeditionary Force, had to be sent for to overcome them. They have added another page to the glories of the Light Division, and the time gained enabled the Graveline waterlines to be flooded and to be held by the French troops.

Thus it was that the port of Dunkirk was kept open. When it was found impossible for the Armies of the north to reopen their communications to Amiens with the main French Armies, only one choice remained. It seemed, indeed, forlorn. The Belgian, British and French Armies were almost surrounded. Their sole line of retreat was to a single port and to its neighbouring beaches. They were pressed on every side by heavy attacks and far outnumbered in the air.

When a week ago to-day I asked the House to fix this afternoon as the occasion for a statement, I feared it would be my hard lot to announce the greatest military disaster in our long history. I thought—and some good judges agreed with me—that perhaps 20,000 or 30,000 men might be re-embarked. But it certainly seemed that the whole of the French First Army and the whole of the British Expeditionary Force north of the Amiens-Abbeville gap, would be broken up in the open field or else would have to capitulate for lack of food and ammunition. These were the hard and heavy tidings for which I called upon the House and the nation to prepare themselves a week ago. The whole root and core and brain of the British Army, on which and around which we were to build, and are to build, the great British Armies in the later years of the war, seemed about to perish upon the field or to be led into an ignominious and starving captivity.

That was the prospect a week ago. But another blow which might well have proved final was yet to fall upon us. The King of the Belgians had called upon us to come to his aid. Had not this Ruler and his Government severed themselves from the Allies, who rescued their country from extinction in the late war, and had they not sought refuge in what has proved to be a fatal neutrality, the French and British Armies might well at the outset have saved not only Belgium but perhaps even Poland. Yet at the last moment, when Belgium was already invaded, King Leopold called upon us to come to his aid, and even at the last moment we came. He and his brave, efficient Army, nearly half a million strong, guarded our eastern flank and thus kept open our only line of retreat to the sea. Suddenly, without prior consultation, with the least possible notice, without the advice of his Ministers and upon his own personal act, he sent a plenipotentiary to the German Command, surrendered his Army and exposed our whole flank and means of retreat.

I asked the House a week ago to suspend its judgment because the facts were not clear, but I do not feel that any reason now exists why we should not form our own opinions upon this pitiful episode. The surrender of the Belgian Army compelled the British at the shortest notice to cover a flank to the sea more than 30 miles in length. Otherwise all would have been cut off, and all would have shared the fate to which King Leopold had condemned the finest Army his country had ever formed. So in doing this and in exposing this flank, as anyone who followed the operations on the map will see, contact was lost between the British and two out of the three corps forming the First French Army, who were still further from the coast than we were, and it seemed impossible that any large number of Allied troops could reach the coast.

The enemy attacked on all sides with great strength and fierceness, and their main power, the power of their far more numerous air force, was thrown into the battle or else concentrated upon Dunkirk and the beaches. Pressing in upon the narrow exit, both from the east and from the west, the enemy began to fire with cannon upon the beaches by which alone the shipping could approach or depart. They sowed magnetic mines in the channels and seas; they sent repeated waves of hostile aircraft, sometimes more than 100 strong in one formation, to cast their bombs upon the single pier that remained, and upon the sand dunes upon which the troops had their eyes for shelter. Their U-boats, one of which was sunk, and their motor launches took their toll of the vast traffic which now began. For four or five days an intense struggle reigned. All their armoured divisions—or what was left of them—together with great masses of German infantry and artillery, hurled themselves in vain upon the ever-narrowing, ever-contracting appendix within which the British and French Armies fought.

Meanwhile, the Royal Navy, with the willing help of countless merchant seamen, strained every nerve to embark the British and Allied troops. Two hundred and twenty light warships and 650 other vessels were engaged. They had to operate upon the difficult coast, often in adverse weather, under an almost ceaseless hail of bombs and an increasing concentration of artillery fire. Nor were the seas, as I have said, themselves free from mines and torpedoes. It was in conditions such as these that our men carried on, with little or no rest, for days and nights on end, making trip after trip across the dangerous waters, bringing with them always men whom they had rescued. The numbers they have brought back are the measure of their devotion and their courage. The hospital ships, which brought off many thousands of British and French wounded, being so plainly marked were a special target for Nazi bombs; but the men and women on board them never faltered in their duty.

Meanwhile, the Royal Air Force, which had already been intervening in the battle, so far as its range would allow, from home bases, now used part of its main metropolitan fighter strength, and struck at the German bombers, and at the fighters which in large numbers protected them. This struggle was protracted and fierce. Suddenly the scene has cleared, the crash and thunder has for the moment—but only for the moment—died away. A miracle of deliverance, achieved by valour, by perseverance, by perfect discipline, by faultless service, by resource, by skill, by unconquerable fidelity, is manifest to us all. The enemy was hurled back by the retreating British and French troops. He was so roughly handled that he did not harry their departure seriously. The Royal Air Force engaged the main strength of the German Air Force, and inflicted upon them losses of at least four to one; and the Navy, using nearly 1,000 ships of all kinds, carried over 335,000 men, French and British, out of the jaws of death and shame, to their native land and to the tasks which lie immediately ahead. We must be very careful not to assign to this deliverance the attributes of a victory. Wars are not won by evacuations. But there was a victory inside this deliverance, which should be noted. It was gained by the Air Force. Many of our soldiers coming back have not seen the Air Force at work; they saw only the bombers which escaped its protective attack. They underrate its achievements. I have heard much talk of this; that is why I go out of my way to say this. I will tell you about it.

This was a great trial of strength between the British and German Air Forces. Can you conceive a greater objective for the Germans in the air than to make evacuation from these beaches impossible, and to sink all these ships which were displayed, almost to the extent of thousands? Could there have been an objective of greater military importance and significance for the whole purpose of the war than this? They tried hard, and they were beaten back; they were frustrated in their task. We got the Army away; and they have paid fourtold for any losses which they have inflicted. Very large formations of German aeroplanes—and we know that they are a very brave race—have turned on several occasions from the attack of one-quarter of their number of the Royal Air Force, and have dispersed in different directions. Twelve aeroplanes have been hunted by two. One aeroplane was driven into the water and cast away, by the mere charge of a British aeroplane, which had no more ammunition. All of our types—the Hurricane, the Spitfire and the new Defiant—and all our pilots have been vindicated as superior to what they have at present to face.

When we consider how much greater would be our advantage in defending the air above this island against an overseas attack, I must say that I find in these facts a sure basis upon which practical and reassuring thoughts may rest. I will pay my tribute to these young airmen. The great French Army was very largely, for the time being, cast back and disturbed by the onrush of a few thousands of armoured vehicles. May it not also be that the cause of civilisation itself will be defended by the skill and devotion of a few thousand airmen? There never had been, I suppose, in all the world, in all the history of war, such an opportunity for youth. The Knights of the Round Table, the Crusaders, all fall back into a prosaic past: not only distant but prosaic; but these young men, going forth every morn to guard their native land and all that we stand for, holding in their hands these instruments of colossal and shattering power, of whom it may be said that

> "When every morning brought a noble chance,
> And every chance brought out a noble knight,"

deserve our gratitude, as do all of the brave men who, in so many ways and on so many occasions, are ready, and continue ready, to give life and all for their native land.

I return to the Army. In the long series of very fierce battles, now on this front, now on that, fighting on three fronts at once, battles fought by two or three divisions against an equal or somewhat larger number of the enemy, and fought fiercely on some of the old grounds that so many of us knew so well, in these battles our losses in men have exceeded 30,000 killed, wounded and missing. I take occasion to express the sympathy of the House to all who have suffered bereavement or who are still anxious. The President of the Board of Trade is not here to-day. His son has been killed, and many in the House have felt the pangs of affliction in the sharpest form. But I will say this about the missing. We have had a large number of wounded come home safely to this country—the greater part—but I would say about the missing that there may be very many reported missing who will come back home, some day, in one way or another. In the confusion of this fight it is inevitable that many have been left in positions where honour required no further resistance from them.

Against this loss of over 30,000 men, we can set a far heavier loss certainly inflicted upon the enemy. But our losses in material are enormous. We have perhaps lost one-third of the men we lost in the opening days of the battle of 21st March, 1918, but we have lost nearly as many guns—nearly 1,000 guns—and all our transport, all the armoured vehicles that were with the Army in the North. This loss will impose a further delay on the expansion of our military strength. That expansion had not been proceeding as fast as we had hoped. The best of all we had to give had gone to the British Expeditionary Force, and although they had not the numbers of tanks and some articles of equipment which were desirable, they were a very well and finely equipped Army. They had the first-fruits of all that our industry had to give, and that is gone. And now here is this further delay. How long it will be, how long it will last, depends upon the exertions which we make in this island. An effort the like of which has never been seen in our records is now being made. Work is proceeding everywhere, night and day, Sundays and week-days. Capital and labour have cast aside their interests, rights, and customs and put them into the common stock. Already the flow of munitions has leapt forward. There is no reason why we should not in a few months overtake the sudden and serious loss that has come upon us, without retarding the development of our general programme.

Nevertheless, our thankfulness at the escape of our Army and so many men, whose loved ones have passed through an agonising week, must not blind us to the fact that what has happened in France and Belgium is a colossal military disaster. The French Army has been weakened, the Belgian Army has been lost, a large part of those fortified lines upon which so much faith had been reposed is gone, many valuable mining districts and factories have passed into the enemy's possession, the whole of the Channel ports are in his hands, with all the tragic consequences that follow from that, and we must expect another blow to be struck almost immediately at us or at France. We are told that Herr Hitler has a plan for invading the British Isles. This has often been thought of before. When Napoleon lay at Boulogne for a year with his flat-bottomed boats and his Grand Army, he was told by someone, "There are bitter weeds in England." There are certainly a great many more of them since the British Expeditionary Force returned.

The whole question of home defence against invasion is, of course, powerfully affected by the fact that we have for the time being in this island incomparably more powerful military forces than we have ever had at any moment in this war or the last. But this will not continue. We shall not be content with a defensive war. We have our duty to our Ally. We have to reconstitute and build up the British Expeditionary Force once again, under its gallant Commander-in-Chief, Lord Gort. All this is in train; but in the interval we must put our defences in this island into such a high state of organisation that the fewest possible numbers will be required to give effective security and that the largest possible potential of offensive effort may be realised. On this we are now engaged. It will be very convenient, if it be the desire of the House, to enter upon this subject in a secret Session. Not that the Government would necessarily be able to reveal in very great detail military secrets, but we like to have our discussions free, without the restraint imposed by the fact that they will be read the next day by the enemy, and the Government would benefit by views freely expressed in all parts of the House by Members with their knowledge of so many different parts of the country. I understand that some request is to be made upon this subject, which will be readily acceded to by His Majesty's Government.

We have found it necessary to take measures of increasing stringency, not only against enemy aliens and suspicious characters of other nationalities, but also against British subjects who may become a danger or a nuisance should the war be transported to the United Kingdom. I know there are a great many people affected by the orders which we have made who are the passionate enemies of Nazi Germany. I am very sorry for them, but we cannot, at the present time and under the present stress, draw all the distinctions which we should like to do. If parachute landings were attempted and fierce fighting attendant upon them followed, these unfortunate people would be far better out of the way, for their own sakes as well as for ours. There is, however, another class, for which I feel not the slightest sympathy. Parliament has given us the powers to put down Fifth Column activities with a strong hand, and we shall use those powers, subject to the supervision and correction of the House, without the slightest hesitation until we are satisfied, and more than satisfied, that this malignancy in our midst has been effectively stamped out.

Turning once again, and this time more generally, to the question of invasion, I would observe that there has never been a period in all these long centuries of which we boast when an absolute guarantee against invasion, still less against serious raids, could have been given to our people. In the days of Napoleon, of which I was speaking just now, the same wind which would have carried his transports across the Channel might have driven away the blockading fleet. There was always the chance, and it is that chance which has excited and befooled the imaginations of many Continental tyrants. Many are the tales that are told. We are assured that novel methods will be adopted, and when we see the originality of malice, the ingenuity of aggression, which our enemy displays, we may certainly prepare ourselves for every kind of novel stratagem and every kind of brutal and treacherous manœuvre. I think that no idea is so outlandish that it should not be considered and viewed with a searching, but at the same time, I hope, with a steady eye. We must never forget the solid assurances of sea power and those which belong to air power if it can be locally exercised.

I have, myself, full confidence that if all do their duty, if nothing is neglected, and if the best arrangements are made, as they are being made, we shall prove ourselves once again able to defend our island home, to ride out the storm of war, and to outlive the menace of tyranny, if necessary for years, if necessary alone. At any rate, that is what we are going to try to do. That is the resolve of His Majesty's Government—every man of them. That is the will of Parliament and the nation. The British Empire and the French Republic, linked together in their cause and in their need, will defend to the death their native soil, aiding each other like good comrades to the utmost of their strength. Even though large tracts of Europe and many old and famous States have fallen or may fall into the grip of the Gestapo and all the odious apparatus of Nazi rule, we shall not flag or fail. We shall go on to the end. We shall fight in France, we shall fight on the seas and oceans, we shall fight with growing confidence and growing strength in the air, we shall defend our island, whatever the cost may be. We shall fight on the beaches, we shall fight on the landing grounds, we shall fight in the fields and in the streets, we shall fight in the hills; we shall never surrender, and even if, which I do not for a moment believe, this island or a large part of it were subjugated and starving, then our Empire beyond the seas, armed and guarded by the British Fleet, would carry on the struggle, until, in God's good time, the new world, with all its power and might, steps forth to the rescue and the liberation of the old.

June 18, 1940

I spoke the other day of the colossal military disaster which occurred when the French High Command failed to withdraw the Northern Armies from Belgium at the moment when they knew that the French front was decisively broken at Sedan and on the Meuse. This delay entailed the loss of 15 or 16 French divisions and threw out of action for the critical period the whole of the British Expeditionary Force. Our Army and 120,000 French troops were indeed rescued by the British Navy from Dunkirk but only with the loss of their cannon, vehicles and modern equipment. This loss inevitably took some weeks to repair, and in the first two of those weeks the battle in France has been lost. When we consider the heroic resistance made by the French Army against heavy odds in this battle, the enormous losses inflicted upon the enemy and the evident exhaustion of the enemy, it may well be thought that these 25 divisions of the best trained and best equipped troops might have turned the scale. However, General Weygand had to fight without them. Only three British divisions or their equivalent were able to stand in the line with their French comrades. They have suffered severely, but they have fought well. We sent every man we could to France as fast as we could re-equip and transport their formations.

I am not reciting these facts for the purpose of recrimination. That, I judge, to be utterly futile and even harmful. We cannot afford it. I recite them in order to explain why it was we did not have, as we could have had, between 12 and 14 British divisions fighting in the line in this great battle instead of only three. Now I put all this aside. I put it on the shelf, from which the historians, when they have time, will select their documents to tell their stories. We have to think of the future and not of the past. This also applies in a small way to our own affairs at home. There are many who would hold an inquest in the House of Commons on the conduct of the Governments —and of Parliaments, for they are in it, too —during the years which led up to this catastrophe. They seek to indict those who were responsible for the guidance of our affairs. This also would be a foolish and pernicious process. There are too many in it. Let each man search his conscience and search his speeches. I frequently search mine.

Of this I am quite sure, that if we open a quarrel between the past and the present, we shall find that we have lost the future. Therefore, I cannot accept the drawing of any distinctions between Members of the present Government. It was formed at a moment of crisis in order to unite all the parties and all sections of opinion. It has received the almost unanimous support of both Houses of Parliament. Its Members are going to stand together, and, subject to the authority of the House of Commons, we are going to govern the country and fight the war. It is absolutely necessary at a time like this that every Minister who tries each day to do his duty shall be respected, and their subordinates must know that their chiefs are not threatened men, men who are here to-day and gone to-morrow, but that their directions must be punctually and faithfully obeyed. Without this concentrated power we cannot face what lies before us. I should not think it would be very advantageous for the House to prolong this Debate this afternoon under conditions of public stress. Many facts are not clear that will be clear in a short time. We are to have a Secret Session on Thursday, and I should think that would be a better opportunity for the many earnest expressions of opinion which Members will desire to make and for the House to discuss vital matters, as I have said before, without having everything read the next morning by our dangerous foes.

The military events which have happened during the past fortnight have not come to me with any sense of surprise. Indeed, I indicated a fortnight ago as clearly as I could to the House that the worst possibilities were open, and I made it perfectly clear then that whatever happened in France would make no difference to the resolve of Britain and the British Empire to fight on, "If necessary for years, if necessary alone." During the last few days we have successfully brought off the great majority of the troops we had on the lines of communication in France—a very large number, scores of thousands—and seven-eighths of the troops we have sent to France since the beginning of the war, that is to say, about 350,000 out of 400,000 men, are safely back in this country. Others are still fighting with the French, and fighting with considerable success in their local encounters with the enemy. We have also brought back a great mass of stores, rifles and munitions of all kinds which had been accumulated in France during the last nine months.

We have, therefore, in this island to-day a very large and powerful miiltary force. This force includes all our best trained and finest troops and includes scores of thousands of those who have already measured their quality against the Germans and found themselves at no disadvantage. We have under arms at the present time in this island over a million and a quarter men. Behind these we have the Local Defence Volunteers, numbering half a million, only a portion of whom, however, are yet armed with rifles or other firearms. We have incorporated into our Defence Forces every man for whom we have a weapon. We expect a very large addition to our weapons in the near future, and in preparation for this we intend to call up, drill and train further large numbers at once. Those who are not called up or employed upon the vast business of munitions production in all its branches—and it runs through every kind of grade—serve their country best by remaining at their ordinary work until they are required.

We also have Dominions Armies here. The Canadians had actually landed in France but have now been safely withdrawn, much disappointed, but in perfect order, with all their artillery and equipment. These very high-class forces from the Dominions will now take part in the defence of the Mother Country. Lest the account which I have given of these very large forces should raise the question why they did not take part in the great battle in France, I must make it clear that, apart from the divisions training and organising at home, only 12 divisions were equipped to fight upon a scale which justified their being sent abroad. This was fully up to the number which the French had been led to expect would be available in France at the ninth month of the war. The rest of our forces at home have a fighting value for home defence which will, of course, steadily increase every week that passes. Thus, the invasion of Great Britain would at this time require the transportation across the sea of hostile armies upon a very large scale and, after they had been so transported, they would have to be continually maintained with all the masses of munitions and supplies which are required for continuous battle, as continuous battle it would be.

Here is where we come to the Navy. After

all, we have a Navy. Some people seem to forget that. We must remind them. For the last 30 years I have been concerned in discussions about the possibilities of oversea invasion, and I took the responsibility on behalf of the Admiralty, at the beginning of the last war, of allowing all Regular troops to be sent out of the country, although our Territorials had only just been called up and were quite untrained. Therefore, this island was for several months practically denuded of fighting troops. The Admiralty had confidence at that time in their ability to prevent a mass invasion, even though at that time the Germans had a magnificent battle fleet in the proportion of 10 to 16, even though they were capable of fighting a general engagement every day and any day, whereas now they have only a couple of heavy ships worth speaking of. We are also told that the Italian Navy is to come to gain sea superiority in these waters. If they seriously intend it, I shall only say that we shall be delighted to offer Signor Mussolini a free and safeguarded passage through the Straits of Gibraltar in order that he may play the part which he aspires to do. There is general curiosity in the British Fleet to find out whether the Italians are up to the level they were at in the last war or whether they have fallen off at all.

Therefore, it seems to me that as far as seaborne invasion on a great scale is concerned, we are far more capable of meeting it to-day than we were at many periods in the last war and during the early months of this war, before our other troops were trained, and while the B.E.F. was already abroad and still abroad. The Navy have never pretended to be able to prevent raids by bodies of 5,000 or 10,000 men flung suddenly across and thrown ashore at several points on the coast some dark night or foggy morning. The efficacy of sea-power, especially under modern conditions, depends upon the invading force being of large size. It has to be of large size, in view of our military strength, to be of any use. If it is of large size, then the Navy have something they can find and meet and, as it were, bite on. Now we must remember that even five divisions, however lightly equipped, would require 200 to 250 ships, and with modern air reconnaissance and photography, it would not be easy to collect such an armada, marshal it and conduct it across the sea without any powerful naval forces to escort it, and with the very great possibility that it would be intercepted long before it reached the coast, and the men all drowned in the sea or, at the worst, blown to pieces with their equipment while they were trying to land. We also have a great system of minefields, recently strongly reinforced, through which we alone know the channel. If the enemy tries to sweep passages through these minefields, it will be the task of the Navy to destroy the minesweepers and any other forces employed to protect them. There should be no difficulty in this, owing to our great superiority at sea.

Those are the regular, well-tested, well-proved arguments on which we have relied during many years in peace and war. But the question is whether there are any new methods by which those solid assurances can be circumvented. Odd as it may seem, some attention has been given to this by the Admiralty, whose prime duty and responsibility it is to destroy any large seaborne expedition before it reaches or at the moment when it reaches these shores. It would not be useful to go into details. It might even suggest ideas to other people which they have not thought of, and they would not be likely to give us any of their ideas in exchange. All I will say is that untiring vigilance and mind-searching must be devoted to the subject, because the enemy is crafty and cunning and full of novel treacheries and stratagems. The House may be assured that the utmost ingenuity is being displayed and imagination is being evoked from large numbers of competent officers, well-trained in tactics and thoroughly up to date, to measure and counterwork novel possibilities, of which many are suggested, some very absurd and some by no means utterly irrational.

Some people will ask why, then, was it that the British Navy was not able to prevent the movement of a large army from Germany into Norway across the Skaggerak? But the conditions in the Channel and in the North Sea are in no way like those which prevail in the Skaggerak. In the Skaggerak, because of the distance, we could give no air support to our surface ships, and consequently, lying as we did close to the enemy's main air power, in those waters we were compelled to use only our submarines. We could not enforce the decisive blockade or interruption which is possible from surface vessels. Our submarines took a heavy toll but could not, by themselves, prevent the invasion of Norway. In the Channel and in the North Sea, on the other hand, our superior naval surface forces, aided by our submarines, will operate with close and effective air assistance.

This brings me, naturally, to the great question of invasion from the air and of the impending struggle between the British and German air forces. It seems quite clear that no invasion on a scale beyond the capacity of our land forces to crush speedily is likely to take place from the air until our Air Force has been definitely overpowered. In the meantime, there may be raids by parachute troops and attempted descents of airborne soldiers. We should be able to give those gentry a warm reception both in the air and if they reach the ground in any condition to continue the dispute. But the great question is, Can we break Hitler's air weapon? Now, of course, it is a very great pity that we have not got an Air Force at least equal to that of the most powerful enemy within striking distance of these shores. But we have a very powerful Air Force which has proved itself far superior in quality, both in men and in many types of machine, to what we have met so far in the numerous fierce air battles which have been fought. In France, where we were at a considerable disadvantage and lost many machines on the ground, we were accustomed to inflict losses of as much as two to two and a half to one. In the fighting over Dunkirk, which was a sort of no man's land, we undoubtedly beat the German air force, and this gave us the mastery locally in the air, and we inflicted losses of three or four to one. Anyone who looks at the photographs which were published a week or so ago of the re-embarkation, showing the masses of troops assembled on the beach and forming an ideal target for hours at a time, must realise that this re-embarkation would not have been possible unless the enemy had resigned all hope of recovering air superiority at that point.

In the defence of this island the advantages to the defenders will be very great. We hope to improve on the rate of three or four to one which was realised at Dunkirk, and in addition all our injured machines and their crews which get down safely—and, surprisingly, a very great many injured machines and men do get down safely in modern air fighting—all of these will fall, in an attack upon these islands, on friendly soil and live to fight another day, whereas all injured enemy machines and their complements will be total losses as far as the war is concerned. During the great battle in France, we gave very powerful and continuous aid to the French Army both by fighters and bombers, but in spite of every kind of pressure we never would allow the entire Metropolitan strength of the Air Force, in fighters, to be consumed. This decision was painful, but it was also right, because the fortunes of the battle in France could not have been decisively affected, even if we had thrown in our entire fighter force. The battle was lost by the unfortunate strategical opening, by the extraordinary and unforeseen power of the armoured columns, and by the great preponderance of the German Army in numbers. Our fighter Air Force might easily have been exhausted as a mere accident in that great struggle, and we should have found ourselves at the present time in a very serious plight. But, as it is, I am happy to inform the House that our fighter air strength is stronger at the present time, relatively to the Germans, who have suffered terrible losses, than it has ever been, and consequently we believe ourselves to possess the capacity to continue the war in the air under better conditions than we have ever experienced before. I look forward confidently to the exploits of our fighter pilots, who will have the glory of saving their native land, their island home, and all they love, from the most deadly of all attacks.

There remains the danger of bombing attacks, which will certainly be made very soon upon us by the bomber forces of the enemy. It is true that the German bomber force is superior in numbers to ours, but we have a very large bomber force also which we shall use to strike at military targets in Germany without intermission. I do not at all underrate the severity of the ordeal which lies before us, but I believe our countrymen will show themselves capable of standing up to it, like the brave men of Barcelona, and will be able to stand up to it, and carry on in spite of it, at least as well as any other people in the world. Much will depend upon this, and every man and every woman will have the chance to show the finest qualities of their race and render the highest service to their cause. For all of us at this time, whatever our sphere, our station, our occupation, our duties, it will be a help to remember the famous lines:

> "He nothing common did, or mean,
> Upon that memorable scene."

I have thought it right upon this occasion to give the House and the country some indication of the solid, practical grounds upon which we base our inflexible resolve to continue the war, and I can assure them that our professional advisers of the three Services unitedly advise that we should do so, and that there are good and reasonable hopes of final victory. We have also fully informed and consulted all the self-governing Dominions, and I have received from their Prime Ministers, Mr. Mackenzie King, Mr. Menzies, Mr. Fraser and General Smuts, messages couched in the most moving terms in which they endorse our decision and declare themselves ready to share our fortunes and to persevere to the end.

We may now ask ourselves, In what ways is our position worsened since the beginning of the war? It is worsened by the fact that the Germans have conquered a large part of the coastline of Western Europe, and many small countries have been overrun by them. This aggravates the possibilities of air attack and adds to our naval preoccupations. It in no way diminishes, but on the contrary definitely increases, the power of our long-distance blockade. Should military resistance come to an end in France, which is not yet certain, though it will in any case be greatly diminished, the Germans can concentrate their forces, both military and industrial, upon us. But for the reasons I have given to the House these will not be found so easy to apply. If invasion becomes more imminent, we, being relieved from the task of maintaining a large army in France, have far larger and more efficient forces here to meet them. If Hitler can bring under his despotic control the industries of the countries he has conquered, this will add greatly to his already vast armament output. On the other hand, this will not happen immediately, and we are now assured of immense, continuous and increasing support in supplies and munitions of all kinds from the United States, and especially of aeroplanes and pilots from the Dominions and across the oceans, coming from regions which are beyond the reach of enemy bombers.

I do not see how any of these factors can operate to our detriment on balance before the winter comes, and the winter will impose a strain upon the Nazi régime, with almost all Europe writhing and starving under their heel which, for all their ruthlessness, will run them very hard. We must not forget that from the moment when we declared war on the 3rd September it was always possible for Germany to turn all her air force upon this country, together with any other devices of invasion she might conceive, and that France could do little or nothing to prevent her doing so. We have, therefore, lived under this danger, in principle and in a slightly modified form, during all these months. In the meanwhile, however, we have enormously improved our methods of defence, and we have learned, what we had no right to assume at the beginning, namely, the individual superiority of our aircraft and pilots.

Therefore, in casting up this dread balance-sheet, contemplating our dangers with a disillusioned eye, I see great reason for intense vigilance and exertion, but none whatever for panic or despair. During the first four years of the last war the Allies experienced, as my right honourable Friend opposite the Member for Carnarvon Boroughs (Mr. Lloyd George) will remember, nothing but disaster and disappointment, and yet at the end their morale was higher than that of the Germans, who had moved from one aggressive triumph to another. During that war we repeatedly asked ourselves the question, "How are we going to win?" and no one was able ever to answer it with much precision, until at the end, quite suddenly, quite unexpectedly, our terrible foe collapsed before us, and we were so glutted with victory that in our folly we cast it away.

We do not yet know what will happen in France or whether the French resistance will be prolonged, both in France and in the French Empire overseas. The French Government will be throwing away great opportunities and casting away their future if they do not continue the war in accordance with their Treaty obligations, from which we have not felt able to release them. The House will have read the historic declaration in which, at the desire of many Frenchmen, and of our own hearts, we have proclaimed our willingness to conclude at the darkest hour in French history a union of common citizenship. However matters may go in France or with the French Government or with another French Government, we in this island and in the British Empire will never lose our sense of comradeship with the French people. If we are now called upon to endure what they have suffered we shall emulate their courage, and if final victory rewards our toils they shall share the gains, aye, and freedom shall be restored to all. We abate nothing of our just demands—Czechs, Poles, Norwegians, Dutch, Belgians, all who have joined their causes to our own shall be restored.

What General Weygand called the "Battle of France" is over. I expect that the battle of Britain is about to begin. Upon this battle depends the survival of Christian civilisation. Upon it depends our own British life and the long continuity of our institutions and our Empire. The whole fury and might of the enemy must very soon be turned on us. Hitler knows that he will have to break us in this island or lose the war. If we can stand up to him all Europe may be free, and the life of the world may move forward into broad, sunlit uplands; but if we fail then the whole world, including the United States, and all that we have known and cared for, will sink into the abyss of a new dark age made more sinister, and perhaps more prolonged, by the lights of a perverted science. Let us therefore brace ourselves to our duty and so bear ourselves that if the British Commonwealth and Empire lasts for a thousand years men will still say, "This was their finest hour."

FIFTY-TWO

POSTWAR FRANCE

World War II produced huge shifts in the power structure of the West, especially with the creation of two superpowers, the Soviet Union and the United States. The Soviet Union aggressively extended its sphere of influence westward with the creation of satellite states in eastern and central Europe. In the ensuing Cold War the United States abandoned its traditional policy of isolation and used its enormous resources to support the European democracies. An uneasy equilibrium of forces resulted. Meanwhile Europe's powers had varying fortunes. East Germany languished under Soviet domination, while West Germany, with American aid, made a spectacular recovery. Britain recovered more slowly, and gradually adjusted to its new situation as a second-class power. In France, as elsewhere on the continent, economic reconstruction presented a major challenge, on the whole successfully met in the postwar years. But France also faced a particularly snarled political situation. France's defeat in 1940 discredited the prewar Radicals. The Vichy regime of 1940–5 thoroughly discredited its mainly conservative supporters, some of whom were monarchists or Fascists. During the German occupation the heroic activity of France's Resistance movement, in which Communists had a leading role, led to an unusually strong Communist vote in the elections of 1945. For the next 13 years, as before the war, France's Fourth Republic had a series of unstable coalition governments until General Charles De Gaulle created the more authoritarian Fifth Republic in 1958. The short life-span of the Fourth Republic revealed both the ineffectiveness of France's multiparty system and the ideological ferment in France's wartime and postwar experience. In his book Crisis and Compromise *Philip Williams analyzes with keen insight and in considerable detail the often bewildering development of politics in France's Fourth Republic.*

PHILIP WILLIAMS

CRISIS AND COMPROMISE: POLITICS IN THE FOURTH REPUBLIC *

World war shook France from the economic stagnation and political paralysis which had marked the last years of the Third Republic. Defeat provided the opportunity for a counter-revolution directed against both the working-class movement and the

* Reprinted from *Crisis and Compromise: Politics in the Fourth Republic,* pp. 17–30, by Philip Williams by permission of Archon Books and of Longmans, Green & Co. Limited (*Politics in Postwar France*). Copyright 1958 and 1964 by Philip Williams.

democratic regime itself. The Resistance was a revolutionary response to this challenge, and its triumph revolutionized the political situation. But the apparent national unity was quickly dissipated. The Communist drive for power forced all groups to take sides. During 1945 and 1946 there proceeded simultaneously a national effort at indispensable economic reconstruction, a struggle over the framing of the new constitution, and a bitter political 'cold war' between the ruling parties. When the Communists went out of office in May 1947 the regime gradually returned to normal and the political practices of the past slowly revived.

1. Political Forces, 1936–45

Before the second world war the Radicals were politically dominant, appealing to all those who 'wore their hearts on the left and their wallets on the right'. The party was so loose in its organization and discipline that members with very different opinions could join; the Radicals in the Senate (such as Caillaux) were far more conservative than those in the Chamber (like the rising young leader Daladier). At elections the latter could usually impose an alliance with the Socialists, but during the course of each parliament's life the moderate wing gradually encouraged their colleagues into coalition with the Right. Its pivotal position gave the party a permanent hold on power; the premiership and ministry of the interior were generally in its hands, and it was able to train many skilful and experienced politicians both in Paris and through its extensive hold on local government.

But the Radicals had the defects of their qualities. The body of opinion represented by them was broad but shallow. This negative, unconstructive and timid following handicapped the party in a period of crisis. Loose discipline allowed it to attract such wide support that it became less a party in the British sense than a social club attached to an electioneering machine. Its hold on power meant that it attracted the careerist politician and the unscrupulous henchman: few were the political and financial scandals in which Radicals were not involved. And in training its young men it sought not to promote strong personalities but to suppress them. Many Radicals positively preferred mediocrity to ability.

Until 1936 the Socialist party sat on the far Left in Parliament. Once revolutionary and anti-militarist, the Socialists had settled down as orthodox defenders of the regime—although they long refused to take office. When they changed their minds in 1936, on becoming the strongest party in the Popular Front majority, they were already feeling the breath of competition on their Left. For at that election the Communist party was accepted as an ally by the Socialists and Radicals. Hitherto badly under-represented by the electoral system, it suddenly leapt from a dozen parliamentary seats to seventy, but in its turn refused office and gave Blum's government only the cold comfort of 'support without participation'.

The Right, like the Socialists, was too weak to win an electoral majority. Much of its strength lay in the support of influential figures like Pétain in the army, Chiappe in the police, Coty in business, Maurras among intellectuals. During the thirties such men became more and more sympathetic towards fascism. At home strong fascist leagues grew up of which *Croix de feu* was the largest (and least extreme). Abroad the entire Right demanded a policy favourable to Mussolini's Italy and to Franco's cause in Spain, and many of its supporters came to see the predominance of Nazi Germany as a lesser evil than the rule of a Jewish Socialist prime minister in Paris.

Fascism did not attract the Right alone. Among its most extreme exponents were the former Communist leader Doriot and the 'Neo-Socialist' Déat. It gained indirectly, too, as Hitler's successive victories sapped the determination and paralysed the will of French leaders—including most Radicals and half the Socialists as well as the Right.

Since at first the Communists stood for resistance to Germany, by the time of Munich anti-Communism had become the main bond between the forces of appeasement and the main motive of governmental policy. Then when the Nazi-Soviet pact was signed the Communists turned defeatist, playing into the hands of those of their enemies for whom the class war at home was more important than the fight against Hitler.

So where the first world war had brought national unity, the second destroyed it. The regime had long been opposed by an extreme Right which felt excluded from government and an extreme Left which felt alienated from society. For some years it had also been losing former supporters who believed it could no longer fulfil its task. The defeat seemed to prove them right. An overwhelming majority conferred full powers upon Marshal Pétain as chief of the French State: the very name of Republic was abandoned. His regime was based primarily on right-wing opinion, which found at Vichy (not of course among the German puppets in Paris) the political leadership it really sought. But the Marshal's first cabinet also included two prominent Socialists, a Radical ex-premier, and an assistant secretary of CGT, the trade union federation. Conversely when General de Gaulle issued his appeal on 18 June 1940 he found followers in all political camps from Socialists to *Croix de feu,* but his support from the Right came from individuals only.[1] In the Resistance inside France the pioneers were usually Socialists, Catholic democrats or army officers. Only after Germany's invasion of Russia did the Communist party play its active part.

Though directed against a foreign occupier, the Resistance was potentially a revolutionary movement; and the Liberation was potentially a revolutionary change. For a few months indeed the new Gaullist authorities shared precarious power with the largely Communist-controlled militia and insurrectionary committees which dominated most of southern France.[2] But at the end of 1944 Thorez allowed his supporters to be disarmed and the Liberation Committees disbanded without resistance. The war was still raging and the party had decided to bid for power by legal means. It knew that the old political leaders as a group (and often as individuals) had suffered a disastrous loss of prestige. The Right was discredited by Vichy; the Radicals were blamed for the events leading up to the war, for their weakness and lack of responsibility in power, and for their rather unheroic part under the occupation. Thus two of the three main forces on the pre-war scene were under a heavy cloud. New men rose to the top who, as in any revolution, included both inexperienced idealists and more or less scrupulous and patriotic adventurers. Wielded into a strong Resistance party they might form a buffer against the Communists; dispersed and divided, they would easily be outmanœuvred by the largest and best-disciplined party.

The Resistance party was never formed. The Communists were bent on hampering any organization they did not control. Some Resisters from the old parties, especially Socialists, were unwilling to lose their former political identity. Christian Democrats who could hope at last to found a major party would not renounce this opportunity for an uncertain fusion with rather reluctant anticlerical partners. Above all General de Gaulle, who in 1943 had revived the discredited old parties by bringing them into the National Resistance Council to strengthen his hand in Washington and London, was in 1944–45 still unwilling to forfeit his position as a national hero by stooping

[1] The Communists denounced him as a hireling of the City of London: cf. Rossi, *La Physiologie du Parti communiste français,* pp. 86–7, 90–3, 220, and his other books cited in the bibliography.

[2] Robert Aron, *Histoire de la Libération de la France* (1959), pp. 573–637; Lüthy, pp. 100–4; Rieber, *Stalin and the French Communist Party,* pp. 150–8, 168–74.

to lead a political party.[3] The attempt to transform the non-Communist Resistance into a political movement was thus stillborn, and instead three parties succeeded in canalizing the new enthusiasm.

The Communists reaped in votes the reward of their Resistance record after 1941, becoming the largest single party; and they contrived through their dynamism, their organizing capacity and their ruthless use of slander and violence to capture control of CGT.[4] Equally spectacular was the sudden emergence of a new party, the *Mouvement républicain populaire* (MRP), based on an old tradition of Catholic democracy which had never before found effective political expression and on a new generation of progressive Christians who had come to maturity in the Resistance. Between these two the old Socialist leaders hoped to rejuvenate their party and make it the link and leader of all the new forces.

In these forgotten years of 1944–45 General de Gaulle was earning distinction at home as the first French premier to bring Communists into his administration, and abroad as the chief advocate of the middle way between Washington and Moscow. Vincent Auriol, later President of the Republic and champion of 'the System' against Gaullism, was the General's chief constitutional adviser and his agent in dealing with the politicians. The Communists were seeking fusion of their party with the Socialists; the voters of the Right could find an electoral home only with MRP; the General was on intimate terms with both Socialists and MRP but sharply divided from the Radicals and Conservatives.[5] And the style of government, in which a national hero of authoritarian temper carried out the revolutionary policies of an insurrectionary committee subject to the criticism of a parliamentary assembly, was one which combined features cherished by the extreme Right, the extreme Left and the moderate Centre.[6]

2. Politics and Constitutional Reform, 1945–47

The Third Republic formally committed suicide on 10 July 1940 when the Chamber and Senate, sitting together as a National Assembly empowered to revise the constitution, voted full powers to Marshal Pétain. The rival government of General de Gaulle established itself at Algiers in 1943. It gradually obtained Allied recognition, and took control in France in 1944. But until 21 October 1945 its authority was based on no formal or legal title.

On that day the French electorate had three decisions to take. They had to choose their parliamentary representatives. They had to decide by referendum whether the new assembly should draft a new constitution: if not, it would simply become a Chamber of Deputies, a senatorial election would take place according to the pre-war procedure, and the new parliament might or might not proceed to revise the constitution in the manner prescribed in 1875. But if the voters gave the new assembly constituent powers (as they did), they would also have to accept or reject a governmental proposal limiting its authority to seven months and requiring its draft constitution to be approved by another referendum. For General de Gaulle was unwilling to confer unlimited

[3] Wright, *Reshaping of French Democracy,* pp. 32–6, 64–78; Matthews, *Death of the Fourth Republic,* pp. 107–11; Fauvet, *La IVe République,* pp. 24–7; H. Michel, *Histoire de la Résistance* (1950), pp. 47–8, 51; M. Granat and H. Michel, *Combat* (1957), pp. 297–306; R. Hostache, *Le Conseil National de la Résistance* (1958), Chapters 2 and 3; Bourdet, no. 27, pp. 1837–62; Frenay, no. 95, pp. 43–8.

[4] Lorwin, *French Labor Movement,* pp. 107–11 (and in Earle, pp. 202–4); Rioux, *Le Syndicalisme,* pp. 75–6; Lefranc, *Les expériences syndicales en France,* pp. 140–1, 151–68; Rossi, pp. 444–5; Rieber, pp. 179–82, 220–4.

[5] The term 'Conservative' is used to denote the small and shifting right-wing groups like PRL (*Pari républicain de la Liberté*), the Peasant party, the Independent Republicans, and the dissident Gaullists: see below, Chapter 11. Without a capital letter, 'conservative' refers to a social and economic outlook which some anticlericals share.

[6] Morazé, p. 141.

power on a single assembly checked by no rival institution.

The referendum produced an overwhelming vote of no confidence in the Third Republic. Only the Radicals advocated returning to the system of which they had been the principal beneficiaries (and only one in three of their two million surviving voters followed them). The Assembly was given constituent status by 18,600,000 votes to 700,000.[7] But this enormous majority divided over the Assembly's powers. Socialists and MRP supported General de Gaulle and called on their followers to vote *OUI–OUI*. The Communists, against whom the restrictions on the Assembly's powers were directed, campaigned vigorously for *OUI–NON*. On the second question they were joined by the Radicals, who disliked plebiscites in principle and General de Gaulle in practice. The General won this vote by nearly 13 million to 6½ million. For the first time France had a Constituent Assembly with limited powers.

The election produced an Assembly unlike any of its predecessors. The three large organized parties, Communists, MRP and Socialists, polled 5, 4¾ and 4½ million votes respectively. These three disciplined groups shared between them in roughly equal numbers nearly four-fifths of the 586 seats in the Assembly. The Radicals were routed; they and their allies polled 2 million votes, but the party held only 24 seats in metropolitan France and many of its leaders were beaten. The different varieties of Conservative did a little better with about 2½ million votes and 64 seats.

For nearly three years after the Liberation the Communists held office and their pressure on the government dominated the political struggle. They pinned their hopes on completing the revolution legally, by electoral victory and infiltration of the state machine. The basis of their strategy was a close alliance with the other great Marxist party; and the reluctance of the Socialist leaders was to be overcome by arousing their followers who still recognized 'no enemies on the Left'. The Radicals were also potential allies, for distrust of political generals had led them to co-operate with the Communists in the 1945 referendum. MRP was to be discredited as the standard-bearer of reaction; in particular the clerical dispute, which many hoped had been buried in the Resistance struggle, was resuscitated in order to prevent any close combination between MRP and the Socialists.[8] But proportional representation, in many ways a help to the Communists, hindered them here: for it allowed each party to fight the electoral battle alone, and so enabled the Socialists to escape being forced into a Marxist coalition which might have alienated them irrevocably from MRP.[9]

Immediately after the election General de Gaulle reconstituted his government and based it on the support of all the main parties. But a few weeks later, on 20 January 1946, he suddenly resigned in exasperation with the quarrels and demands of the parties. Like some other war leaders, he was more interested and knowledgeable in military than in economic affairs; reconstruction of the army was his most cherished objective, and the interference of party politics in this sphere precipitated his departure.[10] He rejected any idea of carrying out a *coup d'état*, and Blum and Auriol advised him against appealing by radio to the public.[11]

His departure inaugurated a year of *tri-*

[7] See Appendix v. Voting figures from Husson, *Les Élections et Référendums* (1945–6, two volumes, cited henceforth as Husson i and ii).

[8] See Hamon, no. 119, pp. 103–5.

[9] Goguel, *Fourth Republic*, pp. 61–2.

[10] The last straw was a large cut in the military budget, moved by the Socialists in order to embarrass the Communist minister responsible but promptly taken up and carried by the Communists themselves. But see below, p. 386; and Rauvet, *IVe*, pp. 64–5.

[11] Wright, *Reshaping*, p. 131; Chapters 4 and 5 give the fullest account of the General's relations with the cabinet and parties. For his rejection of a *coup*, see *La France sera la France* (a collection of his pronouncements published by RPF), pp. 31–3; *Monde*, 13 March 1951; *Rassemblement*, 11 July 1952—but cf. his memoirs: *Le Salut*, pp. 286–7.

partisme, a coalition government of the three main parties, headed at first by the Socialist President of the Constituent Assembly, Félix Gouin. The three parties associated in the government (allied would be too strong a word) could reach no agreement on the constitutional problem. The Socialists, having failed to arrange a compromise, joined the Communists against all the other principal parties in voting the draft constitution on 19 April 1946 and campaigning for it in the referendum. Its opponents attacked the draft itself (which conferred virtually unchecked power on a single chamber); the electoral law associated with it; and the controversial preamble—especially the omission of the right to 'freedom of education', the guarantee of the Catholic schools. But they were even more hostile to the sponsors than to the provisions of the draft. They feared that acceptance would constitute a triumph for the Communists, consolidating both their alliance with the Socialists and their domination of that alliance.

The referendum of 5 May 1946 checked the steady Communist advance. For the first time in French history the electorate answered *NON* in a plebiscite. The draft constitution was rejected by a majority of just over one million votes in a poll of twenty million. Some Socialists had evidently voted against their leaders—who tried to recover the lost ground by a sharp reversal of policy and violent denunciation of the Communists. Nevertheless, in the general election on 2 June the Socialists were the principal losers. The Communists gained a little, MRP gained more. As it emerged as the largest party, its leader Georges Bidault succeeded Gouin at the head of the tripartite government. An equally important shift of power was the replacemen of André Philip, the Socialist minister of finance who favoured a controlled economy, by Robert Schuman, on economic matters one of the most conservative members of MRP.

During the referendum campaign General de Gaulle maintained complete silence and did not even vote.[12] But after the election he emerged from his reserve. At Bayeux on 16 June he denounced the working of the regime, attacked the power of the parties, and expounded his own remedy of strong presidential rule—the so-called Bayeux constitution.[13] His open opposition presented a challenge to MRP, which claimed to be the *parti de la fidélité*. But the MRP leaders believed that an unsatisfactory compromise was better than another controversial draft constitution, another rejection by referendum, and another seven months of provisional government. Until a constitution had been adopted there could be neither relief from the paralysing pressure of imminent elections nor hope of upsetting the coalition with the Communists.

MRP therefore accepted the last-minute concessions offered by the chastened Communists and worried Socialists. But to their vast embarrassment General de Gaulle, in another speech at Épinal, denounced the new proposals.[14] The October referendum proved MRP's fears well-founded. The constitution was adopted by a majority of only 9 million against 8 million; a third of the electorate, 8½ million people, did not trouble to vote. Plainly it was accepted not on its merits but as an escape from provisional government.

The Socialist and Communist parties alone had polled on 2 June half a million more votes than were cast in favour of the constitution on 13 October. Yet since June MRP with its 5½ million voters had joined the *OUI* camp. There was therefore a gap of 6 million between the earlier vote for the three parties and the subsequent vote for the constitution they had framed. General de Gaulle had shown his power. But he was not yet ready to re-enter the political arena, and the general election of 10 November again

[12] *L'Année politique* (henceforth cited as *AP*), 1946, p. 161.

[13] Text of the speech in *ibid.*, pp. 534–9; cf. *La France sera la France*, pp. 36, 51, 167.

[14] Extracts in *ibid.*, pp. 16, 44, 169; text in *AP* 1946, p. 245.

gave nearly three-quarters of the seats to the three main parties. MRP lost the half-million votes which they had gained in June, and the Socialist decline continued. The Communists slightly increased their vote, again becoming the strongest party; but their real power diminished, for the Socialist defeat deprived the Marxist parties of their (theoretical) majority. The groups opposed to *tripartisme* adapted their tactics to the electoral system and divided the constituencies between them; this particularly helped RGR (Radicals and allies) who won 70 seats. The Assembly contained 183 Communists, 166 MRP, 103 Socialists, and 74 Conservatives. It lasted until 1951.

Tripartisme was dying. MRP wanted to demonstrate its anti-Communism to the voters who had deserted it in the referendum; the Communists feared to lose their hold on the working class by staying in office. Since neither party would vote for the other's candidate, Thorez and Bidault in turn failed to secure the absolute majority of the Assembly which they needed to be elected prime minister. The immediate problem was solved by the formation on 16 December of a one-party Socialist government under the veteran Léon Blum. The general public was delighted to find a ministry which knew its own mind; the rival parties were less pleased. In January the constitution was officially inaugurated by the election as President of the Republic of Vincent Auriol, who had succeeded Gouin as President of the Assembly a year before. Blum resigned (as was customary on the election of a new President) and the big parties renewed the coalition under another Socialist, Paul Ramadier. The Radical party, after a year in opposition, now returned to office and began its climb back to power; but its influence was as yet small and the Ramadier ministry rested on the alliance of Socialists and MRP.

The Communists were increasingly uneasy partners. They were opposed to the other parties both on domestic issues, especially wages policy, and on colonial questions (Madagascar and Indo-China were both in revolt). In March their deputies—other than ministers—abstained in a vote of confidence on Indo-China, though the party stayed in office in the hope of influencing French policy during the foreign ministers' conference in Moscow. By May France had aligned herself with the West, and a strike at the Renault works warned the Communists that their trade union influence was threatened: the whole party (including ministers) voted against the government on wages policy. The ministers refused to resign, and were dismissed on 5 May 1947, the most important date in the history of the Fourth Republic.

The Republic had won its 'battle of Prague'. It had taken the risk of admitting Communists into the government, but had escaped the fate of most countries which tried that gamble. The Socialists had not been enticed into an alliance controlled by their rivals. The Communists had neither gained control of the key ministries nor penetrated the governmental machine sufficiently to paralyse it. They were not strong enough either to win a free election or to create a revolutionary situation. Their one great asset was their grip on the trade unions; and France had now to be ruled against the opposition of the largest party and the industrial working class.

A month earlier General de Gaulle had re-entered politics. At Strasbourg on 7 April 1947 he appealed to all Frenchmen to rally to his *Rassemblement du peuple français* (RPF), a new non-party movement to reform the constitution, combat the Communist 'separatists' and regenerate national life. His appeal met with a large response in the country. In the autumn RPF extended its activity to Parliament, setting up an 'intergroup' which all deputies (except Communists) were invited to join while still remaining members of their former parties. But Socialists and MRP forbade their members to adhere, so that the new body consisted of old opponents of *tripartisme* reinforced by a few MRP dissidents who preferred the leadership of the General to that of the party. Gaullists and Communists, whose alliance in 1944 had laid the foundations of the Fourth Republic, were now both bent on its destruction.[15]

3. Social Conflicts

The events of 1947 transformed French politics. Domestically, imperially and internationally there were adjustments and reversals of policy (not all for the better). The working of the regime changed completely. Party cohesion declined as soon as it ceased to be indispensable in defence against Communist pressure. Old individualist habits revived and profoundly affected both political behaviour and constitutional practice.

In the autumn of 1947 the creation of the RPF inter-group and the beginning of active Communist opposition opened a new phase of parliamentary life. The problem of the political regime emerged again into the forefront of controversy. There was massive support in the country for both the drastic solutions, 'people's democracy' leading to Communism, and presidential democracy leading perhaps to authoritarian rule from the Right. Their advocates in the Assembly combined in a negative coalition to make all government impossible, hoping afterwards to fight out their own battle over the ruins of the parliamentary republic. Only by the alliance of all the middle parties, loyal to the classic forms of parliamentary rule, could a system of the familiar type be preserved.

Union of the centre groups was indispensable to the regime's survival and perhaps to their own. But even on the constitution itself they disagreed: Socialists and MRP had created the Fourth Republic, Radicals and many Conservatives still preferred the Third. A graver weakness arose from the clash of party ambitions. The middle parties had a common interest in standing together against the oppositions. But this could neither suppress their rivalries nor prevent the weaker Radical and Conservative groups from pressing continually for a larger share in power as their parliamentary bargaining position improved. Nor was this merely a matter of jobs, for the majority was deeply divided on all questions of policy.

The main cause of division was the economic problem: the distribution of the national income and of the burdens and benefits of government expenditure among different social groups. In the post-Liberation inflation, fixed income groups suffered but small businesses flourished, paying their debts and taxes in depreciated francs. The wage- and salary-earner could not escape direct taxation; but the self-employed defrauded the treasury on a massive scale. Peasants, because of their electoral influence, had always paid far less than their share of taxation.[16] Radical and Conservative politicians passionately advocated a free economy—but insisted on guaranteed agricultural prices and government-supported markets.[17] Moreover, wartime and post-war food shortages meant a golden age for the peasantry. In August 1947—the peak year for farm prices—the average town worker was spending almost three-quarters of his wages on food.[18] Since the supply nearly all came from small farmers, rationing was far less effective than in Britain (where half of it entered through the ports). And the Ger-

[15] Lüthy, p. 137.

[16] Wright, Reshaping, p. 254: 19% of national income, 13% of taxes. For other estimates see Pickles, *French Politics,* pp. 247–8; Goguel, *Fourth Republic,* p. 191; Duverger, *Institutions financières,* pp. 130, 154–6, 168–75; Raymond Aron, *Le Grand Schisme,* pp. 220–1; Meynaud, *Groupes de pression en France,* p. 203 and n.; *Statistiques et études financières, Supplément finances françaises,* no. 18, 1953, p. 202, summarized in *Monde,* 6 to 9 June 1953, and by B. de Jouvenel in *Manchester Guardian,* 6 and 7 July 1953; Shoup, no. 199, pp. 341–2.

[17] See for instance Aron, *Schisme,* pp. 215–16; Siegfried in *AP* 1952, p. xi.

[18] Agricultural prices in relation to the general price level reached 121 in 1947 (1913 parity 100). In the thirties and forties they were nearly always over 100, but they dropped below 90 during the fifties: *Paysans,* p. xxv.

man occupation had reinforced and strengthened old habits of obstruction by making resistance and sabotage a national duty.

For a generation before the war, opposition to taxation had prevented France from balancing her budget. Deputies would not risk electoral disaster by voting adequate taxes; governments would not court parliamentary defeat by proposing them. They paid their way by inflation. Between the wars the monetary problem dominated French politics as unemployment dominated British—largely because of the determination of the better-off to evade their share of the national burdens. Frenchmen were always more reluctant to give their money than their blood.

The remark that 'France is a land of excessive taxation, fortunately tempered by fraud' was as true of the Fourth Republic as of the Third. In 1948 the ministry of finance raised £10,000,000 from Parisians owning American cars, three-quarters of whom had been paying no income tax at all. Officials estimated evasion of one tax at 20%, of another at 30 to 50%.[19] Governments had to rely on indirect taxation which fell most heavily on the poor. This increasing burden on those least able to bear it was the main cause of the recurring political crises; and it could never be tackled effectively because of the conflicting electoral interests of the government parties.

In 1945 Mendès-France, as de Gaulle's minister of economic affairs, had urged an austere policy of controlling the economy, reforming the currency and limiting governmental commitments in order to avoid inflation. He was opposed by bankers and businessmen, peasants and profiteers, conservatives and Communists. The General preferred the more comfortable advice of his finance minister, René Pleven; Mendès-France resigned and the inflation promptly followed. As prime minister in 1946, Georges Bidault called a conference of business, peasant and trade union representatives at the Palais Royal; but they merely agreed to support one another's demands for price and wage increases and so gave the inflation a further impetus. In December Léon Blum formed an all-Socialist government which could at last formulate an agreed economic policy; the other parties allowed it to survive for a month. Significantly, a public opinion poll found that 62% thought it the most successful cabinet since the Liberation.[20]

At the root of the long-term economic problem was the technical inadequacy of France's agriculture and small-scale industry. The Monnet Plan was a bold attempt to lay foundations for modernization. But since the necessary investments were financed mainly through the budget (and Marshall Aid) this policy entailed real sacrifices, which provoked stubborn political resistance and persistent efforts to shift the burden. In one form or another the economic problem destroyed most governments in the first seven years of the Fourth Republic.[21] In November 1947 Ramadier was swept out of office by the repercussions of the month's great strikes. Schuman's first ministry was beaten in July 1948 over the military budget, Marie's broke up in August over price policy, Schuman's second fell in September because the Conservatives objected to the appointment of a Socialist minister of finance.

[19] Cars: René Pleven, *rapporteur* of the finance committee, to a committee on fiscal reform (*Figaro*, 9 December 1948); Jules Moch, minister of the interior, to a Socialist conference (*Bulletin intérieur SFIO*, no. 39, February 1949, p. 69). Percentages: *Figaro*, 12–13 August 1950; Edgar Faure, minister of state for the budget, *JO* 23 May 1950, p. 3814, who quoted an estimate of 3–400 milliards (£3–400 million) for loss through fraud. Ehrmann, *Business*, p. 314, puts it 50% higher. Among small businesses investigated in 1950, the fraud rate was 80%: Duverger, *op. cit.*, p. 168. In 1949 even tax-exempt government bonds proved unsaleable as long as purchasers' names were recorded: M. Wolfe, *The French Franc between the Wars* (New York, 1951), p. 21n. (I owe this reference to Dr. D. Goldey.) For some important qualifications see Aron, *Steadfast*, pp. 49–51; and on the whole subject Shoup, no. 199, pp. 325–44.

[20] *Sondages* 1947, p. 38; also Aron, *Schisme*, p. 189.

[21] 'The movement of the *American* wholesale price index seems to mark the rhythm of French politics': Morazé, p. 146 (cf. p. 139; his italics).

Wages policy split Queuille's cabinet in October 1949 and Bidault's in February 1950; the latter was finally defeated in June over civil service pay. Throughout 1951 economic policy was in constant dispute within the successive governments; in January 1952 the second Pleven ministry was beaten when it tried to economize on the railways, in February the Faure cabinet fell when it proposed increased taxes, in December Antoine Pinay was ousted over his proposals to meet the social security deficit, and in May 1953 René Mayer was overthrown on demanding special powers to economize by decree.

Until 1948 prices rose steadily; either wages rose correspondingly, giving a further twist to the inflationary spiral, or wage stabilization led to strikes and a reinforcement of the Communist party. But in 1949 and 1950 the heavy investments of the post-war years at length began to produce results. The national income rose while prices remained stable—until the Korean war destroyed the equilibrium once again. At the same time some post-war governments made a real if insufficient effort to finance their expenditure by taxes instead of inflation: the proportion of the national income taken by the government rose substantially after the war. The ministries of the Fourth Republic lasted no longer than those of the Third, but they did try to tackle problems that their predecessors had shelved.

Gratitude is not a political sentiment. The modernization programme imposed burdens which were fiercely resented by men on the margin, terrified of proletarianization and unable easily to carry extra liabilities. After 1952 the small businessman lost the advantages of inflation; his customers migrated to the booming industrial areas; and stricter checks on fraud made the high nominal rates of taxation seem intolerable. The peasantry were embittered by the fall in agricultural prices which ended their 'golden age'. For these small men in town and country were often poor; they were a burden on the economy because of their excessive numbers, not their undue individual wealth.[22] Many indeed were barely kept alive by 'that barbed-wire entanglement of protective devices which enables the marginal producer to survive without really enjoying it'.[23] Modernization, however indispensable, threatened their cherished (if unreal) economic independence—and an 'inhuman technocracy' added insult to injury by maintaining that their disappearance would benefit themselves and their country. The exasperation and resentment of 'static France' was the political price paid for Monnet's economic miracle.

4. The Lines of Political Division

The economic problem tended to unite the parties which competed for working-class votes, the Socialists and Communists, against those with no working-class following, Radicals and Conservatives. MRP at first stood with the parties of the Right in the hope of retaining the vast mass of conservative support which it had acquired at the Liberation. But the foundation of RPF won away right-wing supporters of MRP, which was thus thrown back on the Catholic trade unions and from 1948 normally aligned itself in economic controversies with the Socialists. A few years later RPF in turn lost these right-wing supporters to the old-fashioned Conservatives, and from 1950 a tendency developed for some Gaullists to seek working-class votes and join with the Left in support of working-class claims.

The economic problem was not the only cause of division between those centre parties whose union alone kept governments in being. Colonial and military questions often produced a similar alignment of forces, with first Socialists and then members of MRP advocating conciliation of Indo-Chinese or North African nationalism, while most Radicals and Conservatives demanded firm government and the maintenance of French rule. On such issues the Gaullists for years

[22] *Statistiques,* pp. 208–9, 215–16, and summaries (see n. 16).
[23] Wright, no. 227, p. 7.

sided with the Right, and within the majority a 'Fourth Force' of Conservatives and Radicals found themselves more often in agreement on policy with the Gaullist opposition than with their 'Third Force' Socialist and MRP partners.

But this simple division into four groups, authoritarian and democratic conservatives, totalitarian and democratic socialists, omits a major historical factor, the clerical question. To most foreign observers the problem of the church schools seemed trivial, but to many Frenchmen education was as vital an issue as it is to American Catholics, or was to Englishmen half a century ago. It symbolized the attempt to mould the nation's life in either a Catholic or a secular spirit. And even the least ideologically-minded politician knew that in some regions *laïcité* was still the real electoral dividing line.[24]

This cleavage cut right across the social and political divisions, splitting the 'Fourth Force' as well as (though less deeply than) the Third, and uniting most Radicals and all Socialists with the Communists in a common hostility to the claims pressed alike by Conservatives, MRP and RPF. This was the weapon used by the Communists in 1945 to keep Socialists and MRP apart. It split the first Schuman government in 1948, led the Socialists to ally with Radicals instead of MRP in the subsequent local and senatorial elections, and so provoked bitterness which gravely weakened the majority up to the 1951 election. It was by exploiting the church schools question in the new Parliament that RPF alienated the Socialists from their former partners and finally broke the old majority.

Since politics turned on several different conflicts instead of one, there was a coherent majority neither in the country for a single party nor in Parliament for a lasting coalition. Associates on one issue were bitter opponents on others. MRP for example worked with Socialists, Radicals and most Conservatives in defending the regime against Communists and Gaullists. On matters involving working-class interests and sometimes on colonial questions it sympathized with the Socialists and Communists; Radicals, Conservatives and (until 1951) RPF were hostile to its views. But over church schools MRP found its friends (or competitors) among Gaullists and Conservatives, while all Socialists and most Radicals joined the Communists against it. And on Europe it agreed with most Conservatives and Socialists and opposed Communists and RPF, with the Radicals split. So complicated a situation put a high premium on the arts of manœuvre and facilitated other, temporary combinations. Electoral tactics united MRP with the Communists against all the other parties in defence of proportional representation; Socialists and RPF often held very similar views on the problem of Germany.

Most of the peculiarities of French government were thus caused by the country's history. The battle against the Church and the struggle for political freedom were still political issues in the middle of the twentieth century, and they split public opinion on lines different from those imposed by the contemporary social and economic conflict. This persistence of several major political dividing lines was the basic cause of the instability of government, as the bitterness of the conflicts and the recent memories of power abused were the fundamental reasons for its weakness. Strong organizations like the Labour or Conservative parties, each seeking to form a (fairly) homogeneous government to put into practice a (fairly) coherent policy, were impossible in France. The young and dynamic on each side, impatient with the compromise and weakness of coalition government, were consequently tempted into extremist organizations which alarmed more prudent sympathizers and enraged opponents. The democratic parties could not compete effectively because they were at loggerheads over the clerical ques-

[24] It was the only political problem on which voters' views corresponded closely with their party sympathies: Converse and Dupeux, no. 59, p. 19.

tion, which lay between Socialists and MRP, preventing the development of a Labour party, and between Radicals and Conservatives, weakening still further the rudimentary links between the political representatives of the bourgeoisie. No French party could hope to attract a majority of voters or deputies. No French government could be based on a single party which put its policy into practice and then submitted it to the judgment of the electorate. Every ministry was a coalition. Responsibilities were never clearly apportioned; the government parties devoted as much energy to mutual recrimination as to fighting the opposition. The clash of political principles became obscured in the complexity of parliamentary manœvring. The public grew apathetic and cynical; divided ministries, lacking effective support in the country, were too weak to impose necessary sacrifices on any powerful private interest or organized social group. But these undoubted evils had causes deeper than the structure of political institutions, and changing that framework has not done much to cure them.

FIFTY-THREE

THE DRIVE FOR INDEPENDENCE IN AFRICA

One of the most spectacular phenomena on the world scene in the years after 1945 was the rapid and widespread movement for independence among the various African colonies. Here was imperialism in reverse, operating much more rapidly than the original imperial conquests in the generation after 1870. Turmoil and inner conflict accompanied the sudden and successful rise of African nationalism, particularly because it threatened not only ancient tribal groups but also racial minorities of white and Asian settlers. The outcome, of course, remains impossible to predict. But it is certain that after 1945 Africa had a larger part in world affairs than it had before. In her book Independence for Africa *Gwendolen M. Carter traces the rise of nationalism in Africa and analyzes some of its immediate causes and immediate effects.*

GWENDOLEN M. CARTER

INDEPENDENCE FOR AFRICA *

From Cape Town to Tunis, from Dakar to Mombasa, Africans are talking about independence. The word means different things in different places. In West Africa, it means the end of colonial control and the establishment of internal and external sovereignty. In North Africa, the connotation is much the same. In East Africa, Africans demand responsible government, which they interpret as a majority of Africans in the legislative and executive bodies; they also plan a foreseeable end to colonial responsibilities and control. In South Africa, when Africans mention the word "independence," it still implies little more than self-respect, equality before the law, the opportunity for them to organize freely in trade unions and political parties, and the opportunity to change their existing conditions. But wherever one is in Africa, political power and self-determination are the ultimate objective, however impossible they may seem in those areas of the continent where white control is firmly established. "What else," ask Africans, "can bring us the opportunity for self-expression and self-development?"

Throughout the continent the desire for self-government and independence is associated with universal franchise. This is not surprising, since the one thing that Africans have more of than anyone else is numbers. Universal franchise would mean African control in every territory within the conti-

* From *Independence for Africa,* pp. 3–11, by Gwendolen M. Carter. Reprinted by permission of Frederick A. Praeger, Inc., and of Thames and Hudson Ltd. Copyright 1960.

nent. This is why the slogan is the watchword of all African nationalist movements and why it is viewed with such mistrust by most white, or even Asian, minorities.

It is easy to say, as those of us in the West are apt to do, that universal suffrage is no answer to the major problems of Africa. Universal franchise can bring African leaders into power; it cannot keep them responsible to those who have voted for them. Neither can it bring about the economic development which all African countries need and desire so greatly. It cannot provide the technicians to run the secondary or extractive industries on which ultimate prosperity might be based. It cannot produce the schools or the teachers which are so greatly needed. Universal franchise is a means to power. It can neither control the way in which power is used nor create the skills and experience which underdeveloped countries need so sorely.

Yet it is understandable why universal suffrage, majority rule, and legislative omnipotence have a vast appeal to African leaders and to their people. As against colonial officials with their superior training and broad experience, African leaders who are selected by the suffrage of their people can claim to have a far deeper understanding of what those people really want. These African leaders can also argue with great effectiveness that when elections have brought them to power, they will be followed with sacrifice and unremitting effort by those who have placed them where they are. All the arguments which underpin democracy in the Western world can be used by African leaders to counter those of white residents or white colonial administrators whose skill, training, and demonstrated achievement might otherwise seem an adequate basis for retaining ultimate control.

In West Africa, North Africa, and much of Central Africa, the old argument between "good government" and "self-government" is being worked out empirically. That there are dangers involved in independence is beyond dispute. The difficulties which Guinea encountered with the sudden withdrawal of French administrators and advisors have not been without effect on other French West African countries. The way in which Ghana has dealt with the opposition has given pause to canny statesmen in Nigeria. Yet the progress to independence in these areas is hardly slowed down by the problems which may come in its wake. As a former British colonial official once said, "It's no use telling a wave on the edge of Niagara Falls: 'Wait a bit, old chap. It's a hell of a long drop.' "

In some parts of Africa, however, immediate independence is not the objective of African leaders. This is because they realize that the lack of political influence by Africans in the Union of South Africa arises from the fact that, when that country received independence in 1910 as a member of the British Commonwealth of Nations, all political authority was vested in its white minority and has remained so ever since. Thus, any significant political advance for Africans in this situation can result only from a deliberate limitation by the white residents on their own political power, or from extra-constitutional pressures by the Africans, or from international sources. None of these possibilities has yet been effective within South Africa, since the forces against change have so far proved stronger than those working for it.

With the South African situation in mind, Africans within the Federation of Rhodesia and Nyasaland have resisted the granting of independence to that entity for fear that it would mean riveting on them the control of the white minority in Southern and Northern Rhodesia. Should African political advance go ahead quickly in Northern Rhodesia and Nyasaland, the Federation might in time become a genuine racial partnership, exerting a healthy influence on South Africa itself. But it is still uncertain that the Federation can be retained intact. All too few African leaders yet see the potential promise within the situation for their people's advancing influence. From the other side, the whites of Southern Rhodesia, who have long possessed self-government within their own area, might pull their territory out of the Federation if African advancement appeared to threaten their position. The assurance of adequate political power is therefore the primary objective, and independence is feared or welcomed according to how the balance is established.

To establish satisfactory working relations between resident whites and Africans is thus the key in the multiracial territories to major African political influence, if not control. All the more significant, therefore, is the assurance of the 1960 constitutional conference of ultimate African paramountcy in Kenya, an area within which its white residents have long exercised a major political influence. Unlike the Rhodesias, the issue in Kenya is no longer the ultimate balance of power but the adjustments to be made on the way to independence. These can only be made satisfactorily if whites as well as Africans think of themselves and act as Kenyans rather than as members of a particular racial group.

So sudden and so rapid has been the drive for independence in Africa that one may well ask whence it came. Between World War I and World War II, Africans were scarcely articulate. It is true that before World War II there were self-conscious political leaders like Nnamdi Azikiwe (commonly known as Zik) of Nigeria; that the Pan-African movement, though centered outside the African continent, was already talking in terms of independence for African countries; that the British territories had representative institutions which included a few—largely nominated—Africans; that occasionally, as in the Gold Coast in regard to government-enforced cutting out of cocoa trees affected by disease, there were popular outbursts which showed the power of concentrated effort by Africans; that, even in the Union of South Africa, there were strikes by Africans before the end of World War I, although these failed in their objectives and led to increasingly severe restrictions on African labor organization. But quiescence rather than change was then the keynote.

It was during World War II, and more particularly afterward, that the drive for independence got under way. Africans from South Africa and Rhodesia were attached to the fighting forces in North Africa; Africans from Kenya went to Burma; Africans from French West Africa were in France during the onslaught by the Nazi panzer divisions, learning at first hand of France's capitulation. Africans who had been roused by the Italian attack on Ethiopia in 1936 gained a new perspective on the supposed invincibility of white people when they watched rival white armies attack and counterattack each other. Moreover, these Africans underwent new experiences which they inevitably transmitted to their own areas on their return.

Moreover, the American criticisms of colonialism during and after the war, and sharp Soviet attacks on continued colonial control of underdeveloped areas, helped to stimulate the African desire for change. Still more effective were the examples of Asian countries which acquired independence at the end of World War II. Whether it was India, Pakistan, and Ceylon graduating into the Commonwealth of Nations with numbers that transformed it into a multiracial association no longer predominantly "British" in composition, or whether it was the elimination of the Dutch from Indonesia, the fall of colonialism in Asia had a far-reaching impact on the last great area of colonial control: Africa.

The leaders who have powered the recent drive to independence in Africa were for the most part trained abroad. Kwame Nkrumah and Nnamdi Azikiwe were educated both in England and the United States. Léopold Senghor, Félix Houphouet-Boigny, and Sékou Touré secured their professional training in Paris. Tom Mboya and

Julius Nyerere of Tanganyika added English to East African training. The nationalist leaders of South Africa and Southern Rhodesia went predominantly to Fort Hare in the eastern Cape Province of South Africa or to Makerere College in Uganda; at both they received a liberal slant from teachers who had been trained abroad. Only in the Belgian and Portuguese territories and in French Equatorial Africa have there been few leaders with the experience of outside institutions or of centers of higher education which were directed by those who themselves maintained the liberal tradition of the West. It is not surprising to find nationalism less strong in these latter territories and that their handling of self-government—when it arrives—is less successful than in those territories where the educational training of African leaders has been more soundly based.

In an area like Africa, which is emerging into self-government and independence so late and so quickly, not only leadership but also organization has a great effect. Where a nationalist movement secures general support throughout the country before tribalism can be organized to restrain it (as did that of Nkrumah in Ghana or of Nyerere in Tanganyika), its success tends to be assured. The same was true in Guinea where Sékou Touré annihilated any remaining independent power of the chiefs before making his break with France and thereby ensured the control of his political party and trade union organization, unchallenged by sectional rivalries. In other areas, such as the Ivory Coast, where Houphouet-Boigny's political control seems without question because his political party controls all the seats of the legislature, there are sharp ethnic rivalries which have not yet been bridged. These ethnic rivalries and jealousies have already had their impact in driving out "foreign Africans" from the Ivory Coast, despite their contribution to its economic well-being; and these rivalries still complicate the working of its political party machine.

Where nationalist movements scarcely existed, as in the Belgian Congo or French Equatorial Africa, the effect of political representation has been very different. In such areas, political organization often follows tribal lines, and the extension of representation stimulates or even awakens tribal rivalries long dulled or even forgotten. Hence, in the French Congo and in parts of the Belgian Congo and Ruanda-Urundi, sharp, brutal, and bloody conflicts have occurred between rival tribal entities. Sometimes, as in the French Congo, the extension of political representation has given rise to tribal groupings of whose existence even skilled anthropologists had been unaware. Thus, it appears that political representation does not of itself create a spirit of nationalism but may well intensify ethnic separatism.

It is true that when political representation was finally extended to Africans in Kenya, a successful effort was made to establish a transtribal leadership largely through the efforts of Tom Mboya, himself a Luo, and Gikonyo Kiano, an American-educated Kikuyu. Despite this skillful leadership, however, the Kenya African nationalist movement has not been able to avoid divisions which flared dangerously in the latter part of 1959 and which were still evident in mid-1960 despite the temporary united front established at the constitutional conference in January-February, 1960.

In Nigeria, with more than half the population of West Africa (which in itself encompasses approximately the same area as the United States), tribalism and nationalism act as counterbalances to each other. Zik, with his NCNC (National Council of Nigeria and the Cameroons), powered the first nationalist movement in the country. He retains his concern for the unity of Nigeria, even though his own movement is centered around the ubiquitous Ibo, of whom most still remain in the Eastern Region. Chief Awolowo's Action Group, which developed out of a Yoruba cultural association in Western Nigeria, has also transcended its tribal limitations by campaigning vigorously for the support of minorities in other parts of the country. While the Northern Peoples' Congress still concentrates on the northern section of Nigeria, which includes more than half the country's population, the national leadership provided by Alhaji Sir Abubakar Tafewa Balewa is evidence that one of its shrewdest leaders is well aware of the importance of national thinking. It is still possible that the three sections of Nigeria might break apart if rivalries between its three major parties become too strong. It is more likely, however, that the fact of divisions within their own sections, coupled with the need to seek support from other areas than their own, will continue the balance between tribal and national forces within Nigeria which could make it the most stable of all the new countries of Africa.

At the beginning of World War II, there were only three independent countries on the continent of Africa: the Union of South Africa at its southernmost tip; Liberia, founded in 1847 as a home for released slaves and still struggling for survival as a separate entity; and Egypt, more a part of the Middle East than of Africa. By 1957, these countries had been joined by once-independent Ethiopia and Libya, both under Italian control ten years before, and by Morocco and Tunisia, which had established a new relationship with France that enabled them to become independent members of the United Nations. The Sudan had been granted independence by Great Britain in 1956. In 1957, Ghana (formerly the Gold Coast) became the first Negro African state to attain independence from colonial control. Since then, the progression has been rapid. In 1958, Guinea voted *"Non"* on the constitution of the Fifth French Republic and thus summarily broke its ties with France. In 1960, the Federation of Nigeria, Cameroun (formerly the French Cameroons), Somalia, Togoland, the Belgian Congo, the Malagasy Republic (formerly Madagascar), and the Federation of Mali (combining Senegal and Soudan), join the ranks of independent countries. Moreover, recent developments within the Franco-African Community have resulted in other French territories being acknowledged as independent, just as Mali and Malagasy have been, without impairing their association with France in the *Communauté*. Another seven or eight new African states will become independent after 1960. The drive for independence is under way, and nothing seems likely to stop it north of the areas of tight white control.

Americans have commonly thought of independence as a good thing in itself. They have been somewhat disillusioned by developments among certain Latin American states, but this has scarcely impaired their faith that people know best what is best for them. As the number of independent states in the United Nations goes up with extraordinary rapidity (ultimately there may be thirty-four African members, or about one-third of the total membership), they begin to realize some of the problems involved in this breakneck race toward what is still called "freedom." Yet it is far too late now to interfere, even if the West had ever wished to do so.

Before our eyes is taking place one of the great movements of history. In African hands lie the most significant decisions for their continent. Some of the great strains and difficulties to which their countries are subject are illustrated in the following pages. No one can say for sure what the outcome will be. What is sure, however, is that the interest, understanding, and help of Western peoples can be powerful factors in giving Africans the chance to achieve their goals.

FIFTY-FOUR

COMMUNISM IN CHINA

The Communist Party of China seized power in 1949. A number of circumstances contributed to this momentous change. The fall of the Chinese Empire in 1911, the failure of the Chinese Republic, and the devastation caused by Japan's undeclared war (the so-called China Incident) of 1937–45 created tremendous havoc and disillusion. The corrupt Nationalist Chinese regime could not solve China's gigantic problems. Consequently many Chinese leaders, with varying degrees of idealism and opportunism, turned to Marxism and supported a Communist regime patterned, with significant variations, after that of Soviet Russia. Marxism resembled the Confucian system in one important respect. Both the new Communist rulers and the Confucian scholar-administrators demanded full and unchallenged authority and professed to have absolute knowledge of human affairs. In this respect Chinese Communism harmonized with the ancient Chinese way of life and thought. But in other respects Marxism was an alien import from the West. The Communist leaders demanded and obtained, often by ruthless methods, the respect and obedience formerly accorded to the Confucian administrators. The new party leaders, often with only a superficial education, used the prestige of their predecessors, so that both the form and spirit of the old Chinese examination system for civil servants disappeared. In some degree, the message of Marxism transformed Chinese political aspirations from the backward-looking stability of the Confucian state to forward-looking Communism, which preached the necessity for basic and continuing changes in Chinese life. In other respects, Communism has evoked widespread and violent protest from Chinese intellectuals, as evidenced by their bitter criticisms during the Hundred Flowers Campaign of 1957 when for a few weeks they were allowed freedom of speech. In his book Revolution in China, *Charles P. Fitzgerald examines the impact of Communism on the Chinese people and notes the ways in which Marxism both resembles and differs from older Chinese traditions.*

CHARLES P. FITZGERALD

REVOLUTION IN CHINA *

'Those who do not occupy the seats of authority should not concern themselves with the government.' This succinct expression of the non-democratic outlook is an old

* From *Revolution in China,* pp. 143–49, by Charles P. Fitzgerald. Reprinted by permission of Frederick A. Praeger, Inc., and of Cresset Press Ltd. Copyright 1952.

proverbial Chinese saying. It embodies the characteristic authoritarian point of view, the theory upon which the Confucian Empire was governed. The *chün tzu,* the 'aristocratic man', or as some translators have put it, the 'superior man', reserved to himself the functions of administration and the full exercise of political power. As servant of his prince, who in turned ruled by virtue of the Mandate of Heaven, the superior man was educated and trained to govern. No other occupation was worthy of his special talents, no other class was entitled to share his burden or participate in his privilege.

The Empire was overthrown by the republican revolution; the ideals of democracy were introduced to China, misused, abused and cast aside. The Communists triumphed in the civil war, and set up their regime. On that occasion they published a pamphlet giving relevant documents concerning the foundation of the Communist State, and among these, acting as a commentary upon the provisional constitution, is the speech which Mao Tse-tung delivered on the twenty-eighth anniversary of the Chinese Communist Party. Mao in his speech answers his opponents, first fairly stating the criticism which non-Communists made of his party and policy.

> 'You are autocratic' (say the critics). 'My dear gentlemen, you speak truth; we are indeed; . . . having been called upon to put into effect the authority of the People's Democracy, which is the dictatorship of People's Democracy, we shall deprive the reactionary party of the right to speak and only allow that right to the people.' [1]

Once more the superior man is in high honour, and once more his critics may not criticize, since they may not occupy the seats of authority. But the modern superior men are not Confucian scholars, they are 'the people'. This term, however, is neither vague nor all embracing. Those who are to have the right to speak and govern are very clearly defined. Mao Tse-tung does not allow his hearers to go away with any illusions, for orthodoxy is once more enthroned, and doctrine must be plainly proclaimed.

'Who are the people?' says Mao, and answers: 'In China, and in present circumstances, the people are the working class, the peasant class, the small capitalists and the national capitalists. These classes, under the leadership of the working class and the Communist Party, have united and risen to set up their own State, and chosen their own Government which will exercise authority, autocratic authority, even oppression, upon the running dogs of imperialism, the landlord class, the bureaucratic capitalists and the reactionary party of the Kuomintang which represents these classes. We shall not allow them to speak or act wildly; we shall keep them under strict control.' [2]

The comparison between the proverbial expression of the power and authority of the old Empire and the specific claims to similar authority made for the new Communist Republic reveals both the basic similarity of the two systems and their more superficial differences. The Empire was old, long established, universal (in Chinese eyes) and assured. It was not necessary to specify the nature of its enemies. It was the accepted government of the Chinese world. Opponents must either be barbarians who had not yet understood the benefits of civilization, such as the northern nomads, or criminals who sought to overthrow authority in order to enrich themselves. No 'class' of enemies was recognized because it was assumed that every honest and civilized person would naturally accept the rule of civilization, which was that of the Emperor.

The Communists live in a wider world, and in a post-revolutionary age. They cannot yet assume that their system and their regime will be accepted as inevitable, natural and

[1] *The Chinese People's Republic. Documents upon the foundation of the State.* Speech of Mao Tse-tung on July 1, 1949; 'On the dictatorship of People's Democracy'.

[2] *op. cit.*

right. They must still preach their doctrines, repress their enemies, and stigmatize them with opprobrious names so that all may know who are the enemies of the 'people'. But if allowance is made for these temporary expedients of propaganda, it is clear enough that to the Communists, as to the Confucians, there is one truth, one doctrine and one class. This truth alone may be published; this doctrine alone must be the basis of all instruction, and this class alone is entitled to govern.

The new doctrine is of course expressed in terminology which is alien to China. The words of Mao are the language which Stalin uses and which Lenin taught. The Chinese Communist leader recognizes and proclaims this fact. It is made very clear to all that Marxism is not Chinese, but universal, that Lenin is the prophet, and that Lenin was a Russian. The Russian Revolution is the starting-point of the new world, the message of Lenin and Marx came to enlighten the darkness of the Chinese and show them the way out of their troubles. Mao answers his critics who accuse him of inclining to the side of Russia, by openly proclaiming that he does so, must and will do so, because it is from Russia that Communism has come to China, and therefore Russia is the only true friend. Confucianism was a Chinese doctrine, evolved in China to fit Chinese conditions. Marxism is universal, with a strong Russian colouring, and it is not at first sight apparent that it will fit China or Chinese conditions.

When the dogmas of Marx are applied to China it is necessary to make some unadmitted compromises. 'In China and in present circumstances,' Mao is careful to say, and thus tacitly admits that in China and under present circumstances things are not what they were in Russia, or in Western Europe in the time of Marx. The working class, as understood by Europeans, is very small, and very little representative of the nation. So intellectuals, 'brain workers', must be admitted to be workers, and can claim the rights of the sacred working class. This enables the Communist Party to recruit students and literates, essential to the workings of government and to the spread of education and propaganda, but in fact very far from 'working class' in origin.

The peasants, who in Russia proved obdurate opponents of the Communist regime, are the real foundation and chief support of the Chinese Communist Party. So they, in alliance with the 'working class' which means in practice with the intellectuals, are to be among the elite. This again is strange Marxism. But 'in China, and under present circumstances', it is very good sense and wise policy. Still stranger, among the ingredients of the people, the all-wise and virtuous people, are small capitalists and even 'national capitalists'. It is true that these classes are not quite admitted to equality. They are not fit to occupy posts of real authority nor take direction of the Revolution. Mao explains why: these classes, though necessary at present because China's industrialization is still so slight and her economy so backward, are unfitted for executive power, because, rooted in their capitalist rank in society, they lack the qualities of courage, foresight and enterprise which only 'working class' Communists can possess. Then he makes a naïve admission: 'Moreover many of them fear the masses.' In other words they do not believe in Communism.

Here, too, one of the principal differences between the new orthodoxy and the old is revealed. The Confucian system was stabilized and admitted no need of change. It looked backward, in fact, rather than forward. The rule of the sage kings of the remote past was the ideal and all modern government at best an imitation of that ancient model, at worst a degeneration from it. The Communists on the contrary preach change. The present circumstances are but a passing phase. New democracy must be transformed into Socialism and then into Communism, and far off, in the future, lies the true golden age, the classless society, when the party itself and all the organs of the State must perish and give way to 'the higher form of human society'. It is this Messianic quality, this striving towards a distant goal, that mainly differentiates Communist totalitarianism from its Chinese predecessor, the Confucian Empire.

It may well be that therein lies the greatest contribution which contact with Western Europe has brought to China, the reversal of the ancient backward-looking philosophy, which made stability its aim, and the institution of an outlook which sees change as a good, and conceives its ideal as lying in the far-off future. It is certainly not the form which the Western teachers and missionaries expected to see triumph in China. Neither the religion nor the political system of the West could find a secure lodging-place in the Chinese mind, but the idea of progress, of advance towards a new society, thought of in terms of perfection, this very Western idea has taken root in China and become the inspiration of the new regime.

It is often argued in the West that the Communist doctrine of a future classless society, when the power of the State will wither away, is unreal, a mere form of words to cover the actual establishment of a police State. It is always possible that this doctrine, like that of the millennium which it so closely resembles, will be honoured in words and never realized in practice. But it would be probably as inaccurate to suppose that the Communists of the present age are insincere in their profession as to think that the early Christians did not really believe the second coming to be imminent. Whatever may be the present state of belief in Russia, it is obvious to any observer that in China the Communist doctrine has established itself as a religion, and that a great part of its success is the appeal which it makes to men of religious temperament.

The reasons why Communism, as interpreted by Mao Tse-tung, is more successful than was Christianity, even as interpreted by Hung Hsiu-ch'uan, the Heavenly King of the T'ai P'ings, are worth consideration. Under the Empire, in the old Chinese society, there was no institution which ministered to the psychological needs of those who are by nature inclined to rate future bliss more highly than present comfort. The Confucian ideology preached obedience to the ideal of the distant past; Buddhism promised Nirvana to the individual, but saw the world as 'illusion' and as evil. To the former society was degenerate, to the latter irremediable. The Chinese who saw the evils of society, hoped to cure them and planned for a brighter future for posterity got no encouragement from either of the prevailing ideologies. This gave Christianity its opportunity, but it failed because with the Christian doctrine went other things incompatible with Chinese traditions and habits of thought.

The educated classes in China had grown accustomed for many centuries to deride belief in the supernatural as unsophisticated and crude. They could not accept the Christian dogmas, and at the same time were disappointed at the Christian indifference to the world. The world for the Chinese has always mattered more than heaven. It has always been what to do about the government of mankind rather than what to do about the individual soul which has seemed to them important and urgent. To the very many and increasing numbers of Chinese who saw that the world was falling to pieces and that Confucian orthodoxy had no remedy for the catastrophe and no plan for the future, it became necessary to find a doctrine which should speak with the tone of authority and conviction that the Chinese expect from orthodoxy, which should prescribe positive measures for putting the world to rights, and which should not base itself and its claims upon supernatural sanctions and beliefs which the Chinese educated class could not share.

These conditions have been fulfilled by Mao Tse-tung's Communism. The new religion proclaims its own infallibility and the perverse wickedness of its opponents. It makes no pretence of democracy or free will, it does not permit any other view to share its power or dispute with its authority. It announces a programme, taking many years to achieve, which promises a steady improvement in the condition of human life, ending in a paradise: and this paradise will exist here on earth, not in some imagined heaven. This programme is not dependent on the favour of gods but on the efforts of men, and above all on the guidance of the elect, the Communist Party, the incarnation of the leadership of the working class, the most vital element in human society.

This doctrine seems unsatisfying to most Westerners. The ideal of an earthly paradise in the remote future, which will never be seen by those now living, but only enjoyed by posterity, seems unattractive to men who have been brought up to appreciate individualism and the value of the human personality. Many Europeans will not welcome the promised independence from divine protection, even if they could believe that God did not in fact inspire the universe. To most Europeans the suggestion that one group of citizens, because of the nature of their occupation, and irrespective of their moral qualities, are alone entitled to assume leadership and political power is a contradiction of historical experience and a most undesirable ideal. Whether the ruling group are to be workers or landed gentry, the West would not in modern times accept the concept of divine right, and regards any such doctrine as a reversion to more primitive forms of social organization.

It is therefore difficult for the West to believe that the Chinese people can have voluntarily accepted Communism. It is hard to credit the free support given to a regime which denies freedom to some and only hands out a very qualified form to others. And yet there is no real doubt that the new system has obtained the support of the people, has satisfied the aspiration of the literates, and has won to itself the devotion of the men of religious temperament. The Communists in China are dedicated men, selfless and sincere, blind to any criticism of their belief, narrow and devout, hard working, incorruptible and self-assured. They have learned a doctrine and understood its teaching; they practise its virtues, they have no conception that it can have defects. They are fanatics.

FIFTY-FIVE

THE EXPLORATION OF SPACE

It is a truism that historical perspective must diminish as one comes closer to the present. Observers of contemporary events tend to see them "flat," that is, without the extra dimension of elapsed time. Consequently it is all but impossible to find historical significance in contemporary phenomena, if only because, lacking knowledge of the future, no one can know the consequences of a present force or situation. So it is with the exploration of space. This exhilarating development, long forecast by writers of science fiction, had a tentative start with the V-1 and V-2 rockets of World War II and a positive start when Russia launched Sputnik I on October 4, 1957. Where it may lead no one now alive can tell. In a book on space travel published six years before Sputnik I, Arthur C. Clarke speculated on the means, motivation, and possible results of exploring space. Like other scientists of the present, he dreads the prospect of nuclear war. But in the last chapter of his book he sets his dread aside to contemplate the range and depth of creativity that is possible in the conquest of outer space. His book ends with a heart-warming speculation on what a historian of the year 3000 might write about the twentieth century, when humanity left the earth and freed itself from the prison of its planetary existence.

ARTHUR C. CLARKE

THE EXPLORATION OF SPACE *

Even its most enthusiastic supporters do not deny that the conquest of space is going to be a very difficult, dangerous and expensive task. The difficulties must not, however, be exaggerated, for the steadily rising tide of technical knowledge has a way of obliterating obstacles so effectively that what seemed impossible to one generation becomes elementary to the next. Once again the history of aeronautics provides a useful parallel. If the Wright brothers had ever sat down and considered just what would be needed to run a world air-transport system, they would have been appalled at the total requirements—despite the fact that these could not have included all the radio and radar aids which were undreamed of fifty years ago. Yet all these things—and the vast new industries and the armies of technicans that lie behind them—have now become so

* From *The Exploration of Space,* pp. 184–95, by Arthur C. Clarke. Copyright 1951 by Arthur Charles Clarke. Reprinted by permission of Harper & Row, Publishers. Published in England by Temple Press Books Limited.

much a part of our lives that we scarcely ever realise their presence.

The enterprise and skill and resolution that have made our modern world will be sufficient to achieve all that has been described in this book, as well as much that still lies beyond the reach of any imagination today. Given a sufficiently powerful motive, there seems no limit to what the human race can do: history is full of examples, from the Pyramids to the Manhattan Project,[1] of achievements whose difficulty and magnitude were so great that very few people would have considered them possible.

The important factor is, of course, the motive. The Pyramids were built through the power of religion: the Manhattan Project under the pressure of war. What will be the motives which will drive men out into space, and send them to worlds most of which are so fiercely hostile to human life?

It is possible, as we have already seen, to list many excellent practical reasons why mankind ought to conquer space, and the release of atomic power has added a new urgency to some of these. Moreover, the physical resources of our planet are limited: sooner or later sheer necessity would have forced men to travel to the other planets. It may well be a very long time before it is easier—to take an obvious example—to obtain uranium from the Moon than from the Earth, but eventually that time is bound to come.

The suggestion has sometimes been made that the increasing pressure of population may also bring about the conquest of the planets. There might be something in this argument if the other planets could be colonised as they stand, but we have seen that the reverse is the case. For a long time to come, it is obvious that, if sheer *lebensraum* is what is needed, it would be much simpler and more profitable to exploit the undeveloped regions of this Earth. It would be far easier to make the Antarctic bloom like the rose than to establish large, self-supporting colonies on such worlds as Mars, Ganymede or Titan. Yet one day the waste places of our world will be brought to life, and when this happens astronautics will have played a major rôle in the achievement, through the orbital weather stations and, perhaps, direct climatic control by the use of "space-mirrors". When this has happened—indeed, long before—men will be looking hungrily at the planets, and their large-scale development will have begun.

[1] The project which produced the material for the first atomic bomb.

Whether the population of the rest of the Solar System becomes ten million or ten thousand million is not, fundamentally, what is important. There are already far too many people on *this* planet, by whatever standards one judges the matter. It would be no cause for boasting if, after some centuries of prodigious technical achievement, we enabled ten times the present human population to exist on a dozen worlds.

Only little minds are impressed by size and number. The importance of planetary colonisation will lie in the variety and diversity of cultures which it will make possible—cultures as different in some respects as those of the Esquimos and the Pacific islanders. They will, of course, have one thing in common, for they will all be based on a very advanced technology. Yet though the interior of a colony on Pluto might be just like that of one on Mercury, the different external environments would inevitably shape the minds and outlooks of the inhabitants. It will be fascinating to see what effects this will have on human character, thought and artistic creativeness.

These things are the great imponderables of astronautics: in the long run they may be of far more importance than its purely material benefits, considerable though these will undoubtedly be. This has proved true in the past of many great scientific achievements. Copernican astronomy, Darwin's theory of evolution, Freudian psychology—the effect of these on human thought far outweighed their immediate practical results.

We may expect the same of astronautics. With the expansion of the world's mental horizons may come one of the greatest outbursts of creative activity ever known. The parallel with the Renaissance, with its great flowering of the arts and sciences, is very suggestive. "In human records", wrote the anthropologist J. D. Unwin, "there is no trace of any display of productive energy which has not been preceded by a display of expansive energy. Although the two kinds of energy must be carefully distinguished, in the past they have been . . . united in the sense that one has developed out of the other." Unwin continues with this quotation from Sir James Frazer: "Intellectual progress, which reveals itself in the growth of art and science . . . receives an immense impetus from conquest and empire." Interplanetary travel is now the only form of "conquest and empire" compatible with civilisation. Without it, the human mind, compelled to circle for ever in its planetary goldfish-bowl, must eventually stagnate.

It has often been said—and though it is becoming platitudinous it is none the less true—that only through space-flight can mankind find a permanent outlet for its aggressive and pioneering instincts. The desire to reach the planets is only an extension of the desire to see what is over the next hill, or

> Beyond that last blue mountain barred with snow
> Across that angry or that glittering sea.

Perhaps one day men will no longer be interested in the unknown, no longer tantalised by mystery. This is possible, but when Man loses his curiosity one feels he will have lost most of the other things that make him human. The long literary tradition of the space-travel story shows how deeply this idea is rooted in Man's nature: if there were not a single good "scientific" reason for going to the planets, he would still want to go there, just the same.

In fact, as we have seen, the advent of space-travel will produce an expansion of scientific knowledge perhaps unparalleled in history. Now there are a good many people who think that we have already learned more than enough about the Universe in which we live. There are others (including perhaps most scientists) who adopt the non-committal viewpoint that knowledge is neither good nor bad and that these adjectives are only applicable to its uses.

Yet knowledge surely is always desirable, and in that sense good: only insufficient knowledge—or ignorance—can be bad. And worst of all is to be ignorant of one's ignorance. We all know the narrow, limited type of mind which is interested in nothing beyond its town or village, and bases its judgments on these parochial standards. We are slowly—perhaps too slowly—evolving from that mentality towards a world outlook. Few things will do more to accelerate that evolution than the conquest of space. It is not easy to see how the more extreme forms of nationalism can long survive when men have seen the Earth in its true perspective as a single small globe against the stars.

There is, of course, the possibility that as soon as space is crossed all the great powers will join in a race to claim as much territory as their ships can reach. Some American writers have even suggested, more or less seriously, that for its own protection the United States must occupy the Moon to prevent it being used as a launching site for atomic rockets.

This argument (which reflects so faithfully the political paranoia of our times) fortunately does not bear serious examination. The problem of supply—often difficult enough in *terrestrial* military affairs!—would be so enormous as to cancel any strategic advantages the Moon might have. If one wants to send an atomic bomb from A to B, both on the Earth's surface, then taking it to the Moon first would be an extremely inefficient procedure. Moreover, a lunar-launched missile could be detected a good deal more easily than one aimed from the other side of the Earth. A satellite in an orbit a few thousand miles high would seem to possess all the military advantages of the Moon, and none of its disadvantages. It would also be very difficult to locate, if it were covered with light and radar-absorbing paint.

It is one of the tragic ironies of our age that the rocket, which could have been the symbol of humanity's aspirations for the stars, has become one of the weapons threatening to destroy civilisation. This state of affairs has presented a difficult moral problem to those wishing to take an active part in the development of astronautics, for almost all research on rockets is now carried out by military establishments and is covered by various security classifications. The technical problems involved in designing long-range guided missiles are practically identical with those which will be met in the construction of the reconnaissance rockets described in Chapter 4. Separating the military and the peaceful uses of rockets is therefore an even more difficult task than creating atomic energy without atomic bombs.

This particular problem is not, of course, peculiar to rocket research: it can be encountered today in every field of scientific activity—even in medicine, for the power to heal is also the power to kill. It is, however, certainly more acute for the rocket engineer than anyone else except perhaps the nuclear physicist. He can only hope, if he thinks seriously about these matters (and scientific workers are no better and no worse than the rest of us in ignoring uncomfortable facts) that the results of his work will eventually be published and employed for peaceful ends.

This has already happened in the case of radar, which only ten years ago was top-secret yet is now used all over the world to provide safety at sea and in the air. It is true that the rocket has nothing like the immediate "civil" uses of radar. At the moment, indeed, it has only two non-military applications—high-altitude research and take-off assistance for aircraft. The ultimate and revolutionary uses of the rocket are all bound up with astronautics and are therefore still a considerable distance in the future.

There is little doubt that a great many scientists and engineers whose only interest in the rocket is as a means of crossing space have become involved in current military research because in no other way could they find the necessary support. It is worth quoting here some words written by Professor von Braun on becoming an Honorary Fellow of the British Interplanetary Society: "Is it not a shame that people with the same star-inspired ideals had to stand on two opposite sides of the fence? Let's hope that this was the last holocaust, and that henceforth rockets will be used for their ultimate destiny only—space flight!" Dr. Sänger expressed similar views on the occasion of his election: "If the great majority of human beings or the great organisers of human society were thoroughly convinced and enthusiastic about astronautics, then scientists and engineers could direct their research work immediately to space-flight problems. Unfortunately, it is not so. . . . Therefore, I consider the astronautical scientist's task is to turn human mentality slowly towards our target by steps of *fait accompli*. . . . Men are seldom convinced by good reasons, and more often by good facts."

Although, in present conditions, it may still seem a Utopian dream to hope for large-scale support for purely astronautical rocket research, with no military entanglements, it is not impossible that something like this may evolve in the future. When and if the political situation stabilises, and international co-operation on the scientific level is again resumed, the steadily growing astronautical societies in many parts of the world may be able, by their combined efforts, to act as catalysts and so bring about this desired state of affairs. This is one of the long-term plans behind the various International Congresses on Astronautics, the first of which took place in Paris during the autumn of 1950.

It should, however, be made quite clear that no society, as such, can now do effective large-scale research work in rocketry. The cost of a big rocket development programme is many millions of pounds a year: even a single model of a medium-sized liquid-fuel missile may cost several thousand pounds. The function of the astronautical societies, therefore, is not to attempt research and construction themselves—except perhaps into the various subsidiary problems which can be investigated without large budgets. Interplanetary societies will not build spaceships any more than aeronautical societies, *as such,* build aircraft. They will be the specialist organisation—the professional bodies—of the scientists and engineers doing work in this field.

When the time comes to build the first spaceships, the interplanetary societies will be the spearhead of the attack: but their members will probably be acting under government orders—even though they may have had to persuade their governments to issue those orders in the first place!

It has sometimes been said that the main obstacles to interplanetary flight are not technical, but political and economic. There is always an immense resistance to any change and a desire to preserve the *status quo.* Protagonists of space-flight frequently used to meet the remark: "Why go to the Moon? What's wrong with this Earth anyway?" Although the latter statement is seldom encountered these days, it has been succeeded by the query: "Why not devote all this effort to developing our own world before going to others?"

We have already given several answers to this question, pointing out that many of the indirect consequences of space-travel will in fact help us to develop our own world—probably in ways at least as unforeseeable as those in which the American oilfields and farmlands assisted the development of Europe.

There is, however, a much more fundamental reply to this question, and one cannot help thinking that those who ask it have overlooked the facts of human nature. One wonders if they would have asked Pheidias, when he was starting work on the Parthenon frieze, why he was not engaged on something useful like rebuilding the Athenian slums. If he had kept his temper, the artist would probably have answered that he was doing the only job that interested him. So it is, in the ultimate analysis, with those who want to cross space.

There are, it seems, some people who have definite psychological objections to space-flight. In certain cases this has a religious basis—it is a new form of the old feeling that, in some mysterious way, there are things that "Man was never intended to do". We do not know a better way of demolishing this superstition than by referring to the old lady who remarked that aeroplanes were undoubtedly an invention of the Devil, "since men should travel in trains as God intended them to."

Others, one suspects, are afraid that the crossing of space, above all contact with intelligent but non-human races, may destroy the foundations of their religious faith. They may be right, but in any event their attitude is one which does not bear logical examination—for a faith which cannot survive collision with the truth is not worth many regrets.

In the long run, the prospect of meeting other forms of intelligence is perhaps the most exciting of all the possibilities revealed by astronautics. Whether or not Man is alone in the Universe is one of the supreme questions of philosophy. It is difficult to imagine that anyone could fail to be interested in knowing the answer—and only through space-travel can we be sure of obtaining it.

We have seen that there is little likelihood

of encountering intelligence elsewhere in the Solar System. That contact may have to wait for the day, perhaps ages hence, when we can reach the stars. But sooner or later it must come.

There have been many portrayals in literature of these fateful meetings. Most science-fiction writers, with characteristic lack of imagination, have used them as an excuse for stories of conflict and violence indistinguishable from those which stain the pages of our own history. Such an attitude shows a complete misunderstanding of the factors involved.

It has already been pointed out that ours must be one of the youngest cultures in the Universe. An analogy due to Sir James Jeans may help to emphasise this point. Take a penny, lay a postage stamp on it, and put both on top of Cleopatra's Needle.[2] The column then represents the age of the world, the coin the whole period of Man's existence, and the stamp the length of time during which he has been slightly civilised. The period during which life will be possible on Earth corresponds to a further column of stamps certainly hundreds of yards, and perhaps a mile, in height.

Thinking of this picture, we see how very improbable it is that the question of interplanetary warfare can ever arise. Any races we encounter will almost certainly be superhuman or subhuman—more likely the former. Only if we score a bull's-eye on that one stamp—indeed on a fractional thickness of that stamp—in the mile-high column will we meet a race at a level of technical development sufficiently near our own for warfare to be possible. If ships from Earth ever set out to conquer other worlds they may find themselves, at the end of their journeys, in the position of painted war-canoes drawing slowly into New York Harbour.

What, then, if we ever encounter races which are scientifically advanced yet malevolent—the stock villains, in fact, of that type of fiction neatly categorised as "space-opera"? In that event, astronautics might well open a Pandora's Box which could destroy humanity.

This prospect, though it cannot be ruled out, appears highly improbable. It seems unlikely that any culture can advance, for more than a few centuries at a time, on a technological front alone. Morals and ethics must not lag behind science, otherwise (as our own recent history has shown) the social system will breed poisons which will cause its certain destruction. With superhuman knowledge there must go equally great compassion and tolerance. When we meet our peers among the stars, we need have nothing to fear save our own shortcomings.

Just how great these are is something we seldom stop to consider. Our impressions of reality are determined, far more than we imagine, by the senses through which we make contact with the external world. How utterly different our philosophies would have been had Nature economised with us, as she has done with other creatures, and given us eyes incapable of seeing the stars! Yet how pitiably limited are the eyes we do possess, turned as they are to but a single octave in the spectrum! The world in which we live is drenched with invisible radiations, from the radio waves which we have just discovered coming from Sun and stars, to the cosmic rays whose origin is still one of the prime mysteries of modern physics. These things we have discovered within the last generation, and we cannot guess what still lies beneath the threshold of the senses—though recent discoveries in paranormal psychology hint that the search may be only beginning.

The races of other worlds will have senses and philosophies very different from our own. To recall Plato's famous analogy, we are prisoners in a cave, gathering our impressions of the outside world from shadows thrown upon the walls. We may never escape to reach that outer reality, but one day we may hope to reach other prisoners in

[2] For the benefit of those unfamiliar with the Victoria Embankment or Central Park, this obelisk is about 70 feet high.

adjoining caves, where we may learn far more than we could ever do by our own unaided efforts.

Yet space-travel will not, as some fear, destroy the mystery of the Universe. On the contrary, it may indeed increase it. Although many specific problems will be solved, and many doubts settled, our area of contact with the unknown will be enormously magnified. This has always been the case with scientific research: it should never be forgotten that, despite all our knowledge, we live in a far more wonderful and even more mysterious world than did our ancestors. We will not exhaust the marvels of the physical Universe until we have explored the whole Cosmos—and *that* prospect is still, to say the least, satisfyingly remote, if indeed it is theoretically possible. We have scarcely begun a voyage of discovery which may never have an end.

Somewhere on that journey we may at last learn what purpose, if any, life plays in the Universe of matter: certainly we can never learn it on this Earth alone. Among the stars lies the proper study of mankind: Pope's aphorism gave only part of the truth. For the proper study of mankind is not merely Man, but Intelligence.

Our survey is now finished. We have gone as far as is possible, at this moment of time, in trying to assess the impact of astronautics upon human affairs. Beyond this point the imagination can travel where it will, bounded only by the laws of logic.

I am not unmindful of the fact that fifty years from now, instead of preparing for the conquest of the planets, our grandchildren may be dispossessed savages clinging to the fertile oases in a radioactive wilderness. We must keep the problems of today in their true proportions: they are of vital—indeed of supreme—importance, since they can destroy our civilisation and slay the future before its birth. But if we survive them, they will pass into history and the time will come when they will be as little remembered as the causes of the Punic Wars. The crossing of space—even the sense of its imminent achievement in the years before it comes—may do much to turn men's minds outwards and away from their present tribal squabbles. In this sense the rocket, far from being one of the destroyers of civilisation, may provide the safety-valve that is needed to preserve it. Space-flight does not even have to be achieved for this to happen. As soon as there is a general belief in its possibility, that belief will begin to colour Man's psychological outlook.

We stand now at the turning point between two eras. Behind us is a past to which we can never return, even if we wish. Dividing us now from all the ages that have ever been is that moment when the heat of many suns burst from the night sky above the New Mexico desert—the same desert over which, a few years later, was to echo the thunder of the first rockets climbing towards space. The power that was released on that day can take us to the stars, or it can send us to join the great reptiles and Nature's other unsuccessful experiments.

The choice is ours. One would give much to know what verdict an historian of the year 3,000—as detached from us as we are from the Crusaders—would pass upon our age, as he looks back at us down the long perspective of Time. Let us hope that this will be his judgment:

"The twentieth century was, without question, the most momentous hundred years in the history of Mankind. It opened with the conquest of the air, and before it had run half its course had presented civilisation with its supreme challenge—the control of atomic energy. Yet even these events, each of which changed the world, were soon to be eclipsed. To us a thousand years later, the whole story of Mankind before the twentieth century seems like the prelude to some great drama, played on the narrow strip of stage before the curtain has risen and revealed the scenery. For countless generations of men, that tiny, crowded stage—the planet Earth—was the whole of creation, and they the only actors. Yet towards the close of that fabulous century, the curtain began slowly, inexorably to rise, and Man realised at last that the Earth was only one of many worlds; the Sun only one among many stars. The coming of the rocket brought to an end a million years of isolation. With the landing of the first space-ship on Mars and Venus, the childhood of our race was over and history as we know it began. . . ."